THINKING WITHOUT A BANISTER

THINKING

❖ ❖ ❖ WITHOUT A ❖ ❖ ❖

BANISTER

Essays in Understanding, 1953–1975

Hannah Arendt

Edited and with an Introduction by
Jerome Kohn

SCHOCKEN BOOKS, NEW YORK

Excerpts from the poems of W. H. Auden appear courtesy of Edward
Mendelson, Executor of the Estate of W. H. Auden; Random House,
a division of Penguin Random House LLC; and Curtis Brown, Ltd.

" 'As If Speaking to a Brick Wall': A Conversation with Joachim Fest"
originally published, in slightly different form, in Germany as *Eichmann
war von empörender Dummheit: Gespräche und Briefe* by Piper Verlag GmbH,
Munich, in 2011. Joachim Fest's questions copyright © 2011 by Piper Verlag
GmbH. This translation first published as "Eichmann Was Outrageously
Stupid" by Melville House Publishing, New York, in 2013. Translation of
Hannah Arendt's responses copyright © 2013 by Hannah Arendt Bluecher
Literary Trust. Translation of Joachim Fest's questions copyright © 2013 by
Andrew Brown.

"Interview with Roger Errera" originally aired in France as *Un certain
regard* by Office National de Radiodiffusion Télévision Française (ORTF)
in 1974, and subsequently published in *Hannah Arendt Newsletter, #2*
(December 1999). This translation first published as "The Last Interview"
by Melville House Publishing, New York, in 2013. Copyright © 2013 by The
Literary Trust of Hannah Arendt Bluecher. Translation of Roger Errera's
questions copyright © 2013 by Andrew Brown.

Library of Congress Cataloging-in-Publication Data
Arendt, Hannah, 1906–1975.
[Works. Selections]
Thinking without a banister : essays in understanding, 1953–1975 /
Hannah Arendt ; edited and with an introduction by Jerome Kohn.
Includes index.
ISBN 978-0-8052-4215-7 (hardcover : alk. paper).
ISBN 978-1-101-87030-3 (ebook).
1. Philosophy, Modern—20th century. I. Kohn, Jerome. II. Title.
B945.A694 2015 191—dc23 2014046457

www.schocken.com

Jacket design by Linda Huang
Book design by Peter A. Andersen

Printed in the United States of America
First Edition
2 4 6 8 9 7 5 3 1

There's this other thing, which Draenos brought up . . . "groundless thinking." I have a metaphor which is not quite that cruel, and which I have never published but kept for myself. I call it thinking without a banister—in German, *Denken ohne Geländer*. That is, as you go up and down the stairs you can always hold on to the banister so that you don't fall down, but we have lost this banister. That is the way I tell it to myself. And this is indeed what I try to do.

—*Hannah Arendt*

CONTENTS

Contents

INTRODUCTION

Jerome Kohn

The Republic of the United States of America has been in a state of decline for more than fifty years, that is, if the decline is dated from the debacle of the invasion of Cuba at the Bay of Pigs in 1961. More than a century before that, John Quincy Adams already despaired of what he called the "noble experiment," chiefly due to the mordant division of public opinion over the issue of human slavery.

Today, the apathy of public opinion is denounced by politicians of all parties and pundits of all political stripes, for the sake of their own power. But for the people, what does an addiction to polls, however cockeyed their results, signify other than an obsession with public opinion? It will come as no surprise to those familiar with Hannah Arendt's way of thinking that she believed polls, like senseless calls for donations, signify either having lost or been swindled out of one's own opinion. Speaking with a group of students in Chicago in 1963, Arendt said that every one of us "is forced to make up his mind and then exchange his opinion with others. You may remember," she said, "the great mistrust the founders had in public opin-ion, which stands opposed to public spirit. Where public spirit is lacking, public opinion comes in its stead." To Arendt this is a "perversion," and a danger to all republics, perhaps especially those that consider themselves democracies. For (now quoting Madison, *Federalist*, 50) "when men exert their reason cooly and freely on a variety of distinct questions, they inevitably fall into different opinions. . . . When they are governed by a common passion, their opinions, if they are so to be called, will be the same."*

Thomas Jefferson was a "party of one," though not in the sense of *The Loners' Manifesto,*† which would transmogrify loners, political and otherwise, into a group identity! In a letter to Francis Hopkinson written from Paris in March of 1789, Jefferson wrote: "I am not a federalist, because I never submitted the whole system of my opinions to the creed of any party of men whatever in religion, in philosophy, in politics, or in any thing else where I was capable of thinking for myself. Such an addiction is the last degradation of a free and moral agent. If I could not go to heaven but with a party, I would not go there at all. Therefore I protest to you I am not of the party of federalists. But I am much farther from that of the Antifederalists."

If the American Republic has failed, who bears the responsibility? That question can be construed economically or—in various forms—psychologically, which, to Arendt, would bring forth social rather than political answers. To respond politically would require an observer standing at a distance from the certain but ambiguous sociability of men and women. A political response would be to a somewhat different and more precise question: *How have citizens of the United States dissipated the power of their Republic?* Her last public address, delivered in the last year of her life, 1975, in celebration of the approaching two hundredth anniversary of the birth of the American Republic, contains indications of what she might say today. There she emphasized "the erosion of power in this country, the nadir of self-confidence when victory over one of the tiniest and most helpless countries could cheer the inhabitants of what only a few decades ago really was the 'mightiest power on earth' "‡ (referring to the United States in the mid- to late 1940s, after the Allied victory in World War II).

---

* Noteworthy is the fact that Arendt *heard* the founders' words, which temper the element of chance in their actions. Contingency is a *conditio sine qua non* of free action, and at the same time of its manifold interpretations by professional political scientists and historians. Thus Arendt notes the *futility* of action without speech.

† Cf. A. Rufus, *A Party of One: The Loners' Manifesto* (2003).

‡ *Responsibility and Judgment* (New York: Schocken Books, 2003) 257–75.

She next mentions something that, by 1975, seemed to her the "mini-crisis triggered by Joe McCarthy" in the 1950s, which heralded "the destruction of a reliable and devoted civil service . . . probably the most important achievement of the long Roosevelt administration." From that point on there had been a "cataclysm of events, tumbling over one another," and, in words frequently quoted, "cascading like a Niagara Falls of history whose sweeping force leaves everybody, spectators who try to reflect on it and actors who try to slow it down, equally numbed and paralyzed." Now, more than forty years after Arendt delivered that speech, how often do we still hear this country hailed as the world's greatest power, or sole superpower, with even less justification than in 1975? Even more confusing, today this swagger is accompanied by the politically empty economic caveat that somehow America must return to her former "wealth" and "greatness."

The ground beneath Arendt's political thought and speech, the soil that nourished it, was unusually fertile, for better and worse. One matter she almost certainly would be inclined to address today concerns the seemingly relentless political lies at the highest levels of the executive branch—but not only there—of the U.S. government. This lying does not threaten the truth, as the grammatically inept and self-contradictory description of our times as "post-truth" implies, but rather undercuts our ability to believe in the reality of political goings-on as such. If the consequence of the loss of a sense of reality also spells the loss of political power, on the one hand, there is the more crucial matter of how citizens' exercise of freedom *generates* power, on the other. This is why the "freedom to be free," as she states forcefully in this volume, is for Arendt the end or *telos* of political revolution. Of course, none of this is to deny that self-driven financial imbalances, death-ridden racial inequalities, along with other diverse forms of brutality, bureaucratic corruption, and social injustice, deprive us of freedom in ways that are becoming ever more apparent. These are the signs of an encroaching social *totalism*, the more or less complete repression of political freedom in, for example, a republic that has become a bureaucracy. Such totalism need not arrive or result in the terror Arendt perceived as the essence of twentieth-century totalitarianism, but its signs are, I believe, what she cautions us to beware of as "the true predicaments of our time [in] their authentic form."*

Of what does *political* freedom consist? To cast a secret ballot while alone in a voting booth, is that to be free? Is to teach, to write, or to read to be free? For Arendt, the simplest answer appears to be that the capacities to act and to speak—speech as distinct from mere talk—are the conditions *sine qua non* of political freedom. The question that then falls upon us is where and how do acting and speaking together generate power? Unlike military force—including the massed armies and novel weapons of World War II, which still endure—political power for Arendt, at least negatively, is not engendered by men and women talking to their peers about themselves, their families, or their careers. What does relate to power is the speaking out of citizens, their arguing with eloquence in public to persuade other citizens of their opinions. That is the opposite of obedience. Citizens fit words to events that by definition are not their own: no one says "my event," because an event is objective, it stands over against many people, and its consequences affect a plurality of *different* people. The power contained within an event is the potentiality of citizens who recognize their faculty to render it, to a greater or lesser extent, tractable. The condition of that tractability is political *commonalty,* from which the stamp or mold of human inequality is effaced. Political commonalty *is* actualized public space, which Arendt calls "an island of freedom." Such an island has only rarely appeared in a world that for the greater part of its history may be likened to a sea of distrust, malfeasance, and iniquity.

Arendt's letter to Robert Hutchins, included in this volume, is rich with examples of what she recognizes as common political concerns. To some readers, this may suggest the possibility of a common world. How that might develop, and what form of government would best suit it, are fundamental issues raised by attempting to understand such a world. Arendt's view of realizing a common world was never optimistic, and she was reticent to discuss a form of government that had hardly yet, and then only briefly, appeared in the world. Still, on one occasion, when asked about the prospects of a council system of government, she replied:

* *The Origins of Totalitarianism* (New York: Schocken Books, 2004), 593.

"Very slight, if at all. And yet perhaps, after all—in the wake of the next revolution."*

Her conception of council systems of governance is not detailed, for they would be *new beginnings* that cannot be fully grasped in advance. Nevertheless, her vision of them is immense. Arendt saw totalitarianism as "a novel form of government," one of total destruction, and it had no positive counterpart in the sense that monarchy is the counterpart of tyranny, aristocracy of oligarchy, and democracy of ochlocracy. These pairings had remained virtually unchanged since antiquity, until Arendt added the council system as the positive counterpart to totalitarianism and, by extension, to all forms of totalism. Her most extensive account of this system of governance is in her essay on the Hungarian Revolution, which is published here in its entirety for the first time. At the basic level (which is also the basis of power) councils are composed of men and women who have common interests in issues such as fair wages and adequate housing, primary and secondary education, personal safety, and public security. These basic local levels would then elect higher and smaller regional levels of councils whose members would have researched and studied the specifics of resolving these issues. At the top of the pyramid, a governmental or steering council, also elected from below, would direct and organize the conglomerate of common interests within its jurisdiction.

It may be worth mentioning here that Arendt strenuously opposed any notion of "world government," as potentially the greatest tyranny imaginable. In council systems of government the freedom to move, to think, and to act would be present at each level, but *power* would be actualized only in the basic levels' responsibility for the fulfillment of the duties and commitments of the levels above it. Council governments would result in a common world, one literally overflowing with interests that lie between (*inter esse*) the world's plurality of men and women, relating them as acting and speaking individuals while maintaining sufficient space between them for each to address others from his or her unique point of view. This *in-between* space would exist in any one council system and in a plurality of like systems of governance. And it may be added that within council

* *Crises of the Republic* (New York: Harcourt Brace Jovanovich, 1972), 233.

systems citizens would be related as equals in the marketplace not only of ideas but also of products of consumption and utility. The sensuous awareness of political equality would not only prohibit inequity by law but also empower and assure its non-appearance, from bottom to top. One thing is certain, the council system of governance would overwhelm the traditional notion of state sovereignty.

The title of this book, *Thinking Without a Banister,* is Arendt's description—in "Hannah Arendt on Hannah Arendt"—of her own experience of thinking: a world-withdrawn activity that depends on agreement with no one other than oneself. In other words, while withdrawn in the *dialogue* of thinking, the subject divides in two, which Arendt names the "two-in-one." For her to experience the "two-in-one" *is* thinking, as it seems to have been for Plato, Aristotle, Kant, and others whom she names. The activity of thinking enables Arendt, as it did Hegel, to be *reconciled* to the world as it is. The unprecedentedness of the atrocities and destruction of Hitler's and Stalin's totalitarian regimes, however, deprived Arendt, never more so than when she was withdrawn from the world, thinking alone with herself, of any traditional religious, moral, or historical supports. It was in reflection that the burden of her own times weighed heaviest upon her.

To engage in the activity of thinking was, for Arendt, akin to stepping up and down a staircase, caring for the great burden she bore, without the support of a banister on either side. Thinking without a banister complements another of Arendt's metaphors: the abyss that suddenly gaped between past and future when the bridge of traditional norms spanning the passage of time, relating the past to the future, was mocked out of existence by the hitherto unimagined political crimes of totalitarianism. This abyss lacks all spatial dimensions, including depth, for it is bottomless. How giddy is that? W. B. Yeats, the Irish poet whom Arendt greatly admired said it best:

> *Turning and turning in the widening gyre*
> *The falcon cannot hear the falconer;*
> *Things fall apart; the centre cannot hold . . .*

Were Hannah Arendt here today, she probably would share our sense of impending natural and political crises. But would she, as others have done, often in her name, make comparisons to twentieth-century totalitarian movements or their elements? Arendt remembers and describes totalitarian regimes, which for her ended with Stalin's death, in the essay "Authority in the Twentieth Century." There, I trust, she makes clear to readers how far distant from anything comparable we are today. On the other hand, what may be heard as a leitmotif throughout this volume, the specific topic of at least six essays, with echoes in many others, is *revolution*. Arendt's remarks on revolution are timely today because the revolutionary spirit, which flourished at the end of the eighteenth century in France and America, revived the long dormant freedom experienced in action and speech as action. The spontaneous newness of action, the god-like *thaumadzein*, or wonder, with which it endowed the ancient world, I believe, is what originally gave rise to the notion of *amor mundi*, love of the world, frequently associated with Arendt.

The spirit of revolution is fully realized in the world when men and women in action have reached, in Arendt's words, "the point of no return," that is, when it is no longer possible to turn back, like a clock that can be reset. On the contrary, something entirely new is about to be born into the world, and again Yeats, writing in 1916 of a failed action in the struggle for Ireland's independence, says it best:

> *And what if excess of love*
> *Bewildered them till they died?*
> *I write it out in a verse—*
> *MacDonagh and MacBride*
> *And Connolly and Pearse*
> *Now and in time to be,*
> *Wherever green is worn,*
> *Are changed, changed utterly:*
> *A terrible beauty is born.*

By far the more historically influential of the two great eighteenth-century revolutions was the one in France, despite the fact that, unlike the American Revolution, its failure to attain its threefold goal, *liberté, égalité, fraternité*, was an unreserved disaster. Arendt spells out in considerable detail the reasons for the failure of the French and the success of the American revolutions, but what I want to emphasize here is what she says about *amor mundi* regarding the Terror that emerged within the French revolution itself, turning its goals inside out: "What is most difficult is to love the world as it is, with all the evil and suffering in it."

As Yeats says, a *terrible* beauty is born when individual actors fall for the sake of their cause. There is no doubt that a defeated human cause could *please* Hannah Arendt, as it is said not to have pleased the ancient gods, but is that the same as *loving the world as it is*? Arendt is well known for having said she did not love any peoples in the world, only individuals. This corresponds to its obverse: as I will try to show in the second part of this Introduction, Arendt held only individuals responsible for even the most egregious of political crimes, including the crime against humanity. Toward the end of her life—after Heinrich Bluecher (her husband) and Karl Jaspers had died, and the person on whom she most relied after them, her close friend W. H. Auden, who would also die before her, and Martin Heidegger, whom at their last meeting she found enfeebled mentally and physically—Arendt said she felt "free as a leaf in the wind" (*Frei wie ein Blatt im Wind*), a striking image of sheer powerlessness. And since thinking's reconciliation to the world is hardly the same as love, all of this tends to make one a bit skeptical of the worldly wise Hannah Arendt's *amor mundi* in her later years.

At this point it is critical, I believe, to focus on what has frequently been overlooked in Arendt's many accounts of revolution. Resounding clearly within this volume's revolutionary theme of the revival of political freedom and public happiness in the modern age is Arendt's unique insistence that revolutions are of two distinct kinds: those that seek a *new beginning* in the world and those that seek to *renew a past beginning*. For Arendt, the latter is what Virgil describes as Aeneas's founding of Rome, namely, the renewal of the sacked and consumed polis of Troy; her principal example of the former is the absolute new beginning of the Republic of the United States of America. Arendt wants her readers to see and feel the difference. She herself senses it in the change of Virgil's *ab integro saeclorum ordo,* a renewal of what has passed in the order of time, to the words that still appear on our one-dollar bills, *novus ordo seclorum,* signifying a total break in the order of the ages.

Arendt quotes in her beautiful eulogy of Auden, the last essay in this book, his poem written in memory of Yeats, which ends: *In the prison of his days / Teach the free man how to praise.* She goes on to say:

> Praise is the key word of these lines, not praise of "the best of all possible worlds"—as though it were up to the poet (or the philosopher) to justify God's creation—but praise that pitches itself against all that is most unsatisfactory in man's condition . . . and sucks its own strength from the wound.

To Arendt, Auden was the greatest English poet of his time,* and what made him that "was the unprotesting willingness with which he yielded to the 'curse' of his vulnerability to 'human *un*success'—vulnerability to the crookedness of the desires, to the infidelities of the heart, to the injustices of the world." That, too, is not harmonious, to my ear, with *amor mundi.* It is rather the courage of human resolve that Arendt finds in all great poets. And this again brings Virgil to mind, who sang of the founding of Rome as the renewal of his desecrated homeland. In the America of today, with its glorious new beginning more than two hundred years ago, that seems almost the last word of wisdom.

*   *   *

> CLAUDIO: . . . *Death is a fearful thing.*
> ISABELLA: *And shamèd life a hateful.*
>
> Shakespeare, *Measure for Measure* III, i

Hans Jonas said of Hannah Arendt, his friend from their university days, that, however she may be judged in the future, in her lifetime she raised the level of political discourse. In her vast writings that is unquestionable, although there is as yet little sign of its dissemination in the American electorate, or within the bureaus of the public realm, or, where it might be expected, among professional political writers. In its place we have the superficiality of a once reliable newspaper, the glibness that has replaced

---

* This spared her from weighing Auden against Yeats, who was Irish, or T. S. Eliot, who was American.

the wit and intelligence of a weekly magazine, and at best some cerebral puzzles posed by a once portentous book review. A majority of the more competent professionals seems to have agreed that their current audiences are like nothing so much as crabs scurrying across the receding shores of a quasi-literate mass society.

Apart from the quality of political discourse today, Arendt's thought so searches into political events that she found new meaning in political life. Perhaps it is more relevant to say the hallmark of Arendt's work is its demonstration that the activity of thinking is the condition *sine qua non* of understanding events that make less and less sense in their appearance on the surface of the world. Arendt is startled into thinking by surface phenomena, to which her thinking remains bound, circling round and round, penetrating them from a distance, and, in the end, illuminating them from within. The activity of thinking itself, however, *stands under* the event, and, as we like to think, on firmer ground. With knowing wit, T. S. Eliot wrote of Henry James that his mind was so fine that no idea could ever *violate* it. But ideas as such do not violate minds, whereas ideologies of whatever variety or bias *distract* political thinkers from political events, and it is in this sense that the best political writers, from Plato to Hobbes to Arendt, have exercised as active a reproductive imagination as the productive imagination was active in James—which is probably what Eliot was getting at all along.

It is fair to say, in my judgment, that attending the trial of Adolf Eichmann in Jerusalem in 1961 was the most momentous event in Arendt's life during the period covered by this second volume of unpublished and uncollected writings, that is, from the mid-1950s to 1975, whose subtitle is *Essays in Understanding, 1953–1975*. To put it as clearly as I can, the event that most affected Arendt during the first half of her career, which is reflected throughout the first volume of *Essays in Understanding, 1930–1954*, was the appearance, for the first time in two millennia, of a new form of government in the world: totalitarianism. Attempting to understand totalitarianism, of which Hitler and Stalin believed their goals to be identical to those of Nature or History, or some combination of both, and the terror and destruction necessary to reach those goals, literally shifted the ground of the moral, legal, and philosophic tradition—in which Arendt had been raised and educated—from beneath her feet. Years later, the phenomenal presence of Adolf Eichmann in a Jerusalem courtroom, on trial for his life for crimes committed against humanity during World War II, fifteen years earlier, literally took her breath away.* That will be discussed in this part of the Introduction, for *l'Affaire Eichmann* is almost a blueprint of the moral, political, and legal morass in which not only Americans, but also citizens of European states and throughout much of the world, find themselves today.

The most immediate problem may not be the gradual loss of action, which Arendt saw first accelerating and then largely solidifying after the French Revolution.† It may be, rather, the petrifaction of our thinking faculty, which is all too similar to what she first saw in Eichmann as he stood accused of sending innocent men, women, and children to their deaths on a scale never before envisioned or witnessed. But this problem by no means concerns only Arendt's professional worriers who accuse her, in one way or another, of exonerating a Nazi murderer. With far greater incongruity it also includes those of her defenders who at times seem not to realize who or what they are defending. The meaning of what *has* happened, for Arendt, is to help make sense of what *is* happening. And more than that, a sensed *present*—as opposed to merely passing moments—provides the stability from which men and women *can* act together into the unknown future. But when the meaning of the past is indiscernible and its understanding lost, so to speak, in an intellectual fog, how can it be remembered—or judged—in the present? Why are so many intellectuals today convinced that Eichmann was a committed antisemite, or genocidal ideologue, even as they admit his mediocrity? Arendt herself saw this as a *moral* problem well before it was argued or assumed as a self-evident fact. When the trial ended, and shortly after her book *Eichmann in Jerusalem* was published in 1963, Arendt wrote that she had "the feeling that this moral issue has lain dormant because it

---

* Most of the articles Arendt herself wrote about the Eichmann event have been collected in *Responsibility and Judgment*. Her final incomplete and difficult masterwork *The Life of the Mind* (New York: Harcourt Brace Jovanovich, 1978), was inspired by the same event.
† This is the reason, mentioned earlier, that the French Revolution has had far greater influence than the American. In a mainly unpublished manuscript in the Library of Congress, Arendt considers the failure of action after the French Revolution.

was concealed by something about which it is indeed much more difficult to speak and with which it is almost impossible to come to terms—the horror itself in its naked monstrosity." What Arendt means by *the banality of evil* (the subtitle of her book on Eichmann) is simply overwhelmed by the sheer horror of the *event* of the destruction of European Jewry—the only people who as a people survived, against all odds, from antiquity—in comparison with which the fact that nothing can withstand the loss of integrity that flows from, or may be the same as, the loss of the ability to think, remains largely in the shadows.

What she says here is of striking importance. She sees, first, that there is a real difficulty—more than an unwillingness—among intellectuals to face up to the horrors of total domination under totalitarian regimes. It is this that blinds them, and ironically not Arendt, to the moral issues raised by the mediocrity of Eichmann as a participant in the atrocities. Second, she sees that there was nothing—nothing at all—behind the masks that Eichmann wore in Germany, Austria, Hungary, Argentina, or Jerusalem. That explains why the extreme evil he enacted lacked any psychological root or depth, and also why it was capable of spreading like wildfire, or spores in the wind, throughout the human world. The "naked monstrosity" is difficult to "come to terms" with because of the mental struggle required to grasp and bear it. For Arendt, this elusive moral issue requires seeing and understanding bottomless evil, an evil that has no comprehensible end other than sheer destruction, and, moreover, an evil that has no essential connection to antisemitism or any other ideology.*

In the abyss of sheer destruction no reconciliation is possible. This evil defies thinking, and perhaps also the imagination, because without depth—"only the good has depth"—not only is there no support to hang on to, no root to grasp, but there is also no devil, no corruption, nor even stupidity or madness to blame. There *is* a suffocating ordinariness, which

---

* This is not to deny the ideologies of Nature and History of the Nazi and Bolshevik regimes, respectively, which Arendt analyzes at length in *The Origins of Totalitarianism* and elsewhere. But she further understands that a "perfected" totalitarian state would abolish "convictions as a too unreliable support for the system," and to demonstrate "that this system, in distinction from all others, has made man, insofar as he is a being of spontaneous thought and action, superfluous." *Essays in Understanding*, I (New York: Schocken Books, 1994), 353–54.

made it difficult for Arendt not to suspect that Eichmann was a clown! Though such a suspicion would have proved "fatal" to the trial, and in any case "was hard to sustain in view of the sufferings he and his like had caused millions of people . . . [moreover] his worst clowneries were hardly ever noticed and almost never reported." Even today Germans seldom speak of the nonsense of Eichmann's words—Margarethe von Trotta is an exception in this as in much else. Certainly this criminal, Eichmann, committing crimes against humanity, lacked the ability, in his Gestapo bureau, to realize what it was he was doing. It is because the evil he did was not understood by him as evil that it is banal. He was a "desk murderer," who set about his work more diligently than his colleagues, trusting he would be noticed by his superiors and promoted. One can say the reason he had no disgust or revulsion for what he did was because he failed to imagine the lives he was preparing to be worked to death, gassed, and incinerated. He could not even remember them! A question worth considering is how the lack of a sense of disgust is related to the inability to think. That is a moral question, which might open a fruitful inquiry into what Arendt had been searching for since 1933, when she first remarked the presence of evil in the flames of the Reichstag, a search that became ever more complex throughout the war, and culminated in listening to what Eichmann said at his trial in Jerusalem.*

Whether or not Eichmann believed in the necessity of the destruction of European Jewry, he certainly participated in it. Do Arendt's supporters today seriously hold that to *believe* and to *participate* are one and the same? Why not distinguish one from the other, just as these same supporters readily distinguish Eichmann's responsibility for the deaths of millions of Jews from his mediocrity and thoughtlessness? Many who are well disposed toward Arendt draw a portrait of Eichmann, whom they never saw in the flesh, that reveals him as a genocidal, bigoted, *and* banal man. But is that the man Arendt saw on trial for his life in the Jerusalem courtroom? Was Eichmann banal *despite* the evil for which he was responsible, rather

---

* That is not to be gainsaid by anything Eichmann said elsewhere, wearing a different mask and under different circumstances. In the Greek sense of *aisthēsis*—the sensuous apperception of particulars—Eichmann's words as a Gestapo officer are not privileged over those he spoke in court, at least not to those who can hear.

like Christopher Browning's "ordinary men"? Was Eichmann a psychologically normal man who simply went along to get along? Or is this simply the latest version of the old tide against which Arendt swam from the beginning? Does it in any way aid us in conceiving, or better, grasping her judgment that Eichmann should be hanged, not for the perversions of his ambition, but for his responsibility in destroying a discrete part of the world?

Arendt's friends and supporters tend to deal with the question of Eichmann's "conscience" by saying, one way or another, that he "assigned" it to his idol Hitler. Hitler was a little guy who succeeded big-time, and that was reason enough for Eichmann to follow the leader to the letter, while on the road, he assumed, to his own promotion. Arendt, on the contrary, saw with irony that Eichmann's conscience worked conventionally for a few weeks, and then, suddenly, worked the other way around, the Nazi way, and did so energetically throughout his tenure as an expert in logistics for Hitler's plan to exterminate European Jewry. What does this change of conscience mean? Conscience is almost always understood as a voice that speaks to us from within, telling us what *not* to do. Isn't that what we mean when we ask a financial trader who is offering an insider's tip on a stock: "Can you do that with a clear conscience?" Eichmann heard, after a short interval when echoes from his prior life had subsided, only the voices of those of his colleagues who were engaged in the same business as he was. Eichmann had no inner voice; he was not, in Arendt's terminology, two-in-one, which means that he had no thinking partner, no one to speak to in words that pass so fast they cannot be heard, at least not until the thinker reappears in the world as *one*, speaking to others than himself: *Eichmann could calculate, but he could not think.*

Why, one wonders, didn't Eichmann advance in the SS? Why was he considered "small fry" by his peers, unimportant, inferior, and vulgar by his superiors? Is this the company he craved, desiring more than anything to belong and share the fellowship of those who considered themselves so far above him? Such a desire is common enough, in Germany and elsewhere, but Arendt's point throughout is that Eichmann was not like "millions of his countrymen" (in this she agrees with Browning, though for opposite reasons). He was a particular individual, who, because of what he himself had done, was on trial for his life. To think about the role of conscience in such a matter is to realize that the only conscience is a bad one, and that it speaks only to decent men and women. A bad conscience is, indeed, a condition *sine qua non* of human dignity, whereas a clear or clean conscience has no voice, nor needs one.

Perhaps most important of all is that the perpetrators of the Nazi genocide of Jews are said, by some Arendt fans, to have been convinced that what they did, regardless, or perhaps because of how difficult it was, was not only legal but right (*recht*). Did Hitler believe in the "rightness" or "goodness" of the Holocaust? Hitler, to be sure, had "political reasons"—*raisons d'état*, Arendt might have called them with considerable irony—for destroying European Jewry, but did he consider those reasons *morally* justifiable?

Or, on the contrary, was "moral goodness" what Hitler consistently scorned? Why should anyone believe that all perpetrators of mass exterminations are convinced of the moral rectitude of what they do? In *Origins* Arendt wrote: "The ideal subject of totalitarian rule is not the convinced Nazi or the dedicated communist, but the people for whom the distinction between fact and fiction, true and false, no longer exists." She uses the word "ideal" in Max Weber's sense of an "ideal type," and not as referring to the particular man she went to Jerusalem to see in the flesh. Nevertheless, in her account, not being a convinced Nazi,* and not being able to distinguish between fact and fiction, describe Eichmann to a T. This last inability is crucial. For not being able to tell fact from fiction is not at all the same as not knowing the difference between right and wrong. It takes no experience to know that it is right to do what is right, and wrong to do what is wrong. To judge that a particular act is wrong, however, is not a matter of a priori knowledge. It *is* the ability to distinguish between fact and fiction, which is the converse of everyone agreeing that the sky is blue, for then the sky *is* blue, in fact or fiction. If we resist sending Jews to their deaths because they are not in fact polluting the human race, our judgment is not anchored in any standard, but grounded in our own experience of living with or knowing a Jew or Jews. Eichmann may have been an "ideal"

---

* Does Eichmann ever indicate that he understood or believed the Nazi "ideology" of which the extermination of European Jewry was the *telos*?

totalitarian subject, unable to distinguish fact from fiction, *and* responsible for an unprecedented crime against humanity. This is one of the most difficult aspects of Arendt's account of him, a difficulty she herself understood rather better than her commentators, pro and contra.

When Arendt spoke of the banality, or thoughtlessness, of evil she changed her mind from when, in *Origins,* she had called the death factories and the Gulag among the rare appearances of radical evil on earth. Furthermore, it is simply not the case that her two conceptions of evil can be reconciled by suggesting that the acts constituting banal or thoughtless evil are nothing but the theory of radical evil put into practice. There was no one Arendt trusted more than Mary McCarthy, to whom she confessed that she *had* changed her mind about precisely this, namely, that she now thought evil is never radical because it has no root. In no way does this limit evil, but on the contrary, it erases its limits and extends its reach. It is because it has no root that banal or thoughtless evil can spread over the entire surface of the earth. Radical evil may have been a "theory" to Kant—one, to be sure, he never developed—but never to Arendt.*

Prior to going to Jerusalem, Arendt had written of radical evil "about whose nature so little is known, even to us who have been exposed to one of [its] rare outbursts on the public scene. All we know is that we can neither punish nor forgive such offenses and that they therefore transcend the realm of human affairs and the potentialities of human power, both of which they radically destroy whenever they make their appearance."† The *dis*appearance of any root of evil in Eichmann's crimes against humanity has proved more problematic, it seems, to Arendt's supporters than to her detractors. For her the reason Eichmann had to hang was not because he committed a "crime against nature," though many, perhaps even the Israeli judges, may have believed that, and not implausibly. But to Arendt his crime was against human plurality—the essence of the uniqueness of every human being, including himself—which confirms Arendt's previous assertion of a human nature knowable only to God, never to mortals.

---

* The word "radical" does not denote adhering to an ideology, but getting to the root of such a matter as, for example, political antisemitism. The words "radical" and "root" derive from the Latin noun *radix,* meaning root.

† *The Human Condition* (Chicago: University of Chicago Press, 1958), 241.

Eichmann was sentenced to death, not as punishment for what he had done (what possible punishment would be commensurate with his crime?), but because he failed to think what he was doing when he served as an officer in the Gestapo, or when after the war he escaped to Argentina, or when he was taken from there to Jerusalem to stand trial for his acts. Arendt's judgment of Eichmann is that there is no place for such a man in the human world. He could not see that world from anyone else's point of view, noticeably not of those Jews he admired and worked with. That is banal, and (this is the hardest part) the banality of the extreme evil for which *as a human being,* not a monster, he was responsible.

The deeds, as Arendt says, were monstrous, the loading of human freight into boxcars, the "selections" of some to die immediately and others to work as slaves, while their humanity was extracted step by step until they were living corpses; the torture and starvation, the gassing installations and crematoria, the casual piling of corpses upon corpses in ditches, and so on. Eichmann did none of these deeds himself, but he equipped and provided for them, and was thereby more responsible than if he had committed them. The judges held, and Arendt vigorously agreed, that the responsibility of Eichmann increased with his distance from those who wielded the instruments of death. Of course it did, for he was not compelled by the necessity of staying alive that prevailed within the extermination camps.* To see Eichmann's evil as a problem facing all humanity is to see it as what the Hebrew Bible, in the Greek Septuagint, calls a *skandalon* (σκάνδαλον), a stumbling block. It bears some resemblance to what Arendt means by banality, but the differences are considerable: we no longer blame Satan—the brightest of all the angels—who *elected* to quit heaven, and we can see that Eichmann's only language, which he called *"officialese,"* helped dim his mind and mute his conscience. Arendt saw clearly and judged that what humans are capable of doing to humans far exceeds the ancient notion

---

* The kommandos who did the actual killing would themselves have been killed had they hesitated, which was not at all the case with the SS officers who calculated one aspect or another of the "final solution" to the Jewish question. In a somewhat similar train of thought, Primo Levi speaks of those who are "at last flung inside the walls of an indecipherable inferno. This, it seems to me, is the true *Befehlnotstand*, a state of emergency following an order . . . a rigid either/or, immediate obedience or death." *The Drowned and the Saved,* "The Gray Zone," Chapter 2.

of *homo homini lupis* (man is a wolf to men). Politically, the banality of Eichmann reveals no source of determination behind the masks he wore, which changed without consistency or expectation wherever the gales of choice or chance carried him.

We have to agree that Arendt named Eichmann's responsibility for the monstrous acts he himself did not commit "the banality of evil." But what may not yet have been examined sufficiently is that Eichmann, early on in Vienna, slapped the face of a Dr. Josef Löwenherz, a leader in the considerable Viennese Jewish community.* Later, the two collaborated, and Eichmann protected Löwenherz to the extent that throughout the war he could stay on living in Vienna. Nevertheless, Eichmann appears genuinely to regret having slapped Löwenherz, even, or perhaps especially, long after the latter had become, in Arendt's words, "the first Jewish functionary actually to organize a whole Jewish community into an institution at the service of the Nazi authorities." But why examine this story? To see if it reveals some mote of decency, or at least of fellowship, in Eichmann after all? Or what is entirely different, to see that understanding Löwenherz's story underscores the *not-caring,* the *indifference* toward the human victims of the crime against humanity, exhibited by both Löwenherz and Eichmann. To Arendt this indifference is "the greatest danger," even more dangerous than the refusal "to judge at all,"† at least to those who realize the power of judgment. Not fellowship but indifference.

In this volume, in the interview with Joachim Fest, Arendt describes the banality of Eichmann's evil as "a phenomenon that really could not be overlooked" in the "incredible" clichés he repeated endlessly, as if by rote. She then rather abruptly says : "Let me tell you what I mean by banality, since in Jerusalem I remembered a story that Ernst Jünger once told and that I'd forgotten." The story goes as follows: During the war, Jünger comes upon some farmers in the country. One of them had taken in Russian prisoners from the camps who had been starved almost to death. The farmer tells Jünger that these Russian prisoners are "sub-human . . . they

---

* In this volume see the end of Arendt's last interview with Roger Errera.
† *Responsibility and Judgment,* 146.

eat the pigs' food." Arendt then says: "There's something outrageously stupid about this story. I mean the story itself is stupid. . . . The man doesn't see that this is what starving people do. . . . Eichmann was rather intelligent, but in this respect he was stupid. . . . And that was what I actually meant by banality. There's nothing deep about it—nothing demonic! There's simply resistance even to imagine what another person is experiencing, isn't that true?" What is to be noted here is that it is not Eichmann whom Arendt calls "outrageously stupid"—as the original title, *Eichmann war von empörender Dummheit*, implies—but the story. It is through her own reproductive imagination that Arendt can understand that attempting to communicate with Eichmann would be the same as talking "to a brick wall."

If Christian belief had prevailed into the twentieth century, according to Arendt, its fear of Hell would have prevented the horrors of totalitarian domination. But she also sees that Christian belief would have remained an obstacle to knowing ourselves and of what we are capable. Arendt distinguishes between having faith in a credo and true religious trust in the meaningfulness of creation. In the Lord's Prayer, "Give us this day our daily bread" is immediately followed by "Forgive us our trespasses, as we forgive those who trespass against us." Now we can ask, if there is not a full stop between those two entreaties, how are they related? If being given bread every day is not just a matter of consumption and subsistence, but of breaking bread and sharing it with others—of being *copains*, as the French so precisely put it—does human sociability lead not only to peace but also to conflict? Is "every assertion of human freedom equally an assertion of human bondage," in John Calvin's much misunderstood words?

In the deepest pockets of ice in Hell, Dante reveals communion, the holiest of sacraments, transfigured into cannibalism.* In Canto 33, the pil-

---

* See "Dante: He Went Mad in His Hell" by Robert Pogue Harrison, *New York Review of Books*, October 27, 2016. I don't believe for a moment that Dante lost his own mind at the end of *Inferno*, nor, for that matter, that Bach ever evinced "an unruly obsession with God" (cf. Alex Ross, "Bach's Holy Dread," *The New Yorker*, January 2, 2017). One might as well claim the author of *Othello* was paranoid. These three sublime poetic voices—Dante's, Shakespeare's, and Bach's—separated by centuries, produced images in which destruction is not potential of the worlds in which they lived.

grim sees Count Ugolino insatiably gnawing on the neck bone of the Archbishop Ruggieri, whom he calls "neighbor" (*vicino*), since they are locked together for all eternity:

> *con li occhi torti*
> *riprese 'l teschio misero co' denti,*
> *che furo all'osso, come d'un can, forti.*

> (with eyes askance
> He took hold again of the wretched skull with his teeth,
> Which were as strong on the bone as a dog's.) ll. 76–78.

Ruggieri plotted the murder of Ugolino, but not without first seeing that his neighbor-to-be remained alive by eating the dead bodies of his own children. The crime for which Ruggieri was responsible is unspeakable. As far as retributive justice is concerned, is such endless, God-forsaken punishment, *from Dante's God of love,* commensurate with any crime? Regarding Eichmann, Arendt simply quotes Scripture, though the emphasis is hers: "It were better *for him* had he not been born."

Many commentators on Arendt's thought have distinguished the crime against humanity from the criminal who committed it.* But this is not the same at all as distinguishing the monstrosity of the deeds from the banality of the evil for which, according to Arendt, Eichmann was judged and hanged. She clarifies what she means in a thinking dialogue, conducted primarily with Nietzsche. Nietzsche begins by stating "how false" is the idea that the "value" of an act depends on what preceded it in consciousness, which would turn acts into "subjective phenomena." Nor can an act's "value" be equated with its consequences, "which are unknown." So, is the "value" of an act itself unknown? Nietzsche goes on to speak of the "denaturalization of morality," by which he means the separation of the act from the actor, which leads to the notion of contempt against "sin," and the belief that there are "good and bad acts in themselves." Nietzsche opposes to this what he calls the restoration of "nature," implying that any

---

* I remember well an eminent scholar of Arendt's thought exclaiming: "Arendt never claimed that evil was banal." What then does "the banality of evil" mean?

act "in itself is perfectly devoid of value." So far this reminds one of David Hume's impeccably skeptical demonstrations that good and bad are not "matters of fact." The same act can be in one case a privilege, in another a stigma, of which today in governmental and financial affairs we have one example after another. To Nietzsche it is the *self-relatedness* of judges that interprets an act, as well as the actor who performs it, "in relation to its usefulness or harmfulness to themselves."*

Does this accord with Arendt's experience? At first, to her, the total domination of totalitarian governments, that is, their elimination of human freedom, was the appearance of radical evil in the world. Her judgment then was generally approved of and acclaimed. On the other hand, her startling new understanding of the evil of the crime against humanity, and her judgment of its perpetrator Eichmann, were generally denied and condemned. There is no relativism possible here. Plurality itself, including human plurality, is a universal law for Arendt, and whoever infringes upon it, wittingly or not, loses his or her right to live under it. But at the same time this is decidedly not a matter of absolutes. Without standards to judge the unprecedented, the faculty of judgment is fallible in matters of self-interest; it is reliable only in a community of judges, a public entity that discerns the common concerns engendered by, and engendering, public *spirit*. The only valid criteria of a plurality of judges are examples, often misleadingly called precedents, recognized and known to all of them. St. Francis is an example, and so is Bonaparte, and Bluebeard, and in time Arendt's judgment of Eichmann may become exemplary.

* See "Some Questions of Moral Philosophy," in *Responsibility and Judgment.*

ACKNOWLEDGMENTS

Instead of thanking again the many friends, mentors, and helpmates acknowledged in previous volumes of Hannah Arendt's unpublished and uncollected writings—which like this one have been seen into publication by Daniel Frank—here I will mention only a few new names. This by no means implies that my gratitude to those previously cited has diminished; on the contrary, it has grown greater, not least to the few who have since disappeared from the world we shared.

The Hannah Arendt Center for Politics and Humanities at Bard College is a dynamic organization under the direction of the open-minded, generous, and indefatigable Roger Berkowitz. The Center has attracted scholars and students from around the world, creating a sort of international commons in which today's problems and predicaments are discussed and interpreted from a grand diversity of points of view. The Center's activities are frequently anchored in what Arendt wrote and warned of more than forty years ago.

In the north of Germany, the Karl Jaspers *Gesellschaft* is situated in Oldenburg, the city of Jaspers's birth. The head of the imposing Jaspers Haus, Matthias Bormuth, is a psychologist and a philosopher, as was Jaspers himself. Matthias Bormuth has written and spoken of the depth of understanding between Jaspers and Arendt, examining the meaning of the friendship they exemplified with special regard for the millions upon millions—more today than ever before—of the world's uprooted and homeless people. We are all in his debt for that.

Hannah Arendt speaks and writes in a voice that attracts both scholars and those more active in the play of the world. Of course, as no one knew better than she, those are not two entirely distinct classes. It has been my good fortune to have encountered two people inspired by Arendt, one of whom, Thomas Wild, for me chiefly represents scholarship, and the other, Fred Dewey, chiefly represents action. Thomas Wild is the subtlest reader of Arendt I have encountered in many years; his teaching and writings cast new light on her spoken and written words, a light that reveals hitherto unanticipated relations of her way of thinking to the world in and about which she thinks. Fred Dewey, the great grandson of America's premier philosopher, is devoted to Arendt, and, which is rare, finds it urgent to put her thought into action, not in some envisioned future, but amidst the insecurity and instability of the world in which we live now. To that end, he has performed her thinking—no easy undertaking—for audiences whom he regards and addresses as citizens of poleis, in this country and throughout Western Europe. With deepest appreciation this book is dedicated to Thomas Wild and Fred Dewey.

Jerome Kohn

PUBLICATION HISTORY

A listing of original publication information for previously published material and sources for previously unpublished material:

"Karl Marx and the Tradition of Western Political Thought" was originally published in *Social Research*, volume 69, no. 2 (Summer 2002).

"The Great Tradition"

 I. "Law and Power" was originally published in *Social Research*, volume 74, no. 3 (Fall 2007).

 II. "Ruling and Being Ruled" was originally published in *Social Research*, volume 74, no. 4 (Winter 2007).

"Authority in the Twentieth Century" was originally Arendt's contribution to a conference on "The Future of Freedom" in Milan, Italy, in September 1955. The conference was sponsored by the Congress for Cultural Freedom, which was surreptitiously funded by the CIA.

"Letter to Robert M. Hutchins" can be found in the Hannah Arendt Papers, Manuscript Division, Library of Congress, Washington, D.C.

"The Hungarian Revolution and Totalitarian Imperialism" was originally published in slightly different form in the second edition of *The Origins of Totalitarianism* (Cleveland: Meridian, 1958).

"Totalitarianism" was originally published in *The Meridian* (Fall 1958).

"Culture and Politics" can be found in the Hannah Arendt Papers, Manuscript Division, Library of Congress, Washington, D.C.

"Challenges to Traditional Ethics: A Response to Michael Polanyi" can be found in the Hannah Arendt Papers, Manuscript Division, Library of Congress, Washington, D.C. Hannah Arendt presented this paper as a response to Michael Polanyi's "Beyond Nihilism" at the Sixteenth

Conference on Science: Philosophy and Religion in Their Relation to the Democratic Way of Life in 1960.

"Reflections on the 1960 National Conventions: Kennedy vs. Nixon" can be found in the Hannah Arendt Papers, Manuscript Division, Library of Congress, Washington, D.C.

"Action and the 'Pursuit of Happiness'" was originally published in *Commentary* (Fall 1960).

"Freedom and Politics: A Lecture" was originally published, in slightly different form, in *Chicago Review,* volume 14, no. 1 (Spring 1961).

"The Cold War and the West" was originally published in *Partisan Review* (Winter 1962).

"Nation-State and Democracy" can be found in the Hannah Arendt Papers, Manuscript Division, Library of Congress, Washington, D.C.

"Kennedy and After" was originally published in *The New York Review of Books* (December 26, 1963).

"Nathalie Sarraute" was originally published in *The New York Review of Books* (March 5, 1964).

"'As if Speaking to a Brick Wall': *A Conversation with Joachim Fest*" was originally published in *The Last Interview and Other Conversations* by Hannah Arendt (New York: Melville House, 2013).

"Labor, Work, Action" was originally published in English in *Amor Mundi,* ed. J. W. Bernauer (Dordrecht, Netherlands: Martinus Nijhoff Publishers, 1987).

"Politics and Crime: An Exchange of Letters" can be found in the Hannah Arendt Papers, Manuscript Division, Library of Congress, Washington, D.C.

"Introduction to *The Warriors* by J. Glenn Gray" was originally published in the Torchbooks edition of *The Warriors* (New York: Harper & Row, 1967).

"On the Human Condition" was originally published in *The Evolving Society: First Annual Conference on the Cybercultural Revolution,* ed. Alice Mary Hilton (New York: Institute of Cybercultural Research, 1966).

"The Crisis Character of Modern Society" was originally published in *Christianity and Crisis,* volume 26, no. 9 (May 30, 1966).

"Revolution and Freedom" can be found in the Hannah Arendt Papers, Manuscript Division, Library of Congress, Washington, D.C.

"Is America by Nature a Violent Society?" was originally published in an edited version as "Lawlessness Is Inherent in the Uprooted" in *The New York Times Magazine* (1965).

"*The Possessed*" can be found in the Hannah Arendt Papers, Manuscript Division, Library of Congress, Washington, D.C.

"The Freedom to Be Free: The Conditions and Meaning of Revolution" can be found in the Hannah Arendt Papers, Manuscript Division, Library of Congress, Washington, D.C.

"Imagination" was originally published in *Lectures on Kant's Political Philosophy*, ed. Ronald Beiner (Chicago: University of Chicago Press, 1989).

"He's All Dwight" was originally published in *The New York Review of Books* (August 1, 1968).

"Emerson-Thoreau Medal Address" can be found in the Hannah Arendt Papers, Manuscript Division, Library of Congress, Washington, D.C., and was delivered at the American Academy of Arts and Sciences on April 9, 1969.

"The Archimedean Point" was originally published in *Ingenor* 6, College of Engineering (University of Michigan: Spring 1969).

"Heidegger at Eighty" appeared in English in *The New York Review of Books* (October 1971). Originally written and published in German in 1969 for Martin Heidegger's eightieth birthday. Also published in *Letters, 1925–1975, Hannah Arendt and Martin Heidegger,* ed. Ursula Ludz; trans. Andrew Shields (Orlando: Harcourt, 2004).

"For Martin Heidegger" can be found in the Hannah Arendt Papers, Manuscript Division, Library of Congress, Washington, D.C.

"War Crimes and the American Conscience" was originally published in *War Crimes and the American Conscience*, ed. Erwin Knoll and Judith Nies McFadden (New York: Holt, Rinehart, Winston, 1970).

"Letter to the Editor of *The New York Review of Books*" was originally published in *The New York Review of Books* (November 6, 1970) in response to J. M. Cameron's review of *Between Past and Future* and *Men in Dark Times*.

"Values in Contemporary Society" can be found in the Hannah Arendt Papers, Manuscript Division, Library of Congress, Washington, D.C., July 13, 1972.

"Hannah Arendt on Hannah Arendt" was originally published in *The Recovery of the Public World*, ed. Melyvn A. Hill (New York: St. Martin's Press, 1979).

"Remarks" can be found in the Hannah Arendt Papers, Manuscript Division, Library of Congress, Washington, D.C.

"Address to the Advisory Council on Philosophy of Princeton University" can be found in the Hannah Arendt Papers, Manuscript Division, Library of Congress, Washington, D.C.

"Interview with Roger Errera," 1973, a version of which was published in *The Last Interview and Other Conversations*, trans. Andrew Brown (New York: Melville House, 2013).

"Public Rights and Private Interests: A Response to Charles Frankel" was originally published in *Small Comforts for Hard Times: Humanists on Public Policy*, ed. M. Mooney and F. Stuber (New York: Columbia University Press, 1977).

"Preliminary Remarks About the Life of the Mind" can be found in the Hannah Arendt Papers, Manuscript Division, Library of Congress, Washington, D.C.

"Transition" can be found in the Hannah Arendt Papers, Manuscript Division, Library of Congress, Washington, D.C.

"Remembering Wystan H. Auden, Who Died in the Night of the Twenty-eighth of September, 1973" was originally published in *The New Yorker* (January 20, 1975).

THINKING WITHOUT A BANISTER

KARL MARX AND THE TRADITION OF WESTERN POLITICAL THOUGHT

I
The Broken Thread of Tradition

It has never been easy to think and write about Karl Marx. His impact on the already existing parties of the workers, who had only recently won full legal equality and political franchise in the nation-states, was immediate and far-reaching. His neglect, moreover, by the academic, scholarly world hardly lasted more than two decades after his death, and since then his influence has risen, spreading from strict Marxism, which already by the twenties had become somewhat outmoded, to the entire field of social and historical sciences. More recently, his influence has been frequently denied. That is not, however, because Marx's thought and the methods he introduced have been abandoned, but rather because they have become so axiomatic that their origin is no longer remembered. The difficulties that previously prevailed in dealing with Marx, however, were of an academic nature compared with the difficulties that confront us now. To a certain extent they were similar to those that arose in the treatment of Nietzsche and, to a lesser extent, Kierkegaard: struggles pro and contra were so fierce, the misunderstandings that developed within them so tremendous, that it was difficult to say exactly what or who one was thinking and talking about. In the case of Marx, the difficulties were obviously even greater because they concerned politics: from the very beginning positions pro and contra fell into the conventional lines of party politics, so that to his partisans, whoever spoke for Marx was deemed "progressive," and whoever spoke against him "reactionary."

This situation changed for the worse when, with the rise of one Marxian party, Marxism became (or appeared to become) the ruling ideology of a great power. It now seemed that the discussion of Marx was bound up not only with party but also with power politics, and not only with domestic but also with world political concerns. And while the figure of Marx himself, now even more so than before, was dragged into the arena of politics, his influence on modern intellectuals rose to new heights: the chief fact for them, and not wrongly so, was that for the first time a thinker, rather than a practical statesman or politician, had inspired the policies of a great nation, thereby making the weight of thought felt in the entire realm of political activity. Since Marx's idea of right government, outlined first as the dictatorship of the proletariat, which was to be followed by a classless and stateless society, had become the official aim of one country and of political movements throughout the world, then, certainly, Plato's dream of subjecting political action to the strict tenets of philosophical thought had become a reality. Marx attained, albeit posthumously, what Plato in vain had attempted at the court of Dionysios in Sicily.* Marxism and its influence in the modern world became what it is today because of this twofold influence and representation, first by the political parties of the working classes, and, second, by the admiration of the intellectuals, not of Soviet Russia per se, but for the fact that Bolshevism is, or pretends to be, Marxist.

To be sure, Marxism in this sense has done as much to hide and obliterate the actual teachings of Marx as it has to propagate them. If we want to find out who Marx was, what he thought, and how he stands in the tradition of political thought, Marxism all too easily appears mainly as a nuisance—more so than, but not essentially different from, Hegelianism or any other ism based on the writings of a single author. Through Marxism Marx himself has been praised or blamed for many things of which he was entirely innocent; for instance, for decades he was highly esteemed, or deeply resented, as the "inventor of class struggle," of which he was not only not the "inventor" (facts are not invented) but not even the discoverer.

---

* Arendt refers to Plato's legendary voyages to Syracuse, as recounted in the Seventh and Eighth *Epistles.* —Ed.

More recently, attempting to distance themselves from the name (though hardly the influence) of Marx, others have been busy proving how much he found in his avowed predecessors. This searching for influences (for instance, in the case of class struggle) even becomes a bit comical when one remembers that neither the economists of the nineteenth or eighteenth centuries nor the political philosophers of the seventeenth century were needed for a discovery of what was already present in Aristotle. Aristotle defined the substance of democratic government as rule by the poor and of oligarchic government as rule by the rich, and stressed this to the extent that he discarded the content of those already traditional terms, namely, rule by the many and rule by the few. He insisted that a government of the poor be called a democracy, and that a government of the rich be called an oligarchy, even if the rich should outnumber the poor.* The political relevance of class struggle could hardly be more emphatically stated than by basing two distinct forms of government on it. Nor can Marx be credited with having elevated this political and economic fact into the realm of history. For such elevation had been current ever since Hegel encountered Napoleon Bonaparte, seeing in him the "world spirit on horseback."

But the challenge with which Marx confronts us today is much more serious than these academic quarrels over influences and priorities. The fact that one form of totalitarian domination uses, and apparently developed directly from, Marxism, is of course the most formidable charge ever raised against Marx. And that charge cannot be brushed off as easily as can charges of a similar nature—against Nietzsche, Hegel, Luther, or Plato, all of whom, and many more, have at one time or another been accused of being the ancestors of Nazism. Although today it is so conveniently overlooked, the fact that the Nazi version of totalitarianism could develop along lines similar to that of the Soviet, yet nevertheless use an entirely different ideology, shows at least that Marx cannot very well stand accused of having brought forth the specifically totalitarian aspects of Bolshevik domination. It is also true that the interpretations to which his teachings were subjected, through Marxism as well as through Leninism, and the decisive transfor-

* *Politics* 1279b11–1280a3. —Ed.

mation by Stalin of both Marxism and Leninism into a totalitarian ideology, can easily be demonstrated. Nevertheless it also remains a fact that there is a more direct connection between Marx and Bolshevism, as well as Marxist totalitarian movements in nontotalitarian countries, than between Nazism and any of its so-called predecessors.

It has become fashionable during the last few years to assume an unbroken line between Marx, Lenin, and Stalin, thereby accusing Marx of being the father of totalitarian domination. Very few of those who yield to this line of argument seem to be aware that to accuse Marx of totalitarianism amounts to accusing the Western tradition itself of necessarily ending in the monstrosity of this novel form of government. Whoever touches Marx touches the tradition of Western thought; thus the conservatism on which many of our new critics of Marx pride themselves is usually as great a self-misunderstanding as the revolutionary zeal of the ordinary Marxist. The few critics of Marx who are aware of the roots of Marx's thought therefore have attempted to construe a special trend in the tradition, an occidental heresy that nowadays is sometimes called Gnosticism, in recollection of one of the oldest heresies of Catholic Christianity. Yet this attempt to limit the destructiveness of totalitarianism by the consequent interpretation that it has grown directly from such a trend in the Western tradition is doomed to failure. Marx's thought cannot be limited to "immanentism," as if everything could be set right again if only we would leave utopia to the next world and not assume that everything on earth can be measured and judged by earthly yardsticks. For Marx's roots go far deeper in the tradition than even he himself knew. I think it can be shown that the line from Aristotle to Marx shows both fewer and far less decisive breaks than the line from Marx to Stalin.

The serious aspect of this situation, therefore, does not lie in the ease with which Marx can be slandered and his teachings, as well as his problems, misrepresented. The latter is of course bad enough, since, as we shall see, Marx was the first to discern certain problems arising from the industrial revolution, the distortion of which means at once the loss of an important source, and possibly help, in dealing with real predicaments that ever more urgently continue to confront us. But more serious than any of this is the fact that Marx, as distinguished from the true and not the imagined sources of the Nazi ideology of racism, clearly does belong to the tradition of Western political thought. As an ideology Marxism is doubtless the only link that binds the totalitarian form of government directly to that tradition: otherwise any attempt to deduce totalitarianism directly from a strand of occidental thought would lack even the semblance of plausibility.

A serious examination of Marx himself, as opposed to the cursory dismissal of his name and the often unconscious retention of the consequences of his teaching, is therefore somehow dangerous in two respects: it cannot but question certain trends in the social sciences that are Marxist in all but name and the depth of Marx's own thought; and it must necessarily examine the real questions and perplexities of our own tradition with which Marx himself dealt and struggled. The examination of Marx, in other words, cannot but be an examination of traditional thought insofar as it is applicable to the modern world, a world whose presence can be traced back to the industrial revolution on the one hand, and to the political revolutions of the eighteenth century on the other. The modern age presented modern man with two main problems, independent of all political events in the narrow sense of the word: the problems of *labor* and *history*. The significance of Marx's thought lies neither in his economic theories nor in its revolutionary content, but in the stubbornness with which he clung to these two chief new perplexities.

One might argue that the thread of our tradition was broken, in the sense that our traditional political categories were never meant for such a situation, when, for the first time in our history, political equality was extended to the laboring classes. That Marx at least grasped this fact and felt that an emancipation of the laboring class was possible only in a radically changed world distinguishes his thought from that of utopian socialism, the chief defect of which was not (as Marx himself believed) that it was unscientific, but its assumption that the laboring class was an underprivileged group and that the fight for its liberation was a fight for social justice. That the older convictions of Christian charity should develop into fierce passions of social justice is understandable enough at a time when the means to put an end to certain forms of misery were so evidently present. Yet such passions were and are "outdated" in the sense that they had ceased to be applicable to any social group but rather only to individuals. What Marx understood was that labor itself had undergone a decisive change in the modern world: that it had not only become the source of all wealth, and consequently the origin of all social values, but that all men, independent of class origin, were sooner or later destined to become laborers, and that those who could not be adjusted into this process of labor would be seen and judged by society as mere parasites. To put it another way: while others were concerned with this or that right of the laboring class, Marx already foresaw the time when, not this class, but the consciousness that corresponded to it, and to its importance for society as a whole, would decree that no one would have any rights, not even the right to stay alive, who was not a laborer. The result of this process of course has not been the elimination of all other occupations, but the reinterpretation of all human activities as laboring activities.

From the viewpoint of the history of ideas, one might argue with almost equal right that the thread of tradition was also broken the moment that History not only entered human thought but became its *absolute*. Indeed, this had happened not with Marx but with Hegel, whose entire philosophy is a philosophy of history, or rather, one that dissolved all previous philosophic as well as all other thought into history. After Hegel had historicized even logic, and after Darwin, through the idea of evolution, had historicized even nature, there seemed nothing left that could withstand the mighty onslaught of historical categories. The conclusion that Marx quite properly drew from this spiritual (*geistliche*) situation was his attempt to eliminate history altogether. For Hegel, thinking historically, the meaning of a story can emerge only when it has come to an end. End and truth have become identical; truth appears when everything is at its end, which is to say when and only when the end is near can we learn the truth. In other words, we pay for truth with the living impulse that imbues an era, although of course not necessarily with our own lives. The manifold modern versions of an antagonism between life and spirit, especially in the Nietzschean form, have their source in this historicization of all our spiritual categories, that is, in an antagonism between life and truth.

What Hegel states about philosophy in general, that "the owl of Minerva spreads her wings only with the falling of the dusk,"* holds only for a phi-losophy of history, that is, it is true of history and corresponds to the view of historians. Hegel of course was encouraged to take this view because he thought that philosophy had really begun in Greece with Plato and Aristo-tle, who wrote when the polis and the glory of Greek history were at their end. Today we know that Plato and Aristotle were the culmination rather than the beginning of Greek philosophic thought, which had begun its flight when Greece had reached or nearly reached its climax. What remains true, however, is that Plato as well as Aristotle became the beginning of the occidental philosophic tradition, and that this beginning, as distinguished from the beginning of Greek philosophic thought, occurred when Greek political life was indeed approaching its end. The problem then arose of how man, if he is to live in a polis, can live outside of politics; this problem, in what sometimes seems a strange resemblance to our own times, quickly became the question of how it is possible to live without belonging to any polity, that is, in the state of *apolity*, or what we today would call state-lessness.

One could say that the problem of labor indicates the political side, and the problem of history the spiritual side, of the perplexities that arose at the end of the eighteenth century and emerged fully in the middle of the nineteenth. Insofar as we still live with and in these perplexities, which meanwhile have become much sharper in fact while much less articulate in theoretical formulation, we are still Marx's contemporaries. The enormous influence that Marx still exerts in almost all parts of the world seems to con-firm this. Yet this is true only to the extent that we choose not to consider certain events of the twentieth century; that is, those events that ultimately led to the entirely novel form of government we know as totalitarian domi-nation. The thread of our tradition, in the sense of a continuous history, broke only with the emergence of totalitarian institutions and policies that

---

* This famous image appears in the following sentence from Hegel's preface to his *Philosophy of Right: Wenn die Philosophie ihr Grau in Grau malt, dann ist eine Gestalt des Lebens alt geworden, und mit Grau in Grau lässt sie sich nicht verjüngen, sondern nur erkennen; die Eule der Minerva beginnt erst mit der einbrechenden Dämmerung ihren Flug.* (When philosophy paints its gray in gray, then has a shape of life grown old. By philosophy's gray in gray it cannot be rejuvenated but only discerned. The owl of Minerva spreads her wings only with the falling of the dusk.) —Ed.

no longer could be comprehended through the categories of traditional thought. These unprecedented institutions and policies issued in crimes that cannot be judged by traditional moral standards, or punished within the existing legal framework of a civilization whose juridical cornerstone had been the command *Thou shalt not kill.*

The distinction between what can and what cannot be comprehended in terms of the tradition may appear unduly academic. Among the conspicuous reflections of the crisis of the present century—and one of the outstanding indications that it indeed involved nothing less than a breakdown of the tradition—has been the learned attempts by many scholars to date the origin of the crisis. With almost equal plausibility that origin has been seen in historical moments ranging between the fourth century before and the nineteenth century after Christ. Against all such theories, I propose to accept the rise of totalitarianism as a demonstrably new form of government, as an event that, at least politically, palpably concerns the lives of all of us, not only the thoughts of a relatively few individuals or the destinies of certain specific national or social groups. Only this event, with its concomitant change of all political conditions and relationships previously existing on earth, rendered irreparable the various "breaks" which retrospectively have been seen in its wake. Totalitarianism as an event has made the break in our tradition an accomplished fact, and as an event it could never have been foreseen or forethought, much less predicted or "caused," by any single man. So far are we from being able to deduce what actually happened from past spiritual or material "causes" that all such factors appear to be causes only in the light cast by the event, illuminating both itself and its past.

In this sense, then, we are no longer the contemporaries of Marx. And it is from this viewpoint that Marx acquires a new significance for us. He is the one great man of the past who not only was already concerned with predicaments that are still with us, but whose thought could also be used and misused by one of the forms of totalitarianism. Thus Marx seems to provide a reliable link for us back into the tradition, because he himself was more firmly rooted in it (even when he thought he was rebelling against it, turning it upside down, or escaping from the priority of theoretical-intepretative analysis into historical-political action) than we can ever be again. For us totalitarianism necessarily has become the central event of our times and, consequently, the break in tradition a *fait accompli*. Because Marx concerned himself with the few new elementary facts for which the tradition itself did not provide a categorical framework, his success or failure therefore enables us to judge the success or failure of the tradition itself in regard to these facts, even before its moral, legal, theoretical, and practical standards, together with its political institutions and forms of organization, broke down spectacularly. That Marx still looms so large in our present world is indeed the measure of his greatness. That he could prove of use to totalitarianism (though certainly he can never be said to have been its "cause") is a sign of the actual relevance of his thought, even though at the same time it is also the measure of his ultimate failure. Marx lived in a changing world and his greatness was the precision with which he grasped the center of this change. We live in a world whose main feature is change, a world in which change itself has become a matter of course to such an extent that we are in danger of forgetting that which has changed altogether.

The first great challenge to tradition came when Hegel interpreted the world as subject to change in the sense of historical movement. Marx's own challenge to tradition—"The philosophers have only *interpreted* the world . . . the point, however, is to *change* it"*—was one among many possible conclusions that might be derived from Hegel's system. To us it sounds as though Marx were saying: The world the philosophers of the past have interpreted, and that the last of them understood in terms of a continuous, self-developing history, is in fact changing beyond recognition. Let us try to take control of this process and change the world in accordance with our tradition. By "tradition" Marx always understood the tradition of philosophy, to which the one surviving class, representing humanity as a whole, would ultimately become the heir. Marx himself meant that the irresistible motion of history one day would stop, that further change would be ruled out when the world had undergone its last and decisive change. This side of Marx's teaching is usually dismissed as its utopian element: the end in view of a classless society when history itself would come to a

---

* *Theses on Feuerbach*, XI. —Ed.

halt once its motor—class struggle—would have ceased. In fact it indicates that in some fundamental aspects Marx was more closely bound to the tradition than Hegel was. The revolutionary element in Marx's teachings, therefore, is only superficially contained in his version of an end brought about by actual revolution, the outcome of which, according to him, would have coincided rather curiously with the ideal of life associated with the Greek city-states. The really anti-traditional and unprecedented side of his thought is his glorification of labor, and his reinterpretation of the class—the working class—that philosophy since its beginning had always despised. Labor, the human activity of this class, was deemed so irrelevant that philosophy had not even bothered to interpret and understand it. In order to grasp the political importance of the emancipation of labor, and Marx's corresponding dignification of labor as the most fundamental of all human activities, it may be well just to mention, at the beginning of these reflections, the distinction between labor and work that, although largely unarticulated, has been decisive for the whole tradition, and that, only recently, and partly because of Marx's teachings, has become blurred.

Marx is the only thinker of the nineteenth century who took its central event, the emancipation of the working class, seriously in philosophic terms. Marx's great influence today is still due to this one fact, which also, to a large extent, explains how his thought could become so useful for purposes of totalitarian domination. The Soviet Union, which from the moment of its foundation called itself a republic of workers and peasants, may have deprived its workers of all the rights they enjoy in the free world. Yet its ideology is primarily an ideology designed for laborers, and labor, as distinguished from all other human activities, has remained its highest "value," the only distinction it recognizes. In this respect it is, moreover, only the most radical version of our own society, which more and more tends also to become a society of laborers. On the other hand, the Soviet Union's means of domination, unprecedented as they are in political history and unknown to political thought, have frequently (and not altogether wrongly) been called the means of a slave society. Although this term does not do justice to the nonutilitarian character of total domination, it does indicate the total character of the subjection itself. That such subjection is worsened when the utilitarian motive, which had been the chief guarantee of a slave's life, no longer exists, is obvious. But then slavery, at least in Western society, never has been a form of government and therefore never, strictly speaking, has belonged in the political realm. Only those who were not slaves were able to take part in political life under normal, nontyrannical government. But even under tyranny the sphere of private life was left intact, which is to say that there was left a sort of freedom that no slave might enjoy.

But whether Marx, whose influences on politics was tremendous, was ever genuinely interested in politics as such may justly be doubted. The fact is that his interpretation, or rather, glorification of labor, while only following the course of events, in itself could not fail to introduce a complete reversal of all traditional political values. It was not the political emancipation of the working class, the equality for all that for the first time in history included menial workers, that was decisive, but rather the consequence that from now on labor as a human activity no longer belonged to the strictly private realm of life: it became a public political fact of the first order. By this I do not refer to the economic sphere of life; this sphere as a whole always was a matter of public concern. But this sphere is only to a very small extent the sphere of labor.

Labor is necessarily prior to any economy, which is to say that the organized attempt of men living together, handling and securing both the needs and the luxuries of life, starts with and requires labor even when its economy has been developed to the highest degree. As the elementary activity necessary for the mere conservation of life, labor had always been thought of as a curse, in the sense that it made life hard, preventing it from ever becoming easy and thereby distinguishing it from the lives of the Olympian gods.* That human life is not easy is only another way of saying that in

---

* In a July 1953 entry in her *Denktagebuch* (forthcoming from Schocken Books) Arendt writes: *Burckhardt* (Griechische Kulturgeschichte I, 355–56), *macht aufmerksam, dass die griechischen Götter keiner Dienerschaft bedurften: nur die Menschen brauchen Sklaven; die Götter waren frei von irdischer Notdurft, wenn auch dem Schicksal unterworfen. Diese Freiheit hängt mit ihrer Unsterblichkeit zusammen? Jedenfalls sind die griechischen Götter gekennzeichnet durch das "leichte" leben, ihr Dasein ist mühelos.* (Burckhardt remarks that the Greek gods had no need of servants: only men need slaves; the gods are free of all earthly needs, even if they are subject to fate. Is this freedom connected to their immortality? In any case, the Greek gods are characterized by their "easy" life, their existence is *painless*.) This train of thought recurs with a twist in one of the two epigraphs Arendt selected in 1975 for her book *Judg-*

its most elementary aspect it is subject to necessity, that it is not and never can become free from coercion, for coercion is first felt in the peculiarly all-overwhelming urges of our bodies. People who do nothing but cater to these elementary coercive needs were traditionally deemed unfree by definition—that is, they were considered unready to exercise the functions of free citizens. Therefore those who did this work for others in order to free them from fulfilling the necessities of life themselves were known as slaves.

In every civilization labor is the activity that enables the public realm to put at our disposal what we consume. Labor as the metabolism with nature is not primarily productive but consumptive, and its necessity would remain so even if no productivity, no addition to the common world, were ever associated with it. It is because of the connection of all laboring activity to the strictly biological needs of our bodies that it traditionally was deemed to belong to the lower, almost animal-like functions of human life, and as such considered a strictly private matter. Public political life began where this realm of the private ended, or in other words whenever those needs could be transcended into a common world, a world in between men transcending the metabolism with nature of each of its individuals. Politics in the original Greek sense of the word began with the liberation from labor, and in spite of many variations remained the same in this respect for nearly three thousand years; and this, as we know, was first made possible through the institution of slavery. Slavery therefore was not a part of Greek political life but the condition of *politeuein*, of all those activities that for the Greeks fulfilled the life of the citizen. As such it was based on rule over slaves, but was itself not divided into ruling and being ruled; for the early Greeks ruling over slaves was a pre-political condition of *politeuein*, of being political. This original form of politics underwent a decisive change in the period of decay of the Greek polis, a decay that coincided with that culmination of Greek philosophy, which was to become authoritative for all times up to our own. The suspicion and contempt of the philosophers

---

ing, which she did not live to write. Late in the second part of *Faust* Goethe wrote that if one could renounce all magic and stand before nature simply as a human being, then the pain, toil, and labor of being a man would be worthwhile: *Da wär's der Mühe wert ein Mensch zu sein.* —Ed.

concerned the activity of *politeuein* itself but not the basis on which it rested. In the stead of *politeuein*, which had been made possible by liberation from the necessities of biological life, came the ideal of *philosophein*, the activity of philosophizing. From then on the distinction between ruling and being ruled invaded the realm of politics directly; and the rule over the necessities of life became the precondition, not of politics, but of philosophy, that is, ruling over whatever was materially needed to enable man to lead the higher, philosophic life took the place of *politeuein*. In both cases the earlier experience of an activity fulfilling the life of the citizen was all but lost to the tradition. The emancipation of labor, both as the glorification of the laboring activity and as the political equality of the working class, would not have been possible if the original meaning of politics—in which a political realm centered around labor would have been a contradiction in terms—had not been lost.

When Marx made labor the most important activity of man, he was saying, in terms of the tradition, that not freedom but compulsion is what makes man human. When he added that nobody could be free who rules over others he was saying, again in terms of the tradition, what Hegel, in the famous master-servant dialectic, had only less forcefully said before him: that no one can be free, neither those enslaved by necessity nor those enslaved by the necessity to rule. In this Marx not only appeared to contradict himself, insofar as he promised freedom for all at the same moment he denied it to all, but to reverse the very meaning of freedom, based as it had been on the freedom from that compulsion we naturally and originally suffer under the human condition.

Equality for workers and the dignification of the laboring activity were of such tremendous and revolutionary importance because the occidental attitude to labor had been so closely connected with its attitude to life in the purely biological sense. And this sense was stressed even more forcefully than before in Marx's own definition of labor as man's metabolism with nature. The laborers were not only those who were ruled by the free in order not to be enslaved to the sheer necessities of life; they were, psychologically speaking, also those who stood accused of *philopsychia*, of love of life for life's own sake. *Philopsychia* in fact is what distinguished the slave from the free man. In ancient times the free man found his hero in Achilles, who exchanged a short life for the eternal fame of greatness; after the fourth century before Christ the free man became the philosopher who devoted his life to *theorein*, to the "contemplation" of eternal truths, or, in the Middle Ages, to the salvation of his eternal soul. Insofar as the political realm was constituted by free men, labor was eliminated from it; and in all these instances, even those in which the value of political action was most limited, labor was viewed as an activity without any dignity in itself whatsoever.

II
The Modern Challenge to Tradition

At the other end of this position and, as it must appear at first glance, in the most extreme opposition to it, stand three propositions that are the pillars on which Marx's whole theory and philosophy rest: first, *Labor is the Creator of Man;* second, *Violence is the midwife of History* (and, since history for Marx is past political action, this means that violence makes action not only effective but also efficient);* and third, seemingly in contradiction to the other two, *Nobody can be free who enslaves others.* Each of these propositions expresses in quintessential form one of the decisive events with which our own era began. There is first, as a result of the industrial revolution, the full political emancipation of the working class, regardless of property and skill qualifications. Never before had any political organism sought to encompass all those who actually lived in it. If we were to translate this event into the language of the seventeenth and eighteenth centuries, we would have to say that man—even in the state of nature and endowed with nothing but his working or laboring capacity—was accepted as a full citizen.

It is true that in European nation-states this all-encompassing princi-

---

* Elsewhere in these manuscripts Arendt makes the point that Marx was the first to view political history as "made by men as laboring animals. . . . Then it must be possible to make history in the process of labor, of productivity, to make history as we make things. . . . Marx's theory of history sees its decisive movement in the development of the forces of production, and the forces of production are ultimately based on labor as a *force.*" It is to be noted that throughout the Marx manuscripts, Arendt consistently translates *Arbeitskraft* as "labor *force,*" rather than the more usual "labor *power.*" —Ed.

ple was significantly qualified: only people born in a nation's territory or descended from its nationals were recognized as citizens. But this qualification had nothing to do with the new revolutionary principle itself and was not, for instance, applicable in the United States, the only country where the industrial revolution was not hampered by the transformation of feudal states into classes and therefore where the emancipation of the working class could at once achieve its true character. The class system, so greatly overrated by Marx, who knew the industrial revolution only in its European version, is actually a feudal remnant whose curious transformations are swiftly liquidated wherever the industrial revolution has run its full course. The political consequences of the emancipation of labor in America come very close to a realization of the social contract between all men, which the philosophers of the seventeenth and eighteenth centuries still thought to be either a prehistoric fact at the beginning of civilized society or a scientific figment necessary for the legitimacy of political authority.

The industrial revolution, with its unlimited demand for sheer labor force, resulted in the unheard of reinterpretation of labor as the most important quality of man. The emancipation of labor, in the double sense of emancipating the working class and dignifying the activity of laboring, indeed implied a new "social contract," that is, a new fundamental relationship between men based on what the tradition would have despised as their lowest common denominator: ownership of labor force. Marx drew the consequences of this emancipation when he said that labor, the specifically human metabolism with nature, was the most elementary human distinction, that which intrinsically distinguished human from animal life.

Second, there was the tremendous fact of the French and American revolutions. In these events violence had brought about not some haphazard slaughter whose meaning reveals itself only to later generations, or is comprehensible only from the viewpoint of the interested parties, but an entirely new body politic. In its outlines, and in the case of the United States in many details, this body politic had been drawn up by the eighteenth-century *philosophes* and ideologues, that is, by those who perceived an idea that needed nothing but the helping hand of violence to be realized.

Third, the most challenging consequence of the French and American revolutions was the idea of equality: the idea of a society in which nobody should be a master and nobody a servant. All the modern and not so modern objections—that equality and freedom are mutually exclusive, that they cannot exist side by side, that freedom presupposes rule over others, and that equality of all is nothing but the well-known condition of tyranny or leads to it—neglect the great pathos of the eighteenth-century revolutions and their challenge to all previously held conceptions of freedom. When Marx said that nobody can be free who rules over others, he summed up in one great proposition what before him Hegel, as previously indicated, had been intent on proving in the famous dialectic of master and servant: that each master is the slave of his servant, and that each servant eventually becomes his master's master.

The basic self-contradiction in which Marx's whole work, from the early writings to the third volume of *Capital*, is caught (and which can be expressed in various ways, such as that he needed violence to abolish violence, that the goal of history is to end history, that labor is the only productive activity of man but that the development of man's productive forces will eventually lead to the abolition of labor, etc.) arises from this insistence on freedom. For when Marx stated that labor is the most important activity of man, he was saying in terms of the tradition that not freedom but necessity is what makes man human. And he followed this line of thought throughout his philosophy of history, according to which the development of mankind is ruled by, and the meaning of history contained in, the law of historical movement, the political motor of which is class struggle and whose natural irresistible driving force is the development of man's laboring capacity. When under the influence of the French Revolution he added to this that violence is the midwife of History, he denied in terms of the tradition the very substantial content of freedom contained in the human capacity of speech. And he followed this line of thought to its ultimate consequences in his theory of ideologies, according to which all activities of man that express themselves in the spoken word, from legal and political institutions to poetry and philosophy, were mere and perhaps unconscious pretexts for, or justifications of, violent deeds. (An ideology, according to Marx, articulates what somebody pretends to be for the sake of his active role in the world; all past laws, religions, and philosophies are such ideologies.)

From this it follows—and this was already clear in Marx's own historical writings and has become even more manifest in all strictly Marxist historiography—that history, which is the record of past political action, shows its true, undistorted face only in wars and revolutions; and that political activity, if it is not direct, violent action, must be understood as either the preparation of future violence or the consequence of past violence. The development of capitalism is essentially the consequence of the violence of original accumulation, just as the development of the working class is essentially the preparation for the day of revolution. (When Lenin added that the twentieth century was all too likely to become a century of wars and revolutions, he likewise meant that it will be the century in which history comes to a head and shows its true face.) Here again Marx turned at least one strand of our tradition upside down. Since Plato it had become axiomatic that "it lies in the nature of *praxis* to partake less of truth than speech." According to Marx, it is not only *praxis* per se that shows more truth than speech, but the one kind of *praxis* that has severed all bonds with speech. For violence, in distinction to all other kinds of human action, is mute by definition. Speech on the other hand is not only deemed to partake less of truth than action, but is now conceived to be mere "ideological" talk whose chief function is to conceal the truth.

Marx's conviction concerning violence is not less heretical in terms of the tradition than his conviction concerning labor, and both are closely interrelated. The statement *labor created man,* consciously formulated against the traditional dogma *God created man,* has its correlation in the affirmation that violence reveals, which stands against the traditional notion that the word of God is revelation. This Jewish-Christian understanding of the word of God, the *logos theou,* was never incompatible with the Greek conception of *logos* and has made it possible, throughout our tradition, for human speech to retain its revelatory capacity, so that it could be trusted as an instrument for communication between men as well as an instrument of "rational," that is, truth-seeking thought. The basic mistrust of speech, as represented in Marx's theory of ideologies—preceded by Descartes' terrible suspicion that an evil spirit may conceal the truth from man—has proved itself to be a fundamental and efficient onslaught on religion precisely because it is an onslaught on philosophy as well.

As a matter of course Marx takes this position to be the foundation of modern science; science, according to him, "would be superfluous if the appearance and essence of things coincided." That appearance as such was no longer thought capable of revealing essence or (and this is essentially the same) that appearance itself had become mute and no longer spoke to men who mistrusted their senses and all sense perception, is closely connected with the glorification of mute violence. Like the glorification of labor, politically this was an onslaught of freedom, because it implied the glorification of compulsion and natural necessity. But to conclude from this that Marx's longing for the "realm of freedom" was sheer hypocrisy, or that his statement that nobody can be free who rules over others is merely inconsistent, means not only to underrate the relevance of Marx's work, but also to underestimate the objective difficulties and obstacles to all so-called traditional values in the modern world.

Marx's self-contradiction is most striking in the few paragraphs that outline the ideal future society and that are frequently dismissed as utopian. They cannot be dismissed because they constitute the center of Marx's work and express most clearly its original impulses. Moreover, if utopia means that this society has no *topos,* no geographical and historical place on earth, it is certainly not utopian: its geographical *topos* is Athens and its place in history is the fifth century before Christ. In Marx's future society the state has withered away; there is no longer any distinction between rulers and ruled and rulership no longer exists. This corresponds to life in the ancient Greek city-state, which, although it was based on rulership over slaves as its pre-political condition, had excluded rulership from the intercourse of its free citizens. In Herodotus' great definition (to which Marx's statement conforms almost textually), a man is free who wants "neither to rule nor to be ruled." Along with the state, violence in all its forms is gone, and administration has taken the place of police and army; the police are superfluous, because the legislator has become a "natural scientist who does not make or invent laws, but only formulates them," so that man has only to live in conformity with his own nature to remain within the realm of the law. The expectation that it will be easy for men to follow the few elementary rules of behavior discovered and laid down thousands of years ago (as Lenin once strikingly expressed it)* in a society without property conflicts is "utopian" only if one assumes that human nature is corrupt or that human laws are not derived from natural law. But here again there is a striking resemblance to a city-state in which the citizens themselves were supposed to execute death sentences pronounced against them in accordance with the laws, so that they are not killed by special forces trained in the use of the means of violence, but rather helped by guardians to commit suicide. The superfluousness of an army, moreover, follows logically as soon as we assume with Marx that this life of the Athenian city-state has ceased to be confined to the polis and now encompasses the whole world.

Most striking of all is of course Marx's insistence that he does not want to "liberate labor," which already is free in all civilized countries, but to "abolish labor altogether." And by labor Marx here does not mean only that necessary "metabolism with nature," which is the natural condition of man, but the whole realm of work, of craftsmanship and art, which requires specialized training. This realm never fell under the general contempt for the drudgery of labor that is characteristic of our whole tradition and whose degradation specifically characterizes Athenian life in the fifth century. Only there do we find an almost complete leisure society in which the time and energy required for making a living were, so to speak, squeezed in between the much more important activities of *agorein*, walking and talking in the marketplace, of going to the gymnasium, of attending meetings or the theater, or of judging conflicts between citizens. Hardly anything could be more revealing of Marx's original impulses than the fact that he banishes from his future society not only the labor that was executed by slaves in antiquity, but also the activities of the *banausoi*, the craftsmen and artists: "In a communist society there are no painters, only men who, among other things, paint." The aristocratic standards of Athenian life had indeed denied freedom to those whose work still required the exertion of effort. (That effort, and not specialization, was the chief criterion

---

* In *State and Revolution,* Lenin wrote that "people will gradually become accustomed to the observance of the elementary rules of social life that have been repeated for thousands of years" (quoted by Arendt in the first edition of *The Origins of Totalitarianism*). —Ed.

can be seen from the fact that sculptors and peasants, unlike painters and shepherds, were deemed unfree.) In other words, if we insist on examining Marx's thought in the light of the tradition that began in Greece, and of a political philosophy that, either in agreement or opposition, sprang from and formulated the principal experiences of Athenian polis life, we are clearly following the central indications of Marx's work itself.

This "utopian" side of Marx's teachings constitutes a basic self-contradiction, and like all such flagrant inconsistencies in the work of great writers indicates and illuminates the center of its author's thought. In Marx's case the basic inconsistency was not even his own but already existed in clear outline in the three central events that overshadowed the entire nineteenth century: the political revolutions in France and America, the industrial revolution in the Western world, and the demand for freedom for all that was inherent in both. These three events, rather than the work of Marx, were no longer in accord with our tradition of political thought, and it is only after them that, in its brute factuality, our world has changed beyond recognition when compared with any previous era. Even before Marx had begun to write, violence had become the midwife of history, labor had become the central activity of society, and universal equality was on its way to becoming an accomplished fact. Neither Marx nor the spiritual changes that accompanied these revolutionary events, however, can be comprehended apart from the tradition they challenged. Even today our thought still moves within the framework of familiar concepts and "ideals," which are much less utopian than most believe and usually have a very definite place in history, no matter how violently they may clash with the reality in which we live and that they are supposed to grasp.

Marx was not and, as we shall see, could not have been aware that his glorification of violence and labor challenged the traditional connection between freedom and speech. He was aware, however, of the incompatibility of freedom with the necessity that is expressed by labor, and also with the compulsion that is expressed by violence. As he put it, "The realm of freedom in fact begins only where labor, conditioned by need and exterior usefulness, ends." According to the dialectics of history, necessity and compulsion could very well bring forth freedom, except that this solution does not really work if one, following Marx, defines the nature of man—

and not merely the way in which things human happen—in terms of necessity. For the free, laborless man who is supposed to emerge after the end of history would simply have lost his most essentially human capacity, just as the actions of men, once they have lost the element of violence, would have lost their specifically human efficiency.

Marx had a right not to be aware of the intimate relationship between speech and freedom as we know it from the two-sided statement of Aristotle: that a free man is a member of a polis and that the members of a polis are distinguished from the barbarians through the faculty of speech. These two connected statements had already been torn asunder by a tradition that translated the one by declaring that man is a social being, a banality for which one would not have needed Aristotle, and the other by defining man as the *animal rationale,* the reasoning animal. In both instances, the political point of Aristotle's insight as well as his concept of freedom, which corresponded with the experience of the Greek *politēs,* was lost.

The word *politikon* no longer meant a unique, outstanding way of life, of being-together, in which the truly human capacities of man, as distinguished from his mere animal characteristics, could show and prove themselves. It had come to signify an all-embracing quality that men share with many animal species, which perhaps was best expressed in the Stoic concept of mankind as one gigantic herd under one superhuman shepherd. The word *logos,* which in classical Greek usage equivocally meant both word and reason, and thereby preserved a unity between the capacity of speech and the capacity of thought, became *ratio.* The chief political difference between *ratio* and *logos* is that the former primarily resides in, and relates to, a reasoning individual in his singularity, who then uses words in order to express his thoughts to others, while *logos* is essentially related to others and therefore by its very nature political. What Aristotle had seen as one and the same human quality, to live together with others in the *modus* of speaking, now became two distinct characteristics, to have reason and to be social. And these two characteristics, almost from the beginning, were not thought merely to be distinct, but antagonistic to each other: the conflict between man's rationality and his sociability can be seen throughout our tradition of political thought.

This loss of the originally political experiences in the tradition of political thought had already been foreshadowed in the beginning of this tradition itself, which almost but not quite begins with Aristotle; where political thought is concerned it actually starts with Plato. Indeed, in this respect, that is, in affirming in his political philosophy the experience of the polis, Aristotle seems in open conflict with Plato (his political writings are full of polemical remarks against him), whereas the tradition that reinterpreted Aristotle's definition of man eliminated from it all those insights into the nature of politics and man's political freedom that were inconsistent with Platonism.

The chief difference between Plato and Aristotle in their political philosophies is that Plato, writing consciously in opposition to the political life of the decaying Greek city-state, no longer believed in the validity of the kind of speech that accompanied—in the sense of being the other side of—political action. To him, such speech was mere opinion, and as such opposed to the perception of truth, unfit either to adhere to or express truth. Persuasion, *peithein,* the form in which the citizens managed their public affairs among themselves, was to Plato an unfortunate substitute for the kind of unshakable conviction that could spring only from the direct perception of truth, a perception to which the method of *dialegein,* talking a matter through between "two," *autos auto,* "one" talking with one "other," could lead. The philosophical point is that for Plato the perception of truth was essentially speechless and could only be furthered, not attained, by *dialegein.* It is essential in our context that Plato, probably from the impression that the fate of Socrates and the limitations of persuasion so glaringly exposed at his trial made on him, was no longer concerned with freedom at all. Persuasion had become to him a form, not of freedom, but of arbitrary compulsion through words, and in his political philosophy he proposed to substitute for this arbitrary compulsion the coercion of truth. Insofar as this truth was essentially speechless and could be perceived only in the solitude of contemplation, Platonic man was already not a "speaking" but a rational animal, that is, a being whose chief concern and enlightenment lay in himself, in his own reason, and not in the faculty of speech, which by definition presupposed his living among and managing his life together with his equals. When Aristotle connected speech and freedom, he was on the firm ground of a then still existing tradition rooted in experience. Yet in the end

Plato remained victorious because of the fact that the Greek city-state was decaying beyond remedy—something that Plato who, as a full-fledged Athenian citizen, unlike Aristotle, knew and whose influence he suffered severely—and whose ultimate ruin he feared and tried to prevent.

In the entire tradition of philosophical, and particularly of political thought, there has perhaps been no single factor of such overwhelming importance and influence on everything that was to follow than the fact that Plato and Aristotle wrote in the fourth century, under the full impact of a politically decaying society, and under conditions where philosophy quite consciously either deserted the political realm altogether or claimed to rule it like a tyrant. This fact had first of all the most serious consequences for philosophy itself, which hardly needed Hegel to come to believe that not only philosophical thought, but nearly all thought in general, was the indication of the end of a civilization. Even more serious was the abyss that immediately opened between thought and action, and which never since has been closed. All thinking activity that is not simply the calculation of means to obtain an intended or willed end but is concerned with meaning in the most general sense came to play the role of an "afterthought," that is, after action had decided and determined reality. Action, on the other hand, became meaningless, the realm of the accidental and haphazard upon which no great deeds any longer shed their immortal light. The great and conflicting Roman experience remained in this respect without lasting influence, because its Christian heir followed Greek philosophy in its spiritual development and Roman practice only in its legal and institutional history. Roman experience, moreover, never brought forth a philosophical conception of its own, but from the beginning interpreted itself in the Greek categories of the fourth century. When action eventually became meaningful again it was because the remembered story of man's actions was felt to be "in essence incoherent and immoral" (John Adams), so that history's *trostloses Ungefähr* (Kant's "melancholy haphazardness") needed a "ruse of nature" or some other force working behind the back of acting men to achieve any dignity worthy of philosophical thought. The worst consequence, however, was that freedom became a "problem," perhaps the most perplexing one for philosophy, and certainly the most insoluble for political philosophy. Aristotle is the last for whom freedom is not yet "problematic" but inherent in the faculty of speech; in other words, Aristotle still knew that men, as long as they talk with each other and act together in the *modus* of speech, are free.

We have already indicated one of the reasons why Marx's concept of freedom, and his insistence on it as the ultimate goal of all politics, resulted in the basic inconsistency of his teaching. That reason was the early loss of interest in freedom in general as well as the early oblivion of the fundamental connection between speech and freedom, both of which are almost as old as our tradition of political thought. To this, however, must be added one altogether different difficulty, which arises less from the concept of freedom as such than from the change this concept necessarily suffers under conditions of universal equality.

Never before our own times has equality meant in terms of political reality that literally everyone is everyone else's equal—which, of course, does not imply that everybody is the same as everybody else, although the leveling tendencies of our modern society can hardly be denied. Prior to the modern age, equality was understood politically as a matter of equal rights for people of equal status. In other words, it meant that those who were equal should be treated equally, but never that everyone was equal. The Christian notion of the equality of all men before God, so frequently cited as the origin of modern political equality, never intended to make men equal on earth, but on the contrary insisted that only as citizens of a *civitas Dei* could they be considered equal. The shift of emphasis from *civitas terrena* to *civitas Dei* as the ultimate destiny of man did nothing to change the basic inequalities of man's political status on earth, in the framework of which political equality and equity were supposed to operate. The Christian way of life—to live in the world without being of the world—could deny the relevance of earthly distinctions between men in order to affirm the ultimate equality of destiny. But "ultimate" meant beyond this world, leaving earthly distinctions completely intact, and "destiny" referred to a beginning and end, neither of which was rooted in the earth. Because Christian equality before God did not even demand political equality of all Christians, let alone of all men, there is as little justification for praising Christianity for the modern concept of equality as there is for blaming the Church for the equanimity with which it tolerated slavery and serfdom throughout the centuries. Insofar as statesmen were Christians, and not merely statesmen who happened to be of the Christian denomination, they had nothing to do with either.

Originally equals were only those who belonged to the same group, and to extend this term to all men would have been to render it meaningless. The chief privilege inherent in this original meaning was that one's equals, and only they, had a right to judge one's own actions. It is in this sense that Cato in his last trial complained that none of his judges was entitled to judge him, because none of them belonged to his own generation: they were not his equals, even though they were all free Roman citizens. How deeply this distinction between equals and all other men was felt, and how little our own circumstances have prepared us to understand it, can be seen clearly if we once again recall Aristotle's definition of man, *zōon logon echon*, which as a matter of course he meant only for the inhabitants of a polis, for those who were equals, and which we immediately misunderstand as a general statement applicable to all human beings. The reason he defined the specific condition of life in a polis as the content of human as distinguished from animal life was not because he thought it applicable everywhere, but because he had decided that it was the best possible human life.

A more universal definition and concept of man appeared only in the following centuries, during the rise in late antiquity of the condition of *apolity* that so curiously resembles the rise of statelessness in the modern world. Only when the philosophers had definitely (and not only theoretically, as with Plato) broken with the polis, and when political homelessness had become the status of a great many people in the world, did they conceive of man in an entirely unpolitical way, that is, independent from the way in which he lived together with his equals. The late Stoic concept of human equality, however, was as negative as the condition from which it arose. It has as much or as little to do with universal equality in the positive sense in which we live today as the Stoic concept of *ataraxia*, freedom as unmovability, has to do with any positive notion of freedom. In other words, our use today of universal concepts and our tendency to universalize rules until they come to comprehend every possible individual occurrence have a lot to do with the conditions of universal equality under which we actually live, think, and act.

To what extent Marx was aware of and even obsessed by this new universal equality can be seen from his concept of the future as a classless and nationless society, that is, a society where universal equality will have razed all political boundaries between men. What he did not see, and what is so very manifest in Hobbes's magnificent definition of human equality as the equal ability to kill, is that like all frontiers these boundaries give protection together with limitation, and not only separate but also bind men together. Marx's greatness, and the reason for his enormous influence on modern political thought and movements, was that he discovered the positive character of this equality in the nature of man himself, that is, in his conception of man as labor force. He knew very well that this new definition of man was possible only because "the concept of human equality possesses already the solidity of a popular prejudice." Marx's definition of man as *animal laborans* stood in conscious opposition to and challenged the traditional definition of man as *animal rationale*.

Animal rationale, allegedly the translation of *zōon logon echon*, still shared with Aristotle's definition the lack of equal applicability to all men, for not all men are equally "rational," equally capable of theoretical thought. It was the capacity to give and to listen to theoretical reasons, rather than the practical intelligence of men, that the adjective *rationale* primarily aimed at. The later interpretation of the rational part of man as "common sense," despite or perhaps because of its eminently political indications, was never used to define the essence of human nature, even though this common sense was supposed to be equally strong and came to the same conclusions in every single individual. Before Marx only Hobbes—who with Montesquieu was the greatest though not the most influential political thinker of the new era that was beginning—had felt the necessity of finding a new definition of man under the assumption of universal equality. According to Hobbes, this equality was inherent in the original state of nature and "the equality of the ability to kill" defined the most general, common denominator of man. From this basic assumption he deduced the foundations of human political organisms with no less stringent logicality than Marx was to develop, from the assumption of the productive force of labor, the foundations of human society.

Marx's demand that nobody should be called free who rules over others is in complete agreement with the fact of universal equality, a condition in which by definition no one has a right to rule. Yet the elimination of rule, of the age-old distinction between those who rule and those who are ruled, is so far from being the only and sufficient condition of freedom that our tradition even deemed freedom impossible without rulership. Those who were not ruled were deemed free, and this freedom could realize itself solely among equals, indeed only where, just as Marx demanded, the distinction between rulers and subjects did not exist. Yet this freedom based on rule over slaves was a freedom that apart from such basic rulership was inconceivable, not simply because it implied the rule over other human beings but because it entailed control over those basic necessities of life that, if left uncontrolled through emancipation from the labor they require, would render all freedom illusory. Freedom in this original sense was a state of being rather than a faculty; and politics, in any strict sense of the word, was thought to begin when that state had been realized. Political life rested on rulership, but to rule and to be ruled was not its content. Where this was the case, as in the oriental despotisms, the peoples concerned were seen by the Greeks as living under conditions of servitude, that is, as living under pre-political conditions. Freedom therefore was not one of the political "goods," such as honor or justice or wealth or any other good, and it never was enumerated as belonging to man's *eudaimonia,* his essential well-being or happiness. Freedom was the pre-political condition of political activities and therefore of all the goods that men can enjoy through their living together. As such, freedom was taken for granted and did not need to be defined. When he stated that the political life of a free citizen was characterized by *logon echon,* by being conducted in the manner of speech, Aristotle defined the essence of free men and their behavior, not the essence of freedom as a human good.

Universal equality cannot coexist with freedom as the pre-political condition of political life and with the absolute rule over laborers; it is the latter that makes it possible for free citizens to escape the coercive necessities of biological life, at least to the extent that such necessities demand of man's specific activities. Marx's own formulation that freedom is incompatible with rule over others only enhances this difficulty. If it were true, a Greek might have answered him by saying that then freedom is impossible: all men would be slaves of necessity—the necessity to eat and to live, to preserve and regenerate life. Not only are slaves not human, but no man is fully human under these conditions. Nor does the later development of the concept of freedom, which made it one of the most cherished goods within the political realm, change anything in this basic traditional incompatibility between freedom and universal equality. The most important and far-reaching change is already clearly visible in Aristotle, whose definitions of governments are not consistent with his definition of man as citizen. It is as though he himself had already forgotten what the whole tradition after him was bound to let sink into oblivion, namely, the intimate connection between freedom and speech on the one hand, and between rule and necessity on the other. What happened was that rule over others, which originally had been experienced as rule over slaves and therefore as a pre-political condition for the life of the polis, entered the political realm itself and, by dividing men who lived together into those who ruled and those who were ruled, even became its dominating factor. From then on, that is, almost immediately after Aristotle, the problem of power became the decisive political problem, so that this whole realm of human life could be defined, not as the realm of living together, but as the realm of power struggles in which nothing is so much at stake as the question of who rules over whom.

Rule over others very early ceased to be a merely pre-political condition of all political life, for no sooner had it entered the political realm proper than it became at once its very center. This change can best be observed in the definitions of the forms of government, which no longer were understood as various ways of living together but as various forms of rulership among citizens. Kingship and aristocracy, which Plato still defined as resting on distinction (their only minor difference being that the former rests on the distinction of one among the ruling citizens, whereas in the latter several are distinguished), now became monarchy and oligarchy. In monarchy one man, and in oligarchy several men hold power over all others. Plato still thought that these forms of government were plainly perversions, no true *politeiai* but born from some violent upheaval and depending on violence (*bia*). The use of violence disqualifies all forms of government because, according to the older conception, violence begins wherever the polis, the political realm proper, ends. It ends either in the rule over slaves, which makes this realm possible in the first place, or in the defense of the walls of the city, or in the transgression of the boundary of the laws to which all citizens have submitted themselves voluntarily.

Aristotle, who still uses the older concepts of kingship, aristocracy, and polity to indicate the "good" forms of governments, already actually thinks that the question of who rules over whom, or of how many hold power, is the decisive criterion that distinguishes them from each other. In other words, he always describes monarchy as the rule of one, oligarchy as the rule of the few, and democracy as the rule of the majority. However, since the element of violence present in ruling as such would also for him have disqualified these forms of government, he had to introduce the law in an altogether different meaning. The law was now no longer the boundary (which the citizens ought to defend like the walls of the city, because it had the same function for the citizens' political life as the city's wall had for their physical existence and distinctness, as Heraclitus had said), but became a yardstick by which rule could be measured. Rule now either conformed to or overruled the law, and in the latter case the rule was called tyrannical— usually, although not necessarily, exerted by one man—and therefore a kind of perverted monarchy. From then on, law and power became the two conceptual pillars of all definitions of government, and these definitions hardly changed during the more than two thousand years that separate Aristotle from Montesquieu. Since violence in its arbitrary form remained a disqualifying factor, the main question now became whether or not the rule over others conformed to the existing laws, whereas the question of how many actually were in possession of power became less and less relevant. Kant only drew the last consequence from this tradition of political thought when he reduced the number of forms of government to two: to rule over others according to law, which he called republican, and its opposite, rule by lawless, arbitrary power, which he called tyrannical.

In a sense this development is a complete reversal of the earlier Greek political experience, in which an all-important qualification for political life was the pre-political rule over slaves, that is, when only those who held power over others were considered free and fit to participate in politics at all. This early experience, however, was never altogether lost. Politics somehow, though in a very changed way, was still connected with freedom, freedom remained connected with exerting rule, and only rulers were deemed free. This is the context in which freedom could become a "good," something to be enjoyed, closely connected with the power of doing as one pleases, either within or beyond the limits of the law. Freedom remained with the "ruling class," and continued to presuppose others being ruled, even though it was no longer the condition but had become the very content of political life. Thus when universal equality appeared as an unavoidable demand for justice for everyone, for a social and political body in which all were free and no one was ruled, it had all the earmarks of a contradiction in terms: within the tradition of political thought the concept of universal equality could only mean that nobody could be free.

With the anticipated disappearance of rule and domination in Marx's stateless society, freedom indeed becomes a meaningless word unless it is conceived in an altogether different sense. Since Marx here as elsewhere did not bother to redefine his terms but remained in the conceptual framework of the tradition, Lenin was not so wrong when he concluded that if nobody can be free who rules over others, then freedom is only a prejudice or an ideology—although he thereby robbed Marx's work of one of its most important impulses. Marx's adherence to tradition is also the reason for his as well as Lenin's even more fateful error that mere administration, in contrast to government, is the adequate form of men living together under the condition of radical and universal equality. Administration was supposed to be no rule, but it can actually be only rule by nobody, that is, bureaucracy, a form of government without responsibility. Bureaucracy is the form of government in which the personal element of rulership has disappeared, and it is of course true that such a government may even rule in the interest of no class. But this no-man-rule, the fact that in an authentic bureaucracy nobody occupies the empty chair of the ruler, does not mean that the conditions of rule have disappeared. This nobody rules very effectively when looked upon from the side of the ruled, and, what is worse, as a form of government it has one important trait in common with tyranny. Tyrannical power is defined by the tradition as arbitrary power, and this originally signified a rule for which no account need be given, a rule that owes no one any responsibility. The same is true for the bureaucratic rule by nobody, though for an altogether different reason. There are many people in a bureaucracy who may demand an account, but nobody to give it because nobody cannot be held responsible. In the stead of the tyrant's arbitrary decisions we find the haphazard settlements of universal procedures, settlements that are without malice and arbitrariness because there is no will behind them, but to which there is also no appeal. As far as the ruled are concerned, the net of the patterns in which they are caught is by far more dangerous and more deadly than mere arbitrary tyranny. But bureaucracy should not be mistaken for totalitarian domination. If the October Revolution had been permitted to follow the lines prescribed by Marx and Lenin, which was not the case, it would probably have resulted in bureaucratic rule. The rule of nobody, not anarchy, or disappearance of rule, or oppression, is the ever-present danger of any society based on universal equality.

Labor, violence, and freedom indicate the central challenges to our tradition that appeared in the three great events of the modern era, and which Marx attempted to formulate and think through. Compared with them, the one reversal of traditional "values" of which Marx himself was aware, the turning away from "idealism" to "materialism"—by which he believed he had turned Hegel upside down, and for which he has so frequently been praised or blamed—is of minor importance. Such turning operations, however, were characteristic of the new age's conscious rebellion against, and unconscious bondage to, tradition. We are reminded of Kierkegaard's turning the relationship between philosophy and religion upside down; and of Nietzsche's inverted Platonism that, while assuming with Plato that eternal essence and perishable mortal life are contradictions, arrived at the anti-Platonic conclusion that man, insofar as he is a living being, can only be hindered in his being alive through the so-called "essential." This last instance is particularly instructive, since Plato himself already thought he had achieved such a turning operation in teaching that it is not the merely living and hence mortal body but the soul, precisely because it is intangible, which could attain immortality by partaking in true reality, the reality not of the objects of the senses but of the ideas that are seen and grasped only with the eyes of the soul. The *periagōgē*, he demanded, was a turning around by which everything commonly believed in Greece in accordance with the Homeric religion was stood on its head. At least this is quite obviously what Plato himself believed. One may think that Nietzsche, when he reversed Plato, was only returning to a pre-Platonic philosophy; but of course that is not the case, for Nietzsche, like Marx, remained in the framework of the tradition despite all turnings around. To exalt the sensual, as Nietzsche did, one needs the reality of the spiritual, just as Plato needed the brute factuality of the sensual as the given background against which the soul could perform its *periagōgē*, its turning toward the realm of ideas. Plato, whose work is filled with direct and indirect polemical replies to Homer, did not turn Homer downside up, but he did lay the groundwork of a philosophy in which such turning operations were indeed not only a far-fetched possibility, but almost a conclusive necessity. The whole development of philosophy in late antiquity, with its innumerable schools all fighting each other with a fanaticism unparalleled in the pre-Christian world, largely consists of turning operations that were made possible by Plato's *periagōgē*, and for which the Platonic separation of a world of mere shadowy appearances from a world of eternally true ideas had erected the framework.

When in a last gigantic effort Hegel gathered together the various strands of traditional philosophy as they had developed from Plato's original conception, fitting them into one consistent whole, a similar splitting up into two conflicting schools of thought ensued, though on a much lower level: for a short while philosophic thought was dominated by right-wing and left-wing Hegelians. But the three great reversals that eventually were to conclude, at least up to our time, the great uninterrupted tradition of philosophy—Kierkegaard's leap from doubt into belief, Nietzsche's reversed Platonism, and Marx's leap from theory into *praxis*—(though none of them would have been possible without Hegel and his concept of history and in this one all-important respect all three were and remained followers of Hegel), also point to a much more radical break with the tradition than any mere upside-down operation requires. Of these breaks Marx's had the most immediate consequences, simply because it had touched our tradition of political thought and therefore could become directly influential on political developments.

Marx's break certainly did not consist in his "materialism" or in his turning Hegel upside down. Lenin was altogether right when he remarked that no one could understand *Das Kapital* who had not mastered Hegel's *Logik*. In Marx's own opinion, what made socialism scientific and distinguished it from that of his predecessors, the "utopian socialists," was not an economic theory with its scientific insights as well as its errors, but the discovery of a law of movement that ruled matter and, at the same time, showed itself in the reasoning capacity of man as "consciousness," either of the self or of a class. The tremendous practical advantage of Marx's "scientific" over utopian socialism was, and still is, that it liberated the socialist movement from its worn-out moralizing attitudes, and recognized that the class questions in modern society could no longer be solved by a "passion for justice" or on the basis of a slightly modified Christian charity. If labor is the central activity of modern society, it is absurd to think of members of the working class as underprivileged, no matter how oppressed or exploited they may happen to be at any particular moment. The introduction of a dialectical historical movement, according to which the last will be first, at least offered an account of the tremendous power potential of this class, a potential that came to light only several decades after Marx's death. The dialectical movement of thesis, antithesis, and synthesis—which becomes infinite as each synthesis at once establishes itself as a new thesis from which a new antithesis and a new synthesis flow—holds man and matter in its grip and mixes them with each other, then separates them from each other, antithetically, so that they may appear distinct as matter and spirit, only to reunite them synthetically. The foundation of experience on which Hegel's as well as Marx's dialectic rests is the all-encompassing eternal process of nature's metabolism, of which man's metabolism with nature is only an infinitesimally small part, on the one hand, and the fact of human history on the other. The logic of dialectal movement enables Marx to combine nature with history, or matter with man; man becomes the author of a meaningful, comprehensible history because his metabolism with nature, unlike an animal's, is not merely consumptive but requires an activity, namely, labor. For Marx labor is the uniting link between matter and man, between nature and history. He is a "materialist" insofar as the specifically human form of consuming matter is to him the beginning of everything; and he is an "idealist" insofar as nothing ever comes from matter by itself without the consuming activity that lies in the nature of man, which is labor. In other words "materialism" and "idealism" have lost their meaning, although Marx himself seems not to have been aware of this. The greatness of Hegel's system, and the reason why it was so extremely difficult to escape its influence if one wanted to remain within the scope of traditional philosophy at all, lies in his incorporation of the two "worlds" of Plato into one moving whole. The traditional turning from the world of appearance to the world of ideas or, conversely, the turning from the world of ideas back to the world of appearance, takes place in the historical motion itself and becomes the form—although not the content, which is the realization of the Absolute—of the dialectical movement.

Each of the three statements by Marx—*Labor is the Creator of Man, Violence is the midwife of History,* and *Nobody can be free who enslaves others*—is revolutionary in the sense that it follows and brings into articulate thought the three revolutionary events that ushered in the modern world. None, however, is revolutionary in the sense that with it or through it a revolution came to pass. And only the first is revolutionary in the sense that it is in flagrant conflict with the whole of our tradition of political thought. This first statement is also, characteristically enough, the one least suspected of "revolutionary tendencies" in the subversive meaning of the term, and therefore more difficult to understand than the others. The one decisive difference of our own world from all previous ages, the dignification of labor, has already acquired the doubtful status of a commonplace, and this in little more than a century. Marx's prophecies may have been wrong in almost all respects, although he certainly did not err more than is the common lot of social scientists. But in this one respect—in his conviction that the future belongs to man as a laboring animal, to those, that is, who have nothing but their laboring capacity, whom he called the proletariat—he was so right that we, even today, are hardly aware of it. The point is not whether the classical economists, whom Marx in his economic theories followed closely despite all of his criticisms, were right in maintaining that labor is the source of all wealth, but rather that we live in a society of laborers. That is, we live in a society in which men consider all their activities primarily as laboring activities, in the sense that their end is "the preservation of individual life," and themselves primarily as owners of labor force. It is in this sense that those who manifestly do not labor, who do not earn their living through labor, are in a society of laborers judged to be parasites.

Because labor has lost one of its chief characteristics, apparent not only in all traditional definitions of the word but also in its etymological origin in nearly every language, this basic condition of modern life is frequently neglected. Labor has indeed become effortless, just as childbirth tends to become less and less painful. The effort of labor and the pain of birth, both mentioned as the punishment for man's sin in the third chapter of the first book of the Bible, belonged together because both expressed the fact that man was subject to the compulsion of necessity for his very life. Labor and its effort were required for maintaining and preserving individual life, just as birth and its pain were unavoidable for the reproduction of the species. Effort and pain were not just the symptoms, but the *modi* in which the basic necessity inherent in the human condition made itself felt and revealed itself. Labor, namely that activity that is both required for, and inherent in, being alive, does not lose its character of compulsion because it has become easier, although it is true that it is more difficult to perceive coercive necessity in the guise of ease than in the harsh brutality of pain and effort.

What Marx foresaw was that the industrial revolution was bound to "enlarge the realm of natural necessity," that is, the realm of labor, despite all technical developments that tend to make labor effortless. This enlargement is closely bound to the gigantic multiplication of needs, the fulfillment of which is felt to belong to the necessities of life, and the most immediate and tangible result of which has been that the "figure of the laborer" has indeed become the central figure of our society. In this society the old verse "Who does not labor shall not eat" has assumed a direct relevance that stands in opposition to all other periods of human history. The social revolution of our time is contained in the simple fact that until not much more than one hundred years ago, mere laborers had been denied political rights, whereas today we accept as a matter of course the opinion that a nonlaborer may not even have the right to stay alive.

Marx's own hope, nourished by his belief in the dialectical structure of everything that happens, was that somehow this absolute rule of necessity would result in, or resolve itself into, an equally absolute rule of freedom.

That is the only strictly utopian element in his thought. But it is also the only and perhaps desperate conclusion to be drawn from a tradition that holds, in Marx's own words, that the "realm of freedom begins where laboring ends." According to Marx it is foolish to think it possible to liberate and emancipate laborers, that is, those whose very activity subjects them to necessity. When all men have become laborers, the realm of freedom will indeed have vanished. The only thing that then remains is to emancipate man from labor, something that in all probability is just as impossible as the early hope of the philosophers to free man's soul from his body.

Unavoidably, first and foremost the tradition of political thought contains the philosophers' traditional attitude toward politics. Political thought itself is older than our tradition of philosophy, which begins with Plato and Aristotle, just as philosophy itself is older and contains more than the Western tradition eventually accepted and developed. At the beginning, therefore, not of our political or philosophical history, but of our tradition of political philosophy, stands Plato's contempt for politics, his conviction that "the affairs and actions of men (*ta tōn anthrōpōn pragmata*) are not worthy of great seriousness" and that the only reason why the philosopher needs to concern himself with them is the unfortunate fact that philosophy—or, as Aristotle somewhat later would say, a life devoted to it, the *bios theōrētikos*—is materially impossible without a halfway reasonable arrangement of all affairs that concern men insofar as they live together. At the beginning of the tradition politics exists because men are alive and mortal, while philosophy concerns those matters that are eternal, like the universe. Insofar as the philosopher is also a mortal man he, too, is concerned with politics. But this concern has only a negative relationship to his being a philosopher: he is afraid, as Plato so abundantly made clear, that through bad management of political affairs he will not be able to pursue philosophy. *Scholē*, like the Latin *otium*, is not leisure as such but only leisure from political duty, nonparticipation in politics, and therefore the freedom of the mind for its concern with the eternal (the *aei on*), which is possible only if the needs and necessities of mortal life have been taken care of. Politics, therefore, seen from the specifically philosophical viewpoint, begins already in Plato to comprehend more than *politeuesthai*, more than those activities that are characteristic of the ancient Greek polis, for which the mere fulfillment of the needs and necessities of life was a pre-political condition. Politics begins, as it were, to expand its realm downward to the necessities of life themselves, so that to the philosophers' scorn for the perishable affairs of mortals was added the specifically Greek contempt for everything that is necessary for mere life and survival. As Cicero, in his futile attempt to disavow Greek philosophy on this one point—its attitude to politics—succinctly pointed out, if only "all that is essential to our wants and comforts were supplied by some magic wand, as in the legends, then every man of first-rate ability could drop all other responsibility and devote himself exclusively to knowledge and science." In brief, when the philosophers began to concern themselves with politics in a systematic way, politics at once became for them a necessary evil.

Thus our tradition of political philosophy, unhappily and fatefully, and from its very beginning, has deprived political affairs, that is, those activities concerning the common public realm that come into being wherever men live together, of all dignity of their own. In Aristotelian terms, politics is a means to an end; it has no end in and by itself. More than that, the proper end of politics is in a way its opposite, namely, nonparticipation in political affairs, *scholē*, the condition of philosophy, or rather the condition of a life devoted to it. In other words, no other activity appears as anti-philosophical, as hostile to philosophy, as political activity in general and action in particular, with the exception, of course, of what was never deemed to be strictly human activity at all, such as mere laboring. Spinoza polishing lenses eventually could become the symbolic figure of the philosopher, just as innumerable examples taken from the experiences of work, craftsmanship, and the liberal arts since the time of Plato could serve to lead by analogy to the higher knowledge of philosophic truths. But since Socrates no man of action, that is, no one whose original experience was political, as for instance Cicero's was, could ever hope to be taken seriously by the philosophers; and no specifically political deeds, or human greatness as expressed in action, could ever hope to serve as examples of philosophy, in spite of the never forgotten glory of Homer's praise of the hero. Philosophy is further removed from *praxis* even than it is from *poiēsis*.

Of perhaps even greater consequence for the degradation of politics is that in the light of philosophy—for which the origin and principle, the *archē*, are one and the same—politics does not even have an origin of its own: it came into being only because of the elementary and pre-political fact of biological necessity, which makes men need each other in the arduous task of staying alive. Politics, in other words, is derivative in a twofold sense: it has its origin in the pre-political data of biological life, and it has its end in the post-political, highest possibility of human destiny. And since it is the curse, as we have seen, of pre-political necessities to require laboring, we may now say that politics is limited by labor from below and by philosophy from above. Both are excluded from politics strictly speaking, the one as its lowly origin and the other as its exalted aim and end. Very much like the activity of the class of guardians in Plato's *Republic*, politics is supposed to watch and manage the livelihood and the base necessities of labor on the one hand, and to take its orders from the apolitical *theōria* of philosophy on the other. Plato's demand for a philosopher-king does not mean that philosophy itself should, or ever even could be realized in an ideal polity, but rather that rulers who value philosophy more than any other activity should be permitted to rule in such a way that there may be philosophy, that philosophers will have *scholē*, and be undisturbed by those matters that arise from our living together and that, in turn, have their ultimate origin in the imperfections of human life.

Political philosophy never recovered from this blow dealt by philosophy to politics at the very beginning of our tradition. The contempt for politics, the conviction that political activity is a necessary evil, due partly to the necessities of life that force men to live as laborers or rule over slaves who provide for them, and partly to the evils that come from living together itself, that is, to the fact that the multitude, whom the Greeks called *hoi polloi*, threatens the existence of every single person, runs like a red thread throughout the centuries that separate Plato from the modern age. In this context it is irrelevant whether this attitude expresses itself in secular terms, as in Plato and Aristotle, or if it does so in the terms of Christianity. It was Tertullian who first held that, insofar as we are Christians, *nulla res nobis magis aliena quam res publica* ("to us nothing is more alien than public affairs") and nevertheless still insisted on the necessity of the *civitas terrena*, of secular government, because of man's sinfulness and because, as Luther was to put it much later, true Christians *wohnen fern voneinander,* that is, dwell far from each other and are as forlorn among the multitude as were the ancient philosophers. What is important is that the same notion was taken up, again in secular terms, by post-Christian philosophy, so to speak surviving all other changes and radical turnings about, expressing itself in the melancholy reflection of Madison, that government surely is nothing but a reflection on human nature, which would not be necessary if men were angels, and then in the angry words of Nietzsche, that no government can be good about which the subjects have to worry at all. With respect to the evaluation of politics, though not elsewhere, it is irrelevant whether the *civitas Dei* gives meaning and order to the *civitas terrena,* or whether the *bios theōrētikos* prescribes its rules and is the ultimate end of the *bios politikos.*

What matters, in addition to the inherent degradation of this whole realm of life through philosophy, is the radical separation of those matters that men can reach and attain only through living and acting together from those that are perceived and cared about by man in his singularity and solitude. And here again, it does not matter if man in his solitude searches for truth, finally attaining it in the speechless contemplation of the idea of ideas, or whether he cares for the salvation of his soul. What matters is the unbridgeable abyss that opened and has never been closed, not between the so-called individual and the so-called community (which is the latest and most phony way of stating the authentic and old problem), but between being in solitude and living together. Compared to this perplexity, the equally old and vexing problem of the relationship, or rather nonrelationship, between action and thought is secondary in importance. Neither the radical separation between politics and contemplation, between living together and living in solitude as two distinct modes of life, nor their hierarchical structure, was ever doubted after Plato had established both. Here again the only exception is Cicero, who, out of his great Roman political experience, doubted the validity of the superiority of the *bios theōrētikos* over the *bios politikos,* the validity of solitude over the *communitas.* Rightly but futilely Cicero objected that he who was devoted to "knowledge and science" would flee his "solitude and ask for a companion in his study, be it in order to teach or to learn, to listen or to speak." Here as elsewhere the Romans paid a steep price for their contempt of philosophy, which they held to be "impractical." The end result was the undisputed victory of Greek philosophy and the loss of Roman experience for occidental political thought. Cicero, because he was not a philosopher, was unable to challenge philosophy.

The question whether Marx, who at the end of the tradition challenged its formidable unanimity about the proper relationship between philosophy and politics, was a philosopher in the traditional sense or even in any authentic sense, need not be decided. The two decisive statements that sum up abruptly and almost inarticulately his thought on the matter—"The philosophers have only *interpreted* the world . . . the point, however, is to *change* it," and "You cannot supersede [*aufheben* in the Hegelian threefold sense of conserve, raise to a higher level, and abolish] philosophy without realizing it"—are so intimately phrased in Hegel's terminology and thought along his lines that, taken by themselves, their explosive content notwithstanding, they can almost be regarded as an informal and natural continuation of Hegel's philosophy. For nobody could have thought before Hegel that philosophy is only interpretation (of the world or anything else) or that philosophy could be realized only in the *bios theōrētikos*, the life of the philosopher himself. What is to be realized, moreover, is not any specific or new philosophy, not the philosophy, for instance, of Marx himself, but the highest destiny of man as traditional philosophy, culminating in Hegel, defined it.

Marx does not challenge philosophy, he challenges the alleged impracticality of philosophy. He challenges the philosophers' resignation to do no more than find a place for themselves in the world, instead of changing the world and making it "philosophical." And this is not only more than but also decisively different from Plato's ideal of philosophers who should rule as kings, because it implies not the rule of philosophy over men but that men become philosophers. The consequence that Marx drew from Hegel's philosophy of history (and Hegel's entire philosophical work, including the *Logik*, has only this one topic: *history*) was that action, contrary to the philosophical tradition, was so far from being the opposite of thought that it was its true, namely real vehicle, and that politics, far from being infinitely beneath the dignity of philosophy, was the only activity that was inherently philosophical.

THE GREAT TRADITION

I
Law and Power

Since Plato, all the traditional definitions of the nature of the various types of government have rested on two conceptual pillars: law and power. The differences between the various forms of government depended on the distribution of power, whether one single man or the most distinguished citizens or the people possessed the power to rule. The good or bad nature of each of these was judged according to the role played by law in the exercise of power: lawful government was good and lawless bad. The criterion of law, however, as a yardstick for good or bad government was very early replaced, already in Aristotle's political philosophy, by the altogether different notion of interest, with the result that bad government became the exercise of power in the interest of the rulers, and good government the use of power in the interest of the ruled. The types of government, enumerated according to the power principle, did not change in either case: there were always the three basic forms of monarchy, aristocracy, and democracy and the corresponding three basic perversions of tyranny, oligarchy, and ochlocracy (mob rule). Still, modern political thought is liable to overemphasize and misconstrue Aristotle's conception of interest: *dzên kai eudzên* is not yet the rule that "commands the king" (as Cardinal Rohan put it much later), but designate the different concerns of the rich and the poor with which the laws ought to deal according to the principle of *suum cuique*. Rule in the interest of all, therefore, is not much more than a particular interpretation of rule in accordance with *just* laws.

A curious equivocality concerning the relationship between law and power has remained hidden in these well-known clichés. Almost all political theorists without noticing it use two altogether different similes in this regard. On one side, we learn that power enforces law in order to bring about lawfulness; on the other, the law is conceived as the limitation and the boundary of power, which must never be overstepped. In the first case, power could conceivably be understood as a necessary evil, whereas in the second case this role would much rather fall to the function of the law, which seems to owe its existence to the necessity of hedging in an otherwise free and "good" force. Following the traditional category of means and ends, power in the first instance appears as an *instrument* to execute the law, and in the second instance the law appears as an *instrument* to hold power in check. One consequence of this equivocal understanding of the relationship between law and power appears obvious at first glance. If power is only there to enforce and execute the law, it cannot make much difference whether such power resides in one man, or in a few people, or in all of them. There can be only one essential difference—the difference between lawful or constitutional government and lawless or tyrannical government.

The term tyranny, therefore, from Plato onward was used not only for the perversion of one-man rule, but also indiscriminately for any lawless government, that is, any government that in its decisions was bound only by its own will and desires—even if these were the will and desires of a majority—and not also by laws that could not become subject to political decisions. We find the last consequence of this line of thought in Kant's *Zum Ewigen Frieden,* where he concludes that instead of distinguishing many forms of government, one could say that there are only two, namely, constitutional or lawful government, irrespective of who or how many possess power, and domination of despotism. All traditional forms of government are for Kant forms of domination; they are despotic because they are distinguished in accordance with the power principle, and in them whoever possesses power possesses it as a "sovereign," undivided among and unchecked by others. Against monarchy, aristocracy, and democracy, Kant sets constitutional government, where power is always checked by others and which he calls "republican," irrespective of all other criteria.

But if we turn to the second simile in the relationship between law and power, according to which the law is seen as a hedge or wall surrounding powerful men who without this limitation might abuse their strength, the differences between traditional forms of government, between monarchies, aristocracies, and democracies, become all important. The question is now whether only one man, or the most distinguished few, or the whole people should be permitted to exercise power within the limitations of the law. In this context, it is obvious why the rule of one man should be identified with tyranny or, at any rate, be the closest to tyranny, and why democracy should be regarded as the best form of government. Monarchy now comes to mean that only one man is free, aristocracy that freedom is granted only to the best, and democracy alone can be considered free government. We find the last consequence of this line of thought in Hegel's philosophy of History, in which world history is divided into three eras: the oriental despotism where only one was free, the ancient Greek and Roman world where some were free, and finally the Christian Occident in which all are free, because man as such is free. The most striking aspect of this ever-recurring equivocality in the concepts of law and power is that we do not deal here simply with two different strands of our tradition, but that, on the contrary, almost all of the great political thinkers use both similes indiscriminately.

I have enumerated the forms of government in the way they were formulated and defined in the tradition, whose foundation was established not through historical curiosity about the manifold ways of life of different peoples, but through Plato's search for the best form of government, a search that sprang from and always implied his negative attitude to the Athenian city-state. Ever since, the quest for the best government has served to conceptualize and to transform all those political experiences that found their home in the tradition of political thought, which nowhere else perhaps shows its comprehensiveness more impressively than in the astounding fact that not a single novel form of government has been added for 2,500 years. Neither the Roman Republic nor the Roman Empire, neither the medieval kingship nor the emergence of the nation-state was felt to warrant a revision or addition to what was already familiar to Plato. Surprisingly enough in view of its tremendous consequences, the distinction between ruling and being ruled as a condition for all organized society was introduced by Plato in an offhand, almost improvisational manner, while the concept of law assumes its central place as the very content of all political life only in his last treatise, the *Laws*—which, by the way, was lost and rediscovered only in the fifteenth century—and there the laws are understood to be the visible, political translation of the ideas of the *Republic*.

Yet, if in the quest for the best government the question of laws originally played a subordinate role, its role was always major in the definition of tyranny as the worst form of government. The reason for this early constellation lies in the specific political experience of the polis, which Plato as well as Aristotle could not but take for granted. The pre-philosophical Greek political experience had understood law to be boundaries men establish between themselves or between city and city. They hedged in the living space that each was entitled to call his own, and they were sacred as the stabilizers of the human condition, of the changing circumstances and movements and actions of men. They gave stability to a community composed of mortals, and therefore continually endangered in its continuity by new men born into it. The stability of the laws corresponds to the constant motion of all human affairs, a motion that can never end as long as men are born and die. Each new birth endangers the continuity of the polis because with each new birth a new world potentially comes into being. The laws hedge in these new beginnings and guarantee the preexistence of a common world, the permanence of a continuity that transcends the individual life span of each generation, and in which each single man in his mortality can hope to leave a trace of permanence behind him. In this sense, which asserted itself with the rise of the Greek polis, the laws constitute the common public world outside of which, according to the Greeks, human life was deprived of its most essential concerns.

The great advantage of the polis organization of public life was that the polis, because of the stabilizing force of its wall of law, could impart to human affairs a solidity that human action itself, in its intrinsic futility and dependence on the immortalizing of poets, can never possess. Because it surrounded itself with a permanent wall of law, the polis as a unity could claim to ensure that whatever happened or was done within it would not perish with the life of the doer or endurer, but live on in the memory of future generations. Its great merit over kingship, the reason why, mythologically speaking, the Greeks saw in King Theseus's founding of Athens the last and greatest kingly enterprise, was candidly and succinctly given by Pericles, who praised Athens because it did not need a Homer to leave, for better and for worse, "innumerable monuments" of the deeds of its sons.

This early meaning of *nomos* (law) is still present in Plato when he evokes Zeus as the God of boundaries at the beginning of his discourse on the *Laws,* as it was present in Heraclitus when he stated that a people must fight for their laws as they fight for the wall (*teichos*) of their city. Just as a city could come into being physically only after the inhabitants had built a wall around it, so the political life of the citizens, *politeuesthai,* could begin only after the law had been posited and laid down. The fence of the law was needed for the city-state because only here people lived together in such a way that space itself was no longer a sufficient guarantee for assuring each of them his freedom of movement. So much was the positing of the law felt to be a condition of polis life that legislation, lawmaking itself, was not considered a political activity: the lawmaker could be a man called in from the outside or, like Solon, someone who after laying down the law retired from public-political life, at least for a time. So much was law thought to be something erected and laid down by men without any transcendent authority or source that pre-Socratic philosophy, when it proposed to distinguish all things by asking whether they owe their origin to men or are through themselves what they are, introduced the terms *nomô* and *physei,* by law or by nature. Thus, the order of the universe, the *kosmos* of natural things, was differentiated from the world of human affairs, whose order is laid down by men since it is an order of things made and done by men. This distinction, too, survives in the beginning of our tradition, where Aristotle expressly states that political science deals with things that are *nomô* and not *physei.* It is in this context that the tyrant who razes the boundaries of the laws destroys the political realm altogether. He is not a ruler but a destroyer, destroying the walls of the city, the pre-political condition of its existence.

Very early, however, and even before the beginning of our tradition, there already existed another altogether different understanding of law. When Pindar says: *nomô basileus pantôn* we may be justified to translate his words: "the law is the ruler of all things," and understand this to mean that just as the king holds together and gives order to whatever is begun under his leadership, so the law is an order inherent in the universe and governs its motion. This law is not laid down, is not posited by either men or gods; if it is called divine, it is so only because it rules even the gods. This law, obviously, could not be conceived as a wall or boundary erected by men. Laws derived from or nourished by it had a validity that was not restricted to one community, nor to the public realm as such, nor generally to matters that happen *between* men as distinguished from those that happen *within* men. The cosmic law was universal in every respect, applicable to all things and to every man in every situation and condition of life. The distinction between *physei* and *nomô*, between things that grow naturally and things that owe their existence to men, loses its relevance, because one law presides and rules over both. The later concept of natural law, as it was developed in Greek Stoicism, is clearly already indicated, but for an understanding that saw laws in the image of fences and boundaries that hedge in, protect, and establish the various common worlds of the polis, the very term "natural law" would have been a contradiction in terms, since it assumed that things are what they are either by nature or law, but not both.

Of even greater importance for the tradition is that under the assumption that one law rules over all things moral and political, the private and the public realm of life are no longer clearly distinguished, but are both embedded in and ruled over by the eternal order of the universe. Men belong in this universe because, in the words of Kant, "the starry heaven above me" corresponds in its ordered lawful sublimity to "the moral law within me." This law has lost the character of limitation manifest in all positive law codes that contain prohibitions rather than prescriptions, and that therefore leave everything that is not clearly prohibited to the free decision of those who are subject to them. The conflict between private and public morality, between things permitted and demanded in personal intercourse and those that are required by the necessities of political life at the expense of private morality—as for instance in Hobbes who, starting from the public-political realm where power originates, concludes that the nature of man is that of a "power thirsty animal"—or, on the contrary, in conformity with the behavior of each man in his individual privacy, as in the instance of Kant, where the law within me elevates me into a universal legislator. In either case, the universality of one law is saved: those who obey and submit meekly to the laws of power are by nature power thirsty; those who obey the laws of the city recognize in themselves the nature of moral lawfulness.

However, throughout our tradition the distinction between the cosmic law in its universal validity and the rules and prescriptions valid only among a clearly defined group of men was kept, and their relationship was seen more or less in the image that we find for the first time in Heraclitus: "All human laws are nourished by the one divine law; for this holds sway as far as it will, and suffices for all, and prevails in everything" (Frag. 114). It is decisive that our legal tradition also held that positive man-made codes of laws were not only derived from but also depended upon the one universally valid law as their ultimate source of authority. It is this same distinction and relationship that we later find between the *ius civile* and the *ius naturale*, between positive law and natural law or divine command. In each instance, the earlier notion of the law as a fence survives in the codes of posited laws through which the one universal law is translated into human standards of right and wrong.

The one universal law, or later the Command of God, is understood to be eternal and unmovable and from this eternity the positive man-made laws derive their relative permanence through which they can stabilize the ever-changing affairs of men. What happens when this distinction between universal and positive law is no longer upheld—that is, when the universal law in the modern form of a law of development, natural or historical, has become a law of movement which cannot but constantly override positive man-made codes of rules and prescriptions—we have seen in the totalitarian forms of domination. There terror, as the daily execution of an ever-changing universal law of movement, makes all positive law in its relative permanence impossible and drives the whole community into a flood of catastrophes. This danger is latent wherever the old concept of a universal law is deprived of its eternity and, on the contrary, is combined with the modern concept of development as the ever-progressing motions of nature or history. If one considers this process from the point of view of the history of ideas one can easily, albeit fallaciously, come to the conclusion that totalitarian domination is not so much a break with all traditions of Western man as the outgrowth of philosophical "heresy" that culminated in Hegel and was practically applied by Darwin and Marx, whom Engels called the Darwin of history.

The idea of one universal law remained more or less a concern of the philosophers while the jurists, even though they agreed on the necessity of an ultimate (and even transcendent) authority to give their laws legitimacy, continued to think of laws as boundaries and relations between people. This difference is very marked in the twofold origin of natural law that also and independently developed from the Roman *ius gentium*, a law erected between different peoples whose cities prescribed different civil laws. Here, the natural law is neither understood to spring from and operate within each human being nor to preside from above and rule supreme over all happenings in the universe, but as the specific channels of communication and intercourse that are necessary between city and city, between one legal code and another—unless one city wants, in Greek fashion, to live isolated against or destroy another. The Roman influence remained strong in the strictly legal tradition; in the philosophical tradition of political thought, it remained as uninfluential as other Roman experiences.

The standards of right and wrong as they are laid down in positive law have, as it were, two aspects: they are absolute insofar as they owe their existence to a universally valid law, beyond the power and the competence of man; but they are also mere conventions, relative to one people and valid within limitations, insofar as they have been posited and framed by men. Without the second, the universally valid law would remain without reality in the world of men; without the first, the laws and regulations laid down by men would lack their ultimate source of authority and legitimation. Because of this relationship and its twofold aspect, the specific legality of government, which historically is characteristic only for the polis and the various republican forms that are derived from it, could become, in the framework of the tradition, the mainstay of all bodies politic. Enforcement of law finally is seen as the chief duty of government, and lawful government is considered good no matter how many people or how few share in and enjoy the possession of power. At the end of this tradition, we find Kant's political philosophy, where the concept of law has absorbed all others. Here the law has become the criterion for the whole realm of politics to the detriment of all other political experiences and possibilities. Lawfulness is the only legitimate content of human living together and all political activity is ultimately devised as legislation or application of legal prescriptions.

We have sketched this much later development in order to arrive as though through a short circuit at a position where rule and law actually coincide; where constitutional government is no longer one among various possibilities to rule and act within the framework of the law, but a government where the laws themselves rule and the ruler only administers and obeys the laws. This is the logical conclusion of the last stage of Plato's political thought as we know it from the *Laws*.

These considerations seemed necessary for an understanding of the last thinker who, still in the line of the great tradition, inquired into the nature of politics and asked the old questions about the different forms of government. Montesquieu, whose fame rests securely in the discovery of the three branches of government, the legislative, the executive, and the judiciary— that is, in the great discovery that power is not indivisible—was a political writer much rather than a systematic thinker. This enabled him to touch freely on and reformulate almost unintentionally the great problems of political thought as they had come down to him, without encumbering his new insights by making one working whole of them, and without disturbing the inner consistency of his thought with ulterior motives of presentation. His insights are in substance much more "revolutionary" and at the same time more enduringly positive than those of Rousseau, who is his only equal in the weight of sheer immediate impact on the eighteenth-century revolutions and of intellectual influence on the political philosophy of the nineteenth century. His lack of systematic concern, on the other hand, and the loose organization of his material have made it deplorably easy to neglect both the inner consistency of his widely scattered thoughts and the distinct unity of his approach to all political matters, which separates him only slightly less from his successors than from his predecessors.

Hidden beneath the discovery of three branches of government (which only Kant rightly understood as the decisive criterion of truly republican government and which only in the constitution of the American Republic found an adequate realization) lies a vision of political life in which power is completely separated from all connotations of violence. Montesquieu alone had a concept of power that lay absolutely outside of the traditional category of means and ends. The three branches of government represent for him the three main political activities of men: the making of laws, the executing of decisions, and the deciding judgment that must accompany both. Each of these activities engenders its own power. Power can be divided—between the branches of government as well as between federated states and between state and federal governments—because it is not *one* instrument to be applied to *one* goal. Its origins lie in the multiple capacities of men for action; these actions have no end as long as the body politic is alive; their immediate purposes are prescribed by the ever-changing circumstances of human and political life, which by themselves and because they occur within defined communities or given civilizations constitute a realm of public affairs arising between citizens as individuals, binding together or separating them as shared or conflicting interests. Interests in this context have no connotation of material needs or greeds, but constitute quite literally the *inter-esse,* that which is *between* men. This in-between, common to all and therefore of concern to each, is the space in which political life takes place.

Montesquieu's discovery of both the divisible nature of power and the three branches of government sprang from his preoccupation with the phenomenon of action as the central data of the whole realm of politics. His own inquiries led him to make a distinction between the nature of government, *"ce qui le fait être tel,"* and its principle, *"ce qui le fait agir"* (*L'Esprit des Lois,* Book III, Chapter 1). He defined the kinds of government in only slightly changed terms—he neglects the form of aristocracy and states that a republic is constitutional government with sovereign power in the hands of the people, a monarchy a lawful government with sovereign power in the hands of one man, and tyranny a lawless rule where power is wielded by one man according to his arbitrary will. His more profound discovery is his insight that these "particular structures" need each a different "principle" to set them into motion, or in other words, that these structures in themselves are dead and do not correspond to the realities of political life and the experiences of acting men. As a principle of motion, Montesquieu introduced history and historical process into structures that—owing their existence to Greek thought—had originally been conceived as immobile. Or rather, prior to Montesquieu, the only possibility of change had been thought of as change for the worse, the change or perversion that could transform an aristocracy into an oligarchy, a democracy into an ochlocracy, or a monarchy into tyranny. There are of course many more possibilities of such perversion; it was, for instance, noted very early that majority rule also has a particular inclination to end in tyranny. Compared to Montesquieu's principle of action as the driving motor of change, all such perversions are of a physical, almost organic nature. Plato's famous prediction that even the best possible government could not last forever, and his accounting of its eventual doom through some inevitable mistakes in the choice of suitable parents for a desirable offspring, is only the most plausible example for a mentality that could conceive of change only in terms of ruin. Montesquieu, on the contrary, recognized motion as the very condition of history, precisely because he understood that action is the essential factor of all political life. Action does not merely belong to governments, does not only show itself in the recorded deeds of nations, and is never exhausted in the process of ruling and being ruled: "*On juge mal des choses. Il y a souvent autant de politique employée pour obtenir un petit bénéfice que pour obtenir la papauté.*" ("*De la Politique*" in *Mélanges inédits de Montesquieu*, 1892.) He recognizes with the tradition the permanent character of good government founded on lawfulness; but he sees this structure of laws only as the framework within which people move and act, as the stabilizing factor of something which by itself is alive and moving without necessarily developing into a prescribed direction of either doom or progress. He therefore does not only talk about the nature or essence, but also about the structure of government as that which in relative permanence harbors the changing circumstances and actions of mortal men.

Corresponding to his three chief forms of government, Montesquieu distinguishes three principles "which make a community act": these are virtue in a republic, honor in a monarchy, and fear in a tyranny. These principles are not the same as psychological motives. They are rather the criteria according to which all public actions are judged and which articulate the whole of political life. As such, they are the same for both governments and citizens, for rulers and subjects. If the principle of fear inspires all actions in a tyranny, this means that the tyrant acts because he fears his subjects and the oppressed because they fear the tyrant. Just as it is the pride of a subject in a monarchy to distinguish himself and be publicly honored, so it is the pride of the citizen in a republic not to be greater in public matters than his fellow citizens, which is his "virtue." From this it does not follow that the citizens of a republic do not know what honor is, or that the subjects of a monarchy are not "virtuous," nor that all people have at all times to behave according to the rules of the government under which they happen to live. It only means that the sphere of public life is always determined by certain rules that are taken for granted by all who *act*, and that these rules are not the same for all forms of political bodies. If these rules are no longer valid, if the principles of action lose their authority so that no one any longer believes in virtue in a republic, or in honor in a monarchy, or if, in a tyranny, the tyrant ceases to fear his subjects, or the subjects no longer fear their oppressor, then each of the forms of government comes to its end.

Beneath Montesquieu's unsystematic and sometimes even casual observations about the relationship between the nature of governments and their principles of action lies an even deeper insight into the essentials of unity in historically given civilizations. His *"esprit général"* is what unites the structure of government with its corresponding principle of action. As such, it later became the inspiring idea of the historical sciences as well as the philosophy of history. Herder's "spirit of the people" (*Volksgeist*) and Hegel's "world-spirit" (*Weltgeist*) show clear traces of this ancestry. Montesquieu's original discovery is less metaphysical than either of those, and perhaps more fruitful for the political sciences. Writing in the midst of the eighteenth century, he was still blissfully unaware of "world history," which one hundred years later—in Hegel's philosophy and also in the work of the leading historians—will have arrogated to itself the business of world judgment: *"Die Weltgeschichte ist das Weltgericht."* His general unifying spirit is first of all a basic experience of men living and acting together, which expresses itself simultaneously in the laws of a country and in the actions of men living under this law. Virtue in this sense is based on "love of equality" and honor is based on "love of distinction." The laws of a republic are based on equality, and love of equality is the source from which the actions of its citizens spring; monarchical laws are based on distinction, so that love of distinctions inspires the public actions of the citizenry.

Both distinction and equality are basic experiences of all human communal life. We can say with equal validity that men are distinguished and different from each other by birth *and* that all men are "born equal" and are distinguished by social status only. Equality, insofar as it is a political experience—as distinguished from the equality before God, an infinitely superior being before whom all distinctions and differences become negligible—has always meant that, regardless of existing differences, everyone is of equal value because each one received by nature an equal amount of strength. The fundamental experience upon which republican laws are founded and from which the actions of citizens spring is the experience of living together with, and being members of, a group of equally powerful men. Laws in a republic, therefore, are not laws of distinction but of restriction; they are designed to restrict the strength of each citizen so that room may be left for the strength of his fellow citizens. The common ground of republican law and action within it is the insight that human strength is not primarily limited by some superior power—God or nature—but by the power of *equals,* and the joy that springs from it. Virtue as love of equality springs from this experience of equality of power that alone guards men against the dread of loneliness. "One is one and all alone and ever more shall be so," as the old English nursery rhyme dares to indicate to human minds what can only be the supreme tragedy of God.

Distinction, on which monarchies (and all hierarchical forms of government) are based, is no less an authentic and original political experience. Only through distinction can I become truly myself, this one, unique individual that never was before and never will be again. I can establish this uniqueness only by measuring myself against all others so that my role in public affairs will ultimately depend upon the extent to which I can win recognition from them. It is the great advantage of monarchical government that individuals, who have their social and political status according to the distinction they win within their respective walks of life, are never confronted with an undistinguished and indistinguishable mass of "all others," against which the single man can summon up nothing but a desperate minority of one. It is the specific danger of governments based on equality that within the structure of lawfulness—in whose framework the equality of power receives its meaning, direction, and restriction—the powers of equals can cancel each other out until the exhaustion of impotence makes everyone ready to accept a tyrannical government. For good reasons, Montesquieu failed to indicate the common ground for the structure of lawlessness and fear as the principle of actions in tyrannies.

1953

II
Ruling and Being Ruled

If now, in the light of Montesquieu's insights, we reconsider the tradition not from its end but from its beginning and ask ourselves what role the experience of rule played, in what realm of life it was chiefly located, we should remember that the traditional forms of government—enumerated as rule by one, or few, or a multitude, which follow consistently from the division between rulers and subjects, as do their perversions—were always accompanied by an altogether different taxonomy. In the stead of monarchy, we hear of kingship (*basileia*), and monarchy, in this context, is used interchangeably with tyranny, so that one-man rule, monarchy or tyranny, sometimes is called the perversion of kingship. Oligarchy, the rule of the few, is still the perversion of aristocracy, the rule of the best, but instead of the term democracy, majority rule, we find polity, which originally designated the polis or city-state and later became the republic, the Roman *res publica*. Democracy now is seen as the perversion of this polity, an ochlocracy where the mob rules supreme.

Kingship, aristocracy, and polity are praised as the best forms of government or, also very early and later specifically insisted upon by Cicero, a mixture of the three is recommended. But such "mixed government," supposedly embodying the best traits of each form of government, is impossible under the assumption that these governments are essentially distinguished by the rule of one, or the few, or the multitude, because those forms are clearly mutually exclusive. Tyranny, moreover, denounced in this context even more strongly than in the traditional definitions, is not so much condemned for its arbitrary lawlessness as the worst but still a possible form of living together, or as the least desirable but still a comprehensible human attitude toward one's fellow men. The tyrant is rather ruled out of human society altogether; he is considered to be a beast in the shape of a man, unfit for human intercourse and beyond the pale of mankind. In other words, kingship, aristocracy, and polity seem not simply to be the "good forms" of government of which monarchy, oligarchy, and democracy are perversions: the former cannot even be defined within the same framework of categories as the latter.

The descriptions of kingship, aristocracy, and polity rather indicate actual political experiences that crystallized in different forms of people's living together and are embodied in them, experiences that are prior to and not necessarily identical with those that gave rise to the concepts of rule in accordance with law and power. Whether these experiences, which still loom large in the traditional definitions and descriptions of governments, had been conceptualized earlier is a different question. The fact that Thucydides already mentions what was later called a "mixed government" (Book VIII, 97) and that Aristotle alludes to similar theories in his *Politics* (1265b33), seems to indicate that an earlier track of political thought was superseded, absorbed, and partly eliminated with the rise of our tradition. The point is that neither the division between rulers and subjects nor the standards of law and power make much sense when they are applied to the "good forms," which on the contrary change immediately into their "perverted forms" if we try to define them according to that division and those standards.

If kingship were the rule by one man, it clearly would be the same as monarchy, a constitutional monarchy, as we would say today, if in accordance with the laws, and a tyranny if against them. The fact however is that a king (*basileus*) did not have the absolute power of the monarch, that his was not a hereditary office but that he was elected and very clearly never was permitted to be more than *primus inter pares* (first among equals). The moment he is defined in terms of rule as the holder of power, he has already changed into a tyrant. If aristocracy is the rule of the few, who are the best, then the question invariably arises who the best are and how they can be found out—certainly not through self-election—and whether one can make sure that during their rule the best remain the best. The moment the few are identified in accordance with objective standards, they can only be the rich or the hereditary nobility, whose rule Aristotle defined as oligarchy, a perverted aristocracy. Or, if the few are the wisest, then they are according to Plato those who cannot persuade the multitude and must rule over unwilling subjects through violence, which again would be tyranny. Least of all was it possible to define polity or republic in these terms of ruling and being ruled. Aristotle, after having stated axiomatically that "each polis-community is composed of ruler and ruled" goes on immediately to say that in this form of government "it is necessary that all share equally in ruling and being ruled" and that nature itself, by composing cities of the young and the old has indicated for whom it is befitting to rule and for whom to be ruled (*Politics*, VII, 14, 1332b12–36). Obviously, the distinction between ruler and subjects disappears here into the distinction between teacher and pupils, or between father and sons. That the whole organization of polis life did not permit the distinction between ruler and subjects is quite manifest in Herodotus's famous discussion of forms of government where the defender of the Greek polis finally, after he is defeated in a contest, demands to be permitted to retire from political life altogether, because he neither wants to rule or to be ruled. The fact was, of course, that Greek polis life did not know of any such division among its citizens. The rulership on which it was based, as is indicated more than once in Aristotle, was primarily experienced not in the public-political realm, but in the strictly private sphere of the household, whose head ruled over his family and slaves.

This private realm of family and household was constituted by the necessities of life, the necessity of sustaining through labor the individual life and of guaranteeing through procreation and birth the survival of the species. To define the condition for human life in terms of the twofold hardship of labor and birth (not only the English language, but in nearly all European languages the same word, labor, is used for toil and the pangs of birth) and to understand these two as interconnected, corresponding to each other, be it because after man's sin in paradise God decided to make life hard for human beings or be it that this driving necessity is seen in contrast to the "easy" life of the gods, has been one of the few outstanding traits in which the two strands of our past, the Hebrew and the Greek, are in agreement. It indicates the rank of Marx's thought that he, in a time when this fundamental connection was almost forgotten, reestablished it by understanding labor and begetting as the two chief forms of "production of life, one's own life through labor, that is, the means of subsistence, and new life through begetting" (*Deutsche Ideologie*, 17). But while Marx put this production of life through labor at the center of his political philosophy, the whole tradition in complete agreement with the pre-traditional past put labor outside the political realm, making it the merely private concern of each individual of how to solve the problem of staying alive, and held this whole sphere in contempt, not primarily because it was "private," but because it was subject to the necessities inherent in being and keeping alive. Whoever was subject to these necessities, such as laborers and women, could not be free; freedom meant first of all to have become independent of any activities that are necessary for life itself.

The division between ruling and being ruled was first experienced in this private field where it divided those who ruled and those who were subject to necessity. Public-political life rested on this division as its pre-political condition, but the concept of rule itself originally played no role in it. This becomes emphatically true for the city-state and its concept of the equality of citizens, for which freedom is a pre-political condition and neither the content of politics nor a political ideal—but it is already true for an earlier time. Agamemnon was a king of kings, and even in Hesiod's seeming glorification of labor we meet the ever-present slave or servant who executes his master's commands.

In traditional political thought, this elementary freedom from necessity, which can be achieved only through rule over others, is then reflected in the ever-repeated assurances that only a life that aspires to something higher than life itself is worth living, and only an activity whose end is more than the activity itself is worth entering upon. Even the most striking difference between the life of free men in antiquity and the modern age, the enormous amount of ease without which political activity in the Greek and Roman sense, the *bios politikos,* would be altogether impossible, and that rested completely on the fact of slave labor, is for those people's actual experience of freedom less relevant than its seemingly negative counterpart—the freedom from *anagkaia,* the sheer necessities of life.

In other words, the distinction between ruling and being ruled, between rulers and subjects, which the traditional definitions of forms of government assume to be the essence of all political organization, was originally a distinction valid only in private life and therefore only a condition and never the content of politics. The reasons why the philosophers superimposed it on actual political experiences when they began to formalize and conceptualize them, have much more to do with the philosophers' attitude toward politics—an attitude that, to be sure, also had its political reasons and implications—than with any presumably unchangeable traits of the public-political realm itself.

Kingship, aristocracy, and polity or republic are based on this freedom from necessity, which manifests itself in rule over women and slaves, and their distinctness does not lie in the question of how many hold power or of who rules whom. Their distinctness lies in what is understood to be of public concern as such and the relationship between those who are concerned with the public realm. Of public concern in a kingship is first of all a common enterprise that is not a quotidian occurrence but has the outstanding significance of an event that *interrupts* the normal course of everyday life. In order to participate in public affairs at all, the private rulers who follow their chosen leader, the *basileus,* have to leave not only the privacy of their lives but to step out of its daily rhythm altogether.

What Hesiod glorifies over Homer is not labor itself but the dignity of everyday life. As the title *Works and Days* indicates, and as becomes even clearer in the admonitions to the seafaring brother, Hesiod praises staying at home against enterprise and adventure of all kinds. He holds up the quiet beauty of everyday life, characterized no less by the recurring configuration of the days of the year than by the work in the household and field, which also in Hesiod is executed by slaves and only supervised by the head of the household. Hesiod's significance is that he praises a life that keeps away from the common public realm altogether; for him the possibilities of glory and great deeds count for nothing. He is the only Greek who unashamedly praises private life, whose main characteristic for other Greeks was that it did not offer that space or sphere of a common world in which alone one can appear and be seen and therefore become what one is potentially. The reason that the Greek, as distinguished from the Roman, spirit could see in private life not much more than an unavoidable condition for the constitution of a common, public world was that privacy did not offer any possibility for *doxa* in its manifold meanings: appearance and illusion, fame and opinion. And since only that *is* which appears and is seen, Plato's highest idea of the good in its all-embracing and overshadowing reality is *phanotaton*—that is, it shines forth most, has the most shining appearance (*Republica*, 518 C).

The private realm, even if the necessities of life were successfully "ruled" and taken care of, remained a realm of shadowy, inarticulate, and dark matters; private life was deprived of reality because it could not show itself and could not be seen by others. The conviction that only what appears and is seen by others acquires full reality and authentic meaning for man is at the basis of all Greek political life. The principal aim of the tyrant is to condemn men to their private household, which is to deprive them of the possibility of their humanity. The *agon*, the strife of *aristeuein*, of being better than one's fellows and if possible the best of all, is not the competition of "potter with potter, craftsman with craftsman, and beggar with beggar," as Hesiod in his praise of Eris would have us believe (*Works and Days*, 24); it is, on the contrary, the political equation of reality with appearing to others. Only where others were present could a specifically human life begin. Only where one was noticed by others could he, by distinguishing himself, come into his own humanity.

It is therefore not just political life and political experience in the narrow sense of the word, but human life and human experience as such that begin wherever the private household and ruling over it come to an end; the common world, seen by all others in its freely shining public light, then begins. This is equally true for kingship and for the polis, but the advantage of the latter in this respect is that it offers a common world for the daily life of its citizens and not only for sporadic enterprises. By the same token, polis life loses opportunities for the truly extraordinary, and its *doxa* therefore becomes more and more an opinion by which the citizen distinguishes himself in the constant activity of *politeuesthai*, and less the shining glory of immortal fame that follows upon great deeds. What distinguishes kingship from polity and republic is not the relationship between rulers and subjects, and it is not even primarily the different relationship between the citizens, that is, those who live and move together in a common world. The chief historical difference lies in the role action itself plays in these different forms of public organization.

Kingship, probably the oldest, and perhaps the most elementary political form of organization, rests on experience of action in the general sense of beginning something new, of men starting together on a new enterprise. Action is the rallying point of the coming and staying together of heads of private households who have decided to leave behind their private concerns and who form a body politic as long as the enterprise lasts. What drives them together is the appetite for action that never can be satisfied by one man alone; for in distinction to laboring and fabricating, which can be pursued in loneliness or isolation, action is possible only where men join together and act in concert. This concert of action demands and, as it were, creates the king, who, as *primus inter pares* becomes an elected leader whom the others follow out of their own free choice in the spirit of loyalty. Where the element of free engagement is absent, kingship becomes a monarchy and, according to Plato, a tyranny when obedience is not granted voluntarily. The sovereign ruler of regal households who followed King Agamemnon to begin the Trojan enterprise helped him and Menelaos because they hoped to win for themselves "eternal glory," namely, the *doxa* of glorious appearance in the world of mortals, which will survive their deaths. Only in the common world where they themselves and everything they do is seen and noted by others can they hope to overcome their private destiny of mortality, that is, to be born and live and die as one unique, unexchangeable person who, in the privacy of his own concerns, could not hope to leave any trace of his earthly existence behind him.

It is for its utter futility that private existence—the *idiom* of the Greeks and, though to a lesser extent because of the integration of family life into the public political realm, the *res privata* of the Romans—always had the connotation of a life deprived of the most essential human possibilities. Yet something of this futility is also inherent in the great enterprises of the so-called heroic age. The common realm itself, constituted only for the requirements of action, disappears the moment the enterprise has come to an end—when Troy is destroyed, its people killed or distributed as slaves in the private households of the heroes. In a sense, kingship and its enterprises, inspired by the courage to do and to endure—*poiein* and *pathein* have a closer relationship in Greek than in any other language; they are like two sides of the same *pragmata* insofar as they signify the ever-changing and fluctuating fortunes of men—begin what eventually emerges in the polis as a more stable common world of human affairs (*ta tôn anthrôpôn pragmata*). This later common world comprehends and assures survival for everything that men do to, and suffer from, each other, whereby it is understood that human greatness is not restricted to the deed and the doer in the strict sense of the word, but can equally be the share of the endurer and sufferer.

Neither for the Greek polity nor for the Roman Republic was action ever the central political experience. It is the basis of the city-state that people can live permanently together and not merely join together for great enterprises. It is between citizens that political affairs in the more narrow and familiar sense arise, and the central experiences of citizens stem from this living together much more than from acting together. The moment action is required, the polis will revert to the older kingly form of organization, and the citizens will again follow their chosen leader, the *stratêgos,* to lead them in war, either in conquest or defense. But then these actions, which typically take place outside the walls of the city, are also outside of political activity strictly speaking; they no longer constitute, as they did in the early kingship, the only realm in which free men came and lived together. When military action again became the foundation of a form of government, we witness not the restoration of the old kingship but the establishment of monarchy, as when Roman emperors were elected as professional soldiers. The transformation of the *stratêgos* into the monarch, or rather into the Roman *rex*—and the word *rex* in the fifth century BCE had been as abhorrent to Roman republican ears as the word monarch had been to early Greek ears—takes place when wars became an everyday business and military action took predominance over all civil affairs. Only then does one-man rule or monarchy acquire a different status from tyranny. The Greek polis, however, and the Roman Republic are equally removed from the early experience of action as the beginning of an enterprise, on one hand, and from the latest professional soldier's outlook on war as his daily business, on the other.

What determines both Plato's and Aristotle's notion of the essence of politics is the daily living together of many people within the walls of one limited space. What relates these many to each other are two experiences: *equality* and *difference*. The sense of equality, however, as it appeared with the foundation of the polis, was very different from our own belief in universal equality. First, it was not universal but pertained only to those who in actual fact were equals; excluded from it as a matter of course were the unfree, namely, slaves, women, and barbarians. Freedom and equality therefore in the beginning were corresponding notions and no conflict was felt to exist between them. Since equality did not extend to all men, it was not seen against the background of a common human fate, as is the equality of all men before death; nor was it measured against the overwhelming reality of a superhuman being, as is the equality before God. Neither of these senses of equality entered the political realm before the declining centuries of the Roman Empire. What equality originally meant, in a positive sense, was not being alone and not being lonely, for loneliness means to be without equals and the ruler of a rural household had no equals unless he went to war. Gratitude for the fact that not one man but men inhabit the earth found its first political expression in the body politic of the city-state.

There, among equals, not in the solitary supremacy of a rural household, the great Greek passion for *aei aristeuein,* for always striving to distinguish oneself as the best of all, could develop into a way of life and hope to bring forward an aristocracy, not in the sense of rule by the best, but of a constant predominance of the best in polis life. In a famous fragment Heraclitus tells us who the best are and how they are distinguished from the ordinary citizens: "The best prefer one thing, immortal fame, to all mortal things; but the multitude is satisfied with gorging themselves like cattle" (B 29). The need to measure oneself against others in order to come into one's own and show the irrevocable and unexchangeable uniqueness of each man who, because he is mortal, must find and mark out for himself a permanent abode that will survive both the perishable futility of his deeds and the mortality of his person, was certainly one of the strongest motives for the great enterprises of the earlier time of kingship. The great advantage of the polis over kingship is that the common public world, in which alone the deeds of men are seen and remembered, is not confined to the limited time of an enterprise with its beginning and end, but is itself permanent, the permanent abode of posterity. Moreover, the distinguishing activity, the *aristeuein* itself, can now become a daily performance and permeate the whole body politic. As long as the Greek polis was inspired by the agonal spirit, it remained aristocratic no matter whether an oligarchy, as in the beginning, or the multitude in the classical time, holds the power of government. Its aristocratic traits, the reckless individualism of *aristeuein* at any price, eventually brought the polis to its doom because it made alliances between poleis well nigh impossible.

Its exact counterpart is the Roman Republic, based from the beginning on the conclusion of alliances with defeated enemies, where the *salus rei publicae,* the welfare of that which all have in common, was always and consciously put above individual glory, with the result that no one could ever fully become himself. Difference and distinction were secondary to equality, which only there became a working principle, a way of life and not, as in Athens, a sort of springboard from which to start distinguishing oneself above all others. What both Rome and Athens have in common is that the early concept of action as central for political life, and closely connected with the notion of great enterprises, gave way to the notion of an active life consisting of handling public affairs by all citizens at all times. The content of this activity in Rome and Athens was as different as the Latin term *agere* is from the Greek *politeuesthai*. The one consisted chiefly in the never-ending watchful care that the foundation of Rome and her laws, the care for preservation and growth, laid upon the citizens as a burden of eternal responsibility, while the other consisted in constant deliberation and common consideration of all things human, because everything essentially human, according to the spirit of polis life, was bound to appear and show its true face in the public-political realm. But in both cases the citizens who wanted to lead an active life and participate in the highest possibilities their worlds held out to them had to spend as much time as possible among their equals—in the gymnasium or the theater, in the courts or the marketplace, in popular meetings or the senate—and as little time as possible at home as the head or ruler of a household. Their private business, running their households or supervising their craftsmen or watching over their farms, was, as it were, squeezed in between the by far more important matters which they daily attended to in public. The very notion of leisure, therefore, be it *scholê* or *otium,* meant specifically and exclusively leisure from public-political affairs, and not leisure from work, indicating, even before the philosophers demanded it as the prerequisite of the nonactive contemplative way of life, a kind of solitude which neither the polis nor the republic, with the presence of one's fellow citizens, was willing or able to grant.

Seen in the light of actual political experiences, the three forms of government disappear into three different, but not mutually exclusive, ways of living together. Kingship is primarily founded on action in the sense of beginning and seeing through great and single enterprises, and as such was devised for unique occasions, not for everyday life. Kingship occurs in Greek but not in Roman history, which up to the end abhorred the *rex,* because the only experience of one-man rule it ever had was of tyranny. Since Roman political life began after the foundation of Rome, the greatest of all enterprises, it had no experience of enterprises as possible gathering points for men, constituting their own common world. Roman history contained the *res gestae,* the things that Rome had laid upon her citizens and that her citizens had borne (*gerere* means originally to bear) and handled in a great and just spirit.

Aristocracy again is primarily a Greek experience and consists of living together in the modus of *aristeuein,* of winning distinction and measuring oneself constantly against one's equals. Against it, and not necessarily in a different form of government, stands the spirit of the polity that flourished in Rome rather than in Athens. The Roman spirit embodies and exalts—to a degree it is difficult for us to recapture—the great overflowing joy of companionship among one's equals, the tremendous relief from being alone, which must have characterized the first foundation of urban centers and the flocking together of the many from rural occupations in the countryside. Here, the possibility of a "mixed government" is self-evident; it means no more than integrating the three fundamental experiences that characterize men insofar as they live with each other and exist in plurality—the combination of "love of equality" with "love for distinction" (as Montesquieu later put it), and the integration of both in the "royal" faculty of action, the experience that action is a beginning and that no one can act alone.

The exclusion of tyranny as a way of living together, as distinguished from one-man rule or monarchy as the worst among possible forms of government, is no less manifest. The tyrant sins equally against all the fundamental traits of the human condition in its political aspect: he pretends to be able to act completely alone; he isolates men from each other by sowing fear and mistrust between them, thereby destroying equality together with man's capacity to act; and he cannot permit anybody to distinguish himself, and therefore starts his rule with the establishment of uniformity, which is the perversion of equality.

It is this past and its outstanding political experiences that the tradition conceptualized when it defined the forms of government in the framework of ruling and being ruled, of law and power. Nothing, as we pointed out before, could be more alien to these experiences than the division of rulers and subjects, since rule was precisely a pre-political condition of living together and therefore, in terms of antiquity, this could only mean that a category of private life was applied to the public-political realm. As a matter of fact, nothing is so characteristic of the negative aspects of Greek history than the incapacity of the Greeks to rule, which shows itself all the way from the great Trojan enterprise, which ended with the destruction of Troy, the slaughtering of its men and enslavement of its women and children, to the ill-fated behavior of Athens in the Peloponnesian War toward the Melians, and in general toward all the allies. Nowhere were the Greeks ever able to rule over conquered peoples, that is, to establish rulership as a politically valid principle against destruction on one side and slavery on the other. Conquest and destruction could enrich the private realm of the citizens; they could never establish a public realm in which the citizens as citizens would rule over another people, as the heads of households rule over their slaves and women. It is precisely the absence of rule in the public realm that characterizes the specific cruelty of Greek history.

Rome, to be sure, had the greatness to solve this problem. But its solution is not in terms of rule either. *Dominium* as well as *imperium* were based on the Roman faculty to establish *societates*, alliances with former enemies. Roman power expresses itself in establishing specific public realms between Rome and her neighbors, be these enemies or friends, so that a common world comes into being which is neither identical with Rome herself nor with the former political status of the conquered. It is very specifically a world of its own *between* both, founded on Roman law, but again not in the law valid for Roman citizens, but on a law specifically designed to operate in between, the *ius gentium*, a kind of mediator between the different and alien laws of the cities. It was only in her decline that Rome became "the universal master" and then she destroyed the common world, the first great commonwealth, which she herself had built, the *Imperium Romanum* in which power (*imperium*) is supported by *gloria et benevolentia sociorum*, as Cicero says (*De Officiis* III, 88), by the glory of Rome and the goodwill of her allies.

Thus it was only during the decline and after the fall of the Roman Empire that the traditional division between ruling and being ruled as an elementary necessity for all organized communities could base itself on an equally elementary experience in the political realm. During this same period of dying antiquity, the most fundamental distinction on which all political life had rested in the ancient world—the distinction between a world of the free, which alone was political, and the household rule over slaves, which remained private—became increasingly blurred. This was partly because the public realm of free men was breaking down to such an extent that the private realm of each of them almost automatically received a new emphasis, and partly because so many former slaves had been freed that the distinction itself was no longer of such great importance. But from then on, the traditional division between those who rule and those who are ruled kept growing in significance all through the Middle Ages and the first centuries of the modern age. That the whole realm of public political life and the common world in which it moves is essentially structured by this division finally became the basic assumption of the tradition of Western political thought. Wherever this division is lacking, as for instance in the utopian expectations of a future society functioning without the interference of clearly defined state power, the inevitable conclusion is that the whole realm of politics, and not only the state, will wither away.

1953

AUTHORITY IN THE
TWENTIETH CENTURY

I

The rise of fascist, communist, and totalitarian movements and the development of the two totalitarian regimes we know, Stalin's after 1929 and Hitler's after 1938, took place against a background of a more or less general, more or less dramatic breakdown of all traditional authorities. Nowhere was this breakdown the direct result of the regimes or movements themselves, but it seemed as though totalitarianism in the form of regimes as well as of movements was best fitted to take advantage of a general political and social atmosphere in which the validity of authority itself was radically doubted.

The most extreme manifestation of this climate, which, with minor geographical and chronological exceptions, has been the atmosphere of our century since its inception, is the gradual breakdown of the one form of authority which exists in all historically known societies, the authority of parents over children, of teachers over pupils, and generally of the elder over the younger. Even the least "authoritarian" forms of government have always accepted this kind of "authority" as a matter of course. It always has seemed to be required as much by natural needs, the helplessness of the child, as by political necessity, the continuity of an established civilization which can be assured only if those, who are newcomers by birth, are guided through a pre-established world into which they are born as strangers. Because of its simple and elementary character, this form of a strictly limited authority has, throughout the history of political thought, been used and abused as a model for very different and much less limited authoritarian systems.*

It seems that ours is the first century in which this argument no longer carries an overwhelming weight of plausibility; it announced its antiauthoritarian spirit nowhere more radically than when it promised the emancipation of youth as an oppressed class and called itself the "century of the child." We cannot follow up here the implications of this early self-interpretation, which are manifold, nor are we interested now in the various schools of "progressive education" where this principle found its realization. But it may be worth noting that the antiauthoritarian position has been driven to the extreme of *education without authority* only in the United States, the most egalitarian and the least tradition-bound country of the West, where precisely the results of this radical experiment are now, more than any other single political or social factor, leading to a reevaluation of the very concept of authority. Neoconservatism, which has won a surprisingly large following in recent years, is primarily cultural and educational, and not political or social, in outlook; it appeals to a mood and concern which are the direct results of the elimination of authority from the relationship between young and old, teacher and pupil, parents and children.

I mention this strangest, but in other respects least interesting, aspect of the problem of authority in our world only because it shows to what extremes the general decline of authority can go, even to the neglect of obvious natural necessities. For this indicates how very unlikely it is that we shall find in our century the rise of authentic authoritarian forms of government and hence, how careful we must be lest we mistake tyrannical forms of government, which rule by order and decree, for authoritarian structures. Our century, it is true, has seen quite a number of new variations of tyranny and dictatorship, among which we must count the fascist and early communist types of one-party systems. But these differ as much

---

* The first to use this argument seems to be Aristotle, when in his *Politics* he wishes to demonstrate that "every political community is composed of those who rule and those who are ruled" (1332b12). There he says: "Nature herself has provided the distinction . . . [between] the younger and the older ones, of whom she fitted the ones to be ruled and the others to rule" (1332b36).

in institutional structure, type of organization, and political content from authoritarian bodies as they differ from totalitarian domination. Unless we define authority without regard to its historical and verbal content, and identify it with arbitrary orders and total abolition of freedom, i.e., with political realities always thought to be its very opposite, we shall find it hard indeed to speak of a "rise of authoritarian forms of government in our century." The most one can say is that up to now one authentically authoritarian institution has managed to survive the onslaught of the modern age, the Catholic Church, which of course has long ceased to be a body politic properly speaking.

Tyrannies and authoritarian forms of government are very old, the first going back to Greek antiquity and the other having its origin in the spirit of the Roman Republic. Only totalitarian domination is new, as new as the word itself, and the claim to *total*, and not only political, domination. Our knowledge of it is still very limited, the only variety open to our inquiries being the Hitler regime for which documentary material has become available in recent years. No doubt this limitation tempts us to examine the newest body politic in our history with conceptual tools derived from more familiar experiences, except that through such identification—with tyranny on one hand and with authoritarianism on the other—we lose sight of precisely those characteristics and institutions that belong to this and no other phenomenon.

The identification of totalitarianism with authoritarianism is present most frequently in liberal writers. They start from the assumption that "the constancy of progress . . . in the direction of organized and assured freedom is the characteristic fact of modern history"* and look upon each deviation from this course as a reactionary process in the opposite direction. This makes them overlook that there exist differences in principle between the restriction of freedom in authoritarian regimes, the abolition of political freedom in tyrannies and dictatorships, and the total elimination of spontaneity itself, i.e., of the most general and most elementary manifestation

---

* The formulation is Lord Acton's in his "Inaugural Lecture on the Study of History," reprinted in *Essays on Freedom and Power*, New York, 1955, p. 35.

of human freedom, at which only totalitarian regimes aim through various methods of conditioning—for terror and concentration camps are meant not so much to frighten as to condition people. The liberal writer, concerned with history and the progress of freedom rather than with forms of government, sees here only differences in degree, and ignores that authoritarian government, committed to the restriction of liberty, remains tied to the freedom it limits to the extent that it would lose its substance if it abolished it altogether, i.e., would change into a tyranny. The same is true for the distinction between legitimate and illegitimate power on which all authoritarian government hinges. The liberal is apt to pay little attention to it because of his conviction that power corrupts so that the constancy of progress requires a consistent diminishment of power, no matter what its origin may be.

Behind the liberal identification of totalitarianism and authoritarianism, and the concomitant inclination to see "totalitarian" trends in every authoritarian limitation of freedom, lies an older confusion of authority with tyranny and of legitimate power with violence. The difference between tyranny and authoritarian government has always been that the tyrant rules in accordance with his own will and interest, whereas even the most draconic authoritarian government is bound by laws. Its acts are tested by a code which either has not been made by man at all, as in the case of the law of nature or God's Commandments or the Platonic ideas, or at least not by those actually in power. The source of authority in authoritarian government is always external and superior to its own power; it is always this external source that transcends the political realm, from which the authorities derive their "authority," i.e., their legitimacy, and against which their power can be checked.

The modern spokesmen for authority, who even in the short intervals when public opinion provides a favorable climate for neoconservatism remain well aware that theirs is an almost lost cause, are of course eager to point to this distinction between tyranny and authority. Where the liberal writer sees an essentially assured progress in the direction of freedom, which is only temporarily interrupted by some dark forces of the past, the conservative sees a process of doom which was started by the dwindling of authority, so that freedom, after losing the restricting limitation which protected its boundaries, became helpless, defenseless, and bound to be destroyed.* Tyranny and totalitarianism are again identified except that now totalitarian government, if not directly identified with democracy, is seen as its almost inevitable result, that is, the result of the disappearance of all traditionally recognized authorities. Yet the differences between tyranny and dictatorships on one side and totalitarian domination on the other are no less distinct than those between authoritarianism and totalitarianism. The proverbial quiet of the cemetery with which tyrants, from the rulers of ancient city-states to modern dictators, have covered their countries once they have suppressed all organized opposition and destroyed all actual enemies, has never benefited the people living under a totalitarian regime.

Modern one-party dictatorships resemble tyrannies to the extent that their rule rests on parties, and not movements. It is true, though, that already in the case of most fascist dictatorships, it was a movement which brought the dictator into power; but the point is that this movement was frozen into a party after the seizure of power. The very articulate and often repeated criticism the Nazis voiced against Mussolini and Italian fascism, as well as their no less articulate admiration for Stalin and the Bolshevism of the Stalinist era, center around this vital difference between a party dictatorship and a totalitarian movement, or, to use their own language, between the dictatorial head of a normal state and a "world revolution." The totalitarian form of domination depends entirely upon the fact that a movement, and not a party, has taken power, that the rulers are chiefly concerned with keeping the movement moving and preventing it from "degenerating" into a party, so that instead of the tyrant's brutal determination and the dictator's demagogic ability to keep himself in power at all costs, we find the totalitarian leaders' single-minded attention directed to the acceleration of the movement itself. This is the significance of the purges of the Stalin regime, as it is of Hitler's "selection process which should never

---

* It is hardly fair to say that only liberal political thought is primarily interested in freedom; there exists hardly any school of political thought in our history which is not centered around the idea of freedom, much as the concept of liberty may vary with the different writers and according to the different political circumstances. The only exception of any consequence to this statement seems to me to be the political philosophy of Thomas Hobbes, who of course is anything but a conservative. —Ed.

be permitted to come to an end," whose outstanding characteristic it was that it could function only as an extermination process.*

Closely connected with this is the apparently senseless use of terror in totalitarian regimes, which distinguishes them most conspicuously from modern as well as past dictatorships and tyrannies. Terror is no longer a means to frighten and suppress opponents, but on the contrary, increases with the decrease of the opposition, reaches its climax when opposition no longer exists, and directs its full fury never so much against its enemies as against people who are innocent even from the viewpoint of the persecutor. Only the category of "objective or potential enemies," that is, people who have committed no crimes but share certain objective characteristics which at any moment can be decided to be "criminal," is capable of providing enough human material for "purges" or "exterminations" to keep the movement in its constantly increasing motion.

In contradistinction to dictatorships, whose notions of freedom are much less sophisticated, the totalitarian leader justifies all his measures with the very argument that they are necessary for freedom. He is not against freedom, not even for a limitation of it. The trouble is only that his concept of freedom is radically different from that of the nontotalitarian world. It is the historical process of world revolution or the natural process of race selection that need to be "liberated" through purges and exterminations. As in certain seventeenth-century philosophers, freedom is here understood to be a movement unrestrained by external force or impediment, something like the free flow of the water of a river. The unpredictable initiative of men, even if they should decide to support this movement, is as much an impediment to the free-flowing process as laws, traditions, or stable institutions of any sort, even the most tyrannical. A whole school of legal theorists in Nazi Germany tried their best to prove that the very concept of law was so directly in conflict with the political content of a movement as such that even the most revolutionary new legislation would eventually prove to be a

* This formulation occurs frequently in Nazi literature. We quote here from Heinrich Himmler, *Die Schutzstaffel als antibolschewistische Kampf-organisation. Schriften aus dem Schwarzen Korps*, No. 3, 1936.

hindrance to the movement.* And one needs only to read carefully certain speeches of Stalin to realize that he had arrived at very similar conclusions.†

All the dialectical niceties in discussions of the concept of freedom between the dialectical materialists, who are prepared to defend the horrors of the Bolshevik system for the sake of history, and their antitotalitarian opponents, rest ultimately on a simple and nondialectical understanding: What they have in mind when they talk about freedom is the freedom of a process, which apparently needs to be liberated from the meddlesome interfering activities of men, and what we have in mind is freedom of people whose movements need protection by fixed and stable boundaries of laws, constitutions, and institutions.

The task of the totalitarian ruler—to clear the way for the processes of History or Nature and to sweep from the path of his Movement the unpredictable spontaneity of human beings—demands much more radical measures than the mere transformation of laws into decrees, which is characteristic of all bureaucratic forms of tyranny where government and due process of law are replaced by administration and anonymous decision. By the same token, it is only superficially correct to see in the blind devotion of the movement to the Leader a kind of order-obedience relationship as in an army, a relationship which is occasionally carried into political-civil affairs as in the case of a military dictatorship. The Nazis, who especially in later years developed a surprisingly precise terminology, proclaimed that the highest law in Germany is the *will,* not the order, of the Führer.‡

---

* The most interesting item in this literature is Theodor Maunz, *Gestalt und Recht der Polizei*, Hamburg, 1943. Mr. Maunz belongs to the very small number of legal experts in the Third Reich who fully succeeded in cleansing himself from the "prejudice" that the notion of Law has a certain connection to the concept of Justice. His is the best conceptualization of the Nazi "legal" practice.

† Quite characteristic is the speech of Stalin at the occasion of the publication of the Soviet Constitution of 1936.

‡ For the principle: *"Der Wille des Fuehrers ist oberstes Gesetz,"* see for instance Otto Gauweiler, *Rechtseinrichtungen und Rechtsaufgaben der Bewegung*, 1939, p. 10. Also, Werner Best, *Die Deutsche Polizei*, 1941 p. 21: "Der Wille der Führung, gleich in welcher Form er zum Ausdruck gelangt . . . , schafft Recht und ändert bisher geltendes Recht ab." There exist numerous documents which show clearly that there could be a great difference between an order and the will of the Führer. See for instance PS 3063 of the Nuremberg Documents which reports on the pogroms of November 1938: The Order to the SA men in charge of the pogroms demanded that they carry their pistols, but the implication was that "every SA man should know now what he must do . . . , that the Jewish blood should flow, that

What swings the movement into motion and keeps it that way is this ever-changing "will" whose outward manifestations—orders, decrees, ordinances—are so unstable that they are not even officially published and brought to the notice of those whose very life depends upon obeying them.* The motivation for this extraordinary behavior, which indeed far outstrips the most arbitrary whims of tyrants, who at least knew they had to express and make public their "will" in order to be obeyed, is not so much fear of opposition or concern for conspiratory secrecy as it is a well-calculated, conscious misgiving that even such a draconic and "revolutionary" decree as the one with which Hitler started the Second World War—namely, to kill all incurably ill people—could by its very publication become a stabilizing factor and hinder the further development and radicalization of the movement: for example, in this instance the introduction of a national Health Bill with which Hitler after the war intended also to liquidate all those in whose family one member with an incurable lung or heart disease could be found.†

Differences of so decisive a nature must manifest themselves in the whole apparatus of rule and the very structure of the body politic. Such distinctions can be valid only if they can be carried down to the level of technical forms of administration and organization. For brevity's sake, it may be permitted to sum up the technical-structural differences between authoritarian, tyrannical, and totalitarian government in the image of three different representative models. As image for authoritarian government,

---

according to the *will* of the leadership the life of a Jew did not matter" (our italics and translation). A reliable Nazi was not the one who obeyed unquestioningly the orders of Hitler, but who was able to discern Hitler's "will" behind these orders. Needless to say this "will" was always more radical than the orders. In the formulation of Hans Frank, *Die Technik des Staates*, Munich, 1940: "Der kategorische Imperative des Handelns im Dritten Reich lautet: Handle so, dass der Führer, wenn er von Deinem Handeln Kenntnis hätte, dieses Handeln billigen würde."

* The most famous of these decrees is of course the ordinance with which Hitler started the Second World War and which, on September 1, 1939, ordered "allen unheilbar Kranken den Gnadenstoss zu gewähren." But there exist a great many similar decrees, from 1933 onward, which were valid law in the Third Reich and yet were never published. They were collected by Martin Bormann during the war into five large volumes under the title *Verfügungen, Anordnungen, Bekanntgaben*, indicating in the Preface: "Nur für interne Parteiarbeit bestimmt und als geheim zu behandeln." A set of the first four volumes is in the Archives of the Hoover Library, Stanford, California.

† For this plan of Hitler for the postwar period, see the Nuremberg documents published in Vol. 8 of *Nazi Conspiracy and Aggression*, Washington, 1946, p. 175ff.

I propose the shape of the pyramid, which is well known in traditional political thought. The pyramid is indeed a particularly fitting image for a governmental structure whose source of authority lies outside of itself, but whose center of power is located at the top, from which authority and power is filtered down to the base in such a way that each successive layer possesses some, but less authority than the one above it, and where precisely because of this careful filtering process all layers from top to bottom are not only firmly integrated into the whole, but are interrelated like converging rays whose common focal point is the top of the pyramid as well as the transcending source of authority above it. This image can be used only for the Christian type of authoritarian rule as it developed through and under the constant influence of the Church during the Middle Ages, when the focal point above and beyond the earthly pyramid provided the necessary point of reference for the Christian type of equality. The Roman understanding of political authority, where the source of authority lay exclusively in the past, in the foundation of Rome and the greatness of the ancestors, leads into an institutional structure whose focal point would be located in the foundation of the pyramid; but that is of no great importance in our context. In any event, any authoritarian form of government with its hierarchical structure is the least egalitarian of all forms; it incorporates inequality and distinction as its all-permeating principles.

All political theories of tyranny agree that it belongs strictly among the egalitarian forms of government; the tyrant is the ruler who rules as one against all, and the "all" whom he oppresses are all equal, namely equally powerless. If we stick to the image of the pyramid, it is as though all intervening layers between top and bottom had been destroyed, so that the top remains suspended, supported only by the proverbial bayonets, over a mass of carefully isolated, disintegrated, and completely equal individuals. Classical political theory used to rule the tyrant out of mankind altogether, to call him a "wolf in human shape" (Plato) because of this position of One against all, in which he had put himself and which distinguished his rule, the rule of One, which Plato still calls indiscriminately *mon-archy* or tyranny, sharply from various forms of kingship or *basileia*.

In contradistinction to both tyrannical and authoritarian regimes, the proper image of totalitarian rule and organization seems to me to be the structure of the onion, in whose center, in a kind of empty space, the Leader is located; whatever he does; whether he integrates the body politic as in an authoritarian hierarchy or whether he oppresses his subjects like a tyrant, he does it from within, and not from without or above. All the extraordinarily manifold parts of the movement: the front organizations, the various professional societies, the party membership, the party hierarchy, the elite formations and police groups, are related in such a way that each forms the facade in one direction and the center in the other, that is, plays the role of normal outside world for one layer and the role of radical extremism for another. The civilian members of Himmler's General SS, for example, represented a rather philistine facade of normalcy to the SS Leader Corps while they, at the same time, could be trusted to be ideologically more trustworthy and extreme than the ordinary member of the NSDAP.

The same is true for the relationship between sympathizer and party member, between party member and party officer or SA man, between the gauleiter and a member of the secret police, etc.* The great advantage of this system is that the movement provides for each of its layers, even under conditions of totalitarian rule, the fiction of a normal world together with a consciousness of being different rather than more radical from it. Thus, the sympathizers of the front organizations whose convictions differ only gradually from those of the party membership surround the whole movement and provide a deceptive facade of normalcy to the outside world because of their lack of fanaticism and extremism while, at the same time, they represent the normal world to the totalitarian movement whose members come to believe that their convictions differ only in degree from those of other people, so that they need never be aware of the abyss which separates their own world from that which actually surrounds it. The onion structure makes the system organizationally shockproof against the factuality of the real world.

The second advantage of this type of organization is that it permits a kind of double-talk of great importance for the relationship between totali-

---

* Only a detailed description and analysis of the very original organizational structure of totalitarian movements could justify the use of the onion image. I must refer to the chapter on "Totalitarian Organization," in my book *The Origins of Totalitarianism*, New York, 1951.

tarian regimes and the outside nontotalitarian world. In close correspondence with the dual role of each layer—to act as facade in one direction and
as interior center in the other—stands the curious fact that the same official
pronouncements frequently can be understood either as mere propaganda
or as serious indoctrination. Hitler's violently nationalistic speeches, for
instance, which he used to address his officer corps, were meant as indoctrination for the officers of the Wehrmacht; within the higher Nazi hierarchy, however, where the slogan of "Right is what is good for the German
people" had even officially been substituted by "Right is what is good for
the Movement,"* they were nothing but propaganda for an outside world
which was not yet "mature" enough to understand the movement's true
aims. It would lead us too far afield to show how this particular structure
is connected with the fact that totalitarian rule is based on a Movement in
the word's most literal significance, that the Movement is international in
scope, that the rise to power in one country does not mean that the totalitarian ruler cuts himself loose from the interest or goal of the Movement as
a whole, and that, consequently, the country in which he happens to seize
power is much less the seat and the source of his personal power than the
headquarters for the Movement itself.

II

It is obvious that these reflections and descriptions are based on the conviction of the importance of making distinctions. To stress such a conviction
seems to be a gratuitous truism in view of the fact that, at least as far as I
know, nobody has yet openly stated that distinctions are nonsense and that
we can pursue our inquiries in political or any other sciences by simply
ignoring distinctions and proceeding on the assumption that everything
can eventually be called anything else, or that distinctions are meaningful
only to the extent that each of us has the right "to define his own terms."

---

* The formulation: *"Recht ist was der Bewegung nuetzt"* appears very early, see for instance *Dienst-
vorschrift für die P.O. des NSDAP*, 1932, p. 38, which preceded the later *Organisationsbuch der NSDAP*
that carries the same sentence among the "duties of party members" in all its editions.

Yet does not this curious right, which we have come to grant as soon as we deal with matters of importance—as though it were actually the same as the right to one's own opinion—already indicate that such terms as tyranny, authority, totalitarianism have simply lost their common meaning, or that we have ceased to live in a common world where the words we have in common possess an unquestionable meaningfulness, so that short of being condemned to live verbally in an altogether meaningless world we grant each other the right to retreat into our own worlds of meaning and demand only that each of us remain consistent within his own, private terminology? If, under these circumstances, we assure ourselves that we still understand each other, we mean, not that we understand together a world common to us all, but that we understand the consistency of arguing and reasoning, of the process of argumentation in its sheer formality.

However that may be, to proceed under the implicit assumption that distinctions are not important or, better, that in the social-political-historical realm, i.e., in the sphere of human affairs, things do not possess that distinctness which traditional metaphysics used to call their "otherness" (their *alteritas*) has become the hallmark of a great many theories in the social, political, and historical sciences. Among these, two seem to me to deserve special mention because they touch the subject under discussion in an especially significant manner.

I mentioned the first in the beginning when I described the liberal and conservative theories: liberalism, we saw, measures a process of receding freedom, and conservatism measures a process of receding authority; both call the expected end result totalitarianism and see totalitarian trends wherever either one or the other is present. No doubt, both can produce excellent documentation for their findings. Who would deny the serious threats to freedom from all sides since the beginning of the century, and the rise of all kinds of tyrannies at least since the end of the First World War? Who can deny, on the other side, that disappearance of all traditionally established authorities has been one of the most spectacular characteristics of the modern world? It seems as though one need only to fix his glance on either of these two phenomena to justify a theory of progress or a theory of doom according to his own taste or, as the phrase does, according to his own "scale of values." If we look upon the conflicting statements of conservatives and liberals with equal eyes, we can easily see that the truth is equally distributed between them and that we are in fact confronted with a simultaneous recession of both freedom and authority in the modern world. As far as these processes are concerned, one can even say that the numerous oscillations in public opinion—which for more than 150 years has swung at regular intervals from one extreme to the other, from a liberal mood to a conservative one and back again and so on, at times attempting to reassert authority and at others to reassert freedom—have resulted only in further confusing the issues, blurring the distinctive lines between authority and freedom, and eventually destroying the political meaning of either.

Both liberalism and conservatism were born in this climate of violently oscillating public opinion and they are tied together, not only because each would lose its substance without the presence of its opponent in the field of theory and ideology, but because both are primarily concerned with restoration, with restoring either freedom or authority, or the relation between them to its traditional position. It is in this sense that they form the two sides of the same coin, just as their progress-or-doom ideologies are but the two sides in which the historical process, as process, can be understood, if one assumes, as both do, that historical processes have definable directions and predictable ends.

It lies, moreover, in the nature of the image in which History is usually conceived, as process or stream or development, that everything can change into everything else, that distinctions become meaningless because they are obsolete, submerged as it were by the flow of History, the moment they are pronounced. From this viewpoint, liberalism and conservatism present themselves as the political philosophies which correspond to the much more general and comprehensive philosophy of history of the nineteenth century. In form and content, they are the political expression of the historical consciousness of the last stage of the modern age. Their inability to distinguish themselves, theoretically justified by the concepts of history and process, progress or doom, testifies to an age when certain notions, which in their distinctness were clear to all previous centuries, have begun to lose their clarity and plausibility: they have lost their meaning in the public-political reality without, however, losing their significance altogether.

The second and more recent theory implicitly challenging the importance of making distinctions is, especially in the social sciences, the almost universal functionalization of all concepts and ideas. Here, as in the example quoted above, liberalism and conservatism differ not in method, viewpoint, and approach, but only in emphasis and evaluation. A convenient instance may be provided by the widespread conviction in the free world today that Bolshevism and communism are new "religions," their avowed atheism notwithstanding, because they fulfill socially, psychologically, and "emotionally" the same function which traditional religion fulfilled and still fulfills in the free world. The interest of the social sciences does not lie in what Bolshevism as an ideology or a form of government is, nor in what its spokesmen have to say for themselves; the social sciences are not interested in that, and many social scientists believe they can do without the study of what the historians themselves call the sources. Their concern is only with functions, and whatever fulfills the same function can, according to this view, be called the same. It is as though I had the right to call the heel of my shoe a hammer because I, like most women, use it to drive nails into the wall.

It is obvious that one can draw quite different conclusions from such equations. Thus, it would be characteristic of conservatism to insist that after all a heel is not a hammer, but that the use of the heel as a substitute for the hammer proves that hammers are indispensable. In other words, they will find in the fact that atheism can fulfill the same function as religion the best proof that religion is necessary, and recommend the return to true religion as the only way to counter a "heresy." The argument is weak of course; if it is only a question of function and how a thing works, the adherents of "false religion" can make as good a case for using theirs as I can for using my heel, which does not work so badly either. The liberals, on the contrary, view the same phenomena as a bad case of treason to the cause of secularism and believe that only "true secularism" can cure us of the pernicious influence of both false and true religion on politics. But these conflicting recommendations urging free society to return to true religion and become more religious, or to rid ourselves of institutional religion (especially of Catholicism with its constant challenge to secularism), hardly conceal the opponents' agreement on one point: that whatever fulfills the function of a religion, is a religion.

The same argument is frequently used with respect to authority: if violence fulfills the same function as authority, namely makes people obey, then violence is authority. Here again, we find those who counsel a return to authority because they think only a reintroduction of the order-obedience relationship can master the problems of a mass society, and those who believe that a mass society can rule itself like any other social body. Again both parties agree on the one essential point: authority is what makes people obey. All those who call modern dictatorships "authoritarian" or mistake totalitarianism for an authoritarian structure, implicitly have equated violence with authority, and this includes those conservatives who explain the rise of dictatorships in our century by the need to find a surrogate for authority. The crux of the argument is always the same: Everything is related to a functional context, and the use of violence is taken to demonstrate that no society can exist except within an authoritarian framework.

The dangers of these equations, as I see them, lie not only in the confusion of political issues and in the blurring of the distinctive lines which separate totalitarianism from all other forms of government. I do not believe that atheism is a substitute for or can fulfill the same function as a religion any more than I believe that violence can become a substitute for authority. But if we follow the recommendations of the conservatives, who at this particular moment have a rather good chance of being heard, I am quite convinced that we shall not find it hard to produce such substitutes, that we shall use violence and pretend to have restored authority or that our rediscovery of the functional usefulness of religion will produce a substitute religion—as though our civilization were not already sufficiently cluttered with all sorts of pseudo-things and nonsense.

Compared with these theories, the distinctions between tyrannical, authoritarian, and totalitarian systems which we proposed are unhistorical, if one understands by history not the historical space which certain forms of government appeared as recognizable entities, but the historical process in which everything can always change into something else; and these distinctions are anti-functional insofar as the content of the phenomenon is taken to determine both the nature of the political body and its function in society, and not vice versa. Politically speaking, they have a tendency to assume that in the modern world authority has disappeared almost to the vanishing point, and this in the so-called authoritarian systems no less than in the free world, and that freedom, i.e., the freedom of movement of human beings, is threatened everywhere, even in free societies, but abolished radically only in totalitarianism systems, and not even in tyrannies and dictatorships.

III

From this position, whose main negative characteristic is to avoid the frame of reference which stems from the interrelated concepts of historical processes and social functions, arise a number of questions. In the following concluding remarks, I should like to draw your attention to one which, for many reasons, seems to me to be of particular relevance. This is the question of where our occidental concept of authority comes from; which political experiences gave rise to it; and what kind of common, public-political world (I am not speaking of ideas or spiritual developments) came to an end when not this or that specific authority in any particular realm of life, but the very concept of authority lost its validity.

The concept of authority, like the word itself, is Roman in origin. Neither the Greek language nor the manifold political experiences of ancient Greek history knew of it. The closest Greek thought ever came to the notion of authority was, of course, in Plato's political philosophy where he opposed—perhaps without being aware of it—a tyranny of reason to the reality of Greek polis life. The motivation of this philosophy is political; it was caused by the hostility of the polis to philosophy as demonstrated in the trial of Socrates. The reason why Plato in his search for authority arrived at the establishment of tyranny—for a tyranny of reason is no less tyrannical than a tyranny of will and power—lies in the fact that his basis of experience remained entirely negative; his philosophy signifies politically the rebellion of the philosopher against polis life and announces his claim to rule, not for the sake of the polis and politics, but for the sake of philosophy and the existence of the philosopher. There is ample reason to believe that Aristotle was already aware of the resemblance of the philosopher king to a tyrant because both rule in their own interest, which for Aristotle, but not Plato, was an outstanding characteristic of tyrants. The reason Plato may have remained unaware of the tyrannical traits of his philosopher king was that to him, as to the Greek polis in general, the chief trait of tyranny lay in the abolition of the public realm, where a man can show himself, appear and be seen and heard, along with the banishment of the people from the "marketplace" to the privacy of household life which, in the general opinion of the Greeks, meant a cruel deprivation of the most human trait of human existence. To call a *politeia* tyrannical in which the whole of private life is devoured by public concern would have been to Plato a contradiction in terms.

Plato's tyranny of reason is entirely utopian in the sense that no reality and no political experiences have ever corresponded to it. Because of this utopian character we might have omitted this early identification of authority with tyrannical reason from our considerations altogether, if it were not for the fact that the Romans understood their own, entirely different concept of authority in the light of Platonic conceptions. This curious misinterpretation, in turn, has become a fact of prime importance in Western history, which, throughout the centuries following the downfall of the Roman Empire, reinterpreted what were originally Christian religious experiences in the fashion of Roman tradition, that is, in the light of Greek philosophy.

If, the anachronism notwithstanding, we apply the word "authority" to Plato's philosophy, then authority turns out to reside in the ideas which, because they transcend the sphere of human affairs, can be used as standards—measurements and yardsticks—of all that goes on and exists under the sky of ideas. The authority of the ideas, i.e., the quality which enables them to rule over the affairs of men, is by no means a matter of course. The ideas become *ruling* concepts in the full sense of the word only when the philosopher, in fear for his very life, begins to apply them as standards of rule and power. Only under these circumstances, one must understand their transcendence in the same way that one realizes a yardstick must be outside and of a different character from the concrete lengths which it is used to measure. Now the ideas apply to the manifoldness of things in the same way that I apply the one yardstick, the one standard, the one rule to any number of particular things and occurrences. But this applicability, which makes the concept of ideas useful for the political realm, was originally so little inherent in the notion of ideas that Plato had to change the "highest idea," that is, the one which makes all other ideas into ideas, from the idea of the Beautiful in the *Symposium* to the idea of the Good in the *Republic*. This transformation guaranteed the usefulness of the concept of ideas for political purposes, because the word "good" in the Greek language and philosophy implies always "good for," the usefulness and potential excellence of a thing or a man. Because of this change in the concept of the highest idea, the idea of ideas, which occurs in the cave story, the ideas can become rules and measurements in the hands of the philosopher king in the *Republic* and, later, the laws of the *Nomoi*. What appears as the tyranny of the philosopher in the *Republic* becomes finally the tyranny of reason in the *Laws*. The original function of ideas, when conceived with the Beautiful as the highest idea, was not to rule, but to shine and to enlighten the world. Only because Plato found himself in the political predicament of needing a possible application of his teachings to the realm of human affairs as well—which he repeatedly counsels us not to take too seriously—did he endow his ideas with the power to rule, and thereby changed profoundly the very doctrine of ideas itself. But the fact that Plato used his own doctrine for political purposes, as many did after him, does not change the fact that the concept of *idea* is nonpolitical in origin and, though it can be applied to the political realm, does not rest on authentically political experiences.

It may be doubted that Plato's grandiose effort to introduce the concepts of rule, yardsticks, and measurement into the realm of human affairs could ever have lost its essentially utopian character, if the Romans in their never-ending search for tradition had not decided to fall back upon Greek philosophy, and especially the philosophy of the Socratic school, as their recognized authority in all matters of theory and thought. This they did because authority and tradition, in distinction from Greek polis life, already played an all-important role in the political life of the Roman Republic.

In the center of all specifically Roman political life stands the conviction

that the sacredness of foundation is a binding force for all future generations. Political activity in Rome consisted primarily in the preservation of
the foundation of Rome. The Romans, therefore, again in distinction from
the Greek poleis, were unable to repeat this foundation through the establishment of colonies. The foundation of Rome—*tantae molis erat Romanam
condere gentem,* the ever-present meaning of the sufferings and wander-
ings of Aeneas are summed up by Virgil: *dum conderet urbem* (to found the
city)*—together with the equally un-Greek experience of the sacredness
of home and family, the reverent piety for the household gods of hearth
and city, form the political content of the Roman religion. Religion meant
here a state of being bound back (*religare*) to the gigantic, almost superhuman, and therefore legendary effort of laying the foundations. Political and
religious activity were almost indistinguishable; in the words of Cicero:
"There is nothing in which human virtue accedes closer to the holy ways of
the gods (*numen*) than the foundation of new or the preservation of already
established cities."† Religion was the binding power of foundation itself and
it provided, among other things, a dwelling place for the Roman gods, who
resided in the temples of Rome, unlike Greek gods who, though they protected the cities of men and took their temporary abode there, always had
their own home far away from the cities of mortals on Olympus.

Authority in this Roman context rested with those who had founded,
laid the foundations of a beginning, with the ancestors, whom the Romans
called *maiores,* the greater ones. Tradition, by the same token, became
sacred as it never had been in Greece, because it preserved and handed
down authority, the testimony of the ancestors who bore witness as the
authors of the sacred foundation. Religion, authority, and tradition thus
became inseparable, expressing as a trinity the sacred binding power of an
authoritative beginning to which one was bound back through the strength
of tradition. This Roman trinity survived the transformation of the Republic into the Empire and took root wherever the *pax Romana* spread and
formed what eventually was to emerge as Western civilization.

But the full strength of the Roman spirit, or the concept of foundation

* *Aeneid,* Book I, 33, 5. —Ed.
† *De Re Publica,* VII, 12.

as a reliable fundament for the erection of political communities, showed itself only after the downfall of the Roman Empire, when the new Christian Church, the political as well as the spiritual heir of Rome, became indeed so profoundly Roman that it reinterpreted the resurrection of Christ as the new cornerstone on which another permanent institution was to be founded. Called upon by Constantine the Great even before the fall of Rome to win for the declining empire the protection of the "most powerful God," the Church could eventually overcome the strong antipolitical and anti-institutional tendencies of the Christian creed, so manifest in the New Testament, and offer men "in membership of the Church the sense of citizenship which neither Rome nor municipality could any longer offer them,"* because its cornerstone as a public institution was no longer mere Christian faith in resurrection, or Hebrew obedience to God's Commandments, but rather the given testimony of the life, death, and resurrection of Jesus as a historical event. Thus the Apostles could become the "founding fathers," from whom the Church derives its own authority as long as it hands down their testimony as tradition from generation to generation.

With the repetition of the foundation of Rome in the foundation of the Catholic Church, the great Roman trinity of religion, authority, and tradition was carried into the Christian era and resulted in a miracle of longevity for a single institution, which is matched in our history only by the miracle of the thousand-year history of Rome in antiquity.

Although it is true that Roman philosophy had already used Platonic concepts for the interpretation of the Roman political experience, it can nevertheless be stated that these Platonic standards, visible only to the eyes of the mind, by which the visible affairs of men could be judged and measured, now became fully effective politically. What otherwise would have been integrated only with difficulty into the Roman political structure, the revealed Commandments and truths of a truly transcendent authority could now readily be assimilated as part and parcel of the foundation story itself. God's revelation could now be understood politically as the eventual revelation of the standards for human behavior and the measure for political communities; in the words of a modern Platonist in political

---

* See R. H. Barrow, *The Romans*, p. 194.

science, the earlier Platonic "orientation toward the unseen measure was now confirmed through the revelation of the measure itself."* To the extent that the profoundly *Roman* Catholic Church assimilated Greek philosophy into the body of its teachings, it amalgamated the Roman political concept of authority, inevitably connected with a beginning and a foundation in the past, with the Greek philosophical need for standards and transcending measurements—in modern parlance called "values"—without which no order seems possible from the viewpoint of this authority. Eventually nothing was more authoritatively asserted than this amalgamation itself.

Since then, the downfall of any of the three components of the Roman trinity, religion or authority or tradition, has carried with it inevitably the downfall of the other two. It was the error of Luther to believe that his challenge to the mundane authority of the Church could leave tradition and religion intact, as it was the error of Hobbes and the political theorists of the seventeenth century to hope that after the abolition of tradition, authority and religion could remain intact; and as, finally, it was the error of the humanists to think that one could remain within the continuity of Western tradition without religion and without authority.

It is quite noteworthy, in fact highly significant for the overpowering forces with which Greek philosophical concepts—once they had been made sacrosanct by tradition and authority—swept away all the political experiences which did not fit into their frame of reference, that the very notion of foundation has played hardly any role in political thought, even though it alone, politically speaking, made the sanctification of all traditions, including the Platonic one, possible. The only great political thinker in whose work the concept of foundation plays the central and decisive role was Machiavelli. That he could go back to the very origin of the Roman political experience was no doubt due to his contempt for all traditions as they were presented, preserved, and reinterpreted by the Church; but this contempt sprang from absolute incompatibility between a sincerely Christian life and political activity of any sort. He not only believed that a corrupt Church had corrupted political life in Italy, but was convinced that such corruption was inevitable precisely because of the Christian character

---

* Eric Voegelin, *The New Science of Politics*, p. 78.

of the Church. Moreover, he thought that a reformed, noncorrupt Church, though it might be more respectable, would not be less but rather more detrimental to the political realm. All this drove him into the rediscovery of the central Roman political experience, which in its original manifestation was as far removed from Christian "morality" as it was from the Greek concern with philosophy. Following his great masters, he came to believe that a new beginning of Roman history was possible if one repeated the original act of foundation in the establishment of a united Italy, which he hoped could become the same sacred cornerstone of an "eternal" body politic for the Italian nation as the foundation of the Eternal City had been for the Roman people in antiquity.

Since the book of Meinecke, and even before, it has become customary to see in Machiavelli the father of the "*raison d'Etat*" and thereby, implicitly, one of the fathers of the modern nation-state.* This, no doubt, is quite true, but what is even more striking is that Machiavelli and Robespierre very frequently speak the same language. The whole theory of Robespierre about the justification of terror coincides almost word for word with Machiavelli's theory about the necessity of violence for the foundation of new, and the reformation of corrupt, political bodies.

Machiavelli's unique contribution to political thought does not lie in his questionable "realism" or in his being the "father of political science," which he certainly was not. Not even his amoralism would earn him a right to fame, certainly not to greatness, no matter how shocking certain of his statements sound. There is hardly a man among the great political thinkers who has been so unlucky as Machiavelli with his readers and interpreters. When he maintained that in the public-political realm people must "learn how not to be good," he never meant to teach them how to be bad,† but he doubtlessly opposed in this, as in all his other famous statements, consciously and explicitly, Christian political philosophy and the Platonic

---

* The reference is to Friedrich Meinecke, *Die Idee der Staatsräson*, 1924, the first chapter of which deals with Machiavelli.

† This statement which occurs in Chapter 15 of *The Prince* must be understood in the light of the repeated emphatic contempt for "methods [by which] one may indeed gain power, but not glory" (Chapter 8). Machiavelli's concept of goodness was entirely determined through the "revival of religion by Saint Francis and Saint Dominic" which he discusses in its political consequences in the last chapter of the third book of the *Discourses*.

tradition. He fought both concepts of goodness which play such a great role in the tradition of political thought; he was convinced that neither the Platonic concept of the "good for . . ." nor the Christian concept of absolute goodness, which is not of this world, and least of all their amalgamation, is entitled to rule in the public realm, although they may be entirely justified in the sphere of private life. The greatness of his rediscovery of the Roman experience lies in the fact that he not only revitalized a tradition, which lay at the very basis of even those theories which he opposed, but that he had to discover what had never been explicitly stated before him, since the Romans themselves had already thought of their own experiences in terms of a vulgarized Greek rather than an authentically Roman philosophy.

If Machiavelli is the father of anything, he is the father of modern revolutions, all of which have been enacted in "Roman clothes" and were inspired by the Roman pathos of founding a new body politic. From the viewpoint I have tried to sketch in those last remarks, the crisis of the modern age, the famous "decline of the West," reveals itself as the decline of the Roman trinity of authority, tradition, and religion, i.e., as the crisis of the specifically Roman fundament of Western politics.

The only means which this tradition itself provides to mend the broken thread of tradition is the laying of new foundations, that is the repetition of the almost superhuman original Roman effort. Whether this way is still open, nobody can know. Against it speaks the fact that all revolutions of our century have gone wrong and led into totalitarian or tyrannical political bodies; on the other hand, the one successful revolution that occurred at the threshold of the modern world, the American Revolution, in which the Founding Fathers through the Constitution established a genuinely new community, speaks for it. Thus far it has withstood the onslaught of the modern world, even though its specific modernity is unquestionable. Nobody knew any of this better than Machiavelli, whose main political concern was "to lay foundations well": "There is nothing more difficult to carry out, nor more doubtful of success, nor more dangerous to handle, than to initiate a new order of things."*

1956

---

* *The Prince*, Chapters 9 and 6 respectively.

LETTER TO ROBERT M. HUTCHINS*

Hannah Arendt - 180 Morningside Drive - N.Y. 27, N.Y.

27 January 1957

Mr. Robert M. Hutchins, President
The Fund for the Republic, Inc.
60 East 42nd Street
New York 17, New York

Dear Mr. Hutchins:
As I promised at our luncheon a few weeks ago I have thought about the problems you raised and am now writing you my opinion concerning the material Mr. Ferry sent me.

I: Basic Issues

I too believe that empirical investigations are of doubtful efficacy if they are not connected with underlying basic issues. However, I feel that understanding of basic issues should grow out of attempts to understand and cope with concrete issues, which may be acute or latent according to cir-

---

* Robert Maynard Hutchins was an iconoclast who had no patience with words void of meaning or institutions void of purpose. As president of the University of Chicago for twenty-two years, where his influence could hardly have been greater or longer lasting, he once said: "The purpose of a university is nothing less than to procure a moral, intellectual, and spiritual revolution throughout the world." No wonder he and Hannah Arendt became friends. Robert M. Hutchins founded the Fund for the Republic in 1952. —Ed.

cumstances. The reasons why I do not think such investigations should "grow out of attempts to understand the basic issues and ideas" are the following:

a) Study of basic ideas can neither be organized nor commissioned, it can at best be stimulated by an organization such as the Fund for the Republic.

b) An answer to "what the basic issues and ideas are, and what the order is in which they should be studied" is possible only on the basis of an established political philosophy. While a number of such theories undoubtedly exist, none of them can claim enough intellectual authority or generally accepted validity to entitle the Fund to commit itself to it exclusively. Moreover, investigations growing out of such a fore-ordained order will remain lifeless and dry, for the investigators will not feel duty-bound to learn from experience and data themselves, but will be more likely to use facts merely as examples of a preconceived theory.

c) I think it is in the nature of politics that each factual issue of empirical importance discloses its own foundation. Thus, we may be entitled in political research to start from the surface, because every political danger spot is by definition the point where a basic issue breaks the surface. "To operate on the surface," therefore, means not to conduct empirical research in such a way as to remain willfully unaware of the basic issue disclosed by it; and conversely, to go into depth means to connect concretely and explicitly with the underlying basic issue as it is disclosed by experience.

d) I therefore am inclined to believe that the best order to follow is the one drawn up by reality itself, that is, to approach basic issues as indicated in the development of acute and politically relevant issues. By this method, it may be possible to attempt the otherwise forbidding task of reexamining basic ideas and traditionally rooted concepts.

e) From the beginning the scope of operations should be large enough to include issues that have been acute in the recent past or are likely to become acute in a foreseeable future. We are today confronted with a growing number of such latent issues which at any moment may become live and acute. By the same token, it may happen that what we recognize today as an acute issue may temporarily fade from the public scene, which of course should not prevent the Fund's continuing its study.

II: Relationship between basic, latent, and acute issues.

It may be best to illustrate by an example the distinctions and relationships I have in mind. I shall choose Freedom of Religion.

This, in my opinion, is the least acute of the issues mentioned in your outline. It is not endangered by either State or Society, and the mutual tolerance of Churches and denominations in this country has reached an all-time high. As such, therefore, I should not propose to make freedom of religion the topic for a special study. In one respect, however, it may have become a latent issue in recent years, chiefly through the so-called religious revival, which has brought religion and religious formulas back into political discussion. We are told, for instance, that only Christian and God-fearing people can constitute a democracy, or that religion is the only force in the Western world with which to fight communism effectively, etc. I think that this reamalgamation of religion and politics is quite harmful, and even more harmful to religion than it is to politics.

The basic issue involved in freedom of religion is the relationship between religion and politics, or, historically speaking, its severance through the separation of State and Church. Secularization, though it was intended to emancipate politics from religion, had a twofold result: religion lost its political elements, of which the most important was fear of eternal punishment in a hereafter, and politics lost its religious sanction. Secularization liberated and purified both religion and politics, and I personally believe that the advantages of secularism to the potentialities of faith are no less than its more obvious advantages to the purely secular political sphere. Religious freedom, since the rise of Christianity, has involved more than freedom of belief. The new freedom which the early Christians found so difficult to defend against the Roman Empire—religiously the most tolerant body politic we know—was freedom from politics on the grounds of religion. And this freedom was legally guaranteed only by the separation of Church and State.

The dangers arising from secularization are the following: if we think of the government chiefly as an instrument of coercion to make people behave, that is, as an institution which is a "reflection of human nature" and would be superfluous if men were angels (as Madison, I believe, put it), government paid a tremendous price for its severance from the Church; for no fear of death (capital punishment) or pain (torture), nothing indeed that man can inflict upon man, can match the fear of eternal death and eternal pain. Behind the frequent recommendations of God-fearing communities lies, I fear, the very understandable regret that politically we no longer deal with hell-fearing people. Separation of State and Church, in other words, made the concept of government as an instrument of coercion obsolete and open to reexamination.

The latent danger is that religion—because of the perplexities of our age and because our concept of government has not been reexamined in the light of secularization—becomes a means to political ends, an instrument of governments for the purpose of coercion. The temptation to call religion in to help solve purely secular problems—such as the rise of communism and other ideologies, or our inability to define democracy, the aim of government, the nature of politics, etc.—is great but it can only lead to excapism in politics and blasphemy in religion, certainly not to a reintegration on the model of the Middle Ages. The degradation of religion into an instrument of politics certainly endangers freedom of religion, and in this sense this freedom is indeed one of the latent issues.

III: Acute Issues

An enumeration of acute issues can only be tentative; even so it is controversial and stands in need of correction and supplementation. The following may perhaps be counted among them at this moment:

a) *The race issue in the South.*—The basic issues involved are 1. Equality; 2. States' rights versus Federal rights, i.e., the very structure of power and division of power in this country.

1: Equality. An empirical study of the situation will have to bear in mind that equality, in any case one of the gravest and most complicated problems of political science, is first of all an attribute of the public realm, as distinguished from the private sphere of life. What equality is to the content of public affairs, discrimination is to the behavior of people in private matters. In private we live by discrimination, choosing our friends, rejecting certain company, etc., and without such discrimination a private personal existence is inconceivable. The right to discrimination in privacy must be kept intact in any stand one takes against segregation, and the question that legitimately arises concerns the boundary between the private sphere of discrimination and the public sphere of equality.

Practically, greater awareness of the basic issue in this particular case may lead to a revaluation of the steps recently taken to further desegregation. It is, for instance, an open question whether discrimination can be extended to the right to choose one's neighbors. Certainly the most outrageous aspect of segregation lies in the field of public communications, precisely because they are public; discrimination in railroads and buses offends our feeling of human dignity, because it occurs in a sphere where we are all equals. Schools, and education in general, are a borderline area where private and public rights and interests overlap. Thus it may not have been wise to start desegregation in education, it would have been less wise to start it with housing, but it would have been indispensable—as recent events have clearly pointed out*—to end segregation in public communications, and to begin desegregation in the least disputable realm.

2: States versus Federal rights. The whole structure of the country rests on an adequate balance of State and Federal powers. The basic issue here is the nature of power. The idea that power is not indivisible but, on the contrary, can be divided without becoming less powerful, is one of the central concepts of the Constitution. It is precisely divisibility which distinguishes power from strength and force: divided power can mean more power for all concerned, whereas divided force is always less force.

This means practically that the desegregation program must also be judged in terms of the power balance, and that any violation of states' rights, actually guaranteed by the Constitution, would lead to weakening of regional power and ultimately perhaps to a most undesirable weakening of the union as a whole.

b) *Intrusion upon Privacy.*—Several apparently unconnected events have contributed to making this a particularly acute issue today. Although cer-

---

* For example, the Rosa Parks incident in Montgomery, Alabama, in 1955 marked a new beginning of the Civil Rights movement in America. —Ed.

tain personal rights which we thought to be the very essence of the right to privacy have not been noticeably endangered—such as, in my opinion, the rights "to be protected against unlawful searches and seizures" or to own property—other rights which were never mentioned have suddenly been jeopardized by Congressional Committees demanding information concerning one's friends and relatives or reports of opinions uttered in private, by wiretapping, by factory questionnaires inquiring into personal matters, by newspapers, reporters who feel entitled to interviews, etc. It is as though political and social forces were conspiring against the very existence of privacy.

The basic issue here concerns the distinctions and relations among the three realms in which we move constantly: the public realm, in which we are citizens; the social, in which we earn our living; and the private, in which we need to be reasonably free from both public and social and which therefore is hidden from and protected by our four walls. The recent intrusions into privacy offer a welcome opportunity to elucidate issues about which political science has been silent for centuries, and which seem almost buried in never-ending abstract controversies about the right to private property, in which everything is discussed except the problem of what property means in relation to both the public and private realms. The confusion of public opinion in this matter is, partly at least, only a reflection of the inadequacies of learned opinion; the situation may be clarified through an investigation which discloses the unique relevance of each of the three realms in terms of human activities and experiences, some of which need privacy as badly as others need publicity.

c) *The Passport Issue.*—The issue at stake here cannot be clarified through an investigation of the various cases in which passports were refused, because the problem is the recent stand of the Administration that the possession of a passport is a privilege of the American citizens, and not a right. For obvious reasons, this matter is not settled in the Bill of Rights and therefore remains an open question legally speaking. A study of the types of persons who suffered in recent years would lead into endless controversy and only confuse the issue.

Here the basic issue is freedom of movement, which is perhaps the most fundamental, certainly second to no other, of the freedoms we cherish. (One may remember in this context that the Greek formulae for the manumission of slaves enumerated the right to unrestricted movement among the four liberties which together constituted individual freedom—the others being status, personal inviolability, and professional freedom.) In a time when one cannot travel without a passport, freedom of movement is restricted or made a "privilege" if the government is not obliged to give a passport to each citizen who applies for it. The right to refuse applications should be restricted to cases in which freedom of movement is restricted anyhow, such as the cases of criminals or material witnesses or persons subject to arrest but free on bail. For similar reasons, the present inclusion in the application of information on where and for how long the applicant intends to go abroad is quite objectionable. The question that came up recently in the cases of journalists going to China is somewhat different. Since a passport assures its bearer of government protection abroad, the government must have the right to disclaim responsibility for countries with which it does not have normal diplomatic relationships. The question is whether it has the right to go beyond an explicit disclaimer of responsibility and to invalidate passports for those countries.

The present situation can be remedied only through introduction of a Constitutional Amendment, which however would only spell out a freedom guaranteed under the Bill of Rights;* it would not introduce a new idea into the Constitution.

d) *Deprivation of Citizenship as Punishment.*—The helplessness of European countries in dealing with the ever-growing body of stateless people between the two World Wars was one of the unnoticed signals of the decline of the European nation-state system. The issue of statelessness became acute in this country for the first time during World War II, when the government decided to intern and deprive of their constitutional rights citizens of Japanese origin. After this incident, the issue remained dormant until in recent years the government began to deprive naturalized citizens of their citizenship and to deport them as undesirable aliens. The issue became acute

---

* Presumably Arendt refers to the Ninth Amendment. —Ed.

when Brownell* announced his intention to deprive native and naturalized citizens of their citizenship in order to punish them for communist activities.

If this proposition had been carried out, statelessness as punishment would have been incorporated into the very legal structure of this country, thereby putting in jeopardy all citizens, and not only communists. Furthermore, all communists who were native citizens, and a majority of the naturalized, would have become automatically stateless; since such people are undeportable, a situation would have been created for which concentration camps are the only logical answer. Statelessness would at once have become a major legal and political problem in the United States.

The basic issue involved is the following: As long as mankind is nationally and territorially organized in states, a stateless person is not simply expelled from one country, native or adopted, but from all countries—none being obliged to receive and naturalize him—which means he is actually expelled from humanity. Deprivation of citizenship consequently could be counted among the crimes against humanity, and some of the worst recognized crimes in this category have in fact, and not incidentally, been preceded by mass expatriations. The state's right of capital punishment in case of murder is minor compared with its right to denaturalization, for the criminal is judged according to the laws of the country, under which he possesses rights, and he is by no means put outside the pale of the law altogether.

The Brownell proposition was only a glaring illustration of ignorance and thoughtlessness prevailing in a matter which, after all, has been one of the crucial and newest phenomena of the twentieth century. In the light of what we know today about statelessness—its dangers not only due to those concerned, but to the legal structure of any country that harbors a large number of stateless persons—there is every reason to improve even the present United States practice with regard to naturalized citizens. It seems absurd, but the fact is that, under the political circumstances of this country, a Constitutional Amendment may be needed to assure American citizens that they cannot be deprived of their citizenship no matter what they do. The point is that the (unrecognized) right to citizenship is more fundamental than civil rights which a criminal may forfeit through his

* Herbert Brownell, Jr., U.S. Attorney General (1953–57). —Ed.

actions. For the same reasons, it should be made constitutionally impossible to deprive naturalized citizens of their citizenship—which, for various historical reasons, they can now lose more easily in this country than anywhere else—except in cases of dual allegiance (where statelessness anyhow would not ensue) and of fraud about personal identity (name, place, and date of birth, etc.) in the process of naturalization. All other cases of fraud should be punished under law, but not by denaturalization.

e) *The Right to Asylum.*—A last, much less acute and much more complicated issue, which has come up in recent months through events in Hungary and the arrival of Hungarian refugees, is the old demand of the United Nations and international lawyers for a constitutionally guaranteed right to asylum, which despite the turmoil of the twentieth century can nowhere be found in written law, in no constitution or international agreement, or the charters of the old League of Nations or the new United Nations. In a time when political refugees are no longer individual exceptions, but after each major event in any part of the world constitute sizable portions of the population, this demand probably has less hope of fulfillment than ever before. Nevertheless, a cautious and intelligent attempt may be worthwhile even if no immediate results are forthcoming. The moment is favorable, because both the country and the government are anxious to help and rather impatient with legal impediments. If at the moment of the Hungarian Revolution a right to asylum had existed, it would have been possible to accept any number of people temporarily, without committing the country to new immigrants and without changing the quota system. The right to asylum should be limited in time, and extensions to stay should be given under due considerations of changing circumstances in the country of origin. The last three points bring up the question of the wisdom of the Fund's embarking upon an "unofficial constitutional convention to re-examine the Bill of Rights." My personal feeling is that the Fund should rather refrain from comprehensive reconsideration of the Constitution. I do not believe that "the tremendous changes that have occurred since the eighteenth century" make such a reexamination necessary, and it may be dangerous; the Constitution can still take care of these changes through the device of Amendments. Rather than examine the Constitution, I should propose to examine the reasons why Congress, though regularly swamped in all kinds of propositions for Amendments, has shied away from using this method of constitutional legislating for so many years. For this timidity actually is the equivalent to shying away from action in structural issues and to failing to face matters which pose new, unprecedented problems.

IV: Latent Issues

I have already mentioned religious freedom as a latent issue, and I shall not go into detail with respect to others. Generally speaking, it may be as important to relate latent issues to basic ideas as it is to relate acute issues, but it will prove to be much more difficult, and attempts in this direction will be much more exposed to nonpertinent, abstract generalities. It is the very acuteness of an issue that sharpens our eyes for the underlying basic issue. Without this acuteness our only concrete help is history, that is, to remind ourselves of the constellation when the issue was acute; this is very helpful in some instances, as in the religious question, but not so helpful in others.

At this moment all those issues which came to the surface during the McCarthy* crisis are latent—freedom of expression, academic freedom, and other civil rights. Among the latent issues are also certain forms of discrimination and race hatred which were curiously absent in the McCarthy movement but have proved dangerous in the past, such as antisemitism, anti-Catholicism, and other matters which are the specialty of the lunatic fringe in calm times.

In all these instances, a constant watch and control is necessary to determine the moment of danger and its extent, in order to be prepared to face it when it comes. However, on the grounds of past experience and simple common sense, special care should be taken lest those who are commissioned to watch bestow upon their assigned "movements" a momentum the movements themselves do not have. It is natural, nevertheless rather harmful, when a committee for watching antisemitism begins to develop a vested interest in Jew-hatred and to feel frustrated unless it is permitted to exagger-

---

* Joseph McCarthy, U.S. senator from Wisconsin (1947–57), a demogogic anticommunist. —Ed.

ate its findings. The remedy against this danger is smallness in size, complete absence of publicity, employment of especially honest people with good judgment, and sufficient interest in politics to outweigh their job interests.

V: Conclusions

a) *Basic Issues:* The Fund should make public its great concern with basic issues and ideas and promise to do everything to stimulate new thinking. Its best direct approach might be the announcement of a sizable award to be given every year to the best book on basic issues in political theory and philosophy, and a second award to the book in concrete political analysis which is most aware of the basic issues underlying current events.

Apart from these recurring awards, the Fund may see fit to announce special prizes, to be given three years from now, for book-length discussions of those subjects, formulated beforehand, which it deems most worthy of new analysis. One subject that comes to mind is the threat to freedom arising from scientific "progress" in the control of the human mind; the prize-winning book should present a comprehensive statement on attempts in this direction, and results achieved, in such sciences as biochemistry, brain surgery, psychology, social engineering, behavioral science, and others.

A nonnegligible by-product of such awards may be to stimulate individual scholarship and thought which will help to counter the trend toward the institutionalization of thought as well as other areas of life.

b) *Acute Issues:* Several persons in the field should be approached for an enumeration and evaluation of acute issues in terms of basic issues. It may also be advisable to approach a small number of people who were in practical politics in recent years, with the ultimate purpose of bringing both groups together. The function of the latter will be to check the issues of the "thinkers" against their practical, day-to-day experiences, and to help in the translation of ideas into adequate practice on the operational level. I think of people who for instance did the operational work in episodes like the censure of McCarthy.

Those in whom the Fund has confidence should form an advisory committee to consider the best approach to study each issue. It is important not to develop a uniform method for all issues; on the contrary, it should be a principle to treat each topic separately, not only in terms of ideas and basic issues, but also in terms of ways to approach it. To give an example: The study of race relations in the South is probably best conducted along strictly empirical, fact-finding lines. The study of privacy may have to be conducted on three levels; empirical research may have to determine the influence of social pressure, political factors, and police practices; the legal aspects and the impact upon individual psychology will have to be examined in some depth; and the interplay and interrelatedness of the public, social, and private realms may be subject to historical and theoretical studies. The study of the passport situation, on the other hand, should not get involved in fact finding at all, and does not need much theory. It should be put into the hands of experts in various nationality laws, of international lawyers who are to compare the practices and competences of the administration in various countries, and, finally, into the hands of constitutional lawyers to prepare a Constitutional Amendment. The issue of statelessness can be properly handled by international lawyers and people who have been active in refugee work.

Once these studies are completed and decisions how to operate in each case have been reached, groups to do the actual work may be formed. The end result should be a series of works for publication.

c) *Latent Issues* will have to be determined in the same fashion as acute issues, and by the same people. Here the next step should be the establishment of small operational agencies, and the ultimate aim should not be ambitious studies but regular reports to the Fund. The agencies themselves should work without publicity and it should be up to the Fund to decide when and how to use their findings publicly. The employees need not be students of political science and need not have theoretical training. But they must have practical experience, regional knowledge, good judgment, and integrity.

d) *Constitutional Amendments.* A special procedure will probably have to be devised for those issues which could be solved adequately only by Constitutional Amendments. I am hardly the right person to ask to fill in the steps which may eventually lead to Congressional action, but it seems clear to me that the considerations and formulations of legal and political experts in constitutional matters should be followed by discussions in important scholarly bodies. Only after such nonpublic activities have given encouraging results, one should proceed to inform the country at large and to sound out its reaction through the various media of communication, magazine articles, radio, television, etc. The point I want to make is that it probably will be wise to approach Congressmen only after everything has been done to create a favorable climate of public opinion.

Please do not hesitate to call on me if you feel that further discussion and clarification are indicated.

Very Sincerely,
Hannah Arendt

P.S. Due to my haste in preparing this, I regret that I cannot send copies to Mr. Ferry and Mr. Cogley.

1957

THE HUNGARIAN REVOLUTION AND TOTALITARIAN IMPERIALISM

Almost two years have passed since the flames of the Hungarian Revolution illuminated the immense landscape of postwar totalitarianism.* This event cannot be measured by victory or defeat; its greatness rests upon and is secure in the tragedy it enacted. We still see the silent procession of black-clad women in the streets of Russian-occupied Budapest, mourning the dead of the revolution in public. This was the last political gesture of the struggle for freedom, and it was evidently the last act of a tragic event, the like of whose simple urgency has scarcely been seen in recent history. Afterward, in the space of a few weeks and months, the terror drove everyone back into the darkness of their houses, which were not places of safety, but dominated by an ever-present fear. And yet one year after the defeat, the conquered and terrorized people still had enough courage, at least on the anniversary itself, to force themselves out of the darkness and prove that memory was circulating in the houses as well as fear—the remembrance that alone gives permanence to actions, and can ultimately assure their place in history. On the first anniversary of the death of their freedom, the people shunned spontaneously and unanimously all places of public entertainment, theaters, movies, coffeehouses, and restaurants, and sent their children to school with little candles to put in the inkwells of their desks. These actions proved that the events of the revolution were of a sufficient magnitude to qualify them as history. Now it may be up to us to summon up the power of remembrance and reflection that will enter what is worthy of being remembered into the history books.

---

* The Hungarian Revolution started in the last week in October and ended in the first week of November 1956. —Ed.

The context of circumstances within which the revolution happened was of great significance, but it was not compelling enough to release one of those automatic processes that seem almost always to imprison history and which actually are not even historical, if we understand by historical whatever is worthy of being remembered. What happened in Hungary happened nowhere else, and the twelve days of the revolution contained more history than the twelve years since the Red Army had "liberated" the country from Nazi domination.

For twelve years everything had happened exactly according to expectations—the long dreary story of open deceit and broken promises on the one side, and hopes against hope and final disillusionment on the other. The newly conquered territories were prepared for totalitarianism: from the first stage of popular front tactics and a sham parliamentary system, to a one-party dictatorship that quickly liquidated the leaders and members of the formerly tolerated parties, and finally the show trials, which, in true Russian style, got rid of the native communists, whom Moscow rightly or wrongly mistrusted, while power passed into the hands of the most despicable and corrupt elements among the Moscow-trained Hungarian agents.

All this and much more was predictable, not because there were any historical, social, or economic forces pushing developments in one direction, but because all this was part of the known methods of Russian hegemony. It was as though the Russian rulers repeated in great haste all the stages of the October Revolution, up to the emergence of totalitarian dictatorship. The only difference was that what had been a genuine, if catastrophic event in the Russia of the twenties, something that had not been planned out by anybody, not even Stalin, was now set in motion as if it was a program that had to be run through and concluded as quickly as possible. The story of these twelve years, therefore, while unspeakably terrible, is without much interest of its own and varies very little; what happened in one satellite country happened at almost the same moment in all others, from the Baltic Sea down to the Adriatic.

The only exceptions to this rule were the Baltic States on the one hand, and Soviet-occupied Eastern Germany on the other. The former were unhappy enough to be directly incorporated into the Soviet Union, with the consequence that the ceremonious repetition (which did at least slow down developments in the satellites) was dispensed with, and their status was immediately assimilated to that enjoyed by other Soviet nationalities. When up to fifty percent of the population was deported and the loss made good by forced random immigration, it became clear that they had been assimilated to the status of the Tartars, the Kalmyks, or the Volga Germans, that is, to those who had not acquitted themselves well in the war against Hitler. The case of Eastern Germany is an exception in the opposite direction. It never became even a satellite country, but remained occupied territory under a kind of quisling government despite the undeniable zeal of German Moscow agents, with the result that the country, though still miserable enough when compared with the *Bundesrepublik,* has fared much better economically as well as politically than the satellites. This situation may have looked rather different to the Germans living there, but the very fact that it is comparatively easy for them to flee to West Germany whenever they want should make them realize that the Iron Curtain only begins at the Soviet Union's eastern border. They alone still have the ability to take an underground train to West Berlin, a space for personal decision that exists neither in the satellite states nor in the Soviet Union. But these regions are exceptions only because they, too, fall into the orbit of Russian power; they are not exceptions to the satellite system because they have never belonged to it.

Not even the difficulties that began shortly after Stalin's death can be called unexpected, because they reflected so faithfully the difficulties, or rather the controversies, within the top Russian leadership, and these repeated so faithfully the conditions in the twenties, before the streamlining of the international communist movement into its eventual totalitarian shape had been completed, when every Communist Party split into factions that faithfully mirrored the faction-ridden Russian party, and each splinter looked up to its respective Russian leader as to a patron saint—which indeed he was, since the destinies of his protégés all over the world depended utterly upon his own fate. It certainly was interesting that Stalin's death was not only followed by the same succession crisis as Lenin's thirty years before (which, after all, in the absence of any law of succession is rather a matter of course), but that the crisis was met again by the temporary solution of "collective leadership," suggested by Stalin in 1925, with the result that the Communist Parties abroad made one of the collective their leader, and tried to form their faction around him. Thus, Kádár is as much a protégé of Khrushchev as Nagy was a protégé of Malenkov. The victory of Khrushchev over Malenkov not only corresponds to the victory of the Stalinist faction in the twenties; it played out in the same way and had the same consequences in the communist movement outside Russia.

This repetition of historical developments, as if they were an allotted task, seems to be part of the fixtures of totalitarian movements, and frequently borders upon the comical. It occasionally surfaced even during the Hungarian Revolution, since communists played a role there, too: in the despair of defeat, they resorted compulsively to the old tricks, which fitted neither with the style of the events, nor with their own role in them. In one of its last broadcasts, the communist Free Radio Rajk urged comrades to "join the pseudo-Communist Party of Kádár" and turn it into "a true Hungarian Communist Party" from within. For in the same vein, thirty years previously, the early opposition to Stalin had urged the comrades not to leave the party but to use the Trojan horse tactic; and Stalin himself ordered the same tactics for the German communists with respect to the Nazi movement. And these supposedly lofty political exhortations were very much in tune with the secret desires of the modern masses, who, lonely as they are, cannot bear to remain on the sidelines and not join in. The best example of this tendency is perhaps *Gleichschaltung*, or political coordination, in Nazi Germany, where countless people, entirely of their own volition and urged on by nobody, convinced themselves that joining the National Socialist movement was a lofty political act, by which they would change things for the better from within. Each time the result was the same: those who had joined the totalitarian parties for tactical reasons became exemplary Stalinists or Nazis for all practical purposes.

The Hungarian Revolution interrupted these automatic occurrences and conscious or unconscious repetitions, just when the experts on forms of total domination had grown accustomed to them, and public opinion apathetic. The revolution took everybody by surprise; even the events in Poland did not prepare for it. The revolution was unprepared, and nobody anticipated it—those who fought and suffered, no less than those who watched in furious impotence from the outside, or those who went in with armed force to suppress it.* For something was happening here in which nobody believed any longer, if anyone ever had believed in it—neither the communists nor the anticommunists, and least of all those whose mouths were full of high-sounding clichés about the duties of the people to rebel against totalitarian terror, without knowing or caring what price others would have to pay for their empty phrases. If there was ever such a thing as Rosa Luxemburg's "spontaneous revolution," this sudden uprising of an entire people for the sake of freedom and nothing else—spontaneous, and without the demoralizing chaos of a military defeat preceding it, without *coup d'état* techniques, without a closely knit apparatus of professional conspirators and revolutionaries, without even the leadership of a party, something that everyone, conservatives and liberals, radicals and revolutionaries, had discarded as a noble dream—it was then we had the privilege of witnessing it. Perhaps the Hungarian professor was right when he told the United Nations commission that this event was unique in history, as the revolution had no leader. "It was not organized; it was not centrally directed. The will for freedom was the moving force in every action."

Events, past and present—not social forces and historical tendencies, nor questionnaires, public opinion studies, nor any other gadgets in the arsenal of the social sciences—are the true, the only reliable teachers of political scientists, as they are the most trustworthy source of information for those engaged in politics. Once an event of such unusual significance as the spontaneous revolution in Hungary has happened, every policy, theory, and forecast of future potentialities needs reexamination. In its light we must check and enlarge our understanding of the totalitarian form of government as well as of the nature of totalitarian imperialism. The questions that arise here are of a very simple nature. Is it true, as Hugh Seton-Watson believes, that "Orwell's 1984 is only a nightmare" and that "totalitarianism has been overthrown once, and it can be overthrown again"; that, in

---

* Boris I. Nicolaevsky, whose "Battle in the Kremlin"—a series of six articles published in the New York weekly *The New Leader* (July 29–September 2, 1957) —is the most comprehensive and the soundest analysis of developments in Russia after Stalin's death, finds "that the United Nations' report on the Hungarian Revolution has established that the outbreak of violence in Budapest was the result of *deliberate provocation*." I am not convinced; but even if he is right, the result of the Russian provocation was certainly unexpected and went far beyond its own original intentions.

a word, "the Hungarian Revolution could prove to have . . . been Bolshevism's 1905"?*

I
Russia After Stalin's Death

As doubtlessly spontaneous as the Hungarian Revolution was, it cannot be understood outside the context of developments after Stalin's death. As we know today, his death occurred on the eve of a gigantic new purge, so that, whether he died a natural death or was killed, the atmosphere in the party's higher echelons must have been one of intense fear. Since no successor existed, no one appointed by Stalin, and no one was quick enough or felt up to the task, the struggle for succession began immediately, and caused a serious crisis in Soviet Russia and the satellite countries. Even today, almost six years after Stalin's death, we may doubt whether its outcome has really been decided. But one thing is sure: one of the most serious flaws in totalitarian dictatorship is its apparent inability to find a solution to the problem of succession.

The attitude of totalitarian dictators in this matter we knew before: Stalin's carelessness in occasionally appointing his successor, only to kill or demote him a few years later, was matched and supplemented by a few scattered remarks by Hitler on the subject in his "Table Talk" conversations; everything we know suggested strongly that they were convinced the question was only of minor importance: almost anybody would do as long as the apparatus remained intact. To understand this carelessness, one must bear in mind that the choice obviously was limited to a small circle of people who, by the very fact that they were on top *and* alive at the moment of the dictator's death, had already proved their superiority under totalitarian conditions. The risk therefore seems bearable, and is in any case to be preferred over a binding regulation for succession, which would introduce

---

* See Hugh Seton-Watson's introduction to Melvin J. Lasky, *The Hungarian Revolution; A White Book: The Story of the October Uprising as Recorded in Documents, Dispatches, Eye-witness Accounts, and World-Wide Reactions*. Books for Libraries Press, 1970, pp. 23–24. Seton-Watson is credited as the author of the first chapter: "The Historical Background: 1945–1956."

into the totalitarian movement an element of stability alien to and possibly obstructing the needs of the "movement" and its extreme flexibility. If a succession law existed, it would indeed be the only stable law in the whole structure of government, and therefore possibly a first step in the direction of some kind of legality.

However that may be and whatever we may have known, we could not possibly know what would happen in the case of the dictator's death. Only now do we know that succession is an unsolved problem and causes a serious crisis involving the relations among the potential successors themselves, between the various apparatuses on which they rely, and their relationship with the masses. Totalitarian leaders, being mass leaders, need popularity, which is no less effective for being fabricated by propaganda and supported by terror. Thus the first stage in the succession was a popularity contest, for it is in the nature of totalitarian domination that none of the leading contenders for the succession was sufficiently well known, let alone popular— with the exception, perhaps, of Zhukov, who, being an army man, was the least likely to succeed in rising to power. Khrushchev traveled around the country, shaking hands, kissing babies—in short, behaving like an American politician on an election campaign. Beria engaged in an antiwar, appeasement policy whose very extremes were oddly reminiscent of Himmler's efforts during the last months of the war to succeed Hitler by becoming the man the Allied powers would trust enough to conclude peace with. Malenkov and Khrushchev together eventually liquidated Beria, not only because his foreign policy escapades had become dangerous, but also because he was of course the very symbol of popular hatred in Russia as well as abroad—which, again as in the case of Himmler, apparently everybody knew except himself.

This competition for mass popularity should not be mistaken for a genuine fear of the masses. Fear, to be sure, was one of the most potent motives for the establishment of the "collective leadership," but unlike the triumvirate after Lenin's death, these men were not afraid of a people's "counterrevolution," but of each other. Their concern was not to protect themselves collectively from the masses, but to create a mutual assurance that they would not kill each other. And anyone who troubles to look up these gentlemen's past—all of them staunch Stalinists, educated and tested in the decade of party purges and mass murder—will have to admit that this fear was justified, and the steps they took for mutual insurance were only natural.

Fear of the masses, by contrast, would hardly have been justified. At the moment of Stalin's death, the police apparatus was still intact; and even when the mighty police empire was broken up in the wake of Beria's liquidation, and the terror substantially relaxed, there were some boomerang effects from the unrest in the satellite countries—a few student disturbances, one strike in a Moscow plant, some very cautious demands for more leeway in "self-criticism" among the intellectuals—but there were never any serious signs of potential revolts, such as real demands for freedom of expression from the intellectuals, or real unrest.* Moreover, the little show of opposition among intellectuals was not only encouraged by the party, it was probably a direct order; and this, too, far from being a genuine concession, was one of Stalin's tested devices of domination. He used provocation as a tool, to inform himself of the state of public opinion, and to coax any opponents into the open so that he could deal with them appropriately. Khrushchev's speech to the intellectuals, in which he officially announced the end of the "thaw" and informed them that they had indulged in "incorrect understanding of the essence of the party's criticism of the Stalin personality cult," underestimated "the positive role of Stalin," and should go back to "Socialist realism . . . [with its] unlimited opportunities" in developing "their talents to glorify," was not much more than a routine performance.

Another aspect of the same speech is more interesting. For in it Khrushchev announces the establishment of "creative unions," through which "the creative growth of every writer, artist, sculptor, etc." would be subject "to constant comradely concern." Here we find a clue to how he intends to replace the police terror. He seems to be planning a surveillance exerted not

---

* Typical in this respect is the exchange of letters between Ignazio Silone and Ivan Anissimov, editor of the Soviet magazine *Foreign Literature*, which took place during the last months of 1956, when the "thaw" gave hope to writers in the West. They believed there would be another opportunity to enter into conversation with the Russian intelligentsia, and this correspondence shows how terribly unfounded these hopes were. It was published by *Tempo Presente* in Italy and *The New Leader* (July 15, 1957) in the USA, under the title "A Troubled Dialogue."

by an outside (police) body but by recruits from the midst of the people, in this case the writers and artists themselves. This would be an institution-alization of, and possibly an improvement upon, the principle of mutual spying that permeates all totalitarian societies, and which Stalin had ren-dered so effective by making the denunciation of others the only test of loyalty. Another innovation proclaimed by Khrushchev also points in the same direction. His decree against "social parasites" explicitly envisages that these "asocial" elements will be selected for punishment in concentra-tion camps by the populace itself. In other words, Khrushchev proposes to replace certain functions of the secret police with a kind of highly organized and institutionalized mob rule. It is as if the stage has now been reached where the people can be expected and trusted to be their own policemen, and deliver up the victims necessary for the terror.

Similar new developments in the techniques of domination can be dis-covered in the much discussed decentralization projects. For, far from indicating a democratization of Soviet society or a rationalization of the Soviet economy, they were obviously aimed at breaking the power of the managerial class, through the establishment of new economic regions with new men to run them.* The redeployment of Moscow-centralized person-nel to the provinces assured above all their atomization; once they had been shunted off to the provinces, they were now subject to the surveil-lance of local party authorities. And these authorities surely will not fail to exert the same "constant comradely concern with creative growth" that the new unions are to grant to the artists, over every factory and every branch of production. The aim is not new; Khrushchev learned from Sta-lin that every group of people that begins to show signs of class solidarity must be broken up—ideologically for the sake of establishing a classless society, and practically for the sake of an atomized society which alone can be dominated totally and reliably.† But what Stalin only achieved by

---

* Nicolaevsky (see note on page 109) shows that "Khrushchev's fight against the Soviet managerial class . . . goes far back into the past." See also "New Purge in the Kremlin" by Richard Lowenthal, in *Problems of Communism* (September–October 1957, p. 2): "What had started as a drive for more economic reality had turned into a drive for more direct party rule in the economic field."

† The widespread error of thinking that the revolutionary development of the communist move-ment foundered on the birth of a "new class" is shared by Milovan Djilas, in his book *The New Class* (New York, 1957). The error is an old one, and appeared as early as the start of the Stalin regime; it

means of a permanent revolution, with its periodically recurring gigantic party purges, Khrushchev hopes to achieve by less dramatic and destructive means, by building the police function directly into society, and thus ensuring permanent atomization from within, which would make the violent shaking of the country's whole structure superfluous.

Such a reform of the methods and institutions of domination is important enough, particularly as these are not suggestions that came from the period of "thaw." It was quite striking, though it has been hardly noticed, that the bloody crushing of the Hungarian Revolution, terrible and effective as it was, and the police terror that followed in typical totalitarian style, which only really began after peace had been established and has been growing stronger and stronger ever since, does not represent the typical Stalinist resolution of such a crisis.* Stalin most probably would have preferred a police action to a military operation, and he would certainly have carried it through, not merely by execution of leaders and imprisonment of thousands, but by wholesale deportation and by consciously depopulating the country. Nothing would have been further from his mind than to send enough aid to prevent a complete collapse of the Hungarian economy and to stave off mass starvation, as the Soviet Union has done in the last couple of years.

It is too early to tell whether this striking change in methods will prove successful. It may be a temporary phenomenon, a hangover from the time of the collective leadership, of unresolved conflicts at the top with a concomitant relaxation of terror and ideological rigidity. But this seems less likely in view of the fact that in all ideological and all genuinely political

---

stems from a way of thinking that has little interest in the loss of freedom under the dictatorship, but registers each remaining or new inequality with great sensibility and outrage. And as even the real revolutionary vigor of the communist and socialist movements was initially sparked not by political oppression, but by social injustice, we understand only too well that the objective significance of the ruling bureaucracy's disappointing lifestyles—their high salaries, mink coats, automobiles, and villas—is overestimated. But these possessions are not, of course, the sign of a "new class." If, on the other hand, it should be true that such a new class is forming in Yugoslavia, this alone would demonstrate that Tito's dictatorship is not totalitarian—which, indeed, it is not.

* Bela Fabian, the president of the Federation of Hungarian Former Political Prisoners, estimates the number of victims of the terror that started after the army crushed the revolution as follows: 2,140 people were executed, 55,000 are in Hungarian prisons and concentration camps, and 75,000 were deported to Russian concentration camps. See the news item in *Bund* (Bern) of July 24, 1958.

matters, Khrushchev has returned to the reckless employment of Stalin's methods, sealing this retreat with the murder of Nagy—though in this case, the murder itself was not as characteristic of these methods as the fact that it came immediately after a widely publicized promise to Gomulka to spare Nagy's life. This was how Stalin liked to demonstrate his resolve not to bend for the sake of legality or morality: not simply by proclaiming it, but by letting his comrades experience it at first hand. It is all the more striking that in spite of such evident regression to Stalin's methods of domination, Khrushchev has, at least thus far, also refused to abandon the terror in its earlier form, with concentration and extermination camps for large masses of the population. And his reasons for this strategy may have very little to do with the succession crisis. If we consider the position in which Russia has found itself over the last decade, it cannot be denied that there are certain objective factors that must be making the Russian regime very keen to abandon some of the methods we have come to identify with totalitarian rule.

First among these factors is that for the first time in its history, the Soviet Union is suffering from a very real shortage of labor. In this situation, which is chiefly due to the progressive industrialization of the country, the old institutions of slave labor, concentration and extermination camps— which, among their other functions, also had to solve the acute unemployment problem of the thirties—are not only obsolete but positively dangerous. It is quite possible that the Russian political elite feared Stalin's plans for a new super-purge not only because they were concerned for their personal security, but because they felt that Russia was no longer in a position to afford the prohibitively high cost in "human material" involved. This seems to be the most plausible explanation of why the liquidation of Beria and his clique in the police was followed by the partial breakdown of the police apparatus and its enormous economic empire, the transformation of some concentration camps into forced settlements, and the release of a considerable number of inmates.

A second factor, closely connected with the first, is the emergence of communist China, which because of its threefold superiority in population—600 against 200 million—puts Russia at a serious disadvantage in the half-hidden, but very real struggle for ultimate supremacy. Particularly important in this context is that China, its adherence to the Soviet bloc notwithstanding, has thus far refused to follow the Russian (Stalinist) depopulation policy; for as great as the number of victims that the Chinese Revolution has thus far demanded may appear—fifteen million seems a plausible guess—it is not large enough to do serious damage to a population of 600 million, and is insignificant in comparison with the losses Stalin's regime periodically inflicted on the Russian people.* These considerations of sheer numerical force, though they do not necessitate the abolition of the police state or rule by terror, definitely stand in the way of the mass murder of innocents (or, as the totalitarian rulers claim, "objective enemies") that was so highly characteristic of both the Hitler and Stalin regimes.

If the Russian rulers should really take into account such objective factors, which threaten Russia's national existence and international position, then they may even be forced in the direction of a national Bolshevism, which is known to be a heresy among communists, and today seems to have a decisive influence on the policy of both Yugoslavia and China. Of course, it is not surprising that the dictators of smaller countries—Gomulka in Poland, and earlier Rajk and Nagy in Hungary, and Tito in Yugoslavia—should incline to this deviation. Communists who were more than simple agents of Moscow—willing to become ruling bureaucrats of some other country if, for some reason of world revolutionary strategy, the country of their birth should cease to exist—have no other choice. The case is different in China, which could have afforded the price of totalitarian terror even more easily than Russia, and which, in spite of this, deliberately chose a national policy under Mao's leadership. This difference is made clear by China's domestic policy, and is also clearly shown in Mao's famous speech about "inner contradictions," which seems to have been formulated in deliberate contradiction to the official Russian ideology. This speech is without doubt the first serious, ideologically new piece of writing that has

* The best proof of the difference between Mao's and Stalin's rule may be found in a comparison of the population censuses in China and Russia. The last Chinese census, counting close to 600 million people, was higher than statistical expectations, while Russian censuses for decades have been considerably lower than what statistically was expected. In the absence of reliable figures for Russian population losses through the terror of the Stalin period, it became usual to equate the number of those murdered with these millions of people who were "statistically lost."

come out of the communist orbit since Lenin's death, and with it, as has been correctly remarked, the ideological initiative has shifted from Moscow to Beijing.* This, it is true, may harbor momentous consequences for the future; it may even change the totalitarian nature of the Russian regime. But at this moment all such hopes are, to say the least, premature. Zhukov's dismissal, one reason for which was certainly that he was guilty of "nationalist deviations," that, in other words, he started to speak about the "Soviet people" in much the same sense in which Mao tries to reintroduce the concept of the people into communist ideology.

Still, it may be that fear of Chinese competition, in addition to the succession crisis, constituted an important factor in the dramatic relaxation of the mass terror after Stalin's death. If so, it would indeed be more than a mere maneuver or a temporary thaw. But this certainly does not mean that the hopes entertained by so many people today—that this totalitarian domination will reform itself from within over the course of history, ending in a kind of enlightened despotism or a military dictatorship—are justified. The striking thing about the situation at the moment is precisely that the murders and party purges have begun again on a grand scale, but without turning into the kind of mass murder that would decimate the population and ruin the economy. This is more like a tactical retreat, and there have been numerous indications that Khrushchev quite deliberately has left the door wide open for the reestablishment of mass terror and mass murder at any time.

One of these indications I have mentioned already. It is the law against

---

* The complete text of this important speech was published by *The New Leader* (September 9, 1957; Section 2) in a supplementary pamphlet with a valuable commentary by G. F. Hudson. The speech's usual title, "Let a Hundred Flowers Bloom," is quite misleading. Mao's chief concern is to prove and ground theoretically the existence of "contradictions" in communist countries, between classes, on the one hand, and between the people and the government on the other. Of even greater importance is the strong populist note in the speech, as if it had been written by a Narodnik, not a Bolshevist. On the matter of freedom, by contrast, Mao is quite orthodox. Freedom to him is a means to an end, as is democracy; both "are relative, not absolute, they come into being and develop under specific historical circumstances." Editor's addition: This refers to Mao's speech on February 27, 1957, at the extended eleventh plenary session of the Supreme State Conference, entitled "On Correctly Handling Contradictions Among the People" (English translation of the revised speech published in: *The Writings of Mao Zedong, 1949–1976*, Vol. 2, January 1956–December 1957, New York: M. E. Sharpe, 1992, p. 309).

"social parasites" (a term only too familiar to the student of Nazi totalitarianism) by which at any moment any number of people can again disappear into the concentration camps, without having done anything to oppose the regime or committed any other crime. The totalitarian character of the decree is illustrated by the careful omission of criminal acts as defined by criminal law, and lists deportation as the only punishment. It is evidently intended as a lever which will allow Russia to reintroduce the system of concentration camps and slavery if necessary, without any great fuss. If this decree, which admittedly is still only on paper, had received the attention it deserved from the free world, then the talk of a new Soviet legality (which has been refuted by subsequent events) could never have arisen in the first place.

Another indication appears in Khrushchev's speech at the Twentieth Party Congress. The speech was probably originally intended only for the higher echelons of the Russian party and those involved in the "collective leadership." This unusually well-trained audience probably understood immediately that the speech could be interpreted in two altogether different ways. Either Stalin's mental sickness was the cause of all the regime's crimes, and then nobody was to blame—neither those who heard Mr. Khrushchev nor Mr. Khrushchev himself—in which case the mutual fear from which the collective leadership had emerged was completely unjustified: only an unbalanced mind would plot murder. Or, because of his insane suspicions, Stalin had been susceptible to evil influences, and in this case it was not Stalin, but whoever abused his diseased power for his own ends that was to blame. The first alternative remained the official interpretation until summer 1957, when Khrushchev seized power with the help of the army. The second reading became official policy when Khrushchev justified his *coup d'état* by stressing Malenkov's role in the Leningrad affair, alluding to Malenkov's job as head of Stalin's personal secretariat—which had made him the unofficial head of the NKVD. It is common knowledge that the techniques of Khrushchev's *coup d'état* followed closely the pattern set by Stalin in the late twenties for the liquidation of the troika and the right- and left-wing factions of the party, and it therefore seemed only proper that Khrushchev should immediately begin to rehabilitate his old master, and to tell the intellectuals that the "thaw" must come to an end.

Nobody, probably least of all Mr. Khrushchev himself, can know what the course of his future actions will be. Today, everybody knows that the "thaw" is over, and, on the basis of his *coup d'état* speech, it is also certain that Khrushchev could both physically liquidate his exiled former colleagues from the collective leadership at any moment, and let loose a new purge of Stalin collaborators in the party, government, and managerial bureaucracies. But if we are asking ourselves where this is all going, and considering the real outlook for the populations that have come under the system of total domination, we should remind ourselves of the explanation that the Kádár group in Hungary provided a year ago—at a time when Western observers' hopes of a regime reform were still in full bloom. The full double meaning of the "de-Stalinization" process initiated by Khrushchev becomes suddenly obvious when one reads that "the old Stalinist group had not been severe enough in crushing the enemies of socialism," or in "the application of the dictatorship of the proletariat."*

The last of the post-Stalin changes to be mentioned in our context (something to which particularly great hopes of a decisive change in the regime had been attached) is the exchange of positions that has occurred between the army and police, the sudden ascendency of the army and especially the rise of Marshal Zhukov in the Soviet hierarchy at the cost of the police apparatus. These hopes were not entirely unfounded, for it has thus far been an outstanding characteristic of totalitarian government that the army played a subordinate role and could not compete with the police cadres either in power or in prestige. But the hopes were also misguided, because another prominent feature of totalitarian government was left out of account, namely the extraordinary flexibility of its institutional apparatus, which enables it to shift its center of power at almost any time. When one speaks of the monolithic character of the totalitarian power apparatus, one must not forget that the term applies only to the rigid consistency of its ideology, which is matched by an extraordinary opportunism in everyday political matters and the even more extraordinary ability to multiply offices and institutions.

---

* See Paul Landy, "Hungary Since the Revolution," in *Problems of Communism*, September–October 1957.

Moreover, the ascendency of the police over the military apparatus is the hallmark of all tyrannies, and not only totalitarian regimes; it is just that in the latter case, the power of the police does not so much answer the need to suppress the population as validate the claim to global rule. Those who regard the whole earth as their future territory will be of a mind to bring newly conquered territory into line with the motherland, and to rule it using police methods and personnel rather than with the army. Thus the Nazis used their SS troops, essentially a police force, for the rule and even the conquest of foreign territories, putting the army at a considerable disadvantage, with the ultimate aim of amalgamating the police and the Wehrmacht under the leadership of the SS. In view of the flexibility of totalitarianism, it cannot be denied that the same results could be achieved with the opposite approach, and that instead of subordinating the army to the police, military units could be directly transformed into police troops, with the amalgamation of army and police being disguised by the fact that the higher officer corps of the army would also be commanding the police. As long as the party and its ideology retain the initiative, such a development does not necessarily preclude police methods of rule. Only in Germany would this have been impossible, because of the strong military traditions of the *Reichswehr,* which could be broken only from the outside. But of course, even a tradition like this can only remain alive as long as the officer corps is not exclusively chosen from the ranks of the party, and is therefore less reliable and loyal to the party than are the police cadres. Where Russia is concerned, it appears entirely possible that Khrushchev might succeed in replacing the political commissars—who up to now have been forced on the army from without—with control from within the army's own ranks, meaning the party would only need to seek out those officers who wanted to take on this function. Khrushchev is conceivably planning to use the same methods here that he has already tested elsewhere, handing political control of the soldiers to their officers. In any case, under these circumstances the decisive difference between army and police would cease to exist.

When Khrushchev appealed to Zhukov to support his *coup d'état,* the army's ascendency over the police was an accomplished fact. It had been one of the almost automatic consequences of breaking up the police empire, and lasted significantly longer than the temporary strengthening of the managerial group, which for a while had inherited a huge number of factories, mines, and real estate, through the dissolution of the police-controlled share of the economy. It speaks for Khrushchev's shrewdness that he grasped these consequences more quickly than his colleagues, and acted more decisively. The economic aspect was not as crucial as the simple fact that following the liquidation of the police, the army was the only instrument of violence left with which to decide inner-party conflicts. Khrushchev had used Zhukov in the party in exactly the same way Stalin had used his relationships to the secret police more than thirty years previously. And now as then, the supreme power in the state belonged to the party. And just as Stalin realized this power by purging the police apparatus as soon as it had helped him achieve decisive inner-party victories, so Khrushchev did not hesitate to rob Zhukov of the power he had just drawn on for support. Both men acted not only out of their own thirst for power but, most importantly, to restore the power of the party, which for a moment had been so radically shaken that it was necessary to mobilize the organs of violence, the army or police, to rescue it. But even during the short time he had his power, Zhukov never achieved more than minor concessions, such as the assurance of the authority of military commands against interference by political commissars, and these concessions bore an ominous resemblance to those Stalin had made to the population during the war, when military considerations and nationalist propaganda forced the party ideology into the background for a few years. If we compare the Russian development to the Nazi government, it is easy to overlook the fact that in spite of all similarities, Hitler and Stalin handled the war in completely opposite ways. While Hitler deliberately used the war to steer his dictatorship once and for all into the channel of totalitarianism, even accepting military disadvantages to achieve his aim, by contrast Stalin weakened his rule, which had already developed into totalitarianism, toward making Russia a military, one-party dictatorship. Of course, this tactic had the greatest warfare advantage of all; the Russian people really believed they were fighting both against the foreign invader, and for their liberation from total domination.

This last point is decisive. There hardly ever was anything to substantiate hopes that the totalitarian dictatorship would transform of its own accord into a military dictatorship and, from the viewpoint of peace, it is by no means sure that such a transformation was to be desired. But the observation that generals are among the most peace-loving and least dangerous creatures in the world, though quite correct in the Western Hemisphere of the last forty years, does not yet hold true for those who by definition are aggressors. Zhukov certainly was not another Eisenhower, and his rising prestige could point to nothing other than that Russia was preparing for war. This has nothing immediately to do with the Sputniks and the development of an intercontinental rocket, much as these advances show that such a policy would not lack a material basis. More important is Malenkov's statement in 1954 that a nuclear war would spell doom to mankind as a whole. He seems to have meant what he said, for his program of nonmilitary industrial development and increased production of consumer goods was in line with his statement; together, they most likely cost him the support of the army, thereby indirectly helping Khrushchev to his victory. In any case, one year later, when Malenkov had already been shut out of the leadership, Molotov declared that a nuclear war would only spell the end of imperialism and capitalism, but that the communist bloc would profit by it no less than it had profited by the two previous World Wars.

Khrushchev had already expressed the same opinion unofficially in 1956, confirming it officially in 1957 prior to Zhukov's fall: "A new world war could only end in collapse for capitalism. [. . .] Socialism will live on while capitalism will not remain. For despite great losses mankind will not only survive, but will continue to develop." So warlike was this statement, made in an interview for foreign consumption about peaceful coexistence, that even Khrushchev himself felt that "some may think communists are interested in war, since it would lead to the victory of socialism."* This declaration, to be sure, never meant that Russia actually was on the point of starting a war. Totalitarian leaders can change their minds like everyone else, and it stands to reason that the Russian leaders were wavering not only between the hope for victory and the fear of defeat, but between the hope that victory might make them the uncontested masters over the globe, and

---

* See the text of James Reston's interview with Khrushchev in *The New York Times*, October 10, 1957.

the fear that, exhausted by a too costly victory, they be left alone to face the growing power colossus of China. These would be considerations along national lines; if they prevail, Russia may indeed be interested in coming to a *modus vivendi* with the United States.

In any case, Zhukov's demotion may be thanks to, among other things, the fact that Khrushchev changed his mind and decided that, for the moment, war was unlikely and undesirable. The demotion therefore was reassuring from the outset, even if we know too little to be able to judge for sure. Still, it seems likely that Zhukov wanted war, and was justifiably accused of "adventurism," which in communist terminology means warmongering. After a moment's hesitation, Khrushchev obviously decided to follow once more the "wisdom" of his late lord and master, whose ruthlessness in domestic policies always was matched by an extreme caution in foreign affairs. (We cannot be sure, however, for it is also possible that Khrushchev raised his accusations against Zhukov precisely because he himself was toying with the idea of war—just as Stalin accused Tukhachevski of plotting with Nazi Germany when he himself was preparing an alliance with Hitler.) These possibilities, which seem so unnerving and confusing to us, are part of the nature of totalitarian dictatorships, and we should not forget that all such changes are, and are meant to be, of a temporary nature. In Khrushchev's own words: "In life one cell dies and another takes its place, but life goes on." At any event, our interpretation is supported by the fact that Zhukov's dismissal was followed by wholly unusual affirmations of peacefulness toward the Allies, a toast hailing the wartime alliance against Hitler accompanied by a curse on all warmongers— "Let him be damned who thinks of war! Let him be damned who wants war!"—in which Khrushchev, who proposed the toast, was evidently not thinking of the "capitalist and imperialist powers" but rather of his generals at home. These words, too, should of course be enjoyed with caution; they are doubtless meant for propaganda purposes in Russia and the satellite states, where Zhukov's popularity perhaps made a denunciation of him as a warmonger necessary. Unfortunately, one thing is certain: it is highly unlikely that Khrushchev has changed his general opinion on nuclear war.

It is in the terrible nature of these things that our hopes for the maintenance of peace should hang to a considerable degree on the fact that conditions in Russia and its satellites, having fundamentally improved for a number of years, have taken another decisive turn for the worse. It was one of the mainstays of Stalin's politics to combine an aggressive foreign policy with concessions at home, and vice versa: to compensate for a peaceable foreign policy with aggression against his own people, never letting the momentum of the permanent revolution drop. Here, as in everything else, Khrushchev may well follow the advice of his late master.

This is bad enough, but it is not the worst. The worst is that under these circumstances the most important political issue of the nuclear age—the war question—cannot be sensibly raised, let alone solved. As far as the nontotalitarian world is concerned, it is a matter of fact that a war fought with nuclear weapons will harbor a threat of destruction to the existence of mankind, even to the existence of organic life on earth. This, obviously, makes all our traditional ideas about the role of war in politics, its possible justification for the sake of freedom, its role as an *ultima ratio* in foreign affairs, perfectly obsolete. In practice, this puts politics "into a different state of aggregation," the various sides of which Karl Jaspers elucidates in his brilliant book *The Atom Bomb and the Future of Man*. But what is a matter of fact for us, is a matter of ideology for the totalitarian mind. This conflict is not about differences of opinion and the concomitant difficulties in coming to an agreement, but the much more terrifying impossibility of agreeing on facts.* Mr. Khrushchev's off-the-record contribution to the war discussion: "poor men do not mind fire" was truly appalling, not merely because such popular verities of yesterday have become dangerous irrelevancies in today's situation, but because it shows with rare precision that, no matter how folksy or vulgar his expressions may be, he only thinks within the closed framework of the communist ideology, and will not permit new facts to penetrate it.

It has always been an error to measure the threat of totalitarianism by the yardstick of the relatively harmless conflict between a capitalist and a socialist economic order, and to overlook the explosive contradiction

---

* This basic difference of course comes out at once in dialogues between people from the Western and the totalitarian-governed world. Both Mr. Reston's interview and the above-mentioned correspondence between Silone and Anissimov read like object lessons in how totalitarian thought and argumentation manage to avoid giving answers and dissolve facts in ideological talk.

between the totalitarian fiction and the everyday world of factuality in which we live. But it was never as dangerously wrong as it is today, when the same technological discoveries which, taken together, constitute for us a factually changed world, are available to those who in all seriousness regard them as a mere means, as additional tools with which to construct a fictitious world built of lies and based on the denial of facts. Neither the freedom nor the survival of mankind depends upon what we understand by a free market economy; yet freedom as well as survival may well depend upon our success or failure to persuade the totalitarian world to recognize the facts, and come to terms with the new factuality of the world in the atomic age.

II
The Hungarian Revolution

A Russian-American critic quite rightly pointed out that Khrushchev's speech at the Twentieth Party Congress was neither the beginning nor the high point of de-Stalinization; on the contrary, it signaled its end.* But the same speech doubtless led to the rebellion in Poland and the uprising in Hungary. If one regards these events from the perspective of what happened after Stalin's death, one cannot help wondering how this was possible. It is obvious that from the start, this decisive speech was received completely differently in the satellite states than in Russia itself; this was clearly a catastrophic misunderstanding of the speaker's intention. What this misunderstanding expressed was a difference that still exists in the mentality of the satellite states' populations, when compared with the population of the Soviet Union, which has become so uncannily practiced in totalitarian thought.

The sinister ambiguity of the speech was clearly lost on readers in the satellite states, who understood it in the same way as the average reader in the free world. In this naïve reading, it could not but cause a tremendous

---

* Nicolaevsky (see note on page 113) supports this opinion with a careful compilation and analysis of all available information.

relief. For the first time, the leader of the Soviet world was talking like a normal human being about certain sad occurrences that are usual in human life: the sickness, insanity, and crimes creeping into politics and causing great harm to the people. Marxist phraseology and the historical necessity of dialectical materialism were conspicuous by their absence. Had this been the "correct understanding," the speech would have signaled an extraordinary turning point; it would have indicated no less than a conscious break with the methods of totalitarian movements and domination—though that certainly did not mean a break with socialism or dictatorship. It would not have ended the conflict, but it might well have healed the damaging, gaping rift between the two world powers. For Khrushchev would have confirmed the free world's main charge against Stalin's regime: that this was not so much a communist as a crime-ridden government, which ruled undemocratically and unconstitutionally, and without any restriction of power through law whatsoever. If from now on the only problem was that the Soviet Union intended to operate a socialist economy, while America operated a free market economy, then there was no reason why the two main powers, together with their respective allies, should not be able to coexist and cooperate peacefully and in good faith on all issues of world politics.

Several months elapsed before the world learned of the secret speech from *The New York Times*. It also only reached the satellite states via this detour to America. Its immediate consequence was something unheard of: open rebellions in Poland and Hungary, such as there had never been either in the years after Stalin's death, when his name silently but most efficiently vanished from public life, and a number of seasoned Stalinists like Rákosi in Hungary had been removed from power, nor in the years that followed, when some of these Stalinists had been rehabilitated and the police controls retightened. The first point is that the people were roused only by open, clearly spoken words, and not by silent maneuvers—no matter how telling they might have been for the observer—and no amount of ambiguity could alter their inflammatory power. It was not action, but "mere words" that had succeeded, much against the speaker's intention, in breaking the deadly spell of impotent apathy that totalitarian terror and ideology cast over the minds of those they rule.

However, it did not happen everywhere. It happened only in the countries where some old-guard communists, like Nagy or Gomulka, had miraculously survived Stalin's meticulously planned purges, which were intended to rid the parties of everyone who was not a mere agent. In the beginning, the Polish and Hungarian developments were quite similar. In both countries, an inner-party split had occurred between the real communists and the "Muscovites," and the general mood of both countries was also similar, including the stress on national tradition, religious freedom, and violent dissatisfaction among students. One is tempted to say it was almost an accident that what happened in Hungary did not happen in Poland, and vice versa. The point is, however, that by setting the tragic fate of Hungary before the eyes of the Polish people, Gomulka succeeded in stopping the rebellion in its initial stage, so that the Polish people also missed out on the exhilarating experience of the power that comes from acting together. They therefore do not know what can happen when a people unfurls the flag of freedom in plain view.

The third point to remember is that the rebellion in both countries started with intellectuals and university students, and generally with the younger generation, that is, with those strata of the population whose material well-being and ideological indoctrination had been one of the regime's prime concerns. Not the underprivileged, but the over-privileged of communist society took the initiative, and their motive was neither their own nor their fellow citizens' material misery, but exclusively the longing for Freedom and Truth.* This must have been as rude a lesson for Moscow as it was heartwarming for the free world. It showed that bribes in the form of material and social privileges do not necessarily work everywhere, and above all, that the educated classes, the intellectuals, writers, and artists who in our century have shown themselves to be so open to these bribes and so amenable to all kinds of nonsense, can still play a role appropriate to their profession in the politics of our age. The voice from Eastern Europe, speaking so plainly and simply of freedom and truth, sounded like an ulti-

---

* The truly admirable United Nations *Report of the Special Committee on the Problem of Hungary* quotes a young girl student as follows: "Even though we might lack bread and other necessities of life, we wanted freedom. We, the young people, were particularly hampered because we were brought up amidst lies. We continually had to lie. We could not have a healthy idea, because everything was choked in us. We wanted freedom of thought."

mate affirmation that human nature is unchangeable, that nihilism will be futile, that even in the absence of all teaching and under the pressure of incessant indoctrination, a yearning for freedom and truth will rise out of the human heart forever.

Unfortunately, such conclusions need qualification. First, the rebellions happened in countries whose experience with total domination had been quite short-lived. The dictatorships in the satellite states really only become totalitarian around 1949, and the process of their Bolshevization was interrupted in 1953 by Stalin's death and the subsequent period of "thaw." The struggle for succession resulted in the formation of factions, and discussion became inevitable. The cry for freedom was born in the atmosphere of these inner-party discussions; in the language of the communist movement of the twenties, these men were concerned with the reestablishment of inner-party democracy. But this first inner-communist stage of the revolution could only be witnessed in the new, recently conquered countries, not in Russia proper. The word "thaw," the right metaphor for the new party line, may have come from a Russian writer; but Ilya Ehrenburg, an old bohemian and habitué of Left Bank Paris bistros, who may have been nourishing false hope when he coined the term, is rather more typical of Western literary types, whom "the gods have failed," than of the Russian intelligentsia. In any case, Dudintsev's novel *Not by Bread Alone*, probably a product of the encouraged "self-criticism" mentioned above, is not about freedom at all, but the opening of careers to talent. As far as one may speak of a rebellion among Russian intellectuals at all—and the evidence for it is extremely scarce—it seems much rather a yearning for the right to know factual truth than for any right to freedom. One such instance also occurs in Dudintsev's novel, where he recounts the early days of the Nazi invasion. He was watching from a trench a fight between German and Russian airplanes, in which the German Messerschmitts proved victorious although they were outnumbered. "Something snapped in me because I had always been told that our planes were the fastest and the best." Here, Dudintsev tells of one long moment during which the totalitarian fiction collapsed under the weight of fact. The experience of reality could no longer be suppressed by the "historical truth" of the party's argument, in which the sentence "our planes are the fastest and the best" means: in the course of inevitable historical developments, we will have the fastest and best planes, perhaps at the cost of destroying all those who could compete with us in the field of aviation.

The case of Pasternak is quite different. He is unique in being the only great writer from the early revolutionary period who, by some miracle, was not annihilated, and whose poetic substance was not destroyed either, because he found the incredible strength necessary to remain silent for decades. He is the only splendid, living pillar supporting the hopes that "Orwell's 1984 is just a nightmare." These hopes also play host to the extraordinary anecdote about what was apparently the poet's only public appearance under the totalitarian regime. Pasternak, so it is said, had announced he would give a reading in Moscow, to which a tremendous crowd of people had turned up, despite the fact that after all his years of silence, he was known only as the translator of Shakespeare and Goethe into Russian. He read from his poems, and as he was reading an old poem, the paper slipped from his hand. "Then a voice from the hall began to recite the poem from memory. From several corners of the hall, other voices joined in. And the recitation of the poem ended, uninterrupted, in a chorus."* This is the only anecdote I know of that speaks for totalitarian domination not yet having been victorious in Russia itself, and it is undoubtedly of great significance. However, it comes not from the fifties and the period of rebellion in the satellite states, but from 1946, when the greater freedom of the people, which the battle to liberate Russia had forced into being, was still in the air—though there could still be no talk of any rebellion against Stalin's rule.

In light of such a story, particularly when it is held up against recent events, we are naturally tempted to doubt the effectiveness of total domination in generating a specifically totalitarian mentality—and, I fear, to underestimate it. In any case, all our experience with totalitarian conditions indicates that, when they are firmly established, factual reality is a much greater danger to them than a natural human drive for freedom. We know this from shortly after the war, when the Stalin regime deported to concentration camps the returning soldiers of the Russian occupation army

* As reported by Léon Leneman in the French weekly *L'Express,* June 26, 1958.

en masse because they had been exposed to the impact of a reality they had not expected. And we know it from the curiously complete breakdown of Nazi ideology in Germany after Hitler's defeat, which had less to do with "German lack of character" than is generally assumed, and was essentially the result of the dramatic collapse of a fictitious world.

The impact of factual reality, like all other human experiences, needs speech if it is to survive the moment of experience, it needs communication with others to remain sure of itself. Total domination succeeds to the extent that it succeeds in interrupting and destroying all normal channels of communication, those from person to person inside the four walls of privacy no less than the public ones which are safeguarded in democracies by freedom of speech and opinion. Whether this process of making every person incommunicado succeeds, except in the extreme situations of solitary confinement and torture, is hard to say. In any event, it takes time, and it is obvious that the preparation of people for total domination in the satellite countries leaves a great deal to be desired. So long as the terror from outside is not supplemented and supported by the ideological compulsion from within—and it is this compulsion that is made so hideously manifest in the self-denunciations of the show trials*—the ability of the people to distinguish between truth and lies on the elementary factual level remains unimpaired. As long as this is the case, oppression is felt for what it is and rebellions will take place in the name of freedom.

The Hungarian people, young and old, knew that they were "living amid lies," and asked, unanimously and in all manifestos, for something the Rus-

---

* The collapse of the regime in Hungary has yielded one more beautiful example of the motivation and technique of these self-denunciations, by making public the discussion that was to prepare László Rajk for his show trial. This was the little speech that Kádár gave in prison on Rákosi's orders, and which Rákosi secretly recorded, presumably for future use in a show trial against Kádár. The recording was played back at the Central Committee meeting where Rákosi was ousted, and the comrades heard the following: "Dear Laci, I come to you on behalf of Comrade Rákosi. He requested me to come and explain the situation to you. Of course, we all know that you are innocent. But Comrade Rákosi believes that you will understand. Only really great comrades are chosen for such roles. He asked me to tell you that by doing this you will render historic service to the Communist movement." (Quoted from E. M., "János Kádár: A Profile," in: *Problems of Communism*, September–October 1957, p. 16.) This combination of gross flattery and appeal to ideological convictions may be unsurpassable.

sian intelligentsia (judging from their words at the time of the succession crisis—and for a general judgment we can hardly rely on anything else) has even forgotten how to dream of, namely, for freedom of thought. It would probably be erroneous to conclude that the same concern for freedom of thought that gave rise to the rebellion among the intellectuals also transformed the rebellion into a revolution that spread like wildfire, until nobody outside the ranks of the political police was prepared to lift a finger for the regime. A similar error would be to conclude that the revolution was primarily an inner-party affair, a revolt of "true" against "false" communists, just because it was originally sparked by members of the Communist Party. The facts speak an altogether different language. What are the facts?

An unarmed and essentially harmless student demonstration grew from a few thousand people suddenly and spontaneously into a huge crowd, which took it upon itself to carry out one of the students' demands, the overturning of Stalin's statue in one of the public squares of Budapest, and its removal. The following day, some students went to the Radio Building to persuade the station to broadcast the sixteen points of their manifesto. Again, a large crowd immediately gathered, as if from nowhere, and when the AVH, the political police guarding the radio building, tried to disperse the crowd with a few shots, the revolution broke out. The masses attacked the police and acquired their first weapons. The workers, hearing of the situation, left the factories and joined the crowd. The army, called in to support the armed police, sided with the revolution and armed the people. What had started as a student demonstration had become an armed uprising in less than twenty-four hours.

From this moment onward, no programs, points, or manifestos played any role. What carried the revolution was the sheer momentum of a whole people acting together; their demands were so obvious to everyone that they hardly needed elaborate formulation. Russian troops should leave the territory immediately, and free elections should determine a new government. The question was not how various freedoms should be approached— the freedom of thought and speech; the freedom of assembly; the freedom to act and vote—it was how to stabilize a freedom that was already an accomplished fact, and to find the right political institutions for it. If we leave aside the interventions of Russian troops—first of those already stationed in Hungary and then of regular, battle-ready divisions from Russia that finally attacked the country—we may well say that never a revolution achieved its aims so quickly, so completely and with so little bloodshed.* The amazing thing about the Hungarian Revolution is that it was not followed by civil war. The Hungarian army disintegrated in a matter of hours, and the Hungarian government in a matter of days; and after the people made its will known and its voice had been heard in the marketplace, there was no group or class in the whole of Hungary that would have tried to oppose it. The rank and file of the AVH, who remained loyal to the dictatorship to the end, formed neither group nor class; they had been recruited from the dregs of the population and consisted of criminal elements, former Nazi agents, or highly compromised members of the Hungarian fascist party, the higher ranks being composed of Moscow agents, Hungarians with Russian citizenship under the orders of NKVD officers.

The swift disintegration of the country's whole power structure—party, army, and governmental offices—and the absence of internal strife in the developments that followed, are all the more remarkable when we consider that the uprising was clearly started by communists. They very quickly lost the sole initiative, but for that reason, they never for a moment became the object of the people's wrath or vengeance, and nor, when they saw power slipping from their grasp, did they turn against the people. The striking absence of party wrangling and any ideological dispute, and the similarly striking lack of fanaticism can only be due to the ideological superstructure having disintegrated even more swiftly than the organs of the dictatorship themselves. In the general atmosphere of fraternity—and here the word should be understood in the sense of the French Revolution's *fraternité*—which came into being with the first demonstration in the streets, and lasted until the bitter end—beyond the end, in fact—all party ideologies and slogans, not just the communist ones, seemed to have dissolved into nothing, so that intellectuals and workers, communists and noncommunists of every

---

* According to an estimate by the correspondent from the Polish evening paper *Nowa Kultura*, the number of victims of the revolution in Budapest was around eighty. See Seton-Watson (full citation in note on p. 110), p. 24.

stripe really could fight together, for the common goal of freedom.* The one thing brought about by this collapse of ideology was the reality of the revolution itself, and in this negative respect, this sudden change had much the same effect on the minds of the Hungarian people as the sudden collapse of the Hitler regime had on the minds of the German people. (This dramatic collapse of ideologies, triggered by reality, should be recalled if, following another such event, it should yet again occur to somebody to "reeducate" the people. This teaching from outside never reaches the same level of shock created by the event; it therefore either remains wholly ineffectual, or may even cripple the impact of the lesson that reality has just imparted.)

Important as these aspects are, they tell us more about the nature of the regime the Hungarian Revolution rebelled against than about the revolution itself. In its positive significance, the outstanding feature of the uprising was that the actions of people with no leader or any previously formulated program did not result in chaos and anarchy. There was no looting, no trespassing of property, among a multitude whose standard of life had been miserable and whose hunger for merchandise notorious. There were no crimes against life either, for in the few instances where the masses took direct action and hanged senior AVH officers in public, an effort was made to act justly and discriminate, rather than just hanging everyone who fell into their hands. Instead of the lynching and mob rule that might have been expected, revolutionary councils of workers and soldiers appeared immediately, almost simultaneously with the first armed demonstrations. Over the last hundred years, these organizations have emerged with a historically unparalleled regularity whenever the people have been permitted for a few days, or a few weeks, or months, to follow their own political devices without being spoon-fed by a party or steered by a government.

Historically, we encounter these councils for the first time in the revolution that swept Europe in 1848. We meet them again in the Paris Commune of 1871, and during the first Russian Revolution of 1905; but they

---

* This aspect is especially striking when we hear details such as that the insurgents were immediately joined by "800 cadets from the Petöfi Military Academy. These were mostly sons of high Government and Communist Party officials and AVH officers; they had led a privileged life in the Military Academy and had been indoctrinated for years." (United Nations *Report*.)

only emerged clearly and in full force in 1917, in the October Revolution in Russia, and in the postwar revolutions of 1918 and 1919 in Germany and Austria. For those who believe, with Hegel, that "World History is the Final Court of Appeals," the council system is of course finished: it has been defeated every time, and by no means always by the "counterrevolution." The Bolshevik regime deposed the councils—the *soviets,* as they are called in Russian—under Lenin, and attested to their popularity by stealing their name for its own *anti-soviet* regime. In fact, in order to understand the events of the Hungarian Revolution, we must, as Silone remarked in a brilliant article on the events of winter 1956, "first tidy up our language" and realize that "the Soviets disappeared from Russia as early as 1920." The Russian army is not a "Soviet" army, and "the only Soviets that exist in the world [in early 1957] are the Hungarian revolutionary committees."* Perhaps the Russian army struck so quickly and so mercilessly for that very reason, because the Hungarian Revolution was not seeking to restore anything, and was in no way "reactionary"; but in it, the original *soviet* system, the council system that came into existence in the October Revolution and was put down by the Bolshevist party in the Kronstadt uprising, had reentered the stage of history. One might think that today, Russia's totalitarian rulers are more afraid of these "elementary and improvised forms of the people's power" (Silone, ibid.) than of anything else, no matter in what country they might emerge. In Yugoslavia today there are no council system or free workers' councils; but the very fact that Tito sometimes still speaks the old revolutionary language, and the party there still plays with the notion of the councils, is probably enough to make the Russian rulers fearful. But the Bolshevist party is not alone in this fear; it is shared by all parties from right to left, wherever there is some understanding of the council system. Thus in Germany, again, it was not the "reaction" but the Social Democrats who liquidated the council system. And if they had not done it, the communists certainly would have, if they had come into power.

The council system in Hungary, even more markedly than in the case

---

* Silone, who as far as I know was the only writer to have placed this point at the heart of his interpretation of the Hungarian Revolution, is quoted here from his article "After Hungary," in: *The New Leader,* January 21, 1957, p.15.

of earlier revolutions, represented "the first practical step to restore order and to reorganize the Hungarian economy on a socialist basis, but without rigid Party control or the apparatus of terror."* The councils thus were charged with two tasks: one political, the other economic. Though it would be wrong to believe that the dividing line between them was institutional and unblurred, we may assume that the Revolutionary Councils fulfilled mainly political functions, while the Workers' Councils were supposed to handle economic life. In the following, we shall deal only with the Revolutionary Councils and the political aspect; their most immediate task was to prevent chaos and stop criminal elements from gaining the upper hand, and in this they were quite successful. The question of whether economic matters, which are subject to quite different laws from political matters, can be handled by councils—whether, in other words, it is possible to run factories under the management and ownership of their own workers, we shall have to leave open. As a matter of fact, it is quite doubtful whether the political principles of equality and self-rule can readily be applied to the economic sphere. In the political thought of the ancient world, everything economic was bound up with what was needed to sustain life, and therefore with necessity. Antiquity may not have been so wrong in its belief that economics, be it for a household or a state, could only be maintained and prosper under a lord and master, and for this reason could not be allowed to play a role in the polis, the political realm. The principle of government here corresponds to the necessity to which human life is subject, because it is also biological life; a human being is only free because and insofar as he is not just a living being, but a political being. Freedom and equality thus begin only where the interests of sustaining life have been satisfied: outside the household and the slave economy of the ancient world; outside jobs and earning money in our own age. It is important to state that both freedom and equality as political principles are determined neither by a transcendent authority, before which all humans *qua* humans are equal, nor by a general human fate like death, which one day takes all men equally from this world. Rather, they are intrinsically worldly principles, which grow up directly from the coming together of humans, from communal life and joint

---

* This is the evaluation of the United Nations *Report*.

actions. These ancient views, according to which economics has to do with neither politics nor freedom, and therefore cannot be governed with equality in mind, receive some (albeit negative) support from modernity, where all those who have believed that history is primarily the result of economic forces have come to the conviction that man is not free, and that history is the development of necessity over time.

At any event, the Revolutionary and the Workers' Councils, though they emerged together, are better kept apart, because the former were primarily (and particularly in the case of the Hungarian Revolution) the answer to political tyranny, whereas, in Hungary, the latter were the reaction against trade unions that did not represent the workers and their interests, but the party and its interest in keeping the workers down. The demand for new, free general elections in the whole country has been a core part of the councils' program wherever we encounter them in history, whereas the Hungarian demand to restore the multiparty system is not characteristic of the council system, but an almost automatic reaction from the Hungarian people to the shameful suppression and eradication of all parties that had preceded the one-party dictatorship.

In order to understand the council system, it is well to remember that it is as old as the party system itself; it emerged alongside it and has repeatedly been destroyed by it. To this day, the councils represent the only alternative to the party system—that is, the only alternative for a democratic government in the modern age. They are not antiparliamentary; they simply suggest another form in which the people can be represented. But they are inherently antiparty, which is to say, they orient themselves against representation determined by class interests on the one hand, and ideology or *Weltanschauung* on the other. While the historical origin of the party system lies in parliament, the councils were born exclusively of communal action, and the spontaneous demands of the people that arose in this action. They were not deduced from an ideology nor foreseen, let alone preconceived, by any political theory about the best form of government. Wherever they appeared, they were met with utmost hostility from the party bureaucracies, from the extreme right to the extreme left, and with unanimous silence and complete disregard from political scientists and theorists. There is no question that the spirit of the council system is genuinely democratic, but in a sense never seen before and never thought about. All the more characteristic is the curious stubbornness with which this system is suggested each time the people comes to raise its voice. There is real spontaneity here, which comes directly from action and is not influenced by interests or theory from outside the action.

Under modern conditions, then, we know of two alternatives for democratic government: the party system that has been victorious for a hundred years, and the council system that has been repeatedly vanquished over the same period; in many respects they stand in the most acute opposition to each other. Thus, the men elected for the councils are chosen from the bottom by a direct vote, while the party suggests the candidates to the voters from the top down, be it that they offer the voters the choice between various people, or force them to accept a slate of candidates. This gives rise to a completely different method of selecting representatives; for while the naming of a candidate by a party depends on the party program or the party ideology, against which his suitability will be measured, the candidate in the council system must simply inspire enough confidence in his personal integrity, courage, and judgment, for someone to entrust him with representing his own person in all political matters. Once elected, therefore, the representative is not bound by anything other than the duty to justify this trust in his personal qualities, and his pride is "to have been elected by the workers, and not by the government"* or by a party machine.

Once such a body of trusted men is elected, it will of course develop differences of opinion which in turn may lead into the formation of a sort of "parties." But these groups of men holding the same opinion within the councils would not be poltical parties, strictly speaking; they would constitute those factions from which parliamentary parties originally developed. Still, parties do not necessarily have to develop out of such factions, as long as the election of a candidate does not depend upon his adherence to a given faction, but on his personal power of persuasion, with which he is able to present his point of view—in other words, as long as the election continues

---

* Quote taken from *The Revolt in Hungary. A Documentary Chronology of Events,* a compilation of the official and unofficial radio broadcasts from the days of the revolution, published by the Free Europe Committee (undated), p. 17.

to rest on personal qualities. That would mean the councils were controlling the party factions, instead of being their representatives. The strength of any given faction would not depend upon its bureaucratic apparatus, and not even upon the appeal of any *Weltanschauung*, but solely upon the number of trusted and trustworthy men in its ranks. Which is to say, it would depend upon them being popular, in the best sense of the word. The danger this purely personal principle could represent to the dictatorship of a party manifested itself clearly in the initial stages of the Russian Revolution, and the chief reason why Lenin felt he had to emasculate the *soviets* was that the Social Revolutionaries had in their ranks far more men who were trusted by the people than did the Bolsheviks. The power of the Bolshevik party, which had been responsible for the revolution, was endangered by the council system, which had grown out of the revolution.

Remarkable, finally, is the great inherent flexibility of the council system. It seems to need no special conditions for its establishment except the coming together and acting together of a certain number of people on a nontemporary basis. In Hungary, we have seen all kinds of councils: neighborhood councils that emerged from living together, and then grew into city, area, or county councils; revolutionary councils that grew out of fighting together; councils of writers and artists which, one is tempted to think, were born in the cafés; the student and youth councils that came from studying together at school or university; military councils in the army; but also councils of civil servants; workers' councils in the factories; and so on. Wherever people were together in whatever kind of public space, they formed councils, and the councils in each of these quite disparate groups transformed a merely haphazard coming together of people into a political institution. The men elected were a colorful mixture of communists, noncommunists, and members of all parties, simply because party lines played no role whatsoever. The criterion, as a newspaper observed, being solely that there is "none among them who would misuse his power or think only of his personal position." And this was less a question of morality than of personal qualification—of talent. Whoever misuses power or perverts it into violence, or is only interested in his private affairs and without concern for the common world, is simply not fit to play a role in political life. The same principles were observed in the elections when the lower councils had to select men they trusted for the higher organs of government. They were urged to choose representatives "without regard for Party affiliation and with due regard to the confidence of the working people."*

One of the most striking aspects of the Hungarian Revolution is that this principle of the council system not only reemerged, but that in the twelve short or long days it was granted, the Hungarian Revolution also yielded the principle of the council system, managed to mark out a good deal of its range of potentialities in specific detail, and to show the directions in which these could lead. The council members had been scarcely elected by direct vote when these new councils began freely to coordinate among themselves, and to choose from their own midst the representatives for the higher councils, up to the Supreme National Council, the counterpart of a national government. And the initiative for replacing a normal government with a supreme council taken from the councils themselves came from the recently revived National Peasant Party, certainly the last group one might suspect of extreme leftist ideas. While this Supreme Council was never established, due to a shortage of time, the councils did have long enough to take the necessary preliminary steps for it: workers' councils set up coordinating committees and Central Workers' Committees were already functioning in many areas. Revolutionary councils in the provinces were coordinated, and planned to set up a National Revolutionary Committee with which to replace the National Assembly parliament.

We do not know very much more than this. Here, as in all other instances when, for the shortest historical moment, the voice of the people has been heard, unaltered by the shouts of the mob or the bickering of the fanatics, we can do no more than sketch as well as we can a picture of what was tried and what failed, of the physiognomy of the only democratic system in Europe (where the party system was discredited almost as soon as it was born) that has ever really had the people on its side. (Here it is important to keep in mind the decisive difference that has always existed between the continental multiparty system and the Anglo-American two-party system,

* Ibid.

though I cannot discuss that here.)* Thus we do not know whether this system would prove equal to the demands of modern politics in the longer term, the corrections it might require, how sustainable it is as a body politic, and whether council democracy and the voting and election principle on which it is based would be fit to replace the representative democracy in countries with large populations. No theoretical consideration can replace political experience, but more speaks in favor of this system, which is to say for its sustainability, than just its undoubted popularity. After all, it has been tried out once in Russia, one of the modern superpowers, and it did not collapse, but had to be eradicated by force of arms. Nor should we overlook the astounding fact that democracy in the modern world only really seems to function where local organs of self-administration exist, which—like Switzerland's canton system or the town hall meeting in the USA, and similar organs in England and Scandinavia—have an uncanny resemblance to the principle of the council system. At any rate, it was the spontaneous evolution of the council system, and not the attempts to restore the old parties, that gave the Hungarian Revolution the stamp of genuine democratic vigor and the fight for freedom against tyranny. But it cannot be denied that in light of the double development of the Hungarian Revolution, namely the evolution of the council system on the one hand, and the restoration of the multiparty system on the other, it was quite possible that in the end the multiparty system would have been victorious, and the council system would have been destroyed once again.

When we ponder the lesson of the Hungarian Revolution, it may be well to consider how the restored regime proceeded in crushing the unrest. The Russian army in a full-fledged invasion needed three whole weeks to regain control of the country, which indeed speaks well for the solidity of the council regime's newly acquired power. Of the demands made unanimously by the whole people, only one was halfway met: the peasants, who in Hungary as in Poland had spontaneously left the collectives, have not yet been forced back into them, with the result that the whole experiment

* Arendt discusses party systems at length in *The Origins of Totalitarianism* (New York: Schocken, 2004), 320–40. —Ed.

of collective farming practically collapsed, the agricultural output in both countries falling far below the requirements of the national economy. The concession to the peasants, therefore, was important materially as well as ideologically.

The first and most bloody blow of oppression was directed against the Revolutionary Councils, which not only represented the people as a whole, independent of class and other associations, but also were the real organs of action. After the nation had been once more reduced to impotence, a second harsh and uncompromising step could be taken, against the students and intellectuals, and against all organizations that had demanded freedom of thought and expression. Only then followed the dissolution of the Workers' Councils, which the regime regarded more as the successor to the government-controlled trade unions than as a real political body. This order of priority for oppression was not coincidental, as we can see from the fact that it was also observed in Poland, where the Russian rulers did not have to crush a revolution but had only to withdraw certain concessions won in the upheaval of 1956. Here, too, the new Workers' Councils, that is, trade unions independent of party control, were relatively low down the list; they were only abolished in April 1958, and their liquidation followed increasingly severe restrictions on intellectual liberties.

If we translate this order of priority into a conceptual, theoretical language, it follows that freedom of action was considered the most dangerous to total domination, but only slightly more dangerous than freedom of thought. The representation of interests apparently contained too great an element of action to be tolerated; it was also seen as dangerous, but its suppression was less urgent. The only sphere where temporary concessions were deemed possible and wise at a given moment, in spite of all the talk of its absolute primacy in politics, was the economic realm, where nothing more was at stake than laboring and consuming, which obviously are the lowliest of human activities, and in which one is already subject to compulsion, although not of the political kind.

The most remarkable thing about these measures and their prevailing order of priority is perhaps the absence of any materialist ideology. When the Russian rulers were confronted not with ideological debates, but with genuine political action, they grasped surprisingly quickly that freedom resides in the human capacities of action and thought, not in material things, or in labor and earning a living, the activities in which man has to master the material world. Since labor and earning are already subject to the drive to stay alive, it was not very likely that concessions in the economic sphere could open the door wide for freedom. Whatever the free world may think on this matter, however proud it may be that here, even the economy is free, the totalitarian dictators themselves have shown in practice that they know very well that the difference between capitalist and socialist economy, far from constituting the hard core of final disagreement with the free world, represents the only area in which at least temporary concessions are possible.

III
The Satellite System

The last words to come out of free Hungary were spoken over Kossuth Radio, and ended with the following sentence: "Today it is Hungary and tomorrow, or the day after tomorrow, it will be another country; for the imperialism of Moscow knows no bounds, and is only trying to play for time." A few days earlier, the communist station Free Radio Rajk had declared that "it was not only Stalin who used Communism as a pretext to expand Russian imperialism" and that it had been among the goals of the Hungarian Revolution "to present a clear picture of Russia's brutal colonial rule."

We said at the start that the development and expansion of postwar Russia must be seen in the flaming light of the Hungarian Revolution. This light—who would deny it?—is not steady, it flares and flickers; yet we would have nothing to see without this unsteady light. If we want to learn politics from what happens in the world—and there is no other way to learn—our eyes will have to become accustomed to this twilight. The words spoken by men acting in freedom and fighting for it carry more weight and, so we hope, will be taken more seriously than any theoretical reflections, precisely because they are spoken in the excitement and on the spur of the moment.* For such excitement is not hysterical and does not dull the mind; rather, it sharpens and furthers the understanding, just as it increases physical abilities and the intensity of the senses, and strengthens the heart. If, in the heat of battle, those who were fighting said that what they were fighting against was imperialism, then political science must accept the term, although we might have preferred, for conceptual as well as historical reasons, to reserve the word "imperialism" for that epoch of the colonial expansion of Europe that began in the last third of the nineteenth century and ended with the liquidation of British rule over India. Our task now must be to analyze what kind of imperialism developed out of the totalitarian form of government.

Imperialism, both word and phenomenon, was unknown before that last third of the nineteenth century, in which the ever-quickening pace of industrialization in Europe forced open the territorial limitations of the nation-state.† The outstanding feature of the imperialist age was "expansion for expansion's sake," which meant an expansion that was no longer limited by traditional national interests such as military defense of the territory and the desire to annex neighboring lands, or was subject to trade laws. Imperialist expansion was always prompted not by political, but by economic motives, and the only law it followed was that of a constantly expanding economy, wherever foreign capital investment, meaning surplus money within the national economy, or the emigration of unemployable people, meaning those who had become superfluous to the life of the nation, led it. Imperialism thus was the result of the nation-state's attempt to prove itself equal to the demands of the modern world market, under the conditions of a new, industrialized economy, and to survive as a political entity. Its dilemma was that the economic interests of the nation demanded an expansion that could not be justified on the grounds of traditional nationalism, with its insistence on the historical identity of people, state, and territory.

---

* To avoid misunderstandings: I do not mean to attribute the same high significance to reports or theories by eyewitnesses. The presence of terror paralyzes and sterilizes the human capacity for thought even more effectively than it does action. If one does not mind risking one's life, it is easier to act than to think under conditions of terror. For the deadly spell cast by terror over man's mind can be broken only by freedom, not by mere thought.

† A good summary of the historical background is now available in R. Koebner, "The Emergence of the Concept of Imperialism," in the *Cambridge Journal* (year 5, issue 12, September 1952, pp. 726–41).

From beginning to end and for better and worse, the destinies of imperialism—the fate that befell the ruling nations, no less than the lot suffered by their "subject races"—were determined by this origin. Prompted by the natural solidarity of "white men" in alien lands, European national consciousness was perverted into race consciousness, which in turn made the subject races begin to come together and organize themselves along racial lines. But together with racism, nationalism made its inroads into the ancient cultures of Asia and the tribal wilderness of Africa. And if the imperialist-minded colonial bureaucracy could turn a deaf ear to the national aspirations which they themselves had aroused, the nation-state of the mother country could not follow their example without denying the very principle of its own existence. Thus the colonial bureaucracies lived in perennial conflict with their home governments; and while it is true that imperialism posed a serious threat to the nation-state—even undermined it—by cultivating racism and perverting nationalism, the nation-state with its still intact legal and political institutions more or less prevailed, and the worst was almost always prevented. The fear that imperialistic methods of domination could have a boomerang effect on the mother country remained strong enough to make the national parliaments a bulwark of justice for the oppressed peoples, and against the colonial administration.

The old overseas imperialism failed as a form of government for the oppression of foreign peoples, because of the dichotomy between a constitutional government in the mother country, and the methods required to oppress other people permanently. But this failure was due neither to ignorance nor to incompetence. British imperialists knew very well that "administrative massacres" could keep India in bondage forever, but they also knew that public opinion at home would not stand for such measures. Today in particular we must not forget that imperialism could have been a success if the nation-state had been prepared to commit suicide and transform itself into a tyranny. Unfortunately, the French situation provides an all too powerful example of what this would have looked like in practice. For in France's fight for Algeria, there is nothing less at stake than the overthrow of the mother country by the colonial regiment that laid waste to Algeria. It is one of recent European history's few glories that Great Britain, and with it Europe, did not want to pay that price.

Such recollections of this recent past may serve to remind us of how much greater the chances of success are for an imperialism directed by a totalitarian government. Moreover, the control peculiar to the nation-state would not have been expected from Russia: it never was a nation-state; even the czars ruled a multinational empire from the power center of Moscow. The principle of national self-determination, the nightmare of the old imperialists who had to deny to their subject peoples the very principle of their own political existence, still poses no problem for the Moscow rulers. They rule the satellites with essentially the same device they use on the peoples of the Soviet Union: on the one hand making concessions to national culture on the folkloric and linguistic level, and on the other imposing the party line conceived in and directed by Moscow, and Russian as the official language for all nationalities. In a move typical of these relations, at a very early stage of the Bolshevization of the satellite states, Moscow demanded the obligatory study of Russian in all schools. It was just as typical that the demand for its abolition figured prominently in all the programs and manifestos in Hungary and Poland.

No dichotomy of principle, therefore, between home rule and colonial rule will impose restraint on totalitarian imperialism; if it, too, has to fear certain boomerang effects from its imperialist adventures, they have other causes. Thus it cannot be denied that the role of the Red Army in crushing the Hungarian uprising justified Zhukov's hopes of replacing the party dictatorship in Russia with a military dictatorship: events in Hungary had provided compelling evidence that for this kind of foreign rule one could rely neither on party nor police. And in the same vein, the regime's dependence on the reliability of the army, which had never been acknowledged under totalitarian rule, was demonstrated by the swift disintegration of the Hungarian army at the start of the revolution, without which an annoying but harmless show of dissatisfaction could never have grown into an armed uprising. Khrushchev's surprisingly swift and severe reaction against such hopes and aspirations may have sprung from a concern with boomerang effects upon the home government similar to that of the older type of imperialism. But here the danger is only temporary, because of the inevitable time lag in Bolshevization between mother country and colony. The unreliability of satellite armies, which could probably only be deployed with extreme caution even if there were to be a war, proves only that the old military and national traditions still hold some sway, and that the Bolshevization of the army is proceeding more slowly than that of the police, which was built from scratch.

Boomerang effects in totalitarian imperialism, naturally, are different from those of national imperialism, in that they work in the opposite direction: the few stirrings of unrest that we know of or hope for in Russia probably were caused by events in Poland and Hungary. The same goes for the measures the government is forced to take to combat them. For just as European imperialism could never transgress certain limits, even when the effectiveness of extreme measures was beyond doubt, because public opinion at home would not have supported them and a legal government could not have survived them, so totalitarian imperialism is forced to crush all opposition and withhold all concessions, even when it would be wiser to grant them in order to pacify the oppressed countries. Such "mildness" would endanger the government at home and place the conquered territories in a privileged position.

Thus from the start, Russian imperialism's main concern was not how to establish the European imperial distinction between national and colonial areas, but on the contrary how to equalize conditions in the newly conquered countries quickly and radically, to bring their standard of living down to Russia's own. Russia's postwar expansion was not economically motivated, and even the raids by the Russian armies had only a secondary economic aim. The profit motive, which so clearly ruled overseas imperialism, is replaced here by sheer power considerations. But these considerations are not of a national character, and have little to do with Russia's foreign policy interests as such, though it is true that for a decade the Moscow rulers seemed interested in nothing more than robbing their satellites and forcing them into grossly unfair trade agreements. Yet the very neglect with which the Russians used to treat the spoils from dismantled industries in the occupied territories, which were frequently ruined even before being shipped to Russia, indicates that their true aim was much rather to force the satellite's living standards down than to raise their own with the aid of what they had plundered. The trend has now been reversed and large quantities of coal, iron ore, oil, and agricultural products are being shipped to the satellite states, whose needs have become a serious drain on Russian resources and have already caused severe shortages of certain raw materials in the USSR. The goal is again the equalization of conditions, something that not only did not interest overseas imperialism, but which it actively strove to avoid.

However, these and other distinctions between Western national and Russian totalitarian imperialism do not go to the heart of the matter. For the immediate predecessor of totalitarian imperialism is not the British, Dutch, or French version of overseas colonial rule, but the German, Austrian, and Russian version of a continental imperialism that never actually succeeded and therefore is given scant regard by historians of imperialism. In the form of the so-called pan-movements, however—pan-Germanism and pan-Slavism—it was a very potent political force in Central and Eastern Europe before and during the First World War. One of the origins of totalitarianism lies in these pan-movements, and although the former's goal of world domination in principle goes far beyond the limited goals of continental imperialism, its expansion tactics are modeled on the policies of the pan-movements' continental expansion. The expansion strategy of totalitarian imperialism follows geographical continuity, extending from a power center to a widening periphery, so that all newly conquered territory can gravitate toward the old power center. Of course, this continual expansion could never have tolerated a dichotomy between home government and colonial rule; and since the continental imperialism of the pan-movements intended to found its empires in the heart of Europe, its racial thinking was not determined by color. Instead it proposed to treat European peoples as colonials, under the rule of a master race of German or Slavic origin.

But it is only the strategy of geographically continuous expansion that the Russian form of totalitarian imperialism has taken from continental imperialism; it has not adopted the racial, *völkisch* content. The term "satellite" is indeed a very appropriate metaphor for the political entity that comes into being under this strategy. At present, the Russians seem to be concerned neither with acquiring possessions in far-flung lands, nor engineering communist revolutions there. (Russia would probably be no less horrified than America if, through some queer accident of chaotic conditions, the Communist Party should be able to seize power in France.) In spite of its quite extraordinary aggression, Russia's postwar politics as a whole has been restricted to fomenting unrest and, with the help of the Communist Parties, supporting and driving forward the breakdown of outmoded regimes that were already starting to decay. It probably knew better than to join new possessions in far-flung lands to the Soviet Union as colonies, or even to spark a communist revolution in them. This Bolshevist foreign policy is often misunderstood, because the revolutionary unrest among diverse peoples is underestimated and put down to a Russian policy of provocation, or because the role of communists in the more recent revolutions is disregarded, as is the duty of the Moscow agents to crush all revolutions that are indigenous, popular uprisings.

For communist revolutions that are relatively independent of Russia are, in the opinion of the Moscow regime, the most dangerous of all; the "World Revolution" is the step-by-step conquering of the world by the Red Army, steered by Moscow, not the revolution of oppressed peoples spreading from country to country. It is in the interests of totalitarian imperialism not to allow the world to come to rest, to spark unrest everywhere and prevent stabilization; but it is not in its interests to be confronted with independently revolutionary governments, even if they bear the imprint of communism. Moreover, since the expansion is continuous and starts from the national frontier, it can easily hide its ultimate aims behind traditional nationalist claims. Stalin's demands at Yalta would hardly have been granted so easily if the Allied statesmen had not felt he was demanding little more than what Russian foreign policy had been pursuing for centuries. It was the same misunderstanding Hitler profited from at Munich when he claimed to want no more than the annexation of German territory in Austria and Czechoslovakia, and the liberation of German minorities from foreign rule.

The satellite system itself, however, is neither the only nor the only possible form of totalitarian imperialism. It must be seen against the background of Nazi imperialism, with which the Russian model has only one thing in common, the insistence on cohesive expansion; Hitler's lack of interest in former German overseas colonies was notorious. Nazi Germany ruled Western Europe through quislings and corrupt native politicians, and started depopulating the occupied territories in the East using extermination on a grand scale, with the aim of having these emptied lands colonized by elite troops after the war. Moscow's agents in the satellite countries are no quislings, but old and tested members of the communist movement, and as such they are in no worse a position with their Moscow masters than any Ukrainian or White Russian bureaucrat, who is also expected to obey orders and sacrifice the national interests of his people to the demands of the international movement, as Moscow understands it. And not even Stalin, it seems, wanted to exterminate the populations of the satellite states and recolonize the territory. Another, more likely alternative for Russian imperialism would perhaps have been to rule all conquered territories as it did the Baltic countries, without the intermediary of local authorities, incorporating them directly into the Soviet empire, which claims to be a union of federal republics that can be enlarged at will.

The satellite system owes its existence to a compromise, and perhaps only a temporary one. It is the child of that postwar constellation in which the two superpowers, America and Russia, had to agree on their spheres of influence, albeit in an extremely hostile manner. As such, the satellite system is the Russian answer to the American system of alliances, and the sham independence of the satellite states is important to Russia, as the reflection of the intact national sovereignty of America's allies. The metaphor, unfortunately, is again only too appropriate for the real relations here. It corresponds to the fears every country must feel when it enters an alliance with one far more powerful than itself—a fear, that is, not so much of losing its own identity as of becoming a "satellite" whose orbit around the central power is the only thing keeping it alive. And certainly the danger of the coexistence of two hostile superpowers is that any system of alliances initiated by either will automatically degenerate into a satellite system, until every country in the world is sucked into orbit around one power or the other.

American postwar policy has divided the world into communist, allied, and neutral countries, with the aim of preserving the balance between the two superpowers by recognizing in fact, if not *de jure,* their respective spheres of influence and by insisting on the genuine neutrality of all countries outside the two orbits. Only in relation to American foreign policy, it seems to me, can it be meaningful to ask the question that moves us all, of whether the "free world"—America, in this case—could have intervened to aid the Hungarian Revolution. But such an intervention would have contradicted the de facto doctrine of American foreign policy: it would not have been intervening in a neutral territory outside the American and Russian spheres of influence, as in the case of Lebanon, but in a place where Russian hegemony was tacitly recognized. But quite apart from these technical political considerations, which were probably key to Washington's decision to look on and remain neutral, we should still consider what an intervention would have meant for the Hungarian Revolution itself. In all likelihood, given that it would have been carried out by a government, it would have meant first and foremost the restoration of that status quo that the Hungarian people had rejected with an unusual unanimity. It would probably have stifled the political powers that only emerged during the revolution. It might have brought Hungary back into the sphere of influence of the Western world, which we call the "free world," and spared the Hungarian people their terrible suffering; but even this would not have preserved the freedom that the revolution realized in the short weeks of its existence, which sprang directly from communal action. And in principle, this positive freedom was superior to the reality of freedom in the "free world"; for the "free world" (to which Franco's Spain still belongs) is only free when measured against totalitarianism. Measured against the freedom of the Hungarian revolutionaries and freedom fighters, even the "free world" was not free. The only intervention that could really have aided the Hungarian Revolution could have come from those battalions of volunteers from all over the world who are genuinely prepared to fight for nothing but freedom itself. And they, of course, can only come into play if the existing powers allow them to form and give them active support; but we cannot know whether America might have decided to take a different attitude on this occasion to the one it adopted in the Spanish Civil War, because the Russian intervention was so swift and so radical that there was no time for deliberations.

Hypothetical ruminations aside, it seems certain that American foreign policy works on the basis of a kind of balance of power on a global scale, and, no matter how uneasy this balance of power may be, the image of American foreign policy is essentially that of a stable structure. But Russian foreign policy is guided by a different image in which there are no neutral countries to be protected between the superpowers and their spheres of influence. While America instinctively sees the neutral third power in the world as modeled on European states, whose stability is currently well assured, Russia imagines it in the image of the Asian and African countries where, through the collapse of European-style imperialism, everything has begun to move toward revolution. Unfortunately it is hard to deny that the Russian perspective is significantly more realistic than the American. Yet, from the standpoint of the American Republic's relative stability, it is difficult to see that in the twentieth century stability is nothing more than a marginal phenomenon. For the Russians, in any case, the important third part of the world consists of areas—in Asia and Africa—where the national revolution and, according to the communists, the automatic increase of Russia's sphere of influence, is imminent. Insofar as Russian utterances about the possibility of peaceful competition between the two superpowers are more than propaganda talk, it is not a peaceful competition in the production of cars, refrigerators, and butter, but a competition in the cold war enlargement of their respective spheres of influence that is at stake.

However and for whatever reasons the satellite system may have come into being, it is certain that the Russian imperialist methods of conquest and administration are quite in accord with it. In each country, the Russian rulers set in motion a process that must have appeared as if it were not a conquest from outside, but a revolutionary development from within that had taken place, in which the indigenous Communist Party was finally "forced" into power. To this end, already in the later 1940s several different parties began to be tolerated, before being liquidated in favor of a *one-party* dictatorship, which was finally transformed into a *totalitarian* dictatorship. Moscow was not satisfied with importing its own form of domination into the newly conquered territories, but repeated in them the Russian development that had led to totalitarian domination with an exactitude bordering on pedantry. In order to insure against any accidents that might have led the development in an "incorrect" direction, in all countries the ministry of the interior, and with it control of the police, was given over to the communists from the very start, while in the period of popular front tactics, all other ministerial posts were calmly handed over to other parties.

The conquerors' first concern was the police, the core of which was already formed of Soviet police units, which had entered the country with the first Red Army troops. In this one instance, the development of the Russian Revolution was not copied; the police force was organized in totalitarian fashion from the outset. It was held together from within by a spy group, with the most reliable elite elements of the party at its head. This group was charged with spying on the police, while the ordinary members of the police in turn informed on the party members and the population at large. The real Bolshevization of each country was introduced through the familiar show trials of prominent party members, while the less prominent ones quietly disappeared into concentration camps, presumably in Russia. In this way the rug was pulled from under the indigenous Communist Party and its spine broken; the old leaders and the old followers were no longer present, and the party's physiognomy radically altered. The duplication and multiplication of offices and functions so typical of totalitarianism was immediately built into the organization of the police, as the police spy net was duplicated by a similar organization in the Red Army. The only distinction between the two competing bodies was "that they served different masters within one Soviet oligarchy." And like its model in Russia, the police in the satellite countries kept "cadre-cards" for every citizen in the country. They presumably recorded not only compromising information of every sort, but information on everyone's family, friends, and acquaintances, which is much more valuable for totalitarian terror.

Yet, while the police was set up in strict accordance with the Russian model, the device of creating a replica that seemed to be of native origin, and staffing it with native communists, was not followed. The police was the only institution in which Russian advisers did not stay in the background but openly supervised the natives and, as their superiors, prepared and ran the show trials. Something similar now seems to have happened to the satellite armies, which after the Hungarian uprising were put under the command of Russian officers. But while this military control was clearly a reaction against unforeseen developments, the Russian control of the police was planned from the start. It seems that the Russian rulers thought everything would follow automatically once this most important institution of total domination had been established and had set the mechanism in motion.

We should not, however, overlook another more inconspicuous, but no less important, difference between the native Russian rulers and those in the satellite states. It concerns the method of selecting rank-and-file members of the police. Here, too, the Russians had to fall back on methods from the initial stages of totalitarian rule, and recruit members of the secret police from criminal and otherwise compromised elements in the population, who could be asked to do anything at all. Within Russia this has not been necessary for the past twenty-five years; any party member can be brought into the police, just as other citizens are drafted into military service. But this difference may be temporary, arising from the fact that totalitarian rule outside of Russia has not yet been in place long enough to develop all its potential. In any case, in the satellite countries the police is still an "elite" body in the original sense of the word, whose members are not chosen at random, but according to characteristics that distinguish them not only from the ordinary citizen but also from the ordinary party member.

Up to now, this time lag has thwarted Moscow's attempts to create exact replicas of the Russian government in all the countries under its influence. We do not know whether this differential would have become so dangerously noticeable if the succession crisis after Stalin's death had not interrupted normal developments. At any event, it was at that moment that the slavish imitation of the Russian model took its revenge. For the unrest in Poland and Hungary took place in the wake of the de-Stalinization process that was carried out by the satellite dictatorships most loyal to Moscow, without considering that what could be achieved in Russia would not necessarily be permitted everywhere. In this sense it is very instructive to see that in countries like Romania and Albania, Bulgaria and Czechoslovakia, where the Stalinists had succeeded in retaining power, and for a time even began to oppose Moscow, there was no such unrest, and everything stayed as it was, while the "new course continued to be steered in Hungary, as in all other countries of Eastern Europe."*

* Hugh Seton-Watson (see note on p. 110), p. 22f.

It is chiefly this difference in the reaction to developments in Russia from the various Communist Party leaders that explains the present differences in the satellite countries. Though doubtless due to certain failures of totalitarian imperialism, they contain no indication of having definitively broken through the uncanny monotony of the development as a whole. The seriousness of these failures is best gauged by the numbers of Russian occupying troops necessary to keep the peace in these countries—twenty-eight garrisons are stationed in Hungary alone, where Hungarian soldiers, now commanded directly by Russian officers, can still not be trusted with weapons; and the situation is hardly much better elsewhere. The presence of Russian troops is seemingly legalized by the Warsaw Pact, the legality of which could conveniently be modeled on NATO; still, we may hope that they will at least destroy the illusion of independence for the peoples affected, and for the watching world. And this illusion in itself, even disregarding all other atrocities, constitutes a worse hypocrisy than any committed by imperial Europe during its colonial rule. Sitting on bayonets is not only an old-fashioned and rather uncomfortable device of domination, it is a serious setback to the aspirations of the totalitarian rulers, who had naturally hoped to keep the satellites in Moscow's orbit by the sheer force of ideology and terror. It remains to be seen whether this setback is enough to break the spell of attraction this system exerts all over Asia and Africa— that is, in all regions whose political and emotional life is still tuned to the reaction against an older imperialism where foreigners openly assumed power. Unfortunately, these people suffer from a terrible lack of political experience, and find it so difficult to get their bearings in the confusion of modern political methods that they are only too easy to fool. They are apt to conclude that, whatever the faults of this regime, it cannot represent imperialism as they knew it, and that, whatever principles it may violate, it will at least respect and propagate the principle of absolute racial equality. This view is not likely to change so long as the former colonial people are more interested in skin color than in freedom.

However that may be, the failures of totalitarian imperialism should be taken no less seriously than the successes of Soviet technicians and engineers. But one should not conclude from either that a new development is in progress, which could lead to a kind of "enlightened despotism." Neither the failures of 1956, nor the successes of 1957—the year the Soviet Union successfully launched the first artificial satellite, "Sputnik 1," into space, shortly followed by "Sputnik 2," have altered the character of the regime, and if the dramatic events of 1956 demonstrate anything, it is at best the fact that total domination cannot only be shaken from without; it is also threatened from within by the lawlessness and formlessness inherent in the very dynamics of this regime, and so glaringly apparent in its inability to solve the succession problem. As far as we can see, the moment of acute danger for totalitarianism has now passed once again. Khrushchev's victory in the power struggle following Stalin's death was thanks to the careful repetition of all the methods that brought Stalin himself to power in the twenties. We do not know whether this repetition of the relatively bloodless preparatory phase will again be followed by a wave of terror like that of the thirties. More important, we cannot even tell whether the succession crisis would have posed any danger to the regime if it had not happened at a time when Russian imperialism had to annex newly conquered territories in which totalitarianism was not yet fully functioning. It is hard to shake the suspicion that the crisis of totalitarian imperialism was chiefly caused by the coincidence of the succession crisis with an expansion that was not yet fully stabilized.

Still, the danger signs of 1956 were real enough, and although today they are overshadowed by the successes of 1957 and the fact that the system was able to survive, it would not be wise to forget them. If they promise anything at all, it is much rather a sudden and dramatic collapse of the whole regime than a gradual normalization. Such a catastrophic development, as we learned from the Hungarian Revolution, need not necessarily entail chaos—though it certainly would be rather unwise to expect from the Russian people, after forty years of tyranny and thirty years of totalitarianism, the same spirit and the same political productivity that the Hungarian people showed to the world in their most glorious hour.

1958

Postscript

"To the memory of Rosa Luxemburg" was how Hannah Arendt wanted to dedicate this text, whose original German title is "Die Ungarische Revolution und der totalitäre Imperialismus," but, as noted by Ursula Ludz, the publisher raised objections. In a letter written on September 9, 1958, to the publisher, Klaus Piper, and the volume's editor, Hans Rössner, she responded: "If we have to explain in black and white what we mean, we must cut the dedication. It won't work then; one can't explain anything in a dedication. Poor Rosa! She has been dead now for forty years, and still falls between all stools. Of course I understand your reasons. I only ventured to do it in the first place because I was struck by the audience's reaction at my lecture, which also came as quite a surprise to you. Perhaps the young people—and they were the only ones clapping!—know better again; for we are agreed on the fact that they cannot all have been communists—who would have been the very people not clapping! The dedication cannot be rephrased, because one would have to explain that Luxemburg was neither really a socialist nor a communist, but 'only' stood for justice and freedom and revolution as the only possibility for a new form of society and state." The letter is unpublished, and is quoted from the Hannah Arendt Papers in the Manuscript Division of the Library of Congress. —Ed.

TOTALITARIANISM

I am glad of this opportunity to say a few words about the new enlarged and revised edition of *The Origins of Totalitarianism*. My publisher and I both agree on the curious inadequacy of the title, which, by insisting on "origins," seems to disregard the last and largest part of the book. This part is exclusively devoted to the elements of totalitarian movements and governments, while the first two parts on Antisemitism and Imperialism deal with those subterranean streams of modern history in which the origins of these elements may be found.

I am not worried about the title's obvious failure to cover the whole book, for I trust that the reader can easily correct this. What does bother me is that the title suggests, however faintly, a belief in historical causality which I did not hold when I wrote the book and in which I believe in less today. We might have tried to find a title which is closer to my original intentions if we had not felt that seven years of public existence are a bit too long to permit a new name-giving. While I was writing this book, these intentions presented themselves to me in the form of an ever-recurring image: I felt as though I dealt with a crystallized structure which I had to break up into its constituent elements in order to destroy it. This image bothered me a great deal, for I thought it an impossible task to write history, not in order to save and conserve and render fit for remembrance, but on the contrary, in order to destroy. Finally, it dawned upon me that I was not engaged in writing a historical book, even though large parts of it clearly contain historical analyses, but a political book, in which whatever there was of past history not only was seen from the vantage point of the present, but would not have been visible at all without the light which the event, the emergence of totalitarianism, shed on it. In other words, the "origins" in the first and second part of the book are not causes that inevitably led to certain effects; rather, they became origins only after the event had taken place.

The second matter points in the same direction. It is only natural that a book relying so heavily on contemporary events and their documentary sources should need revising more than seven years after its first publication and nine years after the original manuscript was finished. These revisions are mentioned in the Preface to this edition; they are of a technical nature and do not concern the argument or alter the nature of the book. There are, however, two enlargements in this edition which in a sense perhaps change its character. The book originally ended with certain suggestive but consciously inconclusive "Concluding Remarks" which are now replaced with a much less suggestive and more theoretical chapter on "Ideology and Terror: A Novel Form of Government." This chapter seems to me its proper conclusion; but from a more aesthetic viewpoint, it may be argued that the very inconclusiveness of the original ending, showing the extent to which the author was involved and prepared to remain engaged in her subject matter, was better attuned to the mood and style of the whole book.*

From this viewpoint, which is that of the maker and artist and not of the political writer, I have done something which is even worse. I have added a chapter on the Hungarian Revolution in 1956 and thereby introduced a topical interest and a topical controversy which may force open the book's whole frame of reference. There is in this chapter a certain hopefulness—surrounded, to be sure, with many qualifications—which is hard to reconcile with the assumption of the third part that the *only* clear expression of the present age's problems up to date has been the horror of totalitarianism. I know that the reason for my hopefulness sounds strange to most people; only the UN *Report* and Silone in several articles have even noticed the fact that this last of the European revolutions has brought forth once more a form of government which, it is true, was never really tried out, but which one cannot call new because it has appeared with singular regularity for more than a hundred years in all revolutions. I am speaking of the council system, of the Russian *soviets*, which were abolished in the initial stages of

---

* In addition to the new concluding chapter, the original "Concluding Remarks" are included in *The Origins of Totalitarianism* (New York: Schocken Books, 2004). —Ed.

the October Revolution, and the Central European *Räte*, which first had to be liquidated in Germany and Austria before their short-lived and insecure party democracies could be established.

I was not unaware of the importance of the council system when I wrote the *Origins*. I have always been convinced that the turning point of the Russian Revolution was the Kronstadt rebellion and the concomitant crushing of the *soviets* through the Bolshevik party. This was the moment when the much misused metaphor of the revolution devouring its own children actually came true. The revolution-born new institutions of liberty were destroyed and on their ruins the one-party dictatorship was erected. What followed was the establishment of Stalin's totalitarian government, something which no longer belongs to the story of the revolution itself.

Yet, while not unaware of the role which the council system had played in all European revolutions since 1848, I had no hope for its reemergence and therefore left it out of account. The Hungarian Revolution taught me a lesson. If we take into account the amazing reemergence of the council system during the Hungarian Revolution, then it looks as though we are confronted with two new forms of government in our own time, both of which can be understood as only against the bankrupt body politic of the nation-state. The government of total domination certainly corresponds better to the inherent tendencies of a mass society than anything we previously knew. But the council system clearly has been for a long time the result of the wishes of the people, and not of the masses, and it is just barely possible that it contains the very remedies against mass society and the formation of mass-men for which we look everywhere else in vain.

Thus, the last chapter of the present edition is an Epilogue or an afterthought. I am not at all sure that I am right in my hopefulness, but I am convinced that it is as important to present all of the inherent hopes of the present as it is to confront ruthlessly all its intrinsic despairs. In any event, to a political writer, this must be more important than to present the reader with a well-rounded book.

FALL 1958

CULTURE AND POLITICS

I

Whatever it may be that we take to be culture, it is no longer something that we take for granted without question, or without gratitude. The word itself has become cause for discomfort, not only among intellectuals but also among those who create the objects that, taken as a whole, constitute culture. I am afraid that not taking into account this discomfort, which we are presently all aware of, would mean missing both that which is, as well as that which could be.

Culture did not become suspect only yesterday. In Germany the suspicion probably started with the emergence of the "cultural philistinism" (*Bildungsphilisterium*) first described by Clemens Brentano about 150 years ago. For the philistine, culture had become a matter of social prestige and social advancement that became devalued in its eyes precisely because it gained some sort of social utility. We are quite familiar with this dynamic up to the present time: people usually call it the "bargain sale of values" (*Ausverkauf der Werte*), without recognizing that the "bargain sale" began when modern society first discovered the "value" of culture, which is to say, the usefulness of appropriating cultural objects and transforming them into values. The cultural or educated philistine may be a specifically German type; but the socialization of culture—its devaluation in the form of social values—is a more generally modern phenomenon. The philistine in Germany corresponds to the snob in Britain, to the highbrow intellectual in the United States, and perhaps to the *bien pensant* in France, where Rousseau discovered the phenomenon for the first time in the eighteenth-century salons. In Europe these days, those things should be more or less a thing of the past, something to which no one need pay much attention; matters are somewhat different in the United States, where the cultural snobbism of the highbrows is a reaction to mass society. The "bargain sale of values" has been, above all, a "bargain sale" of educational values, and the demand for these values has barely outlasted their declining supply.

The phenomenon of socialization is something else altogether. That which we call "mass culture" is nothing other than the socialization of culture that started in the salons. It is just that the sphere of the social, which first took hold of the upper classes and social ranks, now extends to practically all strata and has thus become a mass phenomenon. All of the features, however, that mass psychology has by now identified as typical of man in mass society: his abandonment (*Verlassenheit*—and this abandonment is neither isolation nor solitude), along with his utmost adaptability; his irritability and lack of support; his extraordinary capacity for consumption (if not gluttony), along with his utter inability to judge qualities or even to discern them; but most of all his egocentrism and the fatal alienation from the world that he mistakes for self-alienation (this, too, dates back to Rousseau)—all of this first manifested itself in "good society," which does not have a mass character. The first people of the new mass society, one might say, constituted a mass to such a small degree (in a quantitative sense) that they were actually able to consider themselves an elite.

Nevertheless, there are considerable differences between the latest phase in the process whereby culture became socialized and the earlier one that produced cultural philistinism. The phenomenon of the entertainment industry may provide the best and most ready example of these differences, for it is the object that by far concerns the educated philistine and the cultural snob the most. The philistine took hold of culture as cultural value, by means of which he secured a higher social position for himself—higher, that is, than the one he occupied, in his own estimation, naturally or by birth. Cultural values were thus what values always are, namely exchange values, and the devaluation that set in almost as a matter of course consisted in the fact that culture was being used or abused for social purposes. By being passed around, cultural values lost their luster and thus the potential—once indigenous to all cultural facts—to captivate in and of themselves. These cultural objects that were denatured to become values were not, however, consumed; even in their most depleted form, they remained a worldly-objective set of things.

Matters are quite different with those objects manufactured by the entertainment industry. They serve to pass the time, as we say; but this means that they serve the life process of society, which consumes them in the same manner it consumes other objects of consumption. The empty time thus consumed is biological time—the time that remains when labor and sleep are accounted for. In the case of the laboring human being, whose only activity consists in maintaining his own vital processes and those of his family, and strengthening them through increased consumption and a raised standard of living, pleasure occupies those parts of life where the biologically determined labor cycle—"the metabolism between man and nature" (Marx)—has created a hiatus. The easier laboring becomes and the less time is taken up by the sustaining of life, the greater the recreational hiatus. The fact that ever more time is freed up that must be filled by pleasure, however, takes nothing away from pleasure being just as much an essential part of the biological process of life as labor and sleep. Biological life, in turn, is always a metabolism that nourishes itself through the ingestion of things, whether it labors or is at rest, whether it consumes or amuses itself. The things offered by the entertainment industry are not values to be used and exchanged; rather, they are objects of consumption as apt to be depleted as any other such object. *Panem et circenses* (bread and circuses)—these two do indeed go together: both are necessary for the life process, for its sustenance and its recovery; both are also swallowed up in this process, that is to say, they both have to be produced and performed time and again if this process is not to come to an eventual halt.

This is all well and good, as long as the entertainment industry produces its own objects of consumption, and one could reproach this industry no more than one could reproach a bakery for creating products of such limited durability that they have to be depleted in the instant of their creation lest they spoil. If, however, the entertainment industry lays claim to products of culture—and this is exactly what happens within mass culture—the immense danger arises that the life process of society, which, like all life processes, insatiably incorporates everything it is offered into the biological circulation of its metabolism, begins literally to devour the products of culture. Of course, this does not happen when cultural products—books or images—are thrown into the market in the form of cheap reproductions and are as a result sold in large numbers; but it certainly does happen when the products of culture are being altered—rewritten, condensed, popularized, transformed into kitsch by means of reproduction—so they may be used by the entertainment industry. It is not the entertainment industry that is a sign of what we call "mass culture," and what should more precisely be called the deterioration of culture. And it is not that this deterioration begins when everyone can buy the dialogues of Plato for pocket change. Rather, it begins when these products are changed to such an extent as to facilitate their mass retailing—a mass retailing that would otherwise be impossible. And those who further this deterioration are not the composers of popular music but the members of the habitually well-read and well-informed intellectual proletariat that is currently attempting to organize and spread culture all over the globe and, in addition, to make this culture palatable to those who actually want nothing to do with it.

Culture relates to objects and is a phenomenon of the world, and pleasure relates to people and is a phenomenon of life.* If life is no longer satisfied with the pleasure derived from the ingestive metabolism established between man and nature—a pleasure that always accompanies struggle and labor because human vital energy can no longer exhaust itself in this process of circulation—then it is free to reach for objects in the world, to appropriate them, and to consume them. Life will then seek to prepare these objects of the world or of culture so that they may become suitable for consumption; that is, it will treat them as if they were objects of nature, which, after all, must also be prepared before they may be merged with the human metabolism. The objects of nature are unaffected by being consumed in

---

* Arendt responded to criticism of her apparent "hostility to life" (*Lebensteindschaft*) thus: "I have opposed the world to life . . . because we live in a time in which there has been, and still is, an enormous overestimation of life. . . . I do not think that I am hostile to life. Life is a magnificent thing but it is not the highest good. Whenever life is considered the highest good, [it] is . . . as soon whisked away. In our society there is a dangerous estrangement from the world and, alongside this, a terrible inability of human beings to love the world." Quoted in *Reflections on Literature and Culture*, ed. Susannah Young-ah Gottlieb (Stanford, Calif.: Stanford University Press, 2007), 332. —Ed.

this way; they continually renew themselves, since man—as long as he lives and labors, struggles and recovers—is also a natural being whose biological circulation is fitted to the larger circulation in which everything natural is moving. But the things of the world produced by man, insofar as he is a worldly and not just a natural being, do not renew themselves. They simply disappear when life appropriates them and consumes them for pleasure. And this disappearance, which first emerges in the context of a mass society founded on alternating labor and consumption, is surely something other than what happens when things wear out within society by circulating as exchange values until their original texture is barely recognizable anymore.

To explain these two processes that are destroying culture in historical or sociological terms, the devaluation of the products of culture within cultural philistinism may be said to exemplify the typical danger of a commercial society, the most important public space of which is the market for goods and exchange; the disappearance of culture within mass society, in turn, may be attributed to a society of laborers who, as laborers, neither know nor need a public, worldly space existing independently of their life process, while, as *persons,* they of course do require such a space and would be able to construct it as soon as any other human beings under different temporal circumstances. A laboring society—which by no means needs to be the same thing as a society of laborers—is, in any event, characterized by understanding and interpreting everything in terms of the function of the individual or social life process. One thing, however, is shared by these anticultural processes that are rather different in and of themselves: both are set into motion when all objects produced in the world are brought into a relation with a society that either uses and exchanges them, evaluates and applies them, or else consumes and ingests them. In both cases, we are dealing with a socialization of the world. The rather common view that democracy is opposed to culture, and that culture may flourish only within aristocracies, is correct insofar as democracy is taken to signify the socialization of man and world—which is by no means how it must necessarily be understood. In any case, it is the phenomenon of society, and that of good society no less than that of mass society, which is threatening to culture.

II

Given that our uneasiness with respect to culture stems from the anticultural phenomena of cultural philistinism and of mass culture—both of which appeared in this century as a result of an all-pervasive socialization—it is of very recent vintage. There is another kind of distrust with respect to culture, however, which is considerably older but perhaps no less relevant. In the context of a reflection on culture, moreover, it has a definitive advantage: instead of being a response to certain degenerative appearances of cultural matters, it was sparked by the very opposite, namely the eminence of culture and the corresponding fear that it might become too overpowering. This distrust is rooted in the political sphere; it is also not unfamiliar to us if we think of our own discomfort with the notion of aesthetic culturedness, or about compound constructions such as *Kulturpolitik*. In either case we become conscious of a tension and a possible conflict between politics and culture, which the aesthete seeks to resolve in favor of culture (clueless as he is about the exigencies of politics), and the politician (unfamiliar with the necessities of cultural production) in favor of politics, that is to say: cultural politics. Our discomfort with such attempts at conflict resolution is, of course, conditioned by modern experiences. The aesthete brings to mind the cultural philistine who likewise believed that that which is supposedly "higher," namely, cultural "values," could only be sullied and degraded by being pulled down into what he believed to be the vulgar and lowly sphere of the political. Even the most liberal cultural politics will recall to us the dreadful experiences with which we have been faced in recent years under a totalitarian regime, where the thing called "politics" has all but annihilated the thing that is generally taken to be culture.

For the purposes of these reflections, I would like to set such typically modern associations aside for the moment and propose to consider a different historical model. Political science cannot operate without such historical models, not only because it is history that supplies it with its objects of study, but also because it is only with the aid of historically sedimented experiences of such things as "politics" and "culture" that we may attempt to broaden our own horizon of experience—forever limited as it is—in order to gain a perspective on general phenomena such as the relationship between culture and politics. As a matter of fact, my proposal to move away from modernity simply acknowledges that the politico-public sphere was of an unparalleled dignity and of much more relevance for people in the life of antiquity. What this implies for political science is that particular elementary phenomena and problems emerge and may be shown much more clearly against this historical backdrop than against that of any subsequent period. With respect to the specific issue before us, the Middle Ages may anyway be disregarded, since its public space in particular was not shaped by primarily secular, earthly forces. Today, the question of the relation between culture and politics is a secular question and therefore cannot be decided from the religious point of view. Modernity, however, poses nearly insurmountable problems to any clarification of political phenomena, since in this period a new sphere has opened up between the familiar spaces of the private and the public, in which the public sphere is in the process of being made private, and its private counterpart is in the process of being made public. The distortion and disfiguration common to all political problems reflected and studied in the medium of society cannot be discussed here.* I only wanted to mention it in order to justify my reference to such a distant past. I would thus ask you to recall that, especially during the classical period, both Greek and Roman antiquity harbored such deep suspicion, if not against culture as such, then at least against all those who produced cultural objects—that is, the artisans and artists—that the prevailing opinion was that this sort of people should not be considered full citizens. The Romans, for example, resolved the conflict between culture and politics in such a clearly one-sided manner in favor of politics that culture ended up appearing in Rome as a Greek import. (Mommsen writes that "singer and poet were lined up right alongside tightrope walkers and jesters," and, as far as the plastic arts were concerned, "even Varro ridiculed the masses and their desire for puppets and icons.") One indicator of this is the fact that the word "culture," which is, after all, of Roman origin, actually denotes "care," which suggests that, in this entire sphere, the

---

* The reader is referred to Part II, "The Public and the Private Realm," in H. Arendt, *The Human Condition* (Chicago: University of Chicago Press, 1958). —Ed.

Romans adopted the role not of producers and creators but of caretakers and guardians.

This is basically the same attitude that also characterized them politically, namely the equally caring retention of beginnings grounded in the past and hallowed by tradition: the founding of the city was to politics what the Greek tradition was to spiritual-intellectual (*geistig*) matters. This attitude may be typical for an agricultural people; it certainly became most productive for the Romans wherever it merged with the incomparably ardent relationship this people had to nature, which is to say: in the shaping of the Roman landscape. Real art, or so it seemed to them, should develop as naturally as the landscape; it should be cultivated nature, and they regarded as the oldest song "the one sung by the leaves to themselves in the green solitude of the woods" (Mommsen). The notion that even agriculture could "yoke" the earth and subject it to violence, and that such violence was evidence of the uncanny greatness of man, as Sophocles tells it in the famous chorus from *Antigone*—"Numberless wonders / Terrible wonders walk the world but none the match for man"—is in exact opposition to what the Romans believed. In short, one could say that the Greeks conceived even of agriculture in terms of *technē* and *poiēsis,* while the Romans conversely experienced even the cultural, world-producing activities of man in terms of the model of labor in which nature is carefully tended to become culture in order to provide man as a natural being with food and a home.

Even though in our use of the word *culture* Roman associations are still present, the Roman model of the relationship between it and politics is not particularly fruitful. The Romans did not take culture seriously until it was ready to become an object of care for them, and thus a part of the *res publica*. In early times they simply stopped artists and poets in their tracks because they believed that such childish play did not conform to *gravitas,* the solemnity and dignity befitting a citizen. They did not think that this kind of productivity would give rise to an activity equal—or perhaps even threatening—to the sphere of the political. The fruitfulness of the Greek model, by comparison, may be gleaned from the fact that, at least in Athens, the conflict between politics and culture never clearly benefited one side or the other, but was also not mediated to the point that either sphere became indifferent to the other. It was as if the Greeks could say in one and the same breath: "He who has not seen the Zeus of Phidias at Olympia has lived in vain" *and*: "People like Phidias, namely sculptors, really should not be granted citizenship."

Thucydides reports a famous saying by Pericles, in which the politically founded suspicion of culture is expressed in an indirect but nevertheless strikingly characteristic way. I am referring to the phrase, all but impossible to translate, *philosophoumen aneu malakias kai philokaloumen met'euteleias.* Here we can clearly hear that it is the polis, the political, which limits the love for wisdom and the love for beauty (both of which are understood, however—and that is what makes the phrase untranslatable—not as states but rather as activities); for it is *euteleia,* the accuracy that prevents excess, which is a political virtue, whereas *malakia,* as reported by Aristotle, was considered a barbaric vice of excess; the primary thing, however, which the Greeks believed elevated them above the barbarians was the polis, the political. In other words, by no means did the Greeks believe that it was their higher form of culture that distinguished them from the barbarians. Quite the contrary, it was the fact that the political limited the cultural. It is difficult for us to grasp this rather simple point of Pericles' words because we tend to believe much more readily—because our tradition has repressed and submerged the political experiences of the West and its worldview in favor of philosophical experiences—that they speak of the familiar conflicts between truth and beauty, on the one hand, and of thought and action, on the other. Our naïve understanding is conditioned by the narrative of the history of philosophy, according to which Plato and the philosophers preceding him wanted to banish Homer and the poets from the republic for telling lies. As it turns out, however, the philosopher Plato was not the only one who felt impelled to put Homer in his place; the politician Pericles did the same thing, in the same eulogy, while citing very different reasons. He explicitly says that the very greatness of Athens consisted in not needing "Homer and his ilk" to make words spoken and deeds done—which constitute the essence of the political—immortal. The power of Athens, he thought, was great enough for the monuments of its fame to grow directly out of action, and thus out of the political itself; great enough, that is, to be able to do without the professional producers of fame; the artists and poets, who objectify the living word and the living deed, turning them into *things* in order to ensure the permanence necessary for their immortal fame.

I believe that the Greek tendency to keep artists and artisans from having any influence on the polis has often been thoroughly misunderstood; it was thought that this tendency could readily be equated with a contempt for the physical labor necessary for sustaining life. This contempt is likewise of an originally political nature: no one can be free who is being forced by life, whose activities are dictated by the necessities of life. The life of the free man within the polis is only possible if he has mastered the necessities of life, which means: he has become a master commanding a household of slaves. The labor that is necessary for bare life, however, stands outside the political and cannot, therefore, come into conflict with it; after all, such labor is not performed in the public sphere but, rather, the private realm of the family and the household. Those who are excluded from the public sphere and confined to the sphere of the private household—the Greek *oiketai* (those belonging to the house) and the Roman *familiares* (those belonging to the family)—are as fundamentally distinct from the craftsmen (who, as their name *dēmiourgoi* indicates, by no means remain at home but, rather, go out among the people to do their work), as they are distinct from the artists, the *poiētai*, whose works serve to educate and to decorate the public space in which political life is situated. A conflict between the political and the cultural can arise only because the activities of acting and producing and their "productions"—products of the deeds and works of men—are situated in public space. The question to be decided regarding this conflict is simply which standards should in the end apply in a public space created and inhabited by people: the standards common to acting or to producing; those that are political in the basic sense of the word, or those that are specifically cultural?

III

We have determined that the conflict between culture and politics is situated in the public sphere, and that this conflict is about whether the public space we all share should be governed by the standards of those who have erected it—that is, by man insofar as he is *homo faber*—or whether its standards should be directly derived from interactions between people, manifest in deeds, words, and events. As we all know, the Greeks chose the latter alternative—and for a good reason, it seems to me. The decision shows itself everywhere. If one wanted to discover it in the usual way that things are evaluated, one could say that the standard of size was primary, compared to all other standards of judgment. If one wanted to see it in terms of political organization, one would do well to remember the phrase, "Wherever you may be you will constitute a polis"—a phrase that was told to all departing exiles, implying that the very organization of the polis was so utterly independent of the singular physiognomy that had been achieved at home that it could be summarily left behind and exchanged as long as the far less tangible relationship established through acting and speaking among human beings remained intact.

The nature of this decision is not only *not* to resolve, once and for all, the conflict between culture and politics—the fight over whether the producing person or the acting person should be privileged—but, rather, to fan its flames even more. The greatness of man, after all, on which the whole question turns, is taken to consist in the human ability to do things and to speak words that are deserving of immortality—that is, worthy of eternal remembrance—despite the fact that human beings are mortal. This exclusively human and purely earthly immortality to which greatness lays claim is called "fame." And the purpose of fame is not only to keep word and deed—which are even more transient and fleeting than mortal human beings—from their immediate disappearance, but even to lend them an immortal permanence. The question posed by Pericles in the citation above really amounts to this: Who is better suited to doing that? The organization of the polis that secures the public space in which greatness may appear and may communicate, and in which a permanent presence of people who see and are seen, who speak and hear and may be heard, thus assures a permanent remembrance? Or else the poets and artists—and more generally, the world-creating, world-producing activities, which obviously provide a considerably better guarantee of fame than acting and political organization, since they consist in the making-permanent and the making-imperishable of that which is by its very nature of the most perishable and the most fleeting kind? It was poetry that taught the Greeks, whose educa-tor was Homer, what fame was and what it was capable of being. And even if poetry, together with music, may be the least materially bound art, it still is a form of production, and it achieves a kind of objectification, the absence of which would make permanence, let alone imperishability, inconceivable.

Furthermore, the dependence of acting upon producing is not limited to that of the "hero" and his fame upon the poet—which is the example mentioned by Pericles. Artistic objectification in general grows out of, and remains beholden to, an already existing world of objects without which the artwork would have no place to exist. The world of objects cannot simply be traced back to the life necessities of man; it is not necessary for bare survival, as the nomadic tribes, the tents and huts of primitive peoples demonstrate. Rather, it derives from a desire to erect a dam against one's own mortality, to place something between the perishability of man and the imperishability of nature that serves as the yardstick for mortals to measure their mortality. What occupies this place is the man-made world that is not immortal but nevertheless considerably more durable and lasting than the life of human beings. All of culture begins with this kind of world-making, which in Aristotelian terms is already an *athanatidzein*, a making-immortal. Outside of such a world—that is to say, outside of what we call "culture" in the broadest sense—acting may not be strictly impossible, but it would leave no trace; no history and no "one thousand stones dug from the bosom of the earth would testify by speaking."

Among the objects of the world we have come to distinguish between things that are used and works of art. Both are alike in that they are objects; that is, they occur not in nature but only in the man-made world, and they are characterized by a certain permanence that extends from the durabil-ity of the common object of use to the potential immortality of the art-work. In this way, both are distinct from consumer goods, on the one hand, the earthly life span of which hardly exceeds the time required for their production, and products of action, on the other hand—in other words, events, deeds, words, and eventually the stories to be derived from them, all of which are themselves so fleeting that they would barely survive the hour or the day of their emergence if memory and the productive capacities of people did not come to their aid. If one looks at objects in the world from the perspective of their durability, it is clear that artworks are superior to all other objects. Even after millennia they have the ability to shine for us, as they did on the day that brought them into the world. That is why they are the most worldly of all things. They are the only ones that are produced for a world supposed to outlast each mortal human being, and that therefore have no function whatsoever in the life process of human society. Not only are they not being consumed like consumer goods, or used up like objects of use; they have to be lifted out of this process of use and consumption altogether; they must be explicitly sealed, so to speak, against the biological necessities of human beings. This may happen in various ways, but culture in the specific sense is only found where it does happen.

I have no idea whether or not it is part of human nature to be a worldly or world-making being. There are worldless peoples just as there are world-less individuals; and human life requires a world only insofar as it needs a home on earth for the duration of its presence. To be sure, every world serves those living in it as an earthly home, but that does not mean that every kind of human making-oneself-at-home amounts to world-making. The earthly home becomes a world only when objects as a whole are pro-duced and organized in such a way that they may withstand the consump-tive life process of human beings living among them—and may outlive human beings, who are mortal. We speak of culture only where this out-living is assured, and we speak of artworks only where we are confronted with objects that are always present in their facticity and their quality, inde-pendent of all functional or utilitarian aspects.

For these reasons, it seems to me, any reflection on culture would do well to take as its point of departure the phenomenon of the artwork. This is particularly true of our present attempt, which tries to investigate the relation between culture and politics with reference to the Greek approach to these things. Artworks in and of themselves have a closer relationship to politics than other objects, and their mode of production has a closer relationship to acting than to any other type of occupation. For one thing, it is a fact that only artworks need the public sphere in order to gain rec-ognition; a similar affinity is expressed in the fact that artworks are spiritual-intellectual objects. In Greek terms, *Mnēmosynē*—remembering and remembrance—is the mother of the muses, which is to say that it is through thinking and remembering that reality is revaluated. This revaluation makes it possible to arrest and objectify the intangible, namely events and deeds and words and stories. Artistic objectification has its root in thought, just like the artisanal kind has its root in use. An event does not become eternal simply by being remembered; but this remembrance prepares it for potential immortality, which is then carried out through artistic objectification. For the Greeks, however, it was potential immortality that was the highest and most profound goal of all politics, and of their very own form of political organization—the polis—in particular. What they sought was not the immortality of the artwork itself but, rather, the potential imperishability, the potentially eternal persistence in memory of great words and deeds: the kind of immortal fame that could be assured by poets through productive objectification, and by the polis through ceaseless narrative commemoration.

IV

Given that Greek thought, especially in its political aspects, was directed so exclusively at the potential immortality of mortals, and thus at the imperishability of what is most perishable, it would seem that no human faculty would have been deemed more important than the productive and art-making one, which is to say, the poetic faculty in the Greek sense of the word *poiēsis*. And if we recall the formidable—and formidably rapid— development of Greek art that begins with a masterwork in order to move from one masterwork to the next in the span of only a few centuries, what is particularly evident is the extraordinary, specifically cultural force sparked by this politically rooted belief in immortality.

Without a doubt, the Greek suspicion of production in all its forms, their suspicion of the danger that supposedly threatened the polis and its political form within the realm of the produced and cultural world, concerns not so much the cultural objects themselves as the attitudes on which production is based—attitudes that typify whoever does nothing but produce things. The suspicion is directed against a generalization of the standards of producers and against their ways of thinking, which intrude upon the political sphere. This explains what may initially be surprising to us, namely that someone could display the greatest receptivity for art and the most ardent admiration of artworks—which, as we know from plentiful anecdotal evidence, was matched by an altogether remarkable self-assuredness on the part of the artists—and yet be constantly considering whether or not artists as persons should be excluded from the political community. The same suspicion is evident in the tendency to regard what were essentially political activities—if, like legislative work or urban planning, these had even the least bit to do with producing—only as pre-political conditions of the political, and thus to exclude them from the polis itself, which is to say, from the realm of essential political activities for which citizenship was required.

This suspicion of production is justified for two factual reasons, both of which may be directly derived from the nature of this activity. First, the latter is essentially impossible without the application of force: In order to produce a table, a tree must be felled, and the wood of the felled tree must in turn be violated to emerge in the form of a table. (When Hölderlin called poetry the "most innocent" activity, he may have been thinking of the violence inherent in all other art forms. But, of course, the poet violates his material as well; he does not sing like a bird living in a tree.) Second, production is always situated within the category of means-ends relations, the only truly legitimate place of which is the sphere of production and fabrication. The process of production has a clearly discernible purpose, namely the end product, for the benefit of which everything that is part of it—the material, the tools, the activity itself, and even the persons involved—becomes a mere means. As the end, the work justifies all means; most of all, it justifies the violence without which those means could never be secured. The producers cannot but regard all objects as means to their ends, and must judge all objects according to their specific utility. If generalized and extended to areas other than that of fabrication, this attitude characterizes *Banausen* (ignoramuses) to this day, one of the few German words borrowed from the Greek that has barely changed its original meaning. The suspicion directed at them stems from the sphere of the political and at one time suggested the desire to keep both the violence and the utilitarian attitude of means-ends rationality out of the public-political space of human community.

Even the most cursory look at the history of political theories or the usual definitions of political action readily reveals that this suspicion has not had the least bit of influence on our tradition of political thought, and that it disappeared just as quickly from the scene, so to speak, as it had emerged in the history of political experiences. Nothing seems more natural to us today than the notion that politics is exactly that space where violence may be legitimate, and this space is usually defined by ruling and being ruled. We cannot even imagine that action could be something other than an activity that pursues a set end by appropriate means, whereby it goes without saying that these means are justified by the given ends. Much to our misfortune we have by now experienced the practical, political consequences of such a belief in the universality of the *banausische* (ignorant) attitude. In any case, what has happened is exactly that which the Greek suspicion of culture sought to avoid—namely, that the political sphere should be overwhelmed and suffused with the categories and the mentality of production. Even though it was not the means-ends category, but originally the in-order-to of production, the political lost its independence; and the public sphere, in which human beings, politically organized, act and talk to one another—that is, the already-made world—was subsumed under the same categories that are first of all necessary to bring that world into existence.

We know from experience how capable a utilitarian means-ends rationality is of giving politics over to inhuman behavior. Still it strikes us as very strange that such inhuman behavior should arise out of the cultural sphere in particular, and that the humanizing element should be the one assigned to the political sphere. This is due to the fact that no matter how much knowledge of, or appreciation for, Greek culture we may possess, our understanding of culture is essentially determined by the Romans, who conceived of this sphere not from the standpoint of the producer of culture but, rather, from that of the loving and careful keeper of the natural and the inherited. To grasp the altogether different Greek view, we need to remember that their discovery of the political rested on the earnest attempt to keep violence out of the community, and that within Greek democracy only the power of *peithō*—the art of persuasion by talking with one another—was considered a legitimate mode of interaction. We must also not lose sight of the fact that the political really refers only to the circumstances internal to the polis. Only because violence as such was considered apolitical and thus beyond the bounds of the polis could the wars among the Greek republics be so terribly devastating. Whatever lay outside of the polis was beyond the law and was thus completely given over to violence; here it really was the case that the strong did what they could, and the weak suffered what they must.

One of the reasons why we find it so difficult to discover an element of violence within culture is that thinking in categories of production has become a given for us, so much so that we take these categories to be universal. In accordance with these categories, we act violently everywhere and in all areas; we then try to stave off the worst by means of laws and agreements. For this reason, however, the domain where these categories are really at home, and where indeed nothing comes to light but through them, appears to us to be the most harmless domain of all—and rightly so. In comparison with the violence that men inflict on one another, the violence they inflict on nature in order to engage in world-making is doubtless innocent. This is why we believe the real danger of the cultural to be enfeeblement, and translate Pericles' mention of *malakia*, cited above, in this sense. But the unmanliness implied by this word, which seemed barbaric to the Greeks, no more excludes violence than it excludes resorting to all attainable means in order to reach the end one is seeking. We who have so often witnessed how a so-called cultural elite of artists and the educated may be won over for a politics of brutality, and how that elite is in awe of the latter for finally having left behind all "never-ending chatter"—that is, reciprocal sharing of convictions—we may be somewhat more attuned to these things, and may come to see in them more than a mere *"trahison des clercs."* To believe in the violence of politics is by no means the sole privilege of brutality. The basis for this belief may also be what the French call a *déformation professionnelle,* an aberration among producers and sponsors of culture that is performed in their own line of work.

The suspicion of means-ends thinking, which in its origins is political as well, hits closer to home. The objection, of course, that may be raised by politics against this type of thinking—necessary as it is for production—is that the end justifies the means, and that perfectly appealing ends may engender altogether terrifying and destructive means. If we follow this line of thinking, which in our century has become all but commonplace, we find that acting in and of itself knows of no ends, or at least is unable ever to realize any end as it has been conceptualized. For all acting is situated in a web of relations in which anything intended by individuals is immediately transformed, and is thus prevented from being brought about as a set goal, such as a purpose, for example. This is to say that in politics the means are always more important than the ends; the same thing could be expressed by saying to oneself, as I did at one time: Every good deed for an evil cause factually makes the world a better place, while every bad deed for a good cause factually makes it worse. But pronouncements like these rely on paradoxes produced by the category of means-ends relations, and in fact convey only that this category is just not relevant to acting. The kind of thinking associated with it assumes a sovereignty in dealing with the purposes one sets for oneself, in dealing with the means necessary for one's own realization of these purposes, or in dealing with other people whom one has to command, so they may simply execute orders to fabricate a preconceived end product. Only the producer can be the master; he is sovereign and may take possession of all things as means and tools to his end. The acting person always remains in a relation to, and dependent upon, other acting persons; he is never truly sovereign. What directly derives from this is the well-known fact of the irreversibility of historical processes, namely those that are rooted in action; this impossibility of reversing that which has been done by no means applies to processes of production, in which the producer may always intervene destructively—that is, reverse the process of production—if he so chooses.

What the Greeks found to be so suspicious about the *Banausen* was this sovereignty inherent to producing displayed by *homo faber,* to whom what we would call a generally utilitarian approach—an estimation of things as means to an end—comes naturally, because he produces things intended for use, and always requires certain things in order to produce others. They supposed, with good reason, that, whenever it is generalized, this way of thinking would necessarily lead to a devaluation of things *qua* things, and that this devaluation would extend to natural objects not produced by man and essentially independent of him. In other words, they feared that the sovereignty and mastery of *homo faber* would end in hubris if this kind of human being were given access to the political sphere. And they further believed that such a "victory" of culture would end in barbarism, because hubris was considered a barbarian vice just as much as *malakia*. At this point I would like to remind you once again of the famous chorus from Antigone: *polla ta deina k'ouden anthrōpou deinoteron pelei*—because it captures in a singular manner the peculiar split in the Greek evaluation of the productive faculties, which inspired them with the highest awe and the most resounding fear at the same time. These faculties remained frightening to them because the hubris they contained threatened the very existence of nature and of the world.

V

The worry about the preservation of the world primarily burdens man insofar as he is not only a producing but also a political being. As such, he needs to be able to depend on production, so that it may provide lasting shelter for acting and speaking in their transience—and for the perishability of mortal life in its perishability. Politics is thus in need of culture, and acting is in need of production for the purpose of stability; yet both need to protect themselves from culture and production, since all production is at the same time destruction.

Insofar as it is culture, the world is supposed to guarantee permanence, and it does so in its purest and most unencumbered form in those objects that we call artworks—objects of culture in an emphatic sense. To fulfill their "purpose," they must be carefully protected from all purposive declarations and existential interests, from being used and consumed; in the present context it is irrelevant when this protection is assured by putting artworks in sacred places—in temples and churches—or by entrusting them to the care of museums and preservationists. In either case, they need the public sphere and find their proper place only in the common, shared world. They do not gain recognition if hidden among private possessions, and they have to be protected from private interests. It is only under the protection of the public that they may emerge as what they are. And whatever emerges in them—which we usually call beauty—is imperishable from the standpoint of the political sphere and its activities, which is the standpoint of acting and speaking in their very transience. Politically speaking, beauty guarantees that even the most transient and perishable things—the deeds and words of mortal human beings—may gain earthly shelter in the human world.

Culture, however, is no less dependent on politics than politics is dependent on culture. Beauty requires the publicity of a political space protected by acting human beings because the public is the space of appearance *par excellence,* in contrast to the private, which is reserved for concealment and security. But beauty itself is not a political phenomenon; it essentially belongs to the sphere of production and is a criterion of the latter, because all objects have an aspect and a shape that is peculiar to their own status as objects. In this way, beauty remains a criterion even for objects of use—not because "functional" objects could ever be beautiful but, on the contrary, because no object, including objects of use, is ever exhausted by its function. Functionality, for its part, is not the aspect in which the object appears; rather, the aspect in which something appears is its form and shape. The functionality of things, by contrast, is that in virtue of which they once again disappear by being used up, consumed, or replaced. *Moreover,* to evaluate any object in terms of its use-value without considering its appearance, we would have to be blind.

Culture and politics are thus dependent on each other, and they have something in common: they are both phenomena of the public would. Even though, as we shall see, this commonality, in the end, outweighs all conflicts and oppositions between the two spheres, what they hold in common concerns only the objects of culture, on the one hand, and acting, political human beings, on the other. This commonality has nothing to do with the producing artist. For *homo faber* does not, after all, stand in the same self-evident relationship to the public sphere that characterizes the objects to which he has given shape and brought to light. In order to keep adding such objects to the world, he himself must be isolated and hidden from the public, whereas political activities—acting and speaking—are all but impossible to perform without the presence of others and therefore without the public sphere of a space constituted by the many. The activities of the artist as well as the craftsman are subject to very different conditions than those that are political. And it is all but self-evident that *homo faber*—as soon as he raises his voice in order to let his opinion of the value of the political be known—will be as suspicious of the political sphere as the polis is suspicious of the mentality and conditions of production.

This side of the coin can only be hinted at here, namely how properly political activities are perceived by the producers of culture with concern and suspicion. What is more important in our present context, however, is that we take notice of one human activity that suggests the common character of culture and politics. I am taking this suggestion from the first part of Kant's *Critique of Judgment,* which contains what is in my opinion the greatest and most original aspect of Kant's political philosophy.

You will recall that Kant's political philosophy in the *Critique of Practical Reason* posits the legislative faculty of reason, and it assumes that the principle of legislation as it is determined by the "categorical imperative" rests on an agreement of rational judgment with itself—which is to say, in Kantian terms, that if I do not want to contradict myself, I must act only on those maxims that could, in principle, also be general laws. The principle of self-agreement is very old. One of its forms, which is analogous to Kant's, can be already found in Socrates, whose central doctrine, in its Platonic formulation, reads as follows: "Since I am one, it is better for me to be in contradiction with the world than to be self-contradictory." This proposition has formed the basis for Western conceptions of ethics and logic, with their emphases on conscience and the law of noncontradiction respectively.

Under the heading "maxims of Common Sense" in the *Critique of Judgment,* Kant now adds to the principle of agreement with oneself the principle of an "enlarged way of thinking," which submits that I can "think from the standpoint of everyone else." The agreement with oneself is thus joined by a potential agreement with others. The power of judgment rests on this enlarged way of thinking, and judging thereupon derives its proper power of legitimacy. This means, in the negative, that it may disregard its own "subjective private conditions." In positive terms it means that the power of judgment cannot prevail without the existence of others from whose standpoint it can also think. The presence of the self is to the law of noncontradiction in logic, as well as the no less formal law of noncontradiction in conscience-based ethics, what the presence of others is to judgment. A certain concrete generality accrues to judgment—a generality (*Allge-*

meingültigkeit) that is altogether different from universal validity (*universelle Gültigkeit*). The claim to validity can never reach farther than another claim, from whose standpoint things are thought in common. Judgment, as Kant says, applies to "every judging person," which means that it does not apply to people who do not participate in the activity of judging and who are not present in the public sphere, where the objects to be judged ultimately appear.

To be sure, the insight that the power of judgment is a *political* faculty in the specific sense of the word is almost as old as articulated political experience itself—a political faculty, that is, in exactly the way in which Kant determines it, namely as the faculty of seeing things not only from one's own perspective but from that of all others who are also present. In this way, judgment is perhaps the basic faculty; it enables man to orient himself in the public-political sphere and therefore in the world held in common. It is all the more surprising, therefore, that no philosopher before or after Kant has ever made it the object of his inquiry; and the reason for this surprising fact may be found in the antipathy toward politics in our philosophical tradition, although this antipathy cannot be discussed here. The Greeks, for one, call this faculty *phronēsis*, and Aristotle's decision to contrast this cardinal ability of the politician with the *sophia* of the philosophers (who are most concerned with truth), is consistent with public opinion in the Athenian polis, as are his political writings generally. Today, we mostly mistake this ability for a "healthy mind-set" (*gesunden Menschenverstand*), which at one time used to be called *Gemeinsinn* in German, and was thus identical with the kind of *common sense* or *sens commun* that the French simply call *le bon sens*—and which could also straightforwardly be called a sense of the world (*Weltsinn*). It alone deserves credit for the fact that our private and "subjective" five senses and their data are fitted to a nonsubjective, "objectively" common world that we may share and evaluate together with others.

Kant's definitions are altogether remarkable: he discovered judgment in all its glory, as he came upon the phenomena of taste and the judgment of taste. He objected to the supposed arbitrariness and subjective nature of *de gustibus non disputandum est* because this arbitrariness was incompatible with his sense of politics. In contrast to these common prejudices, he

insisted that taste actually "assumes that others experience the same pleasure" and that judgments of taste "suggest everyone's agreement." He
therefore understands that taste, like the common sense (*Gemeinsinn*) from
which it is derived, is the exact opposite of a "private feeling," even if the
two are almost always mistaken for each other.

Discussing all of this in detail would take us too far afield. Even our
brief treatment reveals, however, that the specifically cultural behavior of
human beings is here understood as political activity in an emphatic sense.
Both judgments of taste and political judgments are decisions. As decisions,
they have a "foundation that cannot but be subjective." Nevertheless, they
must remain independent of all subjective interests. Judgment issues from
the subjectivity of a position in the world; at the same time, however, it
claims that this world, in which everyone has his or her own position, is an
objective fact, and thus something that we all share. Taste decides what the
world *qua* world is supposed to look and sound like, how it is supposed to be
looked at and listened to, independently of its usefulness or our existential
interest in it. Taste evaluates the world according to its worldliness. Instead
of concerning itself with either the sensual life or with the moral self, it
opposes both and proposes a pure, "disinterested" interest in the world. It
is the world that is primary for the judgment of taste, not man—neither his
life nor his self.

The judgment of taste is also like political judgment in that it carries
no obligations and—in contrast to the cognitive judgment—cannot prove
anything conclusively. All that the judging person can do, as Kant nicely
puts it, is "to woo everyone's agreement" and to hope to arrive at a common
point of view. This courting is nothing other than what the Greeks called
peithein, which is the kind of rhetoric of persuasion that was valued in the
polis as the preferred means of conducting political dialogue. *Peithein* was
not only opposed to the physical violence they despised; it was also clearly
distinguished from the properly philosophical *dialeghesthai*, precisely
because the latter was concerned with cognition, which, like the search for
truth, required conclusive proof. In the cultural and political spheres—
which constitutes the entire sphere of public life—it is not cognition and
truth, but judging and deciding that are crucial: the normative evaluation
and discussion of the shared world, on the one hand, and the decision con-

cerning what the world is supposed to look like and what sort of actions should be taken in it, on the other.

What speaks for this categorization of taste among the political faculties of man, which may perhaps seem odd, is the well-known but little recognized fact that taste commands an organizational power of peculiar strength. We all know that there is nothing comparable to the discovery of agreement in questions concerning likes and dislikes to help human beings recognize one another—and then to feel irrevocably bound to one another. It is as though taste decided not only what the world should look like, but also who belongs together in the world. It is probably not wrong to see this feeling of common belonging, in political terms, as an essentially aristocratic principle of organization. But its political potential may go even further. The belonging together of persons—this is what gets decided in judgments about a common world. And what the individual manifests in its judgments is a singular "being-thus-and-not-otherwise," which characterizes everything personal and which gains legitimacy to the degree that it distances itself from whatever is merely idiosyncratic. But the political, in speech and action, has precisely to do with such personhood—the "who" one is, regardless of one's talents or qualities. For this reason, the political finds itself opposed to the cultural, where quality is always ultimately the decisive factor—the quality, above all, of the produced object, which, under the supposition that something personal is expressed in it, points back to individual talents and qualities rather than the "who" of that very person. The judgment of taste, however, does not simply decide matters of quality; on the contrary, these matters are necessarily evident—even if, in times of cultural decline, only a few should be susceptible to evidence of this kind. Taste decides *among* qualities, and can fully develop only where a sense of quality—the ability to discern evidence of the beautiful—is generally present. Once that is the case, it is solely up to taste, with its ever-active judgment of things in the world, to establish boundaries and provide a human meaning for the cultural realm. All of this is to say: its task consists in de-barbarizing culture.

It is well known that the term *humanity* is of Roman origin, and that no word corresponding to the Latin *humanitas* can be found in Greek. For this reason, I would consider it appropriate to resort to a Roman example to illustrate the way in which taste is the political faculty by means of which culture is humanized. Recall the ancient saying that is Platonic in both its content and its meaning: *amicus Socrates, amicus Plato, sed magis aestimanda veritas* (I love Socrates, I love Plato, but hold truth in higher esteem). This fundamentally apolitical and inhuman principle, which explicitly rejects persons and friendship in the name of truth, should be contrasted with a less well-known statement by Cicero, who once said the following in the context of a disagreement: *Errare malo cum Platone quam cum istis (sc. Pythagoraeis) vera sentire* (I would rather be in error with Plato than experience the truth with the Pythagorians). Granted, this pronouncement is highly ambiguous. It could mean: I would rather err using Platonic reason than to "feel" the truth using Pythagorean nonreason. But if emphasis is put on *sentire,* the phrase means, instead: It is a question of taste to prefer the company of Plato to that of other people, even if Plato should be the reason for my error. Assuming that the latter reading is correct, one might object that neither scientists nor philosophers would ever be able to say such things. It is, however, the way a thoroughly political and cultured human being—in the sense of the Roman *humanitas*—would speak. Most certainly, it is what one would expect to hear from someone who is free in all respects, and for whom the question of freedom is also the most important question in philosophy. Such a person would say: I will not let myself be forced in my interactions with both people and objects—not even if the force happens to be truth.

In the realm of the cultural, freedom is manifested in taste because the judgment of taste contains and communicates more than an "objective" judgment about quality. As a judging activity, taste brings together culture and politics, which already share the open space of the public realm. And taste likewise equalizes the tension between them—a tension that stems from the internal conflict between action and production. Without the freedom of the political, culture remains lifeless: the slow death of the political and the withering away of judgment are the preconditions for the socialization and devaluation of culture with which this essay began. Without, however, the beauty of cultural things and without the radiant splendor in which a politically articulated permanence and a potential imperishability of the world manifest themselves, the political as a whole could not last.

1958

CHALLENGES TO
TRADITIONAL ETHICS: A RESPONSE
TO MICHAEL POLANYI

The title of Mr. Polanyi's paper, "Beyond Nihilism," does not indicate how startling his theory is, but it expresses very precisely the background of sentiment and mood from which the theory itself receives a good deal of its plausibility. The mood is familiar enough. It was first expressed, I think, by such German writers as Ernst Jünger who, in the early fifties, declared that we have arrived "Beyond Point Zero" (*Jenseits des Nullpunkts*) and Romano Guardini who, at about the same time, wrote a pamphlet about "The End of the Modern Age" (*Das Ende der Neuzeit*). Its most recent manifestation may be found in this country in Daniel Bell's *The End of Ideology* with whom Mr. Polanyi, despite a totally different methodological approach, seems to have much in common. Both arrive at the same conclusion: what problems there are in the modern world can and should be solved pragmatically, experimentally, piecemeal; radicalism must give way to a spirit of reforms; the searching and dangerous questions which nihilism raised seem to be unanswerable and should be left in abeyance; and the numberless social and humanitarian philanthropies which so oddly have accompanied the great political and moral catastrophes of our century bear testimony to the wisdom of "a kind of suspended logic." Finally both authors—and this, too, seems to be somehow in tune with the prevalent mood of the past decade—are strangely unconcerned with the most obvious question their own considerations raise, namely, which task or purpose, if any, is left to thinking at all? Mr. Polanyi seems to imply that the activity of thinking itself, once it has been liberated from dogmatic authority, tends to develop radical attitudes and to end in "nihilistic self-doubt." If this tendency is "incurable" because of the logicality inherent in the human mind—its tendency to drive everything into its logical extreme—should we then renounce this faculty altogether, or use it only to the limited extent that it may help to solve immediate practical problems?

The theory of the paper, as distinguished from its mood, is new and startling. Political criminality on a gigantic scale, as evidenced in both the Hitler and the Stalin regimes, is a thing of the past. The horror it inspired, however, the shocked recognition that "everything is possible," the alarmed conclusion that the very foundations of Western morality are no longer secure, that human conscience has lost its compelling power among ordinary people, that "moral insanity," far from being the temporary aber-ration of a nihilistic elite, may be a mass phenomenon—all these reactions were not only exaggerated but mistaken in principle. For the shocking real-ity did not spring from any "moral weakness" but, on the contrary, from an unprecedented "hunger for righteousness" which, for more than two centuries, has intensified moral feelings until the stream of moral passion "broke the dams which contained it and smashed the wheels which har-nessed it." The horrors themselves, therefore, were "moral excesses."

This theory is a theory in the modern sense of the word. Rather than taking its cue from the phenomenal evidence and relying upon a descrip-tion of what actually happened, it is a hypothesis whose "truth" depends on whether it will "work" or not. I think that this hypothesis works all right with one set of historical data which we may identify, roughly, as the modern history of revolution and the formation of a kind of revolutionary character. For this development, the fact that there is such a thing as "moral passion" is indeed decisive. Mr. Polanyi does not tell us in so many words what this passion is, but it seems fair to infer from his paper that he thinks of the passion as perfectionism—an old heresy according to Catholic teach-ing. The psychological image underlying his argument is, I suspect, the notion of the man who sets out to achieve sainthood, then discovers that "no man is good" (just as Socrates discovered that no man is wise), where-upon he decides that under such circumstances the best, namely, the least hypocritical, is to become a villain. We are familiar with this type of nihil-ism from Russian literature, and we are also familiar with another "moral passion" which, I think, has played an even greater role in the making of the "revolutionary," though free of self-doubt, and that is the passion of compassion—"an innate repugnance to see a fellow creature suffer," as Rousseau once put it. That these "moral passions" are essentially boundless and therefore intrinsically extremist, I do not doubt. But is this kind of extremism really the same as the logical extremism of which, as we know, both Hitler and Stalin were possessed? What may be true for Robespierre and Marx, for Lenin and Trotsky, is not necessarily true for Stalin; and as far as Hitler is concerned, we know that *The Protocols of the Elders of Zion* had more influence on his policies than the collected works of all his alleged predecessors from Rousseau to Nietzsche.

The reason why Mr. Polanyi can argue his case with so much plausibility seems to be chiefly due to his method. He relies on the history of ideas and, though without stating this explicitly, on a firm belief in the dialectical nature of historical development. This method is intellectually very satisfactory; it was originally devised by Hegel in an attempt "to reconcile the spirit with reality" (*den Geist mit der Wirklichkeit zu versöhnen*), a reconciliation Hegel called "understanding." The need of the spirit to come to terms with and thus to understand historical reality in its own terms was then something new; prior to the rise of various philosophers of history in the nineteenth century, philosophy had remained relatively unconcerned with the realm of human affairs from whose haphazardness no spiritual meaningfulness was expected to arise. This changed with the advent of the French Revolution because it seemed as though here, for the first time, ideas were making history. The most obvious conclusion from the course of the French Revolution seemed to be that the same rules, which determine the change and development of ideas within the conceptual framework of the mind, determine also the historical and political development in the realm of worldly reality. The trouble with this conclusion is that all ideas, by virtue of being ideas and nothing else, have an extraordinary affinity to each other which is most pronounced where we deal with opposites—such as good and evil or moralism and immoralism. So long as nothing real interferes, immoralism can best be explained as a "moral inversion" and evil as a mere negation of the good. In other words, within the realm of mere ideas one may very well explain Marx in the light of the Marquis de Sade and vice versa, or understand what Hitler and Stalin did in the light of what Rousseau and Nietzsche preached; the result, unfortunately, will always be that one somehow holds responsible the "antibourgeois immoralism" of the twenties for the formation of the SA and SS or the Russian nihilists for the *apparatchiks* of Stalinism.

Negatively speaking, there is an element of truth in this theory. The attraction which Bolshevism as well as Nazism have proved to possess for the European elite can be explained by the rebellion against bourgeois morality and hypocrisy that had started at the beginning of our century and reached a certain climax in the twenties in Germany, as it reached another such climax in the forties and fifties in France. Yet, in order to realize how little this element of truth justifies any generalization, one needs only to recall that each time one of these rebellions of artists and writers took place in our century, it was followed by an extraordinary development of the arts; as a matter of fact, all modern art was born in these repeated rebellions of the elite against society and, more specifically, against bourgeois society. Yet, it was precisely these outbursts of spiritual and intellectual productivity which the totalitarian movements, once they were in power, destroyed and annihilated, and this liquidation did not come about through the artists and writers themselves. If it is true that the Russian intelligentsia welcomed the revolution because it thought—wrongly as it turned out—that any chaos would be better than the prevailing order, and if it is also true that a certain number of German intellectuals welcomed the Nazis because they were convinced that even nonsense would be better than the common sense of bourgeois society, it is no less true that the welcomers were not welcome and that neither the *apparatchiks* of Stalin nor the SS troops of Hitler were recruited from their ranks. In other words, those who, in Mr. Polanyi's terms, were "inverted moralists" were among the first victims of the new order based in crime; they were overcome by something altogether different from what they were themselves, by something for which no training in extreme thought and nihilistic self-doubt could have prepared them.

I mentioned before that theories which explain events according to the dialectical movement of ideas are intellectually very satisfying. One reason for their plausibility lies in the simple fact that they permit us to remain within the range of our intellectual and spiritual tradition; they appeal to intellectuals because they talk about things among which the intellectual feels at home. The trouble is that the "ideas" which prompted the ideological thinking of Stalin and Hitler can hardly be found in the textbooks of intellectual history. These are not respectable, they possess not even the minimum of intellectual respectability which is commonly accorded to such minor, and intellectually speaking, marginal figures as Gobineau or Houston Stewart Chamberlain.* The reason why intellectuals who knew very well how to cope with Lenin and Trotsky were so slow to recognize the political and historical importance of Hitler and Stalin was simply that the latter, in contradiction to the former, did not talk a language which they *qua* intellectuals were equipped to understand. In order to understand Hitler one had to know the history of antisemitism; in order to understand Stalin one needed a certain knowledge of the history of the secret police. Characteristically enough, neither of these histories has ever been treated adequately by the historical sciences.

There exists, however, another possibility to find a link between the "moral excess" and "nihilistic self-doubt" which belong to the recognized history of the modern age and the political disasters which we were forced to witness in our own time. One may indeed argue that a "passion for nihilistic self-doubt" among intellectuals broke the dams by which the quite different passions of the many had been contained. But this argument would lead us back to the "loss of dogmatic authority" as such, that is, to something which, at least politically, has lost its significance beyond any hope of recovery. In our context, another point is more important. If we want to blame our moral disasters upon the loss of dogmatic authority, we shall again find ourselves in the midst of notions which have little if any place in the great tradition of Western thought or in the history of ideas. For politically speaking, it was the fear of hell which acted as the most potent curb upon the potential criminality of human beings. And the idea that a motive of such obvious moral inferiority as the fear of hell should have restrained mankind from the worst crimes is no more palatable than the notion that such an intellectually unspeakably low product as *The Protocols of the Elders of Zion* should have had the power to influence the course of

---

* A. de Gobineau (1816–1882) and H. S. Chamberlain (1885–1927) were theorists of the inequality of the human races. In *The Origins of Totalitarianism* Arendt writes of "the pompous scientificality of both." —Ed.

contemporary events. Yet, I am afraid these very unpalatable notions are closer to the reality with which we were confronted than any dialectic of ideas. It would lead us too far astray now, but I think it can be shown that the belief in hell is the only strictly political element in Western religion, and that this element itself is neither Christian nor religious in origin. If this is true, then it would follow that the politically most momentous consequence of the modern loss of dogmatic authority was the resulting loss of belief in rewards and punishments in a Hereafter.*

To summarize: I am reluctant to follow Mr. Polanyi's argument for two reasons. I do not want to pay those who caused our disasters the undeserved compliment of having been inspired by the great tradition of Western thought; more important, I see in this as in similar attempts a dangerously tempting device to dodge the problem with which these disasters have confronted us, the problem of the human capacity for radical, unmitigated, absolute evil. Mr. Polanyi at one point admits that "moral depravity" has accomplished "moral excess." This moral depravity, I would argue, was no accompaniment, it was the very crux of the whole matter. I admit that I possess no ready solution of the problem; theoretically, I do not even know the answer to the philosophical question: What is radical evil?

Despite my ignorance, I cannot follow Mr. Polanyi in his proposition to find the solution for these problems in his English example, although I agree with him about the astounding decency of English public and private life. He believes that this decency resides in the wisdom of moderation and that it relies on the refusal to engage in generalizing and radicalizing thought; he is convinced of the great virtue of "muddling through." As far as I can see, Mr. Polanyi fails to demonstrate how and why the moral virtue of decency and the intellectual virtue of pragmatic empiricism are interconnected, and he needs indeed no such demonstration because of his conviction that all our misfortunes stem from the misguided fervor to save the world and mankind of which England has been notoriously free. If, however, one does not agree with his basic assumption that an inordinate love of the good is what makes men bad, then this interrelatedness is no

---

* Cf. "What Is Authority," in H. Arendt, *Between Past and Future* (New York: Penguin, 2006), Part V. —Ed.

longer a matter of course. And I may add that, among those who study current history in the light of the history of ideas, there exists a whole school whose members have argued—with no more loyalty to fact, it is true, but with hardly less consistency—that the root of all our evils must be found in the rise of pragmatism and positivism.

Finally, there is one last reason why I think it unlikely that "Europe will repeat the feat" of English history. The general crisis that has overtaken the modern world everywhere and in almost every sphere of life manifests itself differently in each country, involving different areas and taking on different forms. Conversely, no matter how deep the crisis may go, there are always a great number of fundamental issues left which remain virtually untouched and continue to function as though nothing had happened. Thus the morality of work, seriously undermined in most modern countries, has remained virtually intact in Germany and has strangely survived the most vehement nihilistic disintegration of nearly all other moral values. It looks as though not only England and America, but every country is in some respect "happily backward on the road to disaster," even those which in other respects have unhappily progressed on this road very far indeed. If I were to follow Mr. Polanyi's line of thought, I should have to tell Americans that they had better "repeat the feat" of France in their private lives and family relationships and try to recuperate German backwardness when it comes to work and labor; the French, no doubt, could learn a lesson from England and America in the matter of public spirit, and a "reversal" to English decency and fair-mindedness would probably cause a minor revolution in Germany. I could go on almost endlessly; remnants of old-fashioned virtues can be found everywhere in the world. The point is only that if these virtues are nothing more than "old-fashioned," remnants of a happier past—which indeed they mostly are—they are not likely to withstand the onslaught of modernity. Even if we were able to pool and exchange, as it were, our respective backwardness, it is not likely to help us at a moment when, by virtue of a constantly changing reality that is brought about by scientific as well as political developments, we are almost daily confronted with problems about which all our traditions are silent— for the simple reason that they are literally unprecedented.

1960

REFLECTIONS ON THE 1960 NATIONAL
CONVENTIONS: KENNEDY VS. NIXON

Once upon a time, it was the business of national conventions to nominate their candidates for the highest public offices in the country. Then, as now, nominations depended on vote-getting capacity, but this capacity was only one among several factors. Behind the hoopla, the parades, the oratory, there were the smoke-filled rooms where the deals of party bosses were made and where the considered opinions of the delegates could throw their weight into the balance; in case of stalemate, there were the dark horses to be pulled out, to be shown around, and to be built up into national figures through the propaganda of the party machine.

All this and much more is now a thing of the past. The 1960 nominations were foregone conclusions, not because the conventions were rigged but because the vote-getting capacities of the candidates had proved themselves in the primaries and public opinion polls without the help of the party machines. The parties were confronted with accomplished facts, not only because (significantly enough) both candidates had built up their own organizations, but because His Majesty the Voter had already decided with which alternatives he wished to be confronted, instead of waiting patiently for the alternatives to be presented to him by the wisdom of party leadership. This important shift of power is partly due to television plus the fact that we are confronted for the first time with a generation of men who know how to use the new facilities. One of the consequences of this new generation could well be that the voter, having freed himself of the tutelage of the parties in the selection of candidates, will prove much more independent of party affiliation in making up his mind at election time. I am sure that many people, even now, are uncommitted and waiting to see how the two teams will perform on television; the power shift from the party to the electorate probably has increased the ranks of the independent voters.

Whether this is a good or bad thing is an open question. If the parties were what they should be, namely, the breeding grounds of the political elite of the country, I, for instance, might have preferred that candidates be elected by their peers rather than by the people at large. But if anybody might have cherished illusions on this account, the watching of the proceedings of the conventions will have cured him. (All too often one thought how much better informed, more gifted and appealing the commentators and news analysts were than those who made the news and upon whom they had to comment.) It was obvious that these parties, left to themselves, would not have elected the best men; the deadweight of mediocrity bordering on idiocy, of platitudes, of empty rhetoric and amazing unawareness of the issues at stake, was frightening in both conventions—though it was somewhat less heavy in the Democratic than in the Republican Party. The Republican delegates, repeating many times their Thank you Mr. Eisenhower, must have spoken from the bottom of their hearts. What would have happened to this party, the political home not of Mr. Taft but of Mr. Goldwater, if eight years ago it had not been able to draft for itself a savior from outside its ranks? The difference in general climate between the two parties may be gauged by the difference between the wild and futile enthusiasm which greeted Mr. Stevenson in the Democratic convention and the cold indifference amounting to hostility which accompanied Mr. Rockefeller's appearance on the floor of the Republican proceedings. Not that the delegates would have been likely to draft either of them even if they had still been free to do so. But the point of the matter is that the Democrats loved their Mr. Stevenson for exactly the same reasons and qualities for which the Republicans hated Mr. Rockefeller.

It has been suggested that these party conventions, since they have lost the power to nominate, may no longer be needed. I do not think so. The same technical device which contributed to this loss of power, the television screen, has created for them a new significance. Conventions always helped to dramatize political decisions, before the eyes of all concerned, and this offers more than excitement: it gives an unequaled opportunity to get acquainted with those men upon whose day-to-day decisions much of our life will depend. It is not an empty ritual, it is in fact quite impressive, when the roll is called and state after state, delegation after delegation announces more or less formally its choice for nomination, even though—as in the case of the Republicans—there did not exist the slightest chance of surprise. More important, the screen brings into view those imponderables of character and personality which make us decide, not whether we agree or disagree with somebody, but whether we can trust him. This factor will be even more important when the two candidates begin their television debate. If such debates are going to be required of all candidates for the higher office, the future politician will look back upon the old campaigns with whistle-stops, hand shaking, and news conferences as a Ph.D. candidate may look back with considerable nostalgia to the days when he graduated from grammar school.

Without the help of television, I, too, may have fallen for the current clichés about the similarity of the two candidates—their youth, tough-mindedness, organizational talents, ambition, etc.—although I hope I would not have fallen for the similarity of the two platforms which in their final form—after the Republicans had succeeded in emasculating Mr. Rockefeller's propositions—are still enormously different in tone, approach, emphasis, and style. Given the present circumstances and the obvious fact of broad areas of agreement between the parties—an agreement which, incidentally, is neither less nor more decisive than the agreements which bound even the men of the American Revolution together to the amazement of their colleagues in France—what could be more different in style and emphasis than the opening preambles to the platforms, in which the Democrats say, "The common danger of mankind is war and the threat of war," while the Republicans speak immediately of the "thrust of communist imperialism"? The differences between the candidates are even more marked, though, it is true, they have some things in common. They both know how to organize, or at least one hopes they do, since our more recent blunders must be blamed to a large extent upon plain disorganization; they both like work more than play, and they seem to share a healthy respect for efficiency and an equally healthy contempt for homespun platitudes, all of which, after eight years of the Eisenhower administration, does not sound so bad.

However, here the similarity ends. Mr. Nixon, somewhat more at home in his party, one suspects, than Mr. Kennedy among the Democrats, and gifted with a flair for what the average voter is likely to want, has already started to play the role which certainly is best suited for him. He knows that he lacks the glamour of Mr. Eisenhower, who even today is the most popular man in the United States, and he therefore tries to profit from this popularity by embodying the average citizen who admires Mr. Eisenhower. The emphasis, however, is on "average citizen." This was the image bestowed upon Mr. Truman, it was his kind of popularity, and although this kind doubtless never could measure up to Mr. Eisenhower's glamour, Mr. Nixon seems to believe it is the second best thing to achieve. He appeals to, and, I think, consciously relies on the instinct for mediocrity: Nothing dangerous in him; he is just like everybody else, only with more experience and more capacity for hard work, and, therefore, a tremendous success story—from grocery store to presidency, the very incarnation of the current Republican credo, repeated again and again, that "to get ahead" and to improve constantly one's living standards is the quintessence of freedom. No doubt, he does not model himself upon Mr. Eisenhower, which would be disastrous; he models himself on Mr. Truman, Mr. Average Citizen; and he almost admitted it when, in a television interview, he replied to a reporter that in his preference for history books he "was much like Mr. Truman." This seems incredible from a man who less than ten years ago, at a time when "twenty years of treason" was considered legitimate campaign propaganda, had called the same man a "traitor to his country." Since he is doubtlessly intelligent, I do not believe he reckons we all have forgotten. Rather, it is his way of demonstrating his "maturity," and I am not so sure that this notion of maturity does not somehow agree with the idea of those to whom he addresses himself.

Mr. Kennedy, by contrast, neither believes nor wishes us to believe that he is an average person. Eight years of the Eisenhower administration plus six years of the Truman administration may have convinced the citizen that great gifts are not necessary for the presidency; they have failed to convince Mr. Kennedy. He knows this is the most formidable job there is, not only in the United States, but in the world, and he is confident he is cut out to fit it. Yet while this self-confidence may be a bit disturbing, it is not accompanied by the dangerous habit of arrogant men who surround themselves with mediocrities and yes-men. He has so far surrounded himself with the best men available, and his choice of Mr. Johnson was obviously much more than a gesture toward the South. (These choices—Mr. Bowles, Mr. Stevenson, Mr. Galbraith, and, one hopes, Mr. George Kennan in the future—have somewhat counteracted the fact that he rose to power through an organization centered around his family—an extremely dangerous political device for the simple reason that family loyalties are of an entirely different and much stronger nature than political friendship.) Not only does Mr. Kennedy not believe in mediocrity—"the stale, dank atmosphere of normalcy," as he chose to call it—he even believes in greatness. He made by far the best speech of the conventions in which he stressed the few generalities that happen to be true—that "the old era is ending," that "the old slogans and the old delusions" will not do, that a policy pledged to the status quo—and this has been American policy since the end of the Second World War—will go bankrupt because "today there is no status quo" in any part of the world. More important, though less tangible, was the gusto with which he announced, "the problems are not all solved and the battles are not all won," but also his obvious contempt for "private comfort," his use of words such as "pride, courage, dedication," pitted against security, normalcy, mediocrity. If any promising and outpromising was done in these first stages of the election campaign, it was done by Mr. Nixon, who would not have dared to "hold out the promise of more sacrifice instead of more security." And if Mr. Nixon has modeled the image of himself on the virtues of the common man whose appeal for the voter was demonstrated by Mr. Truman in 1948, Mr. Kennedy obviously strives for an image of statesmanship in all its grandeur, destined to recall Franklin D. Roosevelt, although actually modeled on and influenced by the other great statesman of our time, Winston Churchill. This may sound far-fetched, but I think stylistic analysis of Mr. Kennedy's oratory would bear me out on it.

Oddly enough, if one thinks in terms of party politics, while Mr. Kennedy had the merit to put before the nation the only "real question," namely, "Can a nation organized and governed such as ours endure?," it was Mr. Rockefeller's program that in the last analysis came nearest to spelling out Mr. Kennedy's generalities. He, alone in this respect, called for economic growth in terms of a growing population and not as a means to win an economic race with communist Russia—as though political freedom were a matter of free enterprise and differed from tyranny as the owner of two cars differs from the man who owns none. That is dangerous nonsense; tyrannies can be very prosperous indeed, and poverty, under modern conditions, is defeated by technology and industrialization, not by economic systems of political ideologies.

But Mr. Rockefeller's main points concerned our foreign policy. Let me enumerate them briefly. First, he called for "formation of confederations of free nations" in Europe and the Western Hemisphere, eventually also in Africa and Asia. This is the logical consequence of the end of the European nation-state system, and it is perfectly true that the principles which inspired the creation of the American Republic could be of great relevance to the future of other peoples if Americans knew how to translate them into foreign languages, as it were.

The second point, a Marshall Plan for Latin America, seems to me of great urgency; it is certainly the only way to transform the policy of good neighborship from a slogan into a reality.

Thirdly, and perhaps most important, Mr. Rockefeller spelled out the two objectives of a new defense program: to possess a retaliatory power great enough to survive any surprise attack and hence deter any aggression; and, at the same time, to build up an adequate arsenal of conventional weapons for limited nonnuclear warfare. There has been too much talk of Russia's advantage in intercontinental missiles and far too little about her advantage in conventional warfare. The answer to an absolute weapon, as the H-bomb has been rightly called, seems to be an absolute deterrent that could make sure beyond all doubt that victor and vanquished would go down together. With Polaris submarines, we seem to approach this point of absolute weapon answered by absolute deterrent; the result will be the stabilization of the atomic stalemate, which, under present circumstances, is not "cold war," but cold peace and the factual condition for coexistence.

At about the same time, the missile gap will be closed, and this will have the happy result that our foreign policy will be freed from the heavy disabilities our present defense situation imposes on it due to the necessity of foreign bases.

If the conventions served no other purpose than to offer Mr. Rockefeller an opportunity to bring his ideas into the open, their business will not have been in vain. For together with an endorsement of the sit-ins in the South—an endorsement of the people's nonviolent action, taken according to the rules of assembly and association, as distinguished from action by the federal government against the governments of the Southern states—his program would have offered a platform without the ideological nonsense, such as capitalism versus socialism and vice versa, with full awareness of the crucial issues, and outside the hopelessly obsolete framework of both conservatism and liberalism.

1960

Postscriptum

Let me add a few words. I watched the television debate of the candidates—a rather disheartening experience. It got a bit better when they were confronted with concrete questions, but not much better. They got caught in details, did not know how to spell them out in the light of principles; so that Mr. Nixon's "We agree about the goals, we differ only about means," seemed like an understatement. In the direction of an overstatement, one could have said: They agree about everything except a couple of technical details which they should be able to straighten out with the help of some competent economists.

The trouble as I see it was this: Both candidates accepted the rules laid down by Mr. Khrushchev: coexistence means competition between Russia and the United States in economic growth. Moreover, economic growth is to be measured by economic growth in Soviet Russia. This, I think, is totally wrong. Our economic growth is a question of domestic needs of a growing population in the United States. Our attitude to Russia in these matters can only be the same as our attitude to all countries in the world which have not yet reached American conditions of prosperity and abundance. Instead of figuring the growth percentages and entering into this insane competition, we should be able to tell Mr. K and the Russian people:

We shall be glad to see you improve the standard of life of the peoples of the Soviet Union; we always thought it was inexcusably low. We are happy to hear that Russians will soon be able to live as well as we live. We do not share your ideas about how to reach these new levels of well-being, but we are interested in your experiments. We hope you will be interested in what we are doing along these lines in our country. Maybe the time will come when we can learn from each other. This is not yet possible, because you have not yet reached a standard which could compare with ours—for various reasons, most of them not economic, but political.

You want to reach our standard, and we think that by taking our standard of life as your own goal, you have paid us a handsome compliment. We are in no competition with you in this matter for the simple reason that we, according to our principles, cannot but wish the whole world to achieve the material condition *sine qua non* of human dignity. We may remind you: the United States was the first country in world history which held that poverty and misery are not part and parcel of the human condition. Hence, we are not at all disturbed by your boasts that you will reach and surpass us in economic growth. We are disturbed only about one thing: you do not believe in political freedom, and your people, even if they should reach the well-being that prevails in our country, are not likely to receive the blessings of freedom with it. We should like you to boast that in ten years' time you will have reached and surpassed the standards of free speech, free association, free thought, that exist in this country. We are disturbed that you promise only more cars and more satellites. We hope you will be able to make good on the former, as you will undoubtedly be able to make good on the latter. You have paid us the compliment of taking our standard of life to measure your own achievements in this sphere; why do you not take our standard of liberty to measure your own progress in the political sphere as well?

One more word about economic growth. It is true that this, too, is partly an issue of foreign policy. But not in the sense of competition with the Soviet Union as such, but in the sense that we should be able—in addition to planning for an increasing population and for improvement for certain sections of the population—to produce a surplus with which to help underdeveloped areas. In this respect, and this respect only, there does exist a certain competition with Russia as a matter of course. But this competition is not like a horse race; the issue here is not economic growth as such—as though the judges of the economic race were sitting like spectators, scoring the points of the competitors and then making up their minds which system they are going to adopt. This is totally unrealistic. If our increase in wealth does not stimulate productivity and, eventually, prosperity in other parts of the world, especially the backward regions, we shall earn hatred and not admiration for our system.

ACTION AND THE "PURSUIT OF HAPPINESS"

Among the many surprises this country holds in store for its new citizens, especially of European background and origin, there is the amazing discovery that the "pursuit of happiness," which the Declaration of Independence asserted to be one of the inalienable human rights, has remained to this day considerably more than a meaningless phrase in the public and private life of the American Republic. To the extent that there is such a thing as the American frame of mind, it certainly has been deeply influenced, for better or worse, by this most elusive of human rights, which apparently entitles men, in the words of Howard Mumford Jones, to "the ghastly privilege of pursuing a phantom and embracing a delusion." It is not the purpose of the following brief remarks to explore this matter in its full historical and political significance. My purpose is much more modest. It consists in raising the question of a possible relation of action to happiness in an effort to discover the authentic, nonideological background of experience behind this bewildering pursuit.

I

That the phenomenon of action as one of the elementary human activities might contain a clue in this matter was suggested to me by an incident which, though of no great significance in itself, happened to revive certain trains of thought which had lain dormant at the back of my mind for some time. The incident convinced me of the old verity that nothing is more easily overlooked than what lies before everybody's nose. My justification for telling you about it is that I have always believed that, no matter how abstract our theories may sound or how consistent our arguments may appear, there are incidents and stories behind them which, at least for ourselves, contain as in a nutshell the full meaning of whatever we have to say. Thought itself—to the extent that it is more than a technical, logical operation which electronic machines may be better equipped to perform than the human brain—arises out of the actuality of incidents, and incidents of living experience must remain the guideposts by which it takes its bearings if it is not to lose itself in the heights to which thinking soars, or in the depths to which it must descend. In other words, the curve which the activity of thought describes must remain bound to incident as the circle remains bound to its focus; and the only gain one might legitimately expect from this most mysterious of human activities is neither definitions nor theories, but rather the slow prodding discovery and, perhaps, the mapping survey of the region which some incident had completely illuminated for a fleeting second.

It is neither customary nor wise to tell an audience, and least of all a learned audience, about the incidents and stories around which the thinking process describes its circles. It is much safer to take listener and reader along the train of thought itself, trusting to the persuasiveness inherent in the succession of connected things, even though this succession hides as well as preserves the original source out of which the thought process arose and from which it grew. For incidents in themselves are not persuasive; they are isolated instances by definition and thus open to endless interpretation. Moreover, they are often ordinary and common, and although the common and the ordinary must remain our primary concern, the daily food of our thought—if only because it is from them that the uncommon and the extraordinary emerge, and not from matters that are difficult and sophisticated—it is wiser to call attention to such matters by artificially alienating our minds from them in order to repeat the wonder and surprise with which the commonplace, which we constantly and inevitably tend to overlook because of its familiarity, must strike us to assert its true significance.

Alienation as a means to focus attention is common enough in literature and art, especially in modern poetry and painting, where it has received more than its due share of consideration. I think it is no less present in modern philosophy, that is, to the extent that philosophy is still concerned with those elementary plausibilities which are common to all, except the philosopher. Modern philosophy has discovered that interpretation of texts, the art of hermeneutics, can be a very effective means of such alienation, and the frequent complaints about distortion of meaning and violence done to authors bear a strange similarity to the familiar complaints about the distortion of reality in modern painting and writing. The current justification given for this indirect manner of speaking and writing is the "need to go back to the sources themselves," and I do not doubt its legitimacy. However, there are other reasons, less candidly admitted, and, I suspect, of equal relevance. There is first the tendency to present the newest insight as rediscovery of the "oldest truth," and second there is an altogether novel and yet fairly widespread technique of quoting single sentences and sometimes mere words out of context, not with any fraudulent intent, but simply for purposes of insulation, and, as it were, purification so as to prevent any transmission of triteness, the contamination with that atmosphere of empty, banal verbosity, which has infected our language and corrupted the key words of speculative thought—such as truth, freedom, faith, reason, justice, and the like. Metaphorically speaking, it is as though—instead of pouring the new wine into old bottles—the old wine is being used to cause fermentation which, of course, can be done only if first the spirit has been distilled from it. To be sure, this shying away from direct speech and this peculiar use of the treasures of the past have many causes; among them is the insight that in these matters "nothing can be true which is altogether new" (Karl Jaspers), plus the conviction that what only one man says cannot be true either. But this need for support and for company does not tell the whole story; it does not explain the distillation and the distortion which comes from it, this seeming arbitrariness in handling the old texts, or this sudden passion for reading ever deeper and more novel meanings into them. Distillation, then, as the very quintessence of the new art of hermeneutics, plays much the same part, and aims at much the same effects, in modern theoretical writing as alienation in modern art and poetry.

These methods of indirect speech by means of interpretation, though almost unknown prior to our own century, have become by now the expected, though by no means the generally accepted, form for inquiries of a certain type, and I myself shall soon have recourse to what is perhaps the only way of gaining at least a minimum of plausibility for statements which can neither be demonstrated in conclusive argument nor hope to be accepted as self-evident truths. To begin with, telling the anecdote of a real incident is against all the rules of the game; but these rules are not absolute, they are rules of caution rather than laws of thought, and hence can be broken.

The incident, then, which gave rise to the following considerations was as follows: I was engaged in conversation with one of those former radicals—communists, Trotskyites, and the like—whom, I suppose, we all count among our acquaintances and friends, and I was curious how this particular person viewed his own past, how he had come to terms with his former convictions. At the back of my mind, I had the ready-made alternatives into which the answer was likely to fall—Marxism as an ideology provided a convenient framework for thought and argument, for explanation of the past and for prophecy of the future; or, the disgust with institutional religion and the search for a new god whose eventual failure often sent his former adherents in search for newer ones, no less strange as a matter of fact, though thus far less dangerous than the one discarded; or, presumably the best possibility, the old passionate contempt for the prevailing standards of "bourgeois" society, plus the no less passionate but less readily admitted compassion for those whom society persisted to treat unjustly. (The latter, incidentally, the passion of compassion, has been among the strongest psychological motives throughout the history of revolution, from Robespierre down to Lenin and Trotsky. There is a thing as a passionate, unreasoning love of justice as there is such a passionate, unreasoning love for freedom. Those most likely to be caught between the wars were people in whom the passion for justice outbalanced and overruled not only complacency and opportunism but also the passions for either freedom or truth. And in this, they were in no way exceptions from the rules of society as we have come to know it; it is precisely one of the outstanding characteristics of modern society that considerations of justice will tend to outweigh all others.)

In all these instances, revolutions would have been accepted as the only means to bring about a better and happier society—with or without an ideology to guide it, with or without belief in historical necessity and the wave of the future. And if we leave out here the otherwise very important question of using violence in order to achieve universal happiness, it must be admitted that the revolutionist again had little cause to congratulate himself on being free from the commonplace prejudices on which the established society rested. For is it not axiomatic with us that the ultimate end of government and the first law of political action is the promotion of the happiness of society?

To my surprise, the answer of my acquaintance differed from all these expectations. Instead of a straightforward reply, I was told a story, the story of an inveterate gambler who happened to arrive late in a strange town and naturally proceeded forthwith to the gambling place. There a native approached him and warned him that the wheel was crooked, whereupon the stranger replied: "But there is no other wheel in town." The moral of the story was clear: In those days, my acquaintance implied, if you had the itch to do something, you had no other place to go; you went there not for the good of society at large, but for your own sake; and even if you went for other, presumably more honorable motives—such, for instance, as we know from the French Resistance—it could happen to you that once you were in it you would discover that there no longer existed that "*épaisseur triste* between the world of reality and yourself," that trying to save your country, you had first of all saved yourself. Many indeed, if they had the courage, not of their convictions which is relatively easy, but of their experiences should know what the French poet and writer René Char was talking about when during the years of war and desperate action he wrote: "If I survive, I know that I shall have to break with the aroma of these essential years, silently reject (not repress) my treasures, go back to the very beginnings, to my most destitute behavior, when I was in quest of myself without mastery, in naked unsatisfaction, in barely perceptible knowledge and inquiring humility."

But my acquaintance was an American, not a Frenchman, and his experience referred to the early thirties when he, unlike the gambler in the story, might have had other places to go. Even more doubtful is whether in his youth, while still engaged in these activities, he actually knew the wheel was crooked, doubtful, too, whether he then would have dared to own up to his motives, or even whether these really had been his motives at all. What most interests us here is not the truthfulness of a person but the truth of a story, and the story tells us that there exists such intense happiness in acting that the actor, like the gambler, will accept that all the odds are stacked against him. This, I admit, is difficult to believe; what convinced me that I had heard a truth was that the story reminded me instantly of a strange passage in the last letters exchanged between Jefferson and John Adams, when, at the end of their long lives and in a reflective mood, they felt the need to explain themselves to each other. One of the subjects they frequently discussed was death, to which they both looked forward with "more willingness than reluctance," with complete equanimity, in a spirit equally removed from anxiety and from *taedium vitae*. And when in this atmosphere of stillness and quiet the question of life in a hereafter was raised, Jefferson—who perhaps had never shared John Adams's conviction that belief in a future state with rewards and punishment was indispensable for civilized communities—concluded one of his letters as follows: "May we meet there again, *in Congress, with our antient Colleagues,* and receive with them the seal of approbation, 'Well done, good and faithful servants'" (my italics).

To be sure, Jefferson speaks jokingly, or rather with the sovereign irony which old age bestows upon those who are at peace with themselves, whose innate pride has remained intact under life's triumphs and disasters. Yet, behind the irony, there is the candid admission that life in Congress—the joys of discourse, of legislation, of transcending business, of persuading and being persuaded—was as conclusively a foretaste of an eternal bliss to come as the delights of contemplation had been for medieval piety. If we strip these images of life in a hereafter of their religious connotation— which, of course, is more legitimate in the case of Jefferson than in the case of, say, Thomas Aquinas—they present nothing more nor less than various ideals of human happiness. And the point of the matter is that Thomas's *perfecta beatitudo* consisted entirely in a vision, the vision of God, for which the presence of no friends was required (*amici non requiruntur ad perfectam beatitudinem*), whereas Jefferson could think of a possible improvement of the best and happiest moments of his life only by enlarging the circle of his "Colleagues" so that he would be able to sit "in Congress" with the ancients. It is very much in the same spirit and the same mood that

Socrates, in a famous passage about the chances of life after death, frankly and smilingly confessed that all he could ask for was, so to speak, more of the same: no island of the blessed and no life of an immortal soul which would be utterly unlike the life of a mortal man, but the meeting in Hades with his illustrious "antient Colleagues"—Orpheus and Musaeus, Hesiod and Homer—whom he had not been able to meet on earth and whom he would have desired to engage in those unending dialogues of thought of which he had become the master. No doubt, he, too, would have loved to "receive with them the seal of approbation."

But let us return to Jefferson. What makes his statement so remarkably noteworthy is the glaring and somehow innocent discrepancy with the whole body of ancient and modern political theory which Jefferson hardly ever thought of challenging explicitly. In the sentence I quoted the "seal of approbation" is not the common reward for virtue in a future state; it rather belongs together with another passage in which he candidly admitted that there had been a time "when perhaps the esteem of the world was of higher value in my eye than everything in it." Yet Jefferson, too, believed that "the care of human life and happiness . . . is the . . . only legitimate object of good government," that any "happiness" in those who governed was suspect, that it could consist only in an "inordinate passion for power," and that the chief reason the governed must have a share in government was this deplorable "unjustifiable" tendency of human nature (John Dickinson). He would have agreed with Madison that government is but a reflection on human nature, that men, if they were angels, would need no government, and that government, if exercised by angels, would need no Congress and no other institutions of control to check its powers. When he spoke of his public career, he would seldom mention how much he had enjoyed himself; he would rather stress the debt of service he owed to his fellow citizens, "that a tour of duty, in whatever line he can be most useful to his country, is due from every individual." When he spoke of happiness, he, too, would assert that its place lies "in the lap and love of my family, in the society of my neighbors and my books, in the wholesome occupations of my farms and affairs"—in short, in a place as far removed as possible from Congress and in a life upon which the public had no claim.

That these exhortations and reflections are a far cry from the pious banalities, current in nineteenth-century politics and even today still the stock-in-trade of political oratory on its lowest level, I do not deny. But I think that they do not carry much weight in the writing and thinking of the Founding Fathers—little weight in Jefferson's works, and even less in John Adams's. One of the most impressive passages in this respect occurs in an early letter John Adams wrote to his wife from Paris; it reads as follows: "I must study politics and war that my sons may have liberty to study mathematics and philosophy, geography, natural history and naval architecture, navigation, commerce and agriculture, in order to give their children a right to study painting, poetry, music, architecture, statuary, tapestry, and porcelain." These sentences somehow carry conviction because of this amusingly precise enumeration of minutiae; and yet, it is hardly possible to overlook that they contain a theory about the historical development of civilization rather than an indication of a personal yearning for leisure and contemplation. Moreover, and more importantly, the enumeration, which supposedly ascends from a lower to a higher order, actually ends with the most trivial of the proposed occupations—tapestry and porcelain; hence, while Adams obviously set out to write an ascending order in accordance with what tradition and convention had told him was right, he was carried away by his secret convictions, and out came the truth—not his grandchildren, preoccupied with decorating their walls and collecting china, but their grandfather, "loaded down" with public business, had drawn first prize in life's lottery. If we wish to learn something about the authentic experiences behind the commonplace that public business is a burden and a duty, we had better turn to the fifth and fourth centuries BCE in Greece than to the eighteenth century CE of our civilization.

Unfortunately, it is not an uncommon error to mistake the writings of these men of action or even the documents they framed for literary products whose originality, or lack of it, may be judged in accordance with standards valid for ordinary books which, insofar as they are books, do not belong in the realm of action. To be sure, it is not its natural law philosophy which gives significance to the Declaration of Independence, in which case it would indeed be "lacking in depth and subtlety" (Carl L. Becker); nor does it make any sense to look for new ideas in a document whose main notions were so well known that its author thought he had expressed no more than "the common sense of the subject," while at least some of its contemporary readers were aware that these ideas were already rather "hackneyed" (John Adams). Still, the greatness of the document is beyond doubt, and it lies in such facts as that a document was thought to be needed at all out of "respect of the Opinion of mankind," or that a list of very specific grievances against a particular king led to the denial of monarchy, and kingship in general. The grandeur of the Declaration of Independence, in other words, consists in being "an argument in support of an action" (Carl L. Becker), or in its being the perfect way of an action to appear in words. And since we deal here with the written and not with the spoken word, we are confronted by one of the rare moments when the power of action *is* great enough to erect its own monument.

What is true for the Declaration of Independence is even truer for the writings of the men who made the revolution. It was when he ceased to speak in generalities, when he spoke or wrote in terms of either past or future actions that Jefferson came closest to appreciating at its true worth the peculiar relationship between action and happiness to which I am trying to draw your attention. It was only because he was so aware of their being related that he outlined again and again his great and completely forgotten plan of dividing and subdividing republics of the Union into "the elementary republics of the wards" where every man would be able to feel "that he is a participator in the government of affairs," and hence would live in a Congress of his own. He was convinced, and I think rightly, that the republic could not be safe without the establishment of what he even then would call "councils"—certainly without any premonition of the *soviet* and *räte* systems of later revolutions, and most probably without much awareness of the first confused and doomed beginnings of such a system in the sections of Paris during the French Revolution. It is all the more noteworthy that he thought of his universally ignored plan in terms of elementary safety for the existence of the American Republic, for he wrote most emphatically that his "ward system" was his *ceterum censeo Carthaginem esse delendam,** the famous word of concern with the safety of Rome. Jefferson's reason was as follows: "When there shall not be a man in the State who will not be a

* "Moreover, I declare Carthage must be destroyed" (Cato the Elder). —Ed.

member of some one of its councils, great or small, he will let the heart be torn out of his body sooner than his power be wrested from him by a Caesar or a Bonaparte."* The reason, however, why this whole portion of Jefferson's politics, together with similar portions of John Adams's writings, have been buried in oblivion (to the point, incidentally, that the very word "ward" is missing from the indices of current editions) is precisely that no theory could be found to agree with it. The trouble is that, contrary to what Jefferson himself believed, the "common sense of a matter" is by no means always identical with the commonly held beliefs about it.

To put this another way, though Jefferson could write as indignantly as he pleased about "the nonsense of Plato," the truth is that Plato's "foggy mind" has predetermined the categories of political thought to such an extent and has erected a conceptual framework of such stability that Jefferson himself was no more, and perhaps even less, capable of escaping hidden Platonic notions in his political thinking than any avowed admirer of the *Republic*. These notions—to put them as crudely as possible but hardly more crudely than Platonic ideas had become at the end of the eighteenth century—can be enumerated as follows: The ultimate end of politics in general and action in particular is beyond and above the political realm. The goal by which political action must take its bearings, and the standard by which it can be judged, are not political in origin but arise from an altogether different and transcending set of experiences. Action is fundamentally no more than execution of knowledge, and is therefore secondary as well as inferior to it. Hence, it is the "wise man" who is the "good man." Finally, in the Aristotelian version of Platonism, political action and its ultimate goal stand in the same relationship to each other as war and peace, that is, the end of political action is not only different from politics in general, it is its very opposite.

Not much more of this tradition had come down to the eighteenth century's *philosophes* and men of letters than the question which seemingly poses the central problem of all political thought: What is the end of government? But the point to remember is that this question which still haunts the textbooks makes sense only if one takes philosophy as seriously as those did

* Jefferson to J. C. Cabell, February 2, 1816. —Ed.

who for the first time discovered and defined the philosopher's way of life in distinction from, and in opposition to, the political way of life. And neither the Founding Fathers nor the political theorists in England and France from whom they derived their own "philosophy" were willing or even capable of taking philosophy as a way of life seriously enough to reach the origins of their conceptual language. This might have been of small importance if only they had been able to arrive at another comprehensive way of communicating and stating their own experiences. Since this was not the case, they remained unhappily the prisoners of a tradition whose authentic sources lay beyond their scope of experience as well as beyond the grasp of their understanding, and the result was that whenever they thought in general or in theoretical terms, that is, not in terms of political action and the foundation of political institutions, their thought would remain shallow and the depth of their experience would remain inarticulate.

In the last analysis, it was this inarticulate depth which, when it broke through the rigid shell of traditional platitudes, was likely to lead and mislead them into certain grand and dangerous statements—as when Jefferson speaks of "the tree of liberty" which "must be refreshed from time to time with the blood of patriots and tyrants." It was still the same depth of experience and the same inability to clarify and explore with it the conceptual tools of our tradition that led and misled the men of the French Resistance into a philosophy of triumphant "absurdity" when they tried to distill "the aroma of those essential years" for whose trials and sacrifices they were so much better prepared than for the unexpected "happiness" and meaningfulness these years held in store for them.

II

Permit me now to revert from my old-fashioned storytelling to the acceptable method of insulating, distilling, and hence alienating interpretation in order to give more plausibility to what I think these stories have to tell us. I shall first call your attention not even to a sentence but to two words only, which we hardly ever would use together, but which were a current idiom in the eighteenth century. The two words are "public happiness." It is an odd fact which, of course, has often been noticed that Jefferson, when he drafted the Declaration of Independence, changed the current formula in which the inalienable rights were enumerated from "life, liberty and property" to "life, liberty and the pursuit of happiness." It is even stranger that in the debates which preceded the adoption of Jefferson's draft this alteration was not discussed; and this curious lack of attention to a phraseology, which in the course of the following centuries has contributed to a specifically American ideology more than any other word or notion, stands almost as much in need of explanation as the phrase itself. It is quite possible that this original lack of attention was due to the high regard paid to Mr. Jefferson's famous "felicity of the pen"; it is even more likely that the change escaped attention because the word "happiness" occupied a prerevolutionary place in political language so that it sounded quite familiar in its context.

The first source of such familiarity which comes to mind is the conventional idiom in royal proclamations where "the welfare and the happiness of our people" quite explicitly meant the private welfare of the subjects and their private happiness, that is, exactly what the phrase "pursuit of happiness" has come to mean throughout the nineteenth and twentieth centuries. Against this plausibility, however, there stands the fact that it was precisely a highly significant variation in pre-revolutionary America to speak of *public* happiness instead of "welfare and happiness." Thus Jefferson himself, in a paper he prepared for the Virginia Convention of 1774, which in many respects anticipated the Declaration of Independence, declared that "our ancestors" when they left "the British dominions in Europe" exercised "a right which nature has given all men . . . of establishing new societies, under such laws and regulations as to them shall seem most likely *to promote public happiness*" (my italics). If Jefferson was right and it was in quest of "public happiness" that the "free inhabitants of the British dominions" had emigrated to America, then the colonies in the New World must have been the breeding grounds of revolutionaries from the beginning: for "public happiness" meant a share in "the government of affairs," that is, in public power, as distinct from the generally recognized right to be protected by the government even against public power. More importantly in our context, the very combination of the two words "public" and "happiness" indicates strongly that these men knew they were not altogether speaking the truth when they maintained (as did Jefferson in a letter to John Randolph in 1775): "My first wish is a restoration of our just rights; my second, a return to the happy period when . . . I may withdraw myself totally from the public eye, and pass the rest of my days in domestic ease and tranquility, banishing every desire of afterwards even hearing what passes in the world." Only John Adams was bold enough to make the enjoyment of power and public happiness the cornerstone of his political philosophy.

As far as the Declaration of Independence is concerned we doubtlessly are supposed to hear the term "pursuit of happiness" in a twofold meaning even though these meanings can hardly be reconciled either historically or conceptually. In this instance, Jefferson's felicity of pen succeeded only too well in blurring the distinctive line between "private rights and public happiness" (James Madison), which had the obvious immediate advantage that—without antagonizing his colleagues who actually wished to constitute a new body politic, a place for public happiness, where their passion for "emulation," the *spectemur agendo* ("let us be seen in action") in John Adams's phrase, could be realized—his draft formula would also appeal to those in the assembly who wished to give their attention "exclusively to their personal interests" (Cooper), not to be bothered any further with public affairs and a "public happiness" which they neither understood nor desired. And, lest somebody doubt that the Founding Fathers might have had a different notion of the dignity of politics than is currently ascribed to them, let me quote John Adams, who boldly claimed that "it is a principal end of government to regulate this passion [namely, the passion for emulation], which in its turn becomes a principal means of government." In this definition of the "end of government," means and end obviously coincide; the moment one puts the notion of "public happiness" in the place of private rights and personal interests, the very question: What is the end of government? loses its sense.

In order to understand the meaning of this public happiness, it may be well to remember that there existed a very similar and yet significantly different idiom in the political language of pre-revolutionary eighteenth-century France. Tocqueville reports how widespread the "taste" and the "passion for public freedom" was, how predominant in the minds of those who had no conception whatsoever of what we now call revolution nor any premonition of the role they were to play in it. The Americans could speak of public happiness because they had tasted, prior to the revolution, the experience of public freedom in the assemblies of towns and districts, where they used to deliberate upon public affairs and where, according to John Adams, "the sentiments of the people were formed in the first place." They knew that the activities connected with this business constituted no burden but gave those who discharged them in public a feeling of happiness they could acquire nowhere else. Compared to this American experience, the preparation of the French *hommes de lettres* who eventually were to make the French Revolution was theoretical in the extreme; no doubt, the men whom an unfriendly historian with some right has called "the play actors" of the French Assembly also enjoyed themselves, but they certainly had no time, caught in the torrent of revolutionary events they no longer knew how to control, to reflect upon this side of an otherwise grim business.

Which, then, was the background of experience from which the term "public freedom" was coined? Who were the men who, without even knowing it (for "the very notion of a violent revolution had no place in [their] mind; it was not discussed because it was not conceived," as Tocqueville pointed out), were in fact bent upon changing the old order of a whole civilization? The eighteenth century, as I mentioned before, called these men *hommes de lettres,* and one of their outstanding characteristics was they had withdrawn voluntarily from society, first from the society of the royal court and the life of a courtier, and later from the society of the salons. They educated themselves and cultivated their minds in a freely chosen seclusion, putting themselves at a calculated distance from the social as well as the political, from which they were excluded in any case, in order to look upon both in perspective. Living under the rule of an enlightened absolutism where life at the king's court, with its endless intrigues and the omnipresence of gossip, was supposed to offer full compensation for a share in the world of public affairs, their personal distinction lay in their refusal to exchange social consideration for political significance, opting rather for the secluded obscurity of private studies, reflections, and dreams. We know this atmosphere from the writings of the French *moralistes,* and we still are fascinated by the considered and deliberate contempt for society in its initial stages, which was the source even of Montaigne's wisdom, the depth of Pascal's thought, and which left its traces upon many pages of Montesquieu's work.

Moreover, and importantly, no matter to which "estate" the men of letters belonged, they were free from the burden of poverty, and hence in a very similar position to their American colleagues. Dissatisfied with whatever prominence state or society of the *ancien régime* might have granted them, they felt that their leisure was a burden rather than a blessing, an imposed exile from a realm to which they had right of access by virtue of birth, talent, and inclination; and what they missed in this position in which "the world of public affairs was not only hardly known to them but was invisible" (Tocqueville), they called "public freedom."

To put it another way, their leisure was the Roman *otium* and not the Greek *skholē,* it was enforced inactivity, a "languishing in idle retirement" in which philosophy was supposed to deliver "some cure for grief"—a *doloris medicinam,* as Cicero put it. And they were still quite in the Roman style and mood when they began to employ their leisure in the interest of the *res publica* or *la chose publique* as eighteenth-century France, translating literally from the Latin, still called the realm of public affairs. Hence, they turned to the study of Greek and Roman authors, but not—and this is decisive—for the sake of whatever eternal wisdom or immortal beauty the ancient books might contain, but almost exclusively in order to learn about the political institutions to which they bore witness. In eighteenth-century France, as in eighteenth-century America, it was their search of public freedom and public happiness, and not their quest for truth, that led men back to antiquity.

Tocqueville once rightly remarked that "of all ideas and sentiments which prepared the Revolution, the notion and taste of public freedom strictly speaking have been the first ones to disappear." And the same, *mutatis mutandis,* can be said for the notion of public happiness in America where "the pursuit of happiness" was almost immediately used and understood without its original qualifying adjective. There were theoretical as well as historical reasons which caused this fateful disappearance. I mentioned the theoretical insufficiency of our tradition of political thought which, in this instance, turned about the ambiguities in the traditional definitions of tyranny. Tyranny, according to ancient, pre-theoretical under-standing, was the form of government in which the ruler had monopolized for himself the right of action and banished the citizens from the public realm into the privacy of the household where they were supposed to mind their own, private business. Tyranny, in other words, deprived men of pub-lic happiness and public freedom without necessarily encroaching upon the pursuit of personal interests and the enjoyment of private rights. Tyranny, according to traditional theory, is the form of government in which the ruler rules out of his own will and in pursuit of his own interests, thus offending the private welfare and the personal liberties of his own subjects. The eighteenth century, when it spoke of tyranny and despotism, did not distinguish between these two possibilities, and it learned of the sharpness of the distinction between the private and the public, between the unhin-dered pursuit of private interests and the enjoyment of public freedom or of public happiness, only when, during the course of the revolutions, these two principles came into conflict with each other.

Basically, this conflict was the same in the American and the French revolutions though it assumed very different expressions. Theoretically, the briefest way to grasp its significance may be to remember Robespierre's theory of revolution, his conviction that "constitutional government is chiefly concerned with civil liberty, revolutionary government with public freedom." But Jefferson's insistence on some "ward system," his conviction that the revolution was incomplete and the permanence of the republic not assured because it had failed to establish institutions in which the revolu-tionary spirit could be kept alive, point in the same direction. Robespierre's profound unwillingness to put an end to the revolution, his fear lest the end of revolutionary power and the beginning of constitutional government spell the end of public freedom, is essentially akin to Jefferson's halfhearted wish for a revolution in every generation. In terms of the American Revo-lution, the question was whether the new body politic was to constitute a realm of its own for the "public happiness" of its citizens, or whether it had been devised solely to serve and insure their pursuit of private happi-ness more effectively than the old regime. In terms of the French Revolu-tion, the question was whether the end of revolutionary government lay in the establishment of constitutional government which might terminate the reign of public freedom through a guarantee of civil liberties and rights, or whether, for the sake of public freedom, the revolution should be declared in permanence. The guarantee of civil liberties and rights had long been regarded as essential in all nontyrannical rule where the monarch governed within the limits of the law and for the sake of the welfare and the interests of his subjects. If nothing more was at stake, then the revolutionary changes of government that took place at the end of the eighteenth century, the abolition of monarchy and the establishment of republics, must be regarded as accidents, provoked by no more than the wrongheadedness and blunders of the old regimes; not revolutions but reforms, not the foundation of new political bodies but the exchange of a bad ruler for a better one, should have been the answer.

However, the point of the matter is that both the French and the American revolutions, although the men who enacted them on both sides of the Atlantic originally intended no more than such reforms in the direction of constitutional monarchy, were very quickly driven to an insistence on republican government. One of the outstanding characteristics the two revolutions—so unlike each other in most other respects—had in common was the new violent antagonism of monarchists and republicans, and this antagonism was practically unknown prior to the revolutions themselves; it clearly was the result of experiences made in action. Whatever the men of the revolutions might have known or dreamt about before, it was only in the course of the revolutions themselves that they became fully acquainted with public happiness and public freedom, when they became, as the phrase goes, intoxicated with the wine of action. At any rate, the impact of these experiences was sufficiently profound for them to prefer under almost any circumstances—should the alternatives unhappily be put to them in such terms—public freedom to personal interests and public happiness to private welfare. Behind Robespierre's and Jefferson's foredoomed theories and proposals, which foreshadow the revolution declared in permanence, one can discern the uneasy, alarmed, and the alarming question that was to disturb almost every revolutionary after them who was worth his salt: If the end of revolution and the intersection of constitutional government spelled the end of public freedom, was it then even desirable to end the revolution?

It clearly is impossible, within the limitations of this paper, to follow up the twisted trail of these experiences through the history of revolutions from the end of the eighteenth century to the middle of our own. It is even less possible to do justice to the relevance of these experiences for an adequate and truly modern theory of politics. In conclusion, however, I should like to point out the two directions of future considerations which my remarks tried to indicate.

The first of these directions takes us into the dimension of history where, I think, it can be substantiated that the major revolutions of the nineteenth century invariably and spontaneously reproduced Robespierre's drive toward a revolution declared in permanence as well as Jefferson's attempt to establish in "councils," or in the "elementary republics" of a "ward system" a lasting political organization which would preserve, not so much the original goal of the revolution, as the spirit which inspired those who made the revolution and which was unknown to them prior to the course of events.

The second direction takes us into the dimension of theory where, on the ground of historical experience, the relation of action to happiness (which may offer the key to the twofold question: What is Action and what is Virtue?) could be explored. In this second dimension, the meaning of the word "revolution" has to be cleansed of the ideologies of the nineteenth century and saved from its perversion through the totalitarianism of the twentieth century. It then will appear that revolutions have been the time-space where action with all its implications was discovered, or, rather, rediscovered for the modern age—an event of tremendous importance if one remembers for how many centuries action had been overshadowed by contemplation, and the realm of public affairs, in Tocqueville's telling phrase, had been "invisible" to rich and poor alike. It is for this reason that every modern theory of politics will have to square itself with the facts brought to light in the revolutionary upheavals of the last two hundred years, and these facts are, of course, vastly different from what the revolutionary ideologies would like us to believe.

The difficulties in understanding, or even perceiving, these facts are great, because all the tools of traditional political and conceptual thought fail us in such an attempt. The rediscovery of action and the reemergence of a secular, public realm of life may well be the most precious inheritance the modern age has bequeathed upon us who are about to enter an entirely new world. But our position as heirs to this inheritance is far from being untroubled; the trouble was expressed most succinctly by René Char, the French poet and writer whom I quoted before, and who, summing up his experience in the Resistance, said: *"Notre héritage n'est précédé d'aucun testament"* (Our inheritance was left to us by no testament).

1960

FREEDOM AND POLITICS, A LECTURE

I

To speak of the relation between freedom and politics in a lecture is permissible only because a book would be just about as inadequate. For freedom, which only very seldom—in times of crisis or revolution—becomes the direct aim of political action, is actually the reason why such a thing as politics exists in the communal life of man. By freedom, I do not mean that endowment of human nature that the philosophers define one way or another, and like to locate one way or another within human capabilities. Still less do I mean that so-called inner freedom, into which men may escape from external coercion; this is historically a late and objectively a secondary phenomenon. It was originally the result of an estrangement from the world, in which certain worldly experiences and claims were transformed into experiences within one's own self, despite the fact that they came from the outer world and we would have known nothing of them had we not first encountered them as worldly, tangible realities. We first become aware of freedom and its opposite in our intercourse with others, not in intercourse with ourselves. People can only be free in relation to one another, and so only in the realm of politics and action can they experience freedom positively, which is more than *not being forced*.

One cannot speak about politics without also speaking about freedom; and one cannot speak about freedom without also speaking about politics. Where men live together but do not form a body politic—as, for example, in primitive tribal societies or in the privacy of the household—the factor ruling their activities is not freedom but the necessities of life and concern for its preservation. Moreover, wherever the man-made world does not become the scene for political action—as in despotically ruled communities that banish their subjects to the narrowness of the home and private concerns—freedom has no worldly reality. Without a politically guaranteed public realm, freedom lacks the worldly space to make its appearance. To be sure, it may always dwell in men's hearts as a yearning, no matter what their living conditions may be; but it is still not a demonstrable fact in the world. As demonstrably real, freedom and politics coincide and are related to each other as two sides of the same medal.

Yet there is good reason why, today, we cannot take this coincidence of politics and freedom for granted. Since we have become acquainted with forms of total domination, popular opinion holds that nothing is better suited to a complete and total abolition of freedom than the total politicization of life. Seen from the perspective of this most recent experience, which naturally we must always keep in mind for considerations of this sort, we must not only doubt the coincidence of politics and freedom, but also their very compatibility. We are inclined to believe that freedom begins where politics ends, because we have seen that freedom disappeared where politics became endless and limitless. The less politics, so it seems, the more freedom, or: the smaller the space occupied by the political, the larger the domain left to freedom. Indeed, it is quite natural for us to measure the extent of freedom in any given community by the free scope it grants to apparently nonpolitical activities, free economic enterprise, for example, or freedom of academic teaching, of religion, or of cultural and intellectual activities. We believe that politics is compatible with freedom only insofar as it guarantees a possible freedom *from* politics.

This definition of political liberty as a potential freedom from politics that is urged upon us by our most recent experiences has also played a large role in the history of political theory. We find it above all with the political thinkers of the seventeenth and eighteenth centuries, who more often than not simply identified political freedom with security. The purpose of politics was to guarantee security, which, in turn, made freedom possible as something nonpolitical, as a catch-all for activities occurring outside the political realm. Even Montesquieu, though he had a different and much higher opinion of the essence of politics than Hobbes or Spinoza, could still occasionally equate political freedom with security. The rise of the political sciences and political economy in the nineteenth and twentieth centuries even widened the breach between freedom and politics. Government, which since the beginning of the modern age had been identified with the entire domain of the political, was now considered to be the appointed protector not so much of freedom as of the life process and the life interests of society and its individuals. Here, too, security remains the decisive criterion, but what this security is supposed to achieve is not freedom but the uninterrupted process of life. That process, because it is ruled by necessity, has nothing to do with freedom in its real sense. Here freedom has become a marginal phenomenon, in that it forms the boundary that politics is not permitted to overstep, unless life itself and its immediate interests and necessities are at stake.

Thus not only we, who have often become most distrustful of politics when freedom is closest to our hearts, but the entire modern age have separated freedom from politics. Still, I think you all believed you were hearing nothing more than an old truism when I said at the beginning of these remarks that the "reason why" of politics is freedom. The basis for this is historical as well as factual. To the historical belongs what is really an astounding fact, that in all European languages we use a word for politics in which its origin, the Greek *polis*, can still be heard. Not only etymologically, and not only for scholars, this word is drenched with associations stemming from the community where politics in its specific sense was first discovered. It is thanks to this linguistic usage and its associations that, however far we may have distanced ourselves from the polis, in one crucial respect we have never given up its manner of thinking about politics, namely, in the unanimous opinion of all statesmen and all theoreticians of the Western world, that tyranny is the worst of all forms of state. For this opinion is not self-evident, and there is nothing essential about it, apart from the fact that among the classical forms of government tyranny is the only one that in principle cannot be reconciled with freedom. If we really believed, as the theories of the modern age attempt to convince us, that in politics security and life interests are all that is at stake, we would have no reason to reject tyranny; for it can certainly deliver security, and it has often proved itself superior to all other forms of state in protecting mere life. Thus at least in this negative sense, the original coincidence of freedom and politics, which was self-evident to classical antiquity, but not since then, has survived.

Our most recent experiences with totalitarian dictatorships seem suitable to me for confirming anew these oldest experiences with the political. For they have clearly shown us, if one is serious about the abolition of political freedom, that it is not sufficient to prohibit what we generally understand by political rights; that it is not enough to forbid citizens from being politically active, expressing opinions in public, or forming parties or other associations for the purpose of action. One must also destroy freedom of thought, as far as this is possible, and it is possible to a large extent; one must destroy the freedom of the will; and even the harmless-seeming freedom of artistic production. One must take possession of even those areas we are accustomed to regard as outside the realm of politics, precisely because they, too, contain a political element. Or to put it another way: if one wants to prevent humans from acting in freedom, they must be prevented from thinking, willing, and producing, because all these activities imply action, and thereby freedom in every sense, including the political. Therefore, I also believe we entirely misunderstand totalitarianism if we think of it as the total politicization of life through which freedom is destroyed. The exact opposite is the case; we are dealing with the abandonment of politics, as in all dictatorships and despotic regimes, though only in totalitarianism do the phenomena of this abandonment appear in such a radical form as to destroy the element of political freedom in all activities, rather than resting content with stamping out action, the political faculty *par excellence.*

Even this view of things, alienating as it perhaps may be, is still entirely in accordance with traditional political thought. Montesquieu, for example, believes the sign of a free nation is people making any use at all of their reason (*raisonner*), and that, no matter whether they do this well or badly, the fact that they are thinking is enough to bring about freedom. Therefore it is characteristic of a despotic regime that the principle of domination is put in jeopardy as soon as people begin to reason—even if they then try to mount a theoretical justification of tyranny.* This has nothing to do with truth, or any other by-product of thinking; it is the sheer activity of reasoning itself from which freedom arises. Reasoning creates a space between men in which freedom is real. Now, again according to Montesquieu, the curious thing about this freedom that arises from the activity of reasoning is that it provides protection against the results of Reason (*raisonnement*), for where freedom, or rather the space for freedom between people engendered by reasoning, is destroyed, as is the case in all tyrannical forms of state, the results of reasoning can only be pernicious. Which is to say, where freedom has stopped being a worldly reality, freedom as an individual's subjective capacity can only lead to ruin, as modern dictators understand only too well. They cannot permit freedom of thought—as the events following Stalin's death have shown us—even if they want to.

So there is a wealth of associations that come into play when we hear about freedom and politics; these include the oldest historical memories that have deposited themselves in our language, as well as the tradition of political thought, and the experiences of the present that we consciously keep in mind. Taken all together, they make possible an understanding that goes far beyond contemporary political theory and its conceptual framework. They presuppose a different consciousness of freedom and a different concept of politics to those we are accustomed to, and over which we must now tarry for a while.

II

The relationship between politics and freedom is not a matter of free will or freedom of choice, the *liberum arbitrium* that decides between two given things, one good and one evil as, for example, Richard III's "I am determined to prove a villain." Rather it is, to remain with Shakespeare, the freedom of Brutus: "That this shall be or we will fall for it," that is, the freedom to call something into being which did not exist before, which was not given, not even as an object of cognition or imagination, and which

---

* Montesquieu, *De l'Esprit des lois*, Book XIX, Chapter 27.

therefore could not be known. What guides this action is not a future aim that is conceived by the imagination and can then be seized by the will. The action is guided by something altogether different, which Montesquieu, in his analysis of forms of government, calls a principle.* The principle inspires the action, but it cannot prescribe a particular result, as if it were a matter of carrying out a program; it does not manifest itself in any kind of results, but only in the performance of the act itself. In this performance, willing and acting are concurrent, they are one and the same; willing does not prepare for action, it is already the deed.[†] And the action does not execute an act of will; what is manifest is not a subjective will and its end-in-view, but a guiding principle that remains manifest as long as the action lasts. Such principles are honor, glory, or distinguishing oneself above everyone else—the Greek αἰὲν ἀριστεύειν—but also fear, distrust, or hatred. Freedom, by contrast, is not a predicate of these principles, and it is located neither in the will nor elsewhere in human nature; rather, it coincides with the action: men are free as long as they act, neither before nor after; for to *be* free and to act are the same.

To illustrate to you what I mean by freedom as inherent in action, I would like to remind you that Machiavelli rediscovered this aspect of freedom, which was specific to antiquity, before Montesquieu, and formulated it conceptually.[‡] His *virtù,* which answers to the *fortuna* of the world, is not the Roman *virtus,* nor what we understand by virtue. It is perhaps best translated as "virtuosity," that is, an excellence we attribute to the performing arts, where the accomplishment lies in the performance itself, and not to the creative or "making" arts, where an end product outlasts the activity and becomes independent of it. This virtuosity of Machiavelli's *virtù* has much more in common with the Greek ἀρετή, although Machiavelli barely knew the Greeks. He hardly knew they always used metaphors such as flute playing, dancing, healing, and seafaring to describe what was specific to political action, that is, those arts in which virtuosity of performance is the decisive quality.

---

* Montesquieu, *De l'Esprit des lois,* Book III, Chapter 1: "Il y a cette différence entre la nature du gouvernement et son principe, que sa nature est ce qui le fait être tel, et son principe ce qui le fait agir."
[†] In Arendt's last work, *Willing,* the will is specified as the *spring* of action. —Ed.
[‡] Machiavelli, *Il Principe* (The Prince), Chapters 6 and 7.

Because action demands virtuosity and virtuosity is peculiar to the performing arts, politics in general has often been defined as an art. This is completely false if one falls into the common error of taking the word art to refer to the creative, productive arts, and regards the state or government as a work of art—even as the greatest artwork human hands have ever produced. In the sense of the productive arts bringing forth something tangible that both lasts beyond and completely breaks free from the activity that called it into being, politics is the exact opposite of an art—which incidentally does not mean it is a science. The state is not an artwork for the very reason that its existence never becomes independent of the human actions that brought it into being. Independent existence marks the work of art as a product of making; dependence upon further action to keep it in existence marks the state as a product of action. And the similarity between action and the performing arts goes still further. Just as the virtuosity of music making or dancing or theater is dependent upon an audience to experience the performance, action also requires the presence of others in a politically organized space. Such a space is not to be taken for granted wherever men live together in a community. The Greek polis once was precisely that "form of government" necessary for action.

If we understand the political in the sense of the Greek polis—to which were admitted only people who were neither slaves, subject to coercion by others, nor laborers, driven by the necessity of the biological process of life—it represents the space where this freedom as action, properly understood as virtuosity, can appear. In the public, political realm, freedom is a worldly reality, there it can become real in words, deeds, and events that then can be remembered and incorporated into human history. Whatever occurs in this space of appearances is political by definition, even if it has nothing directly to do with action. What remains outside it, such as the great feats of barbarian empires, may be impressive and noteworthy but, strictly speaking, not political. Without such a space established for it, freedom cannot be realized. There is no actual freedom without politics; it simply could not exist. On the other hand, a community that is not a space for the appearance of the endless variations of the virtuosity in which being free manifests itself, is not political.

These conceptions of freedom and politics and their relation to one another seem so strange to us because we usually understand freedom either as freedom of thought or of the will, and because we ascribe to politics the task of providing the necessities of life, which ensure the security of human existence and the safeguarding of its interests. But in this, too, there is a basic conviction that rings very familiar and self-evident, and which is only forgotten when we start to theorize on these matters. It is the age-old conviction that courage is the cardinal virtue in political behavior. Courage is a big word, and I do not mean the foolhardy type of courage that welcomes danger and gladly risks life for the sake of the intense thrill which danger and the possibility of death evoke. Recklessness is no less concerned with life than is cowardice. Courage, which we still believe to be indispensable for political action, does not gratify our individual sense of vitality but is demanded of us by the very nature of the public realm. For in contrast to our private domain where, in the protection of family and the privacy of our own four walls, everything serves and must serve the security of the life process, there stands the public realm, which is common to all, if only because it existed before us and is meant to outlast us, simply cannot afford to give primary concern to individual lives and the elementary interests associated with them. It requires courage in the political sense to step out into this public realm—not because of particular dangers that may lie in wait for us there, but because we have arrived in a realm where care for life has lost its validity. Courage liberates men from their care for life for the sake of the freedom of the world. Courage is required because in politics the primary care is never for life itself, but always for the world, which will outlast all of us, in one form or another.

Those for whom the word "politics" conjures up the idea of freedom therefore cannot feel that the political is only the sum total of private interests and the balancing out of their conflicts; nor that the state's attitude toward the entire population of its territory is the same as that of a paterfamilias toward the members of his family. In both instances, politics is incompatible with freedom. Freedom can be the meaning of politics only if the political designates a realm that is public and therefore not only distinguished from, but also opposed to the private realm and its interests.

In theory, the conception of the public, statelike realm of a political entity, for example a nation, as one vast family, a gigantic household, is very old; however, it has only gained practical significance since modern society pushed its way between the politico-public and the purely private spheres, and blurred the boundaries between them. It is in this social no-man's-land that all of us now live, and modern political theories, whether liberal, conservative, or socialist, are all in essence about society, the peculiar structures of which (though I cannot go into these now)* essentially privatize matters of public interest, and publicize matters of private concern. Furthest advanced along this path are, of course, the totalitarian dictatorships, which, as we all know, boast that they have abolished the difference between public and private life and the conflict between public and private interests, in favor of an instrumentalism of force and terror, which replaces the interests of the social collective as a whole. But in the Western democracies, too, the boundaries between public and private life have become blurred, though in a different way; here the party politicians boast that they represent the private interests of their electorate in the same way a good lawyer represents his clients; as a result, the public realm, the world surrounding us, is again riddled with individual, private interests. The sciences of this society, the social sciences, are familiar to you all, and, from behaviorism to proletarian Marxism, they all aim at one and the same thing, namely, to prevent the acting man in his freedom from interfering in the movement and course of events. In terms of the problem we are considering, it is immaterial whether the socialization of men happens in the sense of behaviorism, which reduces all actions to the behavior of atomized individuals, or in the much more radical sense of the modern ideologies that reduce all political events and actions to a society's historical process and its own laws. The difference between this widely held ideological thinking and total domination is that the latter has discovered the means by which it can absorb men into the social stream of history in such a way that they no longer have any desire to interfere with its automatic flow, but on the contrary, add their own momentum to accelerate it further. The means by which this is achieved are the compulsion imposed by a regime of terror from without, and the compulsion of an ideological way of thinking

* Arendt considers this matter in depth in *The Human Condition* (Chicago, 1958), chapter 6, "The Rise of the Social" and passim. —Ed.

imposed from within. There is no doubt that this totalitarian development is the crucial step toward both the abandonment of politics by men, and the abolishment of freedom; though theoretically speaking, freedom starts to disappear wherever the concepts of society and history have ousted the concept of politics.

III

We have seen that the assertion: "The meaning of politics is freedom" presupposes that the political is concerned with the world as such and not with life, and that freedom begins where concern for life ceases to compel men to behave in a specific manner. And we have seen that this notion of an interdependence of freedom and politics stands in contradiction to the social theories of the modern age. This state of affairs seems like an invitation to try and go back beyond the modern age and its theories and to put our faith in older traditions. But the real difficulty in reaching an understanding of what freedom is arises from the fact that a simple return to tradition does not help us. For my assertion that freedom is, in essence, a political phenomenon, that it is not experienced primarily in will and thought, but in action, and that therefore it requires a sphere appropriate to such action, a political sphere, is in direct contradiction to some very ancient and highly respected concepts. Neither the philosophical concept of freedom as it first arose in late antiquity, where freedom became a phenomenon of thought, nor the Christian and modern notion of free will, are political in nature; indeed, both contain a strongly antipolitical element, which is by no means a foible of philosophers or *homines religiosi*, but is based upon human experience of the highest authenticity in politics itself. We must content ourselves here with recalling that, in answer to our query regarding the relation between politics and freedom, tradition is all but unanimous in saying that freedom begins when a man withdraws from communal life, from the political sphere, and that he experiences freedom not in association with others but in intercourse with himself—whether in the form of an inner dialogue which, since the time of Socrates, we have called thinking, or as a conflict within himself, in the struggle between the I-will and I-can, as Christianity after Paul and Augustine thought to discern the inadequacy and questionable value of human freedom.

As regards the problem of freedom, it is natural for us to examine it and seek our answers within the framework of the Christian tradition. That we must do so is indicated by the simple fact that for the most part, and quite automatically, we think of freedom as free will, that is, as the predicate of a faculty virtually unknown to classical antiquity. For will, as Christianity discovered it, had so little in common with the simple desire to possess some eagerly longed-for object that it could even come into conflict with such impulse. If freedom were actually nothing but a phenomenon of the will, we would have to conclude that it was unknown to the ancients. Such a conclusion, of course, is absurd, but if someone wished to assert it he could argue that the idea of freedom played no role in the works of the great philosophers prior to Augustine. The reason for this striking fact is that in the ancient world freedom was regarded exclusively and radically as a political concept, indeed as the quintessence of the city-state and of citizenship, the βίος πολιτιχός, the political way of life. But our own philosophical tradition, beginning with Parmenides and Plato, was founded in opposition to the polis and the political realm. That ancient philosophy should not have taken up the subject of freedom, which is the most political of all ancient concepts, is entirely understandable. It could not have been otherwise before Christianity discovered in free will a nonpolitical freedom, which could be experienced in intercourse with oneself, and was therefore not dependent upon intercourse with the many.

In view of the extraordinary potential power inherent in the will, we tend to forget that it originally did not manifest itself as I-will-and-I-can, but on the contrary, as a conflict between the two; and it was this conflict that was unknown to antiquity. The conception of the I-will-and-I-can was of course very familiar to the ancients. I need only remind you how Plato insisted that only those who knew how to rule and obey themselves had the right to rule others, and to be free from any obligation to obey them. This self-control, or alternatively, the conviction that self-control alone justifies the exercise of authority, has remained the hallmark of the aristocratic outlook to this very day. And in fact it is a typically political virtue, a phenomenon of virtuosity where the I-will and the I-can must be so well attuned that they practically coincide. But when we separate the I-will and the I-can, we are speaking in contradictory terms from the viewpoint of the Christian conception of free will. Had ancient philosophy known of this separation, it would certainly have understood freedom as an inherent quality of the I-can, rather than the I-will. Wherever the I-can foundered, be it as the result of extraneous circumstance or of individual circumstance, there would have been no talk of freedom.

I chose the example of self-control because to us this is clearly a phenomenon which can be explained only in terms of the will. The Greeks, as you know, gave much thought to the question of moderation and the necessity of steering and taming the steeds of the soul; yet among all those phenomena, which to us are manifestations of the will's strength, the Greeks never discovered the will as a distinct faculty, separate from other human faculties, something, indeed, of a specific and exceptional quality in man. It is a historical fact, which is well worth pondering, that men became explicitly aware of the existence of the will when they experienced its impotence and not its power, and began to say with St. Paul: "For to will is present with me; but how to perform that which is good I find not."* For us, the essential point is that this was not a case of the impotence of man's will in the world. The will was not defeated by some overwhelming force of nature or circumstance, or the conflict of one against many; it was solely the impotence of the will in the individual man. All willing springs from the original conflict in man between his will and the ability to do what he wills; this means, literally, that the I-will strikes back at the self, spurs it on, incites it to action or is ruined by it. This bondage of the will to the self persists, even if a man sets out to conquer the whole world; moreover, and as a matter of principle, it divides the I-will from the I-think—which also implies a self-reflective quality, though in this instance the self is not also the object of the dialogue. Perhaps it is because the will's impotence first made us aware of its existence that it has now become so unusually power-hungry that the will and the will-to-power have become practically synonymous to our ears. Tyranny at any rate, the only form of government that arises from the singularity of the I-will and its absolute egoism, is incomparably more

* Romans 7:18.

greedy and cruel than the utopian governments of reason, with which the philosophers wished to coerce men and which they conceived on the model of the I-think.

I have said that the philosophers first began to show an interest in freedom when freedom was no longer experienced in acting and in associating with others but in willing as intercourse with one's self. The fact that freedom was thus transformed from a primarily political fact into a philosophical problem of the first order naturally did not prevent this new philosophical problematic from subsequently being applied to the political realm. But now that the emphasis had shifted so decisively from action to willpower, the ideal of freedom ceased to be the virtuosity of acting in concert with others and became sovereignty, the independence from others and the ability, if necessary, to prevail against them. Politically, perhaps no other element of the traditional philosophical concept of freedom has proved as pernicious as this equation of freedom with sovereignty that is inherent in it. For this leads either to a denial of freedom—when it is realized that whatever men may be, they are not sovereign—or to the insight, which may seem to contradict this denial but does not, that the freedom of one man or a group can only be purchased at the price of the freedom of others. What is so extraordinarily difficult to understand within this problematic relation is a simple fact, namely, that freedom is only given to men under the condition of nonsovereignty. Moreover, it is as unrealistic to deny freedom because of human nonsovereignty as it is dangerous to believe that one alone—as an individual or an organized group—can be free only if that one is sovereign. Even the sovereignty of a political body is always an illusion which, moreover, can be maintained only by means of violence.

Admittedly, in order properly to understand how unreal and pernicious this identification of freedom and sovereignty is, one must liberate oneself from an old prejudice that goes as far back as the Roman *stoa*. This prejudice is the view that nonsovereignty is the same as dependence, which would mean that the nonsovereignty of human existence would be simply the fact that humans need each other to remain alive. The dependence of human beings upon one another in all questions of mere life is evident; it is sealed in the fact of birth, insofar as humans, as the Greeks say, are born ἐξ ἀλλήλων, out of each other. But *this* dependent quality of human life applies only to the individual; it need not apply to a group that has absolute power over others, or else is powerful and moderate enough to isolate itself from all others. But far more decisive than this dependence of an individual is that man in the singular cannot be imagined, that men's existence as a whole depends upon there always being others of their kind. Were there only *one* man, as we say there is only *one* God, then the concept of humanity as we know it would not exist; if there was only *one* nation on earth, or only *one* people, then of course no man would know what a nation or a people is. Being among one's own kind ends only with death, as the Latin implies so well, equating *inter homines esse* (to be among men) with "life" and *desinere inter homines esse* (to cease to be among men) with "death." Only in death, or in the face of death, can human existence become entirely singular.

Like the sovereignty of the individual, the sovereignty of a group or a political body is, as has been noted, also an illusion, for it can come about only if a great many people behave as if they were *one,* and indeed the *only* one. Such behavior is certainly possible, as we know only too well from the many phenomena of mass society, which also demonstrate that there is no freedom in such society. Where everyone does the same, nobody acts in freedom, even when nobody is directly coerced or compelled. In human relationships, then, which are governed by the fact that there are only *men,* and not *man,* only many peoples, and not a single people, freedom and sovereignty are so little identical that they cannot even exist simultaneously. Where men, whether as individuals or in organized groups, wish to be sovereign, they must abolish freedom. But if they wish to be free, it is precisely sovereignty they must renounce.

To illustrate how difficult it is within the conceptual structure of our philosophical tradition to formulate a concept of freedom that conforms with political experience, I want to look at two modern thinkers who, in terms of both political philosophy and theory, are perhaps the greatest and most profound—namely, Montesquieu and Kant.

Montesquieu is so aware of the inadequacies of the philosophical tradition in these matters that he expressly distinguishes between philosophical and political freedom. The difference is that philosophy demands no more of freedom than the exercise of the will (*l'exercice de la volonté*), independent of circumstances in the world and of attainment of the goals the will sets for itself. Political freedom, by contrast, is the security (*la liberté politique consiste dans la sûreté*) that does not exist always and everywhere, but only in political communities governed by laws. Without security there is no political freedom, for freedom means "being able to do what one ought to will" (*la liberté ne peut consister qu'à pouvoir faire ce que l'on doit vouloir*). As obvious as these sentences make Montesquieu's propensity to juxtapose the philosophical freedom of a willing self with *being* free politically, a worldly, tangible reality, his dependency on the philosophical tradition of free will is no less evident. For Montesquieu's definitions sound as if political freedom is nothing but an extension of philosophical freedom, namely, the freedom that is indispensable for the realization of the freedom of an I-will. If we want to understand Montesquieu's real intentions, however, we must take the trouble to read his sentences so that the emphasis does not fall on the I-*can*—the notion that one must be able to do what one wants or should want—but on the deed. It should be added that actions and deeds are viewed here as considerably more significant than the quasi-automatic fulfillment of the will. Freedom itself is enacted in action, and the security that guarantees the ability to perform them is provided by others. This freedom does not reside in an I-will, which the I-can may either comply with or contradict without bringing man's philosophical freedom into question; political freedom begins only in action, so that not-being-able-to-act and not-being-free amount to one and the same thing, even if philosophy's free will continues to exist intact. In other words, political freedom is not "inner freedom"; it cannot hide inside a person. It is dependent on a free people to grant it the space in which actions can appear, be seen, and be effective. The power of the self-assertion of the will to compel others has nothing whatever to do with this political freedom.

In Kant, the only one among the great philosophers for whom the question "What should I do?" held the same dignity as the specifically philosophical questions: "What can I know? What may I hope?" The strength of the antipolitical tradition in philosophy does not show itself in insufficient formulations as it does in Montesquieu, but in the remarkable fact that in Kant there are two very different political philosophies: the one that is generally accepted as such in the *Critique of Practical Reason,* and the other in the *Critique of Judgment*. The literature on Kant rarely mentions that the first part of the *Critique of Judgment* is actually a philosophy of politics; I believe one can, however, demonstrate that in all his political writings the theme of judgment carried more weight for Kant than did that of practical reason. Freedom appears in the *Critique of Judgment* as a predicate of the imagination, not of the will, and the imagination is most intimately related to that "enlarged mentality," which is the political way of thinking *par excellence,* because through it we have the possibility "to think in the position of everyone else."* Only in this context does it become philosophically clear why Kant was able to say emphatically: "The external force that wrenches away people's public freedom to communicate their thoughts also takes from them their freedom to think."† Here, being unfree retaliates against the "inner" ability to be free and destroys it. Even freedom of thought, as Kant puts it, the inner "conversation with oneself" depends, if it is to issue in thoughts, on the presence of others and thus on the opportunity to "advance our thoughts in public to see whether they agree with the understanding of others."‡

But this concept of freedom as entirely independent of free will has played hardly any role in the reception of Kant's philosophy. And even in Kant's philosophy itself it is overshadowed by that of "practical reason" which ascribes to the will, for good or evil, all power in human affairs, while action itself, as you will remember, no longer falls within the sphere of human power and freedom, but is subordinate to necessity and subject to the law of causality. To be free only as long as one can will, means only as long as the I-will is not opposed by an inner I-can*not,* which in turn means that one becomes unfree as soon as one begins to act. Kant had hardly any doubt about these two fundamental propositions in the narrower sense of his practical-political philosophy.

---

* Kant, *Critique of the Power of Judgment,* ed. Paul Guyer; trans. Paul Guyer and Eric Matthews, Cambridge, 2000, p. 174 (5:294).

† See Kant, "What Does It Mean to Orient Oneself in Thinking?," trans. Allen Wood, in: *Religion and Rational Theology* (The Cambridge Edition of the Works of Immanuel Kant), Cambridge, 1996, p. 16.

‡ Kant, *Anthropology from a Pragmatic Point of View,* Cambridge, 2006, p. 114.

IV

We find it difficult to understand that there may exist a freedom that is not an attribute of the will but of doing and acting. For us, the whole problem of freedom is overshadowed by Christianity and an originally antipolitical philosophic tradition. In order now to define more precisely this freedom that is experienced in the process of acting and nothing else, let us go back once more to antiquity—not for the sake of erudition, or even the continuity of our tradition, but merely in order to grasp the experiences that, although we are all somehow familiar with them, have never again been articulated with the same classical clarity.

The first thing that must strike us is that both Greek and Latin have two words for the verb "to act," which denote two very different processes. The two Greek words are ἄρχειν (to begin, to lead, and to rule) and πράττειν (to carry something through). The corresponding Latin verbs are *agere:* to set something in motion, and *gerere* which is hard to translate and somehow means the enduring and supporting continuation of past acts that result in the *res gestae,* the deeds and events we call historical. In both instances, the first stage of action is a beginning, by which something new comes into the world. The fact that freedom was originally experienced in this ability to make a new beginning, in what since Kant we have come to call spontaneity, can be seen in the range of meanings of the Greek word, where, as I mentioned, beginning is conjoined with leading and finally ruling, the outstanding qualities of the free man. This manifold meaning of ἄρχειν indicates that beginning something new could only fall to someone who was already a ruler, and in Greece this meant a man who presided over a household of slaves, liberating him from the necessities of life, and who was thus free to live in the polis among his peers; but beginning itself coincides with leading others, for only with the help of others could the beginner carry through (πράττειν) whatever he had started to do.

In Latin, to be free and to begin are also interconnected, though in a different way. Roman freedom was a legacy bequeathed by the founders of Rome to the Roman people; their freedom was tied to the beginning their forefathers established by founding the city, and with it Roman history. The descendants had to conduct their forefathers' affairs, bear their consequences (*gerere*), and by the same token augment Rome's foundations (*res gestae*). Roman historiography therefore, though essentially as political as Greek historiography, never was content with commending to the memory of the citizens certain great events and stories, as Thucydides and Herodotus had done; Roman historians were always bound to the beginning of Roman history, because this beginning contained the authentic element that made their history political. Whatever the Romans had to relate, they started *ab urbe condita,* with the foundation of the city, the ultimate guarantee of Roman freedom.

To go one step further, we can say that the intrinsic meaning of the political in antiquity is intimately linked with this ability to begin. There is a good reason why the ancients found it literally impossible to think of the political without the city. Only the founding of a city could provide a beginning and set something in motion, could give rise to the ἄρχειν and *agere*. The city gave the beginning a reliable chance, because the help of others, which is indispensable for carrying something through, the πράττειν and *gerere*, is always on hand in a regulated community of citizens. Thus the citizens of a polis are in a position to do more than people who have become masters of the necessities of life, and can act from time to time: citizens can always be free. It is in the nature of the city-state's development that over time, performance and continuation take on a greater significance for political life than initiation itself, and the consequence of this is that in both Greek and Latin there eventually came to be only *one* verb for acting, namely πράττειν and *gerere*, while ἄρχειν and *agere*, which did not vanish from the languages, no longer retained their full political meaning. Nevertheless, Aristotle, who in his political philosophy otherwise exclusively uses the word πράττειν to designate the whole sphere of human affairs and activities, says that the polis is made up of ἄρχοντες, and not of πράττοντες. The former carries the meaning of both ruling, namely the ruling of slaves, which makes freedom possible, and the positive freedom of beginning.

I have already mentioned that the ancient concept of freedom, precisely because it was exclusively political, played no role in the philosophy of the Socratic school. Roman writers, it is true, rebelled occasionally against the antipolitical tendencies of the Greek philosophic schools, but they did not go further or decisively change either the themes or the way of thinking in the doctrines handed down to them. And of course they never hit upon a theoretical, philosophical formula for the freedom they had experienced in the political realm. We have even less hope of finding a valid political idea of freedom in Christian philosophy, and maybe least of all in the great Christian thinker Augustine, who made the new "inner" freedom of the will, which may have been first experienced by Paul, into one of the cornerstones of traditional Western philosophy. Yet in Augustine we find not only the *liberum arbitrium* that has, as the free choice of the will, become definitive for the tradition, but also a notion of freedom conceived in an entirely different manner, which characteristically appears in his only political treatise, *De Civitate Dei*. In *The City of God*, Augustine, as is only natural, speaks more from his background of specifically Roman experiences than in any other of his writings. Freedom is conceived here not as an inner human disposition, but as a term that characterizes human existence in the world, and he founds this freedom in the fact that man is himself a beginning in the world, an *initium*, insofar as he has not existed as long as the world itself, was not created simultaneously with it, but as a new beginning after the world had come into existence. In the birth of each man this initial beginning is reaffirmed, because in each instance something new comes into an already existing world, which will continue to exist after each individual's death. Because he *is* a beginning, says Augustine, man can begin, and thus be free; God created man so that there was such a thing as a beginning in the world: "[*Initium*] *ut esset, creatus est homo, ante quem nullus fuit.*"*

The strong antipolitical tendencies of early Christianity are so familiar that the notion of a Christian thinker developing the philosophical implications of the ancient political idea of freedom strikes us as almost paradoxical. Yet this second Augustinian concept of freedom had no effect on the tradition of either Christian or modern philosophy, and we begin to find traces of it again only in Kant's writings. Like Augustine, Kant recognizes two concepts of freedom, conceived completely independently of each

---

* St. Augustine, *De Civitate Dei* (The City of God), Book XII, Chapters 20–21.

other:* practical freedom, which he defines as "the independence of the power of choice from necessitation by impulses of sensibility," which therefore is still a negative freedom; and that "spontaneity" which, in his philosophy, is especially fundamental to thinking and cognition, and which he defines as the ability to "begin a series of occurrences entirely from itself." We can see how closely related this Kantian spontaneity is to Augustine's beginning from the fact that he also calls it "freedom in the cosmological sense." If freedom were primarily or exclusively a phenomenon of the will, it would hardly be possible to understand why cognition does not occur apart from the spontaneity of mental concepts, nor why Kant speaks so emphatically about the "spontaneity of thinking."

Be that as it may, the fact that we find a philosophical foundation for politically experienced freedom for the first time in the works of a Roman Christian thinker will seem strange only if we orient our idea of Christianity according to the antipolitical bent of ancient Christian thought, in particular the doctrine of the will in the epistles of St. Paul. Yet I am convinced that this impression would change considerably if we were to look more intently at Jesus of Nazareth—the man and his teachings. Here we find a quite extraordinary understanding of freedom and of the power inherent in human freedom; but the human capacity that corresponds to this power and, in the words of the Gospel, is capable of moving mountains, is not will but faith. The work of faith is the "miracle," a word with many meanings in the New Testament and difficult to understand. We can overlook the difficulties here, however, by referring only to those passages where miracles are not exclusively supernatural events, even though all miracles interrupt some natural series of events or automatic processes, in whose context they constitute the entirely unexpected.

I would like to suggest that, if it is true that action and beginning are essentially the same, it follows that a capacity for performing miracles must likewise be within the range of human faculties. And in order to make this theory a little more palatable, I would like to remind you of the nature of every new beginning: seen from the viewpoint of what has gone before, it

---

* On the following passages, see Kant, *Critique of Pure Reason*, trans. Paul Guyer and Allen W. Wood, Cambridge, 1998, B 561–B 563 (pp. 533–34).

breaks into the world unexpected and unforeseen. Fundamentally, every event seems to us like a miracle, and it may well be a prejudice to consider miracles as supernatural only in religious contexts. And in order to explain this in turn, I may perhaps remind you that the whole frame of our real existence—the earth, the organic life on it, the evolution of mankind out of animal species—rests on a chain of miracles. From the viewpoint of processes in the universe and their statistically overwhelming probabilities, the formation of the earth is an "infinite improbability," as the natural scientists would say—or a miracle, as we might call it. The same is true for the formation of organic life out of inorganic processes, or the evolution of man out of the processes of organic life. In other words, every new beginning becomes a miracle the moment we look at it from the viewpoint of the processes it has interrupted. The crucial thing to remember is that this viewpoint is not special or especially sophisticated; it is, on the contrary, most natural and indeed, in ordinary life, almost commonplace.

I chose this example to illustrate that what we call real is always a mesh of earthly-organic-human reality, which came into being *qua* reality through the advent of infinite improbabilities. Of course the example has its limitations and cannot be applied to the realm of human affairs ingenuously. For in the political realm historical processes confront us—one event follows another—rather than natural developments with their attendant accidents. The result of this is that the miracle of accident and infinite improbability occurs so frequently in human affairs that it seems strange to speak of miracles at all. However, the reason for this frequency is merely that historical processes are created and constantly interrupted by human initiative. If one considers historical processes only as processes, then every new beginning within them, for better and worse, becomes so infinitely unlikely that all large events appear as miracles. Objectively, seen from the outside, the chances that tomorrow will proceed exactly as today are always overwhelming—not quite so overwhelming, but in human proportions nearly as great as the chances that *no* earth would ever rise out of cosmic events, that *no* life would develop out of inorganic processes, and that *no* man would appear out of the evolution of animal life.

The decisive difference between the "infinite improbabilities" on which life on earth and the reality of nature rest, and the miraculous events within human affairs, is that in the latter case there is a miracle worker, which is to say that humans appear to have a highly mysterious gift for making miracles happen. This gift is called action. And insofar as action and beginning are the same, there is an element of action in every human activity that is more than a mere reaction. The simple act of production adds a new object to the world, and pure thought always begins a sequence quite by itself.

V

Finally, let us try to find our way back from these philosophical foundations of a politically experienced conception of freedom, which may help orient ourselves briefly in the field of our present political experiences. We can say that the extraordinary danger of totalitarianism for the future of mankind exists less in the fact that it is tyrannical and does not tolerate political freedom, than that it threatens to kill off all forms of spontaneity, that is, the element of action and freedom in all human activities. It is of the essence of this most horrific form of tyranny that it strives to eliminate the possibility of "miracles" or, to put it more familiarly, to exclude the possibility of events in politics, and thereby deliver us up entirely to the automatic processes that surround us anyhow—in earthly nature as in the universe that surrounds the earth—and by which we ourselves are driven insofar as we are also organic nature. It would be sheer superstition, a negative belief in miracles, to hope for the "infinitely improbable" in the context of these automatic processes, although even this never can be ruled out completely. But it is not in the least superstitious, it is even a counsel of realism, to look for the unforeseeable, to be prepared for and expect "miracles" in the political realm, where in fact they are always possible. For human freedom is not merely a matter of metaphysics; it is a matter of fact, as are the automatic processes within and against which it always asserts itself. On the other hand, the processes set in motion by action also tend to become automatic, which means that no single act and no single event can ever redeem or bring salvation to mankind, or a people, once and for all.

It is in the nature of these automatic processes, to which man is subject and, except for the miracle of freedom would be subjected absolutely, that they can only spell ruin for human life. They are as ruinous as the biological processes that pervade man's entire being and which, biologically, can only lead from birth to death. Only the world and men in the plural can anticipate salvation through the miracle that is possible in all political affairs—at least as long as freedom, the human gift of interrupting ruin, remains intact. No miracle is required to save life as such since by nature it endures with the species, nor can a miracle ever save man in the singular, who must always die as an individual. These ruinous processes can be interrupted only for the world that is common to us all, which outlasts our life or at least can outlast it, and which is the specific concern of politics. From this it follows that, although the ability to begin may be a gift of man in his singularity, he can only realize it in relation to the world and in acting together with his fellow men.

In contrast to thinking and producing, one can only *act* with the help of others and in the world. "[To] act in concert," as Burke puts it,* realizes the ability to begin as *being* free. The difference between acting on the one hand, and producing and thinking on the other, is that in producing and thinking only the beginning is free; the completion, if it is successful, never realizes more than the thought already grasped at the beginning, or the thing conceived beforehand by the power of the imagination, both of which are subject to the processes of production or thought. By contrast, however little an action may achieve, the performance of it remains directed toward the constantly renewed actualization of freedom, with new beginnings constantly flowing into what has once been begun. For the result of action is not an object, which, once it has been conceived, can be produced. The result of action rather has the character of a story, which continues for as long as people continue to act, but the end and the result of which nobody, not even the person who began the story, can foresee or conceive. In the case of action, the beginning and performance are therefore not so separate

---

* Edmund Burke, in his "Thoughts on the Cause of the Present Discontents" (1770), writes: "They believed that no man could act with effect, who did not act in concert; that no man could act in concert, who did not act with confidence; that no men could act with confidence, who were not bound together by common opinions, common affections and common interests." Quoted from the extract in Edmund Burke, *On Government, Politics and Society*, selected and edited by B. W. Hill, New York, 1976, pp. 75–119, here p. 113.

that the person who begins to act knows everything in advance, while those who help him complete the action need only realize his knowledge, follow his orders, and execute his decisions. In action, beginning and performance merge into each other, and, when applied to politics, this means that the person who takes the initiative and thus starts to lead must always move among those who join in to help him as his peers, and neither as a leader among his servants nor as a master among his apprentices or disciples. This is what Herodotus meant when he said that to be free was neither to rule nor to be ruled, and that therefore men could only be free in *ἰσονομία*, as democracy was originally called, in being among one's equals.*

In the state of *being* free, where the gift of freedom, the ability to begin, becomes a tangible worldly reality, the actual space of the political comes into being along with the stories that action generates. This space is always and everywhere that men live together in freedom, without domination or subjugation. But, even if the institutional-organizational framework surrounding it remains intact, this space vanishes immediately if action ceases, and security measures and maintaining the status quo take its place, or if there is a slackening of the initiative to project new beginnings into the processes that action first set in motion. Then the processes that freedom first brought forth also become automatic, and an automatic process produced by men is no less ruinous for the world than automatic natural processes are for the life of the individual. In such cases, historians speak of petrified or declining civilizations, and we know that the processes of decline can go on for centuries. Quantitatively, they occupy by far the largest space in recorded history.

In the history of mankind, the periods of freedom have always been relatively short. By contrast, even in the long epochs of petrification and decline, the sheer ability to begin, the element of freedom inherent in all human activities, can remain intact, and so it is not at all surprising that we tend to define freedom as something that can be realized outside of politics, as freedom *from* politics. Yet this self-understanding is a misunderstanding, which stems from and corresponds to a situation in which everything specifically political has become stagnant or fallen into a presumably inescap-

* Herodotus, Book III, Chapters 80–82.

able automatism. Under such circumstances, freedom is indeed no longer experienced as a positive activity with its own specific "virtuosity." *Being* free then has receded to the gift that only man, among all earthly creatures, seems to have received. Though we find its intimation in nonpolitical activities, that gift can develop fully only where action creates its own worldly space in which freedom can appear.

European man has always known that freedom as a mode of being and a worldly reality can be destroyed, and that only seldom in history has it unfolded its full virtuosity. Now that we are acquainted with totalitarianism we must also suspect that not only *being* free but also the sheer gift of freedom, which was not produced by man but given to him, may be destroyed, too. This knowledge or suspicion weighs more heavily upon us now than ever before, for today, more depends on human freedom than before—on man's ability to tip scales heavily weighted toward disaster, which always happens automatically and therefore always appears irresistible. This time, no less than the continued existence of men on earth may depend upon man's gift of performing "miracles," that is, bringing about the infinitely improbable and establishing it as a worldly reality.

1960

THE COLD WAR AND THE WEST

Wars and revolutions have thus far determined the physiognomy of the twentieth century; and in contrast to the ideologies in the last twenty years, which have more and more degenerated into empty talk, war and revolution still constitute the two major political issues that confront us. In actual fact, the two are interrelated in many ways, and yet for clarification of these matters they must be kept apart. Historically, wars are among the oldest phenomena of recorded history while revolutions in the modern sense of the word probably did not exist prior to the end of the eighteenth century; they are the most recent of all political data. Moreover, revolutions are very likely to stay with us into the foreseeable future whereas wars, if they should continue to threaten the existence of mankind and hence remain unjustifiable on rational grounds, might disappear, at least in their present form, even without a concomitant radical transformation of international relations. Hence—in anticipation of what I have to say—short of total annihilation and short of a decisive technical development in warfare, the present conflict between the two parts of the world may well be decided by the simple question of which side understands better what is involved and what is at stake in revolution.

In the following I would like to take up, almost at random, a few considerations which all seem to point in the same direction.

1. Obviously, Clausewitz's definition of war as the continuation of politics with other means, however appropriate it might have been for the limited warfare of European nation-states in the eighteenth and nineteenth centuries, no longer applies to our situation. This would be true even without nuclear warfare. Since the First World War, we know that no government and no form of government can be expected to survive a defeat in war. A revolutionary change in government—either brought about by the people

themselves, as after World War I, or enforced by the victorious powers through the demand of unconditional surrender and the establishment of War Trials—belongs among the most certain consequences of defeat even if we rule out total annihilation or complete chaos. Hence, even prior to nuclear warfare, wars had become politically, though not yet biologically, a matter of life and death.

At the moment when we are so preoccupied with the threat of total annihilation this may appear irrelevant. But it's not at all inconceivable that the next stage of technical advancement may bring us back to a kind of warfare which, though probably still horrible enough, will not be suicidal and, perhaps, not even spell complete annihilation to the defeated. Such a development seems to be within the range of definite possibilities for the simple reason that our present stage of international relationships, still based upon national sovereignty, cannot function without force or the threat of force as the *ultima ratio* of all foreign policy. Whether we like it or not, our present system of foreign affairs makes no sense without war as a last resort; and put before the alternative of either changing this system radically or making some technical discoveries which would bring war back into the political arena, the latter course may well turn out to be much easier and more feasible.

Politically, the point of the matter is that even under changed technical circumstances it is not likely that governments, no matter how well established and trusted by their citizens, could survive defeat in war, and such survival must be counted as one of the supreme tests of a government's strength and authority. In other words, under conditions of modern warfare, even in its pre-nuclear stage, all governments have lived on borrowed time. Hence the war question—in its most extreme form a question of biological survival—is under any circumstances a question of political survival. Only if we succeed in ruling out war from politics altogether can we hope to achieve that minimum of stability and permanence of the body politic without which neither political life nor political change is possible.

2. Confusion and inadequacy in the discussion of the war question are not surprising. The truth is that a rational debate is impossible as long as we find ourselves caught in a technical stage of development where the means of warfare are such as to exclude their rational use. To try and decide

between "better dead than red" and "better red than dead" resembles nothing so much as trying to square the circle. For those who tell us better dead than red forget that it is a very different matter to risk one's life for the life and freedom of one's country and for posterity than to risk the very existence of the human species. Moreover, the very formula goes back to antiquity and rests upon the ancient conviction that slaves are not human, that to lose one's freedom means to change one's nature and to become, as it were, dehumanized.* None of us, I think, can say that he believes this, least of all those liberals who today try to avail themselves of the old formula. But this is not to say that its reversal has anything better to recommend. When an old truth ceases to be applicable, it does not become any truer by being stood on its head. Within the framework of realities which we face, the slogan "better red than dead" can mean only signing one's own death sentence even before the sentence has been passed.

Insofar as the discussion of the war question moves within the closed circle of these preposterous alternatives, it is nearly always conducted with a mental reservation on both sides. Those who say "better dead than red" actually think: "The losses may not be as great as some anticipate, our civilization will survive"; while those who say "better red than dead" actually think: "Slavery will not be so bad, man will not change his nature, freedom will not vanish from the earth forever." What should alarm us in these discussions is the reckless optimism on both sides—on one side, the readiness to count the losses in the tens and hundreds of millions, due in part, perhaps, to a simple failure of imagination, but also in part to the frightful and frightening increase of population; and on the other side, the readiness to forget the concentration and extermination camps and with them the terrible prospect of freedom vanishing from the earth forever.

The only consoling aspect of this debate seems to be that all concerned by now agree, not only that war as such stands in need of justification, but that its only possible justification is freedom. This is not a matter of course for a number of reasons. First, freedom is implicitly recognized as the very center, the *raison d'être*, of politics by people who fifteen to twenty years ago would have thought this the utmost of political naïveté, if not a

---

* Arendt refers to the ancient practice of enslaving the defeated. —Ed.

prejudice of the lower middle classes. More importantly, perhaps, justifications of war are at least as old as Roman antiquity, but, contrary to what we are inclined to think, it was not freedom but necessity upon which these justifications usually were based. "Just is a war which is necessary, and hallowed are the arms where no hope exists but in them," said Livy; and by necessity he and his successors throughout the centuries understood all the well-known realities of power politics—such as conquest and expansion, defense of vested interests and preservation of power, or conservation of a power equilibrium, etc.—which we today would find quite sufficient to dub a war not just but unjust, although we know, of course, that they were the causes of the outbreak of most wars in history. Even our present-day notion that aggression is a crime has acquired its practical and theoretical significance only after the First World War demonstrated the horribly destructive potentialities of warfare under conditions of modern technology.

3. Since the alliance which achieved victory in the Second World War was not strong enough to achieve peace as well, the whole postwar period has been spent by the two major powers in defining their spheres of interest and in jockeying for position in the rapidly changing power structure of a world in turmoil. This period has been called a "cold war," and the term is accurate enough if we recall that fear of a major war has determined the actual conduct of foreign affairs and preoccupied public opinion more than any other issue. But in actual fact and despite occasional flare-ups, this whole period was much rather a time of cold and uneasy *peace,* and the reason I insist on this is not that I am interested in semantics, but that I feel we should not cry wolf too soon.

In other words, what I am afraid of is that a cold war as a real substitute for a hot war may break out one day because it might constitute the only alternative in our present circumstances, in which we must avoid the threat of total annihilation without knowing how to exclude war as such from the realm of foreign politics. The recent and, let us hope, temporary resumption of nuclear tests has shown how a cold war actually might be conducted. For these tests, unlike those that preceded them, were no longer conducted for the mere sake of the perfection of certain armaments. The tests themselves were meant as an instrument of policy, and they were immediately understood as such. They gave the rather ominous impression of some sort of tentative warfare in which the two opposing camps demonstrate to each other the destructiveness of the weapons in their possession. And while it is always possible that this deadly game of ifs and whens may suddenly turn into the real thing, it is not inconceivable that one day a hypothetical victory and a hypothetical defeat could end a war that never exploded into reality.

Is this sheer fantasy? I think not. We were confronted, potentially at least, with this sort of thing at the end of the Second World War, at the very moment when the atomic bomb made its first appearance. At that time, it was considered whether a demonstration of the potency of the new weapon on a deserted island might not have been enough to force the Japanese into unconditional surrender. The advantages of this alternative have been argued many times on moral grounds, and I think rightly so. The decisive political argument in its favor was that it would have been much more in line with our actual and professed war aims; surely, what we wished to achieve was unconditional surrender, not extermination or wholesale slaughter of the civilian population.

Hypothetical warfare, it must be admitted, rests on at least two assumptions, both of which are actualities in the relationships between those fully developed powers which could enter into a nuclear war at all. It presupposes, first, a stage of technical development where risks can be calculated with almost perfect precision so that very little room is left to chance. Secondly, it presupposes an equality of knowledge and know-how among those who are at war. Thus, a chess game between two equally experienced players will end with one of them conceding defeat or with both agreeing on a stalemate long before all the moves leading to it have been made. The comparison of war with chess is old and has never been true, because the outcome of war depends to a high degree on chance and on personal factors—such as troop morale and military strategy. Technical warfare has eliminated these factors to such an extent that the old simile may unexpectedly acquire its measure of truth. Or, to put this another way, mutual recognition of the results of a cold war, which actually is a war, would not imply a change in human nature; the demonstration of the A-bomb would have *forced* the enemy into unconditional surrender, it would not have *persuaded* him. For the experts, the result of the tests could be as conclusive and as compelling evidence of victory and defeat as the battlefield, the conquest of territory, and the calculation of losses have been for the generals on either side in hot wars.

4. The trouble with these questions* is the same as with other discussions of the war question: they are idle, there is little we can do about the whole business one way or another. Even clarifications and attempts at understanding, though always tempting and, perhaps, necessary for the sake of human dignity, can hardly have any practical or even theoretical results. It is precisely a sense of futility which seems to haunt us whenever we approach this matter.

The same is not at all true for the other great issue confronting us, the issue of revolution. This issue can be clarified in the light of past and present experience, and such clarification is not likely to be futile. Its first prerequisite is to recognize and to understand what seems to be so obvious that no one is willing to talk about it, namely, that the inherent aim of revolution has always been freedom and nothing else. The chief obstacles to such an understanding are of course the various ideologies—capitalism, socialism, communism—all of which owe their existence to the nineteenth century and to social and economic conditions which were utterly unlike our own. We are in no position today to foretell what kind of economic system may eventually prove to be best under the rapidly changing technical and scientific conditions all over the world. But we can say even now that the West has long since ceased to live and to act in accordance with the tenets of capitalism, just as we can see that the chief obstacle to rapid progress in countries ruled by communist dictatorships is precisely their rigid belief in an ideology. The truth of the matter is that West and East are now engaged in all sorts of economic experiments, and this is as it should be. The freer these experiments are from ideological considerations, the better the results are likely to be; and a competition between different economic systems, in view of the enormous objective problems involved, may eventually turn out to be no less healthy than competition has been within the more restricted framework of national economies. Politically, the only

---

* These remarks were occasioned by a series of general questions about the Cold War posed by the *Partisan Review.* —Ed.

issue at stake between West and East is freedom versus tyranny; and the only political freedom within the economic realm concerns the citizens' right to choose their profession and their place of work.

If the ideologies of the nineteenth century constitute a severe handicap in understanding the dangers and the potentialities of the conflict which divides the world today, the two great revolutions of the eighteenth century—which, politically, though not economically, are the origin, the birthplace as it were, of the modern world—may well contain the very principles which are still at stake. Since I cannot possibly hope to argue this matter at all plausibly within the framework of these casual remarks, I shall try to make a few points which seem to me to sum up what came to my mind when I read your questions. First, I must admit that I immediately interpreted or reformulated them until they seemed to be contained in a single question: What are the prospects of the West in the near future, provided nuclear war is avoided and provided, as I believe, revolution will remain the major issue of the century?

My first point would be that every revolution must go through two stages, the stage of freedom—from poverty (which is a liberation from necessity), or from political domination, foreign or domestic (which is a liberation from force)—and the stage of foundation, the constitution of a new body politic or a new form of government. In terms of historical processes, these two belong together, but as political phenomena, they are very different matters and must be kept distinct. My point here is not merely the truism (theoretically interesting enough) that liberation is the prerequisite of freedom and hence entirely different from it, but the practical truth that liberation, and especially liberation from necessity, always takes precedence over the building of freedom because of the urgency inherent in necessity. Moreover, liberation, even if successfully achieved, never guarantees the establishment of freedom; it does no more than remove the obvious obstacle to it.

My second point would be that the whole record of revolutions—if we only knew how to read it—demonstrates beyond doubt that every attempt to abolish poverty, i.e., to solve the so-called social question, with political means is doomed to failure and for this reason leads into terror; terror, on the other hand, sends revolutions to their doom. There has been not a single revolution that ever succeeded in the most important business of revolution, the establishment of a new government for the sake of freedom, except the American Revolution which also was unique in that it was not confronted with mass poverty but conducted, even then, under conditions of an otherwise unknown prosperity.

From this, I would conclude that there would indeed be no great hope that revolution could ever succeed in the world at large, if we were still living under conditions where scarcity and abundance were beyond the scope of human power. The American Revolution, that is, the experience of the foundation on which the republic of the United States rests, would remain what it has been for so long, an exception from an iron rule and an incident of hardly more than local significance. But this is no longer the case. Even though the difficulties standing in the way to a solution of the predicament of mass poverty are still staggering, they are, in principle at least, no longer insurmountable. The advancement of the natural sciences and their technology has opened possibilities which make it very likely that, in a not too distant future, we shall be able to deal with all economic matters on technical and scientific grounds, outside all political considerations. Even today, in the fully developed areas of the West, necessity (and neither political nor humanitarian considerations) is pressing us into all sorts of Point Four* programs for the simple reason that our economy produces abundance and superabundance in the same automatic way as the economy of the early modern age produced mass poverty. Our present technical means permit us to fight poverty, and force us to fight superabundance, in complete political neutrality; in other words economic factors need not interfere with political developments one way or another. This means for our political future that the wreckage of freedom on the rock of necessity which we have witnessed over and over again since Robespierre's "despotism of liberty" is no longer unavoidable.

Short of war and short of total annihilation, both of which I fear will remain actual dangers, the position of the West in general and of the United

---

* The first Point Four program, announced by Harry Truman in 1949, was intended to make "the benefits of our scientific advances and industrial progress available for the improvement and growth of underdeveloped areas." —Ed.

States in particular will depend to a considerable extent upon a clear understanding of these two revolutionary factors: freedom and the conquest of poverty. Technically and economically, the West is in an excellent position to help in the struggle against poverty and misery which is now going on all over the world. If we fail to do our part in this struggle, I am afraid, we shall have occasion to learn by bitter experience how right the men of the French Revolution were when they exclaimed: "*Les malheureux sont la puissance de la terre.*" What we seem to fail to understand—in the West in general and in the United States in particular—is the enormous power of wretchedness, once this *malheur* has come out into the open and has made its voice heard in public. This happened for the first time in the French Revolution, and it has happened time and again ever since. In a sense, the fight against poverty, though to be conducted by technical, nonpolitical means, must also be understood as a power struggle, namely, as the struggle against the force of necessity to prepare the way for the forces of freedom. In the United States the failure to understand the political relevance of the social question may have its roots in the history of the revolution which gave birth to the country's form of government. By the same token, the people of this republic should be in the best possible position to set a new example for the whole world—and particularly to those new ethnic groups and peoples who in rapid succession are now rising to nationhood—when it comes to questions of founding new political bodies and establishing lasting institutions of liberty. There are, I think, two chief reasons why we have been found wanting even there, the one being our failure to remember and articulate conceptually what was at stake in the American Revolution, and this to such an extent that the denial that a revolution ever had taken place here could become, for a long time, a cherished tenet of public as well as learned opinion. The second reason for our failure is perhaps even more serious because it obviously concerns a failing of the revolution itself and of the whole ensuing history of the country—i.e., the inability to solve the race question.

Let me point in conclusion to the last two major revolutions—the Hungarian Revolution, so quickly and so brutally crushed by Russia, and the Cuban Revolution which has fallen under Russian influence. After the American Revolution, the Hungarian Revolution was the first I know of in which the question of bread, of poverty, of the order of society, played no role whatsoever; it was entirely political in the sense that the people fought for nothing but freedom, and that their chief concern was the form the new government should assume. None of the participating groups—and they included practically the whole population—even thought of undoing the profound social change which the communist regime had effected in the country. It was precisely the social conditions which everyone took for granted—just as, in vastly different circumstances, the men of the American Revolution had taken for granted the social and economic conditions of the people. Obviously, the Cuban Revolution offers the opposite example; up to now, it has run true to the course of the French Revolution, and for this very reason has fallen so easily under the sway of Bolshevism. If I reflect on our attitude toward these two recent revolutions, it seems to me that whatever we did, or rather did not do, during the Hungarian crisis—right or wrong—was based upon considerations of power politics but not upon a failure to understand what the whole business was about. In the case of the Cuban Revolution, however, so much closer to us geographically, and yet apparently so much further removed from our sphere of comprehension, I believe our behavior demonstrates that we have not understood what it means when a poverty-stricken people in a backward country, where corruption has been rampant for a very long time, is suddenly released from the obscurity of their farms and hovels, permitted to show their misery, and invited into the streets of the country's capital, which they never saw before. The mistake of the Cuban adventure did not lie so much in wrong information as in a conspicuous inability to comprehend the revolutionary spirit, to grasp what it means when *les malheureux* have come into the open and are told: All this is yours, these are your streets, and your buildings, and your possessions, and hence your pride. From now on, you will yield the road to no one, you will walk in dignity.

Ultimately and short of catastrophe, the position of the West will depend upon its understanding of revolution. And revolution involves both liberation from necessity so that men may walk in dignity and the constitution of a body politic that may permit them to act in freedom.

1962

NATION-STATE AND DEMOCRACY

Of the legitimate forms of state—among which, of course, I count neither the various forms of total domination, nor the imperialist administrative apparatuses—the nation-state is historically and chronologically the youngest. It first came into being in France, in the course of the French Revolution, and to this day it remains that revolution's only undoubted achievement. In itself, this origin proves that the nation-state and democracy have something to do with each other. The marriage into which they entered—like many marriages—looked very promising at the start, at the end of the eighteenth century; but then, as we know, it met a very dismal end. It was the element of democracy in the nation-state—namely the sovereignty of the people, which replaced the sovereignty of the absolute monarch—that, while Napoleon was still in power, very quickly proved extremely fragile. The nation, that is, the people who owed their political emancipation to the nation-state, soon began to show an ill-fated tendency to yield their sovereignty to dictators and leaders of every stripe. The multiparty system, which to this day is the only form in which the sovereignty of the people can be asserted in a nation-state, has been regarded by these people with a degree of mistrust ever since its origin in the middle of the nineteenth century. In many cases—and always with the agreement of the masses in the broadest sense—it has ended with the establishment of a one-party dictatorship and the abolition of the nation-state's specifically democratic institutions. Today, we sometimes forget that long before Hitler seized power, the vast majority of European countries were already under one-party dictatorships, and were thus ruled neither democratically nor dynastically. And we should not forget that then, as may well be the case again today, the dictators could count on the national sentiment of those they had deprived of the right of decision.

These historical reminiscences, as well as contemporary political observations within the nation-state systems, are unsettling for anyone who is serious about democracy. Here, I take democracy to mean the active participation of the people in decisions on public affairs, rather than just the protection of certain basic rights. The experiences of recent decades have shown many times over in numerous countries that, once it has been united as a nation, a people seems prepared to fall under almost any tyranny, as long as its national interests remain protected. Serious resistance is really only to be expected where a foreign government takes the reins. The people, in other words, has deemed its political emancipation, as realized in a fully developed nation-state—its admission to the public realm, in which every citizen has the right to be seen and heard—for the most part to be substantially less important than its government's guarantee of continued permission to live on the territory that history and ancestry have designated its own. The talk of the primacy of foreign policy, and the current popular conviction that only foreign policy truly *is* policy, are another expression of this state of affairs.

The European nation-state, which has received the inheritance of absolutism, rests on the trinity of people, territory, and state. First among its requirements, which are by no means self-evident, is a historically preexisting territory associated with a particular people. From the time this attachment to the native soil came into being until well into our own century, it was represented in the countries of Central and Western Europe by the peasant classes; even for the cities, the peasantry also constituted, so to speak, the model of the affinity of people and soil. The Nazi slogan about blood and soil, like all specifically chauvinist slogans, was coined when this affinity was quite obviously crumbling, and the peasantry had lost its precedence in the structure of society; but still it made a nationalistic appeal to specific feelings about the nation and the nation-state. The second fundamental requirement for a Western nation-state—which is to say, primarily and perhaps even exclusively, a nation-state in the French mold—is that only members of the same people live on the national territory, and that ideally all members of this nation live on this territory. Insofar as people with different national roots also live within the nation, national sentiment demands that they are either assimilated or ejected. However, the criteria for who belongs to one's own people can vary tremendously. The more cultured and civilized the people in question, the more decisive linguistic affiliation will be; the more barbaric the life of the nation, the more valid purely *völkisch* considerations will be. But the principle that one can only be a citizen if one belongs to the same people, or has completely assimilated to that people, is the same in all nation-states. The ultimate result of this is perhaps the most important unspoken precondition for this form of state, which is that the state itself, both as a state under the rule of law or a constitutional state, and as administrative apparatus, can neither reach outside the boundaries of the national territory (the nation-state is incapable of absorbing other countries), nor ensure state legal protection for residents who are not its citizens or do not belong to the same ethnic group.

I would like to explain this a little further. I dare say we are all united on the point that people and nation are not identical, that there are many more peoples than nations, and that we only speak of nations when a people has a public space that belongs to it in common, in a territory that is theirs alone. In this sense, the nation is of course older than the nation-state; nations existed even in the age of absolutism. The nation-state comes into being when the nation takes possession of the state and the apparatus of government.

Furthermore, in this sense neither America nor England is a nation-state. England is not a nation-state in the sense of the model founded in the French Revolution, because a large proportion of the English people lives outside the territory of the United Kingdom. The English people is united in the commonwealth that stretches across the world, and not on the nationally restricted territory of the British Isles. The United States of America were founded in the American Revolution as a federal state system, and this federal principle, which rests on the division of the state powers, and power not being centralized anywhere, was consciously designed and implemented, in contrast to the principle of centralized power that had evolved in Europe in the course of absolutism. And closely connected to this development is the fact that the people of the United States are in fact a mix of peoples, and that nationality is in no way, neither theoretically nor practically, a requirement for citizenship. Nationality—each person's different national origin—has, one might say, become a private matter in the United States—as religious affiliation is in all states where the principle of the separation of church and state is enacted and anchored in law. Thus in America, nationality plays a very great role in the social sphere, which is expressed most clearly in the well-known discrimination there; but politically, even this discrimination is meaningless—except in the case of the Negroes, who constitute a more specific problem.

The extraordinary de facto limitations on how the nationality principle can be applied when states are founded was underlined immediately after the First World War, when the peoples of Eastern and Western Europe were to be organized into nation-states, in accordance with the right to self-determination. In the belt of mixed populations that stretches from the Baltic Sea to the Adriatic, there was neither a historically rooted connection to the native soil, namely the bi-unity of people and territory, nor any homogeneity in the populations to make them a single people. Every state constructed between the two World Wars in this region contained several ethnic groups, each of which laid a claim to national sovereignty, making it impossible to assimilate them. We know that the solution found at this time, to guarantee minority rights to those peoples who had not managed to get their own state, did not prove successful. The minorities were always of the opinion that these rights were simply minor rights, while the people who had been given a state saw the Minority Treaties either as a proviso—valid until the assimilation required in principle by the nation-state had been achieved—or as a concession to the Western powers that would be shed at the first opportunity, in order to do away with the minorities one way or another.

A much more serious development, although it was far less conspicuous and has therefore received hardly any attention, was the advent of mass statelessness between the two World Wars, which shook the very principle of the nation-state. It was the result of refugees flooding out of Central and Eastern Europe who, according to the nation-state principle, never could be naturalized anywhere, meaning that nowhere could they be compensated for the lost legal protection of their homeland. As they stood outside all laws, and were assured of neither the right to settle nor the right to work, they became the prey of the native police apparatus wherever they went, the power of which was thus massively and illegitimately increased in various countries. Once again, the extraordinary limitations of the nation-state principle became apparent, insofar as the constitutionally guaranteed legal protection of the state, and the laws governing the country, quite obviously did not apply to all residents of the territory, but only to those who belonged to the nation-organization itself. The influx of stateless people and the utter lawlessness inflicted on them endangered the nation-state's existence as a state under the rule of law and a constitutional state, thereby threatening its very foundations.

For the essence of the nation-state was that it was constitutional and governed by law, and it could only exist in this form. This fact had been demonstrated in its early history, and would become quite obvious following the Second World War. By the end of the nineteenth century, it was already clear that the modern industrial and economic development of the European peoples had reached a capacity that pointed far beyond national borders. From this contradiction between strictly limited national territory and almost unlimited economic capacity emerged imperialism, whose motto was "expansion for expansion's sake." This growth was not an attempt to conquer or annex any other territory; it was just what happened under the law of a constantly growing economy. Imperialism resulted from the nation-state's attempt to survive as a political entity under the conditions of industry and the modern economy, which were the new conditions in which the peoples of Europe lived, and would very soon come to govern the whole globe. This development caused a dilemma for the nation-state: in practice, the economic interests of the nation necessitated the kind of expansion that could be reconciled neither with the traditional nationalism of this form of state (the trinity of people, state, and historically granted territory), nor its specific legal character, which did not permit the oppression of the people by the state organs. Nor was it compatible with the demands of a consistently imperialist policy. The imperialist experiment posed a very serious threat to the foundations of the nation-state, in particular when this experiment extended and perverted nationalist ideology into an increasingly bestial racial consciousness. But the legal and political institutions of the nation-state still ultimately emerged victorious—at least with regard to overseas imperialism—and almost always prevented the worst from happening, namely the "administrative mass murder" that the English imperialists of the 1920s took to be the only way of retaining control over India.

The European peoples' justified fear that methods of imperialist control could have a boomerang effect on the mother country caused imperialism to founder—which of course does not mean that it remained without consequences. On the contrary: the most significant (and not just disastrous) consequences of the nation-state's imperialist experiment came even as it was foundering. To put it as succinctly as possible, the result, which is not as paradoxical as it might seem, was that in the very moment when Europe itself experienced at close quarters the inadequacy of the nation-state and the dangers of nationalism, it sees itself confronted with non-European and non-American peoples across the world whose greatest ambition still lies in organizing themselves into a European nation-state, and whose strongest political engine is a European, and ultimately a French, brand of nationalism. The fact that the peoples of Africa and Asia can only imagine political freedom in the mold of the already failed nation-state is only the most minor of the dangers that the legacy of the imperialist age has left to us. Much more serious and threatening is the fact that racial thinking, which also stemmed from imperialism, has taken hold of such large strata of recognizably different peoples everywhere.

How do things stand now regarding the question that has been put to us: Is the nation-state an element of democracy? If one takes democracy to mean nothing more than the consistent protection of citizens' basic rights—which may well include the right to the representation of interests, and in particular the freedom of the press, but not the right to participate directly in political decision making—to me there seems to be no doubt that in a historical context, the question must be answered positively. Even the disastrous tendency of the nation-state to sacrifice actual political freedom for the sake of national interests, and to force the people into a unanimous, uniform public opinion in dictatorships of the most divergent kinds and provenances, does not have to mean that in all cases basic citizen's rights are endangered—as we can clearly see in France. But if by democracy we mean a government of the people or, as the word government has lost its real meaning in this phrase, the right for all people to participate in public affairs and to appear in the public realm and make themselves heard, then even historically, democracy in the nation-state has never been in particularly good shape. The European nation-state came into being in the context of a class-based society and, although it is thanks to the nation-state that even the lower strata of the population were emancipated, even in what we might call its classic period there was a ruling and above all a governing class, which took care of the nation's public affairs on its behalf.

But it seems to me that today all these undoubted advantages of the nation-state are things of the past, and are no longer permitted to carry very much weight. The nation-state's unsuitability for life in the modern world has long been demonstrated, and the longer people cleave to it, the more wickedly and recklessly will the ways in which the nation-state and nationalism have been perverted assert themselves. One should not forget that totalitarianism, especially in the form of the Hitler regime, resulted not least from the collapse of the nation-state and the dissolution of the nation's class-based society. With today's power relations, the nation-state's notion of sovereignty, which in any case comes from absolutism, is a dangerous megalomania. With today's transport and population conditions, the xeno-phobia typical of the nation-state is so provincial that a culture with a con-sciously national orientation is liable to sink down very quickly to the level of folklore and *Heimat* kitsch. But there can only be real democracy—and this is perhaps the decisive point in this context—where the centralization of power in the nation-state has been broken, and replaced with a diffu-sion of power into the many power centers of a federal system. Both the individual and the group, which consists of individuals, are almost always powerless against the monopoly of a centrally organized state apparatus, and the powerlessness of the citizen, even when all his rights are protected, stands in basic opposition to democracy in all its forms. Just as today in foreign policy we are everywhere confronted with the question of how we can organize relations between states to eliminate from them the possibility of war as an *ultima ratio,* so in domestic policy we are everywhere con-fronted with the problem of how we can reorganize and split up modern mass society to allow for the free formation of opinion, a sensible exchange of opinions, and thus to the individual taking active responsibility for pub-lic affairs. Nationalism, with its egocentric narrow-mindedness, and the nation-state, with its fundamental inability to transcend its own borders, may well provide the worst imaginable preconditions for this.

1963

KENNEDY AND AFTER

Was this "the loudest shot since Sarajevo"—as a BBC commentator, stunned by impact of the news, said? Does this shot mean that the brief "moment of comparative calm" and "rising hope," of which the dead president spoke only two months ago in an address to the United Nations, will soon be over? Will the day come when we are forced to see in this tragedy a historical turning point? To think in terms of comparisons, to apply historical categories to contemporary events is tempting, for to anticipate the future historian is to escape the terrible reality and naked horror of tragedy that is only too present. And it is misleading; for the future, which depends upon ourselves and our contemporaries, is unpredictable, and history begins only when the story it has to tell us has come to its end.

At this moment when we have been reassured of the continuity of American policy both on the domestic and the international plane, it appears that the country, far from entering a new era, is falling back into its old fold. Unlike Mr. Truman, the new president was not merely Kennedy's running mate, he was a candidate for the presidency, and his chances were good if it had not been for the rather novel and unexpected qualities of the senator from Massachusetts. Time and again during these short days it has been stressed that everything will go on just as before—except that it will be done in a different *style*.

It was the style of everything Kennedy said and did which made this administration so strikingly different—different not in its formulation or pursuit of American policies, but rather in its estimation of politics as such. No doubt, John F. Kennedy thought of politics in what looks, at first glance, like old-fashioned terms, the terms of honor and glory, along with the inescapable highly welcome challenge his generation and his country had been destined to meet. But he was not old-fashioned, and never even tried to "rise above politics," to evade the fierce competitive power struggle which is the essence of party politics. He did not encourage the image of a "great man," waiting to be "drafted" into a position he did not seek. He went after the job, knowing its dangers and its awe-inspiring, solitary responsibility, because it was to him the most desirable thing on earth. He was impatient with convention and protocol because they tended to raise him so high above the common rank of men that he could no longer remain what he intended to be—*primus inter pares,* first among equals.

It was his style which elevated politics, as has been said before, to a new, higher level, and bestowed upon the whole sphere of government a new prestige and a new dignity. The first conspicuous sign of his intentions came as early as the inauguration when he invited many eminent people in the notoriously "unpolitical" fields of the arts and letters. He did not mean to use these poets and artists, musicians, and scholars for any narrowly defined purpose; and I suspect he did not even want, at least not primarily, to make room in the public realm for those who traditionally and conventionally are most alienated from it. It was the other way around; he wanted them to bring splendor and excellence into public affairs which, left to themselves, can only rarely, in times of crisis and emergency, shine by their own intrinsic merits. He looked upon the arts and letters with the eyes of an "intellectual" who, Hamlet-like, feels that his sensibilities may make him unfit for the demands of action and decision.

The spirit which informed and controlled him has been called the spirit of youth (surely not a matter of years, for this never would have been said of Mr. Nixon who is barely three years older). It was the spirit of a very modern man, a completely "contemporary man," as Mr. Stevenson so justly called him. Twice in this century, after the First World War and after the Second, the new generation failed to make its voice heard in the public affairs of its respective countries. Kennedy was perhaps the first modern man in high position to do so. But if his was the voice of youth and of the sixties, it was all the more remarkable that his words and actions displayed the two highest virtues of the statesman—moderation and insight. Most conspicuous in his handling of the Cuba crisis and the civil rights conflict were the extremes to which he did *not* go. He never lost sight of the thinking of his opponents, and as long as their position itself was not extreme, and hence dangerous to what he felt were the interests of the country, he did not attempt to rule it out, even though he might have to overrule it. It was in this spirit, which derived from his ability to grasp his opponents' thinking, that he greeted the student demonstration which picketed the White House after he decided to resume nuclear testing.

There is a curious and infinitely sad resemblance between the death of the two greatest men we have lost during this year—the one very old, the other in the prime of life. Both the late pope* and the late president died much too soon in view of the work they initiated and left unfinished. The whole world changed and darkened when their voices fell silent. And yet the world will never be as it was before they spoke and acted in it.

1963

---

* Pope John XXIII (Angelo Giuseppe Roncalli). —Ed.

NATHALIE SARRAUTE

With the exception of the early *Tropismes,* all of Nathalie Sarraute's books are now available in English. Thanks are due to her publisher and to Maria Jolas who, to quote Janet Flanner in *The New Yorker,* has put her work "into English of such verisimilitude that it seems merely orchestrated in another key." Novels are rarely masterpieces, and this is as it should be; it is even rarer to find a translation that is perfect, and this, perhaps, is not as it should or could be.

When Nathalie Sarraute published her first novel, *Portrait of a Man Unknown,* in 1948, Sartre, in an Introduction, placed her with such authors of "entirely negative works" as Nabokov, Evelyn Waugh, and the Gide of *Les Faux-Monnayeurs,* and called the whole genre "anti-novel." In the fifties, the anti-novel became the New Novel and Sarraute its originator. All these classifications are somewhat artificial and, if applied to Mme. Sarraute, difficult to account for. She has herself pointed out her ancestors, Dostoevsky (especially the *Notes from Underground*) and Kafka in whom she sees Dostoevsky's legitimate heir. But this much is true: She wrote at least her first pair of novels, the *Portrait* and *Martereau* (1953), against the assumptions of the classical novel of the nineteenth century, where author and reader move in a common world of well-known entities and where easily identifiable characters can be understood through the qualities and possessions bestowed upon them. "Since then," she writes in her book of essays, *The Age of Suspicion,* "[this character] has lost everything; his ancestors, his carefully built house, filled from cellar to garret with a variety of objects, down to the tiniest gewgaw, his sources of income and his estates, his clothes, his body, his face ... his personality and, frequently, even his name." Man as such is or has become unknown so that it matters little to the novelist whom he chooses as his "hero" and less into what kind of surrounding he puts him. And since "the character occupied the place of honor between reader and novelist," since he was "the object of their common devotion," this arbitrariness of choice indicates a serious breakdown in communication.

In order to recover some of this lost common ground, Nathalie Sarraute very ingeniously took the nineteenth-century novel, supposedly the common cultural heritage of the author and the reader, as her point of departure and began by choosing her "characters" from this richly populated world. She fished them right out of Balzac and Stendhal, stripped them of all these secondary qualities—customs, morals, possessions—by which they could be dated, and retained only those bare essentials by which we remember them: avarice—the stingy father living with his homely, penny-pinching spinster daughter, the plot turning about her numerous illnesses, fancied or real, as in *Portrait;* hatred and boredom—the closely knit family unit which still survives in France, the "dark entirely closed world" of mother, father, daughter, and nephew in *Martereau,* where the plot turns about the "stranger" who swindles the father out of the money he had wanted to save from the income tax collector; even the hero of the later work, *The Planetarium,* personified ambition (the plot is a familiar one describing his ruthless "rise in social space").

Sarraute has cracked open the "smooth and hard" surface of these traditional characters ("nothing but well-made dolls") in order to discover the endless vibrations of moods and sentiments which, though hardly perceptible in the macrocosm of the outward world, are like the tremors of a never-ending series of earthquakes in the microcosm of the self. This inner life—what she calls "the psychological"—is no less hidden from "the surface world" of appearances than the physiological life process that goes on in the inner organs beneath the skin of bodily appearance. Neither shows itself of its own accord. And just as the physiological process announces itself naturally only through the symptoms of a disease—the tiny pimple, to use her own image, which is a sign of the plague—but needs a special instrument, the surgical knife or X rays, to become visible; so these psychological movements cause the outbreak of symptoms only in the case of great disaster, and need the novelist's magnifying lenses of suspicion to be explored. To choose the intimacy of family life, this "semidarkness" behind closed curtains with its Strindbergian overtones, as a laboratory for this kind of psychological vivisection, instead of the couch, was a sheer stroke of genius: for here, "the fluctuating frontier that [ordinarily] separates conversation from sub-conversation" breaks down most frequently so that the inner life of the self can explode onto the surface in what is commonly called "scenes." No doubt these scenes are the only distraction in the infinite boredom of a world entirely bent upon itself, and yet they also constitute the heartbeat of a hell in which we are condemned to go "eternally round and round," where all appearances are penetrated but no firm ground is ever reached. Behind the lies and pretenses, there is nothing but the vibrations of an ever-present irritation—a "chaos in which a thousand possibilities clash," a morass where every step makes you sink deeper into perdition.

Nathalie Sarraute had become a master of this tumultuous, explosive inner life of an "all-powerful I" before she began her second series of novels, *The Planetarium* (1959) and *The Golden Fruits* (1963), which, despite similarity of technique and style, belong to a different genre. In her essays, written during the first period and published in 1956, as well as in interviews and in numerous passages in the novels themselves, she has explained her intentions with great lucidity, and the reviewer finds it tempting indeed to echo her own insights. She thus has spoken with great abandon of the "psychological movements" which "constitute, in fact, the principal element of my research"; she also has mentioned, though with more restraint, her hope to break through to some domain of authentic *reality*, not Goethe's "the beautiful, the good, the true," but just some tiny, undiluted, undistorted factual matter. Perhaps it will turn out to be "nothing or almost nothing"— "the first blade of grass . . . a crocus not yet open . . . a child's hand nestling in the hollow of my own." But "believe me, that's all that counts." Finally, she quotes a famous line from *The Brothers Karamazov*, which could well be placed as a motto over her whole work: " 'Master, what must I do to gain eternal life?' The Staretz comes a little nearer: 'Above all, do not lie to yourself.' " (In this, as in other respects, she has more in common with Mary McCarthy than with almost any other living writer.)

In an author who has gone to such lengths to explain what she is doing, conspicuous elements she has not mentioned may be all the more noteworthy. First, there is the entirely negative character of her discoveries, which Sartre found so striking. Nothing in either her method or subject matter explains the catastrophic nature of the inner life, the complete or almost complete absence of love, generosity, magnanimity, and the like in her work. Every word, if it is not meant to deceive, is a "weapon," all thoughts are "assembled like a large and powerful army behind its banners . . . about to roll forward." The imagery of warfare is all-pervasive. Even in Kafka, as she herself has noted—but also in Dostoevsky, Proust, and Joyce, the early masters of the inner monologue—there are still these "moments of sincerity, these states of grace," which are absent from her own work. There is, second, and more surprisingly, the fact that she has never elaborated on her enormously effective use of the "they"—what "they say," the commonplace, the cliché, the merely idiomatic turn of phrase—emphasized by many of her reviewers and admirers. "They" made their first appearance in the *Portrait,* moved into the center of the plot in *The Planetarium,* and became the "hero" of *The Golden Fruits.*

In the *Portrait*—which like a Greek tragedy has three main characters: Father, Daughter, and Watcher, the old Messenger in new disguise, who tells the story—"they" form the chorus. Both Father and Daughter are surrounded and supported by a "protective cohort" from the outside world, the father by his "old cronies" whom he meets regularly in a tavern, the daughter by the ceaselessly gossiping elderly women in the doorways of the big apartment houses, who had gathered around her ever since she lay in the cradle, "wagging their heads . . . like the wicked godmothers in fairy tales." Singing out their ageless platitudes, the choruses support the main figures ("children never show any gratitude, believe me") and they form a "firm rampart" of ordinariness behind the fighting line to which the characters betake themselves to regain "density, and weight, steadiness" and to become "somebodies" again. And peace comes when the Daughter, having finally found a commonplace husband, looks forward to joining the chorus: "Piously, I shall mingle my voice with theirs."

This relationship between "I" and "They" is sometimes reversed in the later novels. In both *The Planetarium* and *The Golden Fruits* "they" often appear as the incarnation of the enemy, the cause of all disasters suffered by the "I"—at the first moment of inattention, "they" will come and "appre-

hend, snatch" you without pity, "like dogs that smell in every corner to discover the prey they're going to carry away between their teeth and which,
in a little while, they will lay, all warm and quivering, at the feet" of whom-
ever they happen to recognize as their master at that particular moment.

There is finally the "metamorphosis," the moment of truth, around
which each novel is centered, as Greek tragedy is centered around the
moment of recognition. This is what gives Nathalie Sarraute's writing a
dramatic quality which is, I think, unique in contemporary fiction. (She
probably borrowed the word from Kafka's famous story—in the *Portrait*
she even uses the original message: Father and Daughter confront each
other "like two giant insects, two enormous dung beetles.") The metamorphosis occurs in the rare moments when "sub-conversation" and "sub-
conversation" confront each other, that is, at the moment of descent from
the daylight world of seeming down to "the bottom of a well" where naked,
"clasped to each other," slipping and fighting in a nether world, as private
and incommunicable as the world of dreams and nightmares, the characters
meet in a murderous intimacy that will conceal nothing.

In their ferocious pursuit of truth (this is how you are, do not lie to yourself) the first two novels leave the reader with Strindberg's compassion for
the whole species: "Oh for the pity of men." The family after all is the
most natural human community, and what is revealed in its setting seems
to indicate something about "human nature." The setting of the two later
novels is Society, which is "artificial" in comparison to the family and even
more artificial in this case as it is the society of the literary clique. (The
Planetarium "is not the real sky but an artificial sky," as Mme. Sarraute
explained in an interview with François Bondy in *Der Monat*, December
1963.) Strangely enough, the result of the different settings is that on the
one hand conversation and sub-conversation are more closely interrelated,
and, on the other, everything which has been so desperately sad, almost
tragic, in the earlier work now turns into sheer, hilarious comedy. Here, in
the sphere of the social, there is "nothing sacred. . . . No holy places. No
taboos" to be violated: here "we are all the same, all human beings . . . all
alike" and do not need any intimacy to call each other's bluff: every distinction or even mere difference, "that's an accident, a curious excrescence,
that's a sickness," perhaps even "a little miracle" if it turns out to material-

ize into an object, some work of art "that can't be explained . . . but as for the rest, what a resemblance." (From *The Golden Fruits*.)

The Planetarium still retains a number of "characters," taken from the family—father, aunt, and in-laws—who are by no means "all like," and it has two main characters, Julien Sorel and Mme. de Rênal in modern disguise: the young *ambitieux* has become an ordinary social climber, "a little scoundrel. . . . When he wants something, nothing can stop him, there's nothing he wouldn't do," and the *femme passionnée* of good society has become a literary celebrity. They have no affair, there is no passion left in this society; they are not true protagonists, but more like members of a chorus that has lost its protagonist, the almost accidentally chosen figures of the "they."

The story tells how the newlywed couple-on-the-make obtain the apartment of the young man's aunt (they have an apartment to live in, but they need a new one "to entertain"), who to her own great grief had installed in it a brand-new door in "bad taste," and most of the story's complexities turn about furniture and the unfortunate door. The metamorphosis takes place near the end of the book and, delightfully, concerns the same door: The young man takes the celebrity around for whom he had gone to all the trouble. He is in agony because of the door, but he is saved: While the celebrity is looking around, "in one second, the most amazing, the most marvelous metamorphosis takes place. As though touched by a fairy wand, the door, which, as soon as he had set eyes on it, had been surrounded by the thin papier-mâché walls, the hideous cement of suburban houses . . . reverts to its original aspect, when, resplendent with life, it had appeared framed in the walls of an old convent cloister." Alas, the poor door is not permitted to remain for long in its state of refound grace: there is another embarrassing object in the apartment, a Gothic virgin marred on one side by a restored arm, and the celebrity, oh horror, does not detect it: she "stares fixedly at the shoulder, the arm, she swallows them stolidly, her strong stomach digests them easily, her eyes maintain the calm, indifferent impression of a cow's eyes." This is the moment of truth when everything comes apart in "a breach, a sudden cleavage": The Virgin loses her power to perform miracles and back comes "the oval door . . . floating, uncertain,

suspended in limbo . . . massive old convent door or that of a cheap bunga-
low" to haunt him forever after.

This is one of the most exquisitely funny passages that I know in contemporary literature: it is of course the comedy of our American "other-
directedness" or of the "inauthentic" in French parlance. But how feeble
and pedantic those words sound compared to the miserably grotesque reality of the thing itself! What makes it so comical is that it all takes place in
the milieu of the presumably "inner-directed" elite of "good taste" and
refinement, among intellectuals boasting of the highest standards, who pretend to care about nothing, certainly talk about nothing, but things of the
highest order. When asked to portray themselves they appear as "highly
sensitive and frail beings at odds with a dark and hostile world," as *The
New York Times Book Review,* as though asked to compound the fraud
that *The Planetarium* exposes, said in high praise. But this perhaps is as it
must be, for the truth of the matter is that *The Planetarium* and *The Golden
Fruits* taken together constitute the severest indictment ever meted out to
the "intellectuals." It is as though Sarraute said: *Le Trahison des Clercs?*
Don't make me laugh. What have these creatures got that they could betray
to begin with?

The comedy is at its purest in *The Golden Fruits.* Here, "they" are
among themselves, undisturbed by any "characters" from outside the literary clique. The book tells the story of another book, a novel just published called "The Golden Fruits," from its initial spectacular success to
its quiet downfall into oblivion, and it ends with an outlook into the book's
uncertain future. (Its first reception in France, I am told, was not enthusiastic, perhaps because the reviewers asked themselves how they could possibly consider a work in which every phrase, every turn of smart or idiotic
praise or blame has been anticipated and revealed as mere talk.) We never
learn anything about the book itself—the author is mentioned because he
belongs to the literary clique—for this is the story of Everybook that has
the misfortune to fall into the hands of the literate Everybody, whose whis-
pers and shouts last until Everything has been said.

And indeed everybody is present: the critic; the *maître;* and the admiring ladies; "the culprit" who once had "fallen from grace" by offending

impeccable taste, but has been "disinfected long ago"; the husband who is suspected of not having discovered "The Golden Fruits" by himself, but he has, says his wife; the provincial who far from "them" had found the novel full of platitudes (but it was done "on purpose," and he is convinced); the scholars ("heads heavy with learning") who, having grouped the dead "according to category, lesser, average, great," find a place for the newest arrival; even the doubter, a "mad, exalted creature who goes about the world, barefooted and in rags" disturbing its peace; even "the foreigner, the pariah" (but "you are one of us," there "can be no question of excluding you"). They exhaust all aspects, all arguments and outdo each other with superlatives until they all know: "There will be those who came before and those who come after 'The Golden Fruits.'" There occurs in each one of them this mysterious, delicious process of being "emptied of himself—an empty recipient that will be entirely filled with what they are going to put into it."

And who are "they"? Each one of them is the same "all-powerful I" whose catastrophic inner life was the subject matter of the earlier novels. Each one of them has come out of hell and is afraid of being returned there, remembering only too well how it was when he was still alone, a "poor devil, obscure little fellow, unknown author," always trying to be admitted and invariably beaten down. What could have happened to him had he not clung fast to "another image [of himself] . . . with gigantic proportions, more and more enormous, spreading out on every side"? This is why "they" are all alike and have found in each other's company the medium in which "the weakest vibration is communicated immediately," and "becomes amplified in ever-increasing waves." This kind of society is the macrocosm of the "I," the "I" writ large. Or, perhaps, it is the other way round and the "psychological" inner life, whose trembling fluctuations Sarraute explored, is only the "inner" life of those egomaniacs who, seemingly "outer-directed," are in fact interested in no one and nothing but themselves. Nothing at any rate resembles more closely the disastrous instability of teeming and swarming emotions—from which all loyalty, faithfulness, steadfastness must be absent by definition—than the ups and downs, the tidal waves of fashionable taste by which "they" are thrown hither and thither.

The tide, to be sure, turns; its rise is followed by its fall, and everything quickly crumbles away, though "you never know exactly how." All you know is that from one day to the other everything is in reverse—we hear the same people, the same critic, the same ever-loving wife whose husband now "from the beginning was never taken in," and all the rest of "them," until finally the book is given the *coup de grâce*—"You're still with . . . 'The Golden Fruits'?" "They," to be sure, are not disturbed by this *volte-face*, they remain in the same medium, the same company, they are hardly aware of what happened. And should any one of them even be beset by doubts, he will be told to evoke History, the goddess of change, by which "they [are] borne along . . . as by a superb ocean liner."

This is comedy and like all good comedy is concerned with something deadly serious. The falsity of the intellectual "they" is particularly painful, because it touches one of the most delicate and, at the same time, indispensable elements of common taste for which indeed "no criterion of values" exists. Taste decides not only about how the world should look, it also determines the "elective affinities" of those who belong together in it. The "secret signs" by which we recognize each other, what else do they say but, "We are brothers, aren't we . . . ? I offer you this holy bread. I welcome you to my table." This feeling of natural kinship in the midst of a world, to which we all come as strangers, is monstrously distorted in the society of the "refined" who have made passwords and talismans, means of social organization, out of a common world of objects. But have they really succeeded in ruining it? Shortly before the end, Nathalie Sarraute turns from the "they" and the "I" to the "we," the old We of author and reader. It is the reader who speaks: "We are so frail and they so strong. Or perhaps . . . we, you, and I, are the stronger, even now."

MARCH 5, 1964

"AS IF SPEAKING TO A BRICK WALL"
A Conversation with Joachim Fest

FEST: Frau Arendt, do you think there is any connection between the Eichmann trial and the so-called successor trials in Germany? And in particular, are the reactions in Germany and Israel in any way comparable? People have occasionally suggested that Germans and Jews have in common what is called—in a somewhat inadequate expression—an "unmastered past."

ARENDT: Well, those are actually two questions. Perhaps I might answer the first one first: in my view, the Eichmann trial has really acted as a catalyst for the trials in Germany. Some of these took place earlier, and some arrests were made earlier. But when you look at this from the statistical point of view and bear in mind the date of Eichmann's abduction, not the date of his trial, of course, you'll be overwhelmed, purely in terms of percentages. And I don't want to say here why I think it was like this—it's just a fact.

Now you are quite right to say that the question of the unmastered past is something the Jews and Germans have in common. I'd like to qualify that a bit. To begin with, of course, the actual kinds of unmastered past that they have in common are very different in the case of victims and perpetrators; for even the *Judenräte* were, of course, victims. This doesn't mean they are a hundred percent exonerated, but they obviously stand on the other side—that much is clear.

Now the unmastered past is also something that—I know this from America—Jews and Germans in fact share with almost all countries or all peoples on earth, at least in Europe and America. The very horror that the whole business arouses affects everyone, not just Jews and Germans. What Jews and Germans have in common is the fact that they were the direct participants.

And now you ask, "Is this reaction the same in Germany and Israel?" Look here, a quarter of the population of Israel, twenty-five percent, consists of people who were immediately affected. That's a huge percentage in a population. That they, as victims, obviously react differently from the average German of any generation, who has only one wish—never to hear anything more about it—is clear. But *they* don't want to hear about it either, but for completely different reasons.

Now there's one thing that I've noticed, and that's the attitude of the younger generation in Israel and of course of those born there. There's a lack of interest that's similar in some ways to the lack of interest in Germany. In Israel they also feel, "It's our parents' problem" . . . Only there, of course, it's different: "If our parents want this or that to happen . . . well, of course! They're welcome! But they should please leave us out of it. . . . We're not really interested in that." This was a truly general feeling. So it's a generational problem, in Israel as it is in Germany.

FEST: These trials—like the Nuremberg Trials, to some extent, and the successor trials held mainly in Nuremberg—have brought to light a new type of criminal.

ARENDT: It is indeed a new type of criminal, I agree with you on that, though I'd like to qualify it. When we think of a criminal, we imagine someone with criminal motives. And when we look at Eichmann, he doesn't actually have any criminal motives. Not what is usually understood by "criminal motives." He wanted to go along with the rest. He wanted to say "we," and his going-along-with-the-rest and wanting-to-say-we were quite enough to make the greatest of all crimes possible. The Hitlers, after all, really aren't the ones who are typical in this kind of situation—they'd lack power without the support of these others.

So what's actually going on here? I'd like to concentrate just on Eichmann, since I know his case well. See here, the first thing I'd like to say is that going along with the rest—the kind of going along that involves lots of people acting together—produces power. So long as you're alone, you're always without power regardless of how strong you are. This feeling of power that arises from acting together is absolutely not bad in itself but altogether human. That doesn't mean it's good. It's simply neutral. It's something that's simply a phenomenon, a general human phenomenon that needs to be described as such. In this way of acting there's an extreme feeling of pleasure. I won't start quoting reams of material here—you could go on quoting examples from the American Revolution for hours at a time. Now I'd say that the real perversion of this form of acting is functioning, and in functioning the feeling of pleasure is also always there. Yet everything else in acting together with others, namely, discussing things together, reaching certain decisions, accepting responsibility, thinking about what we are doing, is all eliminated in functioning. What you have there is empty busyness. And the pleasure in this empty functioning was quite evident in Eichmann. Did he seek pleasure in power? I don't think so. He was a typical functionary. And a functionary, who is nothing but a functionary, is really a very dangerous gentleman. Ideology, I believe, in my view, played no great role here. This seems to me decisive.

FEST: When I mentioned a new type of criminal, I meant the following: there was a tendency after the war, both in Germany and in the Allied countries, to demonize the leaders in the Third Reich. The Germans always saw these figures, from Hitler right down to Eichmann, as beasts from the depths and they possibly understood this as a way of creating an alibi for themselves. If you succumb to the power of a beast, you're naturally much less guilty than if you succumb to a completely average man such as Eichmann.

ARENDT: It is also more interesting!

FEST: Really? I guess so. The situation with the Allies was altogether similar. In their case, they found a partial excuse for their lack of resolve, the appeasement policy up until 1939. And on the other hand, victory over this beast from the depths appears as much more glorious, for you're dealing with the Devil incarnate.

ARENDT: The demonization of Hitler, in my view, was much more common among the Germans, including the German émigrés, than among the Allies themselves. In fact, the Allies were appalled, immeasurably and unprecedentedly appalled, when the truth came to light. This is underrated in Germany, catastrophically. For they were shaken profoundly, to the core of their being when they learned of it, when an ordinary soldier saw Bergen-Belsen and so on. . . . I've experienced this in countless conversations. I've lived abroad—so I can say this to you. . . .

Now, demonization itself can help, as you've rightly said, to provide an alibi. You succumb to the Devil incarnate, and as a result you yourself are not guilty. But above all. . . . Look here, our whole mythology, our whole tradition sees the Devil as a fallen angel. And the fallen angel is of course much more interesting than the angel who always remained an angel, since the latter doesn't even provide you with a good story. In other words, evil, especially in the twenties and thirties, played the role of ensuring that it alone had authentic depth, don't you agree? And you have the same situation in philosophy—the negative as the only thing that gives impetus to history, and so on. You can pursue this idea a very long way. And as a result, if you demonize someone, not only do you make him look interesting, you also secretly ascribe to him a depth that other people don't have. The others are too superficial to have killed anyone in the gas chambers. Now I've put it like that deliberately, of course, but that's what it comes down to. Anyway, if there was ever anyone who deprived himself of any demonic aura, it was Herr Eichmann.

FEST: Eichmann was actually such a small figure that one observer asked whether they hadn't caught and put on trial the wrong man. And actually he wasn't a *cruel* man—this emerges quite unambiguously from all the documents. Quite the opposite: he always found it difficult to do what he was instructed to do, and because he always found it difficult, he derived a feeling of worth.

ARENDT: Yes. That's true, and unfortunately it's very common. You think that you can judge what's good or evil from whether you enjoy doing it or not. You think that evil is what always appears in the form of a temptation, while good is what you never spontaneously want to do. I think this is all total rubbish, if you don't mind me saying so. Brecht is always showing the temptation toward good as something that you have to withstand. If you go back into political theory, you can read the same thing in Machiavelli, and even in a certain sense in Kant. So Eichmann and many other people were very often tempted to do what we call good. They withstood it precisely because it was a temptation.

FEST: Yes, you've already indicated that the way we imagine evil, or the way evil is imagined and has been formulated in our culture, in religious, philosophical, and literary terms, has no place for the type of man like Eichmann. One of the main ideas in your book—it already emerges in your subtitle—is the "banality of evil." This has led to many misunderstandings.

ARENDT: Yes, look here, these misunderstandings actually run through the whole polemic, they belong to the small part of it that is genuine. In other words, it's my view that these misunderstandings would have arisen in any case. Somehow, it shocked people enormously, and I can understand that perfectly well; I myself was very shocked by it, too. For me, too, it was something for which I was quite unprepared.

Now, one misunderstanding is this: people thought that what is banal is also commonplace. But I thought . . . That wasn't what I meant. I didn't in the least mean that there's an Eichmann in all of us, that each of us has an Eichmann inside him and the Devil knows what else. Far from it! I can perfectly well imagine talking to somebody, who says to me something that I've never heard before, so it's not in the least commonplace. And I say, "That's really banal." Or I say, "That's just rubbish." That's the sense in which I meant it.

This banality was a phenomenon that really couldn't be overlooked. The phenomenon expressed itself in those unimaginable clichés and turns of phrase that we heard over and over again. I can tell you what I mean by banality since in Jerusalem I remembered a story that Ernst Jünger once told, and that I'd since forgotten . . .

During the war, Ernst Jünger came across some peasants in Pomerania or Mecklenburg—no, I think it was Pomerania (the story is told in *Strahlungen,* "Radiations," the title of Ernst Jünger's collected diaries from the Second World War, first published in 1949). A peasant had taken in Russian prisoners of war straight from the camps, and naturally they were starving—you know how Russian prisoners of war were treated here. And he says to Jünger, "Well, they're subhuman—and . . .

like cattle! It's easy to see: they eat the pigs' food." Jünger comments on this story, "It's sometimes as if the German people were being ridden by the Devil." And he didn't mean anything "demonic" by that. Look here, there's something outrageously stupid about this story. I mean the story itself is stupid. The man doesn't see that this is what starving people do. That anyone would behave like that. Still, there's something *outrageous* about this stupidity. [. . .] Eichmann was rather intelligent, but in this respect he was stupid. It was his thickheadedness that was so outrageous, as if speaking to a brick wall. And that was what I actually meant by banality. There's nothing deep about it—nothing demonic! There's simply resistance ever to imagine what another person is experiencing, isn't that true?

FEST: Would you say that Eichmann, and Höss,* too, are specifically German figures? You mentioned Kant just now, and Eichmann himself occasionally referred to Kant during his trial. He's supposed to have said that he had followed Kant's moral precepts all his life long, and made Kant's concept of duty his guiding principle.

ARENDT: Yes. Quite an impertinent remark, of course, isn't it? On Herr Eichmann's part. After all, Kant's whole ethics amounts to the idea that every person, in every action, must reflect on whether the maxim of his action can become a general law. In other words . . . It really is the complete opposite, so to speak, of obedience! Every person is a lawgiver. In Kant, nobody has the right to obey. The only thing that Eichmann did take from Kant is that fatal business of inclination. And this is, unfortunately, very widespread in Germany. This curious conception of duty in Germany . . . I'll say this to you: Look here, Hitler or sadists such as Boger in the Auschwitz trial—Hitler was probably a plain murderer, a man of murderous instincts. In my opinion, these people aren't typical Germans.

In my view, the Germans as a people aren't especially brutal. In fact, I do not believe in that kind of national characteristics . . . Still, the story I told just now, Jünger's story, is specifically German. I mean this inability, as Kant says, if I can now really quote his own words, "to think

---

* Rudolf Höss, commandant of Auschwitz from mid-May 1940 through November 1943.

in the place of every other person"—yes, this inability . . . this kind of thoughtlessness is like talking to a brick wall. You never can get a reaction, because these people never pay you any attention. That is German. The second thing that strikes me as specifically German is this frankly maniacal way that obedience is idealized. We obey in this sense when we're children, when it is necessary. Obedience is a very important matter then. But this should come to an end at the age of fourteen, or at the latest fifteen.

FEST: Don't you think that behind the references to "oaths," "orders," "obedience" there's more than a mere excuse? Eichmann was forever referring to these words. He explained that he'd been brought up to be obedient from an early age; he asked, "What advantage would I have derived from disobedience? In what respect would it have been of any use to me?" And then he stated that when, in May 1945, no more orders were reaching him, he was suddenly overwhelmed by the feeling that the world was coming to an end.

ARENDT: A life without a führer!

FEST: The problem of obedience runs like a leitmotif through his whole life—you can read it in the trial records, for instance, it's forever cropping up. It's the leitmotif of a completely sham existence.

ARENDT: Yes, this sham existence can of course be seen everywhere. But, you know, he wasn't the only person to refer to all that, was he? To "orders," "oaths," "God," "the duty to obey," and "the virtue of obedience." Also, Eichmann talked about "slavish obedience." In Jerusalem he got into a terrible muddle and suddenly said it was a question of obeying slavishly, there was nothing good about it at all, and so on. Right? So it's forever whirling round and round in people's minds. No, the reference to "oaths," and the idea that responsibility has been taken from you, and so on—you don't find this just with Eichmann, I've also found it in the records of the Nuremberg Trials—there's something outrageously thoughtless about this, too. You see, Eichmann produced these attacks of rage—as did the others—and said, "But they promised us that we wouldn't be held responsible. And now we're left holding the bag, aren't we? And what about the big fish? They've evaded responsibility, of course—as usual." But you know how they evaded responsibility: either they took their own lives, or they were hanged. To forget that when you talk about responsibility is grotesque, and makes the whole question comical! Yes, the fact is they're no longer among the living! When you're unable to imagine that all this is only relevant as long as people are still alive—well, in that case there's no helping you.

FEST: But to what extent is there a deeper problem lurking here? To what extent can people living in totalitarian circumstances still be held responsible? This doesn't apply just to the Eichmann type, it applies in the same way to the *Judenräte* on the other side.

ARENDT: Just a moment before I answer that question. Look, it's a really amazing phenomenon: none of these people expressed any remorse. Yes, Frank* did, obviously; perhaps Heydrich† on his deathbed—so they say; Ley‡ . . .

FEST: Yes, in Frank's case I'd say it was a purely emotional remorse. He retracted it straightaway in his concluding speech to the court.

ARENDT: Yes!

FEST: His was a most ambivalent feeling.

ARENDT: So I can say, "No one expressed remorse."

FEST: Basically, at any rate, it can't be definitely proved in a single case.

ARENDT: And, as is well known, Eichmann said, "Remorse is for little children." No one expressed remorse. On the other hand, we should imagine that when nobody expresses remorse, there ought to be at least one person who stands up for his actions and says, "Yes, actually, we did do it, for this and that reason, and I still think the same way today. We lost. Whether we won or lost doesn't affect the cause itself." In actual fact, the cause collapsed like a wet dishrag. Nobody stood up. Nobody put forward any defense. And this seems quite crucial for the phenom-

---

* Hans Frank, the chief jurist of Nazi Germany and governor-general of the "General Government" territory, which encompassed much of central and southern Poland as well as western Ukraine, during the war. He was tried at Nuremberg for war crimes and crimes against humanity, found guilty, and executed in 1946.

† Reinhard Heydrich, a high-ranking Nazi official and one of the principal architects of the Final Solution. He was attacked in Prague on May 27, 1942, by a team of Czech and Slovak soldiers, sent by the Czechoslovak government in exile, and died from his injuries a week later.

‡ Robert Ley, Nazi politician and head of the German Labor Front from 1933 to 1945. He committed suicide in 1945, while awaiting trial for war crimes in Nuremberg.

enon you touched on just now—obedience. Don't you think? In other words: they just wanted to go along. They're ready to go along with everything. When someone says to them, "You're only one of us if you commit murder"—fine. When they're told, "You're only one of us if you never commit murder"—that's fine, too. Right? That's the way I see it.

FEST: That is so true—indeed, Eichmann stated, when he was imprisoned by the Americans, that he'd been glad to submit to somebody else's leadership again. And the peculiar way he was ready to tell the court or rather the interrogation, the preliminary interrogation, everything he knew, is probably to be interpreted in the same way as his readiness to give absolute obedience to any current authority, right to the limit of what was possible—his readiness to submit to any authority.

ARENDT: Wonderful. He was euphoric in Jerusalem. There's no question about it, is there? The superior was Landau,* everyone could see that, and then came various other ranks down to Herr Captain Less,† whom he used—as Herr Mulisch rightly said‡—as a father confessor. He said, "Captain, I'll willingly say everything." Of course, he wanted to cut a fine figure, too. At any rate, tell his life story. Anyway, the question of responsibility—shall we get back to that?

FEST: Yes, please.

ARENDT: Look here, when we put people on trial, we ascribe responsibility to them. And we have a right to do so, from a legal standpoint . . . We have the right, since the alternative was not martyrdom. There was an alternative on both sides: you didn't have to go along, you could make up your own mind. "Thanks anyway, but . . . I'm not going to do that. I'm not risking my life, I'm trying to get away, I'm trying to see if I can slip off." Isn't that right? "I'm not going along with anyone, and if I should be forced to go along, then I'll take my own life." This possibility existed. It meant not saying "we," but "I"—judging for oneself. And judging for oneself is what people did do, everywhere, at every level of

---

* Moshe Landau, the presiding judge in the Eichmann trial, himself a refugee from Nazi Germany.

† Captain Avner W. Less, a young Israeli police official who interrogated Eichmann for 275 hours in the pretrial interrogations in 1961.

‡ Arendt is referring to Dutch journalist Harry Mulisch's book on the Eichmann trial, *Strafsache 40/61* (Criminal Case 40/61), which she greatly admired.

the populace: religious people and nonreligious people, old and young, educated and uneducated, nobles and bourgeois and a great many workers, an amazing number of workers, especially in Berlin, where I was able to watch it happening.

Those who did go along always justified themselves the same way, as we can see. They always said, "We only stayed on so that things wouldn't get any worse." Right? But, well—this justification should be rejected once and for all—it *couldn't* have got any worse.

FEST: And the American prosecutor Jackson* at the Nuremberg Trials spoke his mind on this in a very apt and characteristic way. Referring to Schacht and Papen,† he said, "If we ask these people why they went along with it for such a long time, then they say it was because they wanted to prevent anything worse. And if we ask them why everything turned out so badly, they say they had no power." At this point, everything really falls apart and their apologia becomes a mere excuse.

ARENDT: Yes. They were all bureaucrats, too.

FEST: Absolutely.

ARENDT: With scruples—they were functionaries with scruples. But their scruples didn't go far enough to show them clearly that there is a boundary at which human beings cease being just functionaries. And if they'd gone away and said, "For God's sake, let someone else do the dirty work!"—wouldn't they suddenly have become human beings again, instead of functionaries?

FEST: Yes. But I'd still like to ask once again what possibilities there were to remain guiltless in a totalitarian regime or within a totalitarian society. Many people are not heroes, and you can't expect them to be. . . . But they are not criminals, either. Sometimes they're just accessories in the sense they knew what was going on.

ARENDT: Yes, you know, it's terrible to be an accessory in that sense. The critical question here is the guilt of people who just looked on, who didn't go along or who at first, and there were many, felt an impulse to go

---

* Robert H. Jackson, the chief U.S. prosecutor at the Nuremberg Trials.

† Hjalmar Schacht, an economist, banker, and politician who served in Hitler's government as president of the Reichsbank and minister of economics; and Franz von Papen, a politician who served as vice-chancellor of Germany under Hitler in 1933 and 1934.

along in solidarity with those who were killed. . . . Jaspers, I believe, has spoken the decisive words about where this being an "accessory" leads. He said, "My guilt is that I'm still alive."* Right? "For we could survive only by keeping our mouths shut." But you see, between this knowledge and the deed there's an abyss. Between the man who sees it and goes away, and the man who stays and does it. . . . So when the person who hasn't done anything, who has only seen and gone away, says, "We're all guilty," he thereby is covering up for the man who actually carried it out—this is what happened in Germany. And so we must not generalize this guilt, since that is only covering up for the guilty. Anyway, I'd like to say a bit more about this, if I may.

FEST: Please do.

ARENDT: We need to realize that in totalitarian circumstances the phenomenon of powerlessness exists, and we need to realize that even in circumstances of absolute powerlessness there are still different ways of behaving. In other words, it doesn't imply that you absolutely have to become a criminal. The phenomenon of powerlessness tips the scales, and this was the situation of all these people. They had become absolutely powerless. There was no possibility of resisting, since they were all isolated, since they didn't belong together anywhere, since not even a dozen people could get together, as it were, and trust one another.

FEST: Would you say, Frau Arendt, that as regards this situation we can get by with the old, simple proposition that it's better to suffer injustice than to commit it?

ARENDT: Look here, this proposition comes from Socrates. In other words, it was formulated before the religious commandments for Christian and Western mankind, taken from the Jews, became authoritative. What Socrates always added, or rather Plato did, is that we can't prove this proposition. For some people, it's self-evident, but you can't prove to other people that it's how they should behave. So what is the reason for the belief of those who view it as self-evident?

---

* Karl Jaspers, *The Question of German Guilt*, 2nd ed. (New York: Fordham University Press, 2000), 66. Jaspers calls this guilt "metaphysical," which he differentiates from moral and political guilt. —Ed.

Now there's another proposition of Socrates', which in my view does provide us with the reason. It's this: "It is better to be out of harmony with the whole world than with oneself, since I am one." For if I am not in harmony with myself, a conflict arises that is unbearable. In other words, it's the idea of contradiction in the moral realm, which is still authoritative for Kant's categorical imperative. This idea presupposes that, in actual fact, I live with myself, and am, so to speak, two-in-one, so that I then can say, "I will not do this or that." For then the only way out, if I do this or that, is suicide, or later, when thought in Christian categories, to change my mind and repent.

Now living with yourself means, of course, talking to yourself. And this talking-to-yourself is basically thinking—a kind of thinking that isn't technical, and of which anybody is capable. So the presupposition behind the idea is: I can converse with myself. And so, there may be situations in which I fall out of harmony with the world to such an extent that I can only have recourse to myself—and perhaps with a friend, too, with another self, as Aristotle so beautifully put it: *allos autos*. This, in my view, is what powerlessness actually is. And some people who walked away without doing anything admitted to themselves that they were powerless and clung to this proposition, the proposition that someone who is powerless can still think.

FEST: Let's get back to Eichmann and the role that bureaucracy played in mass murder. What does it mean for an individual to be embedded in a bureaucratic apparatus? And how far can the awareness of injustice evaporate? Is it maybe that the merely partial responsibility given to a person hides the possibilities for any moral insight? Eichmann said, "I sat at my desk and did my work." And the former gauleiter of Danzig stated that his official soul had always identified with what he did, but his private soul had always opposed it.*

ARENDT: Yes, this is the so-called internal emigration among the murderers—which means the extinction of the whole concept of inner

---

* Fest is referring here to Albert Forster, the gauleiter (party leader of a regional branch of the NSDAP) of Danzig–West Prussia from 1935 to 1945. Forster was directly responsible for the mass murder, resettlement, and forced assimilation of tens of thousands of Jews and nonethnic Germans over the course of his administration.

emigration or inner resistance. I mean there's no such thing. There's only external resistance, inside there's at best a *reservatio mentalis*, right? Those are the lies of a sham existence, transparent and rather nauseating. The bureaucracy, in other words, administered mass murder, which naturally created a sense of anonymity, as in any bureaucracy. The individual person is extinguished. As soon as the person concerned appears in front of the judge, he becomes a human being again. And this is actually what is so splendid about the legal system, isn't it? A real transformation takes place. For if the person then says, "But I was just a bureaucrat," the judge can say, "You listen now, that's not why you're here. You're standing here because you're a human being and because you did certain things." And there's something splendid about this transformation.

Apart from the fact that bureaucracy is essentially anonymous, any relentless activity allows responsibility to evaporate. There's an English idiom, "Stop and think." Nobody can think unless he stops. If you force someone into remorseless activity, or if he allows himself to be forced, then you will always hear the same story. You'll always find that an awareness of responsibility can't develop. It can only happen in the moment when a person reflects—not on himself, but on what he's doing.

FEST: Let's turn for a moment to some of the legal consequences that arise from this whole complex, especially the question that's linked with what we've just been talking about: Does the Eichmann type still belong to the traditional concept of the murderer? Isn't he much more of a functionary in a murderous apparatus than a murderer? And does the partial responsibility he held justify the sense of total guilt?

ARENDT: We've already mentioned the murderer without a motive, I mean without the criminal motives we're familiar with: passion, self-interest, and so forth. . . . Or the perpetrator who commits a crime out of conviction—an intermediate figure. All well and good! So, no, the concepts we've inherited give us no handle on this way of killing from one's desk or in masses. . . . That is, of course, an incomparably more fearsome type of person than any ordinary murderer, since he no longer has any relationship with his victim at all. He really does kill people as if they were flies.

Partial responsibility was, of course, never a ground for partial guilt. Eichmann wasn't commissioned to actually kill, since he wasn't suited for it. But he was part of the killing process! It's not important who actually does this or that. What I mean is . . . when I say "But he's not a typical murderer," I don't mean that he's any better. What I mean is that he is infinitely worse, even though he has no actual "criminal instincts," as we call them. He was pulled into it. But I can imagine murderers whom I might find, if I may say so, much more likable than Herr Eichmann.

FEST: The court in Jerusalem also gave a conclusive answer to this question when it stated that this case wasn't just a mass crime with regard to the victims that was at stake, but also one with regard to the perpetrators. Perhaps at this point I can quote: "Being near to or far away from . . . the man who actually kills the victim [can] have no influence on the extent of the responsibility . . . Rather, the degree of responsibility increases as we draw further away from the man who uses the fatal instrument with his own hands."*

ARENDT: Yes, quite true. I've quoted the same words myself. They come from the closing judgment. I entirely agree.

FEST: But the question is whether the legal norms in place can still grasp the nature of responsibility in this case. Would you say so?

ARENDT: Legal textbooks don't prepare us for administrative mass murder, and nothing prepares us for this type of perpetrator. So can we still exercise justice? Not in accordance with the legal textbooks, as it were, but de facto? In fact, the judges—though they struggle with might and main to deny it—always passed judgment without any hindrance.

Justice leads to two things. First, it should restore the order that has been disturbed. This is a process of healing that can only succeed if the ones who have disturbed the order, the people we're talking about, are condemned. And second, in my view, is what affects us Jews . . . There's a quotation from Grotius that one of the judges used, but which they didn't pay much attention to, alas; he said that it is part of the honor and dignity of the person harmed or wounded that the perpetrator be punished. This has nothing to do with the suffering endured, it has nothing

* See *Eichmann in Jerusalem* (New York: Viking Penguin, 1963), 247.

to do with putting something right. It's really a question of honor and dignity. Look, for us Jews it's a crucial question when we're in Germany. If the German people think they can carry on living quite undisturbed with the murderers in their midst, this goes against the honor and dignity of a Jewish person.

FEST: Let's return to your book, Frau Arendt. In it, you referred to the way that the Eichmann trial laid bare the total nature of the moral collapse at the heart of Europe, among the persecutors and the persecuted alike, and in every country. Does the reaction to your book—a reaction that consisted on the one hand of denying this collapse, and on the other of making a confession of total guilt—indicate precisely what you were trying to prove?

ARENDT: Well, yes, this reaction to my book was for me . . . it was, of course, a test case—but after the event, not in the sense that I had expected it. Let me give you an example, one that I experienced several times . . . This book was read in manuscript by a very great number of people (which is unusual for me), and of those people who read the book in manuscript, at least fifty percent, probably many more, were Jews. Not a single one of them voiced the reaction that came subsequently— they didn't even hint at it! In fact, these include, of course, people who are friends of mine and whom I know well. And one of them, for example, with this book . . . not just one, but several Jews read the book in manuscript and were really enthusiastic, right? Then the campaign started up, and they completely forgot that they'd already read the book in manuscript. If you want to understand this phenomenon better— you know, this is yet another phenomenon—then you really must read *The Golden Fruits* by Nathalie Sarraute;* she depicted it as a comedy. And it is indeed a comedy, it's the comedy of intellectual society, isn't it? The way these opinions swing this way and that, of course under influences. . . . And many more people are subject to these influences than is generally realized. Aren't they? And this has absolutely nothing to do with intelligence. A person can be very intelligent and nevertheless behave like that.

---

* See Arendt's review, "Nathalie Sarraute," in this volume, pp. 265–73. —Ed.

FEST: You mentioned the campaign. There are many reasons behind the resistance to the connections you drew in your book, of course, and some of them—it has to be said—deserve to be treated with respect. This raises the question: Should we tell the truth, even when we come into conflict with certain legitimate interests on the one hand, and people's feelings on the other?

ARENDT: Look here, now you're touching on the only question in the whole controversy that is actually of interest to me.

I don't think that I damaged anyone's legitimate—let me emphasize *legitimate!*—interests. But let's assume that this is a controversial issue and that I did actually damage them. Should I have done so? Well, I think that such is the historian's task, as well as the task of people who live at the time and are independent—there are such people, and they need to be guardians of factual truths. What happens when these guardians are driven out by society, or driven into a corner or put up against a wall by the state—we've seen this happen in the writing of history, for example in Russia, where a new history of Russia comes out every five years. Does the state or society, with their legitimate interests that may come into conflict with the truth, nevertheless have an interest—in principle—with these guardians of factual truth? In this case I'd say yes. What then happens is of course that a whole series of apologias or defenses are brought out and put onto the market just to cover up the two or three truths that are actually quite marginal in this book. It won't succeed—nothing of this kind ever does.

But there's another thing: there are also legitimate feelings. And there's no question about it: I have wounded some people. And you know, it's more unpleasant for me when I hurt people than when I get in the way of organizations and their interests, right? I take this seriously, I must say, while the other thing is only a matter of principle. Well, I have hurt these legitimate feelings—essentially through my style, and I can't say much about that. Look here, it's my view that the legitimate feeling here is sorrow. The *only* one! Not self-congratulation! And very few people understand this. There's nothing I can do about it. In fact, in my opinion people shouldn't adopt a pathetic tone to talk about these things, since that only belittles them. But all of that . . . I also think that you must be able to laugh, since that's a form of legitimate sovereignty. And I feel that all these criticisms of my irony are very unpleasant, indeed, from the point of view of taste. But these are all personal matters. I'm obviously rather unpleasant in the eyes of a great many people. I can't do anything about that. What am I supposed to do? They just don't like me. The style in which people express themselves—well, that's something they themselves aren't aware of.

FEST: One last question, Frau Arendt. There were a great number of people who advised against publishing *Eichmann in Jerusalem* in Germany. They used phrases like "a negative impact on public awareness." How exactly could such a negative impact come about?

ARENDT: Well, the Jewish organizations quite obviously have an odd anxiety: they think that people might misuse my arguments. "That's it," they think, the antisemites are going to say "the Jews themselves were to blame." They say that anyway. But if you read my book, there's nothing useful for antisemites in it. And many people think the German people aren't mature yet. Well, if the German people aren't mature yet, then we'll probably have to wait until the Last Judgment.

1964

LABOR, WORK, ACTION

For this short hour, I should like to raise an apparently odd question. My question is: What does an active life consist of? What do we do when we are active? In asking this question, I shall assume that the age-old distinction between two ways of life, between a *vita contemplativa* and a *vita activa*, which we encounter in our tradition of philosophical and religious thought up to the threshold of the modern age, is valid, and that when we speak of contemplation and action we speak not only of certain human faculties but of two distinct ways of life. Surely, the question is of some relevance. For even if we don't contest the traditional assumption that contemplation is of a higher order than action, or that all action actually is but a means whose true end is contemplation, we can't doubt—and no one ever doubted— that it is quite possible for human beings to go through life without ever indulging in contemplation, while, on the other hand, no man can remain in the contemplative state throughout his whole life. Active life, in other words, is not only what most men are engaged in but even what no man can escape altogether. For it is in the nature of the human condition that contemplation remains dependent upon all sorts of activities—it depends upon labor to produce whatever is necessary to keep the human organism alive, it depends upon work to create whatever is needed to house the human body, and it needs action in order to organize the living together of many human beings in such a way that peace, the condition for the quiet of contemplation, is assured.

Since I started with our tradition, I just described the three chief articulations of active life in a traditional way, that is, as serving the ends of contemplation. It is only natural that active life has always been described by those who themselves followed the contemplative way of life. Hence, the *vita activa* was always defined from the viewpoint of contemplation; compared with the absolute quiet of contemplation, all sorts of human activity appeared to be similar insofar as they were characterized by un-quiet, by something negative, by *a-skholia* or by *nec-octium,* nonleisure or absence of the conditions which make contemplation possible. Compared with this quietude, all distinctions and articulations within the *vita activa* disappear. Seen from the viewpoint of contemplation, it does not matter what disturbs the necessary quiet as long as it is disturbed.

Traditionally therefore the *vita activa* received its meaning from the *vita contemplativa;* a very restricted dignity was bestowed upon it because it served the needs and wants of contemplation in a living body. Christianity with its belief in a hereafter, whose joys announce themselves in the delights of contemplation, conferred a religious sanction upon the abasement of the *vita activa* while, on the other hand, the command to love your neighbor acted as a counterweight against this sanction unknown to antiquity. Yet the determination of the order itself, according to which contemplation was the highest of the human faculties, was Greek, and not Christian in origin; it coincided with the discovery of contemplation as the philosopher's way of life, which as such was found superior to the political way of life of the citizen of the polis. The point of the matter, which I can only mention here in passing, is that Christianity, contrary to what has frequently been assumed, did not elevate active life to a higher position, did not save it from its being derivative, and did not, at least not theoretically, look upon it as something that has its meaning and end within itself. And a change in this hierarchical order was indeed impossible so long as truth was the one comprehensive principle to establish an order among the human faculties, a truth moreover, which was understood as revelation, as something essentially given to man, as distinguished from truth being either the result of some mental activity—thought or reasoning—or as that knowledge which I acquire through making.

Hence, the question arises: Why was the *vita activa,* with all its distinction and articulations, not discovered after the modern break with tradition and the eventual reversal of its hierarchical order, the "revaluation of all values," through Marx and Nietzsche? And the answer, though in actual analysis quite complicated, may be summed up briefly here: it is the very nature of the famed turning upside-down of philosophic systems or hierarchies of values that the conceptual framework itself is left intact. This is especially true for Marx who was convinced that turning Hegel upside down was enough to find the truth—i.e., the truth of the Hegelian system, which is the discovery of the dialectical nature of history.

Let me shortly explain how this identity shows itself in our context. When I enumerated the chief human activities: Labor-Work-Action, it was obvious that action occupied the highest position. Insofar as action related to the political sphere of human life, this estimation agrees with the pre-philosophic, pre-Platonic current opinion of Greek polis life. The introduction of contemplation as the highest point of the hierarchy had the result that this order was in fact rearranged, though not always in explicit theory. (Lip service to the old hierarchy was frequently paid when it had already been reversed in the actual teaching of the philosophers.) Seen from the viewpoint of contemplation, the highest activity was not action but work; the rise of the activity of the craftsman in the scale of estimations makes its first dramatic appearance in Plato's dialogues. Labor, to be sure, remained at the bottom, but political activity as something necessary for the life of contemplation was now recognized only to the extent that it could be pursued in the same way as the activity of the craftsman. Only if seen in the image of work, could political action be trusted to produce lasting results. And such lasting results meant peace, the peace needed for contemplation: No change.

If you now look upon the reversal in the modern age, you are immediately aware that its most important feature in this respect is its glorification of labor, surely the last thing any member of one of the classical communities, be it Rome or Greece, would have thought of as worthy of this position. However, the moment you go deeper into this matter you will see that not labor as such occupied this position (Adam Smith, Locke, Marx are unanimous in their contempt for menial tasks, unskilled labor which helps only to consume), but *productive* labor. Again the standard of lasting results is the actual yardstick. Thus Marx, surely the greatest of the labor philosophers, was constantly trying to reinterpret labor in the image of the working activity—again at the expense of political activity. To be sure, things had changed. Political activity was no longer seen as the laying down of immutable laws which would *make* a commonwealth, having as its end result a reliable product that looked exactly as if it had originated in a blueprint by the maker—as though laws or constitutions were things of the same nature as the table fabricated by the carpenter according to a blueprint he had in mind before he began to make it. Political activity was now supposed to "make history"—a phrase that occurred for the first time in Vico—and not a commonwealth, and this history, as we all know, had for its end product the classless society, which would be the end of the historical process just as the table is indeed the end of the fabrication process. In other words, since on the theoretical level no more was done by the great revaluators of the old values than to turn things upside-down, the old hierarchy within the *vita activa* was hardly disturbed; the old modes of thinking prevailed, and the only relevant distinction between the new and the old was that this order, whose origin and meaningfulness lay in the actual experience of contemplation, became highly questionable. For the actual event which characterizes the modern age in this respect was that contemplation itself had become meaningless.

With this event we shall not deal here. Instead, accepting the oldest, pre-philosophical hierarchy, I propose to look into these activities themselves. And the first thing of which you might have become aware by now is my distinction between labor and work which probably sounded somewhat unusual to you. I draw it from a rather casual remark in Locke who speaks of "the labor of our body and the work of our hands." (Laborers, in Aristotelian language, are those who "with their bodies administer to the needs of life.") The phenomenal evidence in favor of this distinction is too striking to be ignored, and yet it is a fact that, apart from a few scattered remarks and important testimony of social and institutional history, there is hardly anything to support it.

Against this scarcity of evidence stands the simple obstinate fact that every European language, ancient or modern, contains two etymologically unrelated words for what we have come to think of as the same activity: Thus, the Greek distinguished between *ponein* and *ergazesthai*, the Latin between *laborare* and *facere* or *fabricari*, the French between *travailler* and *ouvrer*, the German between *arbeiten* and *werken*. In all these cases, the equivalents for labor have an unequivocal connotation of bodily experiences, of toil and trouble, and in most cases they are significantly also used for the pangs of birth. The last to use this original connection was Marx, who defined labor as the "reproduction of individual life" and begetting, the production of "foreign life," as the production of the species.

If we leave aside all theories, especially the modern labor theories after Marx, and follow solely the etymological and historical evidence, it is obvious that labor is an activity which corresponds to the biological processes of the body, that it is, as the young Marx said, the metabolism between man and nature, or the human mode of this metabolism which we share with all living organisms. By laboring, men produce the vital necessities that must be fed into the life process of the human body. And since this life process, though it leads us from birth to death in a rectilinear progress of decay, is in itself circular, the laboring activity itself must follow the cycle of life, the circular movement of our bodily functions, which means that the laboring activity never comes to an end as long as life lasts; it is endlessly repetitive. Unlike working, whose end has come when the object is finished, ready to be added to the common world of things and objects, laboring always moves in the same circle prescribed by the living organism, and the end of its toil and trouble comes only with the end, i.e., the death of the individual organism.

Labor, in other words, produces consumer goods, and laboring and consuming are but two stages of the ever-recurring cycle of biological life. These two stages of the life process follow each other so closely that they almost constitute one and the same movement, which is hardly ended when it must be started all over again. Labor, unlike all other human activities, stands under the sign of necessity, the "necessity of subsisting" as Locke used to say, or the "eternal necessity imposed by nature" in the words of Marx. Hence, the actual goal of the revolution in Marx is not merely the emancipation of the laboring or working classes, but the emancipation of man from labor. For "the realm of freedom begins only where labor determined through want" and the immediacy of "physical needs" ends. And this emancipation, as we know now, to the extent that it is possible at all, occurs not by political emancipation—the equality of all classes of the citizenry—but through technology. I said: To the extent that it is possible, and I meant by this qualification that consumption, as a stage of the cyclical movement of the living organism is in a way also laborious.

Goods for consumption, the immediate result of the laboring process, are the least durable of tangible things. They are, as Locke pointed out, "of short duration, such as—if they are not consumed—will decay and perish by themselves." After a brief stay in the world, they return into the natural process that yielded them either through absorption into the life process of the human animal or through decay; in their man-made forms they disappear more quickly than any other parts of the world. They are the least worldly and, at the same time, the most natural and the most necessary of all things. Although they are man-made, they come and go, are produced and consumed, in accordance with the ever-recurrent cyclical movement of nature. Hence, they cannot be "heaped up" and "stored away," as would have been necessary if they were to serve Locke's main purpose, to establish the validity of private property on the rights men have to their own body.

But while labor in the sense of producing anything lasting—something outlasting the activity itself and even the life span of the producer—is quite "unproductive" and futile, it is highly productive in another sense. Man's labor power is such that he produces more consumer goods than is necessary for the survival of himself and his family. This, as it were, natural abundance of the laboring process has enabled men to enslave or exploit their fellow men, thus liberating themselves from life's burden; and while this liberation of the few has always been achieved through the use of force by a ruling class, it would never have been possible without this inherent fertility of human labor itself. Yet even this specifically human "productivity" is part and parcel of nature, it partakes of this superabundance we see everywhere in nature's household. It is but another mode of "Be ye fruitful and multiply" in which it is as if nature herself speaks to us.

Since labor corresponds to the condition of life itself, it partakes not only in life's toil and trouble but also in the sheer bliss with which we can experience our being alive. The "blessing or the joy of labor," which plays so great a part in modern labor theories, is no empty notion. Man, the author of the human artifice, which we call the world in distinction to nature, and men, who are always involved with each other through action and speech, are by no means merely natural beings. But insofar as we, too, are just living creatures, laboring is the only way we can also remain and swing contentedly in nature's prescribed cycle, toiling and resting, laboring and consuming, with the same happy and purposeless regularity with which day and night, life and death follow each other. The reward of labor, though it does not leave anything behind itself, is even more real, less futile than any other form of happiness. It lies in nature's fertility, in the quiet confidence that he who in "toil and trouble" has done his part remains a part of nature in the future of his children and his children's children. The Old Testament, which, unlike classical antiquity, held life to be sacred and therefore neither death nor labor to be an evil (certainly not an argument against life), shows in the stories of the patriarchs how unconcerned about death they were and how death came to them in the familiar shape of night and quiet and eternal rest "in a good old age and full of years."

The blessing of life as a whole, inherent in labor, can never be found in work and should not be mistaken for the inevitably brief spell of joy that follows accomplishment and attends achievement. The blessing of labor is that effort and gratification follow each other as closely as producing and consuming, so that happiness is a concomitant of the process itself. There is no lasting happiness and contentment for human beings outside the prescribed cycle of painful exhaustion and pleasurable regeneration. Whatever throws this cycle out of balance—misery where exhaustion is followed by wretchedness or, on the other hand, an entirely effortless life in which boredom takes the place of exhaustion and the mills of necessity, of consumption and digestion, grind an impotent human body mercilessly to death—ruins the elemental happiness that comes from being alive. An element of laboring is present in all human activities, even the highest, insofar as they are undertaken as "routine" jobs by which we make our living and keep ourselves alive. Their very repetitiveness, which more often than not we feel to be a burden that exhausts us, is what provides that minimum of animal contentment for which the great and meaningful spells of joy that are rare and never last, can never substitute, and without which the longer lasting though equally rare spells of real grief and sorrow could hardly be borne.

The work of our hands, as distinguished from the labor of our bodies, fabricates the sheer unending variety of things whose sum total constitutes the human artifice, the world we live in. They are not consumer goods but use-objects, and their proper use does not cause them to disappear. They give the world the stability and solidity without which it could not be relied upon to house the unstable and mortal creature that is man.

To be sure, the durability of the world of things is not absolute; we do not consume use things but use them up, and if we don't, they will simply deteriorate, return into the overall process from which they were drawn and against which they were erected by us. If left to itself or expelled from the human world, the chair will again become wood, and the wood will decay and return to the soil from which the tree sprang before it was cut down to become the material with which men work and build. However, while usage is bound to use up these objects, this end is not planned before, it was not the goal for which it was made, as the "destruction" or immediate consumption of the bread is its inherent end; what usage wears out is durability. In other words, destruction, though unavoidable, is incidental to use but inherent in consumption. What distinguishes the most flimsy pair of shoes from mere consumer goods is that they do not spoil if I don't wear them, they are objects and therefore possess a certain "objective" independence of their own, however modest. Used or unused they will remain in the world for a certain while unless they are wantonly destroyed.

It is this durability that gives the things of the world their relative independence from the men who produced and use them, their "objectivity" that makes them withstand, "stand against" and endure at least for a time the voracious needs and wants of their living users. From this viewpoint, the things of the world have the function of stabilizing human life, and their objectivity lies in the fact that men, their ever-changing nature notwithstanding, can retrieve their identity by being related to the enduring sameness of objects, the same chair today and tomorrow, the same house, at least formerly, from birth to death. Against the subjectivity of men stands the objectivity of the man-made artifice, not the indifference of nature. Only because we have erected a world of objects from what nature gives us and have built this artificial environment into nature, thus also protecting us from her, can we look upon nature as something "objective." Without a world between men and nature, there would be eternal movement, but no objectivity.

Durability and objectivity are the result of fabrication, the work of *homo faber.* It consists of reification. Solidity, inherent in even the most fragile things, comes ultimately from matter which is transformed into material. Material is already a product of human hands that have removed it from its natural location, either killing a life process, as in the case of the tree which provides wood, or interrupting one of nature's slower processes, as in the case of iron, stone, or marble torn out of the womb of the earth. This element of violation and violence is present in all fabrication, and man as the creator of the human artifice has always been a destroyer of nature. The experience of this violence is the most elemental experience of human strength, and by the same token the very opposite of the painful, exhausting effort experienced in sheer labor. This is no longer the earning of one's bread "in the sweat of his brow," in which man may indeed be the lord and master of all living creatures but still remains the servant of nature, his own natural needs, and of the earth. *Homo faber* becomes lord and master of nature herself insofar as he violates and partly destroys what was given to him.

The process of making is itself entirely determined by the categories of means and end. The fabricated thing is an end product in the twofold sense that the production process comes to an end in it and that it is only a means to produce this end. Unlike the laboring activity, where labor and consumption are only two stages of an identical process—the life of the individual or of society—fabrication and usage are two altogether different processes. The end of the fabrication process has come when the thing is finished, and this process need not be replaced. The impulse toward repetition comes from the craftsman's need to earn his means of subsistence, that is, from the element of labor inherent in his work. It also may come from the demand for multiplication on the market. In either case, the process is repeated for reasons outside itself, unlike the compulsory repetition inherent in laboring, where one must eat in order to labor and must labor in order to eat. Multiplication should not be confused with repetition, although it may be felt by the individual craftsman as mere repetition which a machine can better and more productively achieve. Multiplication actually multiplies things, whereas repetition merely follows the recurrent cycle of life in which its products disappear almost as fast as they have appeared.

To have a definite beginning and a definite predictable end is the mark of fabrication, which through this characteristic alone distinguishes itself from all other human activities. Labor, caught in the cyclical movement of the biological process, has neither a beginning nor an end properly speaking—only pauses, intervals between exhaustion and regeneration. Action, though it may have a definite beginning, never, as we shall see, has a predictable end. This great reliability of work is reflected in that the fabrication process, unlike action, is not irreversible: every thing produced by human hands can be destroyed by them, and no use-object is so urgently needed in the life process that its maker cannot survive and afford its destruction. Man, the fabricator of the human artifice, his own world, is indeed a lord and master, not only because he has set himself up as the master of all nature, but because he is master of himself and his doings. This is true neither of laboring, where men remain subject to the necessity of their life, nor of acting, where they remain in dependence upon their fellow men. Alone with his image of the future product, *homo faber* is free to produce, and facing alone the work of his hands, he is free to destroy.

I said before that all fabrication processes are determined by the category of means and end. This shows itself most clearly in the enormous role which tools and instruments play in it. From the standpoint of *homo faber*, man is indeed, as Benjamin Franklin said, a "tool-maker." To be sure, tools and implements are also used in the laboring process, as every housewife proudly owning all the gadgets of a modern kitchen knows; but these implements have a different character and function when used for laboring; they serve to lighten the burden by mechanizing the labor of the laborer. They are, as it were, anthropocentric, whereas the tools of fabrication are designed and invented for the fabrication of things, their fitness and precision dictated by "objective" aims rather than subjective needs and wants. Moreover, every fabrication process produces things that last considerably longer than the process which brought them into existence, whereas in the laboring process, bringing forth these goods of "short duration," the tools and instruments it uses are the only things which survive the laboring process itself. They are useful for labor, and as such not the result of the laboring activity itself. What dominates laboring with one's body, and incidentally all work processes performed in the mode of laboring, is neither the purposeful effort nor the product itself, but the motion of the process and rhythm it imposes upon the laborers. Labor's implements are drawn into this rhythm where body and tool swing in the same repetitive movement—until in the use of machines, it is no longer the body's movement that determines the movement of the implement, but the machine's movement that enforces the movements of the body, and which, in a more advanced state, replaces it altogether. It seems to me highly characteristic that the much discussed question of whether man should be "adjusted" to the machine or the machines should be adjusted to the nature of man never arose with respect to mere tools or instruments. And the reason is that all tools of workmanship remain the servants of the hand, whereas machines demand that the laborer should serve them, adjust the natural rhythm of his body to their mechanical movement. In other words, even the most refined tool remains a servant unable to guide or to replace the hand; even the most primitive machine guides and ideally replaces the body's labor.

The most fundamental experience we have with instrumentality arises out of the fabrication process. Here it is indeed true that the end justifies the means; it does more, it produces and organizes them. The end justifies the violence done to nature to win the material, as the wood justifies killing the tree, and the table justifies destroying the wood. In the same way, the end product organizes the work process itself, decides about the needed specialists, the measure of cooperation, the number of assistants and cooperators. Hence, everything and everybody is judged here in terms of suitability and usefulness for the desired end product, and nothing else.

Strangely enough, the validity of the means-end category is not exhausted with the finished product for which everything and everybody becomes a means. Though the object is an end with respect to the means by which it was produced and the actual end of the making process, it never becomes, so to speak, an end in itself, at least not as long as it remains an object for use. It immediately takes its place in another means-end chain by virtue of its very usefulness; as a mere use-object it becomes a means for, let us say, comfortable living, or as an exchange object, that is, insofar as a definite value has been bestowed upon the material used for fabrication it becomes a means for obtaining other objects. In other words, in a strictly utilitarian world, all ends are bound to be of short duration; they are transformed into means for some further ends. Once the end is attained, it ceases to be an end, it becomes an object among objects which at any moment can be transformed into means to pursue further ends. The perplexity of utilitarianism, the philosophy, as it were, of *homo faber,* is that it gets caught in the unending chain of means and ends without ever arriving at some principle which could justify the category, that is, the utility itself.

The usual way out of this dilemma is to make the user, man himself, the ultimate end to stop the unending chain of ends and means. That man is an end in himself and should never be used as a means to pursue other ends, no matter how elevated these might be, is well known to us from the moral philosophy of Kant, and there is no doubt that Kant wanted first of all to relegate the means-end category and its philosophy of utilitarianism to its proper place and prevent it from ruling the relations between man and man instead of the relationship between men and things. However, even Kant's intrinsically paradoxical formula fails to solve the perplexities of *homo faber.* By elevating man the user into the position of an ultimate end, he degrades even more forcefully all other "ends" to mere means. If man the user is the highest end, "the measure of all things," then not only nature, treated by fabrication as the almost "worthless material" upon which to work and to bestow "value" (as Locke said), but the valuable things themselves have become mere means, losing thereby their own intrinsic worth. Or to put it another way, the most worldly of all activities loses its original objective meaning, it becomes a means to fulfill subjective needs; in and by itself, it is no longer meaningful, no matter how useful it may be.

From the viewpoint of fabrication the finished product is as much an end in itself, an independent durable entity with an existence of its own, as man is an end in himself in Kant's moral philosophy. Of course, the issue at stake here is not instrumentality as such, the use of means to achieve an end, but rather the generalization of the fabrication experience in which usefulness and utility are established as the ultimate standards for the world as well as for the life of acting men moving in it. *Homo faber,* we can say, has transgressed the limits of his activity when, under the guise of utilitarianism, he proposes that instrumentality rule the realm of the finished world as exclusively as it rules the activity through which all things contained in it come into being. This generalization will always be the specific temptation of *homo faber* although, in the final analysis, it will be his own undoing: he will be left with meaninglessness in the midst of usefulness; utilitarianism never can find the answer to the question Lessing once put to utilitarian philosophers of his time: "And what, if you please, is the use of use?"

In the sphere of fabrication itself, there is only one kind of objects to which the unending chain of means and ends does not apply, and this is the work of art, the most useless and, at the same time, the most durable thing human hands can produce. Its very characteristic is its remoteness from the whole context of ordinary usage, so that in case a former object, say a piece of furniture of a bygone age, is considered by a later generation to be a "masterpiece," it is put into a museum and thus carefully removed from any possible usage. Just as the purpose of a chair is actualized when it is sat upon, the inherent purpose of a work of art—whether the artist knows it or not, whether the purpose is achieved or not—is to attain permanence throughout the ages. Nowhere does the sheer durability of the man-made world appear in such purity and clarity, nowhere else therefore does this thing-world reveal itself so spectacularly as the nonmortal home for mortal beings. And though the actual source of inspiration of these permanent things is thought, this does not prevent their being things. The thought process no more produces anything tangible than the sheer ability to use tools produces objects. It is the reification that occurs in writing something down, painting an image, composing a piece of music, etc. which actually *makes* the thought a reality; and in order to produce these thought things, which we usually call artworks, the same workmanship is required that through the primordial instrument of human hands builds the other less durable and more useful things of the human artifice.

The man-made world of things becomes a home for mortal men, whose stability will endure and outlast the ever-changing movement of their lives and deeds, only insofar as it transcends both the sheer functionalism of consumer goods and the sheer utility of use objects. Life in its nonbiological sense, that is, the span of time each man is given between birth and death, manifests itself in action and speech, to which now we will turn our attention. With word and deed we insert ourselves into the human world, and this insertion is like a second birth, in which we confirm and take upon ourselves the naked fact of our original physical appearance. Since through birth we came into being, we share with all other entities the quality of *oth-*

erness, an important aspect of plurality that makes it possible for us to define only by distinction: we are unable to say what anything *is* without distinguishing it from something else. In addition to this we share with all living organisms distinguishing marks that make us individual entities. However, only man can *express* otherness and individuality, only he can distinguish and communicate *himself,* and not merely some affect—thirst or hunger, affection or hostility, or fear. In man, otherness and distinctness become uniqueness, for what he inserts with word and deed into the company of his kind is unique. This insertion is not forced upon us through necessity like labor and it is not prompted by wants and desires like work. It has no such conditions; its impulse springs from the beginning that came into the world when we were born and to which we respond by beginning something new of our own initiative. To act, in its most general sense, means to initiate, to begin, as the Greek word *archein* indicates, or to set something into motion, which is the original meaning of the Latin *agere.*

All human activities are conditioned by the fact of human plurality, that not one man, but men in the plural inhabit the earth and in one way or another live together. But only action and speech relate specifically to this fact that to live always means to live among men, among those who are my equals. Hence, when I insert myself into the world, it is a world where others are already present. Action and speech are so closely related because the primordial and specifically human act must always also answer the question asked of every newcomer: "Who are you?" The disclosure of "who somebody is" is implicit in the fact that speechless action somehow does not exist, or if it exists it is irrelevant; without speech, action loses the actor, and the doer of deeds is possible only to the extent that he is at the same time the speaker of words, who identifies himself as the actor and announces what he is doing, what he has done, or what he intends to do. It is exactly as Dante once said—and more succinctly than I could (*De Monarchia,* I, 13): "For in every action what is primarily intended by the doer . . . is the disclosure of his own image. Hence it comes about that every doer, in so far as he does, takes delight in doing; since everything that is desires its own being, and since in action the being of the doer is somehow intensified, delight necessarily follows. . . . Thus nothing acts unless by acting it makes patent its latent self." To be sure, the disclosure of "who" always remains hidden from the person himself—like the *daimon* in Greek religion who accompanies man throughout his life, always peering over his shoulder from behind and thus visible only to those he encounters. Still, though unknown to the person, action is intensely personal. Action without a name, a "who" attached to it, is meaningless whereas an artwork retains its relevance whether or not we know the master's name. Let me remind you of the monuments to the Unknown Soldier after World War I. They bear testimony to the need for finding a "who," an identifiable some-body whom four years of mass slaughter should have revealed. The unwill-ingness to resign oneself to the brutal fact that the agent of the war was actually *nobody* inspired the erection of the monuments to the unknown ones—that is to all those whom the war had failed to make known, robbing them thereby, not of their achievement, but of their human dignity.

Wherever men live together, there exists a web of human relationships which is, as it were, woven by the deeds and words of innumerable persons, by the living as well as by the dead. Every deed and every new beginning falls into an already existing web, where it nevertheless somehow starts a new process that will affect many others even beyond those with whom the agent comes into direct contact. It is because of this already existing web of human relationships with its conflicting wills and intentions, that action almost never achieves its purpose. And it is also because of this medium and the attendant quality of unpredictability that action always produces stories, with or without intention, as naturally as fabrication produces tan-gible things. These stories may then be recorded in documents and monu-ments, they may be told in poetry and historiography, and worked into all kinds of material. They themselves, however, are of an entirely differ-ent nature from these reifications. They tell us more about their subjects, the "hero" in each story, than any product the human hands ever tells us about the master who produced it, and yet they are not products properly speaking. Although everybody starts his own story, at least his own life story, nobody is the author or producer of it. And yet, it is precisely in these stories that the actual meaning of a human life finally reveals itself. That every individual life between birth and death can eventually be told as a story with beginning and end is the pre-political and pre-historical condi-tion of history, the great story without beginning and end. But the reason why each human life tells its story and why history ultimately becomes the storybook of mankind, with many actors and speakers and yet without any recognizable author, is that both are the outcome of action. The real story in which we are engaged as long as we live has no visible or invisible maker because it is not *made*.

The absence of a maker in this realm accounts for the extraordinary frailty and unreliability of strictly human affairs. Since we always act into a web of relationships, the consequences of each deed are boundless, every action touches off not only a reaction but a chain reaction, every process is the cause of unpredictable new processes. This boundlessness is inescapable; it could not be cured by restricting one's acting to a limited graspable framework or circumstances or by feeding all pertinent material into giant computers. The smallest act in the most limited circumstances bears the seed of the same boundlessness and unpredictability; one deed, one gesture, one word may suffice to change every constellation. In acting, in contradistinction to working, it is indeed true that we can really never know what we are doing.

There stands however in stark contrast to this frailty and unreliability of human affairs another character of human action which seems to make it even more dangerous than we would otherwise assume. And this is the simple fact that, though we don't know what we are doing when we are acting, we have no possibility ever to undo what we have done. The processes of action are not only unpredictable, they are also irreversible, which is to say that in action there is no author or maker who can undo or destroy what he has done if he does not like it or when the consequences prove disastrous. This peculiar resiliency of action, apparently in opposition to the frailty of its results, would be altogether unbearable if this capability had not some remedy within its own range.

The possible redemption from the predicament of irreversibility is the faculty of forgiving, and the remedy for unpredictability is contained in the faculty to make and keep promises. The two remedies belong together: forgiving relates to the past and serves to undo its deeds, while binding oneself through promises serves to establish in the ocean of future uncertainty islands of security without which continuity, let alone durability, of any kind, would ever be possible in the relationships between men. Without being forgiven, released from the consequences of what we have done, our capacity to act would, as it were, be confined to one single deed from which we could never recover; we would remain the victims of its consequences forever, not unlike the sorcerer's apprentice who lacked the magic formula to break the spell. Without being bound to the fulfillment of promises, we would never be able to achieve the identity and continuity which together produce the "person" about whom a story can be told; each of us would be condemned to wander helplessly and without any direction in the darkness of his own lonely heart, caught in its ever-changing moods, contradictions, and equivocalities. But this personal identity, achieved through binding oneself in promises, must be distinguished from the "objective," i.e., object-related, identity that arises out of being confronted with the sameness of chairs and houses, which I mentioned in the earlier discussion of work. In this respect, forgiving and making promises are like control mechanisms built into the very faculty to start new and endless processes.

Without action, without the capacity to start something new and thus articulate the new beginning that comes into the world with the birth of each human being, the life of man, spent between birth and death, would inevitably be doomed beyond salvation. The life span itself would be running toward death, inevitably carrying everything human to ruin and destruction. Action, with all its uncertainties, is like an ever-present reminder that men, though they must die, are not born in order to die but in order to begin something new. *Initium ut esset homo creatus est*—"that there be a beginning man was created," said Augustine. With the creation of man, the principle of beginning came into the world—which, of course, is only another way of saying that with the creation of man, the principle of freedom appeared on earth.

1964

POLITICS AND CRIME
An Exchange of Letters

Having been asked by Merkur *(the German journal for culture and politics) for a discussion of Hans Magnus Enzensberger's book* Politik und Verbrechen *(Suhrkamp 1964), Hannah Arendt responded with the following letter.*

New York, late 1964

I read the book with real enjoyment; I was only familiar with the reportage piece on the murder of the Italian girl that appeared in *Merkur,* which I also liked very much. Enzensberger has an acute sense for the specific and the significant detail. His intention, to tell old stories anew, is a good and important one. And he is often successful, for example with the story about the Russian terrorists. The book's weakest point is the political analyses or inferences. Of these, again, the last essay on treason is quite fine. But he himself surely cannot believe that Auschwitz "laid bare the roots of all politics to date." Did Herr Hitler refute Pericles? Did Auschwitz lay bare the roots of the Athenian polis? This sounds like an empty rhetorical phrase, though I suspect it is not, coming from such an extraordinarily gifted and honest author. In his use of detail, Enzensberger has learned from Walter Benjamin in particular, even stylistically—and I do mean learned, and not copied! This has great advantages, but it can also lead to dangerous misunderstandings. Another example is the facile equation of crime, business, and politics, which was first stated by Brecht. The crimes of the 3rd Reich are not crimes in the sense of the penal code, and the gangsters of Chicago, who situate themselves in the midst of society, are not the forerunners of the Nazis. They still rely, if not exclusively, on the protection that this society affords even to criminals, and they neither intend to, nor really have any interest in, seizing power. The Nazis were not business people, so, though the equation of business with crime may hold, it still is unpolitical: neither Al Capone nor the respectable businessman is political. These errors are quite understandable, when one comes from Marxism, particularly Marxism as reconfigured by Brecht and Benjamin. But it does not contribute to the understanding of political events. On the contrary, it is only a highly cultivated form of escapism: "Auschwitz laid bare the roots of all politics" is like saying that the entire human race is guilty. And where everyone is guilty, nobody is. The specific and the particular are lost in the stew of the general. When a German writes that, it is cause for concern. It means: it was not our fathers, but all people who caused this disaster. Which is simply not true. In addition, there is the dangerous sentiment which is being spread in Germany: if Auschwitz is the consequence of all politics, then we must be grateful that this consequence has finally been brought about. Oh, Felix Culpa!

All this to explain why, after some toing and froing, I will not discuss the book. It would be too difficult for me to separate what is quite excellent in it from what is misguided. I would like to speak with Enzensberger. He should come over here sometime. The Germans' (and not only the Germans') lack of understanding of Anglo-Saxon traditions and American reality is an old story. It can only be cured by visiting, not by reading.

Hannah Arendt

Tjøme, Norway, January 24, 1965

Dear Frau Arendt,

For many years I have read your thoughts, and for many years they have been helpful to me; I therefore owe you thanks; all the more so if some of these thoughts are now directed towards mine, or against them. So please permit me a few lines in response.

The errors of which you accuse me are of differing weights. Insofar as, in your eyes, they are based on Marxism, I would like to let the matter rest. We are working from different premises and arrive at different results. You believe, for example, that the "social question" cannot be resolved by political means; misery, poverty, and exploitation—so it says in your essay on "War and Revolution"*—can be mastered through technology, and technology alone. What was proclaimed two hundred years ago in the American Declaration of Independence, and with a sometimes frightening speed, has "become true," namely that all peoples "among the powers of the earth" will assume a "separate and equal station."

But I do not see the peoples of Africa, South Asia, and Latin America steering their own fate; they enjoy a separate and equal station only in the protocols of state visits; I see billions of people who live in our times, and are abandoned to misery, poverty, and exploitation; and I conclude from this that it will not be easy for me to correct my errors insofar as Marxism is to blame for them. They separate me from you, but this separation is bearable; for it does not result from any kind of misunderstanding, and it does not lead to moral condemnation of one party by the other.

But every word you put to me about Auschwitz, and all thoughts that relate to it, carry much more weight. I cannot bear the idea of standing by your judgment. This judgment rests on the sentence that Auschwitz has laid bare the roots of all politics to date. You interpret this sentence as evasive, as a "form of escapism." I would like to (and indeed I must) defend myself against this.

Let me begin with the conclusion that you suggest: "If Auschwitz is the consequence of all politics, then we must be grateful that this consequence has finally been brought about." This sentence is not scrupulous about justice or logic. It is morally irreconcilable with everything I have written, and it has no logical sense. The most extreme consequence of the development of nuclear devices would be the extinction of all life on earth. If somebody makes this statement, he should never receive the reply that we would have to be grateful if this consequence were finally brought about.

I do not draw this comparison by coincidence. For if I, be it with the insufficient means of a person who is neither an anthropologist nor an historian, consider the history that led to Auschwitz, I do so with regard to its future. It would be escapism, in my eyes, to pretend it was in the past, to act as though it were simply history, over and done with, which is how it is now being made to seem in Germany. Only the feeble-minded could

* Cf. *Merkur,* January 1965.

doubt that it is the Germans, and they alone, who bear the responsibility for the "Final Solution"; but in case my book should be read by the feeble-minded, I have repeated this very clearly three times, explicitly and unmistakably. However, we must think not only of our fathers, but also of our brothers and our sons; not only about the guilt of those who are older than us, but also—indeed, especially—about the guilt with which we burden ourselves. Therefore I say: "the planning of the Final Solution of tomorrow occurs in public" and "In 1964, there are only accessories to the act."* If that is the "general stew," it is not my invention, and the specific that threatens to get lost in it is we ourselves. Today, the vocabulary of "megadeath" sounds from every television screen. It is not a whit better than that of "special treatment." "Posterity attempts to judge those responsible for Hitler's 'Final Solution' and their underlings even while busying itself with the preparation of its own. This is its inconsistency. This inconsistency is our only hope—a tiny one." I should like to stand by this statement. "The Final Solution of yesterday was not prevented. The Final Solution of tomorrow can be prevented."† If that is escapism, then I lay claim to this title.

Allow me please, in conclusion, another remark on your sentence: "When a German writes that, it is cause for concern." I understand this sentence, and I understand why you wrote it. I accept it, from your mouth. But detached from the person who spoke it, it is cause for concern in itself; for it implies that the rightness of a judgment depends upon the nationality of the person proclaiming it.

I have encountered this *argumentum ad nationem* many times. I have met citizens of the Soviet Union who retaliated to any critical remark about their country's conditions by referring to the German attack of 1941. This reaction, too, is understandable. Of course, it does not relate to the conversation itself, but to the prerequisites for it. No dialogue is possible without a minimum of trust. But trust is something that can only be given freely. The

---

* Quotations are taken from the English translation of Hans Magnus Enzensberger's 1964 essay "Reflections Before a Glass Cage," which originally appeared in German in *Politik und Verbrechen*, the book under discussion here, and which contains the passage on Auschwitz. Hans Magnus Enzensberger, "Reflections Before a Glass Cage," trans. Michael Roloff, in: *Critical Essays*, New York, 1982, p. 115. —Ed.

† Ibid, p. 114.

argumentum ad nationem takes back this gift and turns the dialogue into a monologue; for how can somebody speak if his words always founder on his heritage? Everything he says then becomes a simple appendix to his nationality; he can only speak as the "representative" of a collective. He no longer speaks as a person; he becomes a mere mouthpiece for something else, and, like every mouthpiece, is himself dumb and gagged. Therefore I think: a sentence cannot become more of a cause for concern than it already is, through being spoken by a German, a Communist, a Negro, etc. It is either a cause for concern, or it is not. And by the same token—forgive me, I cannot help but say it—for me, the worst thing about the Germans' transgressions is not that Germans committed them, but that they were committed at all, and that they can be committed again.

My ardent hope is that you will understand me. The Germans and the Germans alone are to blame for Auschwitz. Humans are capable of anything. Both sentences are essential, and neither one can replace the other. You should not look for evasions, apologies, excuses from me. What is at stake for me here is not a book, and I know full well that no word exists that can be proved right before the word Auschwitz. With this in mind, I am prepared for you to believe I am in the wrong; I only hope you will not *do* me wrong.

Yours with the greatest respect,
Hans Magnus Enzensberger

New York, January 30, 1965

Dear Herr Enzensberger,

I am glad you have replied to those lines I jotted down rather carelessly, and that we have thus fallen into conversation. Let me say first of all that my intention was not to attack, but to express my misgivings. I did not for a second consider any antagonism, and I naturally assumed the "minimum of trust" of which you rightly speak. Nothing lies further from my mind than to do you wrong or to lump you in with others; the case could not be more different.

It is good that you have accused me of the *argumentum ad nationem*. In the very abbreviated form in which I set it down, of course it does not hold water for a second. But nor is the matter as simple as you make it seem. I would support you on the sentence directed to the "feeble-minded": "The 'Final Solution' of yesterday was the work of one nation: Germany," but not without explaining it. It was, as you write yourself, "Hitler's 'Final Solution,'" to which unfortunately a very large proportion of the German people made themselves accomplices, and none of the guilty parties ever dreamed of laying claim to this "grandiose plan" themselves, or of taking responsibility for it later. Which is to say that it did not need to happen, and it could also have happened elsewhere, albeit not everywhere; and finally, it cannot be explained by German history, in the sense of any kind of causal connection. But the fact is that it did happen in Germany, and thereby became an event in German history, something for which today all Germans must take political, but not moral, responsibility. My misunderstood sentence says: an opinion on the "Final Solution" that, for members of other nations, is nothing more than an opinion, when expressed in Germany has immediate, short-term political implications and consequences. For Germans, it is inevitable that the discussion of these matters brings into play interests that do not exist elsewhere. Only in Germany is Auschwitz a matter for domestic policy, to say nothing of its foreign policy implications, which understandably people often like to ignore. With this caveat I am prepared to agree with you, that *à la longue* the crucial thing is not that the Germans committed such crimes, but that they were committed.

Now to the sentence I took issue with, which basically constitutes the theme of your book: the equation of politics and crime. Let me begin with your logical objection. The logical equivalent of the sentence: Auschwitz is the consequence of all politics, would be: nuclear devices are the consequence of modern technology—and not, as you say: "The most extreme consequence of the development of nuclear devices would be the extinction of life on earth." There are many people today who hold technology as a whole responsible for nuclear weapons, just as you hold politics as a whole responsible for Auschwitz, and I would dispute the one as I would the other. But the matter for debate here is your equation of "megadeath" with the "Final Solution," and I fear that you have simply allowed yourself to be tempted into this equation by the ominous words "Final Solution." Megadeath would in reality be the most definitive solution to all questions,

but the Final Solution was "only" the "Final Solution to the Jewish question." It could be used as a model for the "solution" of similar questions,
and it is also plausible that nuclear weapons might play a role here, but it has
nothing to do with megadeath. The disastrous thing about Auschwitz is the
very fact that a repetition is possible without catastrophic consequences for
all participants.

The *political* consequence inherent in the development of nuclear devices
in warfare is quite simply the abolition of war as a political means—unless
one imputes to the devices themselves a consequence that they can only
have if men bring about that consequence. It is not certain that the political
consequence of warfare's technological development, in your own sense,
will be brought about; I think it very likely, but this is just an opinion,
which one can argue against. What one cannot argue against, as I fear, is
that Auschwitz remains possible, even if people everywhere cease to talk
about nuclear death.

Our concept of politics is pre-formed by Greek and Roman antiquity,
the seventeenth century, and the revolutions of the eighteenth century.
You surely cannot mean that Auschwitz laid bare the roots of this entire
history. And so I assume you meant to say: the roots of all *contemporary*
politics have been exposed there. But even within these limits, you can only
uphold your sentence through the parallel with, in short, Hiroshima. In my
opinion this is a false conclusion, which admittedly immediately suggests
itself, because both events took place almost at the same time in the course
of the war. But it ignores the fact that only Hiroshima and the bombard-
ment of cities, Dresden, for example, were connected to warfare, and in fact
they demonstrated that in a war fought with modern means, the difference
between war and crime cannot be upheld. But Auschwitz had nothing to
do with warfare; it was the start of a policy of depopulation that would only
be halted by Germany's defeat; Hitler, as we know, would have continued
this "eradication" even in peacetime. The policies of the Third Reich were
criminal. Can one therefore say that, since then, the difference between
crime and politics has ceased to exist? One can perhaps say that in a war
conducted with the most modern weapons the difference between war and
crime has ceased to exist, but this seems to me a false analogy.

A last word about evasion. There is an illusory kind of radicalism that does not so much throw the baby out with the bathwater as, through parallels which throw up some common denominator, subsume many particular things under a general thing, downplaying the specific thing-that-happens by making it one case among many. This is what I meant by the word "escapism." We all do this occasionally, as we are swept along, it seems to me, not by the "stream of history," or by justified concerns about the future, but by our process of association. It is a danger of our profession. One can counter it with the constantly renewed attempt to cleave to the specific and not to obliterate differences for the sake of creating constructs.

I hope you take all this as it is meant, which is to say with no offense intended.

Yours sincerely,
Hannah Arendt

INTRODUCTION TO *THE WARRIORS*
BY J. GLENN GRAY

Something strange and disquieting happened to this book when it was published seven years ago. As a rule, very good books don't go unnoticed, just as we hope that only very bad books end up on the junk piles in editorial offices. To be sure, almost everything imaginable can and does happen to the majority of printed matter which must fall between such extremes—neglect, *succès d'estime,* the best-seller list; and since this could hardly be otherwise in view of the flood of publications which, year in and year out, deluge critics and readers alike, much depends upon this rule for the presence of a minimum of standards and intellectual integrity in the general climate of our culture. But exceptions prove this rule, and when we see that Glenn Gray's *The Warriors* is among them, we can only pray that they may be rare. The book was almost entirely overlooked when it first appeared, and yet, by force of sheer availability on the market, it has acquired, slowly and surely, its own circle of not just admirers but lovers, a group of readers in very different walks of life who cherished it as a triumph of personal discovery and, perhaps, for this very personal reason, began to think of its author in terms of affinity, closeness, and affection, which are very rarely felt even in the presence of masterpieces. So let us console ourselves with the hope that such fraternal welcome, unmediated by critical and public opinion, awaits those authors who, for one reason or another, have not been sucked into the dubious mainstream of notoriety.

Moreover, with regard to this book, there is something oddly appropriate to its slow and intimate success. The author, an intelligence officer during the Second World War, tells what he experienced and learnt during more than four years of battle and enemy occupation; and since this particular warrior, of whom a friend even then had "thought of as *the soldier,*" happened to be a philosopher (he received, ironically enough, his induction notice into the Army with the same mail that brought him his doctorate from Columbia University) it took him fourteen years of remembrance and reflection to understand and come to terms with what had happened in those four years. This much time was needed to learn "simplicity" and to unlearn "the simplification of abstract thinking," to become fluent in the art and the language of "concrete" thoughts and feelings, and thus to comprehend that both abstract notions and abstract emotions are not merely false to what actually happens but are viciously interconnected; for "abstract thinking is strictly comparable to the inhumanity of abstract emotions," the love and hatred of collectives—my own people, *the* enemy, especially in wartime, or, finally, in a mood of disillusionment, either hatred of or blind allegiance to "mankind collectively [which] is doubtless as predisposed to injustice as nations are."

Hence, the first lesson to be learned on the battlefield was that the closer you were to the enemy, the less did you hate him—"a civilian far removed from the battle area is nearly certain to be more bloodthirsty than the front-line soldier," unless, of course, the soldier happens to be a killer, and only pacifists who hold abstract notions and emotions about war will mistake the one for the other. Thus, "soldiers who cherished concrete emotions found the moral atmosphere at the front so much more endurable than in rear areas that they willingly accepted the greater strain and personal danger of combat." These soldiers became our author's spiritual brothers for they, too, would agree that Nietzsche was "surely right" when he wrote: "Rather perish than hate and fear, and twice rather perish than make oneself hated and feared." And the second lesson was that no *ism*, not nationalism and not even patriotism, no emotion in which men can be indoctrinated and then manipulated, but only comradeship, the "loyalty to the group is the essence of fighting morale." This self-taught concreteness, an unswerving fidelity to the real, as difficult to achieve for the philosopher, whose formal education had been abstract thought, as for the common run of men who indulge in no less abstract feelings and emotions, is the hallmark of this singularly earnest and beautiful book.

What must strike the reader to begin with in a book about war is its peculiar stillness, the softly reflecting tone of this voice that never teaches or preaches but tells in the greatest modesty what the author remembers. The remembrance begins on the first page; after fourteen years, Gray has begun to reread his war journals and letters. This sets the scene. He finds them "sad and laughable and strange" as they remind him of Plato's description of the people in limbo at the end of *The Republic*. But they also make him aware of how much he has forgotten, of an "absence of continuity between those years and what I have become," and now he is afraid "to continue to forget" since such oblivion might indeed confirm "the deepest fear of my war years . . . that these happenings had no real purpose," that they "might well signify nothing or nothing much." This fear, he confesses, "is still with me." From which we may conclude that he never forgot but that only now the time had come to tell.

Surprisingly enough—as though he did not know how much what he has to tell would go against the grain of fashionable convictions and modern sensibilities in these matters—he begins his tale with "the enduring appeals of battle": the "confraternity of danger"; the "powerful fascination" of the "spectacular"; the "poignancy and intensity" of life in the face of death, for "just as the bliss of erotic love is conditioned by its transiency, so life is sweet because of the threats of death that envelop it"; the "lightheartedness" that comes from being "liberated from our individual impotence and [getting] drunk with the power that union with our fellows brings," a feeling akin to intense aesthetic pleasure when we are so absorbed by its objects that our "ego deserts us" and we feel no longer "shut up within the walls of the self and delivered over to the insufficiencies of the ego"; finally, the wondrous "compulsiveness" of love in wartime when "it falls upon us 'like a mountain wind upon an oak, shaking us leaf and bough,' in the striking simile of the poet Sappho." Gray sums up these enduring appeals, quoting General Robert E. Lee's remark, "It is well that war is so terrible—we would grow too fond of it," in the word "ecstasy" that occurs again and again; for what all these experiences have in common is that men are literally standing, or rather thrown, outside their selves, whether their " 'I' passes insensibly into a 'we' " or they feel so much "part of this circling world," so much alive that, in seeming paradox, death no longer matters to them. It is easy to agree that erotic love is of such an ecstatic nature, but the point of the matter is that comradeship is, too, and that friendship is not just a more intense form of comradeship but its very opposite: "While comradeship wants to break down the walls of self, friendship seeks to expand these walls and keep them intact. The one relationship is ecstatic, the other is wholly individual," the one is amoral (not immoral), the other is guided by moral responsibility. But since all morality depends upon self-awareness, and hence a certain amount of self-love, self-sacrifice is inspired by comradeship rather than friendship; for "friendship makes life doubly dear," and the "unendurable fear that grips friends on the battlefield is at the farthest remove from the recklessness of the soldier-killer" and of the "love for self-sacrifice" which, as we well know, can be aroused with equal ease for good and bad causes.

Rereading the book, one is tempted to quote endlessly and thus deprive the reader of his own discoveries and the great pleasure that goes with them. On the surface of it, this is a book about *Homo furens* and *Homo sapiens*, but in fact it is about life and death, love, friendship, and comradeship, about courage and recklessness, about sensuality and the "surge of vitality," about "inhuman cruelty" and "superhuman kindness," not as stereotypical opposites but as simultaneously present in the same person (for "war compresses the greatest opposites into the smallest space and the shortest time," that is its greatest fascination); and at the end it is about conscience, the very opposite of ecstasy, since conscience means "to set oneself against others and with one stroke lose their comforting presence." To be sure, these are no more nor less than the elementary data of human existence but "unless human beings are pushed to the extreme, we are not so likely to confront simple and primal realities," or to reflect about them.

Opposition to war comes easy today and for Glenn Gray it is a matter of course. It did not need Hiroshima and Nagasaki nor the fact that even in World War II more civilians were killed than soldiers in combat to teach him "the ache of guilt" which to his great surprise has been almost totally neglected in contemporary novels that deal so freely with every other agony of combat. Among the great merits of the book is that it makes opposition to the war forceful and convincing by not denying the realities and by not just warning us but making us understand why "there is in many today as great a fear of a sterile and unexciting peace as of a great war." And to make his point, he tells the story of a Frenchwoman whom he had known in the years of danger and suffering and then met again in peace and comfortable circumstances. She said: "Anything is better than to have nothing at all happen day after day. You know that I do not love war or want it to return. But at least it made me feel alive, as I have not felt alive before or since." Gray comments: "Peace exposed a void in them that war's excitement had enabled them to keep covered up," and he warns of the "emptiness within us," of the exultation of those who feel bound "to something greater than the self." Could boredom be more terrifying than all of war's terrors?

The book, in its undemonstrative subdued fashion, turns about a little episode that happened in the hills of the Apennines. There, not too far away from the front lines, he had encountered an old man, illiterate and apparently a hermit, who was peacefully smoking his pipe in the neighborhood of no living being except his donkey. The soldier was immediately welcomed beside him on the grass because it turned out that the old man was greatly mystified by the din and dust of battle which could be seen in the distance; he did not know that a war was going on. This was strange enough. But it was stranger that the two men, the soldier and the hermit, "began to talk at once of important things as naturally as if we knew one another well." Here our author was again confronted with "simple and primal realities," but now far away from the exultation of war and the extremities of battle, in "peaceableness and sanity," where the "familiar and the evident" seemed no longer remote because two men could share, outside, so to speak, of history, their concern about "the important questions: Who am I? Why am I? What is my function in life?" This was fraternity, and it was possible because one of them, the old man and hermit, was blessed with "the gift of simplicity" and the other, soldier and philosopher, had been stripped of his normal sophistications, of all that is subtly false in what we teach and learn. For this is what had happened: "The professors who had taught me philosophy and for whom I had had great respect and esteem became all at once puny in my imagination. . . . Even the great thinkers of Western civilization seemed suddenly to lose their stature and become only human beings. . . . Their wisdom was almost grotesquely inadequate for the occasion." No such wisdom could be expected from the illiterate peasant beside him on the grass; his company was not inadequate. Both were outside civilization, outside tradition and culture, the soldier because war had thrown him into one of those lonely foxholes with nothing to keep him company but "watching the stars at night," the hermit because it was "as though he had sprung from nature herself . . . her authentic child"; so the one had unlearnt and the other never possessed "the arrogance" that makes men "exaggerate the significance of the human story in relation to the rest of nature's household."

The book concludes as it should with reflections about "the future of war" and the prospects for "eternal peace." Rejecting optimism and pessimism as equally "irrelevant" and convinced that "peace will never occur as a consequence of weakness, exhaustion, or fear" he hopes that the day will come when the strong and the mighty—"a people distinguished by wars and victories," in the words of Nietzsche, quoted by the author—will "break the sword" because they can afford to say "that men ought to choose death twice in preference to being feared and hated," and that "survival without integrity of conscience is worse than perishing outright." Nowhere perhaps than in these passages does one understand better that Glenn Gray's friend thought of him as "*the soldier.*" For they express but the last and, under today's circumstances, inevitable conclusions of the soldier's basic credo—that life is *not* the highest good.

NEW YORK, FEBRUARY 1, 1966

ON THE HUMAN CONDITION

The questions that I am going raise will be asked from a little different viewpoint than that expressed by the other speakers we have heard today, most of whom represented a specific class of citizens—the scientists. Not being a scientist, I shall ask about problems we shall probably face in the near future, and how serious they are, from a general point of view. In other words, I shall try to pose the problems from the point of view of an average citizen of the United States, not as a member of *any* specific class of the population.

First of all, cybernation* *is* a new phenomenon. It must be distinguished from the industrial revolution of the past. The industrial revolution consisted of replacing muscle power, not brainpower. Today machines can take over a certain amount of human activity which we have always identified as the activity of the *human* mind. This calls, in my opinion, for a revaluation of mental activity. What, we must ask, is intellectual activity as such?

This reevaluation of intellectual activity, in itself, is not so new. When I grew up, for example, it was still commonly believed that good chess playing required a great deal of intelligence. If today we know that machines can play a reasonably good game of chess, then, I think, human dignity demands that we say that the chess-playing kind of intelligence apparently has not the same status as other kinds of intelligence, or as other kinds of thinking. In other words, chess-playing intelligence is inherent in something we quite accurately call "brainpower." Brainpower is not the same in different individuals, just as muscle power is not the same, since not everybody has an equal share of either one. But that does not mean anything

---

* "Cybernation" is a word derived from the more common "cybernetics" and refers to the separation of those working with computers from the rest of the working class. —Ed.

about the level at which a human being functions or about his special qualifications as a human being.

Let me cite another example. Mr. Perk talked about the fortunate fact that we can erase memory in the computing machine quite easily, but that is not so easily done in human beings where the process is called brainwashing. I would argue somewhat with Mr. Perk about one point: when it comes to performance, then the human memory, too, is very easily erased. As almost everyone who has ever lost somebody very close to him knows, one can, and usually does, adjust to the situation. One does not continue to feel the loss in such a way that he is prevented from functioning. In effect, that is erasing the event from memory. If human memory were nothing but what either helps us to function or prevents us from functioning, like the erasable memory of a computing machine, it would be a very sad state of affairs.

We know, of course, that remembrance—as distinguished from the simple technical faculty of memory—will stay with us regardless of the functions memory may, or may not, perform. To lose remembrance would indeed deprive us of a whole dimension of human life, namely, the dimension of the past. Similarly, we would have to revaluate and distinguish thought from the technical function of the brain, just as we distinguish remembrance from the technical function of memory.

The Life Cycle

Cybernation has also caused another phenomenon that will require much adjustment. The industrial revolution made life and certain kinds of work easier, but it did not cut (on the contrary, it lengthened) the working day. Many activities—work or labor—though they might have become easier, still consumed at least the same amount of time in the life of the individual. Because man's life, even after the industrial revolution, was still divided between periods of labor and periods of recovering from his labors, nothing was basically changed in the human condition, although the results of our work and our labor were changed very much indeed.

Or to put it differently, the nature of work was changed as the result of the industrial revolution, but the life cycle itself was not interrupted. A man returned to his home from his work, rested, and recovered the energy he would need for the next day's work. That is the cycle of living and laboring, of exhaustion and of recovery. And this cycle has its own rewards. In the Old Testament, a man was meant to labor for his daily bread, to bring it home to his family, and to recover his strength to be able again to earn his daily bread. That is regarded as the life cycle of man, and in the Old Testament it is not regarded as a curse. In the Old Testament we read of the bliss inherent in the natural cycle of laboring, resting, laboring.

Of course, the Greeks believed—and many among us believe—that it is not enough to labor in order to live, and to live in order to labor. But however highly we regard the Greeks—and I regard them highly indeed—the large majority of mankind has lived in the survival cycle that offered contentment, in the rewards of seeing one's children, and then one's own grandchildren, grow to maturity. In the life cycle of the simple things most men have gained their reward and seen their purpose.

Now, all of a sudden, we are to be deprived of this life cycle. Not the few whose ambitions always sought more than survival, but the men who were content and who found a certain dignity in their tasks are to be deprived of that dignity.

The Reversed Pyramid

It has been said that a reversed pyramid will occur, where the few will now work for the many, rather than—as it has always been—the many working for the few. With this reversed pyramid comes the reversal of "social status." Up to now, those who work less have had a higher social status than those who toil hard. But, this is changing rapidly. Those in the executive positions toil as hard as slaves ever toiled in some of the worst eras of history, for example, at the beginning of the industrial revolution.

I took a little poll among my friends recently, and asked them how many hours per day each worked. And I discovered that they work fourteen to fifteen hours per day with—at most—one day off per week. This is a decisive change, a fundamental revolution, which is not often discussed. The less important the job, the more "free" time a person seems to have.

I don't want to call this time off the job "leisure time," because I don't think leisure is the right word. Alice Mary Hilton's distinction between idleness and leisure, which has not been taken up by any of the previous speakers, needs now to be considered. Idleness *is* ugly. It frightens us a little, and it should. We must not think that civilization will simply and all by itself begin to flourish—as if culture can just happen—when there is "free" time. Most of the "free" time we have discussed so far is vacant time—idleness, as Miss Hilton defined it. And idleness, or vacant time, is tragic. Greek culture, where citizens had leisure, as Miss Hilton said, comes to mind. The Greek word for leisure—*scholē*—means an abstention from something else. It is the word from which we have derived the word "school." To have leisure meant that one abstained from certain activities to be free for others. Thus leisure is, as Miss Hilton points out, the very antithesis of idleness.

In ancient Greece, even the artist—the painter and the sculptor—was not recognized as a full citizen, because he was too busy. On the one hand, the freedom of the citizen was not to create the magnificent flowering of Athenian culture but to engage in political activity. On the other, the political tasks and duties of an Athenian citizen—and, in the great times of the Roman Republic, of a Roman citizen—were so all-consuming that he had neither vacant nor idle time.

Vacant Time

The problem of vacant time, of idleness, has only one historic precedent, which was during the decline of the Roman Empire. The Roman plebes had vacant time. And, as you know, the Roman plebes with their vacant time, although it continued through the centuries, did not bring about any flowering of culture. The vacant time of the Roman plebes was "mitigated," at times, by the endless wars waged by the Roman Empire. If I am right, and I hope I am right, we shall never again have such a "consolation." I think that at least traditional warfare as an instrument of foreign policy is probably on its way out.

The revolution we face is profound. Although there has always been a certain class of people who were freed from labor, this class was always on the highest level of society. Our hope now is that we shall all be able to live on so high a level. As a matter of fact, the laborless strata of human society—the aristocrats, to call them by their customary name—were also, for the most part, engaged in war and often developed a rather Spartan code of discipline. They were extremely rigid from fear of deteriorating in their complete freedom from labor and work.

Can We Adjust?

It has been questioned, whether a society can adjust speedily and by its own volition to a completely new set of circumstances. I am very much inclined to say that human beings—conditioned beings as they are by definition—can indeed adjust voluntarily and speedily. Man is not merely conditioned by his environment; he conditions the environment, and the environment then conditions him in turn. This particular cycle, that is now called "feedback," is quite obvious throughout the history of the human race. Man has always adjusted to new conditions more speedily than he thinks himself capable of doing. When the environment has in fact changed, we are conditioned—even if we don't know that we are conditioned, even though we may know very little about the conditions that have molded us.

Those who have had conditioning similar to mine, who have lived through the same changing periods I have seen, will know how adaptable we are. When I was a young child, there were still horse-drawn carriages in the streets. The automobile became the common vehicle for transportation. And then the airplane was invented and perfected. I have adjusted quite well and with little friction in my own lifetime to these very different conditions. And so have millions of others. Considering the changes caused by new methods of transportation and the additional changes caused by political upheavals, I am quite astonished at my adaptability.

But change in a life of vacant time may present a different problem. It is possible that the human species, adaptable though it has always been, may not be able to adapt to vacant time. For vacant time does not condition anything. Vacant time is nothingness.

Our economic problems in the wake of the cybercultural revolution will be relatively easy to solve. There will be many difficulties before we succeed, but our economic problems are soluble. The problem of vacant time, however, challenges some very deep moral commandments, commandments as old as the Judaic-Christian tradition. The precept "he who does not work shall not eat" is as obsolete and open to challenge as the commandment to be "fertile and multiply." Both were admirably suitable for an underpopulated, agricultural society. Both are dangerous for a cybercultural society plagued by a population explosion and affluence. We shall, I am sure, adjust beautifully to buying and selling with a new credit card, and to all the other economic and social changes. The danger is the problem of vacant time. Shall our precept change only from "He who does not work shall not eat," to "He who does not spend energy shall not be able to sleep"? That is, indeed, something altogether different. The change is really fundamental.

The Greek Model

If we want to take the Greeks as a model, then we must consider—before we talk about the flowering of culture—the political institutions of the Greeks. Let us look at the Greek polis and consider whether we want to adopt the institution of the polis, whether we would be able to adopt it, whether we could transpose this original model of political organization that was not even adopted by all the Greeks in the same way. For every polis was an isolated organism, completely separated from the other.

Can we—twentieth-century Americans—devise liberal institutions for our political lives which will fulfill the function the polis fulfilled for the free citizens of Greece? Can we learn to spend our lives in political activity and fill our vacant time with public service? These are the fundamental questions we have asked in our discussion today. And to these questions we must seek proper answers.

1966

THE CRISIS CHARACTER OF
MODERN SOCIETY

Ladies and gentlemen, the invitation to this symposium called upon us, as individuals who have had experience in dealing with particular crises, to recognize that there must be a state of crisis underlying the many crises in almost all fields of human endeavor, a situation of continuous revolution whose analysis should yield some standards, some guidance for action in the field of politics, to answer such questions as to what we should do in Vietnam, how we should deal with the United Nations, the significance of racial unrest, and the like.

Though I certainly share these hopes, I am not too sure that this will actually be the outcome, nor am I at all sure that the Colloquium would be a failure if it were not. Particular questions must receive particular answers; and if the series of crises in which we have lived since the beginning of the century can teach us anything at all, it is, I think, the simple fact that there are no general standards to determine our judgments unfailingly, no general rules under which to subsume the particular cases with any degree of certainty.

The crisis has often been defined as a breakdown of such rules and standards, and this not because we have become all of a sudden so wicked as no longer to recognize what former times have believed to be eternal verities, but, on the contrary, because these traditional verities seem no longer to apply. As Tocqueville noted: when the past ceases to throw its light upon the future, the mind of man wanders in obscurity.

This does not mean, of course, that the past has ceased to exist and to be relevant, but that it has lost its unquestioned validity. And though I very much doubt that the mind of man must then wander in darkness and obscurity, I must admit that the future, by the same token, has lost much of its always very precarious predictability. The simple but significant fact that modern art and modern science began their spectacular careers long before World War I, or before anything dramatic had happened in the political realm, seems to me to demonstrate that for better or worse this break in the tradition—that is, a loss of general standards and rules—cannot be undone.

I think no one has expressed with more concrete precision the impact this breakdown must have on the minds and hearts of men living under such conditions than Churchill. He wrote the following words more than thirty years ago—before Auschwitz, Hiroshima, the hydrogen bomb, etc.: "Scarcely anything materially established which I was brought up to believe was permanent and vital has lasted. Everything I was sure, or was taught to be sure, was impossible has happened."*

Theoretically it is, of course, quite conceivable that one could first define the general rules and standards that have lost their validity, analyze what was wrong with them, and then proceed to think up some other standards we hope will do better, be more adequate to the enormously changed and daily changing realities of our world. Practically speaking, I don't think this is feasible.

On the contrary, it seems to me that whenever we do this—and we are constantly doing it, though most likely without much articulation—we are likely to get ourselves into serious trouble. Obviously, the habit of subsuming particular cases and the adequate human response to them under general rules of behavior will die much slower than the old rules that once had been held valid. Today the general rules are taken from experiences in the thirties. And although I was much gratified to hear this morning an almost unanimous rejection of analogies between the present and Munich or the cold war period under Stalin, the truth of the matter is that our present policy in Vietnam is still by and large justified much too often by such analogies.

Totalitarianism, communism, appeasement have become a kind of negative standards of behavior that can be taken as absolutes. They tell us what

---

* Cf. "Some Questions of Moral Philosophy," in H. Arendt, *Responsibility and Judgment* (New York: Schocken, 2003), ed. J. Kohn, p. 50. —Ed.

to be against. This means that historical events are in danger of becoming substitutes for political rules that were discarded a few decades ago when we were first confronted with the unprecedented. We must try to think and to judge and to act not without taking account of the past but without trusting the validity of any so-called lessons of history. This is difficult and uncomfortable, but it also contains great challenges and perhaps even promises.

But these, some of you may reply, are wrong examples. The guidance for action that the editors of *Christianity and Crisis* had in mind was of a much loftier, more general nature. What we are here to talk about are moral principles. Well, I'm afraid we shall be confronted with similar difficulties.

Moral truth, be it derived from philosophy or from religion, resembles more the validity of agreements than the compelling validity of scientific statements. These agreements determine the action of all when they have become mores, morality, customs with their own standards of conduct that finally become self-evident. We all know how many centuries it took until men could say that all men are born equal, that this is a self-evident truth. This, too, is in fact an agreement; Jefferson said *we hold* this to be true, and he added the word self-evident in the hope of making an agreement—"we hold"—more compelling.

I personally do not doubt that from the turmoil of being confronted with reality without the help of precedent, that is, of tradition and authority, there will finally arise some new code of conduct. And if we are to trust the enormously promising developments in the arts and sciences—developments whose *conditio sine qua non* was the breakdown of tradition—we have no reason to be too pessimistic provided mankind survives at all. And this survival depends in good measure on the insight that such slogans as "There is no alternative for victory" won't do any longer. Although this was entirely right for warfare in former times, such slogans must be discarded once and for all.*

I would agree that, without such exchanges of opinion as this Collo-

---

* According to Arendt, after Hiroshima the struggle against war crimes has become a struggle against war itself, the implication being that the means of modern warfare are themselves criminal. —Ed.

quium provides, little headway can be made in this direction. This is as true of the perplexing questions of today as it has always been with the incomprehensible. Augustine once said that things incomprehensible must be so investigated that one should never think he has found nothing when he has found out how incomprehensible they are, because the one who asks these questions becomes better and better at questioning. And this, curiously enough, was also Socrates' opinion: namely, that though we cannot define goodness or beauty, and have difficulty in persuading men of our opinions in these matters, we become more just and more pious by thinking and talking about justice and piety.

By talking, therefore, about the unprecedented and by making decisions as we must, even though they may one day prove wholly inadequate, I believe we will become better able to deal with the underlying crisis even if we fail to define it, and will eventually lay the groundwork for new agreements between ourselves as well as between the nations of the earth, which then might become customs, rules, standards that again will be frozen into what is called morality. The only condition for progress in such matters (even though I hate the word progress) is that we are and remain aware that our problems are unprecedented and that we do indeed live in a situation of crisis.

1966

REVOLUTION AND FREEDOM,
A LECTURE

I

The following reflections will remind you of the troubled and perplexed state in which the public affairs of the United States of America, and indeed of the world at large, find themselves at the present moment. The title I give them is intended to anticipate my conclusions, for the words Revolution and Freedom seem to me to sum up about all we can see of an uncertain and flickering ray of hope in the otherwise rather dark and threatening prospects of the future.

Before we turn our attention to the uncertainties of hope, permit me to dwell for a few moments on the prospects of legitimate fear without forgetting, however, that they are by no means less uncertain. Immediately upon the close of the Second World War there followed a period we chose to call the "cold war," a term that I think was a misnomer. The fifteen years behind us were a time of uneasy "cold peace" in which the two great world powers have tried, more or less successfully, to define their spheres of influence and to jockey for position in the rapidly changing power structure of a world in turmoil. However, the very fact that we have been calling "cold war" what actually was "cold peace" testifies to our main preoccupation with the fear of war. That we have been far more preoccupied with this fear than with any other issue has been manifest in each of the major crises during this period—the Korean War, the Suez adventure, the Hungarian and the Cuban revolutions; in each of these instances, our conduct was primarily determined by fear of a major war that would be a war with nuclear weapons.

The recent and, let us hope, temporary resumption of atomic tests, on the other hand, may give us an indication of what a cold war actually may turn out to be. For these tests, unlike those that preceded them, have the ominous aspect of a new kind of maneuver in time of peace, involving in their exercise not the make-believe pair of enemies of ordinary troop maneuvers but the pair who, potentially at least, are the real enemies. The nuclear armament race has turned into some sort of tentative, hypothetical warfare in which the opponents demonstrate to each other the destructiveness of the weapons in their possession; and while it is always possible that this deadly game of ifs and whens may suddenly turn into the real thing, it is by no means inconceivable that one day victory and defeat may end a war that never exploded into reality.

Potentially, we were confronted with hypothetical warfare even at the end of the Second World War when many people thought it would have been much wiser, and not only more humane, to demonstrate the new atomic bomb to the Japanese on a deserted island instead of actually dropping it on Hiroshima; the demonstration itself would have forced the enemy into unconditional surrender. Obviously, this play with hypotheses presupposes a stage of technical development in which nearly all risks can be calculated so that there is hardly any room left for chance. It also presupposes an equality in knowledge and know-how among those who play the game. Thus a chess game between two equally experienced players will end with one of them conceding defeat or with both of them agreeing on a stalemate long before all the moves leading up to checkmate or stalemate have actually been made. I use this old comparison of war and chess not because I believe that it has been true in the past, but because it looks as though we were moving into a direction of mastering the technical means of violence in which the old simile might unexpectedly acquire its measure of truth.

Cold war, then, is actually hypothetical war, and hypothetical war, like cold peace, is determined by our justified fear of real war. It sometimes looks as though our only hope lies in the substitution of hypothetical warfare for real war—at least until we arrive at a state of international affairs which rules out the use of the means of violence as a last resort of all policy. To be sure, such a development still lies in a distant future; there exists, however, even now an indication that we may indeed be on our way to it. The indication lies in the rather obvious, though frequently neglected, fact that war can no longer be justified on rational grounds or on the basis of power politics. Of course, this does not preclude the outbreak of war, but it rules out most, if not all, of its time-honored justifications. Neither the ancient wisdom of "better death than slavery" nor the nineteenth-century definition of war as the "continuation of politics by other means" can possibly apply to the kind of wholesale destruction with which we may be confronted. The former, moreover, has its origin in the situation of prisoners in ancient warfare when the victor used to carry home the defeated enemy and sell him into slavery. "Better death than slavery" was meant as an individual decision, although it could involve a whole community if all the citizens individually agreed that they preferred to risk extermination rather than be dispersed into servitude. The decision, however, was based on the ancient conviction that to become a slave meant to cease to be human. To be free and to be human once were identical notions; a person unable to exercise all his faculties, mental as well as physical, was no longer considered a man, and this regardless of whether some kind of necessity, such as poverty and disease, or some man-made violence, such as war and slavery, had deprived him of them.

Do those who today repeat the ancient formula still believe in this coincidence of freedom and humanity? Do people when they hear the slogan "better dead than red" really think of freedom? Don't they rather have in mind a way of life and a standard of living that are the result of abundance and can be enjoyed even in a state of deprivation of freedom? Finally, is it not obvious that it is a very different thing to risk one's own life for the life and freedom of one's country and one's posterity than to risk the very existence of the human species for the same purpose? Even less applicable to our present circumstance is Clausewitz's famous definition of war, because it proceeds from the actualities of war in the nineteenth century and hence does not take into account the possibility of complete annihilation. War is the continuation of politics by other means only in the kind of limited armed contests, conducted according to the rules of the game, that we have known during a relatively brief period of our history. Perhaps this limited warfare can still survive in conflicts between small nations, although I doubt even this. It certainly is inconceivable in a war between the big powers.

In this as in other modern perplexities of a political nature, it seems we are not too well equipped to deal in terms of new thought with troubles that quantitatively as well as qualitatively are entirely new. Those who are ready to accept nuclear warfare as a last, albeit desperate, resort pretend that essentially nothing has changed, that the old justifications still hold, and they try to reassure themselves with the hope that "the losses may not be as great as some anticipate." Yet while we may be rightly alarmed at this optimism, which probably is nothing but lack of imagination, the inability to face the inconceivable, the truth is that those who oppose nuclear warfare on principle have come up with nothing better for *their* justification than their reversal of the old justification: "better red than dead." Hence the whole discussion of the war question, moving within the closed circle of an obsolete alternative, is nearly always conducted with a mental reservation on both sides of the fence. Those who say: better dead than red, actually think: the losses will not be so great, our civilization will survive; while those who say: better red than dead, actually think: slavery will not be so bad, man will not change his nature, freedom will not vanish from the earth forever.

Nobody doubts any longer that the threat of an atomic war is the greatest and the most dangerous of our political predicaments which, however, I am not prepared to discuss here. And even if I were, I am afraid I would not have much to contribute although the war question has been in the back of my mind, as probably in the back of yours, for many years. However that may be, the ray of hope, illuminating this dark background of our everyday worries, seems to be that nearly all concerned by now are agreed that war as such stands in need of justification and that its only possible justification is freedom. Thus the concept of freedom, which for a very long time had somehow disappeared from political discussion in favor of the notion that the end of government is not freedom but the welfare of the people, the happiness of the greatest number, has now returned, though in a somewhat oblique fashion, into the center of statecraft. And freedom is not only one among the many phenomena of the political realm, such as justice, or power, or equality; freedom, though it can be the direct aim of political action only in times of crisis, of war or revolution, is actually the reason that men live together in political organization in the first place. The *raison d'être* of politics is freedom, and without it, political life would be meaningless.

This intrusion of the notion of freedom into discussions of war and of a justifiable use of the means of violence is of relatively recent date. To be sure, justifications of war, even on a theoretical level, are quite old, although, of course, not as old as organized warfare. An obvious prerequisite for such justifications is the conviction that political relations in their normal course do not fall under the sway of violence, and this conviction we find for the first time in Greek antiquity, insofar as the Greek polis, the constitution of the city-state, defined itself explicitly as a way of life that was based exclusively upon persuasion and not upon violence. That these were no empty words, spoken in self-deception, is shown by the Athenian custom of "persuading" those who had been condemned to death to commit suicide by drinking the hemlock cup, thus sparing the Athenian citizen under all circumstances the indignity of physical violation. However, since for the Greeks political life by definition did not extend beyond the walls of the polis, the use of violence seemed to them beyond the need for justification in the realm of what we today call foreign affairs, or international relations, even though their foreign affairs, with the one exception of the Persian Wars which united all Hellas, concerned hardly more than relations between Greek cities. Outside the walls of the polis, that is, outside the realm of politics in the Greek sense of the word, "the strong did what they could, and the weak suffered what they must," as Thucydides tells us. What caused the early downfall of Greece was precisely this, that their polis organization did not find a way to introduce the nonviolent means of politics into the relationships between the poleis, that is, between city-states.

Within the historical framework of civilization, we find the first justifications of war, together with the first notion that there are just and unjust wars, in Roman antiquity. Yet curiously enough, these distinctions and justifications are not concerned with freedom and draw no line between aggressive and defensive warfare. "Just is a war," said Livy, "to whom it is necessary, and hallowed are the arms where no hope exists but in them."

(*Iustum enim est bellum quibus necessarium, et pia arma ubi nulla nisi in armis spes est.*) Necessity, since the time of Livy and through the centuries, has meant many things that we today would find quite sufficient to dub a war unjust rather than just. Expansion, conquest, defense of vested interests, conservation of power in view of the rise of new and threatening powers, and support of a given power equilibrium—all these well-known realities of power politics have perhaps only the remotest connection with a nation's freedom; and yet they were not only actually the causes for the outbreaks of most wars in history, they were also recognized as "necessities," that is, as legitimate motives to invoke a decision of arms. The notion that aggression is a crime and that wars can be justified only if they ward off aggression or prevent it, has acquired its practical and even theoretical significance only after the First World War demonstrated the horribly destructive potential of warfare under conditions of modern technology.

There is, however, another aspect of the war question in which freedom indeed plays the decisive part. From time immemorial, people have risen against the foreign invader, and while these warlike uprisings were never recognized, either in theory or in practice, as the only just wars, they always have been felt to be sacred. If war in our century is at all a justifiable act, then the only precedent to which its defenders might appeal would be such wars of rebellion and liberation. And this is not only a theoretical issue but a matter of recent recorded fact. The Second World War was in all its more important aspects no longer due to power politics in the old sense of the term. You may remember that it was considered by a sizable portion of public opinion to be a kind of civil war raging all over the earth. The extent to which this understanding was right was the extent to which the Spanish Civil War was indeed a kind of prelude to the ensuing World War. To be sure, the issues were confused; totalitarian Russia sided with republican Spain and sent the Spanish revolution together with the republic to their doom. Two years later, the same regime sided with totalitarianism in Germany, and it is certainly thanks to Hitler and not thanks to Stalin that Russia eventually had to fight a war of liberation and to side with those who fought not so much for freedom as against things which are considerably worse than slavery.

Yet no matter how confused and confusing the actual facts, one thing is undeniable, and that is the close interrelatedness of war and revolution. For better and worse, this relation has grown stronger today, and revolution, known to us for almost two hundred years, has been more closely identified with freedom than has any other political phenomenon or occurrence. "The word 'revolutionary,'" as Condorcet summed up what everybody knew in eighteenth-century France, "can be applied only to revolutions whose aim is freedom." If we view the sad political record of our age and if we consider how right Lenin was when he predicted, nearly fifty years ago, that the physiognomy of our century would be determined by wars and revolutions, our consolation may well be that at least it has always been freedom which, in one way or another, sincerely or hypocritically, was at stake. Even the tyrants today are forced to speak of freedom.

We may pursue these reflections a few steps further. The interrelatedness of wars and revolutions is not a novel phenomenon; it is indeed as old as the revolutions themselves, which either were preceded and accompanied by a war of liberation, as in the American Revolution, or which led into wars of defense and aggression, as in the French Revolution. Yet in these eighteenth-century instances, it was the revolutions that touched off the wars, whereas in our own century it has frequently been the other way around. It has been little noticed but is quite noteworthy that since the end of the First World War, we almost automatically expect that no government, and no state or form of government, will be strong enough to survive a defeat in war. (This is not entirely unprecedented; both the Franco-Prussian War of 1870 and the Russo-Japanese War of 1905 were followed by short-lived revolts in the defeated countries. In France there was even a change of form of government—from the Second Empire to the Third Republic—but still these were mere premonitions.) A revolutionary change in government brought about by the people themselves, as after World War I, or enforced from the outside by the victorious powers with the demand of unconditional surrender and the establishment of War Trials, as after World War II, belongs today among the most certain consequences of defeat—short, of course, of total annihilation. Whether this state of affairs is due to a decisive weakening of government as such, to a loss of authority in the powers that be, or whether no state, no matter how well established and trusted by its citizens, could withstand the unparalleled terror of violence unleashed by modern warfare upon the whole population, is an open question. In our context, it must be enough to remember the indisputable fact that even prior to the horror of nuclear warfare, war had become politically, though not yet biologically, a matter of life and death. Or, to put it another way: under conditions of modern warfare, that is, since the First World War, all governments have lived on borrowed time.

The close interrelatedness of war and revolution could be spun out further. These brief remarks are meant to suggest that our present topic, revolution and freedom, may somehow be connected with the as yet unanswerable war question, although it would be folly to expect an answer to the latter from a consideration of the former. We have come to a point of technical development where it looks as though the only choice left to men with respect to war is to abolish it before wars abolish mankind, as Mr. Kennedy recently put it—although it is by no means sure that this will be the last word in the matter. It is quite conceivable that the next stage of technical advance may bring us back to a kind of warfare which, though probably more horrible than the last wars, will not be suicidal and, perhaps, will not even spell complete biological annihilation to the defeated. What is inconceivable, however, is that war will ever again become the relatively benign and limited contest of arms whose outcome is not revolutionary because it leaves intact the political, though not the territorial, integrity of the defeated.

In other words, whatever the outcome of our present predicament may be, if we don't perish altogether (which I somehow think is unlikely despite all the evidence to the contrary), the problem of revolution is likely to stay with us at least into the foreseeable future. Even if we should succeed in changing the physiognomy of this century to the point where it would no longer be a century of wars, it most certainly will remain a century of revolutions. And since revolution has now spread to the four corners of the earth, any peaceful, nonviolent contest between great powers may well be decided by the simple question of which power understands better what is involved and what is at stake in a revolution.

II

In contrast to wars, which are as old as the recorded memory of mankind, revolutions are a relatively novel phenomenon. Prior to the great revolutions at the end of the eighteenth century, the very word was absent from the vocabulary of political theory. Moreover, and this is perhaps of even greater relevance, the word received its modern revolutionary meaning only during the course of these two revolutions; the men who made the first revolutions had no previous notion of either the word or the nature of their enterprise. They were, in the words of John Adams, "called without expectation and compelled without previous inclination"; and what was true for America was equally true for France where, in the words of Tocqueville, "one might have believed the aim of the coming revolution was not the overthrow of the old regime but its restoration."

Restoration, in fact, which we associate with the very opposite of revolution, would be much closer to the original meaning of the word. Revolution, an astronomical term, was introduced into scientific language by Copernicus's *De Revolutionibus Orbium Coelestium* (On the Revolutions of the Celestial Bodies), and when the word first descended from the skies to describe metaphorically what happened on earth between mortal men, it carried the idea of an eternal, irresistible, ever-recurring motion in the haphazard movements, the ups and downs of human destiny, which have been likened to the rising and setting of the sun, moon, and stars from time immemorial. It is true, we find the word as a political term already in the seventeenth century; but it was then used in its strict metaphoric sense to describe a movement of revolving back to some pre-established point, and hence, politically, to indicate a motion of swinging back into some preordained order. Thus, the word was first used not when what we call a revolution broke out in England and Cromwell rose to a kind of revolutionary dictatorship, but on the contrary, in 1660, after the overthrow of the Rump Parliament and at the occasion of the restoration of the monarchy. And even the Glorious Revolution, the event through which, rather paradoxically, the term found its definite place in political and historical language, was not considered a revolution at all, but, on the contrary, a restoration of monarchical power to its former righteousness and glory.

The fact that the word "revolution" meant originally restoration is more than a mere oddity of semantics. You cannot understand the meaning of revolution unless you realize that the first revolutions broke out when restorations were aimed at. We are liable to overlook this paradoxical fact because nothing in the course of the two great eighteenth-century revolutions is more conspicuous and more striking than the emphatic stress on novelty, repeated over and over again by actors and spectators alike—their insistence that nothing comparable in significance and grandeur had ever happened before, that an entirely new story was about to unfold. Yet this entirely new story was initiated, on both sides of the Atlantic, by men who were firmly convinced that they were about to do no more than restore an old order of things that had been disturbed and violated by the existing powers; they pleaded in all sincerity that they desired to revolve back to old times when things had been as they ought to be. Nothing would have been more alien to their mind than eagerness for new things or the present-day conviction that novelty as such could be desirable. The enormous pathos of a new era, of the *novus ordo seclorum,* which is still inscribed on all dollar bills, came to the fore only after the actors, much against their will, had come to a point of no return.

Before we try to ascertain the significance of this strange semantic change, and before we probe deeper into the causes that brought it about, we must turn our attention briefly to another aspect of revolution, which still corresponds to its old astronomic meaning and has not been discarded by modern usage, presumably because the experiences during the actual course of revolutions did not contradict it. As I already indicated, the astronomical term as well as its original metaphorical meaning implied very strongly the notion of irresistibility, namely, that the revolving motion of the stars follows a preordained path that is removed from all influence of human power. We know, or we believe we know, the exact date when the word revolution was used for the first time with an *exclusive* emphasis on irresistibility and without any connotation of a backward-revolving movement; and so important has this emphasis appeared to the historian's understanding of revolutions, that it has become common practice to date the new political significance of the astronomic term from this movement.

The date was the night of the 14th of July, 1789, in Paris, when Louis XVI heard from the Comte de Liancourt* of the fall of the Bastille, the liberation of a few prisoners, and the defection of the royal troops before the massed populace. The famous dialogue that took place between the king and his messenger is very short and very revealing. The king, we are told, exclaimed: *"C'est une révolte,"* and Liancourt corrected him: *"Non, Sire, c'est une révolution!"* Here we hear the word still, and politically for the last time, in the sense of the old metaphor which carries its meaning from the skies down to the earth; but here, for the first time, the emphasis has shifted from the lawfulness of a rotating, cyclical movement to its irresistibility. The motion is still seen in the image of the movements of the stars, but what is stressed now is that it is beyond human power to arrest it, that it is a law unto itself. The king, when he declared that the storming of the Bastille was a rebellion, asserted his power and the various means at his disposal to deal with conspiracy and the defiance of authority; Liancourt replied that what had happened there was irrevocable and beyond the power of kings. It was irresistible.

The storming of the Bastille, as we know, was only the beginning. The notion of an irresistible movement, which the nineteenth century soon was to conceptualize into the idea of historical necessity, echoes from beginning to end through the pages of the French Revolution. Suddenly an entirely new imagery begins to cluster around the old metaphor, and when we think of revolution, we almost automatically begin to think in terms of the images born in the days of the French Revolution—in the days when Desmoulins saw the great "revolutionary torrent" on whose rushing waves the actors were borne and carried away until its undertow sucked them from the surface and they perished together with their foes, the agents of the counterrevolution; when Robespierre spoke of the tempest and the mighty current which, nourished by the crimes of tyranny on one side, by the progress of liberty on the other, increased constantly in rapidity and violence; and when even the spectators believed they were watching a

---

* Arendt means the Duc de La Rochefoucauld-Liancourt. —Ed.

"majestic lava stream which spares nothing and which nobody can arrest," a spectacle that had fallen under the sign of Saturn: "the revolution devouring its own children."

The words I just quoted were not taken from later historical or reflective accounts of what was happening during those fateful years. They were all spoken by the actors themselves and they testify to things heard and seen and witnessed by them, not to things they had done or set out to do on purpose. To be sure, these phrases have by now degenerated into the cliché-ridden stock-in-trade of revolutionary oratory with a demagogic flavor; but even in their degenerated state they point to something real, to something that had never happened before the French Revolution but has happened since at regular intervals, first only in Europe and now in nearly all parts of the earth. Hence it may well be worth our while to ask ourselves what it was that Liancourt was the first to catch a glimpse of. What it was that the actors and witnesses of revolution saw and heard, and thought was irresistible and irrevocable.

The answer, to begin with, seems simple. Behind these words, expressed in entirely new images, we still can see and hear the multitude on their march, how they burst onto the streets of Paris, which then was not merely the capital of France but the capital of the entire civilized world. And this multitude, appearing for the first time in broad daylight, was actually the multitude of the poor and the downtrodden, whom every century before had hidden in darkness and shame. What from then on has been irrevocable, and what the agents and spectators of revolution immediately recognized as such, was that the public realm—reserved, as far as memory could reach, to those who *were* free, namely free of care for the worries that are connected with life's necessity, with bodily needs—should from now on offer its space and its light to the immense majority who are not free but driven by daily needs. Mankind had always known that there existed two aspects of freedom, one negative, namely, to be free from constraint through others, the other positive, namely to be free in action, to actualize not so much the I-will as the I-can. What also always had been more or less understood was that these two were interconnected, that no one could be free to do who was not free from constraint. Hence to the men of the revolution who were still in possession of the ancient wisdom, the road to

343

freedom seemed to be divided into two stages, the negative stage of liberation from constraint (or tyranny, or whatever phrase was used), which then was to be followed by the positive stage of establishing freedom, or rather of building a space where freedom could appear in the words and deeds of free men. The first stage was characterized by violence; the violence of liberation had to be pitted against the violence of tyranny, the violation of human rights and potentialities. But the second stage was supposed to be free of violence. The establishment of a new government, even when it turned out that the recovery of ancient privileges could be secured only by transforming them into constitutional liberties and hence was bound to begin an entirely new story, seemed to be a matter of deliberation, of the application of wisdom and prudence, rather than of violence.

However, this relatively simple scheme of revolutionary events—which in rough outline corresponds to the course of the American Revolution—was found to be entirely inapplicable the moment the French Revolution appeared on the historical scene. It had left out of account the existence of those who never had been admitted to the public realm, whom antiquity had held in slavery, who are found in a state of serfdom throughout the Middle Ages, and to whom even the first centuries of the modern age had granted no more than the very precarious status of the "laboring poor." Hence freedom, it turned out now, had always been a privilege, the privilege of the few, and this not only in the public realm with the rights of citizenship, but in its negative aspect as well: only the few were free to be free. For—and this is decisive—the negative sense of liberty was now seen as consisting of considerably more than being free from constraint by others; it was not only, to use our present terminology, freedom from fear that was involved but most emphatically and even primarily freedom from want.

Freedom from fear is a privilege that even the few have enjoyed only in relatively short periods of history, but freedom from want has indeed been the great privilege by which an infinitely small percentage of men has been distinguished throughout the centuries. Perhaps, one is tempted to add, only those who know freedom from want are in a position to appreciate fully what it means to be free from fear. What has seemed irrevocable ever since the French Revolution was that those who were devoted to freedom could never again be reconciled to a state of affairs where freedom from want was a privilege of the few. Men who had started out to retrieve their own ancient privileges and liberties saw themselves all of a sudden confronted with the enormous task of liberating the people at large, who had never possessed those privileges and liberties. In other words, at least in principle, freedom has been identified with complete equality ever since the revolutions of the eighteenth century; and although it is true that the political theory and practice of antiquity were very well aware of the fact that no one can be free who does not move among his equals, it is no less true that never before had this desire for equality comprehended the whole population of any country. This was the first, and perhaps still is the greatest and most far-reaching consequence of revolution. This is what Robespierre meant when he said the revolution had pitted the grandeur of man against the pettiness of the great, or what Hamilton had in mind when he spoke of the American Revolution having vindicated the honor of the human race, or what Kant finally, taught by Rousseau and the French Revolution, conceived of as the new "dignity of man."

However, as I mentioned before, the actors and spectators of the French Revolution were not only, and perhaps not even primarily, impressed by the irrevocability of what had been done when they had opened the doors to the masses of the poor, but by the irresistibility of the movement itself, by the sense that the revolutionary tempest, though unleashed by men, could not then be arrested by human power. That this was the impression of the king and his messenger may not be very surprising, for they certainly had played no role in bringing forth these events. It is, of course, different with the men of the revolution from whose immediate reactions and their telling imagery I quoted just now. Obviously, they knew they had started something whose consequences and inherent force they themselves had not foreseen and could not control; their action, though aiming at liberty, had liberated something which in its irresistibility they had not known and not seen before. It was only now, when the people of Paris came streaming into the streets, that the very word *le peuple* acquired its revolutionary connotations and thus became the key term of revolutions. What they, as opposed to the king and his messenger, saw as being irresistible was the enormity as well as the pressing urgency of an "unhappiness" that no one before had conceived of as a political factor of the first magnitude.

To illustrate this relationship between the men of the revolution and the multitude in the street, let me quote Lord Acton's interpretative description of the famous women's march to Versailles, one of the turning points in the French Revolution. The marchers "played the genuine part of mothers whose children were starving in squalid homes, and they thereby afforded to motives which they neither shared nor understood the aid of a diamond point that nothing could withstand." The motives neither shared nor understood by the multitude were those of the deputies as they originally arrived and assembled in Paris to represent the "nation" rather than the "people"; what they were concerned with—whether their name was Mirabeau or Robespierre, Danton or Saint-Just—was government, the reformation of monarchy, or, somewhat later, the foundation of a republic. To put it another way, their original goal was freedom, either in the form of retrievance of ancient liberties or in the form of the *constitutio libertatis,* the foundation and constitution of freedom. Paris, however, to their surprise taught them a lesson about the conditions and prerequisites of liberty which mankind has never forgotten since. The lesson, despite its elementary simplicity, was new and unexpected. It said: *"Si vous voulez fonder une république, vous devez vous occuper de tirer le peuple d'un état de misère qui les corrompt. On n'a point de vertus politiques sans orgueil; on n'a point d'orgueil dans la détresse"** (Saint-Just). Freedom, even freedom from constraint, was but an empty word for those who were not liberated from poverty; hence liberation, which must precede freedom, did not merely mean liberation from a tyrannical king or a tyrannical form of government, but meant liberation from want. Once they had been forced to look, and to look in public, upon the immense misery of those whom even Jefferson, the great lover of the people, could call "*la canaille* [riffraff] of the big cities," it was obvious that liberation had to mean first of all "dress and food and the reproduction of the species," as the *sans-culottes* began to distinguish their

---

* "To found a republic you must lift the people from the misery that corrupts them. There are no political virtues without pride; there is no pride in grief." —Ed.

own rights from the lofty language of the proclamation of "the rights of man and of the citizen." Liberation meant provision with life's necessities, the abolition of what then was called "unhappiness," in short, the solution of the social question. Compared to the urgency of these demands, all deliberations about the best form of government appeared irrelevant and futile. "*La République?*" Robespierre was soon to exclaim, "*la Monarchie? Je ne connais que la question sociale.*"* And Saint-Just, at the end of his short life—as though he had forgotten all his earlier enthusiasm for "republican institutions" and public freedom—concluded: "The freedom of the people is in its private life. Let government be only the force to protect this state of simplicity against force itself."

Let me return for a moment to the term "unhappiness" which, because of the altogether different experiences of the American Revolution, does not carry the same weight and the same connotations as the French words, *le malheur, les malheureux*. The unhappy ones, *les malheureux*—this word became in the course of the French Revolution what it had never been before: it became synonymous with the word *le peuple*, the people. "*Le peuple, les malheureux m'applaudissent*"†—this was almost idiomatic in revolutionary oratory. And the point of the matter is that it was precisely this *malheur*, this misery and unhappiness that were felt to be irresistible, the "diamond point which nothing could withstand." What appeared here and was found to be irresistible was necessity, the necessity to which all mortals are bound by virtue of being subjected to their bodies' daily needs and urges, hence a necessity which, prior to the modern age, had always been hidden and protected against the public realm and its freedom, within the relative security of the home and the private life of the family. Once this necessity appeared in public, embodied in the sufferings of the immense majority of the population, it was found that there was no greater force on earth. Hence, in the words of the French Revolution, *les malheureux sont la puissance de la terre.*‡

---

* "Republic? Monarchy? I am aware only of the social question." —Ed.
† "The people, the unhappy, applaud me." —Ed.
‡ "The unhappy are the power of the earth." —Ed.

III

I have dwelt at some length on this lesson drawn from the pages of the French Revolution because the same facts and experiences have appeared in nearly every revolution. It was the French and not the American Revolution that set the world on fire, and it was consequently from the course of the French Revolution, and not from the course of events in America or from the acts of the Founding Fathers, that our present use of the word "revolution" has received its connotations and overtones everywhere, this country not excluded. But if we wish to understand what is involved in revolution, we must not fail to remember that this first fight to give battle to poverty and to deal politically with necessity was lost, and with it the original aim of revolution, the establishment and constitution of freedom, was also lost.

What the course of the French Revolution established once and for all was that the conquest of poverty is a prerequisite for the foundation of freedom; yet what we can also learn from the same revolution is that poverty and necessity cannot be dealt with in the same way as violence, the violation of rights and liberties. Obviously, the tragic mistake of the men of the French Revolution was to pit violence against necessity; but they entered upon this foredoomed path only after they had used and misused necessity, the mighty force of want and misery and destitution, in their struggle against tyranny, that is, when they hoped to add to their own efforts that "diamond point" that would make them irresistible. This "diamond point" then turned against them, until they perished in the same fashion as the old regime whose downfall they had brought about. For, theoretically speaking, if violence pitted against violence leads to war, civil or foreign, violence pitted against necessity has always led to terror. Terror rather than mere violence, or terror let loose after the old regime has been defeated and the new regime established, is what sends revolutions to their doom. The first indication of ruin comes when those newly risen to power begin to forget that the sole aim and end of revolution is freedom. Hence the beginning of the end of the French Revolution came when all participants, moved by the misery of the people, suddenly agreed: *Le but de la Révolution est le Bonheur du Peuple.**

I said that these facts and experiences have appeared in *nearly* every revolution, and the great exception I had in my mind was, of course, the American Revolution. It may be an oversimplification to say that the American Revolution succeeded where all other revolutions failed, but such historical oversimplifications are not only justified but also needed when we try to understand in terms of thought and remembrance. However, if we may say the American Revolution succeeded because the men of the revolution became the Founding Fathers of the American Republic, we must add at once that this success was due almost entirely to the absence, in the American pre-revolutionary scene, of those factors of poverty, misery, unhappiness, and hence of necessity which then were present almost everywhere, and which even today are still decisive factors in the greater part of the world. I must refrain here from quoting the evidence, extant in numerous travelers' reports from America throughout the eighteenth century and reaching back deep into the seventeenth. We have, moreover, the horror-struck accounts of American travelers to Europe, among them, as you know, some of the Founding Fathers themselves, which gave witness to a veritable abyss separating social conditions in this country from those found abroad. America had been a country of prosperity and abundance long before it became, in the eyes of the world at large, the land of the free. And prosperity and abundance, which some among us today believe they owe to a system of free enterprise and to the political institutions of liberty, were of course chiefly due to entirely natural causes, to the immensity of the continent and the enormous wealth of its resources.

Hence, when I said the American Revolution succeeded where all others failed, I did not mean to say that it succeeded in solving the social question, that is, that it found political ways and means to cure a country from the curse of poverty. This is not to deny the enormous and enormously revolutionizing influence of the New World's prosperity upon the events and hopes of the Old World. On the contrary, it is perfectly true that here,

---

* "The end of the Revolution is the happiness of the people." —Ed.

for the first time, men began to see and to believe that misery and want do not have to be part and parcel of the human condition. John Adams said: "I always consider the settlement of America as the opening of a grand scheme and design in Providence for the illumination of the ignorant and the emancipation of the slavish part of mankind all over the earth." But he wrote these words ten years before the outbreak of revolution, in a state of perfect unawareness of such a possibility. In other words, the social question could not very well be solved by revolution in America for the simple reason that at that moment no such solution was required—if we leave out of account, as we must here, the predicament of Negro slavery and the altogether different problem it posed. Therefore, undisturbed by any outside factors the revolution could accomplish its original aim: the establishment of institutions which guarantee liberty for all, and the foundation of a new public realm, called a republic, as opposed to a monarchy, where everybody, in the words of Jefferson, could become a "participator in government."

Before I try to sum up and to draw a few conclusions, permit me to indicate to you as briefly as I can a few of the things which were involved in this *constitutio libertatis*, in the foundation of freedom. First of all, it was a question of political freedom and not civil rights and liberties that could have been obtained through the establishment of a constitutional monarchy—a possibility indeed that was reflected upon and then decided against precisely because it would not have permitted the citizenry to participate in public business. For the absence of freedom under the rule of enlightened absolutism in the eighteenth century did not consist so much in the denial of personal liberties, as in the fact that, in the words of Tocqueville, "the world of public affairs was not only hardly known but was invisible" to anybody outside the king's entourage. What those who made the French Revolution shared with the poor—quite apart and also prior to the role these poor were then to play—was obscurity, namely, that the public realm was invisible to them and that, by the same token, they lacked the public space where they themselves could become visible and be of significance. Hence, love of freedom, for the men of the revolutions on both sides of the Atlantic, comprehended those passions for distinction, emulation, significance, and being seen in action (*spectemur agendo*) whose political, and not psychological, significance John Adams discovered and analyzed in nearly all of his political writings. These passions—which he then summed up in one sentence: "It is in action and not in rest that we find our pleasure"— have been among the decisive and, unfortunately, neglected motives in those who became revolutionists in the nineteenth and twentieth centuries. It is indeed for the sake of action and for the sake of thought that freedom as a political reality is required. This political freedom is distinct from civil rights and liberties, which in all constitutional countries restrain the power of government and protect the individual in his legitimate private and social pursuits. Such rights and liberties are guaranteed by the body politic. Hence, seen from the viewpoint of the political realm, they are negative freedoms, they spell out the limitations not only of government but of the public realm as such. The chief political freedoms, or the chief positive freedoms, are freedom of speech and freedom of assembly. By freedom of speech I understand here not merely the right to speak out freely in private without the government listening in on what I say (which, as you know, is the rule now in all countries under communist domination); this right belongs among the negative freedoms of being properly protected from public power. Freedom of speech means the right to speak and to be heard in public, and so long as man's reason is not infallible, this freedom will remain the prerequisite for freedom of thought. Freedom of thought without freedom of speech is an illusion. Freedom of assembly, furthermore, is the prerequisite for freedom of action insofar as no man can act alone.

Before we entered into these considerations, I said that the conflict that divides the world today—if it is not to be decided by the means of violence and not to end in total annihilation—may well be determined by the extent to which we understand what is at stake in revolution. There are, to sum up, chiefly two things involved: the liberation of the poor and of the oppressed, that is, the solution of the social question and the abolition of colonialism, *and* the foundation of freedom, the establishment of a new body politic. It seems to me that America does not understand liberation very well, and that her statesmen are not very well equipped to deal with it. They lack experience. I mentioned the absence of poverty from the American scene prior to the revolution, and I may add that the War of Independence was not fought against a colonial power in the later imperial sense of the word.

With the foundation of freedom, the constitution of a new political entity, it is altogether different. In this respect, the United States should be able to set an example to the whole world, and more particularly to those new ethnic groups and peoples who in rapid succession are rising to nationhood. I am afraid we have been found wanting even in this, and the reason for our failing lies, of course, in that we deal here with the race question that we have been unable to solve even in our own country. The present nonviolent fight of our Negro fellow citizens for political and civil equality could teach us some elementary lessons about this aspect of revolution and thus become one of our greatest assets in the future instead of the greatest liability of our foreign policy.

However that may be, let us not forget that every revolution must go through two stages, the stage of liberation—from poverty or from foreign domination—and the stage of foundation of freedom. In terms of a political process, these two belong together, and yet as political phenomena they are entirely different and must be kept distinct. What we must try to understand is not simply the theoretical truism that liberation is the prerequisite for freedom, but the practical truth that liberation from necessity, because of its urgency, always takes precedence over the building of freedom. Even more important is to keep in mind that poverty cannot be defeated by political means, that the whole record of past revolutions—if we only knew how to read it—determines beyond doubt that every attempt to solve the social question with political means leads to terror, and that terror sends revolutions to their doom. If we were still living under conditions where scarcity and abundance were entirely natural phenomena, there would indeed be no hope that revolution could ever succeed in the world at large. The great original American experience of foundation on which the republic of the United States rests would remain what it has been for so long, an exception from an iron rule and an incident of hardly more than local significance. But this is no longer the case. Even though the difficulties standing in the way to a solution of the predicament of mass poverty are still enormous, there exists today the very legitimate hope that the advancement of the natural sciences will open, in a not too distant future, possibilities of dealing with these economic matters on technical grounds outside of all political considerations. To be sure, the solution of the social question that technology, and nothing else, holds in store by no means guarantees the eventual establishment of freedom, it would only remove the most obvious obstacle; but even the mere prospect of this solution should once and for all preclude the terrible and terribly dangerous usage of the "diamond point" of necessity for the purpose of ushering in freedom. For technical means in the fight against poverty can be handled in complete political neutrality; they need not interfere with political developments one way or the other. The wreckage of freedom on the rock of necessity, which we have witnessed over and over again since Robespierre introduced his "despotism of liberty," is no longer unavoidable.

In conclusion, let me point to the last two major revolutions—the Hungarian Revolution, which so quickly and so brutally was crushed by foreign domination, and the Cuban Revolution, which has not yet come to its end. The Hungarian Revolution was the only revolution I know of since the American Revolution in which the question of bread, poverty, and the order of society played no role whatsoever. It was entirely political in the sense that the people fought for nothing but freedom—freedom of thought and action, of speech and assembly—and that their chief concern was the form their new government was to assume. Whereby it is important to remember that none of the participants—and they constituted for all practical purposes the entire population—ever thought of undoing the profound social change which the communist regime had effected in the country. It was precisely the social conditions they took for granted—just as, under vastly different circumstances, the men of the American Revolution took for granted the social and economic conditions of their people. The Cuban Revolution, unfortunately, offers the opposite example for very obvious reasons; up to now, it has run true to the course of the French Revolution. And while America's attitude during the Hungarian crisis, right or wrong, was not the result of a failure to understand what was involved in that revolution, I think the same cannot be said with respect to the Cuban Revolution, which only geographically is so much closer to America's sphere of interest and comprehension. While the failure in the case of the Hungarian Revolution can be traced to power politics, the failure in the case of the Cuban Revolution includes a failure to understand what it means when a poverty-stricken people in a backward country, with corruption having been rampant for so very long a time, is suddenly released from the obscurity of their farms and houses, brought out into the streets of a capital they never have even seen before, and told: All this is yours, these are your streets, and your buildings, and your possessions, and hence your pride! Since these people passionately aspire to walk in dignity, without yet knowing what it might mean to act in freedom, it will take them a considerably longer time than it may take a government's so-called experts—those, that is, who think they know everything because they can imagine nothing—to realize that they may have been deceived and pushed onto the road which leads not to freedom but to tyranny.

For those who, without great merit of their own, enjoy the privilege of living under conditions that permit them to walk in dignity and to act in freedom, it would be good to remember that such are the conditions of an island in a very troubled sea. In the long run, it may even be more important to remember that the foundations for this freedom were laid in a revolution, and that this revolution was made by men who valued their *public* happiness and their *public* freedom at least as much if not more than they valued their private well-being and their civil rights.

1961

IS AMERICA BY NATURE A
VIOLENT SOCIETY?

It is highly doubtful that we know anything about the natural virtues and vices of societies, but it seems evident that a country inhabited by a multitude of ethnic groups cannot even be said to possess the nearest equivalent to natural qualities, namely, a national character. If "like attracts like" is as natural for human society as "birds of a feather flock together," one could even say that American society is *artificial* "by nature." Still, it seems true that America, for historical, social, and political reasons, is more likely to erupt into violence than most other civilized countries. And yet there are very few countries where respect for law is so deeply rooted and where citizens are so law-abiding. This was already evident at the time of the American Revolution, and since this central event is not remembered for violence, violence has not the same revolutionary overtones in this country as elsewhere and, precisely for this reason, is more easily condoned.

The reason for this seeming paradox must probably be looked for in the American past, in the experience of establishing law against lawlessness in a colonial country—an experience which culminated, but did not end, with the foundation of a new body politic and the establishment of a new law of the land following the revolution of 1776. For it was a similar experience that came into play in the colonization of the American continent, as well as in the integration of the many waves of immigrants during the last century. Each time the law had to be confirmed anew against the lawlessness inherent in all uprooted people. Americans know some things about the enormous equalizing power of the law, and they know more than enough about the initial stages of criminal violence which always precede—not, of course, the relatively easy assimilation of single individuals—but the integration of a new and alien group.

I think that second peculiarity of American society is more relevant to the present situation. Freedom of assembly is among the crucial, most cherished, and, perhaps, most dangerous rights of American citizens. The number of voluntary associations, organized on the spur of the moment, are still as characteristic of our society as they were when Tocqueville first described them. Their work is usually carried on within the framework of the law, and their pursuit of social, economic, and political goals is normally channeled through pressure groups into the government establishment. But this is not necessarily so, and every time Washington is unreceptive to the claims of a sufficiently large number of citizens, the danger of violence arises. Violence—to take the law into one's own hands—is perhaps more likely to be the consequence of frustrated power in America than in other countries. We have just lived through a period when opposition to our bloody imperialist adventures—voiced first on campuses, on chiefly moral grounds, and supported by an almost unanimous verdict of highly qualified opinion in the country at large—remained not only without echo but was treated with open contempt by the administration. The opposition, taught in the school of the powerful and nonviolent civil rights movement of the early sixties, took to the streets, more and more embittered against "the system" as such. The spell was broken, and the danger of violence, inherent in the disaffection of a whole generation, averted when Senator McCarthy* provided in his person the link between the opposition in the Senate with that in the streets. He himself said that he had wanted "to test the system," and the results, though still inconclusive, have been reassuring in some important respects. Not only has popular pressure enforced an at least temporary change in policy; it has also been demonstrated how quickly the younger generation can become de-alienated, jumping at this first opportunity not to abolish the system, but to make it work again. This is not to deny that the Republic is still in danger of being threatened by a disproportionate growth of presidential power on one side, and by an

---

* Arendt refers to her friend the poet-statesman Senator Eugene McCarthy of Minnesota, who thoroughly opposed America's adventure in Vietnam. Eugene McCarthy was the first to challenge Lyndon Johnson for the Democratic presidential nomination in 1968. —Ed.

even more alarming spread of "invisible government," the transformation of legitimately secret information-gathering agencies into secret policy-making bodies without any legitimacy whatsoever, on the other hand. We must not forget that the Ku Klux Klan and the John Birch Society are also voluntary associations, and who will deny that such groups aid and abet the outbreak of violence? It is difficult to see how this danger can be eliminated without eliminating freedom of assembly. Is that not too high a price to pay for political freedom?

The third factor, racism, is the only one with respect to which one could speak of a strain of violence so deeply rooted in American society as to appear to be "natural." "Racial violence was present almost from the beginning of the American experience," as the splendid *Report of the Commission on Civil Disorders* puts it. This country has never been a nation-state and therefore has been little affected by the vices of nationalism and chauvinism. It has dealt rather successfully with the obvious dangers of domestic violence inherent in a multinational social body by making adherence to the law of the land, and not national origin, the chief touchstone of citizenship, and by tolerating a considerable amount of mutual discrimination in society. But nationalism and racism are not the same, and what has worked with regard to the disruptive forces of the former has not worked with regard to the destructive force of the latter. We often hear it said today that we are called upon to pay the price for slavery, the greatest crime of the American past. But the historical period at stake here is much rather the last one hundred years of Negro *emancipation without integration* than the roughly 250 years of Negro slavery preceding them. Neither in the South nor in the North, neither before nor after emancipation, were free Negroes ever treated as equals. The civil rights movement has been remarkably successful in putting an end to segregation by law in the South, demonstrating once more the tremendous power potential in organized nonviolent action. Even more importantly, it achieved a radical change in the climate of the country with respect to individual Negroes, who, for the first time, were assimilated in pretty much the same way that individuals of other ethnic groups had been assimilated before. "Tokenism" was in fact a step forward, not only because it opened opportunities for individual "exceptions," but also because it demonstrated that at least the educated strata of society were no longer racist. But this assimilation of the few was neither followed nor accompanied by the integration of the many.

In the North, where I think the problem is more acute than in the South, we deal with a group uprooted through recent migration and hence no less lawless than other immigrant groups in their initial stages. Their massive arrival in recent decades has hastened the disastrous disintegration of the big cities, to which they came at a time when the demand for unskilled labor rapidly was declining. We all know the consequences, and it is no secret that racist feeling among the urban population today is at an unprecedented high. It is easy to blame the people; it is less easy to admit the fact that, as things are handled now, those who stand most to lose and are expected to pay by far the greatest part of the cost are precisely those groups who have just "made it" and can least afford it. Impotence breeds violence, and the more impotent these white groups feel the greater grows the danger of violence. Unlike nationalism, which is normally limited by a territory and therefore admits, in principle at least, the existence of a "family of nations" with equal status for each, racism always insists on an absolute superiority over others. Hence, racism is humiliating "by nature," and humiliation breeds even more violence than sheer impotence. Thirty years ago, André Malraux wrote in *Man's Fate* that "a deep humiliation calls forth a violent negative of the world; only drugs, neuroses, and blood consistently shed, can feed such solitudes." Nationalism is on the rise everywhere, and the danger is that, for various reasons, it has become tainted with racism in many parts of the world. The racism inherent in American society for such a long time could indeed become "revolutionary" if the black backlash, in blatant disregard for the Negro people in America, should come under the sway of those extremists who think of it in terms of a world revolution, a worldwide uprising of the colored races.

The Negro violence we are witnessing now is nothing of the sort. It is political to the small extent of hoping to dramatize justified grievances and to serve as an unhappy substitute for organized power. "It is social to the much larger extent that it expresses the violent rage of the poor in an affluent society" where deprivation is no longer the burden of a majority and hence no longer felt as a curse from which only the few are exempt.* Not even violence for the sake of violence preached by extremists—as distinguished from the rioting and looting for the sake of whiskey, color televisions, and pianos— is revolutionary, because it is not a means to an end: no one dreams of being able to seize power. If it is to be a contest of violence, no one doubts who is going to win.

The real danger is not violence but the possibility of a white backlash of such proportions as to be able to invade the domain of regular government. Only such a victory at the polls could stop the present policy of integration. Its consequence would be unmitigated disaster—the end, perhaps not of the country, but certainly of the American Republic.

1965

---

* Cf. *The Affluent Society* by J. K. Galbraith (1958). This influential book showed the growth of American wealth in the private rather than the public sector after World War II. Its stress on the inequality of the distribution of that wealth today seems prophetic. —Ed.

THE POSSESSED

Every masterwork can be read on several levels, but a work is a masterwork only if all the strands are so arranged that they form a consistent whole on each level. Of *The Possessed* we may say that this novel is, on the lowest but indispensable level, a key-novel, a *roman-à-clef*, where everything and everybody can be verified. The plot is lifted right out of the newspapers of the time in which the characters are the center of a real story: Pyotr Verkhovensky is Sergei Nechayev, his father, Stefan Trofimovitch, is a mixture of Granowsky and Kukolnik, Shatov is Dostoevsky, and so forth. Nechayev had returned from Switzerland where he went after some conspiratorial activity in which he collaborated with the police—he always worked for both sides. In Switzerland he had pretended to be the head of a wholly fictitious network of "quintets" covering the whole of Russia. Here he met Bakunin who totally fell for him, and the result of their collaboration was *The Revolutionary Catechism*. Most of the ideas contained in this work are probably Nechayev's. It is the testament of a doomed man without any interests of his own, not even a name. He then returned to Russia and now pretended to be an "emissary from abroad." He organized an actual "quintet" and initiated the murder of the student Ivanov in order to bind the members together by the crime. All five were caught but Nechayev himself escaped abroad. It was at this moment that Dostoevsky wrote *The Possessed* (1869). Nechayev was extradited by the Swiss in 1872, the year the book appeared, and died in prison in 1882. Also melded into Nechayev to form the fictional character Pyotr Verkhovensky were Zaichnevsky, a member of "Young Russia" who possessed extraordinary charm over women, and Tkachev. However Tkachev is perhaps rather the prototype of Shigalov, insofar as he had already proposed to kill everybody over twenty-five to regenerate Russia. Tkachev, incidentally, reviewed the book and declared that these characters were all mentally sick people and not revolutionaries—which shows just how closely Dostoevsky's fiction was connected to the real events of the day.

Also completely realistic is Dostoevsky's description of the government in the provinces, Lembke and the Shpigulin workers. The seemingly incredible incompetence of the entire Russian bureaucracy is expressed with great precision in Lembke's words: "I have so many duties I can't perform one of them, and, on the other hand, I can as truly say that there's nothing for me to do here." There is also the Shpigulin scandal, the strike of the workers for good reasons in which no one of the conspirators has a hand. Dostoevsky's description is entirely realistic: all the strikes from 1896 in Saint Petersburg and then Petrograd were without any outside interference. Insofar as there is a system, no one is of any use; the effect is "as though the ground were giving way under every foot." The workers are the exception to the general rottenness of the society. This remained for some time without consequence, for the sheer oppressive weight of society, its stupidity, complexity, and inefficiency, seemed to render it resistant and impenetrable. But when someone told Lenin, "You're up against a wall," he replied, "Yes, and the wall is rotten."

On the second level, which is generally accepted, *The Possessed* is an explanation or prophecy of what actually happened: the tsarist regime had to fall because of atheism. Atheism undermined a government whose authority was "by the grace of God" and which lost its legitimacy when man no longer believed in God. Shatov declares, "If there is to be a rising in Russia we must begin with atheism." And the same thought is expressed more simply by the bedeviled captain who exclaims, "If there is no God, how can I be a captain?" Furthermore, atheism is connected with Western ideas; the West, already corrupt, is on its way to corrupt Russia—in the form of Marxism. The only resistance is from Slavophiles for whom Russia is the sole hope: the Russian people still believe, even though the intellectuals don't. In spite of his sympathy with this description, Dostoevsky presents a very realistic description of the contempt these lovers of "the people" actually had for the people, and especially the Russian people.

One of the chief representatives of this interpretation is Berdiaev (*Sources and Meaning of Russian Communism*): the revolution first took place within, which indicated the outer revolution was on its way. Since then, Dostoevsky has been granted "a gift of foresight bordering on the demonic." There is at least this much truth in it—atheism eliminates the fear of hell and the fear of hell has been for many centuries the most potent factor in preventing men from doing evil. But the point in Dostoevsky is somewhat different: without belief in God everything *is* permitted. Still, the fact is that Pyotr Verkhovensky–Nechayev shows a strange similarity with Stalin: he "never forgets an offense," he encourages "spying on one another" within the quintet, the "unlimited despotism" of Shigalov's system. The members of the quintet are all potential informers—Liputin with his "marked inclination for police work," Lebyadkin, and especially Verkhovensky himself. As far as Stalin is concerned the resemblance is remarkable, even uncanny—as if it were Nechayev's *Catechism*, which Stalin certainly knew, on which he modeled himself.

On a third level, which was clearly Dostoevsky's own, we approach the same question of atheism but much more seriously: the central question in all Dostoevsky's novels is *not* the question of whether God exists but of whether man can live without belief in God. Before we discuss it we should note that this question carries doubt into belief—not from the outside as it is with the sciences (where the answer is: the sciences neither raise nor answer this question), but from within: if I believe because I can't bear *not* to believe, I clearly don't believe. Dostoevsky knew that, which is his greatness. He did not believe that he or Shatov could bring salvation to Russia or mankind; this can only be done by those people who never had these thoughts, who *simply* believe, the feeble-minded, like Marya, or the Idiot. Dostoevsky's only believer who is not feeble-minded is Aljosha—and that novel he never completed.

In the *Notebooks** the most urgent and central question is: Can one have faith if one is civilized, i.e., European? For faith does not mean some vague notion about a supreme being, but the divinity of Christ. And this means two things which are in fact distinct, but not entirely so in Dostoevsky: a) Morality depends for its legitimacy upon revelation. If one part of rev-

---

* Arendt refers to *The Notebooks for "The Possessed."* —Ed.

elation is destroyed, the whole of Christianity and Christian morality will collapse. If it is impossible to believe, then it is by no means inexcusable to demand total destruction. On the contrary, when long suffering ended by death is set against brief suffering and death, the latter is more humane. Here it follows that Mankind cannot survive without faith. b) The word became flesh in Christ, the incarnation: the possibility of the divine on earth depends upon this event. It is, according to Dostoevsky, the only salvation from despair. The representative of true nonbelief is Stavrogin, the hero who has "neither the feeling nor the knowledge of good and evil." It is precisely this indifference which is his undoing: "life bored him to the point of stupefaction." At the same time he has the feeling of complete freedom. But, for Dostoevsky, morality is understood as the code of a master to whom man subjects himself: the master is God and the example is Christ. Man belongs to somebody (*not* to something) who is both transcendent and superior to him.

The Possessed is more explicitly concerned with this question than with any other; that is, it tries to prove the disastrous consequences of losing faith. It is a negative argument, but since it is a novel, it is no argument, and it is of considerable force because of the truth of the plot and characters. Formulated as an argument, it goes: If you take away God as the one to whom man owes obedience, he is still left to be a servant. Only instead of serving God he now serves ideas; he is no longer owned by God, but *possessed* by ideas which act like demons. These ideas are not something you have, the ideas have you. Stefan Trofimovitch has his whole head full of lofty and noble ideas, and not only produces a son with criminal notions, he himself in his utter thoughtlessness borders on criminality—in the neglect and frauds against his son, in selling Fedka, the criminal, for a gambling debt, and so forth. He is not evil, his ideas have only chased out of his head any ordinary thoughtfulness. Instead of being a servant of a legitimate master, the man becomes a flunky of his ideas—indeed, the "flunkyism of thought" is mentioned more than once by Shatov. This is "the domination of phantoms," phantoms because there is no reality behind them. And this is so for even the noblest of these ideas, the idea of absolute freedom proved by suicide. Kirilov is told by Verkhovensky—who incidentally is not the servant of an idea—"You haven't mastered the idea, but the idea has mastered you." This strange possession comes about because we think ideas not just with our brains; an idea "is felt," and it is "carried out in practice."

The most potent and most fascinating of these ideas which seize man is the idea of total destruction because it arises directly from the vacuum and is the most powerful *inversion* of Creation. And since this vacuum is not just the absence of belief in God but also of faith in the incarnation— the word become flesh—this idea, too, finds its incarnation in living men. "The idea which seizes him dominates him totally, but does not so much rule his thought as use him as the means of its incorporation. And once *incarnated* it demands the immediate transformation into action." For "to change one's conviction is to change immediately one's whole life" (*Notebooks*). This phenomenon, that an idea becomes personified and is acted out, is taken with the utmost seriousness; and is, according to Dostoevsky, what distinguished the Russian ideologues from their Western brethren. Men are *walking ideas*, performing what the idea demands, carrying out its *logic*. Since they have had the true faith, they become all the more dangerous when they lose it. On the other hand, the incarnation of ideas means that their bearers can become *idols*. Such is Stavrogin for Verkhovensky: "Without you I am a fly, a bottled idea; Columbus without America." The idol means that instead of God becoming man, man is to become God. Verkhovensky, who does not believe in progress, is not ruled by an idea as are the others in self-deception. Stavrogin is not ruled by an idea because he "can never lose his reason" to be interested in an idea to that degree." But precisely because of this inability he can become an idol for Verkhovensky. The true opposite to good is not evil or crime, not Fedka, but Stavrogin, who is merely indifferent. The new God would be sheer indifference.

The strength of the book lies not in argument but in the concrete presentation of characters and plots. The most persuasive element, however, is the incontestable grandeur of the content of belief, as contrasted with the shallowness of modern ideas. If men become what they think, wouldn't it be better for them to stick to the notion of Christ even if it were not the truth? As Shatov says to Stavrogin, who had harbored this thought—the thought of an unbeliever!—"But didn't you tell me that if it were mathematically proved to you that the truth excludes Christ, you'd prefer to stick to Christ rather than to the truth?" (It is strange that Dostoevsky never asks himself either how people lived before Christ or in other, non-Christian countries. He seems to believe that each people has its own gods and has to stick to them; emigrants not only lose their people but also their gods. This is, of course, an entirely atheistic thought.)

We have left out of the account an altogether different story, a kind of nonplot—its heros are Stavrogin and Kirilov. You can put the question: What happens when atheism seizes noble natures? And the result on the plane of action is the *acte gratuit*—an action which is entirely unmotivated, as the leading by the nose to the marriage to Marya, "the shame and sense-lessness of it reached the pitch of genius." (The fire and the murders are also called "senseless actions" but they have an aim, to compromise Stavrogin.) Finally there is Kirilov's suicide "without any cause at all, simply for self-will." These are the people who want to be gods—the sin of *superbia*, or pride, which Augustine defines as not serving God but imitating him! This is pure self-will: a will that is entirely unmotivated except by itself, and which affirms only itself. This alone is freedom, because all other acts are motivated and hence affected by something outside themselves.

It follows from such atheism that "to recognize that there is no God and not to recognize at the same instant oneself as God is an absurdity," for the simple reason that we have such a notion as "god." This notion is inherent in life: "Man has done nothing but invent God so as to go on living, and not kill himself." Freedom means freedom from this invented master; once it is realized "man will be sovereign and . . . live in the greatest glory." There is only one hitch: even this glorious being must die. His death is certainly not due to self-will, but if he can make himself *will* his death once, he is free. Thus Kirilov kills himself as the savior of mankind: he is still "a god against my will," he is still unhappy because he "is *bound* to assert my will." Once he has asserted his self-will, the "physical nature of man will change" and he will not need God anymore. But one cannot say that he kills himself *in order to* . . . : not for any specific motive, only to assert his self-will. Absolute freedom is absolute destruction because you are bound to destroy everything that could affect and bind you. The supreme good that *binds* you is life itself. Hence, freedom is self-destruction.

This *acte gratuit* is precisely connected to Stavrogin's indifference. If you take freedom to be the faculty of choosing between two alternatives, e.g., good and evil, you can never be sure that you are free: whichever alternative you decide upon exerts an attractive force on the will, so that will is no longer free. Hence, you show your freedom by complete indifference, like Stavrogin, and commit suicide out of boredom and also out of pride. Out of boredom—for every interest binds you and you become its servant. Or by denying life itself as the last and deepest motive force. The trouble is that once you are *free*, you no longer *are*; hence, this maybe noble act means that man has lost his reason. The second hitch is in the plurality of men; if each man recognizes himself as a god, then the idea is already carried into absurdity. To say all men are gods or to say no man is a god, amounts to the same: How can gods owe obedience to those who are like them? And how could absolute sovereignty be achieved? Stavrogin is aware of this absurdity. He knows that the only alternative on this level is *indifference*. He does not even want to be God like Kirilov. Stavrogin admires Kirilov and first does not want to commit suicide because, far from solving the absurdity of the concept of freedom, it is only a grandiose gesture. Its grandeur may be the overcoming of fear, but Stavrogin does not know fear. He then takes his own life without further ado—he hangs himself, leaves no note, no testament, no confession of faith. He admits he is defeated.

That is where Dostoevsky leaves us and I shall not try to give you solutions to these problems. We would have to raise the question of the Will: Is freedom a property of the Will? The Greeks knew freedom but had no word for what we call will. Instead, please be aware of the unique form of dialogue in Dostoevsky's novels. It is as though naked soul speaks to naked soul in an intimacy approaching telepathy, i.e., the abolition of all distances. What somebody says is answered by: "I understand, I understand, spare your words" as Stavrogin says to Shatov. Again and again we see this response: "I knew it"—when somebody arrives unexpectedly there is always one who did expect the unexpected. Then, there is the degree of intensity, of sheer passion in the intimacy. Compared with it, Western civilized society is hypocritical, full of lies. Here all appearances immediately lead into the interior of the soul; the appearance is never only a facade. Most important, however, is that the world as an objective datum is somehow absent. There are no descriptions of it, and it is not a topic of dialogue;

hence the multitude of perspectives from which you can see the world, as in Balzac, is absent. The topos is not the world but some ultimate concern.

This intimacy can be realized only within one's own people. It is carried along by a knowledge which we find ordinarily only in certain very close family relationships. Hence, Dostoevsky's insistence that you are lost when you lose your people, which is seen in the image of the family, and that you lose God when you leave it. Separation from the people means separation from the entire world, the loss of the distinction between good and evil, along with "boredom and a tendency toward idleness."

1967

"THE FREEDOM TO BE FREE"
The Conditions and Meaning of Revolution

My subject today, I'm afraid, is almost embarrassingly topical. Revolutions have become everyday occurrences since, with the liquidation of imperialism, so many peoples have risen "to assume among the powers of the earth the separate and equal station to which the laws of nature and nature's God entitle them." Just as the most lasting result of imperialist expansion was the export of the idea of the nation-state to the four corners of the earth, so the end of imperialism under the pressure of nationalism has led to the dissemination of the idea of revolution all over the globe.

All these revolutions, no matter how violently anti-Western their rhetoric may be, stand under the sign of traditional Western revolutions. The current state of affairs was preceded by the series of revolutions after the First World War in Europe itself. Since then, and more markedly after the Second World War, nothing seems more certain than that a revolutionary change of the form of government, in distinction to an alteration of administration, will follow defeat in a war between the remaining powers—short, that is, of total annihilation. But it is important to note that even before technological developments made wars between the great powers literally a life-and-death struggle, hence self-defeating, politically speaking wars had already become a matter of life and death. This was by no means a matter of course, but signifies that the protagonists of national wars had begun to act as though they were involved in civil wars. And the small wars of the last twenty years—Korea, Algeria, Vietnam—have clearly been civil wars, in which the great powers became involved, either because revolution threatened their rule or had created a dangerous power vacuum. In these instances it was no longer war that precipitated revolution; the initiative shifted from war to revolution, which in some cases, but by no means all, was followed by military intervention. It is as if we were suddenly back in the eighteenth century, when the American Revolution was followed by a war against England, and the French Revolution by a war against the allied royal powers of Europe.

And again, despite the enormously different circumstances—technological and otherwise—military interventions appear relatively helpless in the face of the phenomenon. A large number of revolutions during the last two hundred years went to their doom, but relatively few were dissipated by superiority in the application of the means of violence. Conversely, military interventions, even when they were successful, have often proved remarkably inefficient in restoring stability and filling the power vacuum. Even victory seems unable to substitute stability for chaos, honesty for corruption, authority and trust in government for decay and disintegration. Restoration, the consequence of an interrupted revolution, usually provides not much more than a thin and quite obviously provisional cover under which the processes of disintegration continue unchecked.* But there is, on the other hand, a great potential future stability inherent in consciously formed new political bodies, of which the American Republic is the prime example; the principal problem, of course, is the rarity of successful revolutions. Still, in the world's present configuration where, for better or worse, revolutions have become the most significant and frequent events—and this will most likely continue for decades to come—it would not only be wiser but also more relevant if, instead of boasting that we are the mightiest power on earth, we would say that we have enjoyed an extraordinary stability since the founding of our republic, and that this stability was the direct outgrowth of revolution. For, since it can no longer be decided by war, the contestation of the great powers may well be decided, in the long run, by which side better understands what revolutions are and what is at stake in them.

It is, I believe, a secret from nobody, at least not since the Bay of Pigs incident, that the foreign policy of this country has shown itself hardly expert or even knowledgeable in judging revolutionary situations or in understanding the momentum of revolutionary movements. Although

* How prescient these words are in regard to the Arab Spring. —Ed.

the Bay of Pigs is often blamed on faulty information and malfunction-
ing secret services, the failure actually lies much deeper. The failure was
in misunderstanding what it means when a poverty-stricken people in a
backward country, in which corruption has reached the point of rottenness, are suddenly released, not from their poverty, but from the obscurity
and hence incomprehensibility of their misery; what it means when they
hear for the first time their condition being discussed in the open and find
themselves invited to participate in that discussion; and what it means when
they are brought to their capital, which they have never seen before, and
told: these streets and these buildings and these squares, all these are yours,
your possessions, and hence your pride. This, or something of the same
sort, happened for the first time during the French Revolution. Curiously,
it was an old man in East Prussia who never left his home town of Königs-
berg, Immanuel Kant, a philosopher and lover of freedom hardly famous
for rebellious thoughts, who at once did understand. He said that "such
a phenomenon in human history will never be forgotten," and indeed,
it has not been forgotten but, on the contrary, has played a major role in
world history ever since it occurred. And though many revolutions have
ended in tyranny, it has also always been remembered that, in the words of
Condorcet, "The word 'revolutionary' can be applied only to revolutions
whose aim is freedom."

Revolution, like any other term of our political vocabulary, can be used
in a generic sense without taking into account either the word's origin or
the temporal moment when the term was first applied to a particular political phenomenon. The assumption of such usage is that no matter when and
why the term itself appeared, the phenomenon to which it refers is coeval
with human memory. The temptation to use the word generically is particularly strong when we speak of "wars and revolutions" together, for wars,
indeed, are as old as the recorded history of mankind. It may be difficult to
use the word war in any other than a generic sense, if only because its first
appearance cannot be dated in time or localized in space, but no such excuse
exists for the indiscriminate usage of the term revolution. Prior to the two
great revolutions at the end of the eighteenth century and the specific sense
it then acquired, the word revolution was hardly prominent in the vocabulary of political thought or practice. When the term occurs in the seven-

teenth century, for example, it clings strictly to its original astronomical meaning, which signified the eternal, irresistible, ever-recurring motion of the heavenly bodies; its political usage was metaphorical, describing a movement back into some pre-established point, and hence a motion, a swinging back to a preordained order. The word was first used not when what we are apt to call a revolution broke out in England and Cromwell rose up as a sort of dictator, but on the contrary, in 1660, on the occasion of the reestablishment of the monarchy, after the overthrow of the Rump Parliament. But even the Glorious Revolution, the event through which, rather paradoxically, the term found its place in historical-political language, was not thought of as a revolution but as the restoration of monarchical power to its former righteousness and glory. The actual meaning of revolution, prior to the events of the late eighteenth century, is perhaps most clearly indicated in the inscription on the Great Seal of England of 1651, according to which the first transformation of monarchy into a republic meant: "*Freedom* by God's blessing *restored.*"

The fact that the word revolution originally meant restoration is more than a mere oddity of semantics. Even the eighteenth-century revolutions cannot be understood without realizing that revolutions first broke out when restoration had been their aim, and that the content of such restoration was freedom. In America, in the words of John Adams, the men of the revolution had been "called without expectation and compelled without previous inclination"; the same is true for France where, in Tocqueville's words, "one might have believed the aim of the coming revolution was the restoration of the *ancien régime* rather than its overthrow." And in the course of both revolutions, when the actors became aware that they were embarking upon an entirely new enterprise rather than revolving back to anything preceding it, when the word "revolution" consequently was acquiring its new meaning, it was Thomas Paine, of all people, who, still true to the spirit of the bygone age, proposed in all seriousness to call the American and French revolutions "counter-revolutions." He wanted to save the extraordinary events from the suspicion that an entirely new beginning had been made, and from the odium of violence with which these events were inevitably linked.

We are likely to overlook the almost instinctive horror manifest in the mentality of these first revolutionists before the entirely new. In part this is because we are so well acquainted with the eagerness of scientists and philosophers of the Modern Age for "things never seen before and thoughts never thought before."*

And in part it is because nothing in the course of these revolutions is as conspicuous and striking as the emphatic stress on novelty, repeated over and over by actors and spectators alike, in their insistence that nothing comparable in significance and grandeur had ever happened before. The crucial and difficult point is that the enormous pathos of the new era, the *novus ordo seclorum*, which is still inscribed on our dollar bills, came to the fore only after the actors, much against their will, had reached a point of no return.

Hence, what actually happened at the end of the eighteenth century was that an attempt at restoration and recovery of old rights and privileges resulted in its exact opposite: a progressing development and the opening up of a future which defied all further attempts at acting or thinking in terms of a circular or revolving motion. And while the term "revolution" was radically transformed in the revolutionary process, something similar, but infinitely more complex, happened to the word "freedom." As long as nothing more was meant by it than freedom "by God's blessing *restored*," it remained a matter of those rights and liberties we today associate with constitutional government, which properly are called civil rights. What was not included in them was the political right to participate in public affairs. None of those other rights, including the right to be represented for purposes of taxation, were either in theory or practice the result of revolution. Not "life, liberty, and property," but the claim that they were inalienable rights of all human creatures, no matter where they lived or what kind of government they enjoyed, was revolutionary. And even in this new and revolutionary extension to all mankind, liberty meant no more than freedom from unjustifiable restraint, that is, something essentially negative. Liberties in the sense of civil rights are the results of liberation, but they are by no means the actual content of freedom, whose essence is admission to the public realm and participation in public affairs. Had the revolutions aimed only at the guarantee of civil rights, liberation from regimes that had

* Cf. H. Arendt, *The Human Condition* (Chicago: University of Chicago Press, 1998), 249. —Ed.

overstepped their powers and infringed upon well-established rights would have been enough. And it is true that the revolutions of the eighteenth century began by claiming those old rights. The complexity comes when revolution is concerned with both liberation and freedom, and, since liberation is indeed a condition of freedom—though freedom is by no means a necessary result of liberation—it is difficult to see and say where the desire for liberation, to be free from oppression, ends, and the desire for freedom, to live a political life, begins. The point of the matter is that liberation from oppression could very well have been fulfilled under monarchical though not tyrannical government, whereas the freedom of a political way of life required a new, or rather rediscovered, form of government. It demanded the constitution of a republic. Nothing, indeed, is more clearly borne out by the facts than Jefferson's retrospective claim "that the contests of that day were contests of principle between the advocates of republican and those of kingly government." The equation of a republican government with freedom, and the conviction that monarchy is a criminal government fit for slaves—though it became commonplace almost as soon as the revolutions began—had been quite absent from the minds of the revolutionaries themselves. Still, though this was a new freedom they were aiming at, it would be hard to maintain they had no prior notion of it. On the contrary, it was a passion for this new political freedom, though not yet equated with a republican form of government, which inspired and prepared those to enact a revolution without fully knowing what they were doing.

No revolution, no matter how wide it opened its gates to the masses and the downtrodden—*les malheureux, les misérables, les damnés de la terre* as we know them from the grand rhetoric of the French Revolution—was ever started by them. And no revolution was ever the result of conspiracies, secret societies, or openly revolutionary parties. Speaking generally, no revolution is even possible where the authority of the body politic is intact, which, under modern conditions, means where the armed forces can be trusted to obey the civil authorities. Revolutions are not necessary but possible answers to the devolution of a regime, not the cause but the consequence of the downfall of political authority. Wherever these disintegrative processes have been allowed to develop unchecked, usually over a prolonged period, revolutions *may* occur under the condition that a sufficient number of the populace exists which is prepared for a regime's collapse and is willing to assume power. Revolutions always appear to succeed with amazing ease in their initial stages, and the reason is that those who supposedly "make" revolutions do not "seize power" but rather pick it up where it lies in the streets.

If the men of the American and French revolutions had anything in common prior to the events which were to determine their lives, shape their convictions, and eventually draw them apart, it was a passionate longing to participate in public affairs, and a no less passionate disgust with the hypocrisy and foolishness of "good society"—to which must be added a restlessness and more or less outspoken contempt for the pettiness of merely private affairs. In the sense of the formation of this very special mentality, John Adams was entirely right when he said that "the revolution was effected before the war commenced," not because of a specifically revolutionary or rebellious spirit, but because the inhabitants of the colonies were "formed by law into corporations, or bodies politic" with the "right to assemble . . . in their own town halls, there to deliberate upon public affairs," for it was indeed "in these assemblies of towns or districts that the sentiments of the people were formed in the first place." To be sure, nothing comparable to the political institutions in the colonies existed in France, but the mentality was still the same; what Tocqueville called a "passion" and "taste" in France was in America an experience manifest from the earliest times of colonization, in fact ever since the Mayflower Compact had been a veritable school of public spirit and public freedom. Prior to the revolutions, these men on both sides of the Atlantic were called *hommes de lettres,* and it is characteristic of them that they spent their leisure time "ransacking the archives of antiquity," that is, turning to Roman history, not because they were romantically enamored of the past as such but with the purpose of recovering the spiritual as well as institutional political lessons that had been lost or half-forgotten during the centuries of a strictly Christian tradition. "The world has been empty since the Romans, and is filled only with their memory, which is now our only prophecy of freedom," exclaimed Saint-Just, as before him Thomas Paine had predicted "what Athens was in miniature, America will be in magnitude."

To understand the role of antiquity in the history of revolutions we would have to recall the enthusiasm for "ancient prudence" with which Harrington and Milton greeted Cromwell's dictatorship, and how this enthusiasm had been revived in the eighteenth century by Montesquieu's *Considerations on the Causes of the Grandeur and the Decadence of the Romans.* Without the classical example of what politics could be and participation in public affairs could mean for the happiness of man, none of the men of the revolutions would have possessed the courage for what would appear as unprecedented action. Historically speaking, it was as if the Renaissance's revival of antiquity was suddenly granted a new lease on life, as if the republican fervor of the short-lived Italian city-states, foredoomed by the advent of the nation-state, had only lain dormant, so to speak, to give the nations of Europe the time to grow up under the tutelage of absolute princes and enlightened despots. The first elements of a political philosophy corresponding to this notion of public freedom are spelled out in John Adams's writings. His point of departure is the observation that "Wherever men, women, or children are to be found, whether they be old or young, rich or poor, high or low . . . ignorant or learned, every individual is seen to be strongly actuated by a desire to be seen, heard, talked of, approved and respected by the people about him and within his knowledge." The virtue of this "desire" Adams saw in "the desire to excel another," and its vice he called "ambition," which "aims at power as a means of distinction." And these two indeed are among the chief virtues and vices of political man. For the will to power as such, regardless of any passion for distinction (in which power is not a means but an end), is characteristic of the tyrant and is no longer even a political vice. It is rather the quality that tends to destroy all political life, its vices no less than its virtues. It is precisely because the tyrant has no desire to excel and lacks all passion for distinction that he finds it so pleasant to dominate, thereby excluding himself from the company of others; conversely, it is the desire to excel which makes men love the company of their peers and spurs them on into the public realm. This public freedom is a tangible worldly reality, created by men to enjoy together in public—to be seen, heard, known, and remembered by others. And this kind of freedom demands equality, it is possible only amongst peers. Institutionally speaking, it is possible only in a republic, which knows no subjects and, strictly speaking, no rulers. This is the reason why discussions of the forms of government, in sharp contrast to later ideologies, played such an enormous role in the thinking and writing of the first revolutionaries.

No doubt, it is obvious and of great consequence that this passion for freedom for its own sake awoke in and was nourished by men of leisure, by the *hommes de lettres* who had no masters and were not always busy making a living. In other words, they enjoyed the privileges of Athenian and Roman citizens without taking part in those affairs of state that so occupied the free-men of antiquity. Needless to add, where men live in truly miserable conditions this passion for freedom is unknown. And if we need additional proof of the absence of such conditions in the colonies, the "lovely equality" in America where, as Jefferson put it, "the most conspicuously wretched individual" was better off than nineteen out of the twenty million inhabitants of France, we need only remember that John Adams ascribed this love of freedom to "poor and rich, high and low, ignorant and learned." It is the chief, perhaps the only reason, why the principles that inspired the men of the first revolutions were triumphantly victorious in America and failed tragically in France. Seen with American eyes, a republican government in France was "as unnatural, irrational, and impracticable as it would be over elephants, lions, tigers, panthers, wolves, and bears in the royal menagerie at Versailles" (John Adams). The reason why the attempt was made nevertheless is that those who made it, *les hommes de lettres,* were not much different from their American colleagues; it was only in the course of the French Revolution that they learned they were acting under radically different circumstances.

The circumstances differed in political as well as social respects. Even the rule of King and Parliament in England was "mild government" in comparison with French absolutism. Under its auspices, England developed an intricate and well-functioning regime of self-government, which needed only the explicit foundation of a republic to confirm its existence. Still, these political differences, though important enough, were negligible compared with the formidable obstacle to the constitution of freedom inherent in the social conditions of Europe. The men of the first revolutions, though they knew well enough that liberation had to precede freedom, were still unaware of the fact that such liberation means more than political liberation from absolute and despotic power; that to be free for freedom meant first of all to be free not only from fear but also from want. And the condition of desperate poverty of the masses of the people, those who for the first time burst into the open when they streamed into the streets of Paris, could not be overcome with political means; the mighty power of the constraint under which they labored did not crumble before the onslaught of the revolution as did the royal power of the king. The American Revolution was fortunate that it did not have to face this obstacle to freedom and, in fact, owed a good measure of its success to the absence of desperate poverty among the free-men, and to the invisibility of slaves, in the colonies of the New World. To be sure, there was poverty and misery in America, which was comparable to the conditions of the European "laboring poor." If, in William Penn's words, "America was a good poor Man's country" and remained the dream of a promised land for Europe's impoverished up to the beginning of the twentieth century, it is no less true that this goodness depended to a considerable degree on black misery. In the middle of the eighteenth century, there lived roughly 400,000 blacks along with approximately 1,850,00 whites in America, and, despite the absence of reliable statistical information, it may be doubted that at the time the percentage of complete destitution was higher in the countries of the Old World (though it would become considerably higher during the nineteenth century). The difference, then, was that the American Revolution—because of the institution of slavery and the belief that slaves belonged to a different "race"— overlooked the existence of the miserable, and with it the formidable task of liberating those who were not so much constrained by political oppression as the sheer necessities of life. *Les malheureux,* the wretched, who play such a tremendous role in the course of the French Revolution, which identified them with *le peuple,* either did not exist or remained in complete obscurity in America.

One of the principal consequences of the revolution in France was, for the first time in history, to bring *le peuple* into the streets and make them visible. When this happened it turned out that not just freedom but the freedom to be free had always been the privilege of the few. By the same token, however, the American Revolution has remained without much consequence for the historical understanding of revolutions, while the French Revolution, which ended in resounding failure, has determined and is still determining what now we call the revolutionary tradition.

What then happened in Paris in 1789? First, freedom from fear is a privilege that even the few have enjoyed in only relatively short periods of history, but freedom from want has been the great privilege that has distinguished a very small percentage of mankind throughout the centuries. What we tend to call the recorded history of mankind is, for the most part, the history of those privileged few.* Only those who know freedom from want can appreciate fully the meaning of freedom from fear, and only those who are free from both want and fear are in a position to conceive a passion for public freedom, to develop within themselves that *goût* or taste for *liberté* and the peculiar taste for *égalité* or equality that *liberté* carries within it.†

Speaking schematically, it may be said that each revolution goes first through the stage of liberation before it can attain to freedom, the second and decisive stage of the foundation of a new form of government and a new body politic. In the course of the American Revolution, the stage of liberation meant liberation from political restraint, from tyranny or monarchy or whatever word may have been used. The first stage was characterized by violence, but the second stage was a matter of deliberation, discussion, and persuasion, in short, of applying "political science" as the Founders understood the term. But in France something altogether different happened. The first stage of the revolution is much better characterized by disintegration rather than by violence, and when the second stage was reached and the National Convention had declared France to be a republic, power already had shifted to the streets. The men who had gathered in Paris to represent *la nation* rather than *le peuple*, whose chief concern—whether their name was Mirabeau or Robespierre, Danton or Saint-Just—had been government, the reformation of monarchy, and later the foundation of a republic, saw themselves suddenly confronted with yet another task of liberation, that is, liberating the people at large from wretchedness: to free them to be

* The French *Annales* School of History and its publication *Annales d'histoire économique et sociale* attempt to rectify this. —Ed.
† Arendt plays with the French word *liberté*, which signifies both liberty and freedom. —Ed.

free. This was not yet what both Marx and Tocqueville would see as the entirely new feature of the revolution of 1848, the switch from changing the form of government to the attempt to alter the order of society by means of class struggle. Only after February 1848, after "the first great battle . . . between the two classes that split society," Marx noted that revolution now meant "the overthrow of bourgeois society, whereas before it had meant the overthrow of the form of state." The French Revolution of 1789 was the prelude to this, and though it ended in dismal failure, it remained decisive for all later revolutions. It showed what the new formula, namely, all men are created equal, meant in practice. And it was this equality that Robespierre had in mind when he said that revolution pits the grandeur of man against the pettiness of the great; and Hamilton as well, when he spoke of the revolution having vindicated the honor of the human race; and also Kant, taught by Rousseau and the French Revolution, when he conceived of a new dignity of man. Whatever the French Revolution did and did not achieve—and it did not achieve human equality—it liberated the poor from obscurity, from nonvisibility. What has seemed irrevocable ever since is that those who were devoted to freedom could remain reconciled to a state of affairs in which freedom from want—*the freedom to be free*—was a privilege of the few.

Apropos of the original constellation of the revolutionaries and the masses of the poor they happened to bring into the open, let me quote Lord Acton's interpretive description of the women's march to Versailles, among the most prominent turning points of the French Revolution. The marchers, he said, "played the genuine part of mothers whose children were starving in squalid homes, and they thereby afforded to motives, which they neither shared nor understood [i.e., concern with government] the aid of a diamond point that nothing could withstand." What *le peuple,* as the French understood it, brought to the revolution and which was altogether absent from the course of events in America, was the irresistibility of a movement that human power was no longer able to control. This elementary experience of irresistibility—as irresistible as the motions of stars—brought forth an entirely new imagery, which still today we almost automatically associate in our thoughts of revolutionary events. When Saint-Just exclaimed, under the impact of what he saw before his eyes, *"Les malheureux sont la puis-*

sance de la terre," he meant the great "revolutionary torrent" (Desmoulins) on whose rushing waves the actors were borne and carried away until its undertow sucked them from the surface and they perished together with their foes, the agents of counterrevolution. Or Robespierre's tempest and mighty current, which was nourished by the crimes of tyranny on one side and by the progress of liberty on the other, constantly increased in rapidity and violence. Or what the spectators reported—a "majestic lava stream which spares nothing and which nobody can arrest," a spectacle that had fallen under the sign of Saturn, "the revolution devouring its own children" (Vergniaud). The words I am quoting here were all spoken by men deeply involved in the French Revolution and testify to things witnessed by them, that is, not to things they had done or set out to do intentionally. This is what happened, and it taught men a lesson that in neither hope nor fear has ever been forgotten. The lesson, as simple as it was new and unexpected, is, as Saint-Just put it, "If you wish to found a republic, you first must pull the people out of a condition of misery that corrupts them. There are no political virtues without pride, and no one can have pride who is wretched."

This new notion of freedom, resting upon liberation from poverty, changed both the course and goal of revolution. Liberty now had come to mean first of all "dress and food and the reproduction of the species," as the *sans-culottes* consciously distinguished their own rights from the lofty and, to them, meaningless language of the proclamation of the Rights of Man and of the Citizen. Compared to the urgency of their demands, all deliberations about the best form of government suddenly appeared irrelevant and futile. "*La République? La Monarchie? Je ne connais que la question sociale,*" said Robespierre. And Saint-Just, who had started out with the greatest possible enthusiasm for "republican institutions," would add, "The freedom of the people is in its private life. Let government be only the force to protect this state of simplicity against force itself." He might not have known it, but that was precisely the credo of enlightened despots which held, with Charles I of England in his speech from the scaffold, that the people's "liberty and freedom consists in having the government of those laws by which their life and their goods may be most their own; 'tis not for having share in Government, that is nothing pertaining to them." If it were true, as all participants moved by the misery of the people suddenly agreed, that the goal of revolutions was the happiness of the people—*le but de la Révolution est le bonheur du peuple*—then it indeed could be provided by a sufficiently enlightened despotic government rather than a republic.

The French Revolution ended in disaster and became a turning point in world history; the American Revolution was a triumphant success and remained a local affair, partly of course because social conditions in the world at large were far more similar to those in France, and partly because the much praised Anglo-Saxon pragmatic tradition prevented subsequent generations of Americans from *thinking* about their revolution and adequately conceptualizing its experience. It is therefore not surprising that the despotism, or actually the return to the age of enlightened absolutism, which announced itself clearly in the course of the French Revolution, became the rule for almost all subsequent revolutions, or at least those that did not end in restoration of the *status quo ante,* and even became dominant in revolutionary theory. I don't need to follow this development in detail; it is sufficiently well known, especially from the history of the Bolshevik party and the Russian Revolution. Moreover, it was predictable: in the late summer of 1918—after the promulgation of the Soviet constitution but prior to the first wave of terror prompted by the attempted assassination of Lenin—Rosa Luxemburg, in a private, later published, and now famous letter, wrote as follows:

> With the repression of political life in the land as a whole . . . life dies out in every public institution, becoming a mere semblance of life, in which only the bureaucracy remains as the active element. Public life gradually falls asleep. The few dozen party leaders of inexhaustible energy and boundless experience direct and rule. Among them only a dozen outstanding heads do the ruling, and an elite of the working class is invited from time to time to meetings where its members are to applaud the speeches of the leaders, and to approve proposed resolutions unanimously. . . . A dictatorship, to be sure; not the dictatorship of the proletariat, however, but of a handful of politicians.

That this is how it turned out—except for Stalin's totalitarian rule, for which it would be difficult to hold either Lenin or the revolutionary tradition responsible—no one is likely to deny. But what is perhaps less obvious is that one would have to change only a few words to obtain a perfect description of the ills of absolutism prior to the revolutions.

A comparison of the two first revolutions, whose beginnings were so similar and whose ends so tremendously different, demonstrates clearly, I think, not only that the conquest of poverty is a prerequisite for the foundation of freedom, but also that liberation from poverty cannot be dealt with in the same way as liberation from political oppression. For if violence pitted against violence leads to war, foreign or civil, violence pitted against social conditions has always led to terror. Terror rather than mere violence, terror let loose after the old regime has been dissolved and the new regime installed, is what either sends revolutions to their doom, or deforms them so decisively that they lapse into tyranny and despotism.

I said before that the revolution's original goal was freedom in the sense of the abolition of personal rule and of the admission of all to the public realm and participation in the administration of affairs common to all. Rulership itself had its most legitimate source not in a drive to power but in the human wish to emancipate mankind from the necessities of life, the achievement of which required violence, the means of forcing the many to bear the burdens of the few so that at least some could be free. This, and not the accumulation of wealth, was the core of slavery, at least in antiquity, and it is due only to the rise of modern technology, rather than the rise of any modern political notions, including revolutionary ideas, which has changed this human condition at least in some parts of the world. What America achieved by great good luck, today many other states, though probably not all, may acquire by virtue of calculated effort and organized development. This fact is the measure of our hope. It permits us to take the lessons of the deformed revolutions into account and still hold fast not only to their undeniable grandeur but also to their inherent promise.

Let me, by way of concluding, just indicate one more aspect of freedom which came to the fore during the revolutions, and for which the revolutionaries themselves were least prepared. It is that the idea of freedom and the actual experience of making a new beginning in the historical continuum should coincide. Let me remind you once more of the *Novus Ordo Saeclorum*. The surprising phrase is based in Virgil, who, in his Fourth *Eclogue*, speaks of "the great cycle of periods [that] is born anew" in the reign of Augustus: *Magnus ab integro saeclorum nascitur ordo.* Virgil speaks of a *great* (*magnus*) but not a *new* (*novus*) order, and it is this change in a line much quoted throughout the centuries that is characteristic of the experiences of the modern age. For Virgil—now in the language of the seventeenth century—it was a question of founding Rome "anew," but not of founding a "new Rome." This way he escaped, in typically Roman fashion, the fearful risks of violence inherent in breaking the tradition of Rome, i.e., the handed-down (*traditio*) story of the founding of the eternal city by suggesting a new beginning. Now, of course we could argue that the new beginning, which the spectators of the first revolutions thought they were watching, was only the rebirth of something quite old: the renascence of a secular political realm finally arising from Christianity, feudalism, and absolutism. But no matter whether it is a question of birth or rebirth, what is decisive in Virgil's line is that it is taken from a nativity hymn, not prophesying the birth of a divine child, but in praise of *birth as such,* the arrival of a new generation, the great saving event or "miracle" which will redeem mankind time and again. In other words, it is the affirmation of the divinity of birth, and the belief that the world's potential salvation lies in the very fact that the human species regenerates itself constantly and forever.

What made the men of the revolution go back to this particular poem of antiquity, quite apart from their erudition, I would suggest, was not only that the pre-revolutionary *idea* of freedom but also the experience of being free coincided, or rather was intimately interwoven, with beginning something new, with, metaphorically speaking, the birth of a new era. To be free and to start something new were felt to be the same. And obviously, this mysterious human gift, the ability to start something new, is connected to the fact that every one of us came into the world as a newcomer through birth. In other words, we can begin something because we *are* beginnings and hence beginners. Insofar as the capacity for acting and speaking—and speaking is but another mode of acting—makes us political beings, and since acting always has meant to set in motion what was not there before, birth or human natality, which corresponds to human mortality, is the ontological condition *sine qua non* of all politics. This was known in both Greek and Roman antiquity, albeit in an inexplicit manner. It came to the fore in the experiences of revolution, and it has influenced, though again rather inexplicitly, what one may call the revolutionary spirit. At any rate, the chain of revolutions, which for better and worse has become the hallmark of the world we live in, time after time discloses to us the eruption of new beginnings within the temporal and historical continuum. For us, who owe it to a revolution and the resulting foundation of an entirely new body politic that we can walk in dignity and act in freedom, it would be wise to remember what a revolution means in the life of nations. Whether it ends in success, with the constitution of a public space for freedom, or in disaster, for those who have risked it or participated in it against their inclination and expectation, the meaning of revolution is the actualization of one of the greatest and most elementary human potentialities, the unequaled experience of *being* free to make a new beginning, from which comes the pride of having opened the world to a *Novus Ordo Saeclorum*.

To sum up: Niccolò Machiavelli, whom one may well call the "father of revolutions," most passionately desired a new order of things for Italy, yet could hardly yet speak with any great amount of experience of these matters. Thus he still believed that the "innovators," i.e., the revolutionists, would encounter their greatest difficulty in the beginning when taking power, and find retaining it far easier. We know from practically all revolutions that the opposite is the case—that it is relatively easy to seize power but infinitely more difficult to keep it—as Lenin, no bad witness in such matters, once remarked. Still, Machiavelli knew enough to say the following: "There is nothing more difficult to carry out, nor more doubtful of success, nor more dangerous to handle, than to initiate a new order of things." With this sentence, I suppose, no one who understands anything at all of the story of the twentieth century will quarrel. Moreover, the dangers Machiavelli expected to arise have proved to be quite real up to our own day, despite the fact that he was not yet aware of the greatest danger in modern revolutions—the danger that rises from poverty. He mentions what since the French Revolution have been called counterrevolutionary forces, represented by those "who profit from the old order," and the "lukewarmness" of those who might profit from the new order because of "the incredulity of mankind, of those who do not truly believe in any new thing until they have experienced it." However, the point of the matter is that Machiavelli saw the danger only in defeat of the attempt to found a new order of things, that is, in the sheer weakening of the country in which the attempt is made. This too has proved to be the case, for such weakness, i.e., the power vacuum of which I spoke before, may well attract conquerors. Not that this power vacuum did not previously exist, but it can remain hidden for years until some decisive event happens, when the collapse of authority and a revolution make it manifest in dramatic calls into the open where it can be seen and known by all. In addition to all this, we have witnessed the supreme danger that out of the abortive attempt to found the institutions of freedom may grow the most thoroughgoing abolition of freedom and of all liberties.

Precisely because revolutions put the question of political freedom in its truest and most radical form—freedom to participate in public affairs, freedom of action—all other freedoms, political as well as civil liberties, are in jeopardy when revolutions fail. Deformed revolutions, such as the October Revolution in Russia under Lenin, or abortive revolutions, such as the various upheavals among the European central powers after World War I, may have, as we now know, consequences which in sheer horror are well-nigh unprecedented. The point of the matter is that revolutions rarely are reversible, that once they have happened they are not forgettable—as Kant remarked about the French Revolution at a time when terror ruled in France. This cannot possibly mean that therefore the best is to prevent revolutions, for if revolutions are the consequences of regimes in full disintegration, and not the "product" of revolutionaries—be they organized in conspiratorial sects or in parties—then to prevent a revolution means to change the form of government, which itself means to effect a revolution with all the dangers and hazards that entails. The collapse of authority and power, which as a rule comes with surprising suddenness not only to the readers of newspapers but also to all secret services and their experts who watch such things, becomes a revolution in the full sense of the word only when there are people willing and capable of picking up the power, of moving into and penetrating, so to speak, the power vacuum. What then happens depends upon many circumstances, not least upon the degree of insight of foreign powers into the irreversibility of revolutionary practices. But it depends most of all upon subjective qualities and the moral-political success or failure of those who are willing to assume responsibility. We have little reason to hope that at some time in the not too distant future such men will match in practical and theoretical wisdom the men of the American Revolution, who became the Founders of this country. But that little hope, I fear, is the only one we have that freedom in a political sense will not vanish again from the earth for God knows how many centuries.

1966–1967

IMAGINATION*

I. Imagination, Kant says, is the faculty of making present what is absent, the faculty of re-presentation: "Imagination is the faculty of representing

* "Imagination" is published in Ron Beiner's edition of Hannah Arendt's *Lectures on Kant's Political Philosophy* (Chicago: University of Chicago Press, 1982), along with the following comment: "The notes on Imagination are from a seminar . . . given during the same semester as the 1970 Kant Lectures. . . . These seminar notes help to elaborate the Kant Lectures by showing that the notion of exemplary validity . . . and the doctrine of the Schematism . . . are linked by the role of the imagination, which is fundamental to both, providing schemata for cognition as well as examples for judgment" (viii). This is enlarged upon, but not altered, in the note immediately preceding "Imagination" (79).

What then is the rationale for republishing these "seminar notes" here? First, they are not "seminar notes." In the first meeting of the seminar—whose dozen or so members were composed of a few advanced students from the lecture course and the rest from those who had followed Arendt's thought for years but did not attend the lectures—Arendt announced that one participant each week would present a paper on a section of the long First Part of Kant's *Critique of Judgment;* moreover, she added, she would attempt to show what she expected by contributing the first paper the following week. "Imagination" is that paper.

Published as a supplement to the Lectures, "Imagination" has been virtually ignored (I can think of one exception). Arendt's fascination with Kant's third *Critique* goes back years before this paper was written; in August and September, 1957, for example, in a flurry of correspondence with Karl Jaspers, she writes of Kant's consideration of common sense, "so often scorned," in which "the phenomenon of taste [is] taken seriously as the basic phenomenon of judgment." She and Jaspers contemplate giving a seminar together "right away" on Kant's understanding of the beautiful "as the quintessence of the worldliness of the world (*die Weltlichkeit der Welt*)."

Finally, and this is only a guess—a guess based in some experience—these few pages offer the best, if not the only, indication of what Arendt's third volume of *The Life of the Mind, Judging,* which has roused so much speculation, might have been like. Arendt died as she was beginning to write it. A few weeks earlier she had asked for my copy of this paper, having misplaced her own, which she found the following day. I am not suggesting that the volume on *Judging* would have begun with this paper; it would be far more likely for Arendt to start with its classical references to Parmenides and Anaxagoras, and in far greater detail. Beginning with a new consideration of the past was her modus operandi throughout *The Life of the Mind*. Most important is the role of the faculty of imagination in Kant, which is highly condensed here. At the time, in 1970, she remarked that "there is something missing in the whole corpus of Kant scholarship, a sustained study of the imagination—reproductive as well as productive—throughout his critical philosophy." —Ed.

in *intuition* an object that is not itself present."* Or: "Imagination (*facultas imaginandi*) is a faculty of *perception* in the absence of an object."† To give the name "imagination" to this faculty of having present what is absent is natural enough. If I represent what is absent, I have an *image* in my mind—an image of something I have seen and now somehow reproduce. In the *Critique of Judgment*, Kant sometimes calls this faculty "reproductive"—I represent what I have seen—to distinguish it from the "productive" faculty—the artistic faculty that produces something it has never seen. But productive imagination (genius) is never entirely productive. It produces, for instance, the centaur out of the given: the horse and the man. This sounds as though we are dealing with memory. But for Kant, imagination is the condition for memory, and a much more comprehensive faculty. In his *Anthropology* Kant puts memory, "the faculty to make present the *past*," together with a "faculty of divination," which makes present the *future*. Both are faculties of "association," that is, of connecting the "no longer" and the "not yet" with the present; and "although they themselves are not perceptions, they serve to connect the perceptions in time."‡ Imagination does not need to be led by this temporal association; it can make present at will whatever it chooses.

What Kant calls the faculty of imagination, to have present in the mind what is absent from sense perception, has less to do with memory than with another faculty, one that has been known since the beginnings of philosophy. Parmenides called it *nous*, by which he meant true *Being* is not what is present, does not present itself to the senses. What is not present is the *it-is;* and the *it-is*, though absent from the senses is present to the mind. Or Anaxagoras' *opsis tōn adēlōn ta phainomena*, "a glimpse of the nonvisible are the appearances."§ To put this differently, by looking at appearances, which are given to intuition in Kant, you become aware, catch a glimpse of something that does not appear. This something is *Being* as such. From it

---

* Kant, *Critique of Pure Reason*, B151 (italics added), trans. N. K. Smith (New York: St. Martin's Press, 1963).

† Kant, *Anthropology from a Pragmatic Point of View*, § 28 (italics added), trans. Mary J. Gregor (The Hague: Nijhoff, 1974).

‡ Ibid., § 34.

§ Hermann Diels and Walther Kranz, *Die Fragmente der Vorsokraiker*, 5th ed. (Berlin), B21a.

comes metaphysics, the discipline that treats of what lies beyond physical reality; and then, still in a mysterious way, what is given to the mind as the nonappearance in the appearances, becomes ontology, the science of Being.

II. The role of imagination for our cognitive faculties is perhaps the greatest discovery Kant made in the *Critique of Pure Reason*. For our purposes it is best to turn to the "Schematism of the Pure Concepts of Understanding."* To anticipate: the same faculty, imagination, which provides schemata for cognition, provides *examples* for judgment. You will recall that in Kant there are two stems of experience and knowledge: intuition (sensibility) and concepts (understanding). Intuition always *gives* us something particular; the concept makes this particular *known* to us. If I say: "this table," it is as though intuition says "this" and the understanding adds "table." "This" relates only to the specific item; "table" identifies it and makes the object communicable.

Two questions arise. First, how do the two faculties come together? To be sure, the concepts of understanding enable the mind to order the manifold of the sensations. But where does the synthesis, their working together, spring from? Second, is this concept, "table," a concept at all? Is it not perhaps also a kind of image? So that some sort of imagination is present in the intellect as well? The answer is: "Synthesis of a manifold . . . is what first gives rise to knowledge. . . . [It] gathers the elements for knowledge, and unites them into a certain content"; this synthesis "is the mere result of the faculty of imagination, a blind but indispensable function of the soul, without which we should have no knowledge *whatsoever*, but of which we are scarcely ever conscious."† And the way imagination produces the synthesis is by "providing an *image for a concept*."‡ Such an image is called a "schema."

The two extremes, namely sensibility and understanding, must be brought into connection with each other by means . . . of imagination, because otherwise the former, though indeed yielding appear-

---

* *Critique of Pure Reason*, B176ff.

† Ibid., B103 (italics added).

‡ Ibid., B180 (italics added).

ances, would supply no objects of empirical knowledge, hence no experience.*

Here Kant calls upon imagination to provide the connection between the two faculties, and in the first edition of the *Critique of Pure Reason* he calls the faculty of imagination "the faculty of synthesis in general [*überhaupt*]." At other places where he speaks directly of the "schematism" involved in our understanding, he calls it "an art concealed in the depths of the human soul"[†] (i.e., we have a kind of "intuition" of something that is *never* present), and by this he suggests that imagination is actually the common root of the other cognitive faculties, that is, it is the "common, but to us unknown, root" of sensibility and understanding,[‡] of which he speaks in the Introduction to the *Critique of Pure Reason* and which, in its last chapter, without naming the faculty, he mentions again.[§]

III. Schema: The point of the matter is that without a "schema" one can never recognize anything. When one says: "this table," the general "image" of table is present in one's mind, and one recognizes that the "this" is a table, something that shares its qualities with many other such things though it is itself an individual, particular thing. If I recognize a house, this perceived house also includes how a house in general looks. This is what Plato called the *eidos*—the general form—of a house, which is never given to the natural senses but only to the eyes of the mind. Since, speaking literally, it is not given even to "the eyes of the mind," it is something *like* an "image" or, better, a "schema." Whenever one draws or builds a house, one draws or builds a particular house, not the house as such. Still, how could one not do it without having this schema or Platonic *eidos* before the eye of one's mind? Kant says: "No image could ever be adequate to the concept of triangle in general. It would never attain that universality of the concept which renders it valid of all triangles, whether right-angled, obtuse-angled, or acute-angled; . . . the schema of the triangle can exist nowhere but in

* Ibid., A124.
[†] Ibid., B180.
[‡] Ibid., B29.
[§] Ibid., B863.

thought."* Yet, though it exists in thought only, it is a kind of "image"; it is not a product of thought, nor is it given to sensibility; and least of all is it the product of an abstraction from sensibly given data. It is something beyond or between thought and sensibility; it belongs to thought insofar as it is outwardly invisible, and it belongs to sensibility insofar as it is something *like* an image. Kant therefore sometimes calls imagination "one of the original sources . . . of all experience," and says that it cannot itself "be derived from any other faculty of the mind."†

One more example: "The concept 'dog' signifies a rule according to which my imagination can delineate the figure of a four-footed animal in a general manner without limitation to any single determinate figure such as experience, or any possible image that I can represent *in concreto*, actually presents—although as soon as the figure is delineated on paper it is again a particular animal!" This is the "art concealed in the depths of the human soul, whose real modes of activity nature is hardly likely ever to allow us to discover and to have open to our gaze."‡ Kant says that the image—for instance, the George Washington Bridge—is the product "of the empirical faculty of reproductive imagination; the schema [bridge] . . . is a product . . . of pure *a priori* imagination . . . through which images themselves first become possible."§ In other words: if I did not have the faculty of "schematizing," I could not have images.

IV. For us, the following points are decisive.

1. In perception of this particular table there is contained "table" as such. Hence, no perception is possible without imagination. Kant remarks that "psychologists have hitherto failed to realize that imagination is a necessary ingredient of perception itself."¶

2. The schema "table" is valid for all particular tables. Without it, we would be surrounded by a manifold of objects of which we could say only "this" and "this" and "this." Not only would no knowledge be possible,

---

* Ibid., B180.
† Ibid., A94.
‡ Ibid., B180–81.
§ Ibid., B181.
¶ Ibid., A120 (note).

but communication—"Bring me a table" (no matter which)—would be impossible.

3. Hence: Without the ability to say "table," we could never communicate. We can describe the George Washington Bridge because we all know "bridge." Suppose someone comes along who does not know "bridge," and there is no bridge to which I could point and utter the word. I would then draw an image of the schema of a bridge, which of course is already a particular bridge, just to remind him of some schema known to him, such as "transition from one side of the river to the other."

In other words: What makes particulars *communicable* is (a) that in perceiving a particular we have in the back of our minds (or in the "depths of our souls") a "schema" whose "shape" is characteristic of many such particulars *and* (b) that this schematic shape is in the back of the minds of many different people. These schematic shapes are products of the imagination, although "no schema can ever be brought into any image whatsoever."* All single agreements or disagreements presuppose that we are talking about the same thing—that we, who are many, agree, come together, on something that is one and the same for us all.

4. The *Critique of Judgment* deals with reflective judgments as distinguished from determinant ones. Determinant judgments subsume the particular under a general rule; reflective judgments, on the contrary, "derive" the rule from the particular. In the schema, one actually "perceives" some "universal" in the particular. One sees, so to speak, the schema "table" by recognizing the table as table. Kant hints at this distinction between determinant and reflective judgments in the *Critique of Pure Reason* by drawing a distinction between "subsuming under a concept" and "bringing to a concept."†

5. Finally, our sensibility seems to need imagination not only as an aid to knowledge but in order to recognize sameness in the manifold. As such, it is the condition of all knowledge: the "synthesis of imagination, prior to apperception, is the ground of the possibility of all knowledge, especially

---

* Ibid., B181.
† Ibid., B104.

of experience."* As such, imagination "determines the sensibility *a priori*," i.e., it inheres in all sense perceptions. Without it, there would be neither the objectivity of the world—that it can be known—nor any possibility of communication—that we can talk about it.

V. The importance of the schema for our purposes is that sensibility and understanding meet in producing it through imagination. In the *Critique of Pure Reason* imagination is at the service of the intellect; in the *Critique of Judgment* the intellect is "at the service of imagination."†

In the *Critique of Judgment* we find an analogy to the "schema": it is the *example*.‡ Kant accords to examples the same role in judgments that the intuitions called schemata have for experience and cognition. Examples play a role in both reflective and determinant judgments, that is, whenever we are concerned with particulars. In the *Critique of Pure Reason*—where we read that "judgment is a peculiar talent which can be practiced only, and cannot be taught" and that "its lack no school can make good"§—they are called "the go-cart [*Gängelband*] of judgment."¶ In the *Critique of Judgment*, i.e., in the treatment of reflective judgments, where one does not subsume a particular under a concept, the example helps one in the same way in which the schema helped one to recognize the table as table. The examples lead and guide us, and the judgment thus acquires "exemplary validity."**

The example is the particular that contains in itself, or is supposed to contain, a concept or a general rule. How, for instance, are you able to judge, to evaluate, an act as courageous? When judging, you say spontaneously, without any derivations from general rules, "This man has courage." If you were a Greek you would have in "the depths of your mind" the example of Achilles. Imagination is again necessary: you must have Achilles present despite his absence. If we say of somebody that he is good, we

---

* Ibid., A118.

† *Critique of Judgment*, General Remark to § 22, trans. J. H. Bernard (New York: Hafner, 1951).

‡ Ibid., § 59.

§ *Critique of Pure Reason*, B172.

¶ Ibid., B173–74.

** *Critique of Judgment*, § 22.

have in the back of our minds the example of Saint Francis or Jesus of Nazareth. The judgment has exemplary validity to the extent that the example is rightly chosen. Or, to take another instance: in the circumstances of French history I can speak of Napoleon Bonaparte as a particular man; but the moment I speak of Bonapartism I make an example of him. The validity of this example will be restricted to those who possess the *experience* of Napoleon, if not as his contemporaries then as heirs of a particular historical tradition. Most concepts in the historical and political sciences are of this restricted nature; they have their origin in a particular historical incident, and then proceed to make it "exemplary"—to see in the particular what is valid for more than one case.

1970

HE'S ALL DWIGHT

When I was asked to write a brief introduction to the reprint edition of *Politics* I was tempted to yield to the rather pleasant melancholy of "once upon a time" and to indulge in the nostalgic contemplation that seems to be the appropriate mood for all recollection. Now that I have carefully reread the forty-two issues which appeared from 1944 to 1949—more carefully, I am sure, than I read them more than twenty years ago—this mood has vanished for the simple reason that so many of its articles, comments, and factual reports read as though they were written today or yesterday or yesteryear, except that the concerns and perplexities of a little magazine with a peak circulation of not much more than five thousand have become the daily bread of newspapers and periodicals with mass circulation. For the issues, far from being outdated, let alone resolved, by the enormous changes in our everyday world, have only increased in urgency.

This is true for the draft card burning, black power (then called "Negroism"), and mass culture; for the military and political futility of "massacre by bombing"; for the military-industrial complex (a "permanent War Economy" was proposed in January 1944 by Charles E. Wilson, then head of the War Production Board, and the atomic bomb was hailed by Harry Truman as "the greatest achievement of the combined efforts of science, industry, labor and the military in all history"); for the breakdown of democratic processes in the democracies (England and the United States); and it is, of course, true for the cold war, which, however, in its beginning "reflected a genuine horror at Russia's record in Europe" (George Woodcock) and was not merely the result of big-power politics. It is especially true for issues that lay dormant for long years, such as the question of responsibility for the horror of Nazi death camps, which came to the fore only much later, in the late fifties, with the new series of war crime trials that culminated in the Eichmann trial in Jerusalem; or for the restoration of the *status quo* in Europe after the liberation from Nazi occupation. The series of articles on Greece, beginning in January 1945, and running through the whole year, is still an excellent introduction to what happened in that country in 1967. For it seems that only now are we beginning to pay the full price for the annihilation of all European underground movements against fascism and Nazism, an annihilation which succeeded because it was one of the very items on which the Allied powers wholeheartedly agreed.

The magazine followed with close and moving attention the half-forgotten tragedy of Warsaw, when for two months Polish resistance fighters rose up against the German Wehrmacht only to be betrayed by the Red Army and finally massacred by the Nazis. This episode was a condition for Soviet rule in East Europe, in much the same way as, in the West, the defeats of the French, Italian, and Greek underground movements served to turn the clock back to political regimes whose bankruptcy had been among the most effective causes, not, perhaps, of the rise of Hitler, but certainly of his conquest of Europe. As Niccolò Tucci said in November 1944: the victors' "job is that of transforming . . . a place of terror and hope into a place without terror and without hope."

I have picked my examples of the magazine's astounding relevance for contemporary political matters almost at random; in fact, there are only two issues of major importance today of which I can find no trace in its back numbers—the rapid disintegration of the big cities and the alarming rise of "invisible government." It has been said of the old *Masses* (1911–1917)—the only magazine I know which bears a certain resemblance to *Politics* and fulfilled a similar function thirty years earlier—that it "seems to have been written in anticipation of a cosmic event which never occurred and in blessed unawareness of the one that did." But whether or not it was "History which destroyed [the *Masses* editors'] frame of reference and made the objects of their concern seem fanciful and unreal," the point of the matter is that the exact opposite is true of *Politics*.

History aside, which of course may well have had its hand in the matter, praise is due exclusively to the editor of this one-man magazine, to his extraordinary flair for significant fact and significant thought, from which followed his flair in the choice of contributors. It is one thing to announce that one wants "to print work by younger relatively unknown American intellectuals" and by even less well-known "leftist refugees," and another to find those who twenty years later will be very well known indeed. Dwight Macdonald's discovery of Simone Weil is the most striking instance; but who then knew the names of Victor Serge, C. Wright Mills, Niccolò Tucci, Nicola Chiaromonte, Albert Camus, or Bruno Bettelheim? For if this was a one-man magazine, it never was the magazine of one man's opinion, not only because of the great generosity and hospitality which made it possible for many voices and viewpoints to have their say but, more importantly, because the editor himself never was a one-opinion man or, perhaps, had ceased to be opinionated when he felt the need to have a magazine of his own.

That Macdonald "is continually changing his mind" (James Farrell) is well known, but what is perhaps less recognized is that this is among his virtues. No one, of course, who is willing to listen to reason and to reality can help changing his mind, but most of us do this imperceptibly, hardly being aware of our changes, whereas Macdonald in a veritable furor of intellectual integrity and moral honesty sets out to hunt down his "mistakes," without ever changing the record in the slightest, his technique being to annotate his earlier articles with refutations of himself. God knows, this is something much more noble than "flexibility."

Politics always prided itself on being radical, which—following a remark of the young Marx—means "to grasp the matter by the root." In line with this aim, stated in the first issue, the editor began to free himself of all formulas—"my 'formula' being to have none," as he puts it later—more specifically, of the Marxist formula with its faith in History and Progress. When this process of liberation was completed, after the bombing of Hiroshima, which occurred at the end of the magazine's second year of existence, he set out for the discovery of new roots in the realm of theory on the one hand, new "Ancestors" such as William Godwin, Proudhon, Bakunin, Alexander Herzen, Tolstoi, etc., and "New Roads in Politics" on the other. The new post-Marxian mood—all contributors were former Marxists— was strongly anarchist and pacifist, and its most important contribution was Macdonald's own series of articles, later published as a book, *The Root*

Is Man. The new creed, if such it was, consisted of a radical humanism for which man was not merely the root, the origin of all political issues, but the ultimate goal of all politics and the only valid standard of judgment to be applied to all political matters.

I personally think that these attempts at arriving at a new political theory have worn less well than comments and reports, but who could not be struck by the fact that the mood of a few lost writers on the Left of twenty years ago has today become the dominant mood of a whole generation firmly convinced in word and deed that "all the genuine problems are moral in nature"—as David Bazelon critically remarked about the socialism of the "New Roads" writers. Radical *humanism* obviously does not follow from being radical, from grasping the matter by the root; like every ism it could even stand in the way of being radical, that is, it could prevent looking for the root in all matters as they present themselves. After a few years' experience, Macdonald reformulated his first program and now wished to do no more than "to seek out the long-range trends in the welter of daily phenomena." In this context, the word radical assumes a different meaning. It points to the fearlessness, unbiased research for those facts in everyday affairs that contain the roots of future developments. In this respect, *Politics*'s radical record is admirable; it was indeed so close to the future that the whole enterprise often looks like a premature dress rehearsal.

In order to avoid misunderstandings, especially by Marxists or former Marxists who equate political intelligence with prophetic powers, I hasten to admit that Macdonald's batting average for short-time predictions was not too good—a failing he shared with Karl Marx who, around 1858, was afraid that *Das Kapital* might not be finished before the outbreak of the revolution. Most of these "mistakes" were irrelevant—for instance, Macdonald's belief in 1944 that the liquidation of the British Empire was "remote." Some were more serious, especially his failure to understand the complex nature of the Second World War, which to him, as to the entire American Left, was simply an "imperialist" war. But this estimate belongs still to his pre-radical, ideological leftist period, and the chief reason he did not revise it after his break with Marxism was his new turn to pacifism, as well as his conviction that "the Soviet System was an even greater threat to what I believe in than Nazism was"—a very debatable statement because it identified the Soviet System with Bolshevism (Lenin's one-party dictatorship) and Bolshevism with Stalinism. Macdonald was clearly wrong when he wrote, three months before Hiroshima, "To say that civilization cannot survive another war is a truism; the question is whether it can survive this one."

The German "economic miracle," the rapid recovery of Japan, the rebuilding of Russia after Stalin's death have all demonstrated that *up to a point* the modern means of production function nowhere better than where the modern means of destruction have first created a kind of *tabula rasa*—provided that the population of the country is sufficiently "modern" and that the production process is not obstructed by the perverse power considerations of a totalitarian dictatorship. (Today it is England, hardly touched by destruction in the war in comparison with Germany, but profoundly unwilling to change her old ways of life, whose fate is in the balance.) Subsequent events proved Macdonald equally wrong when, under the direct impact of Hiroshima, he thought, "We Americans are coming to be hated with an intensity formerly reserved for the Germans." It is, I think, fair to say that, although he once mentioned "the German atrocities in this war [as] a phenomenon unique at least in modern history," he underestimated throughout the horror as well as the outrage inspired by the Nazi extermination factories.

What in retrospect is so remarkable about all this is not the mistakes but, on the contrary, in spite of them and sometimes even because of them, that he could be so uncannily right in detecting the "long-range trends." It may have been a mistake to be against World War II (except on religious grounds, which are always valid because they are nonpolitical); but did not the end of the war, the dropping of the atomic bombs on Hiroshima and Nagasaki, give justification to his misgivings? With the development of nuclear weapons, has not modern warfare indeed begun to threaten with extinction not only civilizations but mankind? And though it was clearly premature in 1945 to fear that Americans would be hated like Germans, it was as if somebody cried "Wolf" when the animal was still so many miles away that no one even believed in its existence. But when twenty-two years later the animal has arrived and Macdonald can write with entire justification, and in words befitting the genuine patriot he is and always has been,

"In the last two years, for the first time in my life, I'm ashamed to be an American," then one can only admire the political instinct of this citizen of the republic who, albeit without being fully aware of it, sensed in Mr. Truman's outrageous jubilation about the Bomb a decisive departure from that "decent respect to the opinions of mankind" which is, as it were, built into the very foundations of this republic.

Politics, then, which counted so many non-Americans among its contributors, was radical in the sense of going back and reviving much that belongs to the very roots of the American tradition as well as much that belongs to the roots of the radical tradition everywhere—the tradition of nay-saying and independence, of cheerful "negativism" when confronted with the temptation of *Realpolitik,* and of self-confidence: pride and trust in one's own judgment. These qualities distinguish the radical, who always remains true to reality in his search for the root of the matter, from the extremist, who single-mindedly follows the logic of whatever "cause" he may espouse at the moment.

In *Politics,* this closeness to reality proved itself, simply and spectacularly, when the magazine decided to embark upon a project of sending packages of food and clothing to the liberated countries at the close of the war. Here, the editor wrote, was "something which those who have criticized the magazine's 'negativism' must admit is positive and constructive." I suspect he wrote this sentence with tongue in cheek, unaware of how literally right he was. Who in Europe at this time would have believed that there existed such a thing as "international fraternity," to which Macdonald appealed, after the fierce political infighting on the Left? (In order to be helped at all you had to belong to some party or, at least, to some splinter group.) But here was a small, independent journal; and its appeal to its readers was such a success that "sometimes it seems that *Politics* is a house organ for the package project rather than a magazine of its own." It was just solidarity with those who had suffered, and nothing else.

This radical mentality as such has remained alive in these pages rather than theories or prophecies, which, right or wrong, are lamentably irrelevant in the long run; no prediction can ever anticipate, and no theory fit, what will *be* once an event has happened. This attitude can be tested on almost every page of *Politics,* and especially where phenomena are presented and analyzed which have no place in the leftist frame of reference. Thus, Macdonald understands that "just as war releases the productive energy of industry from the bonds of property and profit, so it also allows expression to some very fine traits of human nature which have little outlet in peacetime society." And while, after having left the Trotskyites, he still believed in "the yardstick of basic values" with which "to measure month-to-month developments"—all he had left after parting with Marxism—he soon was fearless enough to admit that this yardstick was no less suspect than the verities of the Left, "that our ethical code is no longer *experienced,* but is simply assumed, so that it becomes a collection of mere platitudes."

It was this sensitivity to the long-range, that is, to the crucial issues "in the welter of daily phenomena," which enabled him to raise the "moral" question in our present political predicaments so early—the question of "How may we tell Good from Evil?" The crucial insight, always hidden in the complex welter of appearances, is simple and, once discovered, painfully obvious. Yet nothing is rarer and more precious than the ability to hit upon it. *Politics*'s marksmanship in such matters was very high, not merely among its writers, the editor, and his contributors, but also among its readers. It was a sergeant, stationed in Germany in 1945, who said, "In modern wars there are crimes not criminals. In modern society there is evil but there is no devil." And what could go more directly to the heart of the matter than Mary McCarthy's remark, after the assassination of Gandhi, about political murder in our time: "It is Gandhi who can be killed or Trotski or Carlo Tresca, men *integri vitae scelerisque puri,** while Stalin remains invulnerable to the assassin's bullet"; or Dwight Macdonald's words at the same occasion, perhaps the most fitting epitaph of Gandhi and certainly to be inscribed into the hearts of all true lovers of equality: "He seems to have regarded the capitalist as well as the garbage-man as his social equal."

Politics lasted six years, three as a monthly, one as a bimonthly, and two as a quarterly. It died in 1949 of "the gray dawn of peace," of a time "without terror and without hope." What now came was the political apathy of the fifties, the arrival of "the silent generation," whose imminence Macdonald

---

* Horace, *Ode* 1.22: "whole of life and void of vice." —Ed.

must have felt already early in 1948 when he began "feeling stale, tired, disheartened and, if you like, demoralized." This end is not without tragic overtones. The man who had chosen "politics," this "most unpopular term," to name his magazine, with the intention of restoring it to its ancient dignity, gave up in despair of politics rather than *Politics*. The silent generation, in due time, gave way to the civil rights movement, but the period of a deceptive calm took its definite end only with the assassination of Kennedy. Nearly five years later, *Politics* has found no successor—except, perhaps, *Ramparts*.

While it existed, it was less a one-man magazine than a one-man institution, providing a focal point for many who would no longer fit into any party or group. The feeling of companionship among its readers had something almost embarrassingly personal about it, and it was precisely this personal note that inspired confidence, not in the rightness of any opinions so much as in the reliability of those who wrote for it. Something of this atmosphere is still alive in the extensive letters-to-the-editor columns, many of them attacking and all of them carefully answered, sometimes at considerable length. Among the things that made this magazine an institution—and I think a unique one—was that Macdonald regarded his readers, if he cared to print them at all, as his intellectual equals.

1968

EMERSON-THOREAU MEDAL ADDRESS

Mr. President, Mr. Trilling, Fellows of the Academy,
Ladies and Gentlemen:

I thank you. It is good to be recognized, and membership in this body whose very distinction lies today in its almost unique combination of the arts and the sciences, means recognition that counts since it comes from one's peers. To be honored means perhaps not more, but something different. We may think that we have a claim to recognition; we earn it though we don't necessarily deserve it; but we never earn or deserve an award or an honor. These are gifts freely and gratuitously bestowed, and their meaning, at least to me, is not recognition but welcome. And if it is good to be recognized, it is better to be welcomed, precisely because this is something we can neither earn nor deserve.

To receive the Emerson-Thoreau Medal, however, has still another significance for me. Hermann Grimm once wrote to Emerson: "When I think of America I think of you, and America appears to me as the first country of the world." Not only in the last century, but still in the first third of the twentieth century, Emerson was one of the very few American authors with whom we, who grew up and were educated in Europe, were intimately acquainted before we came to this country. I have always read him as a kind of American Montaigne, and I discovered with great joy, only recently, how close Emerson himself felt to Montaigne. When he first read him in translation, it seemed to him "as if [he] had written the book himself in some former life, so sincerely it spoke my thought and experience" (Journals, March 1843). What Emerson and Montaigne most obviously have in common is that they are both humanists rather than philosophers, and that therefore wrote essays rather than systems, aphorisms rather than books. (This, incidentally, was the reason why Nietzsche, the black sheep among the philosophers, liked Emerson so much.) Both thought chiefly, exclusively, about human matters, and both lived a life of thought. "Life," said Emerson, "consists of what a man is thinking of all day." This kind of thinking can no more become a profession than living itself, hence, this is not the *vita contemplativa,* the philosopher's way of life who has made thinking his profession. Philosophers, as a rule, are rather serious animals; whereas what is so striking in both Emerson and Montaigne is their *serenity,* a serenity that is in no way conformist or complacent—"I like the sayers of No better than the sayers of Yes," said Emerson—a cheerfulness that is pervaded by a quiet, reconciled melancholy—"Every man is wanted, and no man is wanted much." This, as it were, innocent cheerfulness, more innocent in Emerson than in Montaigne, is perhaps today the greatest difficulty for us. When we read in one of Emerson's best poems: "From all that's fair, from all that's foul, / Peals out a cheerful song. . . . But in the darkest meanest things / There alway, alway, something sings. . . . But in the mud and scum of things / There alway, alway something sings," I am sure we feel more nostalgia than kinship. What Emerson dealt out was, as he once remarked about the "true preacher," a "life passed through the fire of thought," and whatever the fire of thought might have done to it, this life itself was still untroubled compared to ours, untroubled, more specifically, by bad thoughts.

Thus, we find in Emerson what former ages called wisdom, and that is something which has never existed in abundance or been in great demand. Embedded in this wisdom there are profound insights and observations which we have lost to our detriment, and which we may be well advised to unearth again now, when we are forced to rethink what the humanities are all about. For this great humanist, the humanities were simply those disciplines that dealt with language (which does not mean linguistics), and in the center of all thought about language, he found the poet, "the Namer or language-maker." Let me in conclusion read to you a few sentences which to me sound like the conclusive and still valid confession of the true humanist. The poet, he writes, names "things sometimes after their appearance, sometimes after their essence, and giving to every one its own name and not another's, thereby rejoicing the intellect, which delights in detachment or boundary. The poets made all the words, and therefore language is *the archives of history,* and, if we must say it, a sort of tomb for the muses. For though the origin of most of our words is forgotten, each word was at first a stroke of genius, and obtained currency because for the moment it symbolized the world to the first speaker and hearer. The etymologist finds the deadest word to have been at once a brilliant picture. Language is fossil poetry."*

APRIL 9, 1969

* Emerson, *Essays: Second Series* (1844), emphasis added. —Ed.

THE ARCHIMEDEAN POINT

I chose a title which perhaps is a little bit surprising, in order to focus the discussion on points of controversy which may be of some relevance in our present debates about the role of the humanities at universities and colleges in general, and at the engineering schools and technological institutes in particular. However, I shall not speak here as a humanist, pleading for more liberal arts courses in the engineering school.

First of all, I am fully aware of the crisis in the humanities as fields of scientific inquiry. The humanities, however you wish to define them, deal with the past, and I think it is a secret from nobody that our attitude to the past and to our tradition has been greatly compromised in this century. Moreover, a recent paper on *The Applied Humanities* by Davenport and Frankel asserts that

> many laymen think it's up to the humanities to prevent technological forces from racing out of control, and that the humanist may well rise to the challenge lest the engineers try to do the applying [of the humanities] themselves.

I believe that the "many laymen" who are quoted here are wrong, and that the engineers, should they try to do what the laymen suggest they may, will soon find out how impossible this whole enterprise actually is.

The logical break against making us slaves of our own inventions are the scientists and engineers themselves, not insofar as they are scientists and engineers, but insofar as they, too, are human beings, citizens, sharing a common world with their fellow citizens (the so-called laymen), possessing in addition the necessary information, or so we hope. Hence, I shall speak here as a layman, and this not only because my ignorance in all scientific matters is complete. What the members of the so-called two cultures share and will always share with each other is the everyday world in which we spend most of our lives, the common world of common sense. Compared to this common world in which we actually move and talk with each other, the men in the laboratory or in the field of pure and applied mathematics live no less, perhaps even more, in a "monastic habitat" than the aloof humanists in their alleged "ivory tower." The present student revolt, in which the natural sciences and engineering schools, are rather conspicuous by their absence, tends to indicate that it is still easier to make activists out of aloof humanists than out of aloof nuclear physicists. There is probably more than one reason for this phenomenon, but the point of the matter is that the activist, whether he comes out of the laboratory or out of the archives and libraries, is first of all a citizen, who tries to persuade other citizens to join him; and a citizen, looked upon from any specialty is, of course, a layman by definition. Despite all the assurances of the psychologists and the believers in social engineering, it is still an open question whether it is possible "to produce"—as people say—good citizens; and assuming that it is possible, who knows which fields of scientific endeavor are most likely to give results in this enterprise? I talk, therefore, as a citizen, as a layman, or simply as a human being.

To begin with, and before I use the Archimedean Point in a more general way, let's remember its origin. Archimedes was a Greek scientist and mathematician in the third century before Christ in Sicily, who was killed by the Roman consul, Marcellus, during the first Punic War. He established the theory of leverage and has been famous for the words, "Give me a place to stand and I shall move the earth." Permit me to stress the obvious. This means that our power over things grows in proportion to our distance from them. To a certain extent, this is true for all cognitive acts. We must always remove ourselves—draw back, as it were—from the obvious object we wish to study. Thucydides, writing the history of the Peloponnesian War, kept himself aloof, quite consciously so, from involvement with the events themselves. He wrote his history during the twenty years of exile from Athens, and he himself said that this gave him an advantageous position for his enterprise. Obviously, no judgment such as Thucydides'—"This was the greatest movement yet known in history"—would have been possible without such withdrawal. But the withdrawal needed for cognitive acts is much more limited than what Archimedes, apparently already thinking about power over things (he will move the earth!), had in mind. And so long as knowledge was thought of as contemplative or experimental, and science was understood as the ordering, interpretation, and explanation of observed phenomena, Archimedes—not only his dreamed-up point outside the earth but his early combination of mechanics and mathematics—was forgotten.

Modern science (that is, the new rise of science, from the seventeenth and eighteenth centuries up to the beginning of the twentieth century—that is, roughly, from Galileo to Einstein) called itself not only a "new science," *scienza nuova*, a term we find already in the sixteenth century, but *scienza activa et operativa*, "an active and operating science." And this science was marked by what historians of science have called a *véritable retour à l'Archimèd*, "a real return to Archimedes." "Modern science," said Alexandre Koyré (whom you perhaps know—I mean the scientists among you),

> substitutes for the mixed world of common sense an Archimedean world of geometry made real, "a universe of measurement and precision."

And to this statement of Koyré's we may add that this science achieved its greatest triumphs after freeing itself from the "shackles of spatiality"—that is, from geometry, which, as the name indicates, depends still on terrestrial measurement and measures and, therefore, on earthbound experience. The Archimedean Point (that is, the point far enough removed from the things of the earth to give power over them, and perhaps to unhinge the earth) was reached, in theory at least, when geometry was subjected to algebraic treatment and a new nonspatial language was devised. Now we all know that this did not remain a matter of theory, or at least not in the twentieth century; and I should like to suggest, to begin with, that it was not a matter of the will-to-power either.

Copernicus's notion of the universe not centered around the earth sprang from sheer force of imagination by virtue of which he lifted himself from the earth into the sun overlooking the planet; and Galileo's use of the telescope merely confirmed what some philosophers had vaguely and speculatively suspected—in antiquity, Aristarchus of Samos, a contemporary of Archimedes, and in the Renaissance, Giordano Bruno. Einstein indeed generalized these early discoveries when he introduced his "observer who is poised freely in space," and not just at one definite point like the sun. It seems to me quite evident that the scientist's strongest intellectual motivation was Einstein's striving after generalizations such as Newton's Law of Gravitation in which the same equation covers the movement of the stars and the motion of terrestrial things; and that if the scientists appealed to power at all, it was the formidable power of abstraction and imagination, not the power over things and men.

The significance of the discovery that neither the earth nor the sun could lay claim to being the center of the universe has been commented upon from the first, but there is hardly any comment on the immense increase in power as a consequence of the new science; the reason for this absence is probably that such an increase in power was never intended. In any event, it took centuries until the new world of the astrophysicist was literally brought down to earth, with the result that the world we live in changed more in a few decades than it had changed in thousands of years. Moreover, the enormous technological consequences which finally gave testimony to the immense power increase of men in the modern age were predicted by no one, neither by the scientists themselves—who even today, I am told, still have an inclination to look down upon engineers as mere plumbers—nor by the historians. (The only predictions came from people like Jules Verne, that is, the predecessors of science fiction.) But, if anyone else should have predicted them, or should have foreseen them, is it not likely that he would have concluded that the increase in human power would be accompanied by an increase in the stature and the pride of man? This, however, has not been the case.

The triumphant mood of the scientists and the men of letters in the early stage of the modern age about things never seen before, thoughts never thought before, the strange pathos of novelty so characteristic of the seventeenth century in all fields of learning, was followed by altogether different comments on the consequences of the Copernican Revolution, comments which then became the stock-in-trade of the humanist. I will give you one quote at the beginning of this period and one quote at its end, and then let's forget about the in-between because it all comes down to the same. Montesquieu writes as follows:

> When I see men crawling about on an atom, I mean the earth, which is only a speck in the universe, and proposing themselves as models of divine providence, I don't know how to reconcile such extravagance with such pettiness!

This was written centuries before the new worldview had become manifest in the actual change of the everyday world we live in. But it was only a matter of decades for this change to occur to when Nietzsche, in the 1880s, at the end of the nineteenth century, roughly 160 years later, still wrote in basically the same vein:

> Has not man's will to diminish himself grown irresistibly since Copernicus? Is it not as though man ever since has been sliding downhill, running away faster and faster from the center?

(He hadn't yet read Yeats!)

> Whence is he going? Into the void? Into a piercing feeling of being nothing? But perhaps this is the straightest road back to the *old* ideal of science. All science, and by no means astronomy alone—concerning whose humiliating effect Kant made a remarkable confession: "It annihilates my importance"—is today inherent in talking man out of his former self-respect, as if this respect had been nothing but a bizarre presumption.

I want to remind you first that Nietzsche thought that this is "the strangest road back to the *old* ideal of science," and I want to explain what he meant by this. Ever since the Greeks, as Nietzsche knew so well, the glory of science has been its objectivity, its disinterestedness, its impartiality in the consequences which its pursuit of truth and knowledge might have. Modern science, indeed in more than one sense, is a return to the old ideal. Its very integrity demands that not only utilitarian considerations but reflections upon the stature of man as well be left in abeyance. It is not without irony that today aloof humanists are accused of indifference to practical questions, that they do not know how to apply the humanities to the needs of the modern world beset by problems of technology. For the pragmatic ideal of science, the ideal of applicability, was originally the ideal of humanists, or rather of their ancestors, namely of the Romans to whom we owe the word *humanitas,* something of which the Greeks were so little aware they had no word for it. The Romans, concerned with *humanitas,* surpassed the Greeks in the technical application of scientific discoveries. But since they measured what we would now call "pure research" with the yardstick of usefulness, of what is good for man in every respect, they killed the development of science. (There is a nice symbolic significance in the fact that it was a Roman who killed Archimedes.)

The objections raised by the Church, the Roman Church, against Galileo were still in the Roman tradition. They are strictly pragmatic ones. "What will be the consequences," the Church asked, "of what you are doing? How will men be able to live with the world you establish?" Now, if it is the greatness of modern science (that is, astrophysics) that, as Planck once remarked, "It has been purged of all anthropological elements," the question arises: How can men live with a worldview that takes so little account of them that it contradicts their sense experience and hence their common sense? And how can they live in a world established and sustained by technological forces which are beyond the ordinary understanding of even the best-informed laymen, which are based, to an extent, upon results obtained by mathematical processes which stubbornly refuse "to be translated back into the language of the world of our senses"—something that Planck, whom I have quoted, still thought absolutely necessary if they are to be of any use to us. "Otherwise," he predicted

the new theories would be no better than a bubble ready to burst at the first puff of wind.

We today, about sixty years after Planck wrote these sentences, know better. The new science returned to the old ideal of Greek sublime indifference to pragmatic concerns, but this was done in a new spirit. No longer contemplative and hence of concern only to the philosophers and scientists, on the contrary, it was active and operative. Thus the new science became finally of tremendous use to us, and it was precisely its usefulness, its applicability, that then confirmed the soundness of the new worldview and inspired new discoveries.

If the gentlemen of the natural science departments and the technological institutes today pride themselves on the applicability of their research and demand a similar pragmatic outlook from the liberal arts faculties, it may perhaps not be totally amiss to ask them to remember that originally it was not science, but, on the contrary, the liberal arts which were supposed to be (I am quoting Cicero) *ad hominem utilitatem*, to be useful for men insofar as they were human, that is, distinguished from mere organic life, and that usefulness as a criterion of the value of scientific research is a rather late development. Let us not forget that such precision instruments as our watches and clocks, which certainly are among the most indispensable tools in the everyday lives of our civilization, were invented for what then (namely, in the seventeenth century) were practically useless purposes—to obtain the exact measurement for the speed of falling bodies.

Thus, the paradox of the development of modern science seems to be that while it enhanced enormously the power of man, it resulted at the same time in a no less decisive diminishment of man's self-respect. Modern man in his search for knowledge and truth, and by sheer force of abstraction, first looked upon the earth and natural processes from a point in the universe, trusting his mental powers rather than his sense experience. He thus acquired the ability to handle nature as though he himself were no longer an earthbound creature, and he began to release those energy processes that ordinarily go on only in the sun; to initiate in a test tube processes of cosmic evolution; and to build machines for the production and control of energies unknown in the household of nature. Yet when he now looked down from this point upon what was going on on earth and upon the various activities of men, including his own, these activities could not but appear to him as though they were what the behaviorists call "overt behavior," which can be studied with the same methods used to study the behavior of rats and apes. Seen from a sufficient distance, the cars in which we travel and which we believe we built ourselves must appear, as Heisenberg once put it, "as inescapable a part of ourselves as a snail's shell to its occupant." Our pride in what we *can* do will necessarily vanish when we discover that we deal actually with a kind of mutation of the human race, and that the whole of technology is not "the result of a conscious human effort to extend man's material power, but rather a large-scale biological process." In the same way, one might add, the coincidence of the population explosion with the invention of nuclear weapons could appear from this distant viewpoint as a phenomenon *in* the household of nature, as a "large-scale biological process" to prevent life on earth from being thrown out of balance.

The "new science" is haunted by a paradox concerning the stature of man: that the more knowledge and the more power man acquires as a scientist, the less respect he can harbor for himself who achieved all this, which was originally discovered by laymen. But laymen, overwhelmed by the very real triumphs of science and technology, are less inclined today to raise such questions than before the technological revolution occurred. Laymen today are worried and sometimes in a mood of rebellion for other, more practical reasons: the enormous destructive potential of modern weapons, or the enormous amounts of money required for the conquest of space, which were perhaps better spent on the conquest of poverty, and the like. The malaise has shifted place.

The scientists themselves are now concerned, because of certain perplexities in their own work. There was, first, the shock of the older generation when they realized that their own time-honored ideals of harmony and necessity were in jeopardy. Einstein's extreme reluctance to sacrifice the principle of causality, as Planck's quantum theory demanded, is well known. His main objection was that with it lawfulness was about to depart from the universe—that it was as though God ruled the universe by playing dice. There was, second, the highly disturbing fact that it proved impossible to translate, as Planck demanded, the results obtained by mathematical processes back into language, not only into the language of our everyday world, but also into any kind of conceptual terminology. The theoretical perplexities that have confronted the new nonanthropocentric, nongeocentric, and nonheliocentric science, because its data refused to be ordered by any of the natural mental categories of the human brain, are well enough known. In the words of Schrödinger,

The new universe is not thinkable. However we think it, it is wrong, perhaps not quite as meaningless as a triangular circle, but much more so than a winged lion.

To be sure, one can say that lawfulness, necessity, and harmony belong among outdated ideals and that all perplexities are caused, as Niels Bohr once thought, by "our necessarily prejudiced conceptual frame" that is unprepared for regularities "of a new kind, defying the deterministic pictorial description," in atomic phenomena. The trouble, however, is that what defies description in terms of the prejudices of the human mind defies description in all conceivable ways of human language. It can no longer be described at all and is being expressed, but not described, by mathematical symbols. Bohr still hoped for the eventual emergence of a widened "conceptual framework" in which all "apparent disharmonies" would disappear. But this hope has thus far not been fulfilled and it is not very likely that it ever will be. The categories and ideas of human reason have their ultimate source in human sense experience, and all terms describing our mental ability as well as a good deal of our conceptual language derive from the world of the senses, and are then used metaphorically. Moreover, the human brain, which supposedly does our thinking, is as earthbound as any other part of the human body; and it was precisely by abstracting from these terrestrial conditions that modern science reached its most glorious and, at the same time, most baffling achievements.

To put it another way, the scientists, in their search for "true reality," lost their confidence in the world of "mere" appearances, in the phenomena as they reveal themselves of their own accord. They began with the invention of instruments which were designed merely to refine the coarseness of our senses and they ended up with instruments to deal with data which, strictly speaking, do not "appear" at all, neither in our everyday world nor even in the laboratory. They make themselves known only because they affect our measuring instruments in certain ways, and still there seems to be no doubt that this *is* "true reality." The soundness of the "new science" became manifest beyond any doubt through the development of modern technology. The trouble is only that the discoverer of "true reality" behind mere appearances remains bound to a world of appearances; he cannot *think* in terms of what he now conceives of as "true reality"; he cannot communicate it in language, and his own life remains bound to a time concept that demonstrably does not belong to "true reality," but is (as Einstein's famous "twin paradox," based on the "clock paradox" established) mere appearance.

This humiliating aspect of modern science is perhaps best illustrated by Heisenberg's discovery of the uncertainty principle and the conclusions he himself drew from it. The uncertainty principle, as you all know, asserts

> that there are certain pairs of quantities, like the position and velocity of a particle, that are related in such a way that determining one of them with increased precision necessarily entails determining the other with reduced precision.

Heisenberg concludes from this fact that

> we decide by our selection of the type of observation employed which aspects of nature are to be determined and which are to be blurred.

He wrote that

> the most important new result of nuclear physics was the recognition of the possibility of applying quite different types of natural law, without the contradiction, to one and the same physical event. This is due to the fact that within a system of law based on certain fundamental ideas only certain quite definitive ways of asking questions make sense, and thus such a system is separated from others that allow different questions to be put.

(I may remark, just incidentally, that if you take these sentences and the perplexity they express out of the physicist's context, you recognize immediately the perplexities of the historical sciences. Almost word for word, what Heisenberg is saying could be said in an introductory course in historiography and the historical sciences. We concentrate on one thing and therefore everything else is blurred. We ask certain questions and therefore can obtain only certain answers. It's exactly the same business! Which really after all should make us a little suspicious.)

Heisenberg concluded that the modern search for "true reality" has led us into a situation in which we have lost the very objectivity of the natural world. Man, wherever he goes in imagination or reality, discovers that he "confronts only himself." Doesn't this mean that there is a definite limit to "purging science of all anthropological elements"? And do not Heisenberg's conclusions come conspicuously close (albeit, of course, on a much more sophisticated level) to the earliest suspicions in the modern age about man's capacity for truth? I am going to quote once more Montesquieu, because I want to leave the philosophers out on purpose. (Montesquieu himself quotes Spinoza, but he doesn't say so. He says, "people have said." Well, there are not many people who said it, it was only Spinoza. But you know that is the way writers operate.) Montesquieu says: "We never judge matters except by the secret return we make on ourselves." This is, by the way, an extraordinarily interesting sentence. It looks so very harmless and inconspicuous. The one who actually discovered what this means was Kant in his *Critique of Judgment,* namely, that you can judge only by this kind of return upon yourself, therefore, according to Kant, this kind of judgment is reflective. Montesquieu goes on, and all this is in the *Lettres Persanes*— that is, not in the *Esprit des Lois* but in the novel he wrote, if you want to call it that:

> I am not surprised that Negroes should paint the devil in blinding white and their own gods black as coal. And some people have said rightly, If triangles were to create a god, they would give him three sides.

(That's where Spinoza comes in.)

The grandeur of Science has always been that it did not pay attention to human interests. Its guideline was: Whatever we *can* discover we *shall* discover; whatever we *can* make we *will* make. However, its results, as we see them today, seem to lead irrevocably to a point where man is reminded of his limitations and, as it were, put back into his place. No matter how great the triumphs of science and its technology in overcoming the limitation of the human sensory apparatus along with its most solid prejudices—"that being and appearance are the same for human beings" (I am quoting Aristotle), and that nothing *is* that does not appear and vice versa—the scientist himself remains a man and subject to precisely these "prejudices." It would be presumptuous for the so-called humanist or any layman to cry hubris. And it would be futile to preach humility. It is only the scientist himself and the engineer who depends upon him, by seeing the perplexities in their own work, who can apply the brakes to technical forces that are threatening to run out of control. And they can do it only because they, too, are laymen and citizens—that is, because in the final analysis, we are all in the same boat.

But let us not fool ourselves. What is at stake is the very ethos, the ethics, of science—the conviction that whatever we *can* discover we *shall,* whatever we *can* make we *must.* And what is further at stake is our current belief in progress. Progress perhaps is not a sempiternal phenomenon. One day there will be an end to it, in one way or another. Quite apart from the question of what we *should* discover and *should* make and what we should perhaps better leave undone, there will certainly appear at some time the limit of what we *can* discover and *can* make. In other words, what I am pleading for here is a new realization of the factually existing limitations of human beings. To be sure, these limitations can be transcended up to a point. Men have always transcended them in imagination, in philosophical speculation, in religious faith, and finally in scientific discoveries. Only by transcending limits, moreover, can we become aware of them.

What I am maintaining here, without being too sure that I am right, is that such limitations have begun to make themselves felt in our scientific enterprise as well as our technicalization of the world. The fact that we are able today to devise a doomsday machine with which to destroy the planet, or at least all organic life on it, seems to present just such an absolute limit to human power. And the same is true for the danger that precisely our know-how to handle processes, which without us would never occur in terrestrial nature, may lead us to let loose irreversible processes. We may let loose what we shall never be able to stop.

Let us take our present space age program, with its built-in limits. All we shall ever be able to do is to explore our immediate surroundings in the universe and those surroundings are infinitely small. The human race could not reach more of the universe even if it were to travel with the velocity of light. The limit will be man's life span and this limitation would hardly change significantly even if we should succeed in doubling the average age of mortals. Moreover, the Archimedean Point, which actually would permit man to know all and to do all, can never be reached. All we can find is the Archimedean Point with respect to the earth, and once arrived there, we obviously would need a new one, and so on *ad infinitum*. In other words, man can only get lost in the immensity of the universe, for the only true Archimedean Point would be the absolute void behind it.

What is called the "conquest of space" today will at best result in a few discoveries in our solar system and the enlargement of the territory, as it were, in which man in contrast to all other living things on earth can be at home—and even this is doubtful. But once this limit is reached, the new worldview that may conceivably grow out of it is likely to be once more geocentric and anthropomorphic, although not in the old sense of the earth being the center of the universe and of man being the highest being in it. It would be geocentric in the sense that the earth and not the universe is the center and the home of mortal man; and it would be anthropomorphic in the sense that man would count his own mortality among the elementary conditions under which his scientific effort, his search for truth and his technical enterprises, the building of his own world, are possible at all. Thank you.

1969

HEIDEGGER AT EIGHTY

Martin Heidegger's eightieth birthday also celebrates the fiftieth anniversary of his public life, which he began not as an author—though he had already published a book on Duns Scotus—but as a teacher. In barely three or four years since that first interesting and solid but still rather conventional study, he had become so different from its author that his students were hardly aware of its existence. If it is true, as Plato once remarked, that "the beginning is also a god; so long as he dwells among men, he redeems all things" (*Laws* 775), then the beginning in Heidegger's case is neither the date of his birth (September 26, 1889, at Messkirch), nor the publication of his first book, but the first lecture courses and seminars which he held as a mere *Privatdozent* (instructor) and assistant to Husserl at the University of Freiburg in 1919. For Heidegger's "fame" predates by about eight years the publication of *Sein und Zeit* in 1927; indeed it is open to question whether the unusual success of this book—not just the immediate impact it had inside and outside the academic world but also its extraordinarily lasting influence, with which few of this century's writings can compare—would have been possible if it had not been preceded by the teacher's reputation among the students, in whose opinion the book's success merely confirmed what they had known for years.

There was something strange about this early fame, stranger perhaps even than the fame of Kafka in the early twenties, or of Braque and Picasso in the preceding decade, who were also unknown to what is commonly understood as the public and nevertheless exerted an extraordinary influence. For in Heidegger's case there was nothing available on which his fame could have been based, nothing tangible except for transcripts of his lectures, which circulated hand to hand among students. These lectures dealt with texts that were generally familiar; they contained no doctrine that could have been learned, reproduced, and handed on. There was hardly more than a name, but the name traveled all over Germany like the rumor of the hidden king. This was something completely different from a "circle" centered around and directed by a "master" (say, the Stefan George circle), which, while well known to the public, still remained apart from it by an aura of secrecy, the *arcana imperii* to which presumably only the circle's members are privy. Here there was neither a secret nor membership; those who heard the rumor were acquainted with one another, to be sure, since they were all students, and there were occasional friendships among them. Later some cliques formed here and there; but there never was a circle and there was nothing esoteric about his following.

Who heard the rumor, and what did it say? In the German universities at the time, after the First World War, there was no rebellion but widespread discontent with the academic enterprise of teaching and learning in those faculties that were more than professional schools, a disquiet that prevailed among students for whom study meant more than preparing for making a living. Philosophy was no breadwinner's study, but rather the study of resolute starvelings who were, for that very reason, all the more demanding. They were in no way disposed toward a wisdom of life or of the world, and for anyone concerned with the solution of all riddles there was available a rich selection of worldviews and their partisans; it wasn't necessary to study philosophy in order to choose among them.

But what they did want they didn't know. The university commonly offered them either the schools—the neo-Kantians, the neo-Hegelians, the neo-Platonists, etc.—or the old academic discipline, in which philosophy, neatly divided into its special fields—epistemology, aesthetics, ethics, logic, and the like—was not so much communicated as drowned in an ocean of boredom. There were, even before Heidegger's appearance, a few rebels against this comfortable and, in its way, quite solid enterprise. Chronologically, there was Husserl and his cry "To the things themselves"; and that meant, "Away from theories, away from books," toward the establishment of philosophy as a rigorous science which would take its place alongside other academic disciplines. This was still a naïve and unrebellious cry, but it was something to which first Scheler and somewhat later Heidegger could appeal. In addition, there was Karl Jaspers in Heidelberg, consciously rebellious and coming from a tradition other than philosophy. He, as is known, was for a long time on friendly terms with Heidegger, precisely because the rebellious element in Heidegger's enterprise appealed to him as something original and fundamentally philosophical in the midst of the academic talk *about* philosophy.

What these few had in common was—to put it in Heidegger's words—that they could distinguish "between an object of scholarship and a matter of thought" (*Aus der Erfahrung des Denkens,* 1947)* and that they were pretty indifferent to the object of scholarship. At that time the rumor of Heidegger's teaching reached those who knew more or less explicitly about the breakdown of tradition and the "dark times" (Brecht) which had set in, who, therefore, were prepared to comply with the academic discipline only because they were concerned with the "matter of thought" or, as Heidegger would say today, "thinking's matter" (*Zur Sache des Denkens,* 1969). The rumor that attracted them to Freiburg and to the *Privatdozent* who taught there, as somewhat later they were attracted to the young professor at Marburg, had it that there was someone who was actually attaining "the things" that Husserl had proclaimed, someone who knew that these things were not academic matters but the concerns of thinking men—concerns not just of yesterday and today, but from time immemorial—and who, precisely because he knew that the thread of tradition was broken, was discovering the past anew. It was technically decisive that, for instance, Plato was not talked *about* and his theory of Ideas expounded; rather for an entire semester a single dialogue was pursued and subjected to question step by step, until the time-honored doctrine had disappeared to make room for a set of problems of immediate and urgent relevance. Today this sounds quite familiar, because nowadays so many proceed in this way; but no one did before Heidegger. The rumor about Heidegger put it quite simply: Thinking has come to life again; the cultural treasures of the past, believed to be dead, are being made to speak, in the course of which it turns out that they propose things altogether different from the familiar, worn-out trivialities they had been presumed to say. There is a teacher; one can perhaps learn to think.

* See "The Thinker as Poet" in *Poetry, Language, Thought,* trans. A. Hofstadter (New York, 1975).

The hidden king reigned therefore in the realm of thinking, which, although it is completely of this world, is so concealed in it that one can never be quite sure whether it exists at all; and still its inhabitants must be more numerous than is commonly believed. For how, otherwise, could the unprecedented, often underground, influence of Heidegger's thinking and thoughtful reading be explained, extending as it does beyond the circle of students and disciples and beyond what is commonly understood by philosophy?

For it is not Heidegger's philosophy, whose existence we can rightfully question (as Jean Beaufret has done), but Heidegger's thinking that has had such a decisive influence on the spiritual physiognomy of this century. This thinking has a digging quality peculiar to itself, which, should we wish to put it in linguistic form, lies in the transitive use of the verb "to think." Heidegger never thinks "about" something; he thinks something. In this entirely uncontemplative activity, he penetrates to the depths, but not to discover, let alone bring to light, some ultimate, secure foundation which as yet had been undiscovered. Rather, he persistently remains there, underground, in order to lay down pathways and fix "trail marks" (a collection of texts from the years 1929 to 1962 had this title, *Wegmarken*). This thinking may set tasks for itself; it may deal with "problems"; it naturally, indeed always, has something specific with which it is particularly occupied, or, more precisely, by which it is specifically aroused; but one cannot say that it has a goal. It is unceasingly active, and even the laying down of paths itself is conducive to opening up a new dimension of thought, rather than reaching a goal sighted beforehand and then aimed at. The pathways may safely be called *Holzwege*, wood-paths (after the title of a collection of essays from the years 1935 to 1946), which, precisely because they lead nowhere outside the wood and "abruptly leave off in the untrodden," are incomparably more agreeable to him who loves the wood and feels at home in it than the streets with their carefully laid out problems where the investigators of philosophical specializations and historians of ideas scurry. The metaphor of "wood-paths" hits upon something essential—not, as one may at first think, that someone has gotten onto a dead-end trail, but rather that someone, like the lumberjack whose occupation lies in the woods, treads paths that he himself has beaten; and clearing the path belongs no less to his line of work than the felling of trees.

On this deep plane, dug up and cleared, as it were, by his own thinking, Heidegger has laid down a vast network of thought-paths; and the single immediate result, which has been understandably noticed, and sometimes imitated, is that he has caused the edifice of traditional metaphysics—in which, for a long time, no one had quite felt at ease in any case—to collapse, just as underground tunnels and subversive burrowings cause the collapse of structures whose foundations are not deeply enough secured. This is a historical matter, perhaps even one of the first order, but it need not trouble those of us who stand outside all the guilds, including the historical. That Kant could with justice, from a specific perspective, be called the "all-destroyer" has little to do with who Kant was—as distinguished from his historical role. As to Heidegger's share in the collapse of metaphysics, which was imminent anyway, what we owe him, and only him, is that this collapse took place in a manner worthy of what had preceded it; that metaphysics was *thought* through to its end, and was not simply, so to speak, overrun by what followed. "The end of philosophy," as Heidegger says in *Zur Sache des Denkens,* but an end that is a credit to philosophy and holds her in honor, prepared by the one person who was most profoundly bound to her and her tradition. For a lifetime he based his seminars and lectures on the philosophers' texts, and only in his old age did he venture to give a seminar on a text of his own. *Zur Sache des Denkens* contains the "protocol for a seminar on the lecture '*Zeit und Sein,*'" which forms the first part of the book.

I have said that people followed the rumor about Heidegger in order to learn thinking. What was experienced was that thinking as pure activity—and this means impelled neither by the thirst for knowledge nor by the drive for cognition—can become a passion which not so much rules and oppresses all other capacities and gifts, as it orders them and prevails through them. We are so accustomed to the old opposition of reason versus passion, spirit versus life, that the idea of a *passionate* thinking, in which thinking and being alive become one, takes us somewhat aback. Heidegger himself once expressed this unification—in a well-documented anecdote—in a single sentence, when at the beginning of a course on Aristotle he said, in place of the usual biographical introduction, "Aristotle was born, worked, and died." That something like Heidegger's passionate thinking exists is indeed, as we can recognize afterward, a condition of the possibility of there being any philosophy at all. But it is more than questionable, especially in our century, whether we would ever have discovered this apart from Heidegger's example of a thinking existence. This passionate thinking, which rises out of the simple fact of being-born-into-the-world and then "thinks recallingly and responsively the meaning that reigns in everything that is" (*Gelassenheit*, 1959, p. 15),* can no more have a final goal—cognition or knowledge—than can life itself. The end of life is death, but man does not live for death's sake, but because he is a living being; and he does not think for the sake of any result whatever, but because he is a "thinking, that is, a sentient being" (ibid.).

A consequence of this is that thinking acts in a peculiarly destructive or critical way toward its own results. To be sure, since the philosophical schools of antiquity, philosophers have exhibited an annoying inclination toward system building, and we often have trouble dismantling the constructions they build while trying to discover what they really thought. This inclination does not stem from thinking itself, but from quite other needs, themselves thoroughly legitimate. If one wished to measure thinking, in its immediate, passionate liveliness, by its results, then one would fare as with Penelope's veil—what was spun during the day would relentlessly undo itself at night, so that the next day it could be begun anew. Each of Heidegger's writings, despite occasional references to what was already published, reads as though he were starting from the beginning and only from time to time taking over the language already coined by him—a language, however, in which the concepts are merely "trail marks," by which a new course of thought orients itself. Heidegger refers to this peculiarity of thinking when he emphasizes that "the *critical* question, what the matter of thought is, belongs necessarily and constantly to thinking"; when, on the occasion of a reference to Nietzsche, he speaks of "thinking's recklessness, beginning ever anew"; and when he says that thinking "has the charac-

---

* *Discourse on Thinking*, trans. J. M. Anderson and E. H. Freund (Harper & Row, 1966), p. 46.

ter of retrogression." And he practices this retrogression when he subjects *Being and Time* to an "imminent criticism," or establishes that his own earlier interpretation of Platonic truth "is not tenable," or speaks generally of the thinker's "backward glance" at his own work, "which always becomes a *retractatio*," not actually a recanting, but rather a rethinking of what already had been thought (in *Zur Sache des Denkens*, pp. 61, 20, 78).

Every thinker, if he lives long enough, must strive to unravel what appear as the results of his thoughts, and he does this simply by rethinking them. (He will say, with Jaspers, "And now, when you want really to begin, you must die.") The thinking "I" is ageless, and it is the curse and blessing of thinkers, so far as they exist only in thinking, that they become old without aging. Also, the passion of thinking, like the other passions, seizes the person—seizes those qualities of the individual of which the sum, when ordered by the will, amounts to what we commonly call "character"—possesses him and, as it were, annihilates his "character," which cannot hold its own against this onslaught. The thinking "I," which "stands within" the raging storm, as Heidegger says, and for which time literally stands still, is not just ageless; it is also, although always specifically other, without qualities. The thinking "I" is everything but the self of consciousness.

Moreover, thinking, as Hegel, in a letter to Zillmann in 1807, remarked about philosophy, is "something solitary," and this not only because the thinker is alone in what Plato speaks of as the "soundless dialogue with myself" (*Sophist* 263e), but because in this dialogue there always reverberates something "unutterable" which cannot be brought fully to sound through language or be articulated in speech, and which, therefore, is not communicable, not to others and not to the thinker himself. It is presumably this "unsayable," of which Plato speaks in the Seventh Letter, that makes thinking such a lonely business and forms each separate wellspring from which it rises up and continually renews itself. One could well imagine that—though this is hardly the case with Heidegger—the passion of thinking might suddenly beset the most gregarious of men, and, in consequence of the solitude it requires, break him.

The first and, so far as I know, the only one who has ever spoken of thinking as a *pathos*, as something to be borne through endurance, was Plato, who, in the *Theaetetus* (155d), calls wonder the beginning of philosophy; he certainly does not mean by this the mere surprise or astonishment that strikes us when we encounter something strange. For the wonder that is the beginning of thinking—as surprise and astonishment may well be the beginning of the sciences—applies to the everyday, the matter-of-course, what we are thoroughly acquainted and familiar with; this is the reason why it cannot be quieted by any knowledge whatever. Heidegger speaks once, wholly in Plato's sense, of the "faculty of wondering at the simple," but, unlike Plato, he adds *and of taking up and accepting this wondering as one's abode*" (*Vorträge und Aufsätze*, 1954, Part III, p. 259). This addition seems to me decisive for reflecting on who Martin Heidegger is. For many—or so we hope—are acquainted with thinking and the solitude bound up with it; but clearly, they do not reside there. When wonder at the simple overtakes them, and, yielding to it, they engage in thinking, they know they have been torn out of their habitual place in the continuum of occupations in which human affairs take place, a place to which they will return in a little while. The abode of which Heidegger speaks lies therefore, in a metaphorical sense, outside the habitations of men; and although "the winds of thought," which Socrates (according to Xenophon) was perhaps the first to mention, can be strong indeed, still these storms are even a degree more metaphorical than the metaphor of "the storms of time." Compared with other places in the world, the habitations of human affairs, the residence of the thinker is a "place of stillness" (*Zur Sache des Denkens*, p. 75).

Originally it is wonder itself which begets and spreads the stillness; and it is because of this stillness that being shielded against all sounds, even the sound of one's own voice, becomes an indispensable condition for thinking to evolve out of wonder. Enclosed in this stillness there occurs a peculiar metamorphosis which affects everything falling within the dimension of thinking in Heidegger's sense. In its essential seclusion from the world, thinking always has to do only with things absent, with matters, facts, or events which are withdrawn from direct perception. If you stand face-to-face with a man, you perceive him of course in his bodily presence, but you are not *thinking* of him. And if you do think about him while he is present, you are secretly withdrawing from the direct encounter. In order to come close, in thinking, to a thing or to a human being, it or he or she must lie, for direct perception, in the distance. Thinking, says Heidegger, is "coming-into-nearness to the distant" (*Gelassenheit*, p. 45).

One can easily bring this point home by a familiar experience. We go on journeys in order to see things in faraway places; in the course of this it often happens that the things we have seen come close to us only in retrospect or recollection, when we no longer are in the power of the immediate impression—it is as if they disclose their meaning only when they are no longer present. This inversion of relation—that thinking removes what is close by, withdrawing from the near and drawing the distant into nearness—is decisive if we wish to find an answer to the question of where we are when we think. Recollection, which in thinking becomes remembrance, has played so prominent a role as a mental faculty in the history of thinking about thinking because it guarantees us that nearness and remoteness, as they are given in sense perception, are actually susceptible of such an inversion.

Heidegger has expressed himself only occasionally, by suggestion, and for the most part negatively, about the "abode" where he feels at home, the residence of thinking—as when he says that thinking's questioning is not "part of everyday life . . . it gratifies no urgent or prevailing need. The questioning itself is 'out of order.'" (*An Introduction to Metaphysics*, pp. 10–11.) But this nearness-remoteness relation and its inversion in thinking pervades Heidegger's whole work, like a key to which everything is attuned. Presence and absence, concealing and revealing, nearness and remoteness—their interlinkage and the connections prevailing among them—have next to nothing to do with the truism that there could not be presence unless absence were experienced, nearness without remoteness, discovery without concealment. Seen from the perspective of thinking's abode, "withdrawal of Being" or "oblivion of Being" reigns in the ordinary world which surrounds the thinker's residence, the "familiar realms . . . of everyday life," i.e., the loss of that with which thinking—which by nature clings to the absent—is concerned. The uplifting (*Aufhebung*) of this "withdrawal" is always paid for by a withdrawal from the world of human affairs, and this remoteness is never more manifest than when thinking ponders exactly these affairs, training them into its own sequestered stillness. Thus, Aristotle, with the great example of Plato still vividly in view, already strongly advised philosophers against dreaming of a philosopher-king who would rule *ta ton anthropon pragmata,* i.e., in the realm of human affairs.

"The faculty of wondering," at least occasionally, "at the simple" is presumably inherent in all humans, and the thinkers well known to us from the past and in the present should then be distinguished by having developed out of this wonder the capacity to think and to unfold the trains of thought that were in each case suitable to them. However, the faculty of "taking up this wondering as one's permanent abode" is a different matter. This is extraordinarily rare, and we find it documented with some degree of certainty only in Plato, who expressed himself more than once and most dramatically in the *Theaetetus* (173d to 176) on the dangers of such residence. There he tells, apparently for the first time, the story of Thales and the Thracian peasant girl, who, watching the "wise man" glance upward in order to observe the stars only to fall in the well, laughed that someone who wants to know the sky should be so ignorant of what lies at his feet. Thales, if we are to trust Aristotle, was very much offended—the more so as his fellow citizens used to scoff at his poverty—and he proved by a large speculation in oil presses that it was an easy matter for "wise men" to get rich if they were to set their hearts on it (*Politics,* 1259a ff). And since books, as everyone knows, are not written by peasant girls, the laughing Thracian child had still to submit to Hegel's saying about her that she had no sense at all for higher things. Plato, who, in the *Republic,* wanted not only to put an end to poetry but also to forbid laughter, at least to the class of guardians, feared the laughter of his fellow citizens more than the hostility of those holding opinions opposed to the philosopher's claim to absolute truth. Perhaps it was Plato himself who knew how likely it is that the thinker's residence, seen from the outside, will look like Aristophanes' cloud cuckoo land. At any rate, he was aware of the philosopher's predicament: if he wants to carry his thoughts to market, he is likely to become a public laughingstock; and this, among other things, may have induced him, at an advanced age, to set out for Sicily three times in order to set the tyrant of Syracuse right by teaching him mathematics as the indispensable introduction to philosophy, and hence to the art of ruling as a philosopher-king. He did not notice that this fantastic undertaking, if seen from the peasant girl's perspective, looks considerably more comical than Thale's mishap. And to a certain extent he was right not to notice it: for, as far as I know, no student of philosophy has ever dared to laugh and no writer who has described this episode has ever smiled. Men have obviously not yet discovered what laughter is good for—perhaps because their thinkers, who have always been ill-disposed toward laughter, have let them down in this respect, even though a few of them have racked their brains over the question of what makes us laugh.

Now we all know that Heidegger, too, once succumbed to the temptation to change his "residence" and "intervene" (as was then said) in the world of human affairs. As far as the world goes, it was even less palatable to him than it was to Plato, for the tyrant and his victims were not located across the sea but in his own country.* As to Heidegger himself, I believe

---

* This episode, which today—now that the embitterment has cooled and, above all, the innumerable canards have been somehow set right—is usually called an "error," has many aspects, among others that of the Weimar Republic, which didn't at all display itself to those who lived in it in the rosy light in which, viewed against the horror of what followed, it is nowadays often seen.

Moreover, the content of Heidegger's "error" differed considerably from the content of the "errors" current at the time. Who in the midst of Nazi Germany could possibly have thought that "the inner truth . . . of this movement" consisted in "the encounter between global technology and modern man" (*An Introduction to Metaphysics*, p. 166)—something about which the vast Nazi literature is entirely silent—except, of course, somebody who had read instead of Hitler's *Mein Kampf* the writings of the Italian futurists who indeed had some connections with fascism, as distinct from national socialism.

There is no doubt that the futurists make more interesting reading, but the decisive point is that Heidegger, like so many other German intellectuals of his generation, Nazis and anti-Nazis, never read *Mein Kampf.* Of course, this misunderstanding of what it was all about is inconsiderable when compared with the much more decisive "error" that consisted in not only ignoring the most relevant "literature" but in escaping from the reality of the Gestapo cellars and the torture-hells of the early concentration camps into seemingly more significant regions. Robert Gilbert, the German folk poet (somehow in the tradition of Heine) and popular songwriter, described even then in four lines of an unforgettable verse what actually happened in the spring of 1933:

> *Keiner braucht mehr anzupochen*
> *mit der Axt durch jede Tür—*
> *die Nation ist aufgebrochen*
> *wie ein Pestgeschwür.*

> *There's no need to give a knock,*
> *With an ax through every door—*
> *For now the nation has burst open*
> *like an abscessed sore.*

that the matter stands differently. He was still young enough to learn from the shock of the collision, which after ten short hectic months thirty-seven years ago drove him back to his accustomed residence, and then to let what he had experienced take root in his thinking. What emerged from this was his discovery of the will as "the will to will" and hence as the "will to power." In modern times and above all in the modern age, much has been written about the will, but despite Kant, despite even Nietzsche, not very much has been found out about its essence. However that may be, no one before Heidegger saw how essentially the will stands opposed to thinking and affects it destructively. To thinking there belongs *"Gelassenheit"*— security, composure, release, a state of relaxation, in brief, a disposition that "let's be." Seen from the standpoint of the will the thinkers must say, only apparently in paradox, "I will non-willing"; for only "by way of this," only when we "wean ourselves from the will," can we "release ourselves into the sought-for nature of the thinking that is not a willing" (*Gelassenheit*, p. 32f [*Discourse on Thinking*, pp. 59–60]).

We who wish to honor the thinkers, even if our residence lies in the midst of the world, can hardly help finding it striking and perhaps exasperating that Plato and Heidegger, when they entered into human affairs, turned to tyrants and Führers. This should be imputed not just to the cir-

---

This escape from reality turned out to be more characteristic and more lasting than all the *Gleichschaltungen* [Arendt refers to the "coordination" or "alignment" of Germans by the Nazis in the 1930s. —Ed.] of those early years. (Heidegger himself corrected his own "error" more quickly and more radically than many of those who later sat in judgment over him—he took considerably more risks than were usual in German literary and university life during that period.) We are still surrounded by intellectuals and so-called scholars, not only in Germany, who, instead of speaking of Hitler, Auschwitz, genocide, and "extermination" as a policy of permanent depopulation, prefer, according to their inspiration and taste, to refer to Plato, Luther, Hegel, Nietzsche, or to Heidegger, Jünger, or Stefan George, in order to dress up the horrible gutter-born phenomenon with the language of the humanities and the history of ideas.

One can indeed say that escape from reality has in the meantime blossomed into a profession, and this in the literature of both the Hitler and the Stalin period. In the latter we still find the notion that Stalin's crimes were necessary for the industrialization of Russia—even though this "industrialization" quite obviously was a gigantic failure—and in the former we still read grotesquely highfalutin and sophisticated theories with whose spirituality the gutter never had anything to do. We move there in a phantom realm of images and "ideas" which has slipped so far away from anything that ever has been or could be experienced into mere "abstraction," that all thoughts, that every thought, even those of the greatest thinkers, lose their solidity, and, like cloud formations, blur and blend into one another.

cumstances of their times and even less to preformed character, but rather to what the French call a *déformation professionnelle*. For the attraction to the tyrannical can be demonstrated theoretically in many of the great thinkers (Kant is the great exception). And if this tendency is not demonstrable in what they did, that is only because very few of them were prepared to go beyond "the faculty of wondering at the simple" and to "accept this wondering as their abode."

With these few it does not finally matter where the storms of their century may have driven them. For the wind that blows through Heidegger's thinking—like that which still sweeps toward us after thousands of years from the work of Plato—does not spring from the century he happens to live in. It comes from the primeval, and what it leaves behind is something perfect, something which, like everything perfect, falls back to whence it came.

1971

FOR MARTIN HEIDEGGER*

"... and if the raging of time too
Profoundly besets my head, and the want and the chimeras
Among mortals unsettle my mortal life,
Let *silence* commemorate me then in *your* depth!"

—Hölderlin, from *Der Archipelagus*, Arendt's italics,
translated by Andrew Shields

On his eightieth birthday, his contemporaries honor the master, the teacher, and—for some surely—the friend. We pause to try to give an account of what this life means for us, for the world, and for our time, this life that in its gathered fullness only now appears *as wholly present in the present,* which is, I suppose, the blessing of old age. Each individual may have a different answer to the question at hand; may each answer do justice, at least to some degree, to the passion of the fulfillment of this life to which the work bears witness.

To me it seems that this life and work have taught us what *thinking* is, and that the writings will remain exemplary of that, and of the courage to venture into the immensity of the untrodden, to open oneself entirely to what is as yet unthought, a courage possessed only by him who turns himself entirely to thinking and its tremendous depth.

May those who follow us, if they recall our century and its people and try to keep faith with us, not forget the devastating sandstorms that swept us all up, each in his own way, and in which such a man as this and his work were still possible.

1977

---

* The following text, translated from the German, was written by Hannah Arendt for Martin Heidegger, and published after his death in *Dem Andenken Martin Heideggers: Zum 26 Mai 1976* (Klostermann, 1977), 9. —Ed.

WAR CRIMES AND THE
AMERICAN CONSCIENCE

I know that the war in Vietnam is not the first and will not be the last unde-
clared war. But I think it is possible to overlook an important point: When a
nation declares war, it implies that it is prepared to play the game according
to the rules. Since the beginning of this century there have been attempts
to lay down certain laws for war. By not declaring war, a nation manages to
evade even these feeble limitations.

1970

LETTER TO THE EDITOR OF
THE NEW YORK REVIEW OF BOOKS
Distinctions

Mr. Cameron's review [of *Between Past and Future* and *Men in Dark Times*, *New York Review of Books*, November 6, 1970]—well-meaning and strange in that it manages to like and to dislike the books under review with almost equal intensity—reads as though he wanted clarification in earnest. In the hope that I am not mistaken, I shall try to comply.

There is the matter of "opacity of style" and "darkness of thought" which according to Mr. Cameron is also "obvious in the work of Kant." This remark is of course terribly discouraging for any attempt at clarification. If Kant fails to satisfy Mr. Cameron on these accounts, who could? That the *Critique of Pure Reason* is not merely one of the greatest but also one of the clearest books ever written in philosophy seems to me "obvious," but how could I convince Mr. Cameron of this—unless we had a chance to spend the better part of a year going over the text? For no doubt the work is difficult; it deals with difficult matters which were very obscure indeed before Kant went to the trouble of clearing them up. Kant's prose is entirely adequate, and the "long-lasting ambiguities," which Mr. Cameron half admires and half complains of, are either due to the subject matter or to the less clear and powerful minds of Kant's commentators and readers.

Mr. Cameron's puzzles are many and to clear them all up would require too much space. I shall select two of them because they appear to me fairly representative. He quotes me, correctly, as proposing "to look upon the past with eyes undistracted by any traditions," and claims that "of course" I myself pay "not the slightest attention to this proposal" and could not if I wanted to because of "the very character of thought and discourse." Thought and discourse are conducted in linguistic terms and "our languages give us the essence of the human past." This statement would be true if Mr. Cameron had left out the "essence"; some past, not necessarily its essence, is indeed alive and present in every form of speech. But the point at issue is not the past but tradition, and the *distinction* between them: Tradition orders the past, hands it down (*tradere*), interprets it, omits, selects, and emphasizes according to a system of pre-established beliefs. Tradition is a mental construct and as such always subject to critical examination. If I say that no tradition can claim validity today, I do not say that the past is dead but that we have no reliable guide through it anymore, from which it follows that tradition itself has become part of the past. To take an example which may be plausible because it involves a good deal of tradition, I can read Aquinas—agreeing or disagreeing with what he has to say—without following the tradition of Thomist thought in the Catholic Church. I also can trace this tradition as part of the past. The result may well be a rediscovery of Aquinas and the destruction of Thomist tradition. Everything turns here on the *distinction* between tradition and past.

Something very similar, the neglect of a distinction in the text, happens when Mr. Cameron cannot "make sense" of my remark that the nuclear processes which we are now able to initiate on earth and which before went on only in the universe surrounding us, for instance in the sun, signify that we no longer "imitate" but "make" nature. (Here, incidentally, Mr. Cameron seems to quote less correctly; the words "make nature" are put in quotation marks in the text because they are taken from Vico's famous remark: *si physica demonstrare possemus, faceremus*, "Mathematical matters we can prove because we ourselves can make them; to prove the physical [i.e., nature] we would have to make it.") The argument again hinges on a distinction, the distinction between the earth and earthbound processes as they occur in the household of nature on one side, and the universe, including the sun, and processes which go on outside the earth on the other. It is the distinction between pre-modern natural science including physics, and astrophysics, which began when Copernicus "imagined he was standing in the sun. . . . overlooking the planets," "reached its classic expression with Newton's law of gravitation, in which the same equation covers the movements of the heavenly bodies and the motion of terrestrial things on earth," until Einstein's "striving after generalization" succeeded in introducing an "observer who is poised freely in space and not just at one definite point like the sun." Nuclear processes have their own habitat outside the earth in the universe surrounding her; they are "universal" processes properly speaking. The science that introduced them into the earth's own nature was "from its very beginnings not a 'natural' but a universal science, it was not a physics but an astrophysics which looked upon the earth from a point in the universe." And insofar as these man-made processes now occur among us—who still are earthbound creatures, moving in the household of nature—they have become part of what is going on on earth, so that it is as though we now "make nature." This is a far cry from "cultivating," "breeding," domesticating wild animals, in brief from agricultural activities where we follow the hints of nature and by "imitating" her prepare the earth for the use of men. Compared to the introduction of processes which without man's intervention would go on only in the sun, these agricultural activities are no less "natural" than the activities of ants or bees which also "change" the earth in order to facilitate their metabolism with nature, to which every living, earthbound organism is subject. Hence, when we use the word "physics" (derived from the Greek *physein*) for present-day astrophysics or the word "natural sciences" (derived from the Latin *nasci,* the exact translation of the Greek term above) for these modern universal sciences, our language no longer gives us "the essence of the past." It rather misleads us into believing that we still live in an unbroken time continuum where the past smoothly develops into the present.

I am afraid that training in "donnish queries" is not the best preparation for making distinctions or for examining terms critically in accordance with matters and issues they are supposed to correspond to. When Mr. Cameron encounters them—in Kant or in some lesser luminaries like myself—he is unaware of their role in the argument and lands himself in puzzles which he then ascribes to the opacity of style and darkness of thought. It is of course entirely possible that he would want to object to the distinctions and the arguments developed from them. (Why should he not wish to hold fast to tradition and maintain for instance that without tradition, the ordering guide to lead us safely through the past, we shall lose our past as well? Why should he not say that the earth is part and parcel of the universe and that therefore my distinction between "natural" and "universal" processes does not hold?) The point is that he does not arrive at the place where controversy could begin.

On the lowest level this kind of misreading appears at the end of Mr. Cameron's review. He concludes with construing as a "dilemma" what actually is a factual description and was meant to be a hopeful one. Since tradition and authority have broken down, I said, we are "confronted anew . . . without the protection of self-evident standards of behavior . . . by the elementary problems of human living-together." Since for him this constitutes a "dilemma"—for me it is no more than a challenge, albeit a serious one—he arrives by association at other, strictly theological dilemmas which he believes "imply that the world is ruled by wicked demons." Let me just assure him I do not believe in them.

Hannah Arendt

1970

VALUES IN CONTEMPORARY SOCIETY*

KNOWLES: A problem that a number of our trustees have perceived, and that all of us are asking about, concerns the moral and ethical framework within which we a working nationally and internationally.

Miss Arendt, in her original introduction to *The Origins of Totalitarianism,* writes:

> This book has been written against a background of both reckless optimism and reckless despair. It holds that Progress and Doom are two sides of the same medal; that both are articles of superstition, not of faith. It was written out of the condition that it should be possible to discover the hidden mechanics by which all traditional elements of our political and spiritual world were dissolved into a conglomeration where everything seems to have lost specific value, and has become unrecognizable for human comprehension, unusable for human purpose. To yield to the mere process of disintegration has become an irresistible temptation, not only because it has assumed the spurious grandeur of "historical necessity," but also because everything outside it has begun to appear lifeless, bloodless, meaningless, and unreal.

She goes on to speak of "the irritating incompatibility between the actual power of modern man (greater than ever before . . .) and the

---

* On July 13, 1972, Kenneth W. Thompson, vice president of the Rockefeller Foundation, invited Hannah Arendt, Paul Freund, Irving Kristol, and Hans Morgenthau to participate in a discussion of values in contemporary society. It was only five days after John H. Knowles, MD, had assumed his position as president of the Foundation; a major signal was intended. The word "value," with its connotation of "equivalence," is not prominent in Arendt's political vocabulary. What follows shows why, and also why talking things through was invaluable to her. —Ed.

impotence of modern men to live in, and understand the sense of, a world which their own strength has established." And then, in the last chapter of the new edition of her book, she speaks of isolation and impotence and how these two have always been characteristic of tyrannies.

It seems to me that isolation and impotence are felt by increasing numbers of people. Therefore, one might conclude that this is fertile ground for tyranny.

ARENDT: All this was written almost twenty-five years ago; at that time it did not correspond to the mood of America. Today, I think, things are uncomfortably close to that mood in this country.

KNOWLES: Yes. Then to conclude from Miss Arendt's preface to her first edition, she said:

> We can no longer afford to take that which was good in the past and simply call it our heritage, to discard the bad and simply think of it as a dead load which by itself time will buy in oblivion. The subterranean stream of Western history has finally come to the surface and usurped the dignity of our tradition. This is the reality in which we live. And this is why all efforts to escape from the grimness of the present into nostalgia for a still intact past, or into the anticipated oblivion of a better future, are vain.

KRISTOL: One of the reasons we are undergoing what we call a "crisis in values" is that we have forgotten a lot of things that previous generations knew.

ARENDT: Values are personal, like spirit. They cannot be manipulated or engineered. I think it would be a great mistake for a foundation to believe that it can solve the basic problems of the era; no single one of us can do that.

But there is something else that one can do, and what a foundation like this could do, and that is to prepare an atmosphere in which things are being talked about. The question is, to what extent do you believe in talk? If you read the early Platonic dialogues, every dialogue is the poetic expression of a problem but none give a conclusion. The arguments always go around in circles and at the end of the argument you are where you began. Then Socrates says very cheerfully, "Let's start all over again"—not meaning that he would now find a solution.

What Socrates apparently believed—I'm not so sure Plato believed in it—was talking about justice makes a man more just. And in talking about courage—even if you don't find any nice definition of what courage is—you may inspire men at a given moment to be courageous. So we create an atmosphere in which we may have a chance, at least, to meet the problems and understand them as they come along.

Right now we live—everybody who teaches knows this—in a moment of great mistrust of science. There is a myth of progress, one of the greatest myths of American civilization, that everything we do should not only be good but must be better. Now, the better excludes the good. The implication is that there is no such thing as good.

This concept of progress, which is not older than the sixteenth and seventeenth centuries, will probably die as a predominant idea, and it will be discovered, first of all in science, that there are limitations, and then that there are limitations, in principle, to human knowledge. We will look differently on our genetic experiments and the idea of going to the moon and to Mars. Perhaps we can go to Mars but not much farther, and compared to the immensity of the universe, that is a limitation.

But to say that these problems are unique is really wrong. We are in an unprecedented era but, as a matter of fact, almost all events in history, when they occurred, were novel. In Christianity, for example, what in God's name, in that day and era, indicated the arrival of Jesus of Nazareth? What indicated the arrival of Paul, which for Western history is much more important? To look to the past in order to find analogies by which to solve our present problems, is, in my opinion, a mythological error. If you cannot read these great books with love and pure motives and just because you are fond of the life of the spirit—the life of the mind—it won't do you any good and it won't do students any good.

As far as unprecedented factors go, I don't think for one moment that reading a particular book throws light on the future mind of man. We come, after all, out of ages which were grounded in certain traditions and certain religious and philosophical beliefs. None of these beliefs is relevant or obligatory any longer. No matter how great you may think these beliefs were, or how meaningful, they are no longer obligatory.

The simple fact that people no longer believe in hell is certainly one of the most decisive changes of the twentieth century. Since the beginning of the modern age, some people didn't believe in hell, but now we have reached the point where almost nobody does, and this is an altogether different proposition. We can no longer threaten people with something ultimate. Capital punishment only hurries up something which is going to happen to us anyhow. . . .

THOMPSON: What about the other side? In addition to not being able to threaten, we can't promise a prosperous and happy life, or prove that success will come with virtue.

ARENDT: Yes, and the belief that success involved an after-life. That the down-trodden will eventually inherit the earth. Now all this you cannot believe either.

THOMPSON: We are faced with the breakdown of the Protestant ethic—the notion that one's present status is proof that Providence has chosen you.

ARENDT: All this has broken down, and I don't think we should be under any illusion that we are going to come here, like a Moses or Hammurabi, with a new decalogue, a new catalogue of laws. I think it would be rather dangerous if we overestimate our real possibilities but, on the other hand, I think it would be very valuable to have an institution encourage and foster talk. Talk, let's say, about fundamentals. Talk about fundamentals as they apply to each specific area—experiments with human beings, and so on—these things are a help, and I think that to talk regularly about them, even though we don't have anything definite to put on the table in the end, could change the whole atmosphere in which the work is done.

THOMPSON: Where would you talk? You mean talk as we are talking now around a table? Do you mean a national forum? Do you mean televised programs?

ARENDT: No, no, no! Not television! Only people who are directly concerned, you know. Not a news conference. On the contrary. The moment you speak for an audience, everything changes. You speak to your peers around a table.

KRISTOL: One teacher can produce six serious thinkers, if he's lucky, in a lifetime. That's a lot. Five teachers can produce thirty. One has to assume that this is for the good. And what a foundation can do—or what something like the National Endowment for the Humanities can do—is try to find these key people. There aren't that many but there are a few dozen in the United States who are genuine believers and authentically superb teachers because they are genuine believers.

ARENDT: I think a problem that really needs to be worked on, and where the foundation may be of help, is that really good teachers are not thought of highly by the academic society. This business of "publish or perish" has been a catastrophe. People write things which should never have been written and which should never be printed. Nobody's interested. But for them to keep their jobs and get the proper promotion, they've got to do it. It demeans the whole of intellectual life. I used to adhere to the principle that a graduate student on a certain level should be independent from me to the extent that he could also, apart from me, choose and establish his own bibliography. This is absolutely impossible today because there is such an amount of sheer nonsense on the market that you cannot ask the student to review it. He will spend years in the library until he finds the few really important books in the field.

KRISTOL: It's true and it's too bad.

ARENDT: The one who really loses is the person who has a passionate interest in matters of the mind, who is an excellent reader, who can establish contact with his students and make them understand that his subject is important, but who will not write. Or, if he is forced to write, will not write well. And, by doing something which he is forced to do because of "publish or perish," he will become a lesser person. I've seen it happen in the places where I have taught.

One might give medals or awards. I know the Danforth Foundation does this. It may not help much but you could do something to raise the prestige, not of the so-called charismatic teacher who is usually a disaster, but of teachers who are truly dedicated. There are not so very many. This is a gift that is very rare, a gift of a very high caliber.

1972

HANNAH ARENDT ON
HANNAH ARENDT

Introduction

In November 1972, a conference on "The Work of Hannah Arendt" was organized by the Toronto Society for the Study of Social and Political Thought sponsored by York University and the Canada Council. Hannah Arendt was invited to attend the conference as the guest of honor, but replied that she would much prefer to be invited to participate. Presented here is a series of her exchanges with and excerpts from some of her longer responses to various participants.*

HANNAH ARENDT: Reason itself, the thinking ability which we have, has a need to actualize itself. The philosophers and the metaphysicians have

---

* C. B. Macpherson at the time was professor emeritus of political economy, University of Toronto;
Christian Bay at the time was professor of political science, University of Toronto;
Michael Gerstein at the time was consultant on Social Services, Halifax, Nova Scotia;
George Baird at the time was an architect and associate professor in the School of Architecture, University of Toronto;
Hans Jonas was professor of philosophy, The Graduate Faculty, New School for Social Research, and an old friend of Hannah Arendt's;
F. M. Bernard at the time was professor of political science, University of Western Ontario, London, Ontario;
Mary McCarthy was a great twentieth-century writer, and Hannah Arendt's closest friend;
Richard J. Bernstein is Vera List Professor of philosophy, New School for Social Research;
Albrecht Wellmer was at the time professor of sociology at the University of Constanz, Germany;
Hans Morgenthau was university professor of political science, the Graduate Faculty, New School for Social Research;
Ed Weissman at the time was associate professor of political science, York University, Toronto.

—Ed.

monopolized this capability. This has led to very great things. It also has led to rather unpleasant things—we have forgotten that *every* human being has a need to think, not to think abstractly, not to answer the ultimate questions of God, immortality, and freedom, nothing but to think while he is living. And he does so constantly.

Everybody who tells a story of what happened to him half an hour ago on the street has got to put this story into shape. And this putting the story into shape is a form of thought.

So in this respect it may even be nice that we lost the monopoly of what Kant once very ironically called the "professional thinkers." We can start worrying about what thinking means for the activity of acting. Now I will admit one thing. I will admit that I am, of course, primarily interested in understanding. This is absolutely true. And I will admit that there are other people who are primarily interested in doing something. I am not. I can very well live without doing anything. But I cannot live without at least trying to understand whatever happens.

And this is somehow the same sense in which you know it from Hegel, namely where I think the central role is reconciliation—reconciliation of man as a thinking and reasonable being. This is what actually happens in the world.

. . .

I don't know any other reconciliation but thought. This need is, of course, much stronger in me than it usually is in political theorists, with their need to unite action and thought. Because they want to act, you know. And I think I understood something of action precisely because I looked at it from the outside, no more or less.

I have acted in my life a few times because I couldn't help it. But that is not what my primary impulse is. And all the lacunae which you would derive from this emphasis I would admit, almost without arguing, because I think it is so very likely that there the lacunae are.

MACPHERSON: Is Miss Arendt really saying that to be a critical theorist and to be engaged are incompatible? Surely not!

ARENDT: No, but one is correct in saying that thinking and acting are not the same, and to the extent that I wish to think I have to withdraw from the world.

MACPHERSON: But to a political theorist and a teacher and a writer of political theory, teaching or theorizing is acting.

ARENDT: Teaching is something else, and writing, too. But thinking in its real purity is different—in this Aristotle was right. You know, all the modern philosophers have somewhere in their work a rather apologetic sentence which says, "thinking is also acting." Oh no, it is not! And to say that is rather dishonest. I mean, let's face the music: it is not the same! On the contrary, I have to keep back to a large extent from participating, from commitment.

There is an old story that is ascribed to Pythagoras, where the people go to the Olympian games. And Pythagoras says: "the one goes there for fame, and the other one goes there for trade, but the best ones sit there in Olympia, in the amphitheater, just to look." That is, those who *look* at it will finally get the gist out of it. And this distinction has to be kept—in the name of honesty, if no other.

· · ·

ARENDT: I do believe that thinking has some influence on action. But on acting man. Because it is the same ego that thinks and the same ego that acts. But not theory. Theory could only influence action in the reform of consciousness. Did you ever think about how many people whose consciousness you will have to reform?

And if you don't think about it in these concrete terms then you think about mankind—that is, about some noun which actually doesn't exist, which is a concept. And this noun—be it mankind or Marx's species being, or the world spirit, or what have you—is constantly construed in the image of a single man.

If we really believe—and I think we share this belief—that plurality rules the earth, then I think one has got to modify this notion of the unity of theory and practice to such an extent that it will be unrecognizable for those who have tried their hand at it before. I really believe that you can only act in concert and I really believe that you can only think by yourself. These are two entirely different—if you want to call it so—existential positions. And to believe that there is any direct influence of theory on action insofar as theory is just a thought thing, i.e., something thought out—I think that this is really not so and in fact will never be so.

.   .   .

ARENDT: The main flaw and mistake of *The Human Condition* is the following: I still was looking at what the tradition calls *vita activa* from the viewpoint of the *vita contemplativa*, without ever saying anything real about the *vita contemplativa*.

Now I think that to look at it from the *vita contemplativa* is already the first fallacy. Because the fundamental experience of the thinking ego is in those lines of the older Cato which I quote at the end of the book: "If I do nothing I am most active and if I'm all by myself, I am at least alone." (It is very interesting that Cato said this!)* This is an experience of sheer activity unimpeded by any physical or bodily obstacles. But the moment you begin to act, you deal with the world, and you are constantly falling over your own feet, so to speak, and then you carry your body—and, as Plato said: "the body always wants to be taken care of and to hell with it!"

All this is spoken out of the experience of thinking. Now I am trying to write about this. And I would take off from this business of Cato. But I am not ready to tell you about it. And I am by no means sure that I will succeed, because it's very easy to talk about the metaphysical fallacies, but these metaphysical fallacies—which are indeed fallacies—has each one of them its authentic root in experience. That is, even as we throw them out of the window as dogmas, we have got to know where they come from. That is, what are the experiences of this ego that thinks, that wills, and judges: in other words, an ego that is busy with sheer mental activity. Now that is quite a mouthful, you know, if you really go at it. And I cannot tell you much about it.

.   .   .

ARENDT: I have a vague idea that there is some pragmatic business in this question "What is thinking good for?," which to me means "Why the hell are you doing all this?" or "What is thinking good for independent of writing and teaching?" It's very difficult to give an answer and certainly more difficult for me than for many.

---

* Cato was a man of action! —Ed.

You see, with the political business I had a certain advantage. I, by nature, am not an actor. If I tell you that I never was either a socialist or a communist—which was absolutely a matter of course for my whole generation, so that I hardly know anybody who never was one or the other—you will see that I never felt the need to commit myself. Until finally *"schliesslich schlug mir mit einem Hammer auf den Kopf und ich fiel mir auf"*: finally somebody beat me over the head and, you can say, this awakened me to the realities. But still, I had this advantage to look at them from the outside. And even in myself from the outside.

But not with thinking. Here I am immediately in it. And therefore I'm quite doubtful whether I will get it or whether I won't. But anyhow I feel that the *Human Condition* needs a second volume and I'm trying to write it.

· · ·

CHRISTIAN BAY: I have a very different conception of the calling of a political theorist from that of Hannah Arendt. I should say that I read Hannah Arendt with pleasure, but out of aesthetic pleasure. She is a philosopher's philosopher. I think it is beautiful to follow her prose, and her sense of unity in history, and to be reminded of all the great things the Greeks have said that are still somehow pertinent today. I think, however, from my point of view, there is a certain lack of seriousness about modern problems in much of her work.

I think perhaps her most serious work is her book on *Eichmann in Jerusalem*: her pointing out with such force how Eichmann is in each of us. I think it has great implications for political education, which, after all, is the ancient Platonic theme of our connectedness with politics. Yet I find this lacking in so much else of Hannah Arendt's work. Perhaps our ability to decentralize and to humanize will depend on the extent to which we find ways of coping with, combating and surpassing Eichmann in ourselves, and become citizens—in a sense so radically different from the customary use of this term.

I get very impatient with abstract discussions at length on how power differs from violence. I would like to know not only what is justice in a world whose injustice we all abhor, but how can the political theorist make us become more committed and more effective in fighting for justice—and for that matter, for human survival, which is the number one problem.

I was disturbed when Hannah Arendt said that her desire is never to indoctrinate. I think that *this* is the highest calling of the political theorist: to attempt to indoctrinate, in a pluralist universe, of course. If we are serious about problems like survival, like justice, then it seems to me our first task is to overcome the sea of liberalism and tolerance, which, in effect, amounts to one opinion having as much justification as another. Unless we passionately care for certain opinions I think we will all be lost insofar as events will continue to be allowed to take their own course: power tending to be ever more asymmetrically distributed, while the liberal institutions permit the economic masters to continue to enrich themselves at the expense not only of the poverty of the rest of us, but of our access to knowledge, to information, to understanding.

I want political theorists of my kind to be men and women of politics first, committed to try to educate ourselves and each other about how to resolve the urgent existential problems that we are up against. And one last point on that. It was possible to say with John Stuart Mill a century ago that in the long run truth will prevail in a free marketplace of ideas. But (a) we don't have much time, and (b) there is no free marketplace of ideas.

Hannah Arendt, what can we as political theorists do to see to it that the existential issues—which sometimes have true and false answers—are brought home to more of our fellow citizens, so that they become citizens in the ancient sense?

ARENDT: I am afraid the disagreement is quite huge and I will just touch on it.

First of all, you like my book *Eichmann in Jerusalem* and you say that I said there is an Eichmann in each one of us. Oh no! There is none in you and none in me! This doesn't mean that there are not quite a number of Eichmanns. But they look really quite different. I always hated this notion of "Eichmann in each one of us." This is simply not true. This would be as untrue as the opposite, that Eichmann is in nobody. In the way I look at things, this is far more abstract than the most abstract things I am said to indulge in so frequently—as long as we mean by abstract not thinking through experience.

What is the subject of our thought? Experience! Nothing else! And if we lose the ground of experience then we get into all kinds of theories. When the political theorist begins to build his systems he is also usually dealing with abstractions.

I don't believe that we have, or can have, much influence in this sense. I think that commitment can easily carry you to a point where you no longer think. There are certain extreme situations where you have to act. But these situations *are* extreme. And then it will turn out who is really reliable—committed—and who is really willing to stick his neck out.

But these other things—that you see in the development in the last years—are more or less things of the public mood. And the public mood may be something which I like, and the public mood may be something which I dislike, but I would not see it as *my* particular task to inspire this mood when I like it, or to go to the barricades when I dislike it.

The unwillingness of people who actually are thinking and are theorists to own up to this, to believe that thinking is worthwhile, but who believe instead that only commitment and engagement are worthwhile, is perhaps one of the reasons why this whole discipline is not always in such good shape. People apparently don't believe in what they are doing.

I cannot tell you black on white, and would hate to try to, what the consequences of this kind of thought which I attempt—not to indoctrinate, but to rouse or to awaken in my students—are in actual politics. I can very well imagine that one becomes a Republican and another becomes a liberal, and a third God knows what. But one thing I would hope is that certain extreme things which are the actual consequence of nonthinking, that is, of somebody who really has decided that he does not want to do what I do perhaps excessively, that he does not want to think at all—that these consequences will not be capable of arising. That is, when the chips are down, the question is how they will act. And then this notion that I examine my assumptions, that I think—I hate to use the word because of the *Frankfurter Schule*—"critically," and that I *don't* let myself get away with repeating the clichés of the public mood matters. And I would say that any society that has lost respect for this is not in very good shape.

MICHAEL GERSTEIN: I wonder, as someone who is or feels himself to be a political actor, how would you instruct me? Or wouldn't you instruct me at all?

ARENDT: No. I wouldn't instruct you, and I would think that this would be presumptuous of me. I think that you should be instructed when you sit together with your peers around a table and exchange opinions. And then out of this comes instruction: not for you personally, but how the group will act.

And I think that every other road of the theoretician who tells his students what to think and how to act is . . . my God! These are adults! We are not in the nursery! Real political action arises as a group act. And you join that group or you don't. And whatever you do on your own, you do not as an actor but as an anarchist.

.   .   .

GEORGE BAIRD: One of the revelations to me in *The Human Condition* was the argument which, as I understand it, sprang partly from Machiavelli: that glory and not goodness is the appropriate criterion for political acts. And, indeed, in *The Human Condition* Miss Arendt argues that goodness may even prove to be radically subversive of the political realm.

Now it seems to me that implicit in all that is a kind of dramatic challenge to the motivations of the political activists as I've understood them typically in the world. On the other hand, Miss Arendt has, in her essay on Rosa Luxemburg, expressed her admiration for what I believe she calls Luxemburg's sense of injustice as the springboard for *her* entry into the political sphere.

It might clarify the discussion vis-à-vis all these pleas for guides to political action if Miss Arendt would try to clarify the relationship between her austere sense of glory—rather than goodness—as the appropriate criterion (which is an extremely tough and unfashionable position in the modern world), and her admiration for Luxemburg. Somewhere there must be a relationship which sustains those distinctions but which clarifies the situation.

ARENDT: This business with goodness was not brought up by me but by

Machiavelli. It has something to do with the distinction between the public and the private. But I can put it differently. I would say that in the notion of wanting to be good, I actually am concerned with my own self. The moment I act politically I'm not concerned with me, but with the world. And that is the *main* distinction.

Rosa Luxemburg was very *much* concerned with the world and not at *all* concerned with herself. If she had been concerned with herself, she would have stayed on in Zurich after her dissertation and would have pursued certain specific intellectual interests. But she couldn't stand the injustice *within the world*.

Whether the criterion is glory—shining in the space of appearances—or whether the criterion is justice, that is not the decisive thing. The decisive thing is whether your own motivation is clear: for the world or for yourself, by which I mean for your soul. That is the way Machiavelli put it when he said, "I love my country, Florence, more than I love my eternal salvation." That doesn't mean that he didn't believe in an afterlife. But it means that the world as such was of greater interest to him than himself, his physical self as well as his soul.

You know that in modern republics religion has become a private affair. And actually Machiavelli was arguing that it *be* private: "Don't let these people into politics! They don't care enough for the world! People who believe that the world is mortal and they themselves are immortal, are very dangerous characters because what we want is the stability and good order of *this* world."

. . .

HANS JONAS: That there is at the bottom of all our being and of our action the desire to share the world with other men is incontestable, but we want to share a certain world with certain men. And if it is the task of politics to make the world a fitting home for man, that raises the question: "What is a fitting home for man?"

It can only be decided if we form some idea of what man is or ought to be. And that again cannot be determined, except arbitrarily, if we cannot make appeal to some truth about man which can validate judgments of this kind, and also the derivative judgments of political taste that crop up in concrete situations—and especially if it is a question of deciding how the future world should look—which we have to do all the time when dealing with technological enterprises that are having an impact on the total dispensation of things.

Now it is not the case that Kant simply made appeal to judgment. He also made appeal to the concept of the good. There is such an idea as the supreme good however we define it. And perhaps it escapes definition. It cannot be an entirely empty concept and it is related to our conception of what man is. In other words, that which has by unanimous consensus here been declared dead and done with—namely metaphysics—has to be called in at some place to give us a final directive.

Our powers of decision reach far beyond the handling of immediate situations and of the short-term future. Our powers of doing or acting now extend over such matters as really involve a judgment or an insight into, or a faith—I leave that open—into, some ultimates. For in ordinary politics as it has been understood until the twentieth century we could do with penultimates. It is not true that the condition of the commonwealth had to be decided by truly ultimate values or standards. When it is a matter, as it is under the conditions of modern technology, that willy-nilly we are embarking on courses which affect the total condition of things on earth and the future condition of man, then I don't think we can simply wash our hands and say: Western metaphysics has got us into an impasse, and we declare it bankrupt, and we now appeal to shareable judgments—when, for God's sake, we do not mean judgments shared with a majority or shared with any defined group. We can share judgments to our perdition with many but we must make an appeal beyond that sphere.

ARENDT: I am afraid that I will have to answer. I am not going to go into the question of Kant's *Critique of Judgment*. Actually the question of the good doesn't arise and the question of truth doesn't arise. The whole book is concerned with the possible validity of particular propositions.

JONAS: But it's not political.

ARENDT: No, but I said of the validity: whether one can transfer it to the political sphere is also one of the very interesting but at this moment side issues. And this, of course, I have done, and I have done it by simply taking into consideration Kant's late writings on politics. One of the main things here is Kant's stance toward the French Revolution. But I am not going to go into that because it would lead us too far away from this question of the ultimates.

Now if our future should depend on what you say—namely that we will get an ultimate which from above will decide for us (and then the question is, of course, who is going to recognize this ultimate and which will be the rules for recognizing this ultimate, and you have really an infinite regress here, but anyhow)—I would be utterly pessimistic. If that is the case then we are lost. Because this actually demands that a new god appear.

The word God is a Christian word, and in the Christian Middle Ages permitted very great skepticism, but one had it in ultimate instances, simply because it was God. But when God disappeared, Western humanity was back in the situation in which it had been before it was saved, or salvaged, or whatever, by the good news—since they didn't believe in it any longer. This was the actual situation. And it was this situation that sent the eighteenth-century revolutionaries back scrambling for antiquity. And not because they were in love with Greek verse or Greek songs, as may be the case with me. But that was not their motivation.

That is, they were in all nakedness confronted with the fact that men exist in the plural. And no human being knows what is MAN in the singular. We know only male and female created he *them:* that is, from the beginning this plurality poses an enormous problem.

For instance, I am perfectly sure that this whole totalitarian catastrophe would not have happened if people still believed in God, or in hell rather, that is, if there were still ultimates. In totalitarian domination there were no ultimates. You know as well as I do: there were no ultimates to which one could validly and with validity appeal. One couldn't appeal to anything or anyone.

And if you go through such a situation as totalitarian domination the first thing you know is the following: you never know how somebody will act. You have the surprise of your life. This goes throughout all layers of society and it goes throughout various distinctions between men. And if you want to make a generalization then you could say that those who were still very firmly convinced of the so-called old values were the first to be ready to change their old values for a new set of values, provided they were given one. And I am afraid of this because I think that the moment you give somebody a new set of values you can immediately exchange it too. And the only thing the guy gets used to is having a set of values, no matter which ones. I do not believe that we can stabilize the situation in which we have been since the seventeenth century in any final way.

F. M. BERNARD: Would you then agree with Voltaire? You raised this question of God and to some extent a metaphysics which one may question *qua* metaphysics but which one may regard as extremely useful socially.

ARENDT: Entirely agree. We wouldn't have to bother about this whole business if metaphysics and this whole value business hadn't collapsed. We begin to question because of the *events*.

· · ·

JONAS: I share with Hannah Arendt the position that we are not in possession of any ultimates, either by knowledge or by conviction or faith. And I also believe that we cannot have this as a command performance because "we need it so bitterly we therefore should have it."

However, a part of wisdom is knowledge of ignorance. The Socratic attitude is to know that one does not know. And this realization of our ignorance can be of great practical importance in the exercise of the power of judgment, which is after all related to action in the political sphere, into future action, and far-reaching action.

Our enterprises have an eschatological tendency in them, a built-in utopianism, namely to move towards ultimate solutions. Lacking the knowledge of ultimate values—or, of what is ultimately desirable, or, of what man is so that the world can be a fitting home for him—we should at least abstain from allowing eschatological situations to come about. This alone is a very important practical injunction that we can draw from the insight that only with some conception of ultimates are we entitled to embark on certain things. So that at least as a restraining force the point of view I brought in may be of some relevance.

ARENDT: With this I would agree.

· · ·

MARY MCCARTHY: I would like to ask a question that I have had in my mind a long, long time. It is about the very sharp distinction that Hannah Arendt makes between the political and the social. It is particularly noticeable in her book *On Revolution,* where she demonstrates, or seeks to demonstrate, that the failure of the Russian and the French revolutions was based on the fact that these revolutions were concerned with the social, and concerned with suffering—in which the sentiment of compassion played a large role. Whereas, the American Revolution was political and ended in the foundation of something.

Now, I have always asked myself: "What is somebody supposed to do on the public stage, in the public space, if he does not concern himself with the social? That is, what's left?"

It seems to me that if you once have a constitution, and you've had the foundation, and you have had a framework of laws, the scene is set for political action. And the only thing that is left for the political man to do is what the Greeks did: make war! Now this cannot be right! On the other hand, if all questions of economics, human welfare, busing, anything that touches the social sphere, are to be excluded from the political scene, then I am mystified. I am left with war and speeches. But the speeches can't be just speeches. They have to be speeches about something.

ARENDT: You are absolutely right, and I may admit that I ask myself this question. Number one: the Greeks did not only make war and Athens existed prior to the Peloponnesian War, and the real flower of Athens came between the Persian Wars and the Peloponnesian War. Now what did they do then?

Life changes constantly, and things are constantly there that want to be talked about. At all times people living together will have affairs that belong in the realm of the public: "are worthy to be talked about in public." What these matters *are* at any historical moment is probably utterly different. For instance, the great cathedrals were the public spaces of the Middle Ages, where men together *worshipped* God. The town halls came later. And there they talked about a matter which is not without interest either: they questioned God. So what becomes public at every given period seems to me utterly different. It would be quite interesting to follow it through a historical study, and I think one could do it. There will always be conflicts. And you don't need war.

RICHARD BERNSTEIN: Let's admit the *negative* side of a persistent thesis in your work. That when men confuse the social and the political there are devastating consequences in theory and in practice.

ARENDT: Okay!

BERNSTEIN: But you know damn well that—at least for us now—one can't consistently make that distinction! Although we can appreciate the distinction, the two are inextricably connected. It's not good enough to answer Mary McCarthy's question by saying that in different times we have to look at exactly what appears in the public realm. It's a question of whether you can dissociate or separate the social and the political consistently now.

ARENDT: I think that is certain. There are things where the right measures can be figured out. These things can really be administered and are not then subject to public debate. Public debate can only deal with things which—if we want to put it negatively—we cannot figure out with certainty. Otherwise, if we can figure it out with certainty, why do we all need to get together?

Take a town hall meeting. There is a question, for instance, of where to put the bridge. This can be done either from above, or, it can be done by debate. In the case that there really is an open question where to put the bridge, it can be done better by debate than from above. I once assisted a town hall meeting in New Hampshire, and I was very impressed by the level of sense in the town.

On the other hand, it seems to me also quite clear that no amount of speeches and discussions and debates—or what is unfortunately taking their place: committees, which are an excuse for doing nothing—that none of these things will be able to solve the very grave social problems which the big cities pose to us.

Or take another example. We have the last remnant of active citizen participation in the republic in the juries. I was a juror—with great delight and real enthusiasm. Here, again, the questions raised were debatable. The jury was extremely responsible, but also aware that there are *different viewpoints*, the two sides of the court trial, from which you could look at the issue. This seems to me quite clearly a matter of *common public interest*.

On the other hand, everything which can be figured out, in what Engels called the administration of things—these are social things in general. That they should then be subject to debate seems to me phony and a plague.

MACPHERSON: Are you telling us what a jury or a town meeting can handle is political, and everything else is social?

ARENDT: No, I didn't say that. I gave these only as examples of where, in everyday life, things come up which are *not* social, and which really *belong* in a public realm. And I gave the town hall meeting and the jury as examples of the very few places where a nonspurious public space still exists.

ALBRECHT WELLMER: I would ask you to give one example in our time of a social problem which is not at the same time a political problem. Take anything: like education, or health, or urban problems, even the simple problem of living standards. It seems to me that even the social problems in our society are unavoidably political problems. But if this is true, then, of course, it would also be true that a distinction between the social and the political in our society is impossible to draw.

ARENDT: Let's take the housing problem. The social problem is adequate housing. But the question of whether this adequate housing means integration or not is *certainly* a political question. With every one of these questions there is a double face. And one of these faces should not be subject to debate. There shouldn't be any debate about the question that everybody should have decent housing.

BAIRD: From an administrative point of view, the British government described as inadequate a huge percentage of the housing stock of Britain in a way that makes no sense to a large population of the inhabitants who actually live there.

ARENDT: I think this example is helpful in showing the double face, which I mentioned in a very concrete way. The political issue is that these people love their neighborhood and don't want to move, even if you give them one more bathroom. This is an entirely debatable question, and a public issue, and should be decided publicly and not from above. But if it's a question of how many square feet every human being needs in order to be able to breathe and to live a decent life, this is something we really can figure out.

. . .

GERSTEIN: It seems to me that one is forced to act politically, to deal with concrete situations and concrete problems. And insofar as one is forced to make those kinds of decisions then the question of class, the question of property, the question of the future of a society becomes a very concrete problem and one can't anymore deal solely in terms of abstractions such as bureaucracy or centralization. This seems to me to reveal the basically de-politicized character of your work which I find very disturbing when I read your work. Hearing you here today disturbs me even further, because fortunately—or unfortunately—we are forced to act in the world and we are going to have to know what the world looks like.

ARENDT: These are the problems of so-called mass society. I say so-called mass society but it is unfortunately a fact.

Now, I would like to know why you believe that words like class and property are less abstract than bureaucracy and administration or the words I use. They are exactly the same. All these belong to the same category of words. The question is only can you point to something real with these words. These words either have a revealing—or disclosing—quality, or they haven't.

If you think that bureaucracy—which means the rule by the bureau, and not the rule by men or the rule of law—has no disclosing quality, then I believe you haven't really lived in this world long enough. But believe me bureaucracy is a reality much more today than class. In other words, you use a number of abstract nouns which were once revealing, namely, in the nineteenth century, and you do not even bother to examine critically whether they still hold, or whether they should be changed, or anything of that kind.

Property is another question. Property is indeed very important, but in a different sense than the one in which you think about it. What we should encourage everywhere is property—of course, not the property of the means of production, but private property strictly speaking. And, believe me, this property is very much in danger, either by inflation, which is only another way of expropriating the people, or by exorbitant taxes, which is also a way of expropriation. These are the sweeter ways to expropriate—instead of pillage and killing. These processes of expropriation you have everywhere. To make a decent amount of property available to every human being—not to expropriate, but to spread it out—then you will have some possibilities for freedom even under the rather inhuman conditions of modern production.

· · ·

MCCARTHY: Actually you do have the tendency now—I am not talking about the Soviet Union—in some of the Eastern states towards private property in exactly the sense you mean: without ownership of the means of production. It seems to me that, so far as I can look ahead, socialism does represent the only force for conservation, and, in fact, represents a conservative force in the modern world.

ARENDT: I said the means of production should not be in the hands of a single man. But who owns it then? The government.

A few years ago, in Germany, the left demanded the nationalization of the Springer Press, the right-wing press. Springer is only one man, and, of course he has a certain amount of power over public opinion through his publications. But he does not have the accumulated power and means of violence which a government has. So the left would have given their government the whole power of Mr. Springer, which, of course, would have been much greater as a government-directed press. I mean even that freedom which Springer must grant because of competition— because there are other newspapers which will tell what he prefers not to tell—even this kind of freedom would have disappeared.

So, if you talk about the ownership of the means of production: the first who inherited it was the government itself. Now the government was, of course, much stronger than any single capitalist. And, if it's a question of the workers, it turned out that they could strike—and the right to strike is, of course, a very precious right—against the single capitalist. But they couldn't strike against the government. So the few rights which the workers movement had actually acquired through long struggle since the middle of the last century, were immediately taken away from them.

MCCARTHY: Consider the situation of the press in the United States: before the last election [1972] some sort of survey was made and I think it was something like ninety percent of the U.S. press supported Nixon. So that you have an amalgam of the press and the government—or, at least the present government of the United States—in the form of the Republican Party; and it looks to me that you have got the same result in the United States at this time as you would have had in Germany had they expropriated Springer.

ARENDT: If you were to expropriate the press you would have not ninety percent supporting the government, but one hundred percent.

MCCARTHY: Not necessarily. For instance, in Holland television is nationally owned. (I think these things probably only work in small countries.) And they have an enormous range of political parties. Each political party has got its own TV channel or piece of a channel. And this functions. It is accepted by the people.

ARENDT: Yes. But there you have laws which force the decentralization of this expropriation, of this accumulative process. The multiparty system in Holland acts as this mitigating factor, which they now try to introduce in some of the Eastern countries. What *we* will have to do, by and large, is experiment.

MCCARTHY: Cheers.

.   .   .

MACPHERSON: Really, two of the statements Miss Arendt has made this morning about power seem to me outrageous. One was that Marx didn't understand power. And the other was that power is not in the bureaucracy.

It seems to me that one can hold that Marx didn't understand power only if you define power in some very peculiar way. And it strikes me that this is part of the pattern of Miss Arendt's thought. She defines a lot of key words in ways unique to herself: you know, social versus political (a rather special meaning to the word "social"), force versus violence (a quite special meaning to the word "force"). . . .

ARENDT: No, power versus violence, I am sorry.

MACPHERSON: Power and violence, sorry. Action (a unique definition of "action"). This intellectual practice—and it's a very enlivening practice, because it starts off, or should start off, all kinds of controversy—is still rather curious: it takes a word that has perhaps more than one meaning in the ordinary understanding and gives it a very special meaning and then proceeds from there to reach striking, paradoxical conclusions.

Well, look, Marx didn't understand power, you say. What he understood, surely, was that power is in any society wielded by the people who control access to the means of production, the means of life, the means of labor. And that, in his terminology, was a class. Would Miss Arendt agree that the only reason a bureaucracy has what power it has—and I wouldn't agree with her that it has anything like the power she attributes to it—because and only insofar as, and only in those countries where it has become a class in Marx's sense, that is, of the people who control access to the means of production?

ARENDT: I would not agree with this. What you consider my idiosyncratic use of words—I think there is a little more to it, of course. We all grow up and inherit a certain vocabulary. We then have got to examine this vocabulary. And this not just by finding out how this word is usually used, which then results in a certain number of uses. These uses are then, so to speak, legitimate. In my opinion a word has a much stronger relation to what it denotes or to what it is than the way it is being used between you and me. That is, you look only to the communicative value of the word. I look to the disclosing quality. And this disclosing quality has, of course, always an historical background.

MACPHERSON: I look at the disclosing quality, too, and that's why I say that such words as Marx's use of class, power, and so on were disclosing concepts.

ARENDT: I didn't say the same about class. You see what I mean is, of course, the so-called superstructure. What Marx means by power is actually the power of a trend or development. This, he then believes, materializes—despite it's being utterly immaterial—in the superstructure, which is the government. Thus the laws of the government as superstructure are nothing but mirrors of the trends in society.

The question of rule Marx did not understand and to a large extent that is in his favor because he did not believe that anybody wants power just for power's sake. This does not exist in Marx. Power in the naked sense that one person wants to rule another, and that we need laws in order to prevent that, this Marx didn't understand.

You know, somehow Marx still believed that if you leave men alone—society corrupts man—and change society man will reappear. He will reappear—God protect us from it: this optimism, runs throughout history. You know, Lenin once said he doesn't understand why criminal law should exist, because once we have changed circumstances everybody will prevent everybody else from committing a crime, as a matter of course, just as every man will hurry up to aid a woman who is in distress. I also thought this example of Lenin so very nineteenth-century, you know. All this we do not believe any longer.

MACPHERSON: But surely Marx saw as clearly as say James Mill that men want power over others in order to extract some benefit for themselves from that power. It's not power for its own sake. It's power to extract benefit.

ARENDT: Yes, but you know this power to extract benefit for profit's sake. . . .

MACPHERSON: Not necessarily for just profit, any benefit.

ARENDT: But we don't know how great a percentage of the population would do it just for fun and without thinking about it. That is, Marx always thought that what we see as human motivations, are actually the motivations of trends. And trends, of course *are* abstractions. And I would doubt whether they exist of themselves. The trend of a white wall is to get dirty with time, unless somebody appears and repaints the room.

MACPHERSON: This is certainly true that Marx was interested in trends, that he was interested in the laws of motion of the society, and so on. But I don't recognize Marx in your picture of him, as having turned the trend into some kind of real force all by itself and then reading it back.

ARENDT: Well, we cannot sit down here and read Marx! But this seems to me quite obvious and it comes, of course, from Hegel. Hegel's world spirit reappears in Marx as man as a species-being. In each case you have ruled out or counted out the plurality of men. There are not many men whose acting together and against each other finally results in history. But there is the one giant noun, and this noun is in the singular and now you ascribe everything to this noun. This I believe, is really an abstraction.

HANS MORGENTHAU: Let me say a word about the basic misunderstanding of power by Marx. Marx connected organically the desire for power with the class division of society. And he believed that with this class division removed in a classless society the struggle for power—the desire for power—would of itself disappear. This is the prophecy of the *Communist Manifesto,* when the domination of man by man will be replaced by the administration of things. But this is a Rousseauist misconception of the nature of man, of the nature of society, and of the nature of power. And what I find particularly interesting is that in this misconception of power, nineteenth-century Marxism and nineteenth-century liberalism are brothers under the skin. They believe the same thing.

. . .

ALBRECHT WELLMER: I have another question concerning the importance of certain distinctions in your work, or, what Mary McCarthy called "the medieval element" in your thinking. It is quite clear that many of these distinctions have proved extremely fruitful with regard to criticizing ideological fixations: particularly those fixations which represent the prevailing nineteenth-century traditions. For instance, in the theory of Marx.

On the other hand, I am puzzled by a certain kind of abstractness of these distinctions. I always have the feeling that these distinctions are designating limiting cases to which nothing in reality really corresponds. I wonder about the nature of these constructs, or ideal types, or concepts, which designate limiting cases.

What I want to say is that there might be a certain Hegelian element missing in your thinking.

ARENDT: Sure!

WELLMER: I want to give a tentative interpretation of the way in which you draw distinctions like work and labor, the political and the social, and power and violence. Could it not be that these alternatives designate not permanent possibilities of mankind—at least, not in the first place—but the extreme limits between which human history extends: namely, the human being as an animal and utopia. So that if, for instance, every labor would have become work, if the social would have become a public or political topic, in *your* sense, and if violence had been abandoned in favor of power, again in *your* sense, then apparently this would be the realization of utopia.

Now, I wonder whether the fact that you are not quite conscious of the utopian element in your thinking explains why you relate in such a strange way to the critical or socialist or anarchist traditions of thinking. I have the feeling that this is precisely the reason why you can never give an adequate account of either of these traditions, or of something like critical theory, and of the relation of your theory to these traditions.

ARENDT: I may be unaware of the utopian element. This is one of the things that strikes me as quite possible. I don't say "yes": I just say it's quite possible. But if I am unaware of it, for heaven's sake, I *am* unaware of it! And no psychoanalysis from the side of the *Frankfurter Schule* will help: I really am not in a position to answer you right now—I have got to think that over.

At least you see one thing which I also see as questionable: namely, if I don't believe in this or that theory, why don't I write a refutation of it? I will do that only under duress. That is my lack of communication. I do not believe that this has anything to do with abstractness.

WELLMER: My question got lost. May I reformulate my question? What would you say to an interpretation of your distinctions according to which one alternative would designate the limiting case of animality and the other limiting case would designate the full realization of humanity?

ARENDT: I would say that by such fancy methods you have *eliminated* distinctions and have already done this Hegelian trick in which one concept, all of its own, begins to develop into its own *negative*. No it doesn't! *Good* doesn't develop into *bad*, and bad doesn't develop into *good*. There I would be *adamant*.

You know, I have a great respect for Hegel. So that's not the issue. Just as I have a great respect for Marx. And I am of course also influenced by others whom, after all, I read.* So don't misunderstand me. But this would be precisely the trap—in my opinion—into which I refuse to go.

· · ·

MORGENTHAU: The question has been raised about centralization, which runs directly counter to democracy if it is pushed far enough.

ARENDT: I think this question is very complicated. I would say on the first level there is almost all over the world a certain rebellion against bigness. And I think this is a healthy reaction. And I myself share it. Especially because this bigness and centralization demands bureaucracies. And bureaucracies are really the rule by nobody. And this nobody is not a benevolent nobody. We cannot hold anybody responsible for what happens because there is really no author of deeds and events, and that is frightening. So I share this to a very large extent. And this, of course, spells decentralization. And I also think that the United States or any country can remain or become powerful only if there are many sources of power. That is, only if power is divided, as it was in the original notion of the Founding Fathers, and before them—not so clear, but still—in Montesquieu.

But if all this is said—and my sympathies are there—and you know I have this romantic sympathy with the council system, which never was tried out: that is, something which builds itself up from the grass roots, so that you really can say *potestas in populo,* that is, that power comes from below and not from above—if all that is said, then we have the following. The world in which we live has to be kept. We cannot permit it to go to pieces. And this means that the "administration of things," which Engels thought such a marvelous idea, and which actually is an awful idea, is still a necessity. And this can be done only in a more or less central manner. And on the other hand, this centralization is itself a danger because its structures are so vulnerable. How can you keep the "administration of things" up without centralization? But with it, the vulnerability is immense.

· · ·

* Here Arendt is surely thinking of Heidegger and Jaspers as well as Jürgen Habermas. —Ed.

ED WEISSMAN: We have just been told that there is this distinction to be drawn between the theorist and the activist in an important way. We've just been told that there is a basic incompatibility between the activist and the theorist. . . .

ARENDT: No, not between the men, between the activities.

WEISSMAN: Right. And implicit in all you've said is a basic intellectual commitment to some sort of idealized picture of the American Constitution and the American experience. This strikes me as the most unshakable sort of a commitment which is basic to so much of what you say that you need not ever bring it up explicitly.

When you do speak of the American Constitution you make what seems to me some assumptions which I would like to ask you about. It strikes me that in some respects you misinterpret the American Constitution in the exact same way that Montesquieu misunderstood the British Constitution. It's the same kind of intellectual transference as well. Basically what he saw in the British Constitution was not, in fact, a real separation of powers at all, but simply a temporary standoff between an old society and a new, which had an institutional reflection. Now you take this notion of the separation of powers and transfer it to the American Republic.

But once you do away with the standoff between the old society and the new, you wind up with the British monarchical situation all over again, when the institutions represent mere interests. So it is no accident that you wind up with the current American administration [1972]. It was inevitable that you'd wind up with an elective king, Nixon, with Kissinger, who, of course, becomes a typical minister to the crown in the old sense of the term.

ARENDT: Well, of course, I did something like Montesquieu did with the English Constitution in that I construed out of the American Constitution a certain ideal type. I tried to back it up a little better than Montesquieu with historical fact, for the simple reason that I do not belong to the aristocracy and therefore do not enjoy this blessed laziness which is one of the main characteristics of Montesquieu's writings. Now whether this is permissible is another question, which would lead us too far here.

Actually we all do that. We all somehow make what Max Weber

called an "ideal type." That is, we think a certain set of historical facts, and speeches, and so forth, through, until it becomes some type of consistent rule. This is especially difficult with Montesquieu because of his laziness; it is much easier with the Founding Fathers because they were extraordinarily hard workers; they give you everything you want.

I do not believe in your conclusions: this inevitability which would lead us from the American Revolution to Mr. Kissinger. I think that even you, schooled in the school of necessity, and trends, and inevitability of historical laws, should see that this is a little abstruse.

. . .

MACPHERSON: I was interested in Arendt's position in relation to traditions. I take it the idea is that she has rejected the tradition of Hobbes and Rousseau, and she has accepted the tradition of Montesquieu and the Federalists. I can understand this, but it raises a puzzle because there is one very important thing that the Hobbes tradition and the Federalist tradition have in common. That is their model of man as a calculating individual seeking to maximize his own interest. Bourgeois man is the model. And the model of society follows when you put in the additional assumption that every man's interest naturally conflicts with everybody else's. Now the question is if Arendt rejects one tradition and accepts the other, what does she do about what they have in common? Does she accept or does she reject the model of bourgeois man?

ARENDT: I do not believe that the model of man is the same for the two traditions. I agree that the model of man which you described is the bourgeois and I agree that this bourgeois, God knows, is a reality.

But if I may, I want to talk about the model of man in this other tradition. The tradition of Montesquieu that you mentioned could really go back to Machiavelli and Montaigne, and so on. They ransacked the archives of antiquity precisely to find a different model of man. And this man is not bourgeois, but the citizen. This distinction between *le citoyen* and *le bourgeois* was current throughout the eighteenth century; it became the central way of talking and thinking about these things during the French Revolution; and it lasted up to 1848.

I think I might express it in a slightly different way. I can say that after the absolute monarchy had become so absolute that it could emancipate itself from all other feudal powers, including the power of the Church, a really great crisis arose. And what then came was the reemergence of real politics, as in antiquity—that's as I see the revolutions.

You see, I only half went back to Greek and Roman antiquity because I like it so much—I like Greek antiquity far more than Roman antiquity. I went back nevertheless because I knew that I simply wanted to read the same books these people had read. They read these books—as they would have said—to find a model for a new political realm they wanted to bring about, and which they called a republic.

The model of man of this republic was to a certain extent the citizen of the Athenian polis. After all, we still have words from then, and they echo through the centuries. On the other hand, the model was the *res publica*, the public thing, of the Romans. The influence of the Romans was stronger in its immediacy on the minds of these men. You know Montesquieu didn't only write *L'Esprit des Lois* but also wrote about *la grandeur* and *la misère* of Rome. These readers were all absolutely fascinated. What did John Adams do? Adams collected constitutions as other people collect stamps. And a large part of his so-called collected works are nothing but excerpts and of no great interest.

They taught themselves a new science, and they called it a new science. Tocqueville was the last who still talked about that. He says for this modern age we need a new science. He meant a new science of politics, not the *nuova scienza* of the previous generations, of Vico. And that is what I actually have in mind. I don't believe something very tangible comes out of anything which people like me are doing, but what I am after is to think about these things, not just in the realm of antiquity, but because I feel the same need for antiquity that the great revolutionaries of the eighteenth century felt.

. . .

BERNARD: I really would like to know what evidence there is for saying that there is this distinction between interests and opinions in the Founding Fathers' vision of democracy.

ARENDT: The distinction is, between the notion of group interests, which are always there, and opinions, where I have got to make up my own mind. This distinction is clear. You have it in the Constitution itself: the legislature was supposed to represent the interests of the inhabitants; the Senate, on the contrary, was supposed to filter these interests and to reach impartial opinions which would relate to the commonweal.

This distinction between the two institutions is of course very old. It follows the Roman *potestas in populo, auctoritas in senatu.* The Senate in Rome was deprived of power. The Roman senator was there only to give his opinion. But this opinion had authority insofar as it was not inspired by the *potestas* of the populace. They were called *maiores* or ancestors. In this sense they represented the constitution of Rome, re-tying it, or connecting it with Rome's past. So the Senate had an altogether different function in the Roman Republic than the populace.

And this is at the back of the thinking of the Founding Fathers, who knew it very well. And this is also one of the reasons why they were so extremely interested in having a Senate—much more interested than any European thinker ever was. They felt that they needed to filter opinions that arise immediately from interested parties through a body which is one step or two steps removed from those interests.

. . .

ARENDT: Now let me talk for a moment about the relationship between Violence and Power. My simile, so to speak, when I talk about power is "all against one." That is, the extreme of power is all against one. Then no violence is necessary to overpower the one. The extreme of violence is the opposite: one against all. The one guy with the machine gun who keeps everybody in a state of perfect obedience, so that no opinion is any longer necessary, and no persuasion.

There is no doubt that violence can destroy power: if you have the minimum of people who are willing to execute your orders then violence can reduce power to sheer impotence. We have seen that many times.

What violence can never do is generate power. That is, once violence has destroyed the power structure, no new power structure springs up. This is what Montesquieu meant when he said that tyranny is the only form of government that carries the seed of its own destruction within itself. After having de-powered everybody in the realm through tyranny, there is no longer any possibility for a new power structure to serve as a sufficient basis for the tyranny to go on—unless of course the whole form of government is changed.

If you look at power without any violence from the subjective side of being forced, then the situation of all against one is probably psychologically even stronger than the other situation of one against all. For example, in the situation in which someone puts a knife to my throat and says, "Your money or I'll cut you," I may immediately obey. But in terms of power I remain as I was because, though I obey, I do not agree. But the situation of all against one is so overpowering that you actually can get at your guy. He can no longer keep his power even though he does not yield it out of violence. So unless limited by laws this would be limitless majority rule.

And the Founding Fathers, as you know, were afraid of majority rule—they were by no means for democracy. Then they found out that power can be checked only through one thing, and that is power—counter-power. The balance of power checking power is an insight of Montesquieu, which the drafters of the Constitution had very much in mind.

. . .

MORGENTHAU: What are you? Are you a conservative? Are you a liberal? Where is your position within the contemporary possibilities?

ARENDT: I don't know. I really don't know and I've never known. And I suppose I never had any such position. You know the left think I am conservative, and the conservatives sometimes think I am left, or I am a maverick or God knows what. And I must say I couldn't care less. I don't think that the real questions of this century will get any kind of illumination by this kind of thing.

I don't belong to any group. You know the only group I ever belonged to were the Zionists. And this was from 1933 to 1943. And after that I broke. This was only because of Hitler, of course. The only possibility was to fight back *as a Jew* and not as a human being—which I thought was a great mistake, because if you are attacked as a Jew you have got to fight back as a Jew, you cannot say "excuse me, I am not a Jew; I am a human being." This is silly. And I was surrounded by this kind of silliness. There was no other possibility, so I went into Jewish politics—not really politics—I went into social work and was somehow *also* connected with politics.

I never was a socialist. I never was a communist. I come from a socialist background. My parents were socialists. But I myself, never. I never wanted anything of that kind. So I cannot answer the question.

I never was a liberal. When I said what I was not, I forgot to mention that. I never believed in liberalism. When I came to this country I wrote in my very halting English a Kafka article, and they had it "Englished" for the *Partisan Review*. And when I came to talk to them about the Englishing I read the article and there of all things the word "progress" appeared. I said: "What do you mean by this, I never used that word," and so on. And then one of the editors went to the other in another room, and left me there, and I overheard him say, in a tone of despair, "She doesn't even believe in progress."

.   .   .

McCARTHY: Where do you stand on capitalism?

ARENDT: I do not share Marx's great enthusiasm about capitalism. If you read the first pages of the *Communist Manifesto* it is the greatest praise of capitalism you ever saw. And this at a time when capitalism was already under very sharp attack especially from the so-called right. The conservatives were the first to bring up these many criticisms, which later were taken over by the left, and also by Marx, of course.

In one sense Marx was entirely right: the logical development of capitalism is socialism. And the reason is very simple. Capitalism started with expropriation. That is the law which then determined its development. And socialism carries expropriation to its logical end without any moderating influences. What today is called humane socialism means no more than that this cruel expropriation, which was started with capitalism, and went on with socialism, is somehow tempered by law.

The whole modern production process is actually a process of gradual expropriation. I therefore would always refuse to make a distinction between capitalism and socialism. For me it is really one and the same movement. And in this sense Karl Marx was entirely right. He is the only one who really dared to think the new production process through—

which crept up in Europe in the seventeenth and then the eighteenth and nineteenth centuries. And so far he is entirely right. Only it is hell. It is not paradise that finally comes out of it.

What Marx did not understand was what power really is. He did not understand this strictly political thing. But he saw one thing, namely, that capitalism, left to its own devices, has a tendency to raze all laws that are in the way of its cruel progress.

Also, the cruelty of capitalism in the seventeenth, eighteenth, and nineteenth century was, of course, overwhelming. And this you have to keep in mind if you read Marx's great praise of capitalism. He was surrounded by the most hideous consequences of this system and nevertheless thought it was great. He was, of course, also Hegelian and believed in the power of the negative. Well I *don't* believe in the power of the negative, of negation, if it entails the terrible misfortune of other people.

So you ask me where I am. I am nowhere, I am really not in the mainstream of present or any other political thought. But not because I want to be so original—it so happens that I somehow don't fit. For instance, this business between capitalism and socialism seems to me the most obvious thing in the world. And nobody even understands what I am talking about, so to speak.

I don't mean that I am misunderstood. On the contrary I am very well understood. But if you come up with such a thing and you take away their banisters from people—their safe guiding lines (they talk about the breakdown of tradition but they have never realized what it means! That it means you really are out in the cold!). Then, of course the reaction is—and this has been my case quite often—that you are simply ignored. And I don't mind that. Sometimes you are attacked. But you usually are ignored, because even useful polemic cannot be carried through on my terms. And you may say that this is a fault of mine.

You said kindly enough that I want to share. Yes, that is true. I do want to share. And I do not want to indoctrinate. That is also true. I do not want anybody to accept whatever I may think. But, on the other hand, this kind of ignoring the main literature in my own field is something that should be held against me at some point. And, well, you know, I don't reflect much on what I am doing. I believe it's a waste of time, and you never know yourself anyhow. So it's quite useless. But this ignoring I think is a real fault, and not just a lacuna. This would cut much deeper if one said why don't you read the books of your colleagues? or why do you do it so seldom?

.   .   .

ARENDT: There's this other thing, which Draenos* brought out. You said "groundless thinking." I have a metaphor which is not quite that cruel, and which I never published but kept for myself. I call it thinking without a banister. In German, *"Denken ohne Geländer."* That is, as you go up and down the stairs you can always hold on to the banister so that you don't fall down. But we have lost this banister. That is the way I tell it to myself. And this is indeed what I try to do.

This business that the tradition is broken, that Ariadne's thread is cut. Well, that is not quite as new as I made it out to be. It was, after all, Tocqueville who said that "when the past has ceased to throw its light onto the future, the mind of man wanders in obscurity." This is the situation since the middle of the nineteenth century, and, seen from the viewpoint of Tocqueville, it is entirely true. I always thought that one has got to start thinking as though nobody had thought before, and then start learning from everybody else.

.   .   .

MCCARTHY: This space that Hannah Arendt creates in her work and which one can walk into with the great sense of walking through an arch into a liberated area, a great part of which is occupied by definitions. Very close to the roots of Hannah Arendt's thinking is the *distinguo*, "I distinguish this from that. I distinguish labor from work. I distinguish fame from reputation." And so on. This is actually a medieval habit of thought.

ARENDT: It is Aristotelian.

MCCARTHY: This habit of distinguishing is not popular in the modern world, where there is a kind of verbal blur surrounding most discourse. And if Hannah Arendt arouses hostility, one reason is because the pos-

---

* The political commentator Stan Spyron Draenos taught at York University in 1972. His essay "Thinking Without a Ground" (1979) is well worth reading today. —Ed.

sibility of making distinctions is not available to the ordinary reader. But to go back to the distinctions themselves—I would say that each one within this liberated area, within this free space—each distinction was like a little house. And, let us say, fame is living in its little house with its architecture, and reputation is living in another. So that all this space created by her is actually furnished.

MORGENTHAU: Sounds like a low-income housing project!

ARENDT: But without any federal subsidy!

MCCARTHY: And I think that the chance of invigoration and oxygenation does combine with some sense of stability and security. And that is through the elaboration, the marvelous, shall we say, unfolding of definitions. Each of her works is an unfolding of definitions, which of course touch on the subject, and more and more enlighten it as one distinction unfolds into another. But there is also the stability in which fame lives in its mansion, or its little house, and labor lives in its, and work in another, and the political is strictly segregated in its house from the social.

ARENDT: It is perfectly true what you say about distinctions. I always start anything—I don't like to know too well what I am doing—I always start anything by saying, "A and B are not the same." And this, of course, comes right out of Aristotle. And for you it comes out of Aquinas, who also did the same.

. . .

ARENDT: I would like to say that everything I did and everything I wrote—all that is tentative. I think that all thinking, the way that I have indulged in it perhaps a little beyond measure, extravagantly, has the earmark of being tentative. And what was so great in the conversations I had with Jaspers was that you could sustain such an effort, which was merely tentative, which did not aim at any results, for weeks.

It could happen to us that I would arrive—I would stay there for a few weeks—and on the first day we hit on a certain subject. One such subject I remember was *"ein guter Vers ist ein guter Vers,"* which I had said. A good line of poetry is a good line of poetry, meaning by this that it has its own convincing force, which he didn't quite believe. And the point for me was to convince him that Brecht was a great poet. This one line was enough for us for two weeks, two sessions every day. And we came back to it again and again.

The disagreement was never quite resolved. But the thinking about such a thing itself became immensely richer, through this exchange "without reservations," as he said, that is, where you don't keep anything back. You don't think "Oh, I shouldn't say that, it will hurt him?" The confidence in the friendship is so great that you know nothing can hurt.

1972

REMARKS*

Gentlemen—are there ladies?—yes—I think you have been exposed to a rather great extent to my views, and I am not going to add much to what has been said. I would like to sharpen what Alan Anderson called the "radicality of the crisis" as I see it. I will try to show you that this in a way applies to both papers.

Now let me first say one thing which, after Mr. Everett's paper, perhaps is not so clear any longer: I am neither a crypto-Baptist nor am I a crypto-Christian! I am by birth a Jew, and as far as religion goes I do not belong to any church, or to any synagogue, or to any denomination. Of course, each time you write something and you send it out to the world and it becomes public, obviously everybody is free to do with it what he pleases, and this is as it should be. I do not have any quarrel with this. You should not try to control whatever may happen to what you have been thinking for yourself. You should rather try to learn from what other people do with it.

The main question would of course be the relationship between religion and politics. And there I am afraid I am too old-fashioned to believe that these two could be interconnected, by no matter what thoughts or considerations. There is no doubt that, as Mr. Everett pointed out, the organizational structure of the American churches has a great resemblance to the political structure of the country. There is no doubt that the notion of covenant itself somehow is biblical in origin. The first to conclude a covenant was Abraham, whom God told to go to other countries, to go abroad, and wherever he went he tried to make a covenant. So that was the first cove-

* The following remarks are Arendt's response to papers on and a discussion of her work by the philosophers and religious thinkers Alan Anderson, William Everett, and Roland Delattre held at the fourteenth annual meeting of the Society of Christian Ethics, convened in Richmond, Virginia, January 21, 1973. —Ed.

nant maker. But the way in which "covenant" then was understood, before the American Revolution, was a covenant between God and his people. And this is of course utterly different from a covenant that relies on mutual pledges, where we mutually pledge "our lives, our property, and our sacred honor." This covenant of mutuality—this covenant which relies only on *mutuality*—cannot possibly be compared to covenants in which one party is God, to whom we owe our existence, who created us, and gave us the Law, while we, on the other hand, pledge only our *obedience*.

As to the covenant that relies on mutual promises—this change can be traced mainly to the theories of John Locke. The biblical notion had been taken over as a covenant between the king and his people, so that the king would give a constitution, and, so to speak, bind himself under certain conditions; but again, the people were only those who pledged allegiance to him. This, I think, is utterly different from the covenant of the American Revolution. I do not believe that the loss of revolutionary spirit can be ascribed to the Constitution of the United States. The distinction between constitutionalism and revolutionary spirit, I would not entirely agree with. I think the Constitution is really the foundation stone of this country, but not in the sense of the written document (I will come back to this point later), but in the sense that constitution *making*, that is, a political *event*, is what founded this country.

You know that from one day to the next this Constitution, which had been debated all over the place and most importantly, of course, in the Federalist Papers, all of a sudden became sacred. Making a constitution is an event, a political event. And this political event is now being forgotten. If this happens, America will have lost, I am afraid, more than its revolutionary tradition.

Now something very similar to this question is the distinction, in my view sharp, between Jesus of Nazareth and Christ. The Christian religion as a religion, as an institution in this world, was not founded by Jesus. It was founded by those who believed in Jesus as Christ. That is, it was founded by Paul. The founder of the Christian religion is Paul, and when I said that this religion became immediately extremely Roman, I meant that Paul founded it on an event, namely on death and resurrection—an event which as you know for many centuries, and even today among certain people, was believed in as a historical fact in which the divine had broken into the purely worldly, secular affairs of men.

The Roman trinity which I mentioned where I said that three things—authority, religion, and tradition—are bound together: may I explain that for a moment? For the Romans, the foundation of Rome was a decisive event, which was then to be augmented by the whole later subsequent history of Rome. This event, as it is depicted in Virgil, actually was a fight between Aeneas and the Romans, or rather, not the Romans, the Italians. And in this fight, what had happened in Troy was turned upside down. It was again due to a woman, but now she was a virgin and not an adulteress. And it was not about Achilles this time, nor did the whole thing end with killing the vanquished or putting them into slavery, but with an alliance. It ended with the alliance of Aeneas and his warriors with the Italians. Virgil tells us we want to rekindle, we want to redo Troy. What happened in Troy we want to undo, and instead of the defeated being killed or enslaved, we want to put an end to the war, not only a peace treaty or a cease-fire, but an alliance. This alliance was the original notion of the Roman *lex*, of Roman law, whose first meaning was that which bound two parties together, whenever men made an alliance. Those who became allies were called in Roman history *societes*, societies (from *societas*, alliance). Now this originary event is what was handed down in tradition. And religion in this Roman sense meant, in perhaps questionable etymology, but one which is found after all in Cicero, religion meant *re-ligare*—to bind yourself back. You find yourself bound back to this originary event.

One of my theses which Alan Anderson outlined roughly is that this sense of authority has broken down. The Christian religion became Roman, was Romanized: it replaced one turning point in history with another—consider our reckoning of time, before and after Christ—and people again bound themselves back, this time to death and resurrection. Now Jesus of Nazareth, I think, is quite different from Christ. The notions of beginning, miracle, and forgiving—very important for political affairs—hardly play any role in Paul. But this is then the condition of the Christian religion and this Christianity, although it binds itself back to a beginning, somehow switched the emphasis, which in Rome lay in the past (so long as the Roman Republic really existed, I mean, not later in the declining centuries of the empire). This stress on the past at the expense of the future was now reversed. Because now—and this I think has been decisive throughout the centuries of the Middle Ages, and we cannot simply throw it out—that man was only a pilgrim on this earth, and what he was actually looking forward to was a life after his death.

If you look at it from the viewpoint of antiquity you can say that the good news was this: you thought you were mortal and you believed in the immortality of the world. Now it turns out that this world diminishes and declines. The idea that the world, which was the only stability which the ancients had, is mortal was enormously strong in these centuries. The good news said: *you* are immortal, and the world is mortal; you yourself are immortal, and therefore a pilgrim on earth, and therefore your present life is like a test for future life—and so on and so forth.

Now if you keep this whole dogmatic structure in view, then there is no possibility for a real dignity of politics. In it politics has dignity only insofar as it saves souls for a future life. That is, you cannot take out the eschatological aspect of Christianity. It is very typical of course that it is taken out today, but the kind of authority we have known throughout our history has recently, in my opinion, definitely collapsed with the arrival of the most Christian, or Jesus-like, pope there ever was—with Roncalli.*

Roncalli, of course, without knowing what he was doing, and because he was what he was, once said that when he was five or six years old, he heard other children say, "I want to become Caesar." He himself said, "I want to become like Jesus," because that was his hero, and that is of course what he actually did! And in doing so, he shows how dangerous politically any religion is which would derive only from Jesus rather than from institutionalized Roman Christianity.

Anyhow, for many years when I wanted to tell students what authority is—which they have great difficulty understanding—I always took as my example the Roman Church. And you know, that's over! It was the only institution that relied to a large extent on the old Roman notion of authority. And there was one other thing with which Christianity some-

---

* Angelo Giuseppe Roncalli was Pope John XXIII from 1958 until his death in 1963. Cf. H. Arendt, "A Christian on St. Peter's Chair," in *Men in Dark Times* (New York, 1968). —Ed.

how ruled on earth or at least was capable of controlling people without having power directly and without using violence, which was of course hell and paradise. Hell and paradise are the actual explanation of what is going to happen in everlasting life. Now this belief actually broke down; it was not shared by many even very faithful Christians in this crude manner; but it was shared by the masses. And now we live for the first time in a world in which the worst you can do to another person is to kill him. And death, as Cicero already said, is something that is going to happen to him anyhow. So you only hurry up the process! But eternal torment is not that. We have attempted to find images of hell in the true sense in the concentration camps. There you have the lingering death which comes closest to the medieval pictures of hell.

But now, for the first time since antiquity, we have got to live, and to live together, on the sheer strength of mutual promises on the one hand, and on what you may call conscience on the other. The latter is a very, very doubtful business, because what your conscience tells you is the worst, somebody else's conscience tells him is the best. It is an anarchic concept. In this respect, we are confronting a situation which we have not confronted since the rise of Christianity. And this is not just for an elite, a few people who permit themselves a certain freethinking and certain notions. You know, even Thomas Aquinas says that the joys of the blessed include their looking down on hell to see how badly off the other fellows are. That offends our moral taste—we don't think that way. But I give you the example of Aquinas because he was a person of great consequence, and that's how he talked about it! How we will get out of this I don't know.

Now let me elaborate—I believe in this business, that to act is to begin. And I want to stress, also, the difficulty, namely, that all beginning—as every one of you knows who ever wrote a paper—has an element of utter arbitrariness. You know the difficulty each one of us has to write the first sentence. And this element of arbitrariness should never be forgotten. But at the same time this arbitrariness somehow mirrors the fact of natality. You know, if you try to think about your own birth in these terms, that whatever is meaningful must be necessary. That is an old notion of philosophy: that only that which cannot *not* be, is meaningful. Yet everything which we live in, every single particular thing, could as well not be. So the only eternity is the all, the whole.

If you think about your own birth, then you know that it was an accident that your mother met your father, and if you go further back, then you have the accident of your grandparents meeting. However far you go back, you will never find an absolute, compelling cause. Augustine said, "that there be a beginning, man was created," and he did not mean by this beginning the same as "in the beginning—*bereshith*—God created heaven and earth." For the first verse of Genesis he used the Latin word *principium*, but for the beginning that *man* was he employed the word *initium*, which is the root of our word "initiative."

What Augustine somehow was saying was that all of this is the price we pay for being free—and now really free to a terrifying extent. And the question we can ask ourselves is, "Do I like being alive, and being a person, so much that I am willing to pay that price?" To believe that we can somehow escape this question seems to me rather doubtful. I don't believe it. I think the crisis is really very deep.

Thinking is one way of confronting this. Not because it gets rid of it, but only because it prepares us ever anew to meet whatever we do meet in our daily lives. So I think that this "thinking," about which I wrote and am writing now—thinking in the Socratic sense—is a maieutic function, a midwifery. That is, you bring out all your opinions, prejudices, what have you, and you know that never, in any of the dialogues, did Socrates discover any child in this midwifery that was not a wind egg. It is true you remain in a way empty after thinking. And this is what I also meant when I said that there are no dangerous thoughts—thinking itself is dangerous enough. On the other hand, I would say that this enterprise of thinking is the only one that somehow corresponds to the radicality of our crisis, which I wanted to bring to your attention. And once you are empty, then (in a way which is difficult to say) you are prepared to judge—that is, without having any book of rules under which you can subsume a particular case, you have to say, "This is good," "This is bad," "This is right," "This is wrong," "This is beautiful," "This is ugly." And the reason I believe so much in Kant's *Critique of Judgment* is not because I am interested in aesthetics but because

I believe that the way in which we say "This is right, this is wrong," is not very different from the way in which we say, "This is beautiful, this is ugly." That is, we are now prepared to meet the phenomena, so to speak, head-on, without any preconceived system. (And please, including any you might attribute to me!)

I would like to come to Mr. DeLattre's paper which I found very interesting; I found both papers very interesting and learned from them. But there is one misunderstanding, namely, in this term "validity in itself." I mean something different by it and probably haven't made it too clear. You see, Aristotle made a very great discovery, which, in a nutshell, lies in the word *energeia*—that is, in activity that has its end in itself. Thus in his *Nicomachean Ethics* Aristotle talks about flute playing. Flute playing is an activity that has its end *only* in itself. It doesn't leave an end product beyond its activity. And such activities, according to Aristotle, are the highest because they are the only ones where the means-end category does not apply. Where there is an end and everything else is considered the means, the end is deprived.

I would think if one talks about art one always should make this distinction between the performing and the productive arts. The productive arts are indeed entirely worldly, that is, they become part and parcel of our habitat, of our world. We can still go to plays and see them and they still speak to us, which is really a miracle. How does it come about? Why do we understand it? Why can we still think it is beautiful? The stability, the imperishability of these works of art is enormous. But over against this stands the instability of the performing arts. At the moment the concert is over, you go home, and those among us who are really musical still hear it, but the thing itself has already disappeared, and can be justified only by itself, that is, by this *energeia,* to have the *ergon* within itself.

Now I would say that if we look at political activity, political activity as *energeia,* it has more to do with performing arts—despite all goal setting—than with the productive arts. I have frequently said, "We don't know what we are doing," and the reason of course is that we can act only in concert. And since we can act only together, we depend upon the goals of our fellow actors. So what we actually wanted, never comes out as we originally conceived it. The curious thing about it is that even though this haphazard, accidental condition prevails in all doing, you later can tell a story. And the story hangs together. This is one of the main problems of all philosophy of history: how is it possible that no matter how chaotic the conditions are, how much the intentions of the actors contradict each other, once they have acted, then all of a sudden something has happened, and it can be told in a story; and the story makes sense. The story has meaning—but only when the action has ended. Before the end things always look rather desperate.

But if you look now at the criterion for this acting, and if I say that this is a virtue of performing activity, then the criterion for politics will be rather virtuosity than virtue. Then the question is *how* and *whether*, while action is going on, it appears as if something else were illuminated. Which is to say that the inspiring principle, which we can never put down as a result, has a chance to shine out, and so become an example for later. That is the way Achilles' courage becomes an example for later generations. That is how you learn about these virtues. The same of course is true of all other great examples in political history.

But these things, again, are very far away from religion, at least as I understand it. You have now a religion, so to speak, without Christ, and Paul has left by the window. I am not personally very . . . I told you I am not a Christian. I don't feel any loyalty to Christ. I may feel a loyalty to Jesus, because what Jesus did, his whole life, the *logoi,* and all the stories, have indeed become exemplary. When someone asked, "What should I do?" he said, "Come on and follow me." But if you do that, then even though Jesus knew what *action* is better than anybody else, he did not know what *institutions* are. I think Luther once said: the word of Jesus still makes the world shake. And this shaking I felt very directly when Roncalli was pope.

So—this is how it can be, but don't forget that: there is no religion without God. And that is a whole dimension of human life which is not political. It is neither private nor public. It is really beyond. And it would be sheer foolishness to claim, no matter which denomination we are dealing with, that this dimension can still prescribe—that we can still derive from this dimension a code of conduct, like the Ten Commandments. This I doubt, not because I doubt the Ten Commandments—on the contrary I think they are really pretty good!—but because people do not believe anymore. And you know, preaching won't help. The most effective sermons were always about hellfire. And to forget that, in this very nice idealism of the Christian churches which are now in crisis, is too easy. Remember not to make life too easy for yourself! I thank you very much.

1973

ADDRESS TO THE ADVISORY
COUNCIL ON PHILOSOPHY AT
PRINCETON UNIVERSITY

Mr. Vlastos* asked me to speak briefly at this occasion on what he called my "own vision of philosophy" and to indicate if possible "its relation to the state of the world today." I now am somewhat apprehensive that what I can say briefly on this matter will disappoint you and sound unduly negative. If to philosophize means to engage, as Plato said, in a silent dialogue between me and myself, it follows that philosophy is indeed, as Hegel remarked, an essentially solitary business; it stands in an inherent opposition to action in which always a *We* and not an *I* is engaged. In other words, the relation of thought to the world—be it the world as it is today or as we wish it to be tomorrow—is always highly problematic. I do not believe that the thought of what Mr. Vlastos calls the "true philosopher" precedes action as the flash of lightning precedes the roar of thunder, as Bergson said, or that, to change the metaphor, once thought has become public and the idea has seized the masses, actuality cannot resist the onslaught of the idea—which Hegel believed was the case in the French Revolution. I'd rather agree with another, seemingly contradictory remark of Hegel's, namely, that philosophy always arrives too late to tell us what the world ought to be like, and this not because the owl of Minerva spreads its wings when dusk is falling—since we cannot recognize the meaning of an historical era before the story itself, in its developmental process, has come to its end and is complete—but because it is in the very nature of thought to be an afterthought.

---

* Gregory Vlastos (1907–1991), classicist and philosopher, developed a Socratic way of thinking within Plato's dialogues. He and Arendt were friends. —Ed.

The chief argument against philosophy has always been that the *sophia* it is in love with is not only difficult or impossible to achieve for mortals, but that philosophy as such is useless; in the normal course of human affairs it is "good for nothing." I believe that we shall never come to grips with the question of what philosophy is all about unless we take this age-old argument seriously. Some kind of thinking, no doubt, is involved in all kinds of activities, scientific, artistic, and last but not least political; moreover, there is plenty of room for teaching and learning how to "think correctly," how to answer arguments, how to read a text, how to analyze a proposition, and so forth. The correct word for this kind of thinking is *deliberation*, and deliberation is concerned with the means to an end; once this end is reached, the thinking process comes to its end. Philosophy, on the contrary, raises questions about the so-called ends, for example it asks: What is happiness? rather than: What are the means to attain it? That this philosophic question can ever find a final answer is more than doubtful. But let us assume for a moment that some philosopher believes he has found a final answer to such a question: Would that stop the urge to think about it either in himself or in all those whom he hoped to convince? And would we be better off, better men, as it were, if we *knew* what justice is and stopped thinking about it? Kant at any rate, believing that thinking corresponds to a "need of human reason," was of a different opinion. He once wrote in his notebooks: "I do not approve of the rule that if the use of pure reason has proved something, this result should later no longer be doubted as if it were a solid axiom. . . . In pure philosophy this is impossible. Our mind has a natural aversion against it." From which it seems to follow that the thirst for knowledge can be quenched once ignorance is dispelled, but the urge to think cannot be stilled, not by my own insights and not by allegedly definite insights of "wise men." The need of reason will be satisfied only through thinking, and the thoughts I had yesterday will be satisfying this need today only to the extent that I am able to think them anew.

This implies that the activity of thinking belongs to those nonproductive, performing activities that have their ends in themselves and are sheer *energeia;* whatever results may come out of it are, from the viewpoint of the thinking ego, mere by-products, liable to be questioned tomorrow and to be subjected again to the thinking process. Hence, the unwillingness of many philosophers to be nailed down on results and their uneasy assertion that the "truth" of which they were aware of so long as the thought process lasted cannot be expressed in words or written down in so inflexible a medium as letters. There is something profoundly right in an occasional remark by Bergson: Every philosopher worth his salt has but one thought which he is unable to say—which is why he usually becomes so loquacious.

Closely connected with this aspect of philosophy, or rather of philosophizing as sheer activity, is the fact that philosophers almost never agree with each other, neither on their results nor even on the subject matter of their curious enterprise. Yet they are in total agreement on one aspect of their activity which, however, they very rarely mention explicitly and, with one exception, as far as I know, never use as an argument to recommend their profession, and that is the great pleasure they derive from it. Aristotle, who is the exception, speaks of the "sweetness" of thought that is greater than any other pleasure and recommends the *bios theoretikos* because it needs no implements and no special place to be engaged in. Nietzsche speaks of it as a kind of intoxication, Kant noticed the swiftness (*Hurtigkeit*) of thought which has no resistance to overcome, not even the materiality of lip, teeth, and tongue as is the case with speech. ("Swift as a thought," sang Homer.) And even Leibniz mentions its *voluptas* ("without novelty and progress there could be no *cogitatio* and hence no delight"). And lest we suspect that we deal here with a deformation of "professional thinkers" (Kant's *Denker von Gewerbe*) let me remind you of old Cato, surely no philosopher, just a Roman, occasionally indulging in thinking when he had withdrawn from ordinary political business. Cato said, "Never am I more active than when I am doing nothing, never am I less alone than when I am by myself." (*Numquam se plus agere quam nihil cum ageret, numquam minus solum esset quam cum solus esset.*) This is spoken in the spirit of Socrates, also no professional philosopher, who loved to raise questions without answering them, who had no doctrine to teach, and who believed that to investigate matters by sheer thinking in the silent dialogue with himself or in the marketplace with others was not just a "way of life" but the only way of being or feeling alive.

This kind of thinking of which the philosopher becomes the expert does not yield any results; it is even dangerous for all results, opinions, customs, and rules. The notion that there exist dangerous thoughts is mistaken for the simple reason that thinking itself is dangerous to all creeds, convictions, and opinions. It is a profitless enterprise as far as results are concerned, and the questions it raises and never answers once and for all arise out of the Platonic "admiring wonder" (*thaumadzein*) that, Aristotle notwithstanding, is not caused by ignorance and does not disappear with knowledge. This wonder, to be sure, is at the root of both the urge to know and the need to think, of science and philosophy; but that does not mean that these two are the same.

Knowledge pursues truth, and the crisis of science today is caused, at least partially, by the fact that scientists, since the beginning of the modern age, have had to be content with provisional verities which will be challenged tomorrow. Philosophy asks the unanswerable questions of what does it mean that everything is as it is, or why is there anything and not rather nothing, and the many variations of these questions. By distinguishing between thinking and knowing, I do not wish to deny that thinking's quest for meaning and science's quest for truth are interconnected. By asking the unanswerable questions of meaning men establish themselves as question-asking beings. Behind all the cognitive questions for which men find answers lurk the unanswerable ones which seem entirely idle and have always been denounced as such. I believe it is very likely that men, if they ever should lose their ability to wonder and thus cease to ask unanswerable questions, also will lose the faculty of asking the answerable questions upon which every civilization is founded. In this sense, the need of reason is the *a priori* condition of the intellect and of cognition. It is the breath of life whose presence, psyche-like, is noticed only after it has left its natural abode, the dead body of a civilization which is no more.

1973

INTERVIEW WITH ROGER ERRERA*

What follows is the text of my filmed interview with Hannah Arendt, which took place in New York in October 1973. She strongly refused to be filmed at home.

The moment was not exactly a calm one, politically speaking. In the Middle East, the October War had just taken place. In the United States, the Watergate affair had begun. It would lead to the resignation of President Nixon in August 1974, under the threat of impeachment. We learned, in the course of our talks, of the dismissal of Archibald Cox, then special prosecutor, and the resignation of Elliot Richardson, then attorney general.

There is more than an echo of these events in the interview. During it, Hannah Arendt was extremely courteous and attentive, fully controlled, at times consulting a few notes (for quotations). It seems to me that she said exactly what she meant to say, correcting herself immediately whenever necessary. No anecdotes, no small talk. With a permanent grace she accepted what was for her neither a familiar nor a relaxing exercise.
—Roger Errera

HANNAH ARENDT: I may need a glass of water, if I could have that.

ROGER ERRERA: You arrived in this country in 1941. You'd come from Europe, and you've been living here for thirty-two years. When you arrived from Europe, what was your main impression?

ARENDT: *Mon impression dominante.* Well you see, this is not a nation-state, America is not a nation-state and Europeans have a hell of a time understanding this simple fact, which, after all, they should know theo-

---

* This version of the interview has considered the original transcript, the French broadcast version, the German translation of that, as well as an inadequate English translation. —Ed.

retically; this country is united neither by heritage, nor by memory, nor by soil, nor by language, nor by the same place of origin. There are no natives here. The natives were the American Indians. Everyone else is a citizen and these citizens are united only by one thing, and that's a big thing: that is, you become a citizen of the United States by consenting to its Constitution. The Constitution—that is a scrap of paper, according to French as well as German common opinion, and you can change it. No, here it is a sacred document, it is the constant remembrance of a sacred act, the act of foundation. And the foundation is to make a union out of wholly disparate ethnic minorities and religions, and still (a) have a union and (b) not assimilate or level down these differences. And all this is very difficult to understand for a foreigner. It's what foreigners never understand. We can say this is a government by law and not by men. To the extent that is true, and needs to be true, the well-being of the country, of the United States of America, of the republic, depends on it.

I would go a little further and I would say that all those who are born in this country have no decisive prerogative over those who like myself arrived only recently. I remember that when I lived in France I asked a French friend how long it takes to become French.

ERRERA: Naturalized?

ARENDT: No, not naturalized, this I knew . . .

ERRERA: Assimilated?

ARENDT: Assimilated in the sense of really recognized as French. And my friend said—she was a good friend and meant nothing against me— "Well, Hannah, I think three generations." Here it takes five years, or even less, and without assimilation. Those who will not part with their original passport don't have the right to vote [this was before the days of dual citizenship —Ed.], and that's about all. Those who take out their first papers and then become American citizens have every right except the right to become president of the United States. And that seems to me a handicap that is not very serious. The first thing is that we don't deal here with a nation. By the same token, this means that the law is much more important in this country than in any other.

ERRERA: Over the last ten years, America has experienced a wave of political violence marked by the assassination of the president and his brother, by the Vietnam War, by the Watergate affair. Why can America overcome crises that in Europe have led to changes of government, or even to very serious domestic unrest?

ARENDT: Now let me try to answer a little differently. I think the turning point in this whole business was indeed the assassination of President Kennedy. No matter how you explain it and no matter what you know or don't know about it, it was quite clear that, for the first time in a very long time, a direct crime interfered with the American political process. And this somehow has changed that process. You know, other assassinations followed, Bobby Kennedy, Martin Luther King, and more. Finally, the attack on Wallace, which belongs in the same category.*

ERRERA: Has American political society today [1973] profoundly changed since 1963?

ARENDT: We don't yet know. We hope that there is some restoration of political responsibility in Congress, in both the Senate and the House. If this should not be the case, then things will go on as before. You know, there are certain things that happen automatically in politics if you leave them unchecked. As long as we have a free press there is a limit to what can happen. The moment the press is no longer free, or when the press is forced to reveal its sources, which, as you know, is now before the courts, then anything can happen. You know, what really makes it possible for a totalitarian or any other kind of dictatorship to rule is that the people are not informed. How can anyone have an opinion who is not informed? On the other hand, if everyone always lies to you, the consequence is not that you believe the lies, but that no one believes anything at all anymore—and rightly so, because lies, by their very nature, have to be changed, to be "re-lied," so to speak. So a lying government which pursues different goals at different times has constantly to rewrite its own history. That means that the people are deprived not only of their

---

* The reference is to the May 15, 1972, assassination attempt on Alabama governor George Wallace, at the time a strong candidate in the Democratic presidential primary race. —Ed.

capacity to act, but also of their capacity to think and to judge. And with such a people you can then do what you please.

Moreover, I think that Watergate—whereby Watergate is not of course a specific break in the headquarters of the Democratic Party, but everything connected with it—has revealed perhaps one of the deepest constitutional crises this country has ever known. And if I say constitutional crisis, this is of course much more important than if I said "*une crise constitutionnelle*" in France. I don't know how many constitutions you have had since the French Revolution. As far as I remember, by the time of World War I, you had had fourteen. And how many you then had—I don't want even to tackle that, every one of you can do it better than I. But, here there is one Constitution, and this Constitution has now lasted for not quite two hundred years. It's a different story. Here, it's the whole fabric of government which actually is at stake.

And this constitutional crisis consists—for the first time in the history of the United States—in a dead-on clash between the legislative and the executive. And here the Constitution itself is somehow at fault, and I would like to talk about that for a moment. The Founding Fathers never believed that tyranny could arise out of the executive office, because they saw this office as the executor of what the legislature decreed. We know today that the greatest danger of tyranny is from the executive. But what did the Founding Fathers—if we take the spirit of the Constitution—think? They thought that they were free from majority rule, and therefore it is a great mistake if you believe that what we have here is democracy, a mistake which many Americans make. What we have here is a republic, and the Founding Fathers were most concerned about preserving the rights of minority voters, because they knew that a healthy body politic depends on a plurality of opinions. They knew that what the French call "*l'union sacrée*" is precisely what one should not have, because this would already be a kind of tyranny, or the consequence of a tyranny, and the tyranny or tyrant could very well be the majority. Hence, the whole government is construed in such a way that even after the victory of the majority, there is always the opposition, and the opposition is necessary because it represents the legitimate opinions of one or more minorities. Now, as you know, about the middle of the nineteenth century, we got the party organizations which were rather novel institutions about whose merits we can very well have different opinions. At that time the common understanding was that there was first a government and second an opposition, and one only. A part of the crisis today is that we have a government without *any* organized opposition.

National security is a new word in the American vocabulary, and this, I think, should be known. National security is really, if I may interpret a bit, a translation of *"raison d'état,"* and this whole notion of reason of state never played any role in this country. This is a new import. National security now covers everything, and it covers, as you may know from the interrogation of Mr. Ehrlichman,* all kinds of crime. For instance, "the president has a right" is now read in the light of "the king can do no wrong"; that is, the president is like a monarch in a republic. He's above the law, and his justification is always that whatever he does, he does for the sake of national security.

ERRERA: In your view, in what way are these implications of *raison d'état*, what you call the intrusion of criminality into the political domain, specific to our time? Is this, indeed, specific to our time?

ARENDT: This is *propre à notre époque*. I really think so. Just as the stateless business is *propre à notre époque*, and repeats itself again and again under different aspects, in different countries, and in different colors. But if we come to these general questions, what is also *propre à notre époque* is the massive intrusion of criminality into political processes. And by this I mean something which by far transcends crimes always justified, rightly or wrongly, by *raison d'état*, because these are always exceptions to the rule, whereas here we are confronted suddenly with a style of politics which in itself is criminal.

Here it's by no means the exception to the rule. It is not that they say because we are in such a special emergency we have to bug everybody and sundry, including the president himself. But that they think that bug-

---

* Arendt is alluding to the testimony of John D. Ehrlichman, President Nixon's adviser on domestic affairs, before the Senate Watergate Committee. —Ed.

ging belongs to the normal political process. And similarly, they don't say we will burgle once, break in to the office of a psychiatrist once* and then never again. By no means. They say this breaking in is absolutely legitimate. When Ehrlichman was asked: "Where do you draw the line? How about murder?" he said he would have to think about that. This entire business of national security comes from *raison d'état*, and as such is a direct European import. Of course, the Germans and the French and the Italians recognize it as entirely justified, because they have always lived under it. But this was precisely the European heritage with which the American Revolution intended to break.

ERRERA: In your essay on the Pentagon Papers[†] you describe the psychology of those you call the "professional problem-solvers," who at the time were the advisers to the American government, and you say: "Their distinction lies in that they were problem-solvers . . . hence they were not simply intelligent, but prided themselves on being 'rational,' and they were indeed to a rather frightening degree above 'sentimentality' and in love with 'theory,' the world of sheer mental effort."

ARENDT: May I interrupt you here? I think that's enough because I have a very good example, precisely from these Pentagon Papers, of this scientific mentality, which finally overwhelms all other insights. You know about the "domino theory," which was the official theory throughout the Cold War from 1950 till about 1969, shortly after the Pentagon Papers. The fact is that very few of the sophisticated intellectuals who wrote the Pentagon Papers believed in this theory. There are only, I think, two or three guys, pretty high up in the administration, but not exactly the most intelligent ones—Mr. Rostow and General Taylor[‡]—

---

* Arendt refers to the burglary of Dr. Lewis Fielding by a covert White House special investigations unit, referred to as "the plumbers," who hoped to find material to discredit Daniel Ellsberg, the former U.S. military analyst who leaked the Pentagon Papers. —Ed.

[†] "Lying in Politics: Reflections on the Pentagon Papers," in H. Arendt, *Crises of the Republic* (New York, 1972), 3–47. —Ed.

[‡] Walt Whitman Rostow, who served as special assistant for national security affairs to Lyndon Johnson from 1966 to 1969, and General Maxwell D. Taylor, chairman of the Joint Chiefs of Staff under Kennedy and Johnson from 1962 to 1964 and ambassador to South Vietnam for a year thereafter. —Ed.

who believed it. That is, they didn't actually believe in it, but in everything they did they acted on it as an assumption. And this not because they were liars, or because they wanted to please their superiors—these people really were all right in those respects—but because it gave them a framework within which they could work. And they took this framework even though they knew—and every intelligence report and every factual analysis proved it to them every morning—that these assumptions were factually wrong. They took it because they didn't have any other framework.*

Good old Hegel once said that all philosophical contemplation serves to eliminate contingency. A mere fact has to be seen by eyewitnesses, who are not the best witnesses. No fact is beyond doubt. But that two and two make four is somehow beyond doubt. And the theories produced in the Pentagon were much more plausible than the facts of what actually happened.

ERRERA: Our century seems to me to be dominated by the persistence of a mode of thinking based on historical determinism.

ARENDT: Yes, and I think there are very good reasons for this belief in historical necessity. The trouble, and it is really an open question, is the following: we don't know the future, everybody acts into the future, and nobody knows what he is doing, because it is the future that is being done. Action is a "we" and not an "I." Only if I were the only one could I foretell what's going to happen from what I do. Now this makes it look as though what actually happens is entirely contingent, and contingency is indeed one of the biggest factors in all history. Nobody knows what is going to happen simply because so much depends on an enormous amount of variables; or, in other words, on *hasard*. On the other hand, if you look back on history, then retrospectively—even though all this was contingent—you can tell a story that makes sense. How is that possible? That is *the* problem for every philosophy of history. How is it possible that in retrospect things always look as though they could not have happened otherwise? The variables have disappeared; reality has such

* Arendt's understanding of "framework" derives from Heidegger's *Gestell*—enframing—which he sees as the essence of technology. —Ed.

an overwhelming impact on us that we ignore what is actually an infinite variety of possibilities.

ERRERA: But if our contemporaries cling fast to determinist ways of thinking, in spite of this being refuted by history, do you think it's because they're afraid of the unforeseen?

ARENDT: *Ja.* Sure. And rightly so. Only they won't say it. If they did, one could immediately start a debate. If they would only say they are afraid, but they are afraid to be afraid. That is one of the main personal motivations. They are afraid of freedom.

ERRERA: Can you imagine a minister in Europe, seeing his policy about to fail, commissioning a team of experts from outside the government to produce a study whose aim would be to find out . . .

ARENDT: It was not *extérieur de l'administration.* They were taken from everywhere and also from . . .

ERRERA: True, but people from outside the government were also involved. So can you imagine a European minister in the same situation commissioning a study of that kind to find out how it all happened?

ARENDT: Of course not.

ERRERA: Why not?

ARENDT: Because of *raison d'état,* reason of state. You know that. He would have immediately started to cover up. On the other hand is the McNamara attitude.* I quoted him: "The picture of the world's greatest superpower killing or seriously injuring a thousand non-combatants a week, while trying to pound a tiny backward nation into submission on an issue whose merits are hotly disputed, is not a pretty one." This is an American attitude. This shows you that things then were still all right, even though they went wrong. But they were still all right because there was still McNamara who wanted to know. He said to his statisticians: find out what happened, find out the reason why everything went wrong—and then the whole mess was uncovered.

ERRERA: Do you think that, at present, American leaders faced with other situations will still want to know?

* Secretary of Defense Robert S. McNamara commissioned the Pentagon Papers in 1967. The following words quoted were selected by Arendt as the epigraph to her essay "Lying in Politics." —Ed.

ARENDT: No. I don't think that a single one is left. I don't know. I take that back. But I think that McNamara was on Nixon's list of enemies—if I am not mistaken, I read it in today's *New York Times*. If that is true, it shows already that this attitude has gone out of American politics on the highest level. It is no longer there. These people already believed in image making, but with a sort of vengeance: Why *didn't* we succeed with image making? And one could say that it was only an image, you know. But now they want everybody to believe their image, and nobody should look beyond it, and that is of course an altogether different political reality.

ERRERA: After what Senator Fulbright calls the "arrogance of power,"* after what we might call the "arrogance of knowledge," is there a third stage that is arrogance pure and simple?

ARENDT: Yes, I don't know whether it's *l'arrogance tout court*. It is really the will to dominate, for heaven's sake, and up to now it hasn't succeeded. I can still sit with you at this table and talk pretty freely. So they haven't yet dominated me; and somehow I am not afraid. Perhaps I am mistaken, but I feel perfectly free in this country. So they have not succeeded. Somebody, I think Morgenthau,† called this whole Nixon enterprise an "abortive revolution." Now, we don't yet know whether it was abortive—it was early when he said that—but there's one thing one *can* say: successful it wasn't either.

ERRERA: But isn't the big threat these days the idea that the goals of politics are limitless? Liberalism, after all, presupposes the idea that political objectives are limited. These days, doesn't the biggest threat come from the rise of men and movements who set themselves unlimited objectives?

ARENDT: I hope I don't shock you if I tell you that I'm not at all sure that I'm a liberal, you know, not at all. I really have no political creed in this sense. I have no political philosophy that could sum up with an *ism*.

---

* Errera is referring to the concept that Arkansas senator J. William Fulbright laid out in his 1966 book *The Arrogance of Power*, in which he took the U.S. government to task for its justifications of the Vietnam War. —Ed.

† Hans Morgenthau, an influential scholar of international relations and foreign policy, author of *Politics Among Nations*, and Arendt's close friend. —Ed.

ERRERA: Of course, but all the same, your philosophical reflections lie within the foundations of liberal thought, with borrowings from antiquity.

ARENDT: Is Montesquieu a liberal? Would you say that all the people whom I take into account as worthwhile are liberal? After all, *"moi je me sers où je peux."* I take whatever I can and whatever suits me. I think one of the great advantages of our time is really what René Char has said: *"Notre héritage n'est garanti d'aucun testament."*

ERRERA: . . . is preceded by no testament: *notre héritage n'est précédé d'aucun testament.*

ARENDT: . . . *n'est précédé d'aucun testament.* This means we are entirely free to help ourselves wherever we can from the experiences and the thoughts of our past.

ERRERA: But doesn't this extreme freedom risk alarming many of our contemporaries who would prefer to find some ready-made theory, some ideology to then apply?

ARENDT: *Certainement. Aucun doute. Aucun doute.*

ERRERA: Doesn't this freedom risk being a freedom of the few, of those who are strong enough to invent new modes of thought?

ARENDT: *Non. Non.* It rests on the conviction that every human being is a thinking being and can reflect just as I do, and therefore can judge for himself, if he wants to. How I can make this wish or need arise in him, this I don't know. The only thing that can help us, I think is to *réfléchir,* to remember and think back. To think in this sense means to subject whatever is thought to a critical examination. Thinking actually undermines whatever there is of rigid rules, general opinions, and so forth. That is, there are no dangerous thoughts for the simple reason that thinking itself is such a dangerous enterprise. But I believe nonthinking is even more dangerous. I don't deny that thinking is dangerous, but I would say not thinking, *ne pas réfléchir, c'est plus dangereux encore.*

ERRERA: Let's go back to René Char's words: "Our inheritance is preceded by no testament." What do you think the inheritance of the twentieth century will be?

ARENDT: We are still in it, you know—you are young, I am old—but we are both still here to leave them something.

ERRERA: What will we leave to the twenty-first century? Three quarters of the century have already gone by . . .

ARENDT: I've no idea. I'm pretty sure that modern art which has now sunk to a rather low level—but after such an enormous creativity as we had during the first forty years, especially in France, this is only natural. A certain exhaustion sets in. So, what we can leave? This whole era, this whole twentieth century, may be known as one of the great centuries in history, but not in politics.

ERRERA: And America?

ARENDT: No. No, no, no . . .

ERRERA: Why?

ARENDT: You know, this country lacks a certain amount of tradition.

ERRERA: There isn't an American artistic tradition?

ARENDT: No, not a great one. A great one in poetry, a great one in novels, in writing, perhaps. But the one thing you might mention is the architecture. The stone buildings are like tents of nomads which have been frozen into stone.

ERRERA: Why is it that Europe is so permeated with innovations that come from America?

ARENDT: Because of their novelty. And if that means progress, then everything new must be better than what went before. But you see, if you want something better, and better, and better, you lose the good. The good can no longer be measured.

ERRERA: In the end our contemporaries have no sense of regression . . .

ARENDT: *Non,* not regression. Why regression? If you think in grand terms about History and want to find a Law of History, then there are only three possibilities. First, the Golden Age, and everything after becomes worse and worse and worse. Not very nice. Second, stagnation, which is boring and not nice at all. And third, progress, which is our Law.

ERRERA: In your work, you've frequently discussed the modern history of the Jews and antisemitism, and you say, at the end of your volume on antisemitism, that the birth of the Zionist movement at the end of the nineteenth century was the only political response the Jews ever found to antisemitism. In what way has the existence of Israel changed the political and psychological context in which Jews live in the world?

ARENDT: Oh, I think it has changed everything. The Jewish people today are united behind Israel.* They feel that they have a state, a political representation in the same way as the Irish, the English, the French, et cetera. They have not only a homeland but a nation-state. And their whole attitude towards the Arabs depends to a large extent on this identification, which the Jews coming from Central Europe made almost instinctively, without thinking, and without reflection; namely, that the state must necessarily be a nation-state.

Now this, that is, the whole relationship between the diaspora and Israel, or what formerly was Palestine, has changed because Israel is no longer just a refuge for the underdogs in Poland, where a Zionist was a guy who tried to get money from rich Jews for the poor Jews. Today the Zionist is the Jewish representative of the Jewish people all over the world. Whether we like that or not is another question, but it does not mean that a Jew in the diaspora has to always be of the same opinion as the government in Israel. It's not a question of the government but of the *state* and so long as the state exists, this is what represents us in the eyes of the world.

ERRERA: Ten years ago, a French author, Georges Friedmann, wrote a book called *The End of the Jewish People?*,† in which he concluded that in the future there would be, on the one hand, a new state, an Israeli nation, and on the other, in the lands of the diaspora, Jews who would be assimilated and would gradually lose their Jewish identities. What do you think of this hypothesis?

ARENDT: *Cette hypothèse* sounds very plausible, and I think it's quite wrong. Look here, in antiquity, while the Jewish state still existed, there was already a Jewish diaspora. Through the centuries, when there were many different forms of government and forms of state, the Jews, the only ancient people that has actually survived these thousands of years, were never assimilated. If Jews could have been assimilated, they

---

* This should be read against the background of the events of the day, i.e., the Yom Kippur War. —Ed.
† Georges Friedmann, *Fin du peuple juif?* (Paris: Gallimard, 1965). —Ed.

would have been assimilated long ago. There was a chance during the Roman period, there was a chance during the Spanish period, there was, of course, a chance in the eighteenth and nineteenth centuries. Look, a people, a collective, doesn't commit suicide. Mr. Friedmann is wrong because he doesn't understand that the intellectuals, who can indeed change nationalities and can absorb different culture, do not correspond to the people as a whole, and especially not a people that has been constituted by laws which we all know.

The "giftedness" of a certain part of the Jewish people is a historical problem, a problem of the first order for some historians. To risk a speculative explanation: we are the only people, the only European people, to have survived from antiquity pretty much intact. We are the only people who have never known analphabetism. We were always literate because you cannot be a Jew without being literate. The women were less literate than the men but even they were much more literate than their non-Jewish counterparts. Not only the elite knew how to read but every Jew had to read—the whole people, in all its classes and on all levels of "giftedness" and intelligence. That means as Jews we have kept our identity.

ERRERA: What does it mean for Jews to be assimilated into American society?

ARENDT: Well, in the sense in which we spoke of assimilated Jewry, by which we meant assimilation to the surrounding culture, it doesn't exist. Would you kindly tell me to whom the Jews should assimilate here? To the English? To the Irish? To the Germans? To the French? To whoever came here?

ERRERA: When people say that American Jews are very Americanized, not just Americans but Americani*z*ed, what are they getting at?

ARENDT: One means their way of life, and all these Jews are very good American citizens. So it signifies their public life, not their private life, not their social life. Their social and their private life is today more Jewish than it ever was before. The younger generation in great numbers learn Hebrew, even if they are from parents who don't know any Hebrew. But the main thing is really Israel, the main question is: Are you for or against Israel?

Take, for example, the German Jews of my generation who came to this country. They became in no time at all very nationalistic Jews, much more nationalistic than I ever was, even though I was a Zionist and they were not: I never said I'm a German, I always said I'm a Jew. They are now assimilated. But to what? To the Jewish community. They were used to assimilation so they assimilated to the Jewish community of America, which means of course that they then, with the fervor of converts, became extra-specially nationalistic and pro-Israel.

ERRERA: Throughout history, what has ensured the survival of the Jewish people has been, mainly, a religious kind of bond. We are living in a period when religions as a whole are going through a crisis, where people are trying to loosen the shackles of religion. In these conditions, what, in the current period, comprises the unity of the Jewish people throughout the world?

ARENDT: I think you are slightly wrong with this thesis. When you say religion, you think, of course, of the Christian religion, which is a creed and a faith. This is not at all true of Judaism, which is a national religion where nation and religion coincide. You know that Jews, for example, don't recognize baptism; for them it is as though it didn't happen. That is, a Jew never ceases to be a Jew according to Jewish law. So long as somebody is born from a Jewish mother—*la recherche de la paternité est interdite*—he is a Jew. Thus the notion of what religion is, is altogether different, more a way of life than a religion in the particular, specific sense of Christianity. I remember, for instance, I had Jewish instruction, religious instruction, and when I was about fourteen years old, of course I wanted to rebel and say something shocking to our teacher, so I got up and said, "I don't believe in God." Whereupon he said, "Who asked you?"

ERRERA: Your first book, published in 1951, was called *The Origins of Totalitarianism*. In this book you tried not just to describe a phenomenon but also to explain it. Hence this question: In your view, what is totalitarianism?

ARENDT: *Oui, enfin.* Let me start with making certain distinctions upon which other people are not agreed. First of all, a totalitarian dictatorship is neither a simple dictatorship nor a simple tyranny. Totalitarianism begins in contempt for what we have. The second step is the notion: "Things must change—no matter how. Anything is better than what we have. Totalitarian movements organize this kind of mass sentiment, and by organizing it articulate it, and by articulating it somehow make the people desire it. This is the much talked about *Gleichschaltung*—the coordination process. You are coordinated not with the powers that be, but with your neighbors, that is, coordinated with the majority of the populace. But instead of communicating with the others, you are now glued to them. And you feel of course marvelous. You were once told, Thou shalt not kill. Now you are told, Thou shalt kill; and although you think it very difficult to kill, you do it because it's become your code of behavior. You learn whom to kill and how to kill and how to do it together. Totalitarianism appeals to the very dangerous emotional needs of people who have lived in complete isolation and in fear of one another.

When I analyzed a totalitarian government, I tried to analyze it as a new form of government, one that was never known before; therefore I tried to enumerate its main characteristics. Among these, I would like to remind you of one which is entirely absent from all tyrannies, yesterday or today, and that is the role of the innocent, the innocent victim. Under Stalin you didn't have to do anything to be deported or to be killed. You were given your role according to the dynamism of history and played this role regardless of what else you did or did not do. With respect to this, I said no government before has killed people for saying yes. Usually a government or tyrants kill people for saying no. Now, I was reminded by a friend that something very similar was said in China many centuries ago, namely that men who have the impertinence to approve are no better than the disobedient who oppose. And this of course is the quintessential sign of totalitarianism, of the total domination of men by men. Now, in this sense there is no totalitarianism today, even in Russia, which may be one of the worst tyrannies ever known. Today in Russia you have to do something to be sent away into exile, or to a forced labor camp, or to a psychiatric ward.

It may be of some interest to note that totalitarian regimes arose when the majority of European governments were under dictatorships. Dictatorship, if the concept is taken in the original sense of the word, is not a tyranny. A dictatorship temporarily suspends the laws in the case of an emergency, usually during a war, or civil war, or suchlike. But a dictatorship is intended to be limited in time and a tyranny is not.

ARENDT: When I wrote *Eichmann in Jerusalem,* though I didn't know this line from Brecht, *Der Schoss ist fruchtbar noch, aus dem das kroch,** one of my principal intentions was to destroy the legend of the greatness of evil, of the demonic force, to relieve people of the admiration they have for great evil characters like Richard III or Macbeth, and so forth. I had found in Brecht the following remark: "The great political criminals must be exposed and exposed especially to laughter. They are not great political criminals, but people who committed great political crimes, which is something entirely different. The failure of his enterprises does not indicate that Hitler was an idiot." See here, that Hitler was an idiot was, of course, a prejudice of the whole opposition to him prior to his seizure of power. And therefore a great many books tried to justify Hitler and to make him a great man. So Brecht says: "That he failed does not indicate that Hitler was an idiot and the extent of his enterprises does not make him a great man." That is, neither the one nor the other; this classification of idiocy and of greatness has no application. "If the ruling classes," says Brecht, "permit a small crook to become a great crook, he is not entitled to a privileged position in our view of history. That is, the fact that he becomes a great crook and that what he does has great consequences does not add to his stature." And speaking generally, he adds to these rather abrupt remarks: "One may state that tragedy deals with the sufferings of mankind in a less serious way than comedy."

This, of course, is a shocking statement. I think that at the same time it is entirely true. What is really necessary is—if I want to keep my integrity under these circumstances—then I can do it only if by remembering my old way of looking at such a thing and say: No matter what he does, if he killed ten million people, he is still a clown.

ERRERA: When you published your book on the Eichmann trial, it aroused some very violent reactions. Why were there such reactions?

---

* "The womb he crawled from is still fertile." —Ed.

ARENDT: Well, as I said before, this controversy was partly caused by the fact that I attacked bureaucracy, and if you attack a bureaucracy, you had better be prepared, for this bureaucracy to defend itself, and counterattack; it will attack you, will try to make you appear intolerable and everything else that goes with it. That is, more or less, a dirty political business. Now, with this I really had no quarrel. But suppose they had not done it, suppose they had not organized this campaign, the opposition to this book still would have been strong, because the Jewish people were offended, and now I mean people whom I really respect. And therefore I can understand it. They were offended chiefly by what Brecht referred to, by laughter. My laughter, at the time, was kind of innocent. I did not reflect on my laughter. What I saw was a clown.

Eichmann was never bothered by anything which he had done to the Jews as a whole. But he was bothered by one little incident: he had slapped the face of the then president of the Jewish community in Vienna during an interrogation. God knows many far worse things were happening to Jews than being slapped in the face. But this he never condoned himself for having done, and he thought this was very wrong, indeed. He had lost his cool, so to speak.

ERRERA: Why do you think we are seeing the emergence of a whole literature that, when it comes to Nazism, for instance, often describes its leaders and their crimes in a novelistic way and tries to humanize them, and thereby indirectly to justify them? Do you think that publications of this kind are purely commercial, or do they have a deeper significance?

ARENDT: I think this literature has the *signification* that it shows what happened once can happen again, and this, I believe, is entirely true. Look here, tyranny was discovered very early in human history, and identified very early as inimical to political life. Still, it has never in any way prevented any tyrant from becoming a tyrant. It did not prevent Nero, and it did not prevent Caligula. And the cases of Nero and Caligula have not prevented a much nearer example of what the massive intrusion of criminality into political processes means for *human* life.

1973

PUBLIC RIGHTS AND
PRIVATE INTERESTS
A Response to Charles Frankel

The area of agreement between Charles Frankel* and myself is large, and so the questions I shall raise will be of a general nature concerning matters on which there exists an almost universal consensus. It is that consensus I would like to challenge.

The first question concerns the title of this section of papers, a title Frankel borrows from his essay "Private Rights and the Public Good," which assumes that our rights are private and our obligations are public—as though there were no rights in the public realm. It is true that this has been the standard rhetoric in the West for many centuries, even into our own, but it is an assumption I must challenge. For it is necessary, I think, to distinguish the *private* rights we have as individuals from the *public* rights we have as citizens. Every individual in the privacy of his household is subject to life's necessities and has the right to be protected in the pursuit of his private interests; but by virtue of his citizenship he receives a kind of second life in addition to his private life. These two, the private and the public, must be considered separately, for the aims and chief concerns in each case are different.

Throughout his life man moves constantly in two different orders of existence: he moves within what is his *own,* and he also moves in a sphere that is *common* to him and his fellow men. The "public good," the concerns of citizens, is indeed the common good because it is localized in the *world* which we have in common *without owning it.* Quite frequently, it will be

* Charles Frankel (1917–1979) was a social philosopher, assistant secretary of state under Lyndon B. Johnson, and founding director of the National Humanities Center. —Ed.

antagonistic to whatever we may deem good to ourselves in our private existence. The reckless pursuit of private interests in the public-political sphere is as ruinous for the public good as the arrogant attempts of governments to regulate the private lives of their citizens are ruinous for private happiness.

In the eighteenth century, this second life in the common world was characterized as being capable of affording "public happiness," that is, a happiness which one could attain to only in public, independent of his private happiness. The possibility for enjoying "public happiness" has decreased in modern life because during the last two centuries the public sphere has shrunk. The voting booth can hardly be called a *public* space, as it accommodates only one; indeed, the only way in which a citizen today can still function as a citizen is as a member of a jury.

Hence, my first question may be put: Assuming that the private individual and the citizen are not the same, do we still exercise our public rights? The Constitution provides for one such right in the First Amendment, which concerns the "right of the people peaceably to assemble"—a right deemed cognate to the right of free speech and equally fundamental. This right still survives in "voluntary associations," of which the civil disobedience groups of the sixties were an outstanding example, but it has also degenerated into lobbying, that is, into the organization of *private* interest groups for the purpose of public, political influence.

It should be clear that my distinction between private and public depends on the locality where a person moves. No one will doubt, for instance, that a physician has different rights, obligations, liberties, and constraints in the hospital, on the one hand, and at an evening's social gathering, on the other. Or take the case of a juror. Once made member of a jury, a person all of a sudden is supposed to be impartial and disinterested, and we assume that every individual is capable of this impartiality regardless of background, education, and private interests. To constitute a jury, a number of persons must be *equalized,* for people are not born equal and they are not equal in their private lives. Equality always means the equalization of differences. In society, for example, we often speak of law as the great equalizer: we are equal before the law. In religion, we speak of God before whom all are equal. Or we say that we are equal in the face of death, or that the human condition in general equalizes us. When we talk about equality, we must always ask what equalizes us.

Jurors are equalized by the task and the place. Though drawn from quite different backgrounds and social strata, through their task as jurors they are made to act not as party members or as friends but as peers. They deal with something which is of no private interest to them at all; they are interested in something in regard to which they, as private individuals, are disinterested. Jurors share an interest in the case before them—something outside themselves; what is common to them is something that is not subjective, and this I think is quite important.

My second question is connected with the first. The working premise of this second series of essays was that the enduring challenge of society is to care for the public good without violating the rights of individual citizens and that, happily, the two interests often coincide. This coincidence is indeed the basic presupposition of any "harmony of interests." The assumption is that "enlightened self-interest" automatically reconciles opposed private interests.

If we understand "enlightened *self*-interest" as the "interest in the common good," I would argue that such a thing does not exist. The principal characteristic of the common good with respect to the plurality of individuals who share it is that it is much more durable than the life of any one individual. There is an intrinsic conflict between the interests of individual mortals and the interest of the common world which they inhabit, and the source of this conflict lies in the overwhelming *urgency* of individual interests. To recognize and embrace the common good requires not enlightened self-interest but *impartiality;* such impartiality, however, is resisted at every turn by self-interests, which always appear more urgent than the common good. The reason for this is very simple: such urgency protects that which is most private, the interests of the life process itself. For us as individuals, the privacy of our own life, life in itself, is the highest good, and alone can be the highest good.

Until very recent times, whatever belonged to life's necessities was hidden in the obscurity of privacy. But we seem to have decided of late—how wisely I am not sure—that everything should be made public. The life process, however, particularly the process of raising children, requires a certain obscurity. Whatever advantages it may have, public space exposes one mercilessly, in a way none of us could stand all the time. We need a private space in order, among other things, to hide; we need it for all our private affairs, with our families and our friends. And we have acquired, since the eighteenth century, an enormous space of intimacy which we consider sacrosanct. And rightly so. Yet it is precisely this space which we are asked to sacrifice when we act as citizens.

Public interest always demands a sacrifice of individual interests which are determined by life's necessities and by the limited time which is given to mortals. The necessary sacrifice of individual interests to the common weal—in the most extreme case, the sacrifice of life—is compensated for by public happiness, that is, by the kind of "happiness" which men can only experience in the public realm.*

My second question then, is this: What about the private rights of individuals who are citizens? How can one's private interests and rights be reconciled with what one is entitled to demand as a citizen? Among the most important private rights is "the right to be let alone" (Brandeis). This right is by no means a matter of course. It is Christian in origin: "Render unto Caesar the things that are Caesar's" (Matthew 22:21); "No thing is more alien to us than the public thing, *res publica*" (Tertullian); or, simply, "Mind your own business." For the Christians were those who minded their own business. Their reason, to be sure, is no longer our reason. Their reason was that saving one's soul required all the time one could spare so that politics to them was a luxury. And indeed, freedom, political life, the life of the

---

* In an earlier essay Arendt distinguishes the public realm from "the perspective of truth," just as here she distinguishes "public rights" from "private interests." In both cases she purposefully omits spelling out the gravitational human attraction to public life. In the earlier essay she takes notice of her omission, which may bear repeating here: "Since I have dealt with politics from . . . a viewpoint outside the political realm, I have failed to mention . . . the greatness and the dignity of what goes on inside it. . . . From this perspective we remain unaware of the actual content of political life—of the joy and the gratification that arise out of being in company with our peers, out of acting together and appearing in public, out of inserting ourselves into the world by word and deed, thus acquiring and sustaining our personal identity and beginning something entirely new." ("Truth and Politics," in H. Arendt, *Between Past and Future* (New York: Penguin, 2006), 258–59. —Ed.

citizen—this "public happiness" I've been speaking of—*is* a luxury; it is an *additional* happiness that one is made capable of only after the requirements of the life process have been fulfilled.

So if we talk about equality, the question always is: How much do we have to change the private lives of the poor? In other words, how much money do we have to give the poor to make them capable of enjoying public happiness? Education is very nice, but the real thing is money. Only when they can enjoy public life will they be willing and able to make sacrifices for the public good. To ask sacrifices of individuals who are not yet citizens is to ask them for an idealism which they do not and cannot have due to the urgency of the life process. Before we ask the poor for idealism, we must first make them citizens: and this involves so changing the circumstances of their private lives that they become capable of enjoying public life.

But many people today, and not merely those who care about the salvation of their souls, demand to be left alone. This is, in fact, a new freedom that is being demanded—the right to be free from any mandatory participation in public life, be it something so basic as the duty to vote or to serve as a juror. If we wish to spend time painting pictures and let the whole community rot, we feel we have this freedom. But again, this freedom is by no means a matter of course, and perhaps not even a matter by which we can judge the relative freedom of governments. Consider, for example, the case of Aleksandr Solzhenitsyn.* Solzhenitsyn didn't mind his own business and for that reason came into conflict with his government. In other words, the Soviet Union is no longer Stalinist. Under Stalin, if one minded his own business, he was sent to a labor camp (they were actually extermination camps), just as if he had opposed the government. Indeed, Stalinist terror acquired its full momentum only after all political opposition had been liquidated. In Soviet Russia today, however, the private individual who minds his own business can live without any conflict with the government. The government remains tyrannical—that is, it does not permit political life; but it is no longer totalitarian—that is, it has not liquidated the whole

* Russian author (1918–2008) whose *One Day in the Life of Ivan Denisovich* (1962) and later works were of great importance to Arendt. —Ed.

sphere of privacy. Solzhenitsyn's difficulties arose when he demanded *political* rights, not private rights.

The notion that private rights are sacrosanct is Roman in origin. The Greeks distinguished between the *idion* and the *koinon,* between what is one's own and what is held in common. It is interesting that the former term has become in every language, including the Greek, the root for the word *idiocy.* The idiot is one who lives only in his own household and is concerned only with his own life and its necessities. The truly free state, then—one that respects not only certain liberties but is genuinely free—is a state in which no one is, in this sense, an idiot; that is, a state in which everyone takes part in one way or another in what is common.

But the Romans were the first to claim, through the tall walls demarcating their properties, the sanctity of the private sphere; the notion that private rights are sacrosanct sprang from the Roman concern for home and hearth, their insistence that the private cult of hearth and home be as sacred as a public cult. Indeed, only he who owned his own home was deemed able to participate in public life; that is, private ownership was the condition *sine qua non* for entering into public affairs. This implies two things: (1) life's necessities are private, not fit to be seen in public, and (2) life is sacrosanct. The chief quality of this life was precisely that it was protected from the glaring lights of the public realm. Whereas the chief quality of the public is illumination; it is like light that exposes everything to all sides so that, for example, all sides of a question can be seen. It is the opposite of the obscurity of privacy. Both these qualities are basic to a good society, whereas obscurity is a necessary condition of life itself. As the public realm has shrunk in the modern age, the private realm has been very much extended, and the word that indicates this extension is, as has been noted, *intimacy.* Today the whole of privacy is very much threatened again, and the threats appear to arise rather from society than from government. But while governments threaten our public rights—our right to public happiness—our private interests and rights, given the necessities of modern production, are so organized that they effectively influence the public realm. The primary condition for privacy is ownership, which is not the same as property. Neither the capitalist system nor the socialist system respects ownership any longer—inflation and devaluation of currency are capitalist modes of expropriation—although both, in different ways, respect acquisition. Hence, one of our problems is to find a way to restore ownership to private individuals under the conditions of modern production.

What is necessary for freedom is not wealth. What is necessary is security and a place of one's own shielded from the claims of the public. What is necessary for the public realm is that it be shielded from the private interests which have intruded upon it in the most brutal and aggressive form.

1974

PRELIMINARY REMARKS ABOUT
THE LIFE OF THE MIND*

The series of lectures which I proposed for the fall term of this year was originally prepared for and partly delivered on another occasion, where I was required to speak as a "philosopher."[†] That is, I was required to speak as someone who is fond of thinking but who "knows that he knows nothing," as Merleau-Ponty put it ("In Praise of Philosophy," 17), hence as someone who—Socrates-like—has nothing to teach. And this enterprise, unacademic in every sense of the word, calls for a few remarks because it touches upon the very relationship between you, who supposedly have come here to learn, and myself, who clearly am supposed to teach.

There are indeed quite a number of legitimate ways in which philosophy can be taught and learned, and schools for this purpose have existed since antiquity. Since the rise and flourishing of medieval universities this schooling has consisted chiefly in the interpretation of the great thinkers—theologians and philosophers—or in logical exercises of which the analytic schools of our own day are the last, or latest, successors. In these fields there is indeed much to be taught and much to be learned, and someone "who knows that he knows nothing" does not belong there. Yet philosophy, even in these legitimate ways of inquiring, remains a curious subject matter. Plato, certainly foremost among all those whose texts have been taught and learned throughout the centuries, once said: "Every one of us is like a man who sees things in a dream and thinks he knows them perfectly,

---

* The following is an edited version of unpublished remarks made by Hannah Arendt to students and others enrolled in her lecture course on "Thinking," given in the fall of 1974 at what was then known as the Graduate Faculty of the New School for Social Research. Perhaps nowhere more personally does Arendt consider her work as a "teacher." —Ed.

† Arendt refers to the Gifford Lectures in Edinburgh, Scotland. —Ed.

and then awakens and finds that he knows nothing" (*Statesman*, 277D). Although I am not erudite enough to document my point, I'd guess—after all, an educated guess—that there is no one among the great thinkers who, at the end of his life, would not have agreed with Plato on this as on so much else.

In brief, those of you who might have come here to be taught and to learn will be disappointed. Don't be deceived by the bibliography.* It would be sheer madness to expect anyone to read all these books during one term; I drew this list up only to indicate the books I found especially helpful in my enterprise, hoping that you are already familiar with quite a number of them. I put them in alphabetical order, instead of chronological, to indicate that we shall leap freely over the centuries, without paying attention to the suspicions of the historians of ideas who assume that ideas, handed down from generation to generation, develop according to their own intrinsic nature.

To the extent that we are mindful of our leaps, we shall take our bearings from the history of *events* rather than the history of ideas, and this political history of Western civilization is full of gaps, caused by sudden changes in the world, the rise and fall of empires, nations, and cultures. The story that leads from classical antiquity to the first centuries of the Common Era, from the decline of Rome to the Barbarian invasions and the rise of Byzantium, from the fall of Rome to the truly Dark Ages, from there to the long centuries of the Middle Ages and the Renaissance, followed rather abruptly by the Modern Age, which as abruptly has come to an end in our time—well, Hegel and Marx notwithstanding, this story cannot be told in a single breath, as if it followed a uniform Law of History with inexorable necessity. And still this story, beset as it is by so many discords and sheer accidents, is certainly not entirely void of continuity. This continuity, insofar as it is a fact and not a theoretical assumption, is called *Tradition*, which is Roman in origin, the deliberate mental product of the last centuries of the Roman Republic. Its resiliency has proved to be extraordinary, nour-

---

* Instead of printing her bibliography here, anyone interested in it is advised to visit Arendt's personal library, happily housed in Bard College's Stevenson Library. Arendt weeded out her collection of books, giving away hundreds of volumes, a few years before she died. Those she kept comprise, and amplify, the bibliography for this course. —Ed.

ished throughout the intervening ages by ever-repeated revivals of ancient learning, of which what is referred to as "the Renaissance" in textbooks is but the last episode, closing and still intimately connected with a similar preceding revival called Scholasticism, which in its turn developed out of the Carolingian Renaissance after the Dark Ages. In other words, the only guarantee for continuity in history is Tradition, which is first of all an academic matter. It depends on *learning*.

You will have guessed by now that I am neither a Hegelian nor a Marxian, and that I do not believe in any Law of History. More important for our purpose here is that I think that Tradition, the mental continuity of occidental history, has broken down and that the rupture of its thread, for better and worse, is irreparable. This, God knows, has many disadvantages: our intellectual ambience is increasingly overcrowded by an enormous amount of sheer nonsense, which would be folly to refute, not only because of the limited time of a man's life, but also because of the absence of generally recognized criteria with which right can be distinguished from wrong. There is, on the other hand, hardly a century that has been as rich and fecund in art and science as ours [the twentieth century], at least in its first fifty years, when artists and scientists suddenly began to discard a great number of their traditional concepts. Something very similar began also in philosophy, which I'll briefly discuss in the first introductory lecture.

In these preliminary remarks I wish to stress only one thing, namely, that this course of lectures will be organized by a question concerning the nature and experience of *thinking*. Taking a hint from the elder Cato— *numquam se plus agere quam nihil cum ageret, numquam minus solum esse quam cum solus esset*—my question is simply: What are we doing when we are *thinking*, that is, when we are *active* without *doing* anything at all? Where are we when we are alone without being lonely? To raise such questions one might discard all traditional answers, and of course Cato himself was a statesman, not a philosopher. Still, it would be reckless to rely only on one's own experiences and fail to consult those whom Kant called *Denker von Gewerbe*, "professional thinkers." But you will see that I went farther in my consultations. I felt entirely free, free of Tradition and chronological order, and also liberated from any so-called field of expertise. I consulted poets and scientists as well as philosophers, and am quite aware of the chief objection which may be raised to my unmethodological approach, namely, that I make use of only what confirms my own experience in these matters. I do not think this objection is valid because I make no claim for the general validity for what I have to say; it is not as if my propositions were scientific statements capable of being verified.

Finally, since I am much older than you, I have read of course many more books, and since I am quite willing and even eager to discuss with you my own text—something that, as those among you who know me know I never have done before—it is quite possible that you may learn here a little something, bits of knowledge, perhaps, and pick up some information. But this will be incidental and marginal to what we are about.*

1974

---

* These preliminary remarks conclude with a few "technicalities," including the participation expected of students, certain preferences given to registered students over auditors (including former students and interested parties of all ages and occupations, a large number of whom always audited Arendt's lecture courses), the availability of a free pro-seminar, and the requirements for students attending the lectures for academic credit. These students would be given an examination, consisting of many quotations to identify by author and century (a favorite practice of Arendt, who understood that knowing the Tradition was the condition *sine qua non* of realizing it had ended), and an essay to be written on one or more of those quotations. The examination, as well as the bibliography mentioned in the third footnote to these remarks, can be found among Arendt's papers in the Manuscript Division of the Library of Congress in Washington, D.C. —Ed.

TRANSITION*

In the second series of these lectures I shall deal with willing and judging, the two other basic mental activities. Seen from the perspective of these time speculations, they concern matters which are absent either because they are not yet or because they are no more; but in contradistinction to the thinking activity that deals with the invisibles in all experience and with universals; they deal always with particulars and in this respect are much closer to the world of appearances. If we wish to placate our common sense that is so decisively offended by the need of reason to pursue its purposeless quest for meaning, an activity which obviously is "good for nothing," it is tempting indeed to justify this need to think solely on the grounds that thinking is an indispensable preparation for deciding what shall be and for evaluating what is no more and therefore submitted to our judgment, whereby judgment, in turn, would be a mere preparation for willing. This is indeed the perspective, and, within limits, the legitimate perspective of man insofar as he is an acting being.

But this last attempt to defend the thinking activity against the reproach of its practical uselessness does not work. The decision at which the will arrives can never be derived from the mechanics of desire or the delibera-

---

* The manuscript of "Thinking," the first volume of Arendt's posthumously published *Life of the Mind,* ends with a section called "Transition." For reasons unknown, this was changed in the published edition of 1978 to "Postscriptum" and shortened from ten to four pages. Though it was tempting simply to print the deleted pages here, it was judged preferable to print the entire "Transition" as Arendt wrote it, and in which material from the four previously published pages is interspersed. The principal reason for doing this—and also a possible rationale for the earlier editing—is the growing interest in what Arendt was prevented by her death from writing on "Judging," which may well have turned out to be a third volume of *The Life of the Mind.* The following "Transition" certainly says more about the activity of judging in relation to the activities of both thinking and willing than the previously published "Postscriptum." —Ed.

tion of the intellect that may precede it. The will is either an organ of free spontaneity that interrupts all causal chains of motivation, which would bind it or it is nothing but an illusion; with respect to desire on one hand and to reason on the other, it acts like "a kind of coup d'état," as Bergson once said, and this implies of course that "free acts are exceptional," and that "although we are free whenever we are willing to get back into ourselves, it seldom happens that we are willing."* In other words, it is impossible to deal with the willing activity without touching on the problem of freedom, and it is entirely true that this problem "has been to the moderns what the paradoxes of the Eleatics were to the ancients."†

The most obvious and also the most plausible way out of all difficulties is to declare that the will, in distinction from other faculties of the mind, is a mere illusion of consciousness, an "artificial concept," corresponding to nothing that has ever existed and creating useless riddles like so many of the metaphysical fallacies. This is the considered opinion of Gilbert Ryle, who believes he has refuted "the doctrine that there exists a Faculty . . . of the 'Will,' and, accordingly, that there occur processes, or operations, corresponding to what it describes as volitions." And in support of his argument he quite correctly draws our attention to "the fact that Plato and Aristotle never mentioned [volitions] in their frequent and elaborate discussions of the nature of the soul and the springs of conduct," because they were still unacquainted with this "special hypothesis [of later times] the acceptance of which rests not on the discovery but on the postulation of [certain] ghostly thrusts."‡

This suspicion that such eminently important concepts, like will and freedom, of which we find almost no trace in ancient philosophy, are mere illusions is much older than modern philosophy. Spinoza as well as Hobbes firmly believed that they are due to a kind of optic delusion, to a trick played on us by the fact of consciousness and our ignorance of the causes that actually move us. Thus, a stone, having received "from the impulsion of an external cause a certain quantity of motion" and unable to detect the

---

* Bergson, *Time and Free Will*, pp. 142, 167, 169, 240.
† Ibid.
‡ *Concept of the Mind*, ch. 3, pp. 62ff.

original external cause would, if it only is not "indifferent" to being moved, "believe itself to be completely free, and would think that it continued in motion solely because of its own wish."* And in almost the same terms, Hobbes speaks of "a wooden top that is lashed by the boys. . . . [This top] if it were sensible to its own motion, would think it proceeded from its own will, unless it felt what lashed it."† As John Stuart Mill put it: "our internal consciousness tells us that we have a power, which the whole outward experience of the human race tells us that we never use."‡ In the same vein, Kant spoke of "the fact of freedom," which reason can never prove or refute.

I propose to take this internal evidence, the "immediate datum of consciousness" (Bergson) seriously, and since I agree with Ryle—and many others—that this datum and all problems connected with it were unknown to Greek antiquity, I must accept what Ryle rejects, namely, that this faculty was indeed "discovered" and that we can date this discovery historically, whereby we shall find that this discovery coincides with the discovery of human "inwardness" as a specific region of our life. In brief, I shall analyze the faculty of the will in terms of its history, and this in itself has its difficulties.

Are not the human faculties, as distinct from the conditions and circumstances of human life, coeval with the appearance of man on earth—as I asserted before of man's faculty and need of thinking? To be sure, there is such a thing as the "history of ideas" and our task would be easier if we traced the idea of freedom historically—how it changed from being a word indicating a political status, that of a free citizen and not a slave, and a physical fact, that of a healthy man whose body was at the command of his mind and who was not paralyzed—to indicating an inner disposition by virtue of which a man could *feel* free when he actually was a slave or unable to move his limbs. Ideas are mental artifacts and their history presupposes the unchanging identity of man as artificer. To assume that there is a history of the mind's faculties as distinguished from the mind's products is like assuming that with the invention of new tools and even implements that

---

* Spinoza, Letter LXII.

† Hobbes, "The Questions Concerning Liberty, Necessity and Chance," English Works, London, 1841, vol. V.

‡ "An Examination of Sir William Hamilton's Philosophy."

can serve as full-fledged substitutes for tools, the human body, which is a toolmaker's and a tool user's body, would also be subject to change. And still, there is the fact that prior to the rise of Christianity we find nowhere any notion of a mental faculty that corresponded to the "idea" of freedom as the faculty of the intellect corresponded to truth, and the faculty of reason to things beyond human knowledge or, as we have said, to meaning.

We shall follow the experiences men had with this paradoxical and self-contradictory faculty (every volition since it speaks to itself in imperatives produces its own counter-volition) from the Apostle Paul's early discovery of the impotence of the will—"I do not what I want, but I do the very thing I hate . . . I can will what is right but I cannot do it"*—through the Middle Ages, beginning with Augustine's insight that what is "at war" here is not the spirit and the flesh but the mind as will with itself, man's "inmost self" with itself. I shall then proceed to the modern age which, with the rise of the notion of progress, exchanged the old philosophical primacy of the present over the other tenses for the primacy of the future, a force that in Hegel's words "the now cannot resist" so that thinking is understood "as essentially the negation of something being there" ("*in der Tat ist das Denken wesentlich die Negation eines unmittelbar Vorhandenen*").† In the words of Schelling, "In the final and highest instance there is no other Being than Will,"‡ an attitude which found its final climactic and self-defeating end in Nietzsche's "will to Power."

At the same time we shall follow another parallel development in the history of the will according to which this is the inner capacity by which men decide about "Who" they are going to be, in what shape they wish to show themselves in the world of appearances. In other words, it is the will, whose subject matter are *projects,* not *objects,* which in a sense creates the *person* who can be blamed or praised and anyhow held responsible not merely for his actions but also for his whole "being," his *character.* "For Will is in itself the consciousness of personality or of everybody as an individual."§ The

---

* Letter to the Romans, 5:15–19.
† *Jenenser Realphilosophie,* Philosophy of Nature, I A, "The Concept of Motion."
‡ *On Human Freedom* (1809), translation by James Gutman (Chicago, 1936), p. 8.
§ Hegel, *Phenomenology of Mind,* Baillie edition, p. 601.

Marxian and existentialist notions which play such a great role in twentieth-century thought and pretend that man is his own producer and maker, rest on these experiences, despite the fact that I certainly did not "make myself" or "produce" my existence; this, I think, is the last of the metaphysical fallacies, corresponding to the modern age's emphasis on willing as a replacement of thinking.

I shall conclude this second series of lectures with an analysis of the faculty of judgment, and our chief difficulty will be of an altogether different kind, consisting of the curious scarcity of sources which could provide us with authoritative testimony. It was not before Kant's *Critique of Judgment* that this faculty became a major topic of a major thinker. My main assumption in singling out this faculty will be that judgments are not arrived at by either deduction or induction, that, in brief, they have nothing in common with logical operations—as when we say: All men are mortal, Socrates is a man, therefore, Socrates is mortal. The first to be aware of such a separate faculty was, as far as I know, Cicero, who, wondering how the "crowd of the unlearned" could be receptive to and hence persuaded by the highly sophisticated rhetorical devices of orators, said as follows:

> Everybody discriminates [*diiudicare*] between right and wrong in matters of art and proportion by some *silent sense* without any knowledge of art and proportion . . . and [people] display this [discrimination] much more in judging . . . words since these are fixed [*infixa*] in *common sense* and in these things nature did not want anybody not to be an expert. . . . It is remarkable how little difference there is between the learned and the ignorant in judging while there is the greatest difference in making"* (my italics).

We shall be in search of this "silent sense," which—if it was dealt with at all—has always, even in Kant, been thought of as "taste" and therefore as belonging to the realm of aesthetics; in practical and moral matters it was called "conscience" and conscience did not judge; it told you, as the divine voice of either God or reason, what to do, what not to do, and what to

* In *De Oratore*, III, 195–197.

repent of. Whatever the voice of conscience may be, it cannot be said to be "silent" and its validity depends entirely upon an authority which is above and beyond all merely human laws and rules.

Kant had been concerned with the phenomenon of taste in his youth and he had failed to elaborate on this concern because the "critical business," the desire to inquire into the "scandal of reason," intervened and kept him busy for more than ten years. When he returned to his early concern, which for him was rooted in the "sociability" of man, in the fact that man is a social [geselliges] being for whom nothing would make any sense if he were unable to share it with others, he changed his youthful project and wrote not a Critique of Taste but a Critique of Judgment, perhaps because he had discovered, while busy with the Critique of Pure Reason, this special faculty for which "general logic contains no rules"; even then, he counted this faculty together with intellect and reason among the "higher faculties of the mind."* In the context of the Critique of Pure Reason, judgment has the function of naming the particular under general rules, and for this task, Kant found, there are no rules to instruct the mind "whether something does or does not come under them"; and even if there were such rules, "for the very reason that [they are rules they would] again demand guidance from judgment."† Thus judgment emerges as "a peculiar talent which can be practiced only, and cannot be taught."

Judgment deals with particulars, and when thinking, moving among generalities emerges from its withdrawal and returns to the world of particular appearances, it turns out that the mind needs a new "gift" to deal with them. And Kant adds: "Deficiency" in this gift "is ordinarily called stupidity, and for such a failing there is no remedy. An obtuse or narrow-minded person . . . may indeed be trained through study, even to the extent of becoming learned. But as such people are commonly still lacking in judgment, it is not unusual to meet learned men who in the application of their scientific knowledge betray that original want, which can never be made good."‡ For the only help to "sharpen" this peculiar talent of the mind

* B169 and 171.
† B172.
‡ B173.

"are examples," the "go cart of judgment," and in order to find the right examples one needs, of course, again judgment. Such is the case for what Kant calls the determinate judgment about which he has little to say; the *Critique of Judgment* then deals with "reflexive judgment" which appears in the *Critique of Pure Reason* only in a footnote;* here judgment in matters of the beautiful is said to be *"the proper test of the correctness of the rules,"* which is only another way of saying that in the last instance the particular decides, sits in judgment, as it were, on the validity of the general.

And this seems logically impossible. If judgment, "the faculty of *thinking* the particular," has nothing to rely on but other particulars "for which the general has to be found,"† it lacks all standards or criteria by which to judge. The standard cannot be borrowed from experience and cannot be derived from the outside. I cannot judge one particular by another particular: in order to determine its worth or its value, I need a *tertium comparationis*, something related to the two particulars and yet distinct from both. In Kant himself, it is reason with its "regulative ideas" which comes to the help of the faculty of judgment, but if the faculty is separate from other faculties of the mind then we shall have to ascribe to it its own *modus operandi*, its own way of proceeding.

And this is of some relevance to a whole set of problems by which modern thought is haunted, especially to the problem of theory and practice and to all attempts to arrive at a halfway plausible theory of ethics. Since Hegel and Marx these questions have been treated under the perspective of History and under the assumption that there is such a thing as Progress of

---

* Kant's footnote to B35–36 in "The Transcendental Aesthetic" of *The Critique of Pure Reason* reads as follows: "The Germans are the only people who now employ the word 'aesthetics' to indicate what others call the critique of taste. At the foundation of this term lies the disappointed hope, which the eminent analyst Baumgarten conceived, of subjecting the criticism of the beautiful to principles of reason, and so of elevating its rules into a science. But his endeavors were in vain, for the said rules are, in respect to their chief sources, merely empirical, consequently never can serve as determinate laws *a priori*, by which our judgment in matters of taste is to be directed. It is rather our judgment which forms the proper test of the correctness of the rules. On this account it is advisable to give up the use of the term as designating the critique of taste, and to apply it solely to that doctrine, which is true science—the science of the laws of sensibility—and thus come nearer to the language and the sense of the ancients in their well-known division of the objects of cognition into *aisthēta kai noēta*, or to share it with speculative philosophy, and employ it partly in a transcendental, partly in a psychological signification." —Ed.

† Introduction to the *Critique of Judgment*, part IV.

the human race. Finally we shall be left with the only alternative there is in these matters: we either can say with Hegel: *Die Weltgeschichte ist das Weltgericht,* leaving the ultimate judgment to Success, or we can maintain with Kant the autonomy of the minds of men and their possible independence of things as they are or as they have come into being. In which case we still shall have to concern ourselves with the concept of history, but we may then be able to reflect on the oldest meaning of this word, which, like so many other terms of our political and philosophical language, is Greek in origin and derived from *historein,* to inquire, to say what is, *legein ta eonta,* in Herodotus. But the origin of the verb *historein* is to be found in Homer— *Iliad* XXIII—where the noun *histor* occurs, the "historian" as it were, and this Homeric historian is a *judge.** If judgment is our faculty to deal with the past, the historian is the man who by saying what is sits in judgment over it. In which case we may reclaim our human dignity, win it back as it were from the pseudo-divinity of the modern age, called History, not denying its importance but denying its right to being the ultimate judge. Old Cato with whom I started these lectures—"never am I less alone than when I am by myself, never am I more active than when I do nothing"—has left us a curious phrase which is apt to summarize the political principle implied in this enterprise. He said: *Victrix causa deis placuit sed victa Catoni:* The victorious cause pleased the gods, but the defeated one pleased Cato.†

1974

---

* In *Iliad,* Canto 23, the funeral games—chariot racing, boxing, foot racing, throwing, archery— are judged by the *histor,* who awards prizes justly, and disqualifies participants suspected of cheating.
—Ed.

† In fact this is not the same "old Cato" quoted earlier, but his great grandson, Cato the Younger (95–46 BCE), as imitated by the poet Lucan in his epic *Pharsalia,* I, 128. Arendt makes this error consistently, as far back as the 1930s. It is a curious error for someone of her proficiency in scanning classical verse. It is, perhaps, the exception that proves the rule. —Ed.

REMEMBERING WYSTAN H. AUDEN, WHO DIED IN THE NIGHT OF THE TWENTY-EIGHTH OF SEPTEMBER, 1973

I met Auden late in his life and mine—at an age when the easy, knowledgeable intimacy of friendships formed in one's youth can no longer be attained, because not enough life is left, or expected to be left, to share with another. Thus, we were very good friends but not intimate friends. Moreover, there was a reserve in him that discouraged familiarity—not that I tested it, ever. I rather gladly respected it as the necessary secretiveness of the great poet, one who must have taught himself early not to talk in prose, loosely and at random, of things that he knew how to say much more satisfactorily in the condensed concentration of poetry. Reticence may be the *déformation professionnelle* of the poet. In Auden's case, this seemed all the more likely because much of his work, in utter simplicity, arose out of the spoken word, out of idioms of everyday language—like "Lay your sleeping head, my love, Human on my faithless arm." This kind of perfection is very rare; we find it in some of the greatest of Goethe's poems, and it must exist in most of Pushkin's works, because their hallmark is that they are untranslatable. The moment poems of this kind are wrenched from their original abode, they disappear in a cloud of banality. Here all depends on the "fluent gestures" in "elevating facts from the prosaic to the poetic"—a point that the critic Clive James stressed in his essay on Auden in *Commentary* in December 1973. Where such fluency is achieved, we are magically convinced that everyday speech is latently poetic, and, taught by the poets, our ears open up to the true mysteries of language. The very untranslatability of one of Auden's poems is what, many years ago, convinced me of his greatness. Three German translators had tried their luck and killed mercilessly one of my favorite poems, "If I Could Tell You" (*Collected Shorter Poems 1927–*

1957), which arises naturally from two colloquial idioms—"Time will tell" and "I told you so":

> Time will say nothing but I told you so,
> Time only knows the price we have to pay;
> If I could tell you I would let you know.
>
> If we should weep when clowns put on their show,
> If we should stumble when musicians play,
> Time will say nothing but I told you so. . . .
>
> The winds must come from somewhere when they blow,
> There must be reasons why the leaves decay;
> Time will say nothing but I told you so. . . .
>
> Suppose the lions all get up and go,
> And all the brooks and soldiers run away;
> Will Time say nothing but I told you so?
> If I could tell you I would let you know.

I met Auden in the autumn of 1958, but I had seen him before, in the late forties, at a publisher's party. Although we exchanged not a word on that occasion, I had remembered him quite well—a nice-looking, well-dressed, very English gentleman, friendly and relaxed. I did not recognize him ten years later, for now his face was marked by those famous deep wrinkles, as though life itself had delineated a kind of face-scape to make manifest "the heart's invisible furies." If you listened to him, nothing could seem more deceptive than this appearance. Time and again, when, to all appearances, he could not cope anymore, when his slum apartment was so cold that the plumbing no longer functioned and he had to use the toilet in the liquor store at the corner, when his suit—no one could convince him that a man needed at least two suits, so that one could go to the cleaner, or two pairs of shoes, so that one pair could be repaired: a subject of an endless ongoing debate between us throughout the years—was covered with spots or worn so thin that his trousers would suddenly split from top to bottom—in brief, whenever disaster hit before your very eyes, he would begin to more or less intone an utterly idiosyncratic version of "Count your blessings." Since he never talked nonsense or said something obviously silly—and since I always remained aware that this was the voice of a very great poet—it took me years to realize that in his case it was not appearance that was deceptive, and that it was fatally wrong to ascribe what I saw of his way of life to the harmless eccentricity of a typical English gentleman.

I finally saw the misery, and somehow realized vaguely his compelling need to hide it behind the "Count your blessings" litany, yet I found it difficult to understand fully why he was so miserable and was unable to do anything about the absurd circumstances that made everyday life so unbearable for him. It certainly could not be lack of recognition. He was reasonably famous, and such ambition could anyhow never have counted for much with him, since he was the least vain of all the authors I have ever met—completely immune to the countless vulnerabilities of ordinary vanity. Not that he was humble; in his case it was self-confidence that protected him against flattery, and this self-confidence existed prior to recognition and fame, prior also to achievement. Geoffrey Grigson, in the *Times Literary Supplement*, reports the following dialogue between the very young Auden and his tutor at Oxford. "Tutor: 'And what are you going to do, Mr. Auden, when you leave the university?' Auden: 'I am going to be a poet.' Tutor: 'Well—in that case you should find it very useful to have read English.' Auden: 'You don't understand. I am going to be a great poet.'"

His confidence never left him, because it was not acquired by comparisons with others, or by winning a race in competition; it was natural—interconnected, but not identical, with his enormous ability to do with language, and do quickly, whatever he pleased. When friends asked him to produce a birthday poem for the next evening at six o'clock, they could be sure of getting it; clearly this is possible only in the absence of self-doubt. But even this did not go to his head, for he did not claim, or perhaps even aspire to, final perfection. He constantly revised his own poems, agreeing with Valéry that a poem is never finished, only abandoned. In other words, he was blessed with that rare self-confidence which does not need admiration and the good opinion of others, and can even withstand self-criticism and self-examination without falling into the trap of self-doubt.

This has nothing to do with arrogance but is easily mistaken for it. Auden was never arrogant except when he was provoked by some vulgarity; then he protected himself with the rather abrupt rudeness characteristic of English intellectual life.

Stephen Spender, the friend who knew him so well, has stressed that "throughout the whole development of [Auden's] poetry . . . his theme had been love"—had it not occurred to Auden to change Descartes' *"Cogito ergo sum"* by defining man as the "bubble-brained creature" that said "I'm loved therefore I am"?—and at the end of the address that Spender gave in memory of his late friend at Christ Church in Oxford he told of asking Auden about a reading he had given in America: "His face lit up with a smile that altered its lines, and he said: 'They loved me!'" They did not admire him, they *loved* him: here, I think, lies the key both to his extraordinary unhappiness and to the extraordinary greatness—intensity—of his poetry. Now, with the sad wisdom of remembrance, I see him as having been an expert in the infinite varieties of unrequited love, among which the infuriating substitution of admiration for love must surely have loomed large. And beneath these emotions there must have been from the beginning a certain animal *tristesse* that no reason and no faith could overcome:

> The desires of the heart are as crooked as corkscrews,
> Not to be born is the best for man;
> The second-best is a formal order,
> The dance's pattern; dance while you can.

So he wrote in "Death's Echo," in *Collected Shorter Poems*. When I knew him, he would not have mentioned the best any longer, so firmly had he opted for the second-best, the "formal order," and the result was what Chester Kallman has so aptly named "the most dishevelled child of all disciplinarians." I think it was this *tristesse* and its "dance while you can" that made Auden feel so much attracted to and almost at home in Berlin of the twenties where *carpe diem* was practiced constantly in many variations. He once mentioned as a "disease" his early "addiction to German usages," but much more prominent than these, and less easy to get rid of, was the obvious influence of Bertolt Brecht, with whom I think he had more in common than he was ever ready to admit. In the late fifties, with Chester Kallman, he translated Brecht's *Rise and Fall of the City of Mahagonny*—a translation that was never published, presumably because of copyright difficulties. To this day, I know of no other adequate rendering of Brecht into English.

In merely literary terms, Brecht's influence can easily be traced in Auden's ballads—for instance, in the late, marvelous "Ballad of Barnaby," the tale of the tumbler who, having grown old and pious, "honoured the Mother-of-God" by tumbling for her; or in the early "little story / About Miss Edith Gee; / She lived in Clevedon Terrace / At Number 83." What made this influence possible was that they both belonged to the post–First World War generation, with its curious mixture of despair and *joie de vivre*, its contempt for conventional codes of behavior, and its penchant for "playing it cool," which expressed itself in England, I suspect, in the wearing of the mask of the snob, while it expressed itself in Germany in a widespread pretense of wickedness, somewhat in the vein of Brecht's *The Threepenny Opera*. In Berlin, one joked about this fashionable inverted hypocrisy, as one joked about everything: *"Er geht böse über den Kurfürstendamm"*—meaning, "That is probably all the wickedness he is capable of." After 1933, I think, nobody joked about wickedness anymore.

In the case of Auden, as in the case of Brecht, inverted hypocrisy served to hide an irresistible inclination toward being good and doing good—something that both were ashamed to admit, let alone proclaim. This seems plausible for Auden, because he finally became a Christian, but it may be a shock at first to hear it about Brecht. Yet a close reading of his poems and plays seems to me almost to prove it. Not only are there plays *Der Gute Mensch von Sezuan* and *Die Heilige Johanna der Schlachthöfe* but, perhaps more convincingly, there are these lines right in the midst of the cynicism of *The Threepenny Opera:*

> *Ein guter Mensch sein! Ja, wer wär's nicht gern?*
> *Sein Gut den Armen geben, warum nicht?*
> *Wenn alle gut sind, ist* Sein *Reich nicht fern.*
> *Wer sässe nicht sehr gern in* Seinem *Licht?*

To be good! Yes who wouldn't want that?
To give all you've got to the poor, why not?
When all are good, His kingdom is not far.
Who wouldn't sit gladly in His light?

[Cf. H. Arendt, *Men in Dark Times*
(New York, 1968), 235–36 N47. —Ed.]

What drove these profoundly apolitical poets into the chaotic political scene of our century was Robespierre's *"zèle compatissant,"* the powerful urge toward *"les malheureux,"* as distinguished from any need for action toward *public* happiness, or any desire to change the world.

Auden, so much wiser—though by no means smarter—than Brecht, knew early that "poetry makes nothing happen." To him, it was sheer nonsense for the poet to claim special privileges or to ask for the indulgences that we are so happy to grant out of sheer gratitude. There was nothing more admirable in Auden than his complete sanity and his firm belief in sanity; in his eyes all kinds of madness were lack of discipline—"Naughty, naughty," as he used to say. The main thing was to have no illusions and to accept no thoughts—no theoretical systems—that would blind you to reality. He turned against his early leftist beliefs because events (the Moscow trials, the Hitler-Stalin pact, and experiences during the Spanish Civil War) had proven them to be "dishonest"—"shamefully" so, as he said in his foreword to the *Collected Shorter Poems,* telling how he threw out what he had once written:

History to the defeated
may say alas but cannot help nor pardon.

To say this, he noted, was "to equate goodness with success." He protested that he never believed in "this wicked doctrine"—a statement that I doubt, not only because the lines are too good, too precise, to have been produced for the sake of being "rhetorically effective" but because this was the doctrine everybody believed in during the twenties and thirties. Then came the time when

In the nightmare of the dark
All the dogs of Europe bark . . .

Intellectual disgrace
Stares from every human face—

the time when it looked for quite a while as if the worst could happen and
sheer evil could become a success. The Hitler-Stalin pact was the turning
point for the left, now one had to give up all belief in history as the ultimate
judge of human affairs.

In the 1940s there were many who turned against their old beliefs, but
there were very few who understood what had been wrong with those
beliefs. Far from giving up their belief in history and success, they simply
changed trains, as it were; the train of Socialism and Communism had been
wrong, and they changed to the train of Capitalism or Freudianism or some
refined Marxism, or a sophisticated mixture of all three. Auden, instead,
became a Christian; that is, he left the train of History altogether. I don't
know whether Stephen Spender is right in asserting that "prayer corresponded to his deepest need"—I suspect that his deepest need was simply
to write verses—but I am reasonably sure that his sanity, the great good
sense that illuminated all his prose writings (his essays and book reviews),
was due in no small measure to the protective shield of orthodoxy. Its
time-honored coherent meaningfulness that could be neither proved nor
disproved by reason provided him, as it had provided Chesterton, with an
intellectually satisfying and emotionally rather comfortable refuge against
the onslaught of what he called "rubbish"; that is, the countless follies of
the age.

Rereading Auden's poems in chronological order and remembering him in
the last years of his life, when misery and unhappiness had grown more and
more unbearable without, however, in the least touching either the divine
gift or the blessed facility of the talent, I have become surer than ever that
he was "hurt into poetry" even more than Yeats: "Mad Ireland hurt you
into poetry." Despite Auden's susceptibility to compassion, public politi-

cal circumstances were not necessary to hurt him into poetry. What made him a poet was his extraordinary facility with and love for words, but what made him a great poet was the unprotesting willingness with which he yielded to the "curse" of vulnerability to "human *un*success" on all levels of human existence—vulnerability to the crookedness of the desires, to the infidelities of the heart, to the injustices of the world.

> Follow, poet, follow right
> To the bottom of the night,
> With your unconstraining voice
> Still persuade us to rejoice;
>
> With the farming of a verse
> Make a vineyard of the curse,
> Sing of human unsuccess
> In a rapture of distress;
>
> In the deserts of the heart
> Let the healing fountain start,
> In the prison of his days
> Teach the free man how to praise.

Praise is the key word of these lines, not praise of "the best of all possible worlds"—as though it were up to the poet (or the philosopher) to justify God's creation—but praise that pitches itself against all that is most unsatisfactory in man's condition on this earth and sucks its own strength from the wound: somehow convinced, as the bards of Ancient Greece were, that the gods spin unhappiness and evil things toward mortals so that they may tell the tales and sing the songs.

> I could (which you cannot)
> Find reasons fast enough
> To face the sky and roar
> In anger and despair

At what is going on,
Demanding that it name
Whoever is to blame:
The sky would only wait
Till all my breath was gone
And then reiterate
As if I wasn't there
That singular command
I do not understand,
Bless what there is for being,
Which has to be obeyed, for
What else am I made for,
Agreeing or disagreeing?

And the triumph of the private person was that the voice of the great poet never silenced the small but penetrating voice of sheer sound common sense whose loss has so often been the price paid for divine gifts. Auden never permitted himself to lose his mind—that is, to lose the "distress" in the "rapture" that rose out of it:

No metaphor, remember, can express
A real historical unhappiness;
Your tears have value if they make us gay;
O Happy Grief! is all sad verse can say.

It seems, of course, very unlikely that the young Auden, when he decided he was going to be a *great* poet, knew the price he would have to pay, and I think it entirely possible that in the end—when not the intensity of his feelings and not the gift of transforming them into praise but the sheer physical strength of the heart to bear them and live with them gradually faded away—he considered the price too high. We, in any event—his audience, readers and listeners—can only be grateful that he paid his price up to the last penny for the everlasting glory of the English language. And his friends may find some consolation in his beautiful joke beyond the grave—that for more than one reason, as Spender said, "his wise unconscious self chose a good day for dying." The wisdom to know "when to live and when to die" is not given to mortals, but Wystan, one would like to think, may have received it as the supreme reward that the cruel gods of poetry bestowed on the most obedient of their servants.

1975

INDEX

persuasion, 24, 137–8, 182, 336
Petőfi Military Academy, 133*n*
peuple, le, 345, 347, 377, 379
Phidias, 168
philanthropy, 185
philistines, 160
philosopher kings, 42, 85–6, 428
philosophy:
 alienation as theme in, 203
 ancient roots of, 9, 14, 34, 39–42
 Arendt's vision of, 485–8
 and contingency, 495
 isolation as habitat for, 425–30
 pleasure of, 487
 and politics, 181
 shortcomings of, 485–6
 teaching and learning of, 513
 three reversals in, 34
 see also specific philosophers and schools
physics, 435–6
Picasso, Pablo, 419
Pindar, 46
Piper, Klaus, 156
Planck, Max, 411, 413
Planetarium, The (Sarraute), 266, 267,
 268–71
Plato, xviii, 19, 163, 183, 318, 390, 419, 421,
 430*n*, 431, 440, 495, 518
 Jefferson's criticism of, 210
 on law, 43–5
 political thought of, 4, 5, 9, 24–5, 27, 30–1,
 33–4, 38, 40–2, 50, 58, 62, 64, 77, 84–6,
 168, 284, 447
 on thinking, xiv, 425–9, 446, 514
 see also specific works
Platonism, 33–4, 36, 61, 72, 88–9, 184, 210,
 293, 420, 488
 dialogue in, 439–40
pleasure, 162–3
"plumbers," 494*n*
plurality:
 action and, 66, 233, 303–4
 of human beings, 233, 304, 366, 463
 law of, xxix
 of opinions, 492

poets, poetry:
 alienation as theme of, 202
 American, 499
 ancient Greek, 171, 173
 Emerson on, 404–5
 judgment of, 474–5
 as most innocent art form, 174
 Pasternak's recitation of, 129
 Plato on, 428
 political content and themes in, 529–31
 and remembrance, 173
 stories recorded in, 305
 and truth, 168–9
 see also specific poets and works
pogroms, 75*n*–6*n*
Point Four programs, 252
Poland, 116, 140, 500
 rebellion in, 125–7, 141, 146, 153, 396
Polanyi, Michael, 185–91
police:
 in Hungarian Revolution, 119, 152–3
 in totalitarian dictatorships, 112–13, 115–21
polis, 23–4, 46, 58, 84, 167–8, 181, 222, 226,
 236, 292, 308, 336
 question of modern relevance of, 327
political activism, 450–1, 466
political commonality, xii–xiii
political freedom, elements of, xii, 234
political parties, 73
 council system vs., 137
 historical perspective of, 136–7, 493
 ideal vs. reality of, 193
 multi-party system of, 139–40, 255, 460
 in 1960 National Conventions, 192–200
 totalitarian elimination of diversity of, 73,
 106, 121, 136, 151, 159, 223, 255
 two-party system of, 139–40, 255
political theorists, role and responsibility of,
 447–50, 466
politics:
 action and, 52–4, 62–5, 293, 482–3
 and crime, 308–15
 and culture, 160–84
 degradation of, 39–40
 dignity of, 479